The E-business (R)evolution

Living and Working in an Interconnected World

ISBN 013067039-1

90000

9 780130 670397

Hewlett-Packard® Professional Books

OPERATING SYSTEMS

Diercks	MPE/iX System Administration Handbook
Fernandez	Configuring CDE: The Common Desktop Environment
Lund	Integrating UNIX and PC Network Operating Systems
Madell	Disk and File Management Tasks on HP-UX
Poniatowski	HP-UX 11i System Administration Handbook and Toolkit
Poniatowski	HP-UX 11.x System Administration Handbook and Toolkit
Poniatowski	HP-UX 11.x System Administration "How To" Book
Poniatowski	HP-UX System Administration Handbook and Toolkit
Poniatowski	Learning the HP-UX Operating System
Poniatowski	UNIX User's Handbook, Second Edition
Rehman	HP Certified, HP-UX System Administration
Roberts	UNIX and Windows 2000 Interoperability Guide
Sauers, Weygant	HP-UX Tuning and Performance
Stone, Symons	UNIX Fault Management
Weygant	Clusters for High Availability: A Primer of HP Solutions, Second Edition
Wong	HP-UX 11i Security

ONLINE/INTERNET

Amor	The E-business (R)evolution: Living and Working in an Interconnected World, Second Edition
Greenberg, Lakeland	A Methodology for Developing and Deploying Internet and Intranet Solutions
Greenberg, Lakeland	Building Professional Web Sites with the Right Tools
Klein	Building Enhanced HTML Help with DHTML and CSS
Werry, Mowbray	Online Communities: Commerce, Community Action, and the Virtual University

NETWORKING/COMMUNICATIONS

Blommers	OpenView Network Node Manager: Designing and Implementing an Enterprise Solution
Blommers	Practical Planning for Network Growth
Bruce, Dempsey	Security in Distributed Computing: Did You Lock the Door?
Lucke	Designing and Implementing Computer Workgroups

ENTERPRISE

Blommers	Architecting Enterprise Solutions with UNIX Networking
Cook	Building Enterprise Information Architectures
Missbach/Hoffmann	SAP Hardware Solutions: Servers, Storage, and Networks for mySAP.com
Pipkin	Halting the Hacker: A Practical Guide to Computer Security
Pipkin	Information Security: Protecting the Global Enterprise
Thornburgh	Fibre Channel for Mass Storage
Thornburgh, Schoenborn	Storage Area Networks: Designing and Implementing a Mass Storage System
Todman	Designing a Data Warehouse: Supporting Customer Relationship Management

PROGRAMMING

IMAGE PROCESSING

OTHER TITLES OF INTEREST

The E-business (R)evolution

Living and Working in an Interconnected World

Daniel Amor

Hewlett-Packard Company

www.hp.com/hpbooks

Prentice Hall PTR
Upper Saddle River, New Jersey 07458
www.phptr.com

Library of Congress Cataloging-in-Publication Data

A CIP catalog record for this book can be obtained from the Library of Congress.

Editorial/production supervision: *Mary Sudul*
Cover design director: *Jerry Votta*
Cover design: *DesignSource*
Manufacturing manager: *Maura Goldstaub*
Acquisitions editor: *Jill Harry*
Editorial assistant: *Richard Winkler*
Marketing manager: *Dan DePasquale*

Publisher, Hewlett-Packard Books: *Patricia Pekary*

© 2002 by Hewlett-Packard Company

Published by Prentice Hall PTR
Prentice-Hall, Inc.
Upper Saddle River, New Jersey 07458

Prentice Hall books are widely used by corporations and government agencies for training, marketing, and resale.
The publisher offers discounts on this book when ordered in bulk quantities. For more information, contact Corporate Sales Department, Phone: 800-382-3419; FAX: 201-236-7141;
E-mail: corpsales@prenhall.com
Or write: Prentice Hall PTR, Corporate Sales Dept., One Lake Street, Upper Saddle River, NJ 07458.

Other product or company names mentioned herein are the trademarks or registered trademarks of their respective owners.

Printed in the United States of America

10 9 8 7 6 5 4 3 2 1

ISBN 0-13-067039-1

Pearson Education LTD.
Pearson Education Australia PTY, Limited
Pearson Education Singapore, Pte. Ltd.
Pearson Education North Asia Ltd.
Pearson Education Canada, Ltd.
Pearson Educación de Mexico, S.A. de C.V.
Pearson Education — Japan
Pearson Education Malaysia, Pte. Ltd.

To Sabine,

for her love, patience
and understanding

Contents

FOREWORD BY PAOLO GLISENTI

In the years to come, readers of Daniel Amor's book will look back with mixed feelings at the time when it was first published. That was the period, many will then surely remember, when the world of Internet went through its first phase of consolidation and cleansing. Few even dared to speak of an imminent "Internet led recession". It was undoubtedly an opportune moment for this book to appear. After hundreds of enthusiastic and somehow naive hymns followed by fictional Cassandra's prophecies of an early Doomsday for the Web, Daniel Amor took us all back to what we really required to make sense of our destiny on the longer term. A diligent *tableau de bord* intentionally aimed at entrepreneurs and managers badly in need of a working tool to take their companies sailing in unchartered waters towards the promised land of the new economy; but even more interestingly, in my view, a practical guide for anybody just willing to understand the profound implications of the (r)evolution on the Internet.

Many will read this book thinking that its added value would be the privilege of getting at first hand an insider's look provided by a celebrated consultant of many large and small companies engaged in e-commerce and intranet projects. Flicking back and forth through the pages of this thick book, I formed a different opinion about Amor's work, for three different reasons.

Firstly, it is of some significance that today's most comprehensive "manual" to e-business should be the work of a European. It's in some way a telling sign of the present time, as Europe is in sight of definitely closing the gap with America and even of gaining important competitive advantages in certain areas where the convergence of enabling Internet technologies and mobile communication systems is more likely to happen. We have been used to the idea that meaningful texts on the e-economy would be mainly "imported" from the United States and only occasionally adapted to European standards and common practises. With Daniel Amor's book, the intellectual and scientific process is now for the first time visibly reversed.

Secondly, this book is not about the techniques but about the usages of Internet technologies and applications. It's the business idea that you should be looking for, not so much the technological vision. Otherwise, even a perfect IT infrastructure, Amor tells us, would never be sufficient. Nothing is more relevant—is Amor's thinking—than understanding the functional changes that are at hand. More important: what counts in today's world is grasping the profound motives for introducing Internet technologies and services in our lives. These motives are seldom explained clearly. Daniel Amor's book is therefore not for insiders. Neither is it directed to "electronic entrepreneurs". Far from it. I would not recommend it to information systems managers. Rather, it should find its place on the desk of any CEO and CFO, irrespectively of his or her mission and role. Perhaps, it might even be of use to heads of human resources as they are getting more and more occupied with continuous organizational changes and creative compensation policies in order to attract talents from the outside and nurture strategic skills internally.

Thirdly, I believe that the most impressive result of Amor's work is a first time "how to" book which contains a long term vision of the strategic options we will have to face eventually. Manuals of this kind, as much as they are based on solid direct operational experience, usually remain a "cold" working instrument. Rational and well structured at best, they are never compelling and intriguing as you consult the various chapters. Not in this case. For example, take Amor's view of the different degree of convergence between media and you will develop a new line of thinking about consumer product innovation. Furthermore, take Amor's view of the potential implications of the tremendous pervasiveness of Internet technologies and applications and you will probably start to evaluate alternatives in deciding which operational and navigational system you want to adopt. He advocates a world order based on open systems, open sources, open services. To read his warnings that the pressure exercised by large corporations keen on imposing universal technological and software standards might entail a deadly loss of creativity and ingenuity across the board is, I think, surprising given his close working relations with some of the same companies he implicitly refers to. It's an act of true intellectual honesty and professional rigor for which any independent business consultant should take credit.

One last thought. Try what I did when I got my copy of this book. Put it on your bookshelf among the many others dedicated to the narration of this fantastic first phase of the e-business revolution. It will show the real gap between the development of the e-technologies and their actual use. Not in theory nor under macroeconomic scenarios, but in real day to day practices. As this gap opens up and is reduced every moment, depending on our company's dynamics, Amor's book should be consulted to measure the changing distance between dreams and reality. The introduction of Internet applications is a long chain of motives and reasons which moves and adapts itself to the needs of individual companies and entrepreneurs. Day after day. Day after day. Endlessly.

And when you have finished reading Chapter 8 it's probably time to go back to Chapter 1. An evolution rather than a revolution. This is what it's all about.

Paolo Glisenti
Freelance E-Business and Internet Author
Roma, Italy, December 10th, 2000

INTRODUCTION

The New Paradigm

Over the last few years the Internet has evolved from a scientific network into a platform that is enabling a new generation of businesses. The first wave of electronic business was fundamentally the exchange of information. But, with time, more and more types of businesses have become available electronically. Nowadays we can buy goods online, book vacations or have texts translated over the Internet in an instant. Home banking, for example, is one application that is already provided by most banks around the world. Looking up an account balance, transferring money and performing other transactions are done every day by millions of people. Public administration has discovered the Internet as a means to talk to the general public at election times. And it will not be long before we see general elections decided on the Internet.

The reason I have called this book *The E-business (R)evolution* is twofold. Technology has revolutionized the way we can do business, but business itself is only slowly adapting to the new possibilities. The New Economy needs a new paradigm, but the process of conversion will take some time to complete. The necessary technology is ready and waiting. The *e-business* in the title is not the same as IBM uses it; it is much more, as you will discover by reading this book. There is a reason why the "B" in e-business is not written in capital letters, as in IBM's case.

The Internet is changing the concept of programming applications. We are moving toward pervasive computing and electronic services. Jini technology is one of the first implementations of what one could call "one world, one computer." Jini allows every device to talk to every other device in a common language (a device in this case can be anything with a silicon chip inside it and an Internet connection). Other companies have started to develop similar paradigms, technologies and visions, such as IBM's T Spaces technology and Hewlett-Packard's E-Services strategy.

You have probably already heard of the empty refrigerator that sends an e-mail to the grocery with a request for fresh milk to be delivered to the doorstep before breakfast in the morning. Prototypes have already been built. A bar-code reader is able to detect which products are put into the fridge and taken out afterward. For many people, this may not be a necessity. The grocery store is more than just a place where people can buy food. It is a social place where people meet, which cannot be simply replaced by two chips. But for those who do not have the time to do the shopping, or are not able to walk to the store, this may become a valuable option.

New technologies are emerging slowly. In Helsinki, for example, it is already possible to pay for a soft drink with a cellular phone. Instead of inserting coins into the vending machine it is possible to call the machine with a cell phone, using a special number that in turn releases a can of soda. In Europe more people have cellular phones than computers, therefore the crossover of communication technology and information technology is on the verge of happening. Through cell-broadcast people with GSM cellular phones are able to receive news flashes, which can keep them up-to-date on the latest political and financial developments. The future of computing lies in devices—not stand-alone personal computers.

Other applications may be more useful to all of us, but the Internet is generally not designed to be a mass medium such as television or radio. The Internet is an infrastructure for many mass and niche markets. Two applications, which may be suitable for many car owners, are the following:

1. **Cost Saving**—Imagine your car sending a request to all gas stations within ten miles to find out which one is the cheapest. The navigational system of the car will then direct the driver to that gas station.

2. **Life Saving**—After an accident the car is able to detect how severe the crash was and will call an ambulance and the police, if appropriate.

Pervasive Computing

Pervasive computing is therefore the next logical step in the evolution of computers. The Internet has enabled the connection of computers and allowed them to exchange information. Connecting all types of devices will create a network that is thousands of times larger than the current Internet, offering more than a simple exchange of information. It will enable businesses to offer services, which can be as basic as, "print something onto the nearest printer" or as complex as, "create a short document on the financial situation within the company."

In such an interconnected world everything becomes part of one huge system. This may sound like the evil Borgs in the *Star Trek* saga, who say: "You will be assimilated." The Borgs are a civilization that work and live in a collective; they have only one mind. Without the other members of the collective they are lost. Their mission is to assimilate all other cultures and to incorporate all other technologies into their own. They believe that resistance to change is futile.

Hopefully the introduction of new technologies will not be based on pressure, but on agreements, understanding and cooperation. It would be very worrisome if this goal were achieved on propriety standards, and it could be totally superfluous if this goal were achieved by wasting useful resources. But it can also mean a leap into the future if this New World is built on open systems, open sources, open standards and open services. It remains to be seen if Jini will succeed, but the general direction is set, and everybody will have to follow it over the next few years in order not to fall behind.

Pervasive computing is only just getting off the ground, but getting to know all about it will give you the edge over your competitors when it comes to implementing it. But before getting into pervasive computing, one should think about one's business idea. In order to be successful on the Internet it is necessary to get that right first, otherwise the best IT infrastructure will not be of any help.

Business on the Net Today

If you look at the current situation, you can divide the Internet presence of enterprises into six phases:

- **Phase 1: "Hello, I'm online, too"**—In this phase, the company has set up a Web page. However, no real structure is provided. There is no search engine, there is only some of the product information, and there is no link to the current stock price and no way to communicate with people within the company.

- **Phase 2: "Structured Web site"**—The Web site now has a decent structure; you can use a search engine to search for keywords, see all the company information, and exchange messages within the company.

- **Phase 3: "Trying e-commerce"**—The company is trying to sell information, goods, etc., online, but the system is not connected to the real databases on the company intranet. It is slow, costs a lot of money and is not really secure. There is no way to hook up your company's back-end system to the back-end of another company.

- **Phase 4: "Doing e-business"**—Your Web site has a direct link into the legacy systems of your intranet, allows retrieval of information from internal databases, and uses secure protocols to transmit data between your company and the customer or another business. You are able to save costs and start making a profit from your online business.

- **Phase 5: "Pervasive e-business"**—Using any device that contains a chip (cellular phone, car, etc.) people are able to connect to your data and transmit or receive the desired information to do e-business.

- **Phase 6: "One world, one computer"**—All chip-based devices are interconnected and create one huge information resource. The devices are able to interchange any type of information on an object-oriented level. Applications are transparent to these devices. Users won't know where the answer to their problems came from.

Most companies nowadays are somewhere near or between phase 2 and phase 3. Most of them are moving toward phase 4. One important part of this book is to show what will happen after phase 4. Pervasive computing is the most likely thing to happen. This book will show what such a world could look like and what the alternatives are. It tries to identify the standards and the owners, and tries to find out what the Internet will be like in five years time.

Who Should Read This Book

This book is intended for the electronic entrepreneur who is either thinking about setting up an e-business or has already set one up. It provides you with a checklist of all the important items in the e-business arena. You can check immediately how much of your business is ready to go online. After having read this book you will be able to build up your own e-business or enhance it dramatically to make it not only yet another Web page, but also a real financial stronghold for your company.

This book is the basis for your e-business decisions. The information given in this book is not technological hype that will evaporate next year; it will be the basis for your e-business over the next few years. The book covers all the topics required for a complete and secure e-business solution. It goes into great depth in each topic, so that you will be competent enough to decide which of the solutions described fits your needs best.

The major question for all technologies in this book is: "Why should I use it?" There are enough books on how to use a technology and many people know how to do it, but many people forget to ask why. Sometimes it makes sense to avoid new technologies, as it may only add extra overhead to the work that needs to be done. So, whenever people come up to you and explain a new technology, do not ask how it can be done, but why it should be done.

This book contains many examples and links to Web pages. As the Internet is changing every day, it cannot be guaranteed that every link will be available at the time of reading. As a convenience to the readers, a Web site has been set up that contains a list of all examples used in the book. The list on the Web site will be updated at regular intervals. In addition, the Web site will contain links to other e-business sites and more information on the topics in the book.

How This Book Is Organized

The book is divided into four parts. The first part is the foundation for online activities. It introduces the reader to the basic concepts of the Internet and how to do business via the Internet. It takes both technology and business into consideration, and does not forget to talk about the legal aspects of doing business via the Internet. Finally, it explains how marketing on the Web should be done in order to be successful. Without marketing, your online business will lack the visibility it requires to succeed.

The second part talks about how e-business applications are used for Internet-, intranet- or extranet-based applications. It looks at the questions from all perspectives: client software, middleware, and back-end systems. Its focus is on search engines, portals, shopping and ORM sites. Customer relationship management, content management and knowledge management are such important parts of an e-business solution that I created an extra chapter for these topics. Last but not least, one chapter is dedicated to communication possibilities via the Internet. Using this information you are prepared to go online and discover other businesses, what they offer and how they did it.

The third part explains the technologies that are below your applications. This is done from the technical and business points of view, to show you the business cases that are viable right now. Each chapter contains a set of business cases that are evaluated, and it is explained how Internet technologies help to resolve issues with the business cases and how to extend one's business through new technology.

The fourth part is an outlook into the future of electronic business, and gets into more detail on how software and hardware will be developed in the future. The Open Source model is explained, as well as how pervasive computing has been implemented. The last chapter of the book explores future possibilities.

Appendix A offers a glossary of e-business terms used throughout the book. In case you do not understand a certain term, look here. Appendix B describes how a business can be moved to the Internet, and what is required to do so. It not only lists the ideas, and the required hardware and software, but also goes into detail regarding costs and the benefits. Appendix C is a short list of my favorite Web sites, ordered by subject areas. Appendix D enters the world of localization and internationalization of Web sites and Appendix E offers some insight on the death of dot.coms.

Acknowledgments

There are many people I would like to thank who helped me to make this project a reality. This book is dedicated to Sabine, the woman I love. I thank her for her love, support and understanding. I really tried to write as much of the book as possible while she was asleep, but especially in the end I had not much time left for her. I worked on this book besides my real job as a consultant and project manager for Hewlett-Packard. Sabine, I want to tell you that I love you.

I also want to thank my family for their support and their suggestions. Although being half-English (father) and half-Czech (mother) I wrote this book for an American publisher in U.S. English. I still tried to keep the balance between U.S. American interests and the rest of the world. Although some reviewers complained that the book did not only provide American examples, I did not want to create a U.S. only book, as the world out there is much bigger and showing all ideas is so much more interesting.

I want to thank all readers of the first edition. Although some complained about the lack of editing (which had been resolved soon after the first reprints), many readers liked the way the book was organized. That was probably the reason why it got translated into so many languages. The book has been published in Bulgarian, Chinese, Dutch, English, French, German, Italian, Japanese, Korean, Russian, Spanish, with more languages to come. I appreciated the readers writing to me with suggestions and complaints and hope that this will continue with the second edition of the book.

I owe Hewlett-Packard, my managers—Isabelle Roux-Buisson and Albert Frank—and my colleagues a big thank you for their support and the many general discussions on business on the Internet that were conducted in coffee breaks and during meetings that made me change some parts of the book while writing it. A special thank you goes out to Susan Wright and Pat Pekary at HP Press for managing the internal HP publication processes. I also want to thank Rosie Chiovari, Phil Mindigo and Peter O'Neill in the United States for supporting the crazy European writing a book on business on the Internet.

The people at Prentice Hall were also very responsive and helpful and I want to thank them for the continued support during the writing of the book, without which this book would not have been possible. I want to thank Jill Pisoni, Linda Ramagnano, Gail Cocker, Camille Trentacoste and Vincent Janoski for the production of the first edition and Jill Harry (former Pisoni), Justin Somma and Jennifer Blackwell for the production of the second edition.

And last, but not least, I want to thank Uta Winter of MediaTechbooks[1] and Samantha Shurety of IBM[2] for reviewing my book at various stages of the development, and for their invaluable support, ideas and suggestions.

E-Business Is Dead, Long Live E-Business

This section has been written for the second edition. In the second half of 2000 many startup companies went bankrupt and the stock exchanges around the world sank to record lows. Some people thought that this would be the end of e-commerce and e-business, just to be proved wrong. In April 2001 I

---

[1]http://www.mediatechbooks.de/

[2]http://www.ibm.com/

started revising the *The E-Business (R)Evolution* although there was still a lot of bad press regarding the Internet and E-Business. Despite the bad press the Internet platform had been established at that time. More and more people use the Internet on a daily basis and it has become a commodity that can be used all around the world. During my last holiday in Asia I visited the United Arab Emirates, Malaysia and Singapore. In all of these countries I was able to find an Internet cafe within five minutes, connect to my mail server and check for new e-mails. But not only did the Internet work, also my mobile phone worked flawlessly. The GSM mobile phone standard makes it so I can use it almost all over the world (except for the United States).

At the same time more and more companies have realized that there is a need for a digital presence. The online retailers who survived the battlefield that was the year 2000 are emerging stronger, smarter and more competitive.

A Shop.org[3] study, called "The State of Online Retailing 4.0" conducted by The Boston Consulting Group shows that in April 2001, 72 percent of catalogers, 43 percent of store-based retailers and 27 percent of Web-based retailers are profitable at an operating level. Despite the dot-com shakeout, online retailers overall were able to reduce losses as a percentage of revenues. Operating losses decreased as a percentage of revenue, from 19 percent in 1999 to 13 percent, or 5.6 billion U.S. dollars, in 2000.

Customer acquisition costs for all online retailers fell from an average of 38 Dollar/Euro in 1999 to 29 Dollar/Euro in 2000, the report says. Web-based retailers, in particular, were able to bring customer acquisition costs down from a high of 82 Dollar/Euro to 55 Dollar/Euro over the same period. Indeed, the best performing Web-based retailers (the top 50 percent) reduced acquisition costs to an average of 14 Dollar/Euro per customer, rivaling the performance of catalog-based retailers.

If I look at the number of e-business projects we did in the E-Solutions Division Europe of Hewlett-Packard, I can see a clear increase in 2001, although 2000 was the year of hype. During 2000 many people talked about e-business, but only very few did something. This was one of the major factors that resulted in the crash of the stock market. Now more people really do something and talk less about it, reducing the expectations in these companies and increasing their stock value.

To make it easier for many of you to understand the reasons why so many companies failed, I have added Appendix E to the book, which contains a lot of information about famous dot.coms that failed. The second edition of *The E-Business (R)Evolution* is based on the reader's input and the changes in the market. I appreciate any input from readers and look forward to incorporate it into the next edition of the book.

The book contains a lot of common software products and interesting Web sites. The software packages and Web sites are most likely to change, so please

---

[3]http://www.shop.org/

use the references as a guide and indicator, and use a search engine or portal site to get more information about a Web site, if it is not available anymore.

Daniel Amor
danny@ebusinessrevolution.com
http://www.ebusinessrevolution.com
Stuttgart, Germany, June 16th, 2001

Part I

The Foundation

Chapter 1

INTRODUCTION TO INTERNET BUSINESS

1.1 Being Online

1.1.1 The Basics

Flashback. When I first connected to the Internet in 1992 it was still a quiet place. Apart from sending and receiving email, downloading software via FTP, or chatting via IRC, "talk," and "nn," there was not much else to do. Programs like Archie and Gopher were in vogue, and using the Internet required a lot of UNIX knowledge. All I had at that time was an ASCII-text terminal connected via Telnet to a Hewlett-Packard Apollo Workstation. I did not have a Web browser, since no browser software had been invented yet. Besides the Internet, there were other computer networks, such as the Fidonet, that were far more attractive at the time because they had colorful interfaces.

When I wrote the first edition of this book back in 1999, I had to start up my laptop and use a Web browser to connect to the Internet, either via the Local Area Network (LAN) at work or via the modem at home. I was able to do all I did in 1992—and more. Fidonet[1] is still around, but its popularity has decreased a lot since the early days, and most of it has been incorporated in the Internet over the last few years, as have most other old computer networks, like BitNet and MausNet.

In 2001 things have become even simpler. Using my laptop, I connect via wireless LAN (WLAN) to the next wireless hub that is connected to the Internet. Both my HP laptop at work and my iBook at home can easily exchange information, and I no longer have to use any cables. Some HP offices have WLAN hubs already installed (the rest will soon follow), which means that I can walk into the office and have instant intranet/Internet connectivity without setting up a network configuration. The same is true at home. I can easily use my HP laptop to connect from home to the HP intranet and can exchange files with my

---

[1]http://www.fidonet.org/

3

iBook without having to connect them physically. WLAN hubs have been set up at various airports, providing instant Internet connectivity throughout the airport. Helsinki and Singapore are two of the airports that support WLAN. Although not yet common, the demand is huge, and many companies are working, using the same IEEE standard (802.11) to ensure that interoperability can be guaranteed. The ELSA AirLancer[2] card on Windows 2000 works without trouble with Apple's AirPort[3] card on Mac OS X. And this is true for many other hardware vendors and software platforms as well. WLAN increases the compatibility across platforms and makes the exchange of information and services even easier than before.

With a simple-to-use browser, I am able to do my emailing, upload and download software, use online chats, and search for keywords on the Internet. I am able to check my balance at the bank and buy flowers online. All services can be accessed with this single piece of software, making it easy for the layperson to access different services, as all are provided through the same interface. Technical complexities are hidden from the user by technologies that provide a seamless, easy-to-understand interface for many different situations and processes. The software has become so easy to use that even nontechnical people have email addresses.

If we look at the Internet demography in detail we can see that the online buying and selling practices of Internet users are representative of the practices of the general public. Exact figures are not available for the Internet, and so we do not know exactly how many people are online, nor do we know how many businesses there are. This is because of the structure of the Internet. It is different than anything we have seen before. Traditional methods of measuring audience just do not work. With all other types of media the number of offerings is limited by region; for example, 40 television stations or five larger newspapers for Tuscany, Italy. Counting viewers or sales is relatively easy, as the number of newspaper stands and televisions is limited in the region. This makes it easy to define prices advertisers have to pay for the advertising sections. On the Internet we have unlimited space and resources. People from Tuscany may choose from one of the 40 TV stations, or choose *any* location in cyberspace. And anybody who wants to *appear* as someone who lives in Tuscany can do it easily by choosing another virtual identity.

For the first time, a mass media has more offerings than it has potential users. More importantly, for the first time, everybody is able to interact. People are able to change content, add information, and link resources to logical structures and offer them to others. On TV, we have a limited set of channels; on the Internet, users have their own channels, moving through cyberspace at their own pace and in their own direction, guided only by their interest and curiosity. On TV, you can normally watch one program at a time; on the Internet,

---

[2]http://www.elsa.de/
[3]http://www.apple.com/

you can watch multiple Web pages at a time. Sometimes I have more than 40 browser windows open and flip through them while searching for specific information. There is no way to determine how much time I spend on a particular page.

It will be just a matter of years before almost everyone will be connected to the Internet. The fear that it will replace real life is unnecessary. Just as TV has not replaced radio or books, the cyberworld won't replace the real world. But it will add a new dimension to human life, no doubt. The dream of the global village will eventually become a reality. Everything and everyone will be only a click away. Prices for hardware and software are dropping, making them available even to the poorer people in the world.

1.1.2   Distance Learning

The University of Amsterdam has already created special online lectures for people who are not able to attend the regular lectures in Amsterdam. The Network University (TNU)[4] is a large-scale project that aims to provide highly interactive, innovative, Internet-based distance learning to a global audience that opts for the advantages of a new form of academic education. The target groups for this service are physically disadvantaged students and students from overseas, mostly from Africa and Asia, who are able to pay for the lectures, but may not be able to pay to live in Europe, or may not be able to get a visa for the Netherlands. Through new Internet communication technologies and standard Web pages, the virtual lecturer talks to the students, who in turn are able to communicate with the lecturer via the Internet and telephone.

The master's degree programs offered by TNU are rooted in an interdisciplinary approach to the social sciences. The programs are distinguished by their full use of the Internet as a medium, providing access to vast amounts of information as well as a channel of communication that facilitates new ways of learning. The participants of TNU are not at the receiving end of a one-way communication process but, through the mediation of technology, actively contribute to the content and future development of the program. The online learning process is supported by access to an Internet-based *content call-center* that will offer 24-hour supervision and feedback. This feedback is offered in different languages.

Interactivity, global reach, the multilingual and multicultural approach, and the nearly 100 percent availability are the keys to success in this project— especially for students from all over the world who live in many different time zones.

---

[4]http://www.netuni.nl/

1.1.3 Space and Time on the Internet

The reasons for an organization's success on the Internet are radically different from what we have seen in the past. It is not the bigger fish swallowing the smaller fish, nor is it the faster runner beating the slower runner. In the information society, the more knowledgeable people are making more deals than the less informed. Knowledge is quality, and this is where business is heading.

Nicolas Hayek, president of the Swatch Group,[5] which produces the highly successful "Swatch"[6] watch, has created a new time standard for the Internet age. Instead of dividing the day into 24 hours, a day is divided into 1,000 Swatch Beats. The Internet time uses its own meridian, the Biel Mean Time (BMT), named after a town in Switzerland. One Swatch Beat equals 86.4 seconds.

Although many people may think that the Internet time is a gag, it reflects the way work is done in the digital age. Instead of being served from nine to five, customers are served around the clock, whenever they need a product or service. Time zones and geographical boundaries no longer have importance. Once someone has gone digital, his or her concerns are in the here and now. Although time zones are important for people to communicate with each other, they have become irrelevant for business. It does not matter if it is five o'clock in Boston or ten o'clock in Nairobi; the customers on the Internet want to receive the goods, information, or service they have requested—now.

Through the Internet, everything moves closer together, resulting in nearly automatic response time. As the Internet is getting faster every day through new inventions and new programs—such as the Internet 2[7] initiative in the United States—every company will be as fast as its competition and just as near to the customer as the competition. Distance, size, and speed become irrelevant. In order to be successful, the service needs to be *better* than the competition. Quality of service becomes the ultimate success factor. Due to new technologies, speed becomes less relevant.

Through the Internet, many businesses can offer their services at maximum speed (converging to a delivery time of zero). New technologies such as DSL and cable modems allow customers to surf at very high speeds. As everyone is able to reach maximum speed, it does not make sense for businesses to try to be faster than the competition. Purchasing decisions today are less frequently based on convenience of location and more frequently based on brand, quality, and price. This simplifies the lives of the customers. Instead of choosing the objective best product, they choose the subjective best product.

The Internet reduces the three dimensions and time of our physical world to a single point, to the here and now of the customer. Each customer has his or her own universe, which needs to be addressed when offering goods,

---

[5] http://www.theswatchgroup.ch/

[6] http://www.swatch.com/

[7] http://www.internet2.edu/

information, or services online. Through personalization, the universe of the Internet appears differently to everyone. The Internet is constantly changing; making *change* the only constant you can count on. Products, ideas, and prices, for example, are changing much faster than ever before.

1.1.4   The Web Is Not the Internet

Many people confuse two terms that are related but not identical in meaning: the Internet and Internet Protocol (IP). The Internet, which evolved from the military ARPANet, has its roots in the 1960s. Its basic idea was to create a network that would continue to work as a whole, even when parts of it collapse. The Internet refers to a network infrastructure that is built on certain standards—Internet standards—that are used by all participants to connect to each other. The specification of the IP does not specify which type of information, services, or products should be exchanged. The IP defines how the flow of information is organized. Chapter 3 contains more information on IP and related standards.

These specifications reside on a layer above the Internet layer, and one of these protocols for the exchange of information is the hypertext transfer protocol (HTTP), which is utilized by the World Wide Web. In addition to HTTP are other protocols that enable people to communicate via email (POP3, SMTP, IMAP), online chat (IRC), and newsgroups (NNTP). The Web offers the exchange of documents via HTTP (mainly in the HTML format), allowing browsers to correctly display the content.

The World Wide Web is just one of the numerous services offered on the Internet and does not specify if a particular Web page is available on an intranet, extranet, or the Internet. It provides a simple-to-use interface that allows people with very little computer knowledge to access Web services all over the Internet. These Web services include content, products, and services, which can be viewed or ordered through the Web browser. The Web browser is a synonym to the first generation of the commercial Internet. It allows customers to serve themselves over the Web. The second generation of commercial Internet usage will move away from "do it yourself" to "do it for me." This new paradigm, also known as *pervasive computing*, will automate many processes that customers have been using via Web browsers. Pervasive computing is still a vision and will take quite a while to become a reality. Therefore, browsers will continue to remain important over the next few years.

But one trend can be seen, the move away from a computer-based Internet. Today, mobile phones, TV sets and kiosks are used to access the Internet and new browsers need to be created to support these devices and new web pages need to be created that support the output on these devices. The Internet is diversifying not only in the content area, but also in the technology and business area.

1.2 Defining E-Business

1.2.1 Overview

One of the first companies to use the term *e-business* was IBM,[8] back in 1997. At that time, the company launched its first thematic campaign built around the term. Until then, *e-commerce* had been the buzzword. The shift in terminology also meant a shift in paradigm. To that point, selling was the only experience that people could reproduce on the Web. Broadening the approach to allow more types of business on the Web created the new term *e-business*. E-commerce is just one aspect of e-business, like e-franchising, emailing, and e-marketing. E-business is about using convenience, availability, and worldwide reach to enhance existing businesses or creating new *virtual* business. IBM defines e-business as "a secure, flexible and integrated approach to delivering differentiated business value by combining the systems and processes that run core business operations with the simplicity and reach made possible by Internet technology."

IBM's e-business is what results when you combine the resources of traditional information systems with the vast reach of the Web and connect critical business systems directly to critical business constituencies—customers, employees and suppliers via intranets, extranets, and the Web. By connecting your traditional IT systems to the Web, you become an e-business. Most companies deploy applications on the Internet that make it easier to do the things you already do.

Forward-thinking organizations are beginning to automate, organize, standardize, and stabilize the services offered in order to create and maintain sustainable computer-mediated relationships throughout an e-business life cycle. At about the same time, other companies such as Hewlett-Packard,[9] also started to offer complete solutions for e-business, including software and hardware bundles and e-business consulting. In April 1999, Hewlett-Packard launched a new marketing campaign: "Hewlett-Packard—The E-Service Company." More and more hardware companies are moving their business away from hardware and starting to offer consulting services and software as well as hardware is not very profitable anymore.

You may be surprised to learn that the concept of electronic business was invented before the Internet ever became popular. In the 1970s, e-business was already popular among financial networks that used propriety hardware and software solutions. Electronic Data Interchange (EDI) was also available long before the Internet was used for it. But without the Internet, e-business would not have been possible on such a large scale. Private networks used in the 1970s and 1980s cost too much for smaller enterprises and were not accessible for private use.

---

[8]http://www.ibm.com/
[9]http://www.hp.com/

Remember, the Internet is not just another application; it is neither software nor hardware. It is the environment for the business and communications of the future. The Internet combines many existing technologies into one framework. Computer networks and communications networks, such as fax, telephone, and pager, are already integrated into the Internet. Sending a fax via the Internet is just as easy as receiving a voice mail. Not only are different types of communication possible via the Internet, but so is the conversion between them. For example, it is possible to convert a fax to an email or an email to a message for a cell phone. This enables businesses that use different methods of communication to come together more easily. In addition, it is possible to translate the communication text from one language to another, on the fly, not only between human languages like English and Russian, but also between programming and database languages. Using these interfaces, it is possible to connect a wide range of different types of hardware and software.

1.2.2 Communication Gateways

Hotels all over the world offer an example of the integration of technologies. They use the Internet without having a direct link to it. They use email to fax gateways. People can go to the Web site of the hotel and send an email to one of the hotels. The emails are collected at the Internet provider where the Web site is located and sent via fax to the hotel. This is all done automatically. The hotel can then either respond via traditional fax or telephone or can respond via fax to the email gateway. Suddenly, people from all over the world can reach that particular hotel, book rooms, or get information for the cost of a local phone call—a fraction of what the cost used to be. Instead of calling or sending a fax to the hotel, which may be located in another country, customers can dial in to their local Internet provider to connect to the Internet and send off a request.

Although this is clearly not the best way to communicate with your clients over the Internet, it is probably the cheapest, as you do not have to invest in new equipment. All you have to do is Internet-enable your existing devices, using gateways. This is the first step many companies take when they are unsure about whether or not to embark on an online venture.

E-business, the Internet, and globalization all depend on each other. The more global players that exist, the more e-business they want to do. The more e-business is online, the more people will be attracted to get direct Internet access. And the more people online, the more global players will arise.

E-business can be divided into three areas. It can be within the organization using an intranet or business-to-employee (B2E) infrastructure. An intranet uses Internet standards for electronic communication, allowing people to see organization-specific Web sites. These Web sites are separated from the outside world by firewalls and other security measures. People from outside the organization are not able to see these private pieces of information.

Apple,[10] for example, built an intranet Web site to sell older Apple systems and accessories to its employees. Before that, Apple emailed special promotion details to employees, who then ordered the products over the telephone. The intranet Web site now allows employees to obtain current information and place orders online, eliminating time-consuming phone calls.

IBM[11] is using its "Refurbished Computer Warehouse" Web site to sell PCs coming off leases. The site allows employees to view the machines' specifications and then purchase them online with credit cards or through traditional methods such as the telephone. These offerings are restricted to employees, and are not accessible nor visible to the outside world.

Since employees get special prices, offering these prices to the public would put pressure on the company to reduce the prices for the rest of the world. Depending on the security policies of the organization or company, people may be allowed to connect over the Internet via virtual private networks (VPNs) to the intranet, using encryption lines and strong authentication for identification purposes.

The second e-business area concerns the business-to-business (B2B) deals conducted over an extranet. An extranet consists of two intranets connected via the Internet, whereby two organizations are allowed to see confidential data of the other. Normally, only small parts of information are made available to the partner, just enough to enable the business. Business-to-business networks existed long before the Internet. Many organizations had private networks to talk to their partners and customers, but maintaining them was very expensive. Through the use of the Internet, the costs have been cut dramatically. In most cases, VPNs are used to keep the business transactions private.

The third area of e-business is the business-to-consumer (B2C) area. This is the most prominent, and one which most people have already seen. The Web sites of Quelle,[12] a German fashion retailer; Discolandia,[13] an online CD shop; and Megazine[14] offer goods and services to anybody who comes to their Web sites. Traditionally, this is what most people know as e-commerce: selling products on the Web. But as we will discover, B2C e-business involves much more.

No matter in which of the three areas you want to do business, it is important to ask the right questions before going online. Just having a Web page or the infrastructure for an intranet, extranet, or the Internet is no solution. You need to decide on your target group and think about the processes involved.

Technically speaking, there is no difference between an intranet, an extranet, and the Internet. Extranets and intranets (which can be viewed only by certain groups) are subsets of the Internet. Therefore, this book does not

---

[10]http://www.apple.com/

[11]http://www.ibm.com/

[12]http://www.quelle.de/

[13]http://www.discolandia.com/

[14]http://www.megazine.ch/

make a distinction between the three forms of networks, as electronic business can be conducted in basically the same way over all three. With a restricted group, it is easier to force certain technical standards, but otherwise they are very similar. The differences will be specified when appropriate.

1.2.3 E-Business Statistics

Presentations, talks, and books about e-business will give you statistics on the Internet, its users, and prospective businesses. There are problems with many of these statistics, so they are basically avoided in this book; instead, we'll focus on the things that really matter.

If you look at the numbers of online users, you will see they are increasing. Depending on which statistics you believe, the numbers are increasing either faster or slower, but the point is clear: They are growing. The same applies to business. Every day more business is done via the Web. But how much exactly, nobody knows. Even if we could determine the statistics in a given moment, the numbers would be outdated in the next. With millions and millions of servers and clients connected to the Internet, it is almost impossible to get precise data. There is no precise definition of what an Internet user is or what business on the Internet means. An Internet "user" can be anything ranging from a browser window, a cookie session, a real person, or a Web proxy. It all depends on your view of the world. If I connect from work to a certain Web page, I have to use a Web proxy server that relays my request and saves the pages in a cache, just in case somebody else in my company needs the same information. The Web server sees only the proxy address, so those 6,000 people working at my company can appear to be one user.

Although many people use statistics to show how successful the Internet is, the numbers aren't often used. Figures for such a fast-changing medium look outdated immediately, even if they were once correct. There is no doubt that the Internet is a success and can be used in a highly successful manner for your company. Therefore, this book contains a lot of real-world (or even better, cyber-world) examples from the Internet, both of companies that are successful and those that have failed.

Once you have built a Web site, it will be useful to create statistics on the use of the Web pages, but those statistics will help you only with your Web site and will never give you an idea of the Internet as a whole.

The Internet is the first mass medium that allows true real-time interaction. Radio, television, newspapers, and catalogs deliver information to your home, but there is no way of direct communication back to the others involved in a certain process. You can send an order back to the catalog company or send a letter to your newspaper, but this is not what you get when you go in a shop or walk into the newspaper office. There, you get an immediate reaction on behalf of your request, and this is exactly what the Internet provides. It moves everyone together; every piece of information, every service, and every business, is instantly available, anytime. The dream of the global village becomes true.

The winners of the Internet today are the UPSs and Federal Expresses of the world. Since many products for sale on the Internet are not digitized, someone needs to ship the products from the online merchant to the customers. This will change somewhat in the future, as books, music, and videos—the best sellers so far—are digitized easily.

1.2.4   Internet Demographics

There are some statistics worth mentioning in relation to a change in the demographics on the Internet. A few years ago the white male young academic in the United States was the prime user of the Internet. These days, a change towards a more diverse Internet has taken place. There is probably no ethnic group in the world that has absolutely no connection to the Internet. While Internet presence in the United States is still probably the overall highest, most European countries are following suit and South America and Asia are not far behind. Several Web sites have started to deal with this subject, such as the CyberAtlas from Internet.com[15]. See Figure 1.1.

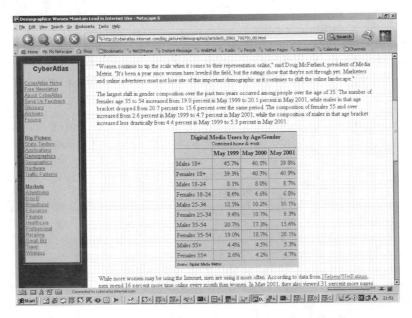

Figure 1.1. Information on Internet Demographics

Brazil is such an example, and in some areas Brazil is even leading the increase in Internet presence. More than 90 percent of Brazilian taxpayers

---

[15]http://cyberatlas.internet.com/

complete their tax statements over the Internet or on a floppy disk. Twelve million Brazilian regularly go online, and that translates into about 70 percent of the Latin-American Internet population. This accounts only for the rich southern portion of the country. In stark contract, the north has millions of poor farmers who have to fight for electricity and clean water.

In Southern Brazil, even the *Favelas*—the slums in Rio de Janerio and Sao Paolo—provide Internet cafes for educational purposes. The government is trying to lead the way and an electronic government initiative has already been put in place. Everything is linked together digitally and the government promotes the rollout of a countrywide fibre network. Many schools are now equipped with an Internet connection. Teachers are being trained over the Net. Other countries, like Mexico and Malaysia, offer Internet cafes even in small towns and villages. The Internet has evolved and has become a truly global entity.

While many countries have been involved in the *The E-Business (R)Evolution* over the past few years, there are still some countries reluctant to open up to the Internet. One of these countries is Cuba. Cuba uses the Internet mainly as a propaganda tool and to tell its version of history. For the Cuban people, the Internet is still mostly a no-go. In Cuba, only the government, some parts of the university, and foreign companies have access to the Internet, and companies have to pay extremely high fees. Cubans are not allowed to own a computer or a mobile phone. To make sure that tourists are not cut off from their email, there are now some Internet cafes, but the price for going online is extremely high. Going online for one hour is about half of the monthly income of a Cuban worker.

As you can see, the Internet is not welcomed in every country, since it provides a window into every dimension of life. Some governments fear that the free exchange of information will destroy their power base, and they have good reason to believe so. If someone can get hold of an Internet connection it is possible to exchange any type of information. Encryption technologies make it virtually impossible to break the seal of the information. These governments lose control over their people.

One important conclusion drawn from this discussion is that the Internet has diversified itself over the years. It provides a real global infrastructure to host the information, products, and services of any community on this planet and beyond. Information, communication, and transactions are conducted in any language, using any local customs that are desired. This means that it is not possible to target a global audience with one Web site. It is necessary to create local or virtual offerings for local or virtual communities. The trend of globalizing products and services has not been successful, at least so far. As a result, companies like MTV[16] have stepped down from providing one single music channel to the world and now provides localized versions for the different

---

[16]http://www.mtv.com/

markets. MTV Germany, MTV Italy, and MTV India are just three spin-offs of the global brand in local language, airing local music and starring local veejays.

A few years ago it was feared that the Internet would destroy languages and cultures because English was the predominant language. Today many think exactly the opposite. The Internet enables the preservation of languages and cultures that were about to extinct. There are no limits as language barriers are torn down.

1.2.5 Strategies for Digital Business

Going online simply because all of your competitors are online is the wrong strategy. There are many reasons to go online, so choose your primary goal. Otherwise it will be difficult to measure the success of your online venture. See what your competitors are doing and look out for new competitors that are now closer to you through the Internet.

In order to set realistic goals for your e-business, it is necessary to find out what portion of the overall business will be conducted via the Web in the next one to two years. Although you are most likely not getting the figures right—as the Internet is moving far too fast to be able to deliver reliable forecasts—these figures *can* indicate a trend. Where do you want to be within that timeframe? Do you want to go fully digital and use the Internet as the main channel for the business, or is it "just" the fourth channel for your existing business? This leads to the question of how fast you are planning to grow your company. Many Internet startups have managed to grow very quickly in a very short time. In order to do so, you need a working intranet based on the same key technologies as the Internet (e.g., TCP/IP). Only if your business is fully digitized are you able to grow at the rate at which eBay[17] or Yahoo![18] grew in 1998—more than 1,000 percent. This is essential, because the design of the electronic business and the support infrastructure must be able to handle growth effortlessly over time. Otherwise, the company may lose valuable time and money re-engineering a site after just a few months.

The expectations within the company need to be set right; otherwise, the online venture will not maximize your revenues. It takes much longer than was once thought to get a return on investment (ROI), and therefore your company needs some good financial backing.

Amazon.com took five years to recoup the investments it made. If the Internet is used for cost reduction, it is necessary to measure the costs for every single item upfront, which may cost more than using the Internet. In most cases, the reengineering of the business processes will help more than will using new technology. And since in many cases less staff time is required to perform a task, the staff's new "free time" can be used to implement new business processes without additional cost.

---

[17]http://www.ebay.com/
[18]http://www.yahoo.com/

Some of the most important reasons that a company needs to be on the Internet include the following:

- **Expand market reach**—Collect experience with a new customer segment.

- **Visibility**—Generate more visibility in your target market and gain "mind share."

- **Responsiveness**—Increase responsiveness to customers and partners.

- **New services**—Provide new services for customers and partners.

- **Strengthening business relationships**—Real-time data increases the profit for every partner involved.

- **Cost-reduction**—Reduce cost of product, support, service and estate.

- **Channel conflicts**—Prevent and resolve channel conflicts.

Table 1.1. Reasons for Going Online

Table 1.1 contains a short list of good reasons a company needs to go online. In the following section, each of these reasons is explored in more depth, and online examples are used to verify the reasoning. There are more reasons to go online, of course, but most companies will relate to one or more listed here. But be careful; do not let your competitors drive you to this decision. Be there *before* the competition, or take your time to develop a full business plan.

Once you have decided on the goals, you need to find criteria for measuring success. Cost reduction, for example, may not be truly measurable. If a printer manufacturer is offering printer drivers on its Web page, measuring the cost reduction may be difficult, as the company may not have measured the costs before the introduction of the online service. Sending out floppy disks and CD-ROMs would have cost more, but were part of the price for the printer. Measuring parts of the product separately may become difficult. Although measuring the cost reduction may not be possible, the introduction of the online service will reduce costs for more products, as they require your company to put a price tag on the various parts of a product.

1.2.6   Strengths and Advantages of E-Business

The strengths of e-business depend on the strengths of the Internet, the preferred infrastructure today and probably in the future as well. The Internet is available all over the world, 24 hours a day, 7 days a week. It is simple to use and the transaction costs for the end-user are low. The costs are also extremely low for the vendors on the Internet, compared to traditional distribution channels. The Internet allows two-way communications and is built around open standards. The two-way communication allows customers to provide direct feedback, and the open standards offer interoperability between companies, Web sites, and services. It is fairly easy to integrate processes, services, and products, once they have been digitized.

Using the latest software from BroadVision[19] and others, it is possible to customize your entire Web site for every single user, without incurring any additional costs. The masscustomization allows us to create Web pages, products and services that suit the users' requirements. A customized Web page includes not only the preferred layout of the customer, but also a preselection of goods the customer may be interested in. Internet pricing becomes irrelevant, as all prices drop to the lowest possible level. The only chance to distinguish your products from your competitor's is to add services that increase the value of the product without increasing its price (or increasing it just slightly).

Although many people are afraid of security breaches on the Internet, encryption, digital signatures, firewall software, and secure procedures all help to prevent them. This allows companies to offer private information to their customers and business partners without fearing an unauthorized person is able to see that particular information. Banks, for example, are able to allow customers to look at their account balance in real time without having to worry that a hacker will be able to break into the bank's computer system. This is achieved through the use of security components, and these same measures also allow trade on the Internet to expand.

Companies need to protect their customer profiles, as this information is very private and should not be passed from one organization to another. Customers should never get the feeling that they are being followed around on the Web site and that their every click is saved in a database. Providing a link to the privacy policy from the home page is a must for all electronic entrepreneurs, but only few have done it so far.

Table 1.2 provides a list of advantages of e-business. A Web site is a good opportunity for an organization to reduce the cost of labor. By using a Web site to answer your customers' questions, you will be able to offer 24-hour assistance and still reduce the number of calls to your service number. Your call center will be reduced, and those employees can be used to build an online database, helping customers to find even more answers online. This can go so far that only one or two people are needed to talk to customers on the phone, since

---

[19]http://www.broadvision.com/

Getting into electronic business has several advantages:

- **Global accessibility and sales reach**—Businesses can expand their customer base, and even expand their product line.

- **Closer relationships**—Business-to-business sellers can grow closer relationships.

- **Free samples**—Products can be sampled via the Web fast, easily and free of charge.

- **Reduced costs**—Businesses can reduce their costly production by dynamically adjusting prices.

- **Media breaks**—The Internet reduces the number of media breaks that are necessary to transport information.

- **Time to market**—Shorter time to market and faster response time to changing market demands.

- **Customer loyalty**—Improved customer loyalty and service through easier access to the latest information and a never-closing site.

Table 1.2. Advantages of E-business

most customers will get their answers from the company's Web site. Especially in tough economic times, it is very important to have low fix costs and labor is very expensive.

Companies that want to invest in electronic business are not restricted to the publishing, entertainment, information, and software industries, as you might imagine. Every company will need to invest in new technologies, as electronic business is more than just selling things online; it means moving processes and communications online, and this affects every company.

Today many work and communications processes have to deal with media breaks. A media break is a transition of information from one media to another, such as moving information from a fax to a database. This costs a lot of time. Consider this: A customer is calling a shop to order some products. The shop assistant will take the order and pass it on to the person who is responsible for booking it. This person may type in the order and send out the goods. This simple process already has two media breaks: phone to paper and paper to computer. The information did not change, but the medium that carried the information did. Electronic business drives the information onto one digital platform that can be shared by all the participants in the business process without the risk of losing parts of the information in a conversion process. Digital information is not only more convenient, but it allows new applications that were not possible before. For example, online tracking has become quite successful. This application could only be implemented because all relevant information is available electronically.

1.3   Reasons for Going Online

1.3.1   Expanding Market Reach

One of the major advantages of the Internet is its global availability. If you have a small company, it is now quite simple to expand your market reach beyond your geographic location and your current customer segments. Although this may relieve some of the pressure you experience in your current target market, it will mean new pressure from competitors who are already on the Internet and are trying to get into your markets. The first phase of expansion would be to collect experience with a new customer segment and the new Internet medium.

Barnes & Noble,[20] one of the largest chains of bookshops in the United States, was forced to open a "branch" on the Internet because it felt the pressure of Amazon.com.[21] Amazon sells books only over the Internet and attracts more and more of the people who traditionally went into the shops of Barnes & Noble. The online venture started small for Barnes & Noble, in order to gain experience, but grew fast after the initial pilot and has since become number two in the online bookselling market.

Tupperware, on the other hand, decided to ban all activities on the Internet for a long time. The Tupperware Web site[22] contained only marketing information. According to the CEO of Tupperware, in 1999 the Internet was used as a marketing medium only and they did not want to use it for anything else. The personal contact in the form of Tupperware parties is part of the company culture. It seems, though, that Tupperware was losing a huge opportunity, especially with people who just wanted to order another Tupperware container or replace one. These customers had to go to the next Tupperware party, which took up a lot more of the customers' precious time than some were willing to spend. It should be no surprise that in the beginning of 2000 Tupperware changed its mind and started to offer online shopping on its U.S. Web site (see Figure 1.2), allowing people to buy Tupperware products without having to attend one of their famous Tupperware parties.

---

[20]http://www.barnesandnoble.com/

[21]http://www.amazon.com/

[22]http://www.tupperware.com/

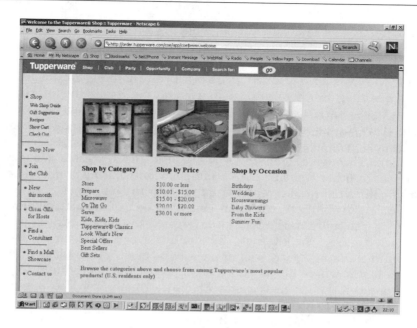

Figure 1.2. Online shopping at Tupperware.

On the Internet, every company that offers goods, services, or information is reduced to the same size: the size of the customer's browser window. Therefore, it is easy for a small online-translation service, for example, to compete with a large one. The customer will see differences in pricing, service, and the way the company presents itself on the Web. This, combined with what other people say about the online service, is the basis for the customer's decision on where they want to do business.

Marketing for the Web site is important. Many people choose a Web site because others are talking about it or because they have seen advertisements for it. If you had the choice between visiting Barnes & Noble's Web site or MediaTechBooks'[23] Web site, you would probably visit the first one because the brand name is well known. On the Internet, customers will also visit the second one to double-check prices and offerings, which is different from traditional shopping. Moving from one bookshop to another online takes only a few seconds and the customer does not feel the pressure of a sales associate, who traditionally may help the customer make his or her decision.

1.3.2 Generating Visibility

Another important goal, especially for small and medium-sized enterprises (the so-called SMEs) is to gain more visibility. The Internet allows a company to

---

[23]http://www.mediatechbooks.de/

present itself at very low cost. Although buying a computer and setting up an Internet connection may not be cheap, once you have incurred these costs, setting up new Web pages and adding prices, products, and information costs very little, and the costs for reproduction are practically nothing. You do not need to replicate a catalog, brochure, or flyer. You simply put it onto the Internet and it replicates itself. Each user generates his or her own copy when accessing your Web site. This is especially true when you use one-to-one marketing tools that allow the customer to see a personalized view of your products, services, and information. Through co-branding, you are also able to present your products and services on other Web sites. Co-branding means sharing brand names with other companies to provide greater trust towards the consumer.

Generating visibility is crucial for every company. The better known your company is, the more people will be interested in doing business with you. In the early years of the Internet, being online was a synonym for being cool and forward-thinking, but it was in no way a "must." Today it is difficult to find an industry where this is still true. Missing the opportunity to present your company on the Internet, even with only a simple Web site, is something nobody can afford to do today. Several years ago the Security First Network Bank[24] wanted to become the first Internet bank in the U.S. Now it is one of the largest electronic banks in the Internet business.

Early adopters have the advantage of getting to know technology in advance of competitors. Therefore, new technology enables small startups to become large organizations. Dell,[25] which began by selling computers over the phone, wanted to become the biggest computer retailer on the Internet. There is no doubt that they have achieved this goal. For Dell, it was easy to move from telephone business to Internet business. As they do not have a channel that involves shops and retailers, they did not have to resolve a potential channel conflict. All they did was move from one communications platform to another that offered them more possibilities.

With the traditional telephone business, Dell had to send out catalogs to its customers. Using the Internet, they have a 24/7 Web site with a lot of technology but few human resources behind it. Once the Web site was set up, Dell could accept orders and offer instant help without any user interaction. And since they still have their traditional telephone business their call center can now also be used to help Web customers.

1.3.3 Strengthening Business Relationships

Implementing B2B communication on the Internet has huge potential. In the past, many industries used EDI to simplify business processes and reduce the cost of communication between business partners. Through EDI, suppliers, manufacturers, distributors, and retailers are able to share information on the

---

[24]http://www.sfnb.com/
[25]http://www.dell.com/

inventory and enhance the flow of information and goods through the supply chain. Passing on the information electronically reduces the cost of communication and the number of errors.

The disadvantage of EDI is that it is very expensive and time consuming to implement; therefore, many SMEs do not use it. Once a company has introduced it, every partner that uses it needs it as well. Even if two companies have an existing EDI infrastructure, the special connection between these companies needs to be developed. Consider a manufacturer with 50 suppliers; the costs are enormous for the manufacturer if it has to implement 50 EDI infrastructures.

While the paradigm of EDI is good, the technology was too expensive. With the Internet, it has become accessible for all companies. Costs that have been reduced by 50 times are not infrequent, and EDI on the Web allows for more content. Exchange of multimedia information has been made possible and fosters much tighter relationships among participants. The real-time capabilities of the Internet provide a sense of teamwork and shared goals. EDI via the Internet enables all components and systems of a virtual value chain to communicate with each other automatically.

Early EDI implementations on the Web were proprietary standards, but more and more implementations of EDI via the Web use XML documents. For further information on XML, see Chapter 10.

1.3.4 Responsiveness

The Internet can easily support increased responsiveness to your customers. Increasing responsiveness to customers and partners is very important to tie customers to a company. Being responsive gives customers the feeling that they are being treated well. For example, Trans-O-Flex[26], a logistics and shipping company in Germany, gives customers the ability to check the location of their shipments at any time. Although this feature is now a must for all companies, it was revolutionary a few years ago.

Responsiveness also means that when customers email your company via email addresses that you have provided, their emails should be answered quickly and competently. If an employee does not know how to respond to an email request, he or she should know whom to ask within the company. As a rule of thumb, email should be responded to within one working day, even if you do not have the answers ready. Send a short notice that you have received the email and that you will try to help to resolve the queries.

Offering up-to-date information on your company to partners is also very important. GemPlus,[27] one of Europe's leading smart-card manufacturers, provides partners with sensitive, up-to-date information via a secure Web connection, using basic authentication and Secure Sockets Layer (SSL) encryption.

---

[26]http://www.trans-o-flex.de/

[27]http://www.gemplus.fr/

Partners are able to see this information by using their logins and passwords. This part of the Web site is GemPlus's extranet area.

As you can see, there is no difference technically between extranet and Internet, except for the limitations placed on the viewers.

1.3.5   Offering New Services

Offering new services is also a reason to go online. Introducing new services in traditional markets is difficult and expensive. The Internet, on the other hand, offers the possibility to introduce new services with very few startup costs. New services can be provided for customers and partners and for employees as well. A service for employees could be a search engine on an intranet. The larger a company grows, the harder it is to find relevant information on an internal network. Of course, a search engine is only helpful if all employees put their documents online. Even if they are not able to create HTML documents, it is fairly easy to upload existing documents to the intranet, which can then be indexed by the search engine. The search hit-rate for non-Web documents is lower than with HTML documents, but still much higher than if they were not online at all.

Hewlett-Packard's new service provides specific configuration bundles to resellers over its order@hp.com Web site.[28] Previously, Hewlett-Packard did not offer preconfigured bundles online. The next step was to offer an online configurator where partners, resellers, and end customers are now able to configure their PCs and UNIX servers using a simple Web page. Complex configurations need special configurator tools. More information on configurator tools can be found in Chapter 7.

AutoByTel,[29] the "Dell of the car industry," offers a complete set of car services online. It is possible to buy, rent, insure, and lease a car from a single Web site. AutoByTel, as the name suggests, used to sell cars via telephone, so moving to the Web was a natural thing to do.

MWG Biotech[30] is one of the leading biotech companies in Europe and one of the pioneers on the Internet. On the MWG Biotech Web page, you can find information about the company, products, and services, and can even use a tracking mechanism to find out about pending orders. In 1994 the company automated its DNA synthesis process, which allows individual control of the complete ordering, production, and delivery of oligonucleotide, a specialized tool used in biomedical research.

Once an oligonucleotide has been ordered, an order number and a tracking code is issued for each oligonucleotide. Using the order number and tracking code, customers can follow their orders from the actual ordering until the actual delivery. By 1999, 90.5 percent of all orders were placed electronically,

---

[28]http://euros.external.hp.com/

[29]http://www.autobytel.com/

[30]http://www.mwg-biotech.com/

via either email or the Web. In 2000 this figure rose to 95.5 percent. Through this innovative service, the number of order-related calls are significantly reduced and the sales department of MWG Biotech can work on the needs of the customers more efficiently. Figure 1.3 shows the Oligo Tracking application.

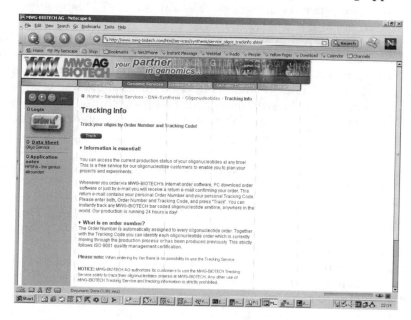

Figure 1.3. Oligo Tracking at MWG Biotech.

The expanding areas of genomic services, genomic instruments, and genomic discovery also have dedicated e-business solutions enabling customers to access the complete product palette via the Web. These additional services differentiate MWG Biotech from its competitors that offer similar products. These services not only increase customer satisfaction, but also reduce the cost of service significantly.

1.3.6 Cost Reduction

The cost for real estate, service support, and production can be reduced greatly through the use of the Internet, another very good reason to move toward e-business. Printer manufacturers, such as Canon[31] and Epson,[32] use the Internet to distribute printer drivers and updates. The cost for replicating floppy disks or CD-ROMs is not very high per piece, but because of the high volume of printers they sell, it is a very large sum in the end. The replication cost on

---

[31]http://www.canon.com/
[32]http://www.epson.com/

the Internet is nearly zero. Although downloading the driver does not cost anything, the infrastructure to do this does need to be paid for. By generating new business on the Internet, these infrastructure costs become irrelevant to these companies, as they are generating additional business by offering an instant solution to missing printer drivers as one new service. This results in more content customers and less overhead.

The ExhiBit Gallery[33] in Pisa, Italy—a small gallery focusing on contemporary paintings—closed down its showrooms shortly after it moved to the Internet. The costs for the showroom and staff were too high to maintain. The gallery received few visitors, but reducing its business hours was not a practical solution. Moving to the Internet provided the ideal solution. The showrooms are now open 24 hours a day, and about 400 people from all over the world are visiting the online gallery every day.

Customer service costs can also be reduced by offering frequently asked questions (FAQ) pages, where customers can find answers about a product or service. Newsgroups, where customers can ask questions, can also be very helpful. Other customers may be able to share their experiences and reduce the workload for the customer service center. In addition, companies can support employees and business partners over their corporate intranets, keeping them informed and soliciting their feedback.

A company Web site can also help to reduce inventory costs by shortening the sales and supply cycles. By distributing information in electronic form, you can reduce material costs by saving on paper, printing, and manual distribution. In actuality, the customer is taking over parts of the distribution costs.

Still, cost reduction should not be seen as the primary goal in the long term. In the long term, everybody will have saved money and increased profits. Remember that in order to survive, it is necessary to have a meaningful relationship with your customers. This will allow you to charge more money for a service than others do, because service quality, not the base product, is what matters in the end.

1.3.7 Just-in-Time Inventory

As pressure for lower prices is very high on the Internet, it is necessary to reduce operating costs by reacting much faster to demand, as demand is created in real time. Therefore, it is necessary to cut down inventory to reduce the cost and adapt more dynamically to the wishes of the customers. The longer it takes to reach suppliers, the more inventory a company needs to hold to account for errors and delays.

Holding large quantities of one product is not helpful if your customers have highly dynamic demand for certain products. Therefore, it is necessary to build stronger relationships with your suppliers and integrate them into your digital ordering process. Estimates on the product sales for the next day, week, or

---

[33]http://www.gallery-net.com/individuals/

month (depending on your inventory cycle) also help to keep the overhead low. Therefore, digital communication between factories, marketing, and purchasing departments becomes essential.

In the United States an initiative called *Collaborative Planning Forecasting Replenishment*[34] (CPFR) has been set up by retailers, wholesalers, and manufacturers to define standards and guidelines for better forecasting. Using this system, retailers and suppliers are able to exchange their forecasts electronically and in real time in order to change orders or production. Online bookshops such as Amazon.com have very limited stocks. They rely totally on their suppliers to deliver the books in real time, which they then pass on to their customers.

1.3.8   Preventing Financial Loss

This leads us to the last reason to go online—preventing financial losses, which is also one of the most important reasons. Although the Internet may pose a financial threat to a company, it also means a great opportunity. In their first few years of business, many new online companies need to invest heavily in a new infrastructure. But once a company has broken even, it is much easier to resist changes of the future. Amazon.com was in the red, financially speaking, until 1999, and only then was a break-even reached. Although highly successful, marketing and infrastructure have cost more than the company received in revenues. In order to grow, Amazon.com needed to invest a great deal in new customer segments.

One of Germany's largest shopping malls, My-World,[35] had to relaunch its Web site in early 1998 because it wasn't as successful as originally anticipated. But since its relaunching, it has become an important online shopping portal for Germany. IBM's WorldAvenue[36] had to be closed down, as it generated no revenue. These two examples show quite clearly that it is not sufficient to convert existing environments to the Internet. They need to be adapted to have an impact and to be a success. In Chapter 7 we will see how shopping malls can be transformed to portal sites and become highly successful.

The Internet may pose a financial risk to your company, but not investing in e-business will kill your company almost for sure. As your competition will be seeing the benefits of e-business they can reduce costs and prices more easily. In order to make your e-business venture a success, the guidelines in this book may be helpful. As with most guides, this is not the only way to conduct business—but it is a way that balances risks and investments so that you will be highly likely to succeed.

---

[34]http://www.cpfr.org/
[35]http://www.my-world.de/
[36]used to be http://www.worldavenue.com/

1.3.9   Relevance to IT

Although your IT department should not need to be the driver for your business decisions, without them you are nobody on the e-business side of life. Your IT group needs to adapt to understand the new needs for the New Economy. The department needs to employ Internet experts without reducing staff who have knowledge of the systems currently used. The IT department can gain experience in the Internet world by implementing an intranet first. If you do not have an IT department, or you do not want to invest directly into Internet technologies, then you should consider outsourcing the whole operation. If you have your own IT department and want to implement your own e-business strategy, keep in touch with them to learn what can be done and how much it will cost. For some new services, it may be better to outsource the development and just maintain it on your network. Your existing IT infrastructure should be able to cope with the changes that come along with the Internet. The Internet is changing all the time, so you need the right people with the right skills to move in the right direction.

As more traditional electronic services—such as email, remote access, and Web server hosting—have become commodities, these services can be out-sourced to third-party services that specialize in these areas. This frees up resources in your IT department to deal with new services and technologies that are not yet commodities. Part of the IT department would start to act as a broker for services between the internal customers and the external service providers. This would allow IT to maintain control over the services, without having to keep up operations on a daily basis.

1.3.10   Concerns About Going Online

Traditional companies have established processes and channels, and going on-line would require additional investments for the digital age. Many conservative companies are reluctant to invest in new technologies, processes, and ideas, as they are successful in their businesses and fear that the investment will do more harm than good.

Employees fear that with the introduction of the Internet they may lose their jobs, as they are not qualified to work on the Internet. The Internet drastically changes the work of many employees. It requires the employee to adapt to the ever-changing Internet. Lifelong learning becomes more important in order to keep up with the latest developments on the Internet. Unlike traditional business, where change comes slowly, technology and paradigms on the Internet change quickly.

In 1997 "push" technology was expected to take off and become the next big thing. Many companies were heavily investing in this technology—and it disappeared soon after. By 1998 nobody knew why there had been such a fuss about it. Push technology is still being used, but it has been integrated into many products, such as newsfeeds and automatic software updates that are triggered by the server, not by the user (which is called "pull"). The certainty that many businesses relied on in the past is gone. Only the companies that are prepared to invest will survive the challenges of the 21st century.

Resellers and merchants fear that disintermediation will ruin their business. Through the Internet, it has become easy for a manufacturer to get in direct contact with the end customer. But most manufacturers cannot do this without conflict between the company and the traditional channels. Therefore, to prevent a channel conflict, manufacturers may be reluctant to go online. More forward-thinking manufacturers may use the Internet, but not to reach out for the end customers; rather, they may want to increase their relationships with their retailers.

Companies offering information and soft products on the Internet are concerned about copyright issues. Compact disc sales are dropping even though more people are listening to music. The reasons for this are CD recorders, which make it easy to duplicate audio CDs, and the file format MP3, which allows transfer of songs over the Internet in a highly compressed way. Typical files in the MP3 format are compressed at a ratio of 1:10, resulting in a 3-minute song that is 3 MB instead of 30 MB. New appliances such as the Rio MP3[37] player replace the Discman. Although unauthorized copying of music over the Internet is illegal, many sites offer the files. If you search for your favorite music, you can be almost certain you will find something that interests you.

A successful online business needs to be accepted by the customers. If none of your customers have access to the Internet, then providing an online service is not practical, especially if your company is not targeting new customers. Providing your current customers with Internet access and Internet-enabled equipment may cost too much. In order to move your customers to the Internet, you need to offer additional services that are not available elsewhere. For example, online ordering should offer customers the option of tracking their order, which would not be possible without the Internet.

Without global consent on the legal framework that needs to be implemented on the Internet, many companies are reluctant to invest, as they are not sure what the consequences may be for them.

1.4   Differentiating between E-business Categories

1.4.1   Overview

Electronic business is a superset of business cases, which have been digitized and now work on the Internet. An e-business category is defined by the business case and not by the technology used to implement it. Over time, more and more types of business will be converted to a digital form. Any kind of business

---

[37]http://www.diamondmm.com/

When going online people have many concerns. If you want to provide a solution, you need to take their concerns into account.

- **Channel conflict**—Disintermediation may happen.

- **Competition**—The competition is growing from a local competition to a worldwide competition.

- **Copyright**—Once information has been published on the Internet, it becomes easy to copy.

- **Customer acceptance**—Many companies are afraid that their customers won't accept the new channel.

- **Legal issues**—There is no legal framework for the Internet that is binding on a worldwide basis.

- **Loyalty**—The Internet is less personal, so people are not bound to a certain vendor.

- **Pricing**—The New Economy makes it easier to compare prices. Prices will drop, so quality and add-on services become more important.

- **Security**—Most companies are very concerned about security on the Internet.

- **Service**—A customer can compare the offerings of a certain company with those of another one much more easily.

- **Viability**—Many companies are unsure about the viability of their digital business case.

Table 1.3. Concerns on the Internet

will be connected, sooner or later. Even though this seems unlikely, technology is moving fast enough to make things possible tomorrow that seem impossible today.

Though many other categories exist, the following have been selected because of their proven success on the Internet. In order for one of these categories to be successful, it needs to interact with the other categories. Commerce, for example, without marketing and communications, does not make a lot of sense. These categories need to work together, both offline and online.

The Internet offers incredible possibilities for integrating the categories and automating the interaction between the processes.

1.4.2   E-Auctioning

Auctioning on the Internet has become a new dimension. In traditional auctions, a number of people turned up at the auction house and some people were allowed to bid over the phone. Getting to the auction house or bidding over the phone involved costs that sometimes were higher than the value of the goods. Auctions were restricted to a location or to a very exclusive circle of people.

The Internet makes auctions more democratic, allowing everyone with an Internet connection to bid for any good offered. Everyone is able to go to the auction Web site with a click, no matter where the server is physically located. The Internet also speeds up the bidding process. In the real world, it can take quite a while until a final bid has been made. On the Internet, most live bids are over in a few seconds. During the live bid, an auctioneer registers the bids and hands over the goods to the highest bidder.

Besides the advantage of the live bid, the larger auction sites offer the opportunity to view present goods on a Web page. These private auctions are not live—bidders place their bids on the Web page and the auctioneer waits until a certain value has been reached or a time limit has been passed and then "hands out" the goods to the lucky one. See Chapter 7 for more information on auctions.

eBay,[38] QXL[39] and Ricardo[40] offer visitors the opportunity to become either a bidder, an auctioneer, or both (see Figure 1.4). The Web site becomes an infrastructure for exchanging goods based on the auction model, which works basically by setting the prices by demand.

The whole Internet is transforming the fixed price structures to more dynamic pricing. Auction Web sites are only the beginning. In a few years' time, individual prices based on customer demand will be on every Web site offering goods, information, or services. A detailed description on the business models and technologies can be found in my book Dynamic Commerce[41].

1.4.3   E-Banking

Electronic banking is one of the most successful online businesses. E-banking allows customers to access their accounts and execute orders through a simple-to-use Web site. There is no special software for customers to install (other than a Web browser), and many banks do not charge for this service. Some banks even lower costs for online transactions versus onsite banking transactions. Electronic banking saves individuals and companies time and money. All

---

[38] http://www.ebay.com/
[39] http://www.qxl.co.uk/
[40] http://www.ricardo.de/
[41] http://www.dynamiccommerce.org/

Figure 1.4. Internet auctions.

around the world, banks such as the Banco Nacional de Bolivia,[42] the Banco Continential de Panama[43] and the Banco Hipotecario del Uruguay[44] have discovered the Internet.

Online banking puts the power of banking into the hands of the customer and allows the customers to choose self-service for all their banking needs. With online service, customers can view their account details, review their account histories, transfer funds, order checks, pay bills, reorder checks, or get in touch with the customer service department of the bank. The only transaction that currently can't be done online are cash deposits and withdrawals, but banks are working to solve this problem. In the meantime, ATMs will have to do.

To get started, the virtual banking customer needs a computer or embedded device connected to the Internet and a browser. Depending on the security strategy by the online bank, the customer may need to install a plug-in or enable Java to increase the level of security in the browser. The plug-in or Java applet is used to increase the level of encryption to make sure nobody can intercept banking transactions. More sophisticated systems use smart-card technology to allow secure access for customers. Smart cards are like credit cards, but with a chip. Another option to make banking more secure is a list

---

[42]http://www.bnb.com.bo/

[43]http://www.bcocontinental.com/

[44]http://www.bhu.net/

of transaction numbers (TAN), which are one-time passwords that can be used for a single transaction.

Many people use PC banking software, such as Quicken,[45] and other personal financial management software packages, although these are not the same as electronic banking. The major difference is that with PC banking, software is loaded onto your computer and all your transactions are handled through a third-party vendor, adding security issues to the e-banking service.

Electronic banking is an online service that allows customers to perform the same banking functions as in Quicken, except that they can access their accounts directly over the Internet.

1.4.4   E-Commerce

If we look back, commerce in the pre-Internet age was very restricted compared to the possibilities the new information technologies and the infostructure (information infrastructure) offer. The major limiting factors were time and space. Even if shops were open 24 hours a day, only a limited number of customers could come to the location of the shop. The shop can also offer only a limited selection of goods, as space is limited on the premises.

A shop on the Internet is unlimited in space and time. There are no limits on the number of products a shop can offer. Amazon.com offers more than 4.7 million books. Imagine a bookshop with 4.7 million books in stock. The comparison may not seem fair, as Amazon does not stock the books, but orders them on demand. But Amazon.com does offer information on every single book.

Online retailers (sometimes also called e-tailers) offer either more products than traditional retailers or more service, for the same products. On the Internet, books, compact discs, and tickets are outselling their traditional counterparts, as these products are bought because of their content and not because of their design. The look and feel of an airline ticket is not important; the price and the service are what really matter. New technologies make the Internet also attractive for goods that are bought on an emotional basis, because of their design and not their content, such as cars and clothing.

The Internet is changing the traditional sales model, which is tactical in nature. The companies used to produce a deliverable—either a product, service, or piece of information—and then employ the 4 P's of marketing (price, product, promotion and placement) as the foundation of their efforts to sell it. Internet commerce, on the other hand, is far more strategic. While most companies view their products purely in terms of the demand conversion stage, Internet commerce will increasingly force them to view the entire sales cycle (market development, demand creation, fulfillment, customer support, and customer retention) as their product. In the tactical model, these phases in the sales cycle are just extras that aid in pre-sales and post-sales. In a strategic model, however, they are building blocks of the entire sales message.

---

[45]http://www.quicken.com

Many people think that e-commerce is the same as e-business, but as defined here, e-commerce is only a subset. E-commerce was one of the first business types to become digitally available, but the Internet offers more than just the buying and selling of products and services.

1.4.5   E-Directories

Directories have always played an important role in finding a particular service or product. Telephone directories—the white pages for private telephone numbers and the Yellow Pages for businesses—have been essential in locating a person or business. In addition to the directories in book form, the telephone companies allowed people to call in to ask for information.

These two functions have migrated to the Internet. The database is located in a single place, providing centralized functionality, but offering it to anyone at any time, making it a decentralized solution.

The Internet offers the possibility to replicate phone directories without much hassle, but it can do more than just allow users to search for a name and receive a phone number. On the Internet, for example, it is possible to conduct a "reverse lookup," entering a phone number and getting the telephone subscriber's name. Moreover, new directories can locate the Web pages and email addresses of people and businesses.

The Internet makes the retrieval easier and more difficult at the same time: The means of searching are more powerful, but finding a particular piece of information has become more difficult as the amount of information has increased dramatically.

1.4.6   E-Engineering

Engineering has also changed dramatically over the last few years. Just a few years ago, engineers working on a draft all needed to be in the same office to work effectively. If a design needed to be sent out to another location, large prints had to be made and sent via postal service to the other location. There, the design was refined, checked, or processed. All these processes involved a lot of manual work, making them slow and error-prone.

The Internet changed the speed of design. It enabled electronic collaboration to a much higher degree than was ever before possible. The location of the engineers no longer matters. Everyone with an Internet connection is able to take part in the development. New tools for concurrent development have been developed to support the possibilities of the Internet.

Through the Internet, it has also become possible to develop continuous engineering by letting engineers from all over the world participate. Open source development is done that way, and very efficiently. Open source development, managed and promoted by the Open Source Initiative (OSI, a nonprofit organization), is a movement among programmers to develop and distribute free, reliable software. In a cooperative effort, programmers write and contribute pieces of code, which are used to develop new software or to improve upon existing software.

1.4.7 E-Franchising

In the past, big traditional franchising companies like McDonald's[46] and Benetton[47] have made their money by vending their products and brands to retailers who exclusively sell the products of the franchising company. These retailers are called franchising partners. By offering a set of products and brands, the franchising company guarantees a certain success for the retailer, as people like buying these products because the brands are well known. The advantage for the franchising companies is that they do not need to invest in shop personnel, for example. The franchising partner is responsible for the employees and the financial success of the single outlet.

Electronic franchising works very similarly and has actually become much easier on the Internet. Moving digital products, processes, and brands is extremely easy. The affiliation programs of the large booksellers on the Internet are one example. They are not truly franchisers, as the large booksellers have their own stores. But they allow franchising partners to exclusively distribute their products on the partners' Web sites. The advantage of this system is that there are no distribution costs involved. It is possible to link to the original products without letting the customers know. Quelle,[48] for example, is selling books on its Web site. Books are not part of its core product set, but in cooperation with Libri,[49] Quelle is able to offer more than 1.5 million books.

1.4.8 E-Gambling

Although there may be moral issues related to gambling, it is one of the most profitable businesses on the Internet. In the real world, gambling is restricted by many laws, making it difficult to access the casinos. The owners of the games often need to pay high taxes to the state, which makes it difficult to create competition, and only a certain number of casinos are allowed per state.

This has changed dramatically on the Internet. Gambling is still not legal in some states, and the taxes are still high in these states, but the business has moved to places where gambling is legal and only low taxes need to be paid. Most gambling Web sites have moved to the Caribbean or South America, where no laws on gambling have been implemented.

The companies that operate the gambling Web sites are able to operate the full program of games, without any restrictions. As the owners have their companies in countries where gambling is legal, they are able to operate without

---

[46]http://www.mcdonalds.com/
[47]http://www.benetton.com/
[48]http://www.quelle.de/
[49]http://www.libri.de/

fearing government intervention. But unlike real-world casinos, which are restricted to geographical locations, online casinos are able to attract gamblers from all over the world with a mouse click. Companies such as 123Gambling,[50] SlotMachines,[51] and CasinoPlace[52] attract hundreds of thousands of gamblers every day.

1.4.9   E-Learning

The constant change on the Internet also requires a change in learning. In the Industrial Age, the subjects and the content taught did not change a lot. Changes to the curriculum did occur over the years, but compared to the Information Age, change was extremely slow. Having a job for 40 years in a steel plant, for example, is no longer likely. Fluctuation between jobs is much higher, which requires a readjustment of the job focus. New technologies appear in Internet time, which requires continually learning new technologies, paradigms, and processes. Lifelong learning has become a necessity, as teachers need to learn a new subject just as much as the pupils do. As knowledge becomes a major income factor, people may find it necessary to use alternatives to classroom learning.

Computer-based training (CBT) was introduced a few years ago, making it possible to learn via computer. Software is used to explain the subject and then test the pupil. Although this is an effective way of learning some subjects, there is no one to question in the case of a misunderstanding.

Electronic learning—sometimes also called Internet-based training (IBT)—offers a new dimension in digital learning. Instead of an executable file, which is used to explain and test a subject, the material is presented online. Tests are executed in real time, and the pupils are able to exchange ideas and questions. In addition, an online teacher can be present—a real teacher, who may explain topics to anyone attending a course, no matter where the students are located. Instead of waiting for the next hour, the students can connect to the learning network whenever they want, making the learning experience more individualized by allowing people to learn at their own pace.

An IBT session can also be offered to students before the complete course is available. For hot topics, the course can be developed at the same time that the students are beginning to learn.

1.4.10   Emailing

Many people do not think about email when talking about digital business, but communication is truly the basis of all business. The Internet breaks into the traditional communication markets. Postal services and telecommunications

---

[50]http://www.123gambling.com/

[51]http://www.slotmachines.com.ar/

[52]http://www.casinoplace.com/

companies are losing market share to electronic communication, especially to email. Email combines the strengths of phone calls and letters. The advantage of a phone call is its immediacy, and the letter has the advantage that everything is in written form. The Internet enables instant communication in written form, either by email or online chat.

More and more businesses are talking digitally to each other. Unlike a phone call, emails can contain more than just the text. It is possible to attach files, which may, for example, contain formatted documents, presentations, images, or sounds. Information can be shared much more easily.

Email also changes the way people communicate. Instead of writing down every aspect in a single letter, thoughts may be spread over multiple emails. The advantage is that a thought may evolve through instant response, but it also means that you expect instant response to every email that has been sent out, just as everyone expects a response from you.

1.4.11 E-Marketing

Traditional marketing focused on target groups and presenting a positive product image to that particular group. Communication in advertising was one-way only. The marketing team could not get immediate results on the customer reaction. In the pre-Information Age society, this was fine, as there was time to conduct surveys and publish the results that influenced the company strategy and the products.

In the Information Age, everything has started to flow. Products, strategies, prices—everything depends on the customers' needs. Everything becomes much more customer-centric. The demands of the customer directly affect product design, marketing strategies, and pricing. As marketing traditionally has direct ties to the customer, the information flowing back from the customer in real time needs to be passed on to the appropriate department within the company in order to react in real time to the ever-faster changing demands of the customers.

The Internet allows companies to react to individual customer demands. One-to-one marketing has become the standard way of dealing with customers over the Internet. Remember, one-to-many marketing does not work in Internet time.

1.4.12 E-Operational Resources Management

Besides the goods needed for production, companies need to buy operational resources. These are the nonproduction goods and services that are required and managed on a daily basis to run the day-to-day business. The areas for operational resources include capital equipment (such as computer equipment), maintenance, repair, and operating (MRO) supplies (such as office supplies), and travel and entertainment (T&E) (such as travel services).

The process of acquiring operational resources involves many organizations and departments within the company, which deal with many different suppliers. The suppliers are providing services, goods, and information. Although the operating resources do account for a large amount of company spending, the buying process is often not well organized and managed. In many cases a paper-based process is used for ordering new pencils and phone lines. Due to the decentralized approach of ordering supplies in many companies, every department is able to handle the operational resources on an individual basis, which results in higher prices than if companies used a central buying organization. Once a central buying organization has been put in place, the paper-based process needs to be digitized in order to automate, control, and leverage it. As long as the process is not digitized, the company is not able to control the spending and the suppliers involved in the process.

Operational Resources Management (ORM) allows companies to manage operational resources more strategically by using the Internet and its connectivity to provide a communication infrastructure in which buyers and suppliers can work together on a direct basis without losing control over the spending. Actually, the company gets more control over the spending through the electronic management system. Introducing ORM does not require additional hardware or software to be installed, as many systems run on standard Web browsers, which can be run on any computer platform. Through the use of electronic communication, the cost per transaction can be lowered significantly as the process is automated.

1.4.13 E-Research

The Internet itself has been the foundation for many new areas of research; it has also propelled research activities in general. Biology, chemistry, astronomy, and all other areas of interest have found a fruitful platform to form worldwide research teams. The World Wide Web was invented because the nuclear physics community wanted to share information and provide a simple means for studying research data. Many scientific publications appear only on the Web (such as JITTA[53]), because publishing them in a magazine is prohibitively expensive. Through the Internet, many more people are able to review and comment on recent studies and findings.

This approach also has some disadvantages, as more people publish unverified results to claim ownership, resulting in the publication on the Internet of some questionable material. Before a research paper is published in a print magazine, it is normally verified; on the Internet it is up to the user to verify the integrity of information. But the advantages of the Internet are much greater than the problems related to it. The Internet enables poorer countries to participate in high-technology research by contributing ideas and concepts to the research community without having to invest in expensive technology.

---

[53]http://www.jitta.org/

1.4.14 E-Supply

Numerous independent companies and customers form a supply chain. Manufacturers, logistics companies, senders, receivers, and retailers all work together to coordinate the order-generation and order-taking. Order fulfillment and distribution of the products, service, or information is organized through the supply-chain management. By digitizing the products, the processes, and the communication, the Internet offers great potential in linking and managing these organizations. Although EDI was able to link up the companies, it never really took off, as small and medium-sized companies could not afford an EDI link to each partner they worked with.

The Internet significantly reduced the cost for starting up digital B2B communication. Through the use of open standards—such as XML and Java—supply-chain partners are able to share and exchange information more easily and with lower costs involved. The supply-management process may even be contracted to a third party instead of an organization developing its own applications and investing in separate systems. In this intermediated market, sophisticated logistics management and automated supply-chain management are available almost universally.

1.4.15 E-Trading

Before the Internet, buying and selling stocks was restricted to people with access to financial networks in order to buy and sell the stocks at the right moment. Others could get the stock quotes only in the newspaper.

The Internet has changed the way stocks are traded. E-trading, also often called e brokering, offers real-time stock prices to every desk throughout the world. People are able to react in real time to changes in the stock market. Everyone with an Internet bank account is able to buy and sell stock. This enables anyone to participate in the stock market and earn money by investing. Although computer-based trading makes the stock market riskier than ever, it does offer access and opportunities for people who, just a few years ago, did not even know what a stock option was.

1.4.16 E-Travel

One of the hottest markets on the Internet is online travel agencies. In 1998, 9 percent of Internet users had used the Internet to make travel reservations. In 2000, more than 60 percent of Internet users booked travel arrangements over the Internet. The convenience of the Internet is considered responsible for the growth. People who enjoy travel love the flexibility and convenience of the Internet.

Travel companies that are not yet selling most of their services online may have to develop a plan for transitioning to the Internet or attempt to partner with other online services that are already established. Middle-tier companies are the most at risk and must take immediate action, while lower tier companies may be capable of selling some services through online auctions or reseller sites.

While more people are purchasing airline tickets online, people will most likely buy them from leading travel agents, such as as Travelocity.com,[54] Rumbo.com,[55] and Expedia[56] and not from airline Web sites, such as AmericanAirlines[57] or Lufthansa.[58]

This shift will be due to the fact that airline sites simply aren't offering the kind of comprehensive services, travel packages, and technology backbone that consumers are demanding. As a response, airline Web pages are teaming up with hotel and rental car chains to offer a more complete solution.

1.5   Using the New Paradigm of E-Business

1.5.1   The Interoperable Network

In the early 1990s, a strong concentration appeared on the computer market, the so-called Wintel (composed of the Windows[59] software and the Intel[60] hardware) monopoly. In order to exchange information with business partners, everyone was forced to use the same operating system, word processor, and hardware.

With the introduction of the Internet, incompatible devices have learned to talk to each other. This allows interchanging products and integrating processes. This is achieved through the use of digital technologies based on open standards. Moving everything to the same basis started to converge networks, markets, products, technologies, and business processes.

The convergence of the networks was the first segment. Telephones, broadcast, satellite, and wireless networks are now all able to send and receive digital signals. Sending information from a mobile phone to a standard telephone network is possible. It has become totally transparent to the user which networks are used to route a phone call. A phone call from the United States to Asia may be routed through satellite networks, the Internet, and normal telephone networks.

Through the Internet, several regulated monopolies face competition from those who used to be in different markets. Suddenly, telephone companies, cable television operators, and power supply companies have become competitors to offer access to the Internet, and Web site owners and television broadcast-

---

[54]http://www.travelocity.com/

[55]http://www.rumbo.com/

[56]http://www.expedia.com/

[57]http://www.aa.com/

[58]http://www.lufthansa.com/

[59]http://www.microsoft.com/

[60]http://www.intel.com/

ers have begun to offer competitive products. Market boundaries are breaking down, just as geographical boundaries have started to collapse.

More and more products are now available in digital form: audio signals, such as voice and music; video signals, such as television and video broadcasts; textual information, such as books, magazines and news and some companies experiment with digital perfumes. All these pieces of information from other media have been moved to a new medium, the computer platform, where databases, computer software, and games were already in use. Through the use of networks, which all evolved into the Internet, all these types of information can easily be transmitted to any place in the world.

Different types of technologies, such as printers, computers, cameras and mobile phones, are moving closer together to offer users a wider variety of appliances. Using a mobile phone to communicate with a digital camera and a printer without a computer as an intermediary is already possible, thanks to the Internet.

By digitizing processes, different types of processes in a value chain are integrated into a seamless process. A digital process can be mass-customized more easily by using digital feedback from the customer. Through the feedback mechanism, it is also possible to streamline processes much more easily than would have been possible in the real world.

The convergence brings many new opportunities for startup companies and many uncertainties for established companies. Startups will use the new technologies to implement new processes and products, while many traditional companies will try to convert their current success to the digital world without enhancement. A dictionary in book form and on the Internet will use the same data, but presentation and functionality will be very different than if a company just replicates the book by providing a Web site with all the content. The Internet-based dictionary will have search and link capabilities that exceed the cross-indexing features a book can provide. Some companies do not add these new functionalities, because their current set of features are satisfying the needs of their customers. Startups will see their opportunity to get into the dictionary market and will win market share by offering new digital products. These new products mean new uses, new customers, and new ways of doing business. Traditional companies focus on the opportunity to expand their business, but startups focus on the novelty of the Internet and its possibilities.

1.5.2 The New Economy

Digital business is causing an upheaval that is shaking the foundations of traditional business. More and more companies now recognize the opportunity the Internet offers and have started to establish an online presence with a sound business model behind it. Increased revenues and additional customers who return voluntarily to the company are incentives that make more and more companies digitize their offerings. Through the Internet, it is possible to invent new and innovative ways to add value to existing products and services without necessarily spending a lot of money.

Over the last few years, the Internet has established itself as a mainstream medium. With the publication of the Starr report on Monica Lewinsky,[61] first released on the Internet, everyone in the traditional media was forced to turn to the Internet for the information. Television news broadcasts were showing online excerpts, as no other information was available, and many sites replicated the report and newspapers reprinted parts of it.

Internet technologies are advancing to support commercial transactions, and new commercial transactions have been invented by these new Internet technologies. Companies need to move fast in this New Economy. But speed is not the only factor that is important for achieving success in electronic business. Careful planning and execution are just as important as moving quickly. This requires the combination of a variety of skills and disciplines, many of which are new and unfamiliar. Computer companies, advertising agencies, Internet providers, and service providers come together and act on an equal level of expertise. In the Industrial Age, every company had expertise in one field. In the Information Age, every company has a lot of expertise in its own field and at least some expertise in the fields of the others.

1.5.3 Delivery of Goods

Even though every piece of the business may be digitized, most businesses require a traditional delivery of goods at the end of the transaction. It is important to note that poor delivery can break an e-commerce operation. As delivery is not done digitally, it requires other processes and technologies. The most frequent complaints by e-commerce customers were related to poor delivery and a poor returns procedure. The trouble is that a lot of e-commerce companies have spent all their time and money on attracting customers to their operations, and selling them goods, but have invested little in getting those goods to the customer quickly, efficiently, and at the customer's convenience.

The reality of selling over the Internet is that customers are no longer willing to wait the inevitable 28 days for delivery, which is still commonplace with traditional mail-order companies. Customers have placed the order quickly, paid quickly, and want it delivered next day. In the cut-throat world of e-commerce, only those companies which can do this will survive and prosper.

The desire for quick, if not instant, delivery among cyber shoppers is one reason why sales of MP3 files and software downloads are booming. You pay your money and get the goods within minutes. It is also the reason why e-commerce companies like Amazon.com are so successful; unless otherwise stated, it will deliver a book to a customer the next day. E-customers are impatient customers; they will give you only one chance, especially since the competition is only a mouse click away.

---

[61]http://www.house.gov/icreport/

One of the problems with selling over the Internet is that one can easily overtrade. With a traditional shop or mail order business, the number of potential customers can be calculated with reasonable accuracy. But with its global marketplace, such calculations on the Internet are impossible.

The problem lies in the different degrees of scalability of the sales and marketing operation, on one hand, and the supply, logistics, and administration aspects on the other. The cost of reaching potentially vast numbers of customers on the Internet is little more than the cost of reaching just a few. This is a far cry from traditional advertising and marketing, where there is a definite relationship between the size of the potential market and the amount of money spent on advertising.

The conclusion to be drawn from this observation is that anyone contemplating setting up an e-commerce business should invest more funds and spend more management time on the delivery aspect of the operation than on the sales and marketing side. But this is exactly the opposite approach as that being taken by all too many e-commerce high flyers, many of whom are now heading for disaster. Remember this, and you will surely stay ahead of the game.

One way around the problems associated with getting the goods to the customer, problems which can be particularly acute for a startup company, is to outsource as much of the operation as possible to one of the many specialist logistics companies. There are companies that will do everything from stock control and warehousing delivery to administration and handling returns.

A typical example of a company able to handle the complete outsourcing of the logistics is iForce[62] in the UK or Deutsche Post[63] in Germany. These companies can handle all the tasks of a full e-commerce business except for choosing the products and selling them to the customer.

Outsourcing is also very flexible and can, at least in theory, handle the scalability problem mentioned earlier. However, full outsourcing is expensive, and therefore requires high margins and a high sales volume, factors which tend to preclude its use by smaller e-commerce businesses.

Some companies may decide not to outsource everything, but just that element which would prove very expensive to set up: the delivery function. But if they take this route, they must make sure that the chosen delivery company can be relied upon to deliver the goods pleasantly and efficiently at the promised time.

This approach means that the company will have to set up a warehousing and order fulfillment operation. The design of such an operation is very important. It must, above all, aim to have every order dispatched the same day it is received. This means two things: the operation must be fully computerized and integrated with the order-taking system and the delivery company and the

---

[62]http://www.iforce.co.uk/

[63]http://www.deutschepost.de/

operation must be sufficiently scalable to cope with the worst-case scenario, a flood of orders over just a few days, as is common during the pre-Christmas period.

This is no easy task. It requires skill and expertise as well as money, and it is one reason why outsourcing could still be the best solution. However, very small e-commerce businesses operating in niche markets might well find that installation of a few racks and bins in a post room will be sufficient warehousing, a simple bit of software to print out mailing labels and mailing slips may prove sufficient for the administration, and if there is a rush, the manager can just call upon everyone to help.

Delivery is often forgotten in e-business, as startups often don't know how to do it properly, and established brick-and-mortar companies think that they can use their existing delivery methods for their Internet customers. Both approaches will fail, as the Internet has its own rules. Speed and ease are the most important issues to consider.

1.5.4 Multichannel E-Business

The Internet added an important channel to existing businesses. This led to cannibalization of traditional channels, but it is better to cannibalize your own company than to wait until a competitor, a small Internet startup or an established company that has already taken the Internet plunge, does it for you. Many companies tried to spinoff the Internet activity in order to avoid channel conflicts in the past. This led to a huge reinvention of the market, but did not solve the problem.

But an alternative has emerged: the so-called multichannel e-business. This is a revolutionary new framework that will enable large organizations to seize opportunities in both digital and land-based marketplaces. Companies that deploy this framework combine Web and traditional channels to deliver the best and most profitable service, depending on the individual customer, the kind of product, and the type of interaction. Moreover, because these mixed channels can be linked together electronically, the customer can experience continuous, uniform service even when they interact with multiple channels. Another plus is that companies can learn a great deal about customer behavior and needs.

Unlike with a spin-off, companies do not have to build a complete organization around the new Web sales channel. Instead, they separate value-adding pieces of traditional business models from nonproductive ones and recombine them in new ways using Web technology. Companies that adopt a multichannel e-business strategy can realize tremendous benefits at the bottom line, including discontinuous increases in revenues and a dramatic reduction of costs.

Customers should be treated equally well, no matter if they call in using their mobile phone, use a Web terminal, or send in a fax. The same information about the customer should be available for the sales representative dealing with the customer. The customer should have the same services, product, and information offerings and the same look and feel for the company. Through multichannel e-business, it can be guaranteed that the customer is handled consistently and that feedback is stored in a central location. To ensure such consistency, it is necessary to have a central content management system, a central customer relationship management system, and a central knowledge management system. Since these are critical, this book includes a new Chapter 8, dedicated to these technologies.

As a result, many organizations that have attempted to merge electronic business activities into the front office have experienced inconsistent levels of integration, at best. In one common scenario, customers find themselves on the phone, repeating information they've already submitted in an email or via the Web. At the same time, call center employees must search through multiple applications to manually piece together the customer's history as it relates to a particular issue or order. Inevitably, customer satisfaction declines, as does employee productivity. Multichannel e-business helps to reverse this trend by consolidating customer touch points, incorporating email response management, and providing a single view into integrated self-service and self-sales portals.

Multichannel e-business solutions make it also very easy to add another channel to an existing business. Adding a mobile channel is very easy for companies that have already implemented a multichannel e-business architecture.

Now that you have an overview of the possibilities e-business can provide, let's further explore the options the Internet can offer. The deeper you delve into this book, the more detailed information you will find about the technologies and business processes mentioned here.

Chapter 2

PREPARING THE ONLINE BUSINESS

2.1 Competitor Analysis on the Internet

2.1.1 Locate your Competition

Your competition may already have a functioning Web site and may already be doing business via the Web. In order to be successful on the Internet, it is essential to regularly check out your competitors on the Web and to identify what they are doing. Some may be aggressively pursuing electronic business, while others may just have a simple marketing Web site up and running.

Learn what they are trying to achieve and how they stay in contact with their customers, and then use their ideas in your online initiatives. Find out if they are only extending their existing offerings to the Internet or if they are creating new business. Don't copy your competitors, but use their ideas as a basis for new online ventures for your company. Don't forget to look at companies that may be in a totally different business—they may also offer some new ideas on how to make your online business even more successful.

Although current competitors are a threat, this threat is more or less quantifiable when you have had time to get to know your competition. Digital startup companies are the unknown variables in business because they are the companies that find new ways to deconstruct and reconstruct traditional value chains. One bright idea may propel them in front of the established competition by using the Internet for their business, especially with competitors that simply move their existing business processes to the Internet.

The Internet offers new possibilities in competitor analysis. Every company that goes digital becomes transparent as they do so, as every company needs to show what it is doing; otherwise, the customers cannot compare their choices and make informed decisions. This basic feature of the Internet can also be used to monitor the competition.

In most cases your competitors offer similar products, services, or information. Therefore, they also have similar customers and objectives. This competition is normally very tough, as every company tries to gain more customers and market share. Therefore, it is necessary to understand the competitors. The difference between profit and loss is small in today's economy, so discovering how to take the lead and leave the competition behind is an important factor. Even a small advantage over the competition may lead to a larger market share. Finding out the little secrets of your competitors is crucial for business survival. The Internet has facilitated this information retrieval. The Web sites of competitors offer a lot of useful and valuable information. Only by comparing your strategies with those of the competition can you win. By knowing the competitors, you can predict their next moves, exploit their weaknesses, and undermine their strengths.

2.1.2 Collecting Competitive Information

With the Internet, collecting information about the competition has become much easier than it was in the past. You can gather information directly from the Web sites of competitors and even from customers. Conduct regular customer surveys on your Web site, and ask customers what they think about your products compared to your competitors'. Use traditional methods to gather information as well. Salespeople, for example, can use customer visits to learn about the competition. All these pieces of information need to be categorized, interpreted, and analyzed, and using e-business technologies can speed this process along. The collected intelligence can then be used to stay ahead of the competition.

Some companies collect business information and offer these pieces of information as a service on their Web sites. On its financial pages,[1] Yahoo! offers information about many companies around the world. Another company, Dun & Bradstreet,[2] has information on more than 35 million companies. Another important area to monitor is research and development, so checking out the number of patents a company delivers each year will help you find out what is going on in that particular company.

Monitoring the competition and adapting your own enterprise to be ahead of the market are crucial things to do, especially in the interconnected world we have today. Competition should always be operated within the law. Engaging hackers to break into the systems of your competitors may give you an edge, but it is highly illegal. Any illegal activity will immediately result in bad publicity and loss of revenue. The Internet enables your competition to show your errors to your customers in an instant, and there is no way to hide anything anymore. And don't expect any favors from your rivals.

Besides news services, online surveys, and competitive Web pages, there are other means of gathering intelligence about your competition. Subscribe to your competitors' mailing lists and listen to what their customers are talking

---

[1]http://finance.yahoo.com/
[2]http://www.dunandbrad.co.uk/

about. You may discover some new ideas for your organization, and you may find out about errors your competitors have made and learn how to avoid them.

2.2   The Fourth Channel

2.2.1   Understanding the Fourth Channel

Channels are a set of independent organizations that are involved in the process of making a product or service available for use or consumption by the consumer or business. Traditionally, buyers and sellers conducted trade through three channels: face-to-face, through the mail, and by phone.

Wholesalers and retailers provide essential services in the physical market. Imagine needing to visit the factory of every manufacturer to buy a certain product. By going to a local store, you save traveling costs but pay the margins for distributors. In many businesses, that margin for wholesalers and retailers is extraordinarily high. A more efficient way of distributing goods would lower prices and increase consumer benefits.

On the Internet, customers can visit manufacturers' Web sites and order goods directly. There are no physical or geographical obstacles for the direct factory-to-consumer interactions. Therefore, at least that portion of the markup (distribution costs) will disappear. Intermediaries won't be able to get margins from passing on a certain good or service.

The Internet has become the fourth channel for trade. Internet trade is booming, and this can create conflicts with the other channels. The Internet allows businesses to sell more and at lower cost. The sales forces and distribution partners may not be able to keep up with the pace of the Internet. As we've already seen, some companies have been forced to withdraw their Internet venture in order to prevent the total collapse of the other channels.

The Internet offers several advantages over traditional channels. Information can be exchanged on a worldwide basis without the need to respect time zones or holidays. The distribution of content can be done at a much lower cost, and products, information, and services can be customized to meet the requirements of the customer.

Companies with well-established channels need to be careful before launching their electronic business, as this can create problems with their existing channels. Before launching the new channel, it is important to find a way to resolve the channel conflict. If online sales reduce the sales volumes in the existing channels, then it needs to be determined what the impact will be and what can be done to prevent it. One solution would be to redefine the role of all channels by splitting up the market into four different segments or by creating new businesses for certain channels. Partners should always be incorporated into the online venture, and new business should be distributed over the Internet. The Internet can support the ordering process between producers, distributors, and end customers.

Unlike traditional methods of doing business, the value chain is also used to give customers access to products regardless of the location of the manufacturer. Without this system, a car could only be bought directly at the factory, requiring everyone to go to a single location, which would be inconvenient for the car manufacturer and the customers. Because of the Internet, things are changing rapidly. Customers are able to choose their preferred company, no matter how near or far. This gives you the opportunity to change the way you supply your customers and deal with your suppliers.

The Internet allows a more direct communication at all levels along the value chain, allowing more detailed information to be passed on without additional cost. Through the use of technology, it is possible to reduce costs for communication and delivery, and every company instantly becomes a global player if the software used for the Web site is internationalized and the processes are in place to handle international orders.

2.2.2 Preventing Channel Conflicts

A myth about the Internet is that it will cause the disappearance of the physical distribution chains as people move from buying through distributors and retailers to buying directly from manufacturers. Disintermediation was proposed by many in the early years of the Internet, but Web experience has shown that this is not the case. The reality is that the Internet is transforming the distribution chain, but is not eliminating it.

The traditional value chain is linear (see 2.1). The manufacturers build the products; distributors buy products from multiple manufacturers and bring them through several levels of distribution in small lots to retailers who deal directly with consumers. The value-add of the distribution chain lies in shipping, warehousing, and delivering products.

Some channel partners are not prepared for the Internet and can create channel conflicts. Channel conflicts arise if manufacturers sell goods on their Web sites (even though they have a network of retailers) and alienate their sales forces along with the stores that sell their products. A similar channel conflict may arise if the larger resellers go online to sell directly to the end customers. The Internet allows every partner in the value chain to contact the end customers. If the channel conflicts are not resolved, partners in the value chain may decide to leave the chain. Let's have a look at two examples where things went wrong in the past.

A few years ago, Levi Strauss & Co.[3] started to sell women's jeans on its Web site to North American customers. This Web site effectively bypassed the traditional retail value chain with shops all over the United States. They were actually so successful that jeans shops started to boycott the producer as retail sales dropped. Levi Strauss had to remove the offering from its Web site and had to think about a new strategy. A story about the company's new strategy

---

[3]http://www.levistrauss.com/

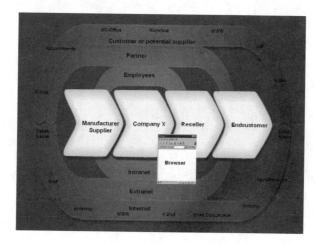

Figure 2.1. Typical value chain.

appeared in the *International Herald Tribune*[4] in February 1999. Levi Strauss decided to reopen their online shop with a much wider selection of jeans than is available at department stores and banned all retailers from selling its brands on the Internet. Every Web site that was offering Levi's jeans had to remove the offering.

KLM,[5] the Dutch airline, had a similar problem when it started to sell space on cargo planes directly to end customers. Resellers of KLM's services and large customers that also act as resellers of cargo space decided they were losing a lot of money and their market share was reduced. These companies started turning to other airlines for their business. KLM had to close down this particular business and had to rethink its strategy.

The most important thing is to contact all partners in the value chain and decide who sells what to whom. If *everybody* targets the end customers, nobody wins, as all partners try to have the lowest prices for the same product, competing for the same customer. So organizations need to find constructive ways around this. For example, manufacturers may retail to end customers via the Web, but only if they sell to customer segments that are not in the reach of the retailers. Ideally, manufacturers will use the Web to receive orders of the retailers, just as retailers receive orders of the shops. This keeps the value chain intact, but no revenue in any of the existing channels is compromised, and as a side effect, the costs per order are lowered.

---

[4]http://www.iht.com/, February 9, 1999, "Virtual Stores, Real Clout, Cyberspace Sales Pressure Traditional Retailers."

[5]http://www.klm.com/

2.2.3   High Emotions

Emotions run high when a channel conflict arises and the relations between the channel partners are damaged. A channel conflict damages the business of all channel partners. Even the end customers can become confused, looking to competitors to satisfy their needs. Interestingly, the channel conflict is not only an Internet problem. It existed long before the Internet and is a standard business concern. A channel conflict can be tolerated only until the competition becomes unfair, meaning that a company is cannibalizing the business of other members in the same value chain. If the partners stick to the rules, the best one will win and the customer will see this in lower retail prices.

Some retailers worry that low-cost Internet operations of manufacturers will undercut traditional store sales and hurt their online business. At least for now, most manufacturers that are online are selling at or near retail price. This keeps most retailers happy.

The difficulty lies in understanding the difference between fair and unfair competition. Preventing a channel conflict will result in a stable or growing market share position. In order to resolve the channel conflict, you need a clear market segmentation for all channel partners. To reduce the damage that unfair competition creates, there are some steps that can be taken. All channel partners need to be able to deal with a channel conflict in order to survive. Just complaining about the threat won't resolve the problem.

Manufacturers who have until now dealt with retailers and dealers should not use the Internet to remove the intermediaries to the end customer. The reasons manufacturers used to deal with intermediaries are easily explained and are still applicable today. Intermediaries are often more efficient in making goods available to particular markets. Through their contacts, experience, specialization, and scale of operation, intermediaries usually offer more than a manufacturer could achieve on its own. Retailers and dealers play an important role in matching supply and demand. Most manufacturers have narrow assortments of goods, yet the end consumers want a broad range of choices. Still, the Internet is starting to blur the differences between manufacturers and retailers.

By going online, a manufacturer is not automatically able to take over these varied functions. Manufacturers that are selling directly can make more profit per sold item, as there is no need to give a percentage to the channel. The disadvantage of this is that many manufacturers are not in the position to handle end customer requests as efficiently as the local channel partner can; those manufacturers therefore need to invest in a customer support organization.

Still, many manufacturers decide to sell their products online. If done correctly, this will increase the overall volume of sales without hurting the channel partners. Manufacturers should never use their advantage to offer lower prices than their channel partners. Instead, they could use the new medium to reach new target groups and pass them on to the channel.

Channel conflicts are a natural thing in business. The following
checklist should help all intermediaries to handle and resolve
a channel conflict.

- **Market check**—Retailers and vendors should regularly
  check each other's target markets and talk to each other
  in order to determine if the channel conflicts can be resolved.

- **Channel strategy**—Prepare a strategy for channel conflicts and look out for partners in case you lose in the
  channel conflict.

- **Conflict documentation**—Document the circumstances of a conflict. This helps you to remain calm and
  not get emotional about the unfair competition.

- **Time limit**—Define a limit. If the partner in the channel
  conflict does not respond to your complaints, abandon the
  product set.

Table 2.1. Resolving the Channel Conflict

2.2.4   Reconstructing the Value Chain

In order to prevent channel conflict, it is necessary to change the model of distribution and adapt it to the possibilities the Internet can offer. Through the
use of the Internet, distribution models are being deconstructed and reconstructed in a different manner, into so-called value Webs.

During the construction of the value Web, a new class of intermediaries
arises. Unlike the traditional chains, where additional value is created through
sophisticated logistics, in the New Economy, value is created by adding information. Consumers come to value Web sites looking for information and opportunities to purchase.

New intermediaries, such as flug.de,[6] easytravel,[7] TISS,[8] and Travel Overland,[9] are selling flight tickets over the Internet and are becoming part of a
new value chain. They are changing the traditional model of selling goods and

---

[6]http://www.flug.de/

[7]http://www.easytravel.cu/

[8]http://www.tiss.com/

[9]http://www.travel-overland.de/

services. On the Internet, everybody is able to easily become an intermediary. The chances for traditional companies and Internet startups are about the same. For a manufacturer, the Internet offers the possibility of breaking up old structures and creating relationships with new intermediaries. In order to be a successful intermediary on the Internet, it is necessary to add real value to the core product, as the Internet offers many more possibilities to compare product and service offerings of different online businesses. Have a look at the homepage of TISS in Figure 2.2.

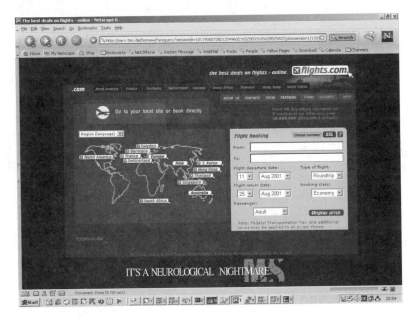

Figure 2.2. TISS Homepage

Resolving the channel conflict is possible. Libri,[10] one of Germany's largest online bookshops, is also one of the largest retailers of books. Instead of selling the books directly to the customers, the orders from the online customers are redirected to the nearest bookshop in Germany. The customer is then able to pick up the books at the bookshop or the books will be sent to the customer via mail. As you can see quite clearly from this example, the channel has not been cannibalized. Libri could have sold the books directly to the customers online, with the result that the bookshops would have chosen another distributor. Instead, the bookshops are taking part in the Internet experience of the distributor and everybody is gaining new customers through the Web site.

Instead of bypassing the traditional retailers to contact the end customers directly, manufacturers should treat their immediate partners as customers.

---

[10]http://www.libri.de/

Offer them a dedicated Web site where they can order their products, and allow them to customize the appearance of the Web site, just as you would expect an end-customer Web site to look.

Many surveys show quite clearly that the fourth-channel Internet not only attracts customers from traditional markets, but also generates new business, which then can be brought back to the traditional markets. The Web offers a great opportunity to expand the business.

Michael Dell, the owner of Dell Computers,[11] said once—when asked about how to resolve the channel conflict—that the Internet posed no threat to the traditional channels. All that was needed to keep everyone happy was to increase the number of orders.

By implementing new processes and opening up communication, the supply chain is converted to a true demand-pull supply of goods and services that removes the traditional channels. The Internet may remove the need for intermediaries in the current form, but new intermediaries will be necessary—as we have seen earlier in this section.

By failing to recognize the significance and the possibilities of the Internet, many businesses will be forced out of traditional value chains, while their customers and suppliers start to communicate in a more direct way and experience increased margins by dealing directly with each other. By embracing the Internet, its technologies, and the new ways and means of dealing with others, every company is able to offer a better service to existing customers and build profitable new businesses.

2.2.5   New Intermediaries

Retailers offering undifferentiated, high-priced products will rapidly disappear over the next few years. At the same time, new players will quickly emerge, as the Internet has very low barriers to entry. Information-based services are the key to success for becoming an intermediary for the New Economy. Information and appropriate processes can help to increase response time. The Internet is fast becoming an important factor in business decision-making. New players appear, such as IndustryNet,[12] one of the representatives of the new emerging industrial marketplace. Suppliers are using the Internet for presenting their products and pricing. New intermediaries will aggregate information from various locations into a central location. This allows the new intermediaries to offer greater customer convenience while pushing product prices down.

Let's examine some examples in the United States. A new intermediary is Food.com,[13] a matchmaking service for online pizza buyers and sellers. Rather than searching for an appropriate online pizza shop, customers can order pizza directly through the Cyberslice.com Web site. The system locates the shop

---

[11]http://www.dell.com/
[12]http://www.industry.net/
[13]http://www.food.com/

located nearest to the customer and sends an automated voice message to the pizza service. The restaurant uses touch-tone prompts to take the order, paying Cyberslice.com a small fee in commission for every pizza transaction. A similar service is provided by Bodegon Consta Azul.[14]

Two types of intermediation will survive on the Internet: those who extend services from the physical world and those who evolve from the new capabilities of the New Economy. The first group will implement services such as digital telephone directory services and certification authorities, which are identity-issuing agencies on the Internet.

The second group includes the real new intermediaries and will be based on knowledge and connectivity. Products will be bought on demand for customers who are interested in a service. The product itself becomes less valuable if no service is associated with it, driving costs for products down to nearly zero. In Germany, for example, costs for mobile phones are nearly zero. For about 50 cents, it is possible to buy a mobile phone. But in order to use the phone, the customer needs to buy services for it, such as a prepaid phone card or a GSM card that is debited on a monthly basis.

2.3   Paradigms in the New Economy

2.3.1   The One-to-One Enterprise

This section describes two paradigms that change the way business is done. The impact of the one-to-one marketing paradigm and the dynamic trade idea do not halt at the frontiers to the real world, but will eventually be part of the overall economy.

As we will see in Chapter 5, a one-to-one marketing strategy needs to be implemented in order to make your company successful on the Internet. Mass customization is a must on the Internet as more and more companies make this a standard.

In order to support one-to-one marketing, you must transform your whole company to support the new paradigm. Therefore, it is necessary to look at the products, services, and information your company is offering right now and decide which of them gain value through the one-to-one approach. Digital goods, such as news services, are easy to customize to the individual reader, unlike products such as perfumes, which cannot be customized—this would cost far too much. But this may change in the near future; therefore, it is necessary to repeat this step of evaluating the assets of your company. The vision of the dynamic enterprise needs to be updated on a regular basis to encompass more and more customized products. Though it may not seem likely right now, even products such as gas from a gas station may be customized in the future.

---

[14]http://www.skema.com.ve/costa-azul/

The dynamic enterprise is a long-term goal for most established companies, as it requires many organizational changes within the enterprise. The major difference of the one-to-one approach is that there are no target groups or product segments anymore, but instead, individuals who want products designed to their own needs and not the needs of the average customer.

In the real world this is not possible, as it would take up far too many resources, but in the digital world it is possible for a company to build truly individual relationships with each of its customers. Most companies just use the Internet as a one-to-one marketing vehicle but forget to use the data that they have gathered when talking in real life to the customer.

As the dynamic enterprise does not have target groups, it is not possible to measure success for a certain product with traditional means. Instead of measuring success by product segments or target groups, the success is measured for every customer individually. How successful the company has been in dealings with a particular customer is what really matters, not how many units of a certain product have been sold.

This change of focus may result in lower product sales, but this should not worry you too much. The focus on the customer has a lot of advantages. By collecting more detailed information on customers, you will easily be able to adapt to their needs. Customers are willing to spend more on a certain product and its associated services if it is customized to their specifications. Mass customization will keep the costs down while customer satisfaction will rise—this will eventually increase the profits.

Traditionally, many companies use "standard" marketing for 95 percent of their customers and one-to-one marketing for the other 5 percent. The traditional one-to-one marketing meant that a dedicated person would build up a relationship with the customer and would adapt the products to the needs of the customer. This is extremely cost-intensive both for the companies and the customers; only very large customers could afford this type of marketing, and companies have had no interest in extending the personal marketing initiative.

With the Internet and the new possibilities in one-to-one marketing, companies are able to extend the customized approach to all customers and reduce the cost for information technology at the same time. Typically, businesses won't allow everybody to be part of the one-to-one marketing offensive at one time, but offer these capabilities over time to more customers. Therefore, the shift is performed by steadily moving one target group after the other to the new paradigm.

The biggest obstacles to overcome are convincing everyone in the company to adhere to the new paradigm and convincing the customers that this new paradigm is the best for them as well. One-to-one marketing and production perfects the trend to mass customization.

2.3.2 Dynamic Trade

The digital economy is driven by several factors that constantly change the
Internet environment. Customer demand is changing. As soon as one site offers an added value to its services and products, customers expect that added
value from all others as well; otherwise, they will abandon a particular Web
site. The pressure from customers has increased, as they are more willing to
change than companies are. The growing globalization is also a driving factor
on the Internet and works both ways. The more the economy is globalized, the
more the Internet is used for business transactions. The same is true the other
way around. The more the Internet is used for business transactions, the more
global the economy becomes. The Internet ubiquity, new technologies, and intermediaries are also driving forces on the Internet that constantly change the
conditions in which companies operate.

Waverly Deutsch of Forrester Research[15] stated in a speech[16] that the constant change on the Internet is creating a New Economy that Forrester calls
dynamic trade. This dynamic trade is "leveraging technology to satisfy current
demand with customized response." Unlike traditional shops, where prices are
decided in advance, the Internet offers the possibility of creating highly dynamic prices for a certain point in time, customized to the request of a certain
customer. As comparing prices has become easy on the Internet—especially if
customers use shopping agents—fixed pricing does not work anymore.

Dynamic trade will change relationships between organizations (especially
between buyers and sellers) and alter the processes used to do business. Established organizations will surely change in the near future. Instead of static
organizations, more and more virtual organizations will appear. A virtual organization can be set-up ad hoc for certain tasks and broken up when the task
has been executed.

The constant change alters the way business is done over the Internet. Instead of using a price list, the *market* decides on the price of a product. Product
attributes become buyer-selected instead of seller-selected, as in the traditional
market. The production of goods in the era of dynamic trade is initiated after
the sale has been completed, as the product is highly customized and cannot be
produced before the customer has ordered the goods. Customer relationships
are strongly customized, and the company asset is the customer database with
detailed information on the customers' preferences. The customers get much
more power through the dynamic economy.

That said, this also requires more flexibility from your partners. Instead
of having one partner that delivers a certain service or product, you will more
likely have a few of them delivering the same product or service and will choose
the one that has the best price at a certain point in time. Contracts become
more flexible and do not contain fixed pricing.

---

[15]http://www.forrester.com/

[16]Forrester Forum, "Preparing for Dynamic Trade in the Internet Economy," Amsterdam, 1999.

In the dynamic economy, added value is provided in the form of services. The core product becomes less important, while the services around the product become more important, both for the company selling it and for the customers buying it. By linking real-time demand into production, the supply chain has become highly dynamic as well. The production therefore moves closer to the customer and is able to respond to demand much faster and more exactly.

The real change comes from the new pricing model, which now matches market conditions. This pricing model is based on the auction and bid model, which is already used by some companies on the Internet.

Today, airlines already offer all seats at dynamic prices. If there is a lot of interest in getting tickets for a certain flight, the prices will go up for the seats. For flights where many seats are still empty, the prices will drop, as it is better for the airlines to have a fully booked flight. It happens quite often that people who sit side by side in an airplane paid totally different prices, depending on the time they bought the tickets. Last-minute sales already work this way and have for some years.

Another industry that is already highly dynamic is the telecom industry, where capacity on international carriers is sold at a dynamic price. Depending on the time of day and the number of interested companies, the price for a one-minute phone call may go up or down.

In order to prepare your company for dynamic trade, a flexible execution environment is required. Therefore, your strictly hierarchical company needs to reorganize to a hyperarchical company, which consists of many virtual teams that are able to reorganize at any time. A fluid restructuring of internal and external processes will become the goal. A corporate process audit team will be necessary to monitor all ongoing activities and to establish process metrics with partners.

2.4   Return on Investment

2.4.1   Main Categories

No matter what you want to achieve in the long run with your e-business initiative, part of a good business plan is a solid return on investment (ROI) calculation. In the past this has often not been the case with Internet startups, and that was one of the many reasons why they failed. The ROI is a clear way to determine whether a company is earning a profit on its technology investment. The biggest challenge with ROI calculations is that there is no single path. Actually, there are almost as many paths to take as there are companies doing business on the Internet.

The calculation of e-business ROI can be divided into three main categories: those that develop their own measurement practices; those that use off-the-shelf ROI products; and those that hire consultants to develop a custom ROI measurement. Many companies, including the big five consulting companies

(Accenture,[17] Deloitte & Touche,[18] Ernst & Young,[19] KPMG,[20] and PricewaterhouseCoopers,[21]) offer ROI measurement products and services.

Companies that have started with ROI calculations in the past have quantifiable results today and can drive their business more easily into the right direction. Why? Simply because they have a better basis for their assumptions on future business. Companies that have started their e-business initiatives without an ROI in mind have difficulties today in determining what direction they need to take to correct possible issues.

Gauging an IT project's ROI has never been easy, but Web projects present a new set of challenges for business and IT managers. Before the Web, IT projects were typically measured by the cost savings or efficiencies they brought to a company. But e-business is different. The goals of a Web project are often strategic and involve many areas of a company. As a result, Web project investments affect areas that are more difficult to measure, such as total revenue and customer relationships.

Demonstrating ROI for Web initiatives is climbing fast on the list of business priorities. IT and e-commerce managers are striving to find effective metrics to determine if the payback they'll get justifies the investment. Measuring ROI has become critical for e-business ventures because they compete for funding with other projects that are easier to measure, such as opening a new branch or launching a new product.

Measuring returns on Internet technology and e-commerce projects can be challenging for a number of reasons. Predicting customer behavior is difficult because the concept of using the Web to do business is still relatively new to many consumers and businesses, and that means forecasting sales and profits is imprecise at best.

Also, many of the economic benefits of the Internet and e-commerce are intangible and therefore difficult to measure. E-business projects may also include hidden costs, such as planning, procuring, project management, and operations.

2.4.2 Methodologies

The complete coverage on ROI is too complex to handle within this book, but some example methodologies will be described in this subsection. Businesses are using a variety of metrics for e-business, many of which have already been used to measure the financial payback of such IT endeavors as data warehousing, Enterprise Resource Planning (ERP), desktop hardware and software upgrades, and network expansions.

---

[17]http://www.accenture.com/

[18]http://www.deloitte.com/

[19]http://www.ey.com/

[20]http://www.kpmg.com/

[21]http://www.pwcglobal.com/

The most common methodology is what is known as simple ROI, a standard cost/benefit analysis that compares the costs of implementing a system with the financial benefits it provides over time.

A more complex methodology is called Economic Value Added (EVA), which measures the payback of technology and other investments within a company. EVA has been developed by management consultant Stern Stewart & Co. and calculates after-tax operating profit minus the capital used to generate the profit.

EVA is applied to any investment evaluated by management as standard company policy. Although there are certain areas in e-business where it's hard to do a precise calculation, and managers have to rely on their instinct, it helps to calculate the ROI in a much better way.

In addition to EVA, companies are using net present value (the value of the net benefits of an investment that are realized over time, measured in current dollars) and weighted scoring methods (which evaluate investments relative to a company's overall IT strategy or its e-business strategy).

Some companies are using technology such as data warehousing to analyze and conduct historical comparisons of activity at their Web site in order to measure payback. Many other solutions exist, but it is difficult to determine which solution is the best for your business. In the following subsection some examples are provided, but it is important to get a consulting company involved to define the best way to measure the ROI for your e-business.

2.4.3   Examples

Last year Vitro Corp.,[22] a glass manufacturer based in Mexico City, began using EVA for any IT investment exceeding $20,000, following a directive from the company's CFO. Vitro applied EVA measures to ERP, distributed networks, customer relationship management, network upgrades, and most recently, Internet-based procurement of supplies.

The ROI studies have helped the IT department make decisions on whether to go ahead with project launches and to track performance of those that get the green light. It also helps prioritize the initiatives according to the projected benefits and the risk involved.

CoolSavings.com,[23] a direct marketing service that offers consumers discounts on goods from leading manufacturers, used another approach to ROI. Instead of measuring internal returns, the company measured customers' returns on online advertising. The company has used the measuring services of comScore Networks, Inc.,[24] to track the returns. This helped the company to find out the number of marketing dollars it has to put out to attract and retain a customer.

---

[22]http://www.vitro.com/
[23]http://www.coolsavings.com/
[24]http://www.comscore.com/

Another company using Web-oriented ROI to help establish business priorities is Ryder System, Inc.,[25] a trucking and transportation company. The company rolled out a product developed with consulting help from IBM. The tool, dubbed Return on Web Investment (ROWI), was fashioned to quickly assess and prioritize e-business initiatives that may come up. The company recognized that traditional cycles of planning did not work on the Internet because they took too long. ROWI is a framework that lets the company evaluate Web opportunities.

As part of its ROWI calculations, Ryder has developed what it calls a strategy tree to identify certain priorities, such as customer satisfaction and financial performance, that can further these objectives. Ryder used the information it gathered to create a scorecard that lists objectives, goals, and indicators, and their correlation to financial performance. The scorecard is then applied to proposed projects.

Individual.com[26] is a company that provides customized news and information services over the Internet. It is using a data warehouse hosted by Primary Knowledge to track activity on its Web site and the effectiveness of its online advertising campaign. Primary Knowledge aggregates all customer data in a scalable, secure data warehouse and enables companies to act on it with report packages, analysis tools, and targeting applications.

Another example is Sunstone Hotels,[27] a 72-hotel chain, using homegrown ROI methods with a primary focus on assessing its cost structure. Sunstone's e-procurement unit, BuyEfficient, buys more than $60 million worth of goods yearly through an online marketplace designed by PurchasePro.com.[28]

More advanced e-business sites become more difficult to measure, as they contain a complex set of relationships, such as supply chain partners, fulfillment houses, and logistics partners that complicate efforts to measure costs and returns. These partnerships have become an asset for the company, but there is no traditional way to measure the value. Although there is no universal measurement available today, it is important to understand that these measurements are necessary in order to control the company as accurately as possible. The more companies understand that they must work to tailor these measures to their businesses, the more successful those measures will be.

2.5   Driving Business Process Reengineering

2.5.1   Changing Business Processes

With the introduction of high-speed networks, businesses are able to execute much faster without having to change their existing business processes. One

---

[25]http://www.rydersystem.com/

[26]http://www.individual.com/

[27]http://www.sunstonehotels.com/

[28]http://www.purchasepro.com/

example is the processing of electronic data exchange (EDI) messages. The Internet has made it possible to deliver EDI much faster. EDI is communicated in a store-and-forward principle that can take up to a day to arrive at the computer of the recipient. An email over the Internet arrives at the destination, in most cases, within seconds. EDI is used, for example, to notify manufacturers that their shipment has arrived, but if the information arrives the next day, its usefulness is limited. Replacing private EDI networks with EDI over the Internet speeds up processes significantly without requiring a change of the process and without increasing turnaround times.

EDI is a standard format for exchanging business data. The standard is approved by the American National Standards Institute X12 (ANSI)[29] and it was developed by the Data Interchange Standards Association. ANSI X12 is either closely coordinated with or is being merged with an international standard, EDIFACT. An EDI message contains a string of data elements, each of which represents a singular fact, such as a price, product model number, and so forth, separated by a delimiter. The entire string is called a data segment. One or more data segments framed by a header and trailer form a transaction set, which is the EDI unit of transmission (equivalent to a message). A transaction set often consists of what would usually be contained in a typical business document or form.

Through the increased speed of traditional business processes, the economy has been put into a position to offer real-time delivery of processing information. Customers expect to see results 24 hours a day, seven days a week, no matter where the company is located. The expectation of a rapid response means that there is less time for organizational navigation through a company. Direct questions require direct responses, and customers want direct access to those responses. They want to be able to access an enterprise system directly or speak to the responsible person directly. Real-time processing is becoming a major factor in the market, while the number of batch process systems decreases.

2.5.2 Introduction to Business Process Reengineering

The general idea of business process reengineering (BPR) is to provide the means for optimizing and enhancing business processes, both in the production area and in the administration. Using information technology in general—and the Internet in particular—many processes can be streamlined, reducing time and costs for every single step. By digitizing the information flow, for example, costly media breaks can be prevented. A media break occurs every time information is moved from one medium to another, requiring cost for the conversion. A handwritten document that needs to be typed into a computer is one example.

---

[29] http://www.ansi.org/

In the early 1990s, many consulting companies started to use the term *business process reengineering*, especially after James Champy and Michael Hammer[30] wrote a bestseller on the topic. In order to explain what is needed to reengineer a business, they used a set of terms to describe the needs for BPR: "radical," "fundamental," "business process," and "increase by factors."

Radical means that it is not enough to scratch at the surface and modify existing processes, but that it is necessary to create completely new processes to deal with the change. BPR questions existing processes, rules, and structures and replaces them with completely new processes, rules, and structures to increase the revenues or effectiveness by factors.

Fundamental means that the reasons for the business are questioned: Why are things done in a certain way? What are the reasons for using a certain process? Do we need this product or service?

The term *increase by factor* means that the goal of BPR is not to enhance existing processes and increase revenues by five percent, but that effectiveness and revenues are supposed to jump by factor two (100 percent) or higher as a result of the business process reengineering.

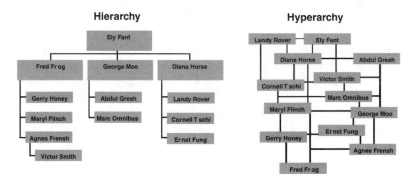

Figure 2.3. A typical hierarchy compared to a hyperarchy.

BPR's focus is to reorganize companies to fit the new processes. Instead of creating organizations based on products or location, the organizations are defined by the business process. The business processes are defined in a customer-centric way. Every person in the process who receives input from you needs to be considered a customer, and every person giving you input is viewed as a supplier.

In many companies the employees seem to be working very efficiently within their organization, but viewed from a customer's standpoint, the results are very inefficient. The problems are the coordination of resources for a process and the management of information. Even simple processes involve several departments of a company in order to be executed. Instead of adhering to the

---

[30]M. Hammer and J. Champy, *Re-engineering the Corporation*, Harperbusiness, New York, 2001.

structure of these departments, the BPR tries to reorganize the departments to fit the process. In many cases virtual organizations fit best, as the processes change without necessarily changing the work for the single employee.

In order to make organizations more flexible, it is necessary to get rid of the strict hierarchical organization and move on to a hyperarchical system, which allows every department to communicate directly with every other deparment. Decisions are made by the person who is collecting and evaluating all the relevant information. Figure 2.3 shows the differences between a hierarchy and a hyperarchy. The World Wide Web is the best example of a hyperarchical system. There is no root page from which everything starts. Each single Web site may decide to have a hierarchical system for its documents, but between Web sites there is no hierarchy. Every Web site has the same priority on the Web.

2.5.3 Methods of Reorganization

There are two possible ways to reorganize a business. A change can be initiated either by the employees or by the structure of the company. In order to get the maximum benefit out of the reengineering process, both approaches should always be combined and executed at the same time, as both have the same goal but come from different angles.

Changing processes through the employees means that it is necessary to influence key persons throughout the company. A more positive work environment is created through the training of these people, which results in a more friendly atmosphere that enables the employees to work more efficiently. The goal is to build a team out of several individuals working for the same department. Only if these people are able to communicate the necessary information within the department can the work be done in time. As a result, the structure of the company is changing.

The structural approach works the other way around. By applying structural changes within the company, employees are moving from their actual position to another position that fits better into the new structure of the company.

2.5.4 Planning Systems

Manufacturing resources, planning systems, and material requirement planning software can compute the actual requirements for material and resources in a highly dynamic way. In order to do these calculations, they need detailed and accurate input data. So far, this has been difficult, and many systems have failed, as it was not possible to keep all the systems up to date because data was delayed for one reason or another. This resulted in inconsistent systems and forced people to manually change requirements to meet the demand. Human interaction is often inaccurate and leads to more delays, as humans are much slower in moving data. The data on demand was coming from many different sources, in many different formats, on many different types of media, forcing people to convert information manually.

The advantage of electronic business is that all information on customer demand is already in digital form and can be easily sent to the inventory management system. The necessary data can be gathered, formatted, and presented easily by the inventory system, which can handle the data and deliver the right output. If the two computers are directly linked, the inventory system can be fed with real-time information. But even if the systems are not directly connected—because of security concerns, for example—the data fed into the inventory system has a much higher quality than from other sources. The reasons include the technical possibilities and the consistent media, but also the direct contact to the customer, which enables you to receive detailed information.

In order to use the full impact of the Internet for the digital planning systems, new processes need to be put in place that replace or enhance the old processes, structures, and resources.

2.5.5   Just-in-Time

The ultimate goal of every digital company is to move to just-in-time (JIT) inventory management. Software companies that distribute their goods over the Internet have already achieved this goal. The product is created in the instant a demand for the product is generated. In the case of the software company, it would be the moment a customer has paid for the software. Other companies, such as a digital bookshop, will try to avoid any inventories and pass on the order from their customers on a JIT basis to the publisher. The publisher then sends out the books to the virtual bookshop, which in turn passes the goods on to the customers. In this process the publisher still has to produce books in advance of demand.

In order to make every part of the value chain JIT, it is necessary to change the way external relationships are managed and requires the change of many internal processes. In order to implement a JIT environment, an effective exchange of information between supplier and purchaser is required. Organizations need to become much more tightly integrated in order to achieve this level of cooperation and meet the requirements for the input and output. Electronic shopping systems are the first step in that direction, as they are able to facilitate the level of interaction and exchange information at a fraction of the cost of the proprietary systems developed and used by the major retailers before the worldwide introduction of the Internet. With the worldwide deployment of electronic business, businesses are able to take all the advantages of the digital era to implement complex JIT systems.

Suppliers, on one hand, will benefit from the frequent and direct communications with customer organizations and feed the incoming information directly into the production systems: first, to make production predictions better, and later, to create a real JIT environment. Through strong relationships with your customers, you are able to adopt even more demanding supplier performance criteria that result in higher levels of service to your (potential) customers and propel your company ahead of the competition. Companies that supply others with products that are easily digitized—such as software and music—will be able to deliver the products directly and immediately to their customers. Inventory, production, and shipping costs go literally down to zero.

Purchasers, on the other hand, are able to manage the supply chain more easily as a result of the introduction of the electronic business. More information about the customers is becoming available and a more accurate demand-forecasting is possible. The demand from customers can be fed easily into the inventory control system, and the demand is passed directly on to the suppliers. The whole process of ordering can be automated and can accelerate not only the inventory management process, but the overall process throughout the new virtual value chain.

By connecting purchasers and suppliers directly to each other, purchasers will be able to automate the order process and the delivery schedules by routing the orders automatically, based on the customer's demand. The purchaser is also able to check inventory levels both inhouse and at the supplier sites, offering customers a far better service. Companies that are not willing to adapt to this new paradigm will have a tough life in the future.

2.6   Designing, Developing, and Deploying the System

2.6.1   Identifying the Online Business

After the World Wide Web was developed, information sellers saw the opportunity to distribute their goods on a worldwide basis without spending much money on infrastructure. These businesses were the first to open a Web site and start doing business over the Internet. Slowly but steadily, more and more businesses that do not sell or provide information were doing business over the Internet. Information providers offered their information for free in the beginning, as the Internet had been designed for the exchange of scientific information.

First of all, in order to make the right decision, it is necessary to identify the type of business you are in. There is no single solution for all industries. Companies can be divided into three categories: providers of "soft" goods, providers of "hard" goods, and service providers. Soft goods are products that can be easily digitized—such as software and information—and delivered over the Internet. Hard goods, on the other hand—such as food and toys—are not easily digitizable and need traditional methods of delivery. Service providers offer products—such as translations or advertising—that can be done both online and offline. Depending on the type of product your company sells, a different strategy is necessary to be successful on the Internet.

If the company is in the soft goods business, the Internet can become a sales and distribution channel. You must evaluate if the Internet business can become the fourth channel. If so, then it should help to reduce costs. Companies that deal with hard goods won't see the Internet as their primary goal for expansion, as it is not possible to digitize these products, but the Internet still can help reduce costs for these companies. Manufacturers, retailers, and online shops can reduce costs by digitizing the value chain and the orders between the partners.

Set realistic goals for your online business. The online business can help to reduce presale costs, such as marketing, and postsale costs, such as customer care. Online marketing can be much more direct than traditional marketing, and the success of marketing can be measured more easily. But the main cost reduction will come from the sales costs. Online distribution of goods can reduce these costs to almost zero. The order costs will also go down to nearly zero. The order information is provided by the customer in digital form and can be easily processed by your company.

Direct revenues from your online business may come from point-of-sale revenues, subscriptions to online services, and revenues from advertisers. Traditional business will not want to base their revenues on advertising online, but many startup online businesses live off of only banner advertising until they are profitable enough to base their income on actual product sales.

Depending on the size of your company, you should decide if you want to host your Web site inhouse or if you should outsource the server or even the whole business. The advantage of outsourcing is the lower costs, but you may lose control over your business. As most companies today need an intranet, putting Web servers in front of the firewall would not increase costs largely. Outsourcing online business may be useful if your company does not have the resources to implement and maintain the solution. A section in Chapter 5 is dedicated to finding the right ISP.

Next, you will need to design the appropriate online experience. Online shoppers want an efficient and easy-to-use Web site that offers the lowest prices possible, without decreasing the service. Online business will want direct access and integration to the databases of the partners and cooperation between the legacy systems.

To better understand the needs of your customers, track the visits of the customers on your Web site and save the information. This profiling helps to improve the business, the navigation on the Web site, and can help to find new areas of business that can change or extend the focus of your company.

Unlike traditional business that was restricted to national laws, online businesses need to keep up with international laws. You'll find that online businesses that restrict business to only one or very few countries will not work very well. Your company will receive many requests from customers in other countries asking why the Web site is restricted, resulting in an overload for the customer care center and harming the online image of the company.

Before launching your electronic business on the Internet, it is necessary to analyze the situation that your company is in.

- **Identification**—Identify the type of business you are in.

- **Evaluation**—Evaluate the Internet as your sales and distribution channel.

- **Goals**—Set realistic goals for your online venture.

- **Reduction**—Use the Internet to cut costs.

- **Sales**—Use the Internet to make sales.

- **Location**—Place your site either at your Internet connection or at the ISP.

- **Shopping**—Design the appropriate shopping experience for your customers.

- **Profiling**—Get to know better the needs of your customers.

- **Public relations**—Advertise and promote your site.

- **Payment**—Accept online payment.

- **Laws**—Keep up with international laws.

Table 2.2. Electronic Business Analysis

2.6.2 Developing a Business Plan

In order to develop a successful e-business plan, it is necessary to embed the e-business strategy into the overall enterprise strategy. More forward-thinking organizations will work to make the e-business strategy the overall enterprise strategy in the end. Several issues need to be taken into account, which we will explore here.

E-business over the Internet is not just a platform that enables existing customers, but will also result in new customers. Although these new customers are very important to your business, you also need to take care of existing customers. They already have business relations with your company and can also benefit from your move to the Internet. Therefore, they need to move from physical channels into the electronic channel. This move does cost money; depending on the type of company, it may range from installation of new software to buying hardware and hooking up an Internet connection. Therefore, it is necessary to add value to the electronic channel. If your customers do not gain anything from it, it is not very likely that they will use it.

If you are an Internet startup or are only concerned with new customers, this won't be that important. Be forewarned, however, that this approach is risky since you do not know your customers yet. Relying on strong relationships and moving the communication between the partners involved will result in much higher revenues, but only if all parties are of the same opinion.

It is necessary to do some research and ask your customers what they really need and how the existing service can be improved. The use of the Internet will most probably require you to create new processes and, depending on these new processes, people will accept the online offering or reject it. Technology should be used to improve existing processes or create new ones, but business should not be driven by technology, as it makes the business case much too dependent on one piece of software or hardware.

A sound business plan can be implemented in several ways, which are interchangeable and do not restrict the business to the policies of a software vendor, for example. Another important issue to consider when relying on technology is that in the Internet world, technology and user preferences change very quickly. A technology that is "in" today can be out tomorrow. It is not possible to plan 12 or 18 months in advance. The business case must be flexible enough to adapt to the expectations of the customers and the evolving technologies on the Internet.

New companies appear on the Internet rapidly, creating a vast supply of new choices. Any business plan for the Internet needs to take into account that not only are technology and customers' expectations changing very quickly, but so is the competition. There is no time to do extensive competition analysis by comparing your company to other existing companies. It is necessary to compare ideas instead of companies. We will see how competition analysis is done on the Internet later in this chapter.

In order to implement such a business case, the management, the employees, and the business partners need to be aware of this shift; you must get their input if the processes involved are supportable by them. It is also important to understand how areas such as performance reviews and sales targets are affected.

One of the primary tasks is to define the customer segment your e-business wants to target. Depending on the type of network you are using to create the e-business, the target group will be different. If you are using your company intranet as the foundation for the proposed e-business, you will have an internal audience, such as marketing, sales, finance, and any other internal department. If the business plan is to communicate with partners, suppliers, or retailers in order to exchange information, products or services over a network, creating an extranet will resolve the technical issues. When using the Internet, you will most likely reach external customers. Depending on the target audience, you can start to implement the e-business system, as this element in the business plan has an effect on many other areas, ranging from interface design to marketing.

In order to make the e-business system attractive to the target group, it is necessary to develop an effective online marketing campaign. All departments involved in running the system need to understand the target audience: who they are and how they spend their time on the Web site. In order to develop a sound business plan, it is necessary to know what factors are important for the target audience. You should also identify the needs and expectations of the customers, as well as how the company and its services and products can address these needs and services more effectively than the competition.

There are, of course, risks involved, as with any business initiative. Therefore, it is important to identify these risks in advance and create backup plans to relieve negative effects that may impact your company. The electronic world usually has some very special risks—such as a defective Web server or a dead connection to the Internet—that in itself may not be difficult to resolve, but that can bring down your whole business if the problem cannot be resolved in a short time. The main risk comes from security breaches, from people who try to steal, delete, or change information that is the basis of your business. Although most people think that an Internet connection makes your company vulnerable, the biggest security risk comes from within the company. Security technology is able to secure the access from the Internet, but with the simple click of an email, employees are able to send information to outsiders (such as competitors).

The business plan should also evaluate possible channel conflicts by investigating attitudes and perceptions in existing channels and then providing solutions on how to resolve the conflicts.

Another important property of the business plan is to provide a road map listing with all major milestones for all phases of the project, from the design phase to the operating phase, from the strategic level to the tactical level. It should cover the next 12 to 18 months in detail, as this is the maximum time for deploying a new electronic business. A project that takes longer to deploy will most probably have difficulties succeeding, as the technology is moving far too fast to make a project competitive using technology older than two years. Defining milestones for the next few years will make sense on a business level, but should not incorporate any dependencies on a specific hardware or software technology, as this will be superseded by something else in no more than two years' time.

The business plan needs to address the issue of integrating the new e-business processes with the old real-world processes and the processes of your partners and customers. Only if this is addressed in a reasonable manner is it possible to create a complex network of business processes. In the end, the goal of your e-business initiative will be to integrate all communications and move them to the Internet to make them more automatic and direct.

Inventory, accounting, sales forecasting, order processing, customer information, and operational resources management will be integrated into your digital business, and therefore the business plan needs to state when and how these services can be integrated into the overall plan. Only if it is possible to integrate the existing services and partners into the e-business will it be truly successful, as the viability and profitability depend on the efficiency of the value-chain-wide system implementations.

2.6.3 Preparing for the Electronic Revolution

When implementing electronic business in your company, you should get all departments in your company involved. Electronic business will transform the way you conduct business; therefore, it is necessary to include each employee in this process. They need to support the Internet initiative and to support the necessary redesign of the business processes.

For the three major phases—design, development, and deployment—every department needs to be involved to understand what impact the Internet will have on their daily business. Marketing, sales, customer service, engineering, operations, and information technology will benefit from the decision if implemented correctly. The departments are able to assist in reengineering the business processes with their specific knowledge, and by asking them to send a representative to the project team, they will be more willing to participate in the changes in the company. The project team provides ideas and input for the functionality and the design requirements of the future digital business. In order to make the project team work effectively, everybody should have some knowledge of the Internet. Provide introductory courses for employees who haven't had contact with the Internet in order to make their contributions more valuable and reduce their fear of the new medium. The course should give them a feeling for the possibilities, along with some basic applications such as email and creating HTML pages.

In order to survive in the Internet Age, technology should be able to support heterogeneous systems architectures. Therefore, it is necessary to use component technology to build new applications by reusing existing building blocks. Every application needs to be Internet-enabled, and connections to the applications of your partners need to be established, just as if they were your own systems.

Your employees' computers should be connected to each other so that people are able to exchange files, information, and emails. One or more intranet servers should be set up, that run not only a mail service, but also a Web server with company information and departmental information. Through the introduction of an intranet, all employees have the opportunity to experiment with technology while at work. This reduces the amount of time spent introducing new technologies. Technology is changing fast; every day, updates of existing programs or completely new programs appear. Therefore, the business plan needs to discuss the paradigm and how the company is able to cope with the rapid change.

In order to foster the vision of the Internet business, it is necessary that every employee understands the impact. Every single employee not only needs to know how to browse Web pages and send email, but should have a personal Web page up and running, both on your intranet and on the Internet. Although it may seem drastic, it is a good idea to get rid of all people who are not able to utilize the Web. Designing a Web page is simple—anyone can learn how to do it. Do not expect that everyone will have an extensive Web site up and running, but a single page should be done by everyone. This should apply to the managers as well!

2.6.4   Design and Development

Technical aspects and business processes need to be combined during the design phase. In order to deal with other businesses and customers, it is necessary to exchange data. Therefore, security has the highest priority. In most cases, it is necessary to reveal some data to customers and business partners, but a company needs to be sure that the right data goes to the right person. Protecting the sensitive information becomes a critical issue in the design and development phase.

In order to provide a valuable service to your customers, the data presented should be up-to-date. Mission-critical information is the most valuable to the customer, but requires you to add some extra protection to your company intranet, as the information can easily be used against you.

The project teams need to determine which technologies can be used to implement the business processes and which business processes need to be reengineered to become more valuable. If Internet technologies are already used on the intranet, you must determine how your company can connect your intranet to the Internet.

The visual presentation on the company's Web site is also very important. Marketing should develop a visual strategy for the Web site that takes into account the needs of the customers and the business processes of the company.

To succeed in the electronic world, the employees in your company are required to adopt new skills, knowledge, and expertise in three disciplines: creativity, strategy, and technology. Unlike normal business, the digital business employees need to constantly update their knowledge, as technology is changing all the time. Lifelong learning becomes a must for everyone involved in the Internet. Only if everyone is up-to-date about the latest technology can new creative business models be created and an ever-changing strategy be developed. It is no longer possible to create a long-term strategy, since new competitors and technologies emerge and constantly change the business model.

Strategic planning needs to be approached very differently because of the dynamic nature of the Internet. Using the Internet to start investigations on the competition has been made easier, not only for your company, but also for any other company. The existing business processes need to monitored and analyzed around the clock and need to be adjusted to the changing environment by the introduction of new business models and new technologies. Many existing processes can be streamlined and enhanced by Internet technologies.

It is obvious by now that Internet technologies are rapidly evolving every day. In order to keep pace with the new breakthroughs, it is necessary to have a core team of experts who are able to understand the hardware and software solutions and evaluate new technologies. Technologies for site development, systems integration, and security issues also need to be addressed by this group, which must consist of technical and business people.

The creative team needs to understand more than just design in order to develop an appealing user experience. This requires the creative department to understand the business models and the technical implications of emerging standards. They also need to understand what customers see on a Web page and how to use it. User tracking has become easy and helps companies to evaluate business processes and to streamline the process and the Web design. The Web design will also have impact on the audience development activities, as it will drive Web-surfer traffic to the Web site. Although not necessarily the target customers for a company, surfers are prospective customers who may be willing to try out a new business; therefore, they need to be taken care of.

Marketing and promotional techniques that are effective in traditional media don't always translate well into the online marketplace. The creative area involves understanding the most effective online marketing techniques and applying the ones that make the most sense for the specific product and the audience. The best technologies need to be evaluated in your business plan.

As most businesses do not have inhouse expertise in all disciplines, it may be helpful to have a partner for the startup phase. This will reduce the delay for developing and deploying the electronic business, and the advantage competitors may gain through a delay is reduced. The partners are able to provide skills, knowledge, and expertise in the area of electronic business and the Internet. Many companies offer consulting in this area, and depending on the size of the consulting firm, the direction will be different. The big five consulting companies are more focused on strategic planning and concentrate less on technical details. Many companies get the big five involved for developing a strategy but retain smaller companies as soon as they start the design, development, and deployment of the solution, as the big five lack the in-depth Internet expertise and the creativity that are necessary to build up an electronic business.

For many companies, the big five are too expensive, and so they will choose smaller consulting companies. In order to find the right one, look for a company that is able to provide reference projects and experience in strategy, creativity, and technology. Depending on the knowledge within your company, the consulting firm should be able to support the electronic business through its entire life cycle, from planning to deployment and operation. Depending on your plans, the company should also offer the possibility to hand over the project at the time you are ready to implement it. Having a partner that is able to support the entire life cycle will offer you a fallback strategy in the event of problems, even though you decided to outsource only a part of the business.

In order to succeed with your Internet business, the following steps may be helpful:

- **Find a champion**—Get management involved and explain the benefits.

- **Plan for change**—Technology will change the corporate culture.

- **Define a pilot project**—Don't try to change everything at once.

- **Estimate the costs**—Training, maintenance, and support will be the majority of costs.

- **Measure productivity**—Measure it before and after the pilot has been implemented.

- **Reengineer business processes**—Make technology part of the business reengineering process, but don't let it dominate.

- **Learn as you go**—Make adjustments while you implement.

- **Prepare for resistance**—People don't change overnight, and organizations are even slower.

Table 2.3. Implementation Strategies

2.6.5 Building a Pilot

Once the design has been completed and the first implementation has taken place, it is a good move to start with a pilot, which proves the integrity and the effectiveness of the design concept. During the pilot phase, the departments and some selected customers should test the system and provide feed-back about the quality and usefulness of the system. A feedback form on the system should allow users to report bugs and logical errors. Performance issues should be resolved during the pilot phase, and the seamless integration into legacy systems needs to be checked. Another important point is to see if the system is scalable or if it crashes with 50 users online at the same time, and the effectiveness of the processes defined on the system needs to be verified.

During the pilot phase, it is possible to bring more customers into the system if you see that it works, but be careful about letting everyone from the public in without extensive testing. Although a few months of piloting may seem like a long time and a waste of money, it is still cheaper than going into full production with a faulty system. If you let all customers in, mark the site clearly as "beta" so that nobody associates your beta site with your brand.

There are no rules about how long a pilot phase should take. It depends on the size of the project and its importance. If you just plan to set up a few Web pages to inform your customers about your company, this can be done with a short pilot phase, as the information can be exchanged rather easily or the server can be switched off without doing real harm. If you plan to digitize complex business processes and want to rely on that service, then it is necessary to do extensive testing, which will take some months' time. More and more companies decide not to do a pilot phase, but go directly online with a beta version of their site and then let the general public test the site. Although this provides your company with zillions of bug reports, it may not be the best way of handling things. A system that takes too long to fix will ruin your company's image.

2.6.6   Going into Production

Once the feedback from the pilot phase has been evaluated and modifications have been introduced to the pilot system, your company is ready to deploy the complete system to the public. Although all departments will still be involved, the IT department will be responsible for the roll-out of the service. It will also be responsible for the availability of the service, and needs therefore to be trained in the technology used for building the business. It is also important to train the IT department on the business itself to better understand the requirements of the customers and users. This is necessary to maintain the system and the components involved and is necessary to extend the system based on the upcoming requirements of the users. Therefore, costs and goals for the IT personnel need to be included into the business plan. For some services, it may make sense to outsource the service operations. Calculations for both scenarios should be made. There is no simple rule to decide for or against outsourcing; the calculation will provide the answer.

In order to generate service awareness, the marketing staff needs to develop an audience. The audience then needs to be attracted to the site, and customer relationships need to be fostered. The key success factor is to create customers who return to the site, do business, and increase the number of visitors and customers through the awareness campaign. Unlike traditional businesses, the increase of customers does not automatically mean that you need to increase resources, such as employees or machines. The virtual business can expand by adding new hardware in the simplest case, and the customers won't notice a delay or disruption of service because the company is growing.

To accomplish a growth in customers and business, the marketing and communications department needs to use a combination of proven audience development techniques, such as special promotions, PR campaigns, and advertising (both online and offline), that leverage the unique characteristics of the Internet. This could include special prices for ordering online and up-to-date information. The marketing paradigm on the Internet is different than in print and broadcast media. The Internet has its own specialized promotional tools, which we will get to know in detail in Chapter 5. In order to be successful, a company needs to create online communities and always be on the cutting edge. Further, the subtle complexities of the online culture need to be appreciated and leveraged. Activities such as spamming are not acceptable on the Internet and are a factor for losing market share. The business plan needs to create a vision for the development of new marketing strategies on the Internet and for handling the risks associated with going online.

2.6.7   Connecting Your Intranet

In order to be successful on the Internet, you should first have a working intranet. An intranet allows companies to digitize internal business processes and also allows communication between all employees of a company. This is extremely helpful, especially if your company has several sites that are geographically separated. The experience the company and employees get from the intranet is very valuable for getting to know new technologies and new processes. It enables the employees to digitize existing processes and to invent new processes to simplify the work. It also enables new ways of communication, via email and chat between employees, and prepares them for the Internet.

As soon as your company goes online, employees will start to talk to their clients via email and chat. Just putting up some Web pages will most probably not return any investment. Only when you and your company start to digitize your processes will you see the revenues from the Internet flowing back into the company. Much of this depends on the company culture and the ability of each employee to accept and understand the importance of electronic communication in order to adapt his or her working habits to accommodate radically revised ways of working. An intranet that is readily adopted often becomes a seat of innovation and the development of new and better business practice, much of which will be related to internal company communication rather than the business of trading.

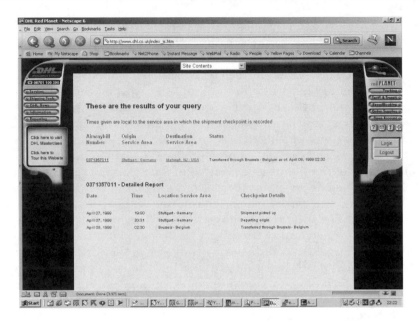

Figure 2.4. Order tracking at the DHL Web site.

Federal Express[31] built a very successful tracking and tracing functionality into its external Web page for their customers. Instead of calling FedEx, customers enter a tracking number to find out exactly where their package is at a given moment. After a short while, employees noticed how useful this service was to them. They started using it, and it soon replaced the old process that existed within the company. Now, everybody—customers, partners, and employees—is using the same system. They may see different views of the same data—the employee may see all shipping records, while the customers can only see their own—but using only a single data source reduces costs massively. Once FedEx offered this new service to customers and partners, it gave FedEx an edge over the competition. Customers suddenly preferred FedEx to other services. UPS and the other companies had to implement a tracking service as well to stay in business. See Figure 2.4 for the order-tracking system of FedEx rival DHL.[32]

2.6.8   Verifying the Results

As the Internet is changing constantly, it is not possible to find a single point in time to verify the results of your electronic business. The results are changing just as fast as the building blocks of the business. Therefore, a new paradigm

---

[31]http://www.fedex.com/
[32]http://www.dhl.com/

for verification is necessary: constant verification. As soon as your electronic business becomes visible to customers, you will be able to detect signs of the success and failure of the service.

Unlike traditional business, where you check results once a year, once a month, or once a week, it is possible to detect change in your online business in an instant of change. You can also adjust the business process to minimize the loss or increase the profit. Constant monitoring of the highly dynamic business has become a must. Therefore, a mission-critical operations center is something larger companies cannot afford to do without. Smaller companies may not be able to afford a 24-hour operations center, and they will rely on algorithms that adjust their business processes to the needs of the changing environment.

It is important to understand that a company that is not represented on the Internet will have difficulties in the future. Although not a must today, more and more companies expect to communicate and trade electronically. By starting as soon as possible with e-business, companies can reduce costs easily and increase profits, which should be the major drivers for every company.

Chapter 3

SELECTING
THE TECHNOLOGY

3.1   Internet Networking

3.1.1   The Internet Infrastructure

Over the last few centuries governments played a key role in building and regulating the transportation, communications, and energy infrastructures. Technology was driven by politics. Although it helped to move society from agriculture to industry, it now hinders the transition from the industrial society to the information society. Technology is driven nowadays by the private sector, and governments have more and more trouble keeping in touch with the latest developments in order to create appropriate regulations.

Many industries—such as transportation (airlines and railways), communications (mail services and telephone companies) and energy (power plants and gas stations)—have been privatized over the last few decades, splitting politics from economics, and vice versa.

Four key technological areas play a large role in future expansion of the Internet: the traditional telecommunications companies, satellite technology vendors, wireless networks providers, and cable companies.

The traditional telecommunications companies are moving quickly from providing simple services—such as phone calls—to becoming more technological, providing solutions for all types of customers. They are developing new technologies for higher bandwidth communication across existing networks, such as xDSL technologies and faster switches. In addition, software companies have developed new types of compression technologies to reduce the amount of data sent over the network. In addition to enhancing existing networks, new types of networks are being set up. Fibre-optic networks, which use optical amplification and photonic switches, are more powerful and more efficient. Telecommunications companies are not alone in laying these new fibre cables; electric utility companies spend a lot of money in providing fibre-optic Internet backbone.

New broadband networks with a global reach are being set up by satellite companies that work closely together with electronic and aerospace corporations to get the satellites up and running. These new broadband networks will connect people who live in areas where telephone service over normal copper wire is not available. These networks will be much faster than today's technology, at a much lower price, making network access available to people with very little income.

Most of the industrial countries have spent a lot of money and effort in building up cable networks for television over the last decades. The cable wires can be used for more than just television; many cable providers started to prepare the networks for two-way Internet traffic by introducing set-top boxes, which act as converters and separators for the inbound and outbound traffic (which, incidentally, includes more than just voice and video).

Wireless networks are the latest type of network being converted for Internet use. Local wireless networks will soon be found in every household, where all devices will be able to communicate via wireless Internet protocols. New standards for mobile phones will increase the throughput, and it is already possible for mobile phones to receive and transmit voice, data, and Internet traffic. The older generation of mobile phones can only pass the Internet traffic on to a computer, but newer ones are able to process the data themselves, allowing users to receive and send email and browse the Web.

3.1.2 The Internet Architecture

The Internet is actually a network of computer networks. It does not consist of just one network, but of many, which are physically separate and linked together only at very specific points. Every network that wants to participate in the Internet needs to adhere to a set of communication protocols, known as Internet Protocol (IP).

A network consists of nodes and channels that provide the basic communication infrastructure. Two different type of nodes are available: end nodes and intermediary nodes. The end nodes are servers and clients in most cases, either providing a set of services or requesting a set of services. Clients are most likely computers, from which users communicate to other nodes, and servers are centralized service providers that offer services for the clients, such as Web server and mail server functionalities.

Intermediary nodes are normally scaled-down computers that forward traffic between network segments. These devices are called routers and bridges. Sometimes they offer the option of filtering certain requests out and restricting access to certain devices within a network, but neither clients nor servers can access any service an intermediary node offers.

End nodes and intermediary nodes do not necessarily need to be different devices. Servers can also be clients at the same time, just as they can be a router simultaneously (and vice versa; a client can become a server or router).

Every node has a unique identifier called an IP address. Larger systems may have even more than one IP address. Normally, a domain name is assigned to the IP address, as a domain name is easier to remember.

The channels required for the communication between nodes can be implemented by many different means. In most cases a piece of cable is used to connect end nodes via intermediaries. The cable can be either coaxial, fibre optic, or good old copper wire. Depending on the type of cable used, you will get different connection speeds, but as the protocols for transmission are the same, the applications do not need to be rewritten for the different transmission channels. In addition to physical connections, wireless transmissions can be conducted. These electromagnetic transmissions are done at different frequencies, such as infrared transmissions, microwave links, cellular phone communication, and communication over a satellite link.

In general, it can be said that any node is able to communicate with every other node on the Internet. As this behavior is not always desired, intermediary nodes can refuse connections to particular nodes. These firewalls, as they are called, protect company-only networks (intranets) from the general public. As intranets use the same set of protocols, anybody would be able to get access to internal data that is company-confidential. Firewalls are also used to protect governmental data and any other set of information you want to make available to only a certain group over a network.

You may already know the Internet evolved from ARPANet. ARPANet was created by the U.S. government. Its basic idea was to create a network that would continue to work as a whole, even when parts of it collapsed (due to a nuclear attack, for example). In order to make this work, the network could be based on a hierarchical structure. Redundancy is the key to this type of network. Neither ARPANet nor the Internet provide rules on how nodes need to be connected. In most cases clients will have only a single link to other nodes, but servers and routers will have more than just one link. Through this "chaotic" structure, the Internet remains stable even though some nodes may drop out, as two nodes can be interconnected by more than one route. In case one intermediary node fails, the connection can be rerouted over other network segments, without any user interaction. The network is able to reorganize itself.

The Internet Protocol Suite, which needs to be implemented on every node, enables every pair of nodes to communicate directly without needing to know much about each other, except for the IP address or the domain name. The protocols are pieces of software that run on every node.

As the Internet apparently does not belong to anyone in particular, it seems astonishing that it still works so perfectly. One reason for this is that networks are not connected directly to each other anymore, but use backbones. These backbones are high-speed connections that link network segments that are physically separated and offer connection to networks that belong to others through interchange points, or gateways. The Internet backbones can really be called the "Information Highway." The local networks are more like cities, where the roads are more crowded and narrower.

The basic protocols on the Internet are planned and controlled in a hierarchical manner. Although anybody can contribute to the development of new technologies and protocols, only very few organizations influence what will be in the set of Internet protocols.

The Internet Engineering Task Force (IETF)[1] is the driving force for new standards. It is an open international community of companies that design and operate networks, research new technologies, and sell products based on these technologies. Although it is open to anyone, the task force is driven by companies that try to agree on new standards, which enable new services on the Internet. Internet standards proposed by the IETF are called Request for Comments (RFCs).[2] For historical reasons, the RFCs that are drafts keep their names when they become standards.

The Internet Engineering Steering Group (IESG)[3] is responsible for technical management of IETF activities and the Internet standards process.

The third group able to influence new standards is the Internet Society (ISOC),[4] which is an organization of Internet experts who comment on policies and practices. It oversees a number of other boards and task forces dealing with network policy issues.

The well-known World Wide Web Consortium (W3C)[5] has no direct influence on Internet standards. This organization is responsible for Web standards, which are built on top of the Internet standards.

3.1.3 The Internet Protocol Suite

In order to keep up communications, a set of rules has been established that takes care of the communications between the nodes connected to the Internet. The rules contain a wide number of functions that are grouped into protocols. This family of protocols is called the Internet Protocol Suite (IPS) or sometimes just TCP/IP.

The protocols are based on the OSI/ISO model of layers. The lower layers of the OSI/ISO model perform deep-nested, technical functions, while the layers in the middle are used by applications and rely on the fact that the functions in the lower layers work flawlessly. The upper layer protocols are based on the functionality an application requires, reducing the complexity of the applications drastically. A connection over the Internet can be established easily by any application without having to know anything about the hardware used to access the Internet, such as modems or routers.

---

[1] http://www.ietf.org/

[2] http://www.ietf.org/rfc/

[3] http://www.ietf.org/iesg.html

[4] http://www.isoc.org/

[5] http://www.w3.org/

Unlike the complete OSI/ISO model, which consists of seven layers, the IPS model uses only four of those layers: the link, network, transport, and application layers. The link layer is the lowest layer and is responsible for the network access. It connects the node and the channel and specifies how the node connects to the communication channel. It results in a signal being transmitted on a channel. The signal has been converted from packets that are made of a series of bits that contain the information. The signal is transmitted through a physical port (such as a parallel or RJ-11 port) onto a channel, which can be a fibre-optic cable or a copper wire. Typical protocols for the link layer are FDDI (Fibre Distributed Data Interface), which is used to create Ethernet networks and PPP (Point-to-Point Protocol) for token ring networks. The software for the link layer is also known as the device driver and is normally embedded on the network card.

The network layer is the next layer above the link layer. It is responsible for data addressing and the transmission of information. The protocols define how packets are moved around on the network—that is, how information is routed from one start node to the end node. Information is represented in segments and packets. A packet is composed of a set of bits or bytes. The protocol used for the network layer is the Internet Protocol (IP). Another protocol used at this level is responsible for multicasting, which sends out a single message to multiple recipients, reducing the required bandwidth for sending out the information. This protocol is used for audio and video broadcasts over the Internet and is called Internet Group Management Protocol. (IGMP)

The next level, the transport layer, is responsible for the delivery of the data to a certain node. It ensures whether and how the receipt of complete and accurate messages can be guaranteed. Information is represented in messages and segments. Messages are composed of a group of packets. The transport layer breaks down larger messages into segments, which then can be transported. On this layer, two protocols are of importance. The Transmission Control Protocol (TCP) is the key protocol and provides a reliable message-transmission service. The User Datagram Protocol (UDP) offers a stateless, unreliable service that works with the paradigm of best effort. Best effort means that no service can be guaranteed.

The application layer ensures the delivery of data to a certain application from another application that is located on the same or on another node in the network. This layer uses messages to encapsulate information. The protocols on this level include the Hypertext Transfer Protocol (HTTP), which ensures the transmission of HTML documents; the Simple Mail Transfer Protocol (SMTP), which is able to transfer mail from one node to any other; and the File Transfer Protocol (FTP), which transfers files between nodes.

Although this structure may seem complicated, it actually simplifies the implementation of the whole IPS. By segmenting information in messages, packets, bytes, bits, and signals, depending on the layer, it becomes easier to develop software that incorporates the required protocol more easily. Every layer can be implemented separately without knowledge of the other layers, making the software more simple and robust. It also makes it easy to integrate software from different vendors into a single solution, even if they operate on different levels. Through the use of the common protocol, they can be used transparently.

3.1.4 The Domain Name System

As we have seen, the network layer is responsible for addressing the nodes and for how they are connected. Every node on the Internet has a unique IP address. As IP addresses are difficult to remember, domain names have been put on top of the IP addresses. For most people, it is far easier to remember www.hp.com than its corresponding IP address (192.151.11.13). Actually, hp.com has more than one IP address assigned; through what is called a round-robin mechanism, customers are delegated to one of four machines to keep CPU load levels on all computers more or less equal. A round robin is an arrangement of choosing all elements in a group equally in some rational order, usually from the top to the bottom of a list and then starting again at the top of the list and so on. A simple way to think of round robin is that it is about "taking turns."

Every domain name maps to one or more IP address, and every IP address can map to one or more domain names. If there is more than one IP address per domain name, this means that there are several servers at the same location that share the incoming load of requests. If several domain names point to a single IP address, then most likely several customers are sharing one large Web server at the site of an Internet Service Provider (ISP).

In order to map the domain names to the IP address, a specialized service called the Domain Name System (DNS) is required. The hierarchical name space of the DNS is used to map domain names to IP addresses and vice versa. A name space is a document that identifies the names of particular data elements or attributes used within the DNS structure. It consists of a sequence of names, from the most specific to the most general (left to right), separated by dots (e.g., www.ferrari.it).

As you can see in Figure 3.1, the root of the system has no name. Below the root, there is a set of top-level domain names (TLDs), which either consist of the two-letter country codes (as described in ISO-3166) or are of a more generic nature, such as .edu, .com, .net and .org. Most countries, such as Germany (.de) do allow the registration of individual organizations directly below the TLD, which makes the hierarchy flat. For other countries, such as the United Kingdom (.uk), there is an additional layer of generic categories below the TLD, reflecting the generic TLD. In the United Kingdom, for example, these second-level domains are .ac for academic institutions, such as universities; .co for commercial companies (such as www.netcraft.co.uk); .org for all sorts of organizations; and .gov for governmental sites. The TLD .us, for the United States,

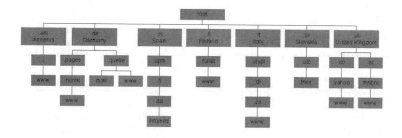

Figure 3.1. The DNS hierarchy.

is based on geographical second-level domains. The .us domains tend to become very long and unusable. For example, the domain www.tpwd.state.tx.us is the Texas Parks and Wildlife site, which is very difficult to remember, as you do not only have to remember a TLD, but also .tx for Texas and .state for state department.

Nodes that are connected permanently to the Internet do not change their IP address or domain name over time. But many people connect over modems to the Internet and do not require permanent connections. As the number of addresses using the Internet Protocol is limited, dynamic connections do not get assigned a permanent IP address, but use dynamic addresses as well. Every time you connect via modem to the Internet, you will get an IP address from the pool of addresses your ISP owns. This allows ISPs to connect thousands of people with only a few hundred IP addresses, as not everybody is online at the same time.

During the early years of the Internet, the DNS system was stored in a single master file from which all nodes had to download from time to time to keep up to date. As more and more nodes were connected to the Internet, it became quite clear that this solution doesn't scale at all. Therefore, a new decentralized approach needed to be implemented.[6] Instead of getting the information from one resource only, the decentralized approach enabled the information to be retrieved from thousands of servers connected to the Internet.

The new system allows the direct query between the source DNS and the target DNS. When looking up a Web page located at the domain www.rus. uni-stuttgart.de from a computer with a domain name tmbbvaf1.bbn.hp.com, the node with the host name tmbbvaf1 sends a request to the local DNS server. The DNS server is able to see that the domain name is not a local address and passes the request on to the authoritative server for the .de domain. By the way, domain names in the bbn.hp.com domain can be resolved locally and do not need a connection to the outside world. The authoritative servers for all

---

[6]http://www.ietf.org/rfc/rfc1034.txt

TLDs are the only files that are distributed from a central point and are highly unlikely to change over time. The .de server passes the request on to the DNS server of the University of Stuttgart (uni-stuttgart.de), which then passes the information on to .rus.uni-stuttgart.de, which is able to return the IP address to tmbbvaf1.bbn.hp.com.

Although this seems highly complicated, the IP address is within fractions of a second at the client. The process is sped up by keeping a local cache of IP address information. If you try to connect to a certain site and someone else from your local network wants to do the same a little bit later, the local DNS will hold a copy of the request in memory. This reduces the network load and speeds up the process even further.

3.1.5 IPv6

The Internet is currently based on the Internet Protocol version 4 (IPv4), which is able to address about 4 billion IP addresses. In 1990 about 20 percent of the available IP addresses were already assigned and the number of assignments was doubling every 14 months. Without changes in paradigms, the complete range of IP addresses would have already been exhausted in 1994, when work on IPv6 began.

In 1999 most of the Internet still used IPv4 and there are still IP addresses available. The reason is the introduction of dynamic IP addresses for Internet users who are not connected all day to the Internet. My first ISP gave me a static IP address, which was great at that time, but today would be impossible. The advantage of static IP addresses is that if the connection breaks down and you reconnect, you can continue with all your activities as if nothing has happened; downloads, for example, were put on hold, but not stopped. Today ISPs use a range of IP addresses assigned to users at the time of the login. Another reason that the IP address range is still not exhausted is that most companies use network address translation (NAT). NAT means that the company's intranet uses a certain range of IP addresses that may be used by someone else on the Internet. These internal IP addresses are not visible to the outside world. At the company firewall, the internal IP addresses are translated to Internet IP addresses, which the company purchased. This further reduces the risk of a break-in because attackers never see the original IP address, as the complete internal network architecture is hidden by this mechanism.

Hewlett-Packard is one of the few companies that bought a complete Class A network, which includes the complete IP range starting with 15.*. A company today buys parts of a Class C network and hides the rest of the required IP addresses behind a NAT service. A short explanation of what Class A, Class B and Class C networks are can be found in Table 3.1.

Although it is not expected that there will be a shortage of IP addresses in the near future, there are still many valid reasons for implementing the next

The IP address range was originally subdivided into three different classes, depending on the size of the company. Today most companies get only small fractions of a Class C network.

- **Class A networks**—A Class A network gives access to 16,777,216 (2^{24}) IP addresses.

- **Class B networks**—A Class B network gives access to 65,536 (2^{16}) IP addresses.

- **Class C networks**—A Class C network gives access to 256 (2^8) IP addresses.

Table 3.1. Networks in IPv4

generation of the Internet Protocol. The IPv6 standard is defined in RFC1726.[7] As we have seen, the original reason for creating IPv6 was limited IP address space. With IPv6, address space has increased from 2^{32} (4,294,967,296, a number with 11 digits) to 2^{128} (a huge number with 39 digits), allowing support for 10^{12} nodes and 10^9 networks. In order to enhance the flexibility of the network topology, the routing algorithm should have no knowledge of how the network has been made. In IPv4 each node needs to be connected to the other with less than 256 devices in between (the so-called *hops*). Another important requirement is that the performance should not decrease with the introduction of a new protocol, and the robustness of the service should not degenerate.

In order to make the transition to IPv6 possible, it is necessary that IPv6 supports and accepts IPv4 packets. The new protocol needs to be backward compatible to allow older systems and devices to work on the new protocol stack. In order to make IPv6 a viable solution for the future, it needs to be independent of the network media. No matter if the transmission is done over a high-speed network with 500 Gbps or low-speed networks with 300 bps, it should be possible, just as with IPv4.

As IPv4 allows not only TCP but also UDP, it is necessary for IPv6 to support this unreliable datagram service as well. This will allow applications using this protocol to work on IPv6. The configuration, administration, and operation of IPv6 should become easier than with IPv4, and security needs to be introduced, as this is a requirement for electronic business.

As IPv6 has such a large IP address space, one of the goals is to use every IP address only once. The basic multicast features introduced in IPv4 need to

---

[7]http://www.ietf.org/rfc/rfc1726.txt

be enhanced to support better broadcasting over the Internet, such as radio and television streams. Packet headers should be extensible to hold additional information required for the particular transmission, and the data structure should be independent of the actual protocol. As a result, it would become possible to create new types of packets and network services, which are able to implement quality of service (QoS). QoS means that packets belonging to different applications will get a different priority on the transit via the Internet. Voice may have a higher priority than email, for example.

The current implementation of the Internet protocol is based on the premise that devices and networks are immobile. But more and more mobile devices such as cell phones are connecting to the Internet, and even complete networks are becoming mobile. A car stuffed with a mobile phone, computers, printers, and scanners, such as the MegaCar,[8] forms a highly mobile network. MegaCar uses up to 16 multiplexed GSM-mobile phone channels to connect to the Internet. Although international roaming will keep the car connected no matter which country you enter, the price will go up, since you will pay international phone-call rates back to the ISP in the originating country. An automatic switch over to a local provider would greatly reduce costs, but would require a reconnect.

Through mobility, devices and networks need to connect to different hosts in different locations in order to keep costs low and to have the maximum speed available. Therefore, the connection to the Internet needs to be highly dynamic. With IPv4 it is necessary to disconnect and reconnect. In order to have better control over the network, the new IPv6 protocol should support debugging and control protocols.

Based on this proposal, most companies involved in network technologies have created software or devices that support IPv6. The Internet 2 project[9] in the United States is based on the new protocol stack to allow the introduction, development, and testing of new services and applications.

In 2001 IPv6 is slowly becoming more common on the Internet. Most hardware and software solutions support IPv6, making the migration easier. Some universities have already switched over completely to IPv6, and it is just a matter of time before ISPs and company networks will follow. The advantages are obvious and through a good set of tools now available, it is possible to mix IPv4 and IPv6 environments and make the transition easier.

3.1.6   ATM Networks

Another interesting technology that has emerged over the last few years is the Asynchronous Transfer Mode (ATM), a new networking technology designed especially for next-generation, multimedia communications, just like telephony, video or computer-generated data.

---

[8]http://www.megacar.com/
[9]http://www.internet2.edu/

In addition to TCP/IP, ATM offers new protocols that are especially designed to handle time-critical data, such as video or audio. These new protocols are able to provide a homogeneous network for all types of traffic and are independent of the content that is transported.

The information is transported in constant-sized cells that permit rapid switching so that time-critical data can be sent over the same network as computer network traffic. Instead of providing a fixed data rate, each application can decide how much bandwidth is required and request it on the network. Bandwidth on demand has now become possible.

The ATM protocols are very scalable. Although ATM is used mostly for backbones, it is currently based on fibre cabling. It is possible to implement ATM over OC-48, which offers a bandwidth of 2.488 Gbps. But ATM is not restricted to fibre-optic cabling. If implemented properly, ATM can run over any medium.

The ATM protocols are developed and maintained by the ATM Forum,[10] an international nonprofit organization formed with the objective of accelerating the use of ATM products and services through a rapid convergence of interoperability specifications. Once a standard has been developed and approved, it is presented to the International Telecommunications Union (ITU).[11]

There are many reasons ATM will be the networking technology in the near future and beyond. One reason is that it has been engineered in a manner to proactively address the problems when switching to next-generation networks.

As multimedia applications proliferate, a technology like ATM has a good chance to succeed, as it is able to handle all aspects of multimedia, video, audio, and information. Another reason is that this networking technology will provide for sufficient improvements in capability to justify the expense of the investment in new technology. The scalability in bandwidth allows for true Gbps networks, and is much more scalable in a number of network nodes because of the switched network architecture.

The most important reason for the success of ATM in the future is that this technology is standards-based. Standards and interoperability are the most important factors behind internetworked communications. Networking standards that are technically sound and rigidly followed are more important than many technical limitations within a system.

3.2   Exploring the IT Infrastructure

3.2.1   The Platform

The Internet is continuing to place new pressures on IT infrastructures. Nevertheless, businesses are looking to harness the power of Internet technology to transform their relationships, their value-creation processes, and even their

---

[10]http://www.atmforum.com/

[11]http://www.itu.int/

entire industries. There are new ways to buy and use IT services which enable new flexibility and increased capacity (e.g., utility computing, service-centric computing).

Companies need to compete and thrive in the new Internet-enabled economy. Therefore businesses need power for their always-on Internet infrastructures. Service providers must quickly create profitable revenue streams, deliver on SLAs (service level agreements), and deliver a satisfying customer experience. Enterprises must build customer loyalty, create competitive advantage, and grow revenue while streamlining processes and reducing costs. SMEs (small to medium enterprises) must rapidly and continuously scale to meet growing customer demands and build infrastructure simply, quickly, and cost-effectively, while focusing on business rather than technology.

Choosing the right platform can become a religious war within the IT department. No matter which platform you choose, you will find strong supporters and also people who will fight the decision. Although not quite logical, choosing a computer platform is often not based on facts, but on feelings. Remember the clashes between user groups of the Commodore 64 and the Atari 800, between Commodore Amiga and Atari ST, between Windows 3.1 and Macintosh, and more recently between Windows NT and Linux?

In many companies the hardware dictates the solutions, because people in the IT department are not willing to support another platform. Although it is easier to maintain a homogeneous network, the problem with this is that it may not be possible to get the best solution for a given problem. But, on the other hand, it does not help to have the perfect platform for the solution if the people who are responsible for running it are unwilling to do so. Although such behavior is not professional, it happens all over the world. Another issue with homogeneous networks is that if an error occurs on one system, it is highly likely that all other systems will also fail. Hackers and viruses also have much greater impact on homogeneous environments.

The Internet has changed the face of applications dramatically. It does not matter anymore which hardware and software are used to implement a solution. In order to be Internet-ready, the output needs to be platform-independent. Many companies have acquired different software and hardware platforms in the past because of a missing or changing platform strategy. Internet technologies enabled these platforms to talk to each other and exchange information and services.

Two types of platforms are interesting for electronic businesses. They are high-end commercial UNIX systems and low-cost Intel/Motorola-based operating systems (including Linux, Windows NT, FreeBSD, Mac OS X, and NetBSD). Windows 95/98 and Mac OS, highly popular among end customers, are not suited for hosting electronic services.

Internet startups are most likely to buy a low-cost solution that is easily extensible. Building a complex solution can be done either by creating a server farm of low-cost platforms or by using one or a few high-end systems. The advantage of many cheaper computers is the higher availability and reliability of the whole system. If one cheap computer has a downtime because of a software or hardware problem, the service can continue to run (if configured well). If only one large computer is available, a downtime of this server will cause the provided service to stop. The disadvantage of many computers is the highly complex system management that is required to run the service. Have a look at Figure 3.2 to see the effect of a system that has not been highly available in the past.

Figure 3.2. Downtime on the Lufthansa site.

Remember that every platform has its advantages and disadvantages. If you need arguments for or against a certain platform, then choose among the thousands of papers on the Internet explaining why a certain platform is the best. Just to name some examples, the unix-vs-nt[12] homepage is for UNIX fans, and DHBrown Associates[13] has published a paper on why Linux is not as good as Windows NT. But this is not the place to convert you to a particular operating system. The right operating system is the one that supports the needs of the user, so this depends on the expectations and requirements of every single user. The operating system is just as good as the person using it. This book, for example, has been written in LaTeX, making it totally OS independent. The files were kept on a server, used to add text on any platform

---

[12]http://www.unix-vs-nt.org/
[13]http://www.dhba.com/

that supports Internet connectivity, files, and text editors, no matter where I happened to be.

We'll now explore some of the major advantages and disadvantages of each group of platforms, but keep in mind that the platform should not be your major issue. Get the business idea right, implement the business processes, and *then* get the platform that suits your needs best. By using Java and XML, it is possible to create applications and services that do not depend on a certain platform, but can run from any platform depending on the requirements of the electronic service.

The high-end UNIX systems are the most expensive investment upfront but offer some features that other platforms will not be able to deliver. For these reasons, the large majority of Web servers connected to the Internet are running on UNIX servers. People who need scalability will be delighted by the prospect of starting with a single processor machine and ending with up to 64 processors in a single box. As commercial versions of UNIX scale very well over several processors, it is possible to reach the maximum boost for your online venture. New technologies such as non-uniform memory access (NUMA) allow you to share resources over a set of computers, creating a very tightly integrated cluster.

NUMA is a method of configuring a cluster of microprocessor in a multiprocessing system so that they can share memory locally, improving performance and the ability of the system to be expanded. NUMA is used in a symmetric multiprocessing (SMP) system. An SMP system is a "tightly-coupled," "share everything" system in which multiple processors working under a single operating system access each other's memory over a common bus. SMP and NUMA systems are typically used for applications such as data mining and decision support system in which processing can be parceled out to a number of processors that collectively work on a common database

Today the UNIX world already offers 64-bit operating systems, such as HP-UX 11, which increase the amount of addressable memory and enlarge the file system size. These systems also provide support for large disk arrays and clustering. This offers a high availability solution which is critical for most electronic businesses. The concept of clustering means that you are running not one computer but several servers as if they were one, sharing processing load and providing automatic redirection of traffic if one of the servers goes down. While the low-end systems require additional software and hardware for clustering, the high-end UNIX systems provide built-in support for clustering.

If UNIX knowledge is already available within the company and among the administrators, these systems make a lot of sense, as the cost for running the system is very low. They also are fast, stable and cause few problems. If no knowledge is available on UNIX, consider a system you already know or send your administrators for extensive training. A misconfigured UNIX system will give you just as much pain as any other system, and it may have cost a lot more to set it up in the first place. During the startup phase, the hardware vendor should provide a consultant who will check the installation and performance of the system. This will help to avoid future financial problems.

It is also important to mention that an administrator who is able to administer one flavor of UNIX will need training for the other flavors. This training will be much shorter than for the newcomer, but is necessary because of the subtle differences between the UNIXes. For example, threading is implemented in totally different ways on Solaris and HP-UX. In order to get the maximum out of each system, the administrator needs to fine-tune the settings, which are different for each of the systems.

Low-cost servers, based mainly on PowerPC and Intel architectures, have the advantage that more people are able to get these computers and create software that will run on one of these platforms. Anyone buying a low-cost computer today can choose from a series of operating systems and is able to contribute to the large pool of software, either commercially or by putting software into the public domain.

There is a lot of discussion on which operating system is most suitable for the PowerPC/Intel architecture, and there is no right answer to this discussion. It seems Linux,[14] Mac OS X,[15] Windows NT,[16] FreeBSD[17] and BeOS[18] are similar in function and reliability. Whether a system works for your online venture depends on how much knowledge you have about the platform and about the products you are using. Standard products, such as Web servers, databases, word processors, HTML editors, mail servers, firewall software, antivirus software are available for these platforms. The operating systems provide a multi-threaded kernel and offer modern graphical user interfaces, which make them easy to administer. Even less experienced users are able to administer a digital business running on such a system.

These operating systems also offer limited support for symmetric multiprocessing (SMP), allowing them to put more than one processor into a box. However, these operating systems do not scale well over more than one processor. Clustering possibilities are reduced, and these operating systems provide less stable service than the previously mentioned high-end systems. This leads to a less scalable solution, since more boxes need to be managed.

Most commercial applications are available for Microsoft's Windows NT and Apple's Mac OS X operating systems, but the other operating systems are catching up. Oracle[19] and SAP,[20] for example, have started to support Linux.

The size of your online business will dictate the size of the server you need. The service you want to offer will decide which solution and platform is needed

---

[14] http://www.linux.org/

[15] http://www.apple.com/macosx/server/

[16] http://www.microsoft.com/ntserver/

[17] http://www.freebsd.org/

[18] http://www.be.com/

[19] http://www.oracle.com/

[20] http://www.sap.com/

to implement it, and if you ask five different companies, you will get (at least) five different answers. There is no simple answer to your Internet business platform requirements and to find the optimal solution, pilots should be in place to test the availability and reliability of the proposed service, instead of putting it untested into production and risking an image loss.

3.2.2 Basic Internet Software

The Internet protocols described in the last section are required for the basic Internet software that is running on most computers today. This subsection gives a short overview on the available software and its use on the Internet. E-mail and Web clients are the most prominent pieces of basic software customers are using each day to conduct business over the Internet. This software connects to email and Web servers for the exchange of information and can be run on all Internet nodes, including servers and intermediating hosts, acting as clients. Actually, any network-enabled device can be both client and server. Pervasive computing makes this possible (see Chapter 16 for more information on pervasive computing).

Internet protocols are implemented by software that runs in all Internet nodes, including workstations, hosts and intermediating nodes. In some cases, the software that implements a particular protocol may be a standalone tool; in others, it may be a function within application software; and yet in others, it may be embedded within systems software. Moreover, a particular piece of software may implement protocols in only one layer or in several.

On the lowest layer, the data-link layer, the Point-to-Point Protocol (PPP) is most widely used to connect to the Internet via modem. This piece of software is embedded in all modern operating systems, and setting up a connection has been made easy. A phone number, a login name, and a password are all that is required by modern PPP implementations.

The protocols on the network and transport layer (TCP/IP) are also embedded into the operating system and work transparently in the background. People who want to communicate via the Internet do not need to know how the TCP/IP works. On some systems, it is necessary to add information for these protocols manually (namely the IP address, the DNS server, the default gateway, and the netmask). A new type of protocol, Dynamic Host Configuration Protocol (DHCP) is able to resolve all this information from a server, making human interaction for setting up the Internet connection superfluous.

On servers and routers, additional commands are implemented that allow you to configure routings and other rules related to the network. These tools are very powerful, but not required for nontechnical people to set up an Internet connection.

On the application level, the end-user programs are written and use the above-described protocols. Services that you offer to your customers are running on this communication layer. Computers that run Web servers (such as

Apache[21] or Roxen[22]) use HTTP to distribute their documents. A file server (built into all UNIXes by default) uses FTP to allow access to files, and mail servers use SMTP, POP3, and IMAP4 to service mail to customers.

On the client side, the customers need applications that connect to the services offered by the server. Email clients (such as Eudora[23]) pick up the customers' mail using the same protocols the mail servers use (SMTP, POP3 and IMAP4). A Web browser (such as Netscape Communicator[24] or Internet Explorer[25]) uses HTTP to download HTML documents, and FTP clients use FTP to upload and download files to and from a server. More in-depth information on browsers can be found in Chapter 10.

In order to provide a valuable, well-accepted service to your customers, you should try to determine which protocols are supported by the installed software base of your clients. If you are writing an application that requires a new protocol, then try to integrate the new protocol into a Java applet that can be executed from within a Web browser before offering a standalone solution, which needs to be downloaded and installed separately by the user. Customers are often reluctant to install another piece of software, since not everyone knows how to do this, and installation of new software always involves risk.

3.3 Deciding on the Enterprise Middleware

3.3.1 Mail and Collaboration

We can see two users of mail and collaboration on the Internet: private mail systems, which are used in companies and run by themselves, and public mail systems, which are used by individuals and are mainly hosted by Internet service providers. While the functionality of the mail and collaboration software is similar, we see totally different products in both areas. The private mail systems are dominated by Lotus Notes, Microsoft Exchange, Novell, Hewlett-Packard's OpenMail, and Netscape's Mailserver, and the public mail systems are often run by Software.com's InterMail,[26] Netscape, Sun SIMS, Sendmail, and MCIS.

More than one-third of the Internet's public mailing is handled through InterMail. This mailing system offers a Web-based front end, which has become very popular over the last few years. Instead of using applications such as Eudora, Pine, Elm, or even Netscape Messenger, which is part of the Netscape browser, more and more people have started to use Web-based email programs. The major advantage is that the email client is very easy to use. Anybody who

---

[21]http://www.apache.org/
[22]http://www.roxen.com/
[23]http://www.eudora.com/
[24]http://www.netscape.com/
[25]http://www.microsoft.com/windows/ie/
[26]http://www.software.com/

is able to use a browser is able to send and receive email, without any of the configuration required by all other types of email clients.

The second advantage is that the email can be read from any terminal that has a Web browser installed and is connected to the Internet. This feature appeals to business people who travel a lot and need their email. Therefore, we anticipate a convergence between corporate and private mailing systems, resulting in unified mailing solutions that allow both Web-based and email client access, depending on where the user is.

Web-based mailing has already become the preferred method of reading and sending email for individuals and traveling business people accessing the Internet. More and more companies are searching for solutions to allow their employees secure access to their internal mailing. Today many employees forward their mail to Excite,[27] MyOwnEmail[28] or any other of the thousands of free Web mailing services on the Internet. This poses security risks, since email is transported to less secure servers and is not necessarily protected, as your corporate email service should be.

While InterMail, in its standard configuration, is more appropriate for traditional Web mail that meets the needs of the service providers and their customers, OpenMail Anywhere[29] sets a new standard in secure Web access to corporate mailboxes.

InterMail is the standard for carrier-class messaging because of its massive scalability, high performance, and a host of features designed to ensure reliable operation, uninterrupted access, smooth administration, and customized integration with other systems and services. Three different versions are available to meet the needs of the service provider, ranging from 25,000 customers to unlimited customers.

The InterMail software is designed to enable consumer, business, and Webmail messaging services within a single integrated architecture. Service providers are able to create and customize classes of service at varying price points for consumers and business customers. Service providers can further differentiate their products by offering SLAs. These capabilities help service providers to expand market share, retain subscribers, lower total cost of ownership, and derive increased profits.

While InterMail is built on efficiency, it lacks a secure integration into the corporate mailing infrastructure. OpenMail Anywhere, on the other hand, offers a tight integration into HP's trusted Web platform Virtual Vault, which makes it easy to allow employees to access their email either from within the company through their standard mailing application or over the Internet through a Web browser.

The integration of OpenMail and Virtual Vault eliminates the need for remote users to rely on dial-up networking or to carry a laptop to access email

---

[27] http://www.excite.com/
[28] http://www.myownemail.com/
[29] http://www.openmail.hp.com/

from remote locations. OpenMail users simply access an SSL-secured URL from any device with an Internet browser, including PDAs, Web phones, walk-up terminals, and PCs. The browser accesses OpenMail Web client software located on a Virtual Vault server. The server then connects users to their Open-Mail accounts on OpenMail servers inside the corporate firewall.

With this solution, companies can reduce their investment in remote-access systems, private networking, and associated support and help-desk staff. Virtual Vault uses trusted mandatory security mechanisms to block sophisticated attacks on the OpenMail client, the boundary Web server, and internal corporate OpenMail servers. Attackers cannot modify Web pages nor can they modify legitimate application code.

3.3.2 Network and Systems Management

Today companies face enormous challenges in managing their infrastructures. There are three reasons why this is happening. First of all, the existing infrastructure is growing rapidly; the Internet and its services require new devices and new software, which become part of the business within a very short time. The second reason is that technological approaches to networking, database, application, hardware, and software platforms continue to diverge. And finally, business success in today's economy is predicated on keeping costs in line while delivering more timely and better targeted goods and services than the competition. These reasons require you to have a solid network and a systems management solution in place.

This effective network and systems management architecture allows you to manage all networks and systems centrally. This means that you are able to control every single system and every component of the network and will also receive immediate response from the system in case of an error, so that it can be corrected either over the network or locally, if need be. This prevents errors, such as the one in Figure 3.3.

Such a solution should support open systems, multivendor environments, and multiplatform infrastructures, meaning that all types of hardware and software should be able to be managed through this central interface, including all operating systems and all network protocols. Better systems are also able to manage not only the infrastructure, but also applications and complete solutions. Ideally a management solution should support the lines of business (LOB). It is quite uncommon to find a company that is exclusively running one type of hardware and one type of operating system. Over time, legacy systems have been introduced into the company and cannot be replaced easily with newer systems, as they have become mission-critical. Changing strategies of the company will lead to different hardware and software equipment over time. Therefore, the network and management solution needs to take this into account.

The management system should integrate all necessary functions, such as

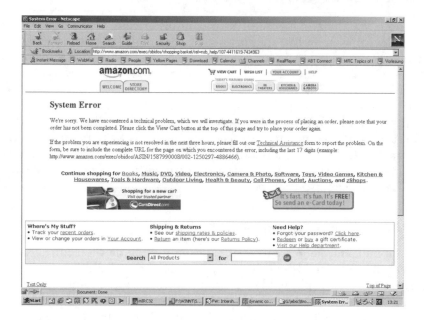

Figure 3.3. Error on Amazon.com.

inventory, storage, scheduling, and security. It needs to be open to extension
by third parties and allow customization by the enterprise staff as well as service providers. Comprehensive control of the enterprise requires end-to-end
management of the entire IT infrastructure. Issues in enterprise management are not bound by specific technologies. Therefore, an end-to-end management system must address all types of resources: systems, networks, desktops,
databases, and applications.

A consistent user interface will help the administrators easily detect anom-
alies on the network and on the systems and take the appropriate action, if
necessary, to resolve the problem. A global view of the network should also
be provided, which can also be drilled down to single components to make it
easy to find the problem. An early warning system should also be integrated
to support the problem management module to notify administrators in case of
problems.

Over the years, Hewlett-Packard's OpenView software has established itself as the industry standard. More than half of the servers on the Internet
are managed through OpenView systems, as it is a proven product and easily tailored to the needs of each organization. OpenView meets the needs of
troubleshooters, help desks, and administrators and supports distributed heterogeneous environments. It expands the effectiveness and productivity of IT
organizations by increasing the uptime of networked systems and by decreasing problem resolution time. The OpenView system collects, consolidates, and

selectively presents only the most critical information to the central management system.

Besides OpenView, there are two other highly successful products on the market. Unicenter TNG[30] by Computer Associates and Tivoli Enterprise[31] by IBM both provide a similar functionality.

Tivoli Enterprise is a suite of management applications that gives you the power to manage your entire enterprise application architecture, including your data center, your distributed system, and even your laptops. Tivoli Enterprise unites these disparate environments and enables you to manage them together as a single business system, treating each as a strategic component of your complete enterprise.

Tivoli Enterprise is an open, object-oriented framework that includes a set of managers, brokers, and agents that conform to the CORBA specification. CORBA technology allows differences between computer operating systems to be hidden from the Tivoli Enterprise user, and it allows services to be encapsulated in objects that can be used by multiple management applications. The Tivoli management framework provides platform independence, a unifying architecture for all applications, and the ability for third-party vendors to adapt to, or plug into, the framework. It also provides a set of application program interfaces (API) and services. This enables customers to write new applications that also plug into, or leverage, the Tivoli management framework and can be monitored over the network.

Unicenter TNG (The Next Generation) is a comprehensive, open and scalable solution that provides the management of all IT resources in an enterprise. It delivers a rich set of management functions, which are built on top of an object-oriented, open architecture and a highly scalable, manager/agent infrastructure. Unicenter TNG allows IT organizations to manage all of their enterprise resources through a single management interface, which encompasses heterogeneous networks, systems, applications, databases, and even non-IT devices, such as door openers. The network management function in Unicenter TNG uses the common object repository to store information. This shared repository is instrumental in ensuring uniform enforcement of management policies, user interface, and interaction.

Besides the big three in network and systems management (Tivoli, Unicenter TNG, and OpenView), there are many smaller solutions that work exclusively on the Simple Networking Management Protocol (SNMP) level. Many applications use this protocol to output management data, which can be collected by these SNMP-savvy applications and can be processed to inform the administrator about the status of these applications and devices. The big three do understand SNMP as well. Depending on the size of your company, you should decide if you need a simple solution, based on SNMP only, which is

---

[30]http://www.cai.com/unicenter/
[31]http://www.tivoli.com/

not secure, or if you should go for a full-blown management system, such as
OpenView.

3.3.3 Security Software

Communication over the Internet is by default open and uncontrolled, and conflicts with the business needs of digital businesses. Privacy, confidentiality, and
integrity of the business transactions are problems for the Internet if no additional security layers are implemented. The growing demand for e-business
also raises the awareness for security issues and concerns about achieving this
goal. The news is full of reports on Internet security that are hypercritical and
increase fear. Network-based fraud is growing dramatically and has made Internet security a business issue—not just a technical issue to be resolved in the
IT departments of companies considering an Internet business strategy.

Today technology is able to make a system secure, but more than pure technology is required. Many security problems have been reported in the past,
and it is certain that we will see even more incidents in the future. But if
you look more closely at the problems behind the attacks, you will often find
human error, missing procedures, and incorrectly configured software are the
main problems. These errors can't be eliminated by technology; instead, they
require intensive training for every employee.

Security is often not a technical issue, but a political and process-related
issue. The software solutions for ensuring privacy, confidentiality, and integrity
are available and have proven themselves over the last few years, but often
companies forget the human component in their security strategy. The weakest
link in the chain will break, no matter how strong the other links are.

Therefore some measures need to be taken to protect a company from these
threats. To protect your company information from hackers, it is necessary
to have a firewall solution. The solutions in the market range from free software products (FreeBSD[32] has some basic firewall functionality built in and
FreeStone,[33] offers a fully functional freeware implementation of a firewall) to
highly complex multilayered solutions (using software such as Firewall 1 by
CheckPoint[34]) depending on the needs and financial situation of your company.
Still, hackers can easily steal information from within your company by sending an email to one of the employees and requesting a certain document. If the
employees have not been educated about social engineering and other forms of
attack, the best software solution will not be able to protect your intellectual
property.

The HP Praesidium firewall[35] provides a boundary protection environment.
This provides control for allowing or denying all network connections into or

---

[32]http://www.freebsd.org/
[33]http://www.soscorp.com/products/Freestone.html
[34]http://www.checkpoint.com/
[35]http://www.hp.com/go/security/

out of a particular network. It provides for active online authentication of who is getting through, using either the strong techniques of multifactor authentication using token cards or weak passwords to establish sessions. The firewall also provides an audit of all activity that ensures nonrepudiation and detection of misuse events. The firewall runs on a conventional operating system that has been strengthened by the removal and disabling of many applications and services that are not required on a firewall. For example, the sendmail or the finger daemons are not run on the firewall machine; actually, everything has been disabled to the outside except for the firewall service. This makes it more difficult for attackers to get in.

The Praesidium firewall provides for network connections with a single solution that gives access to the LAN and to the perimeter (the DMZ) and provides remote access using the VPN. The Praesidium firewall provides access to basic backend services, and it can reside in parallel with a Praesidium Virtual Vault, providing access to more sensitive mission-critical environments on the inside.

IBM's eNetwork Firewall[36] contains all three critical firewall architectures in one product. Filtering, proxy, and circuit-level gateways provide customers with both a high level of security and flexibility. The virtual private network support is based on the IPSec standard and offers a high level of security (see Table 3.2 for an explanation of IPsec). There are many other firewall products, and the software you choose should fit your security concept—not the other way around.

If you have the right procedures and technologies in place to protect intellectual property, you are in shape to try to set up a true e-business on the Web with a connection to your internal data. Remembering the phases from the introduction to this book, we are moving toward phase four, "Doing E-Business". Your Web site has a direct link into the legacy systems of your intranet, allows retrieval of information from internal databases, and uses secure protocols to transmit data between your company and the customer or another business. You are able to save costs and start making a profit from your online business

Information security is necessary to prevent unauthorized access to electronic data. The result of unauthorized access can be disclosure, alteration, substitution, or destruction of information.

Once the company intranet is secure, it is possible to start communication over the Internet. Organizations and people describe their needs for information security and trust in terms of five major requirements: confidentiality, integrity, availability, legitimate use, and nonrepudiation. Confidentiality is necessary to control who gets to read the information and to conceal the information to all others. Integrity needs to assure that information and programs are changed only in a specified and authorized manner and that the data presented is genuine and was not altered or deleted during transit. Availability

---

[36]http://www.software.ibm.com/security/firewall/

The Internet Protocol Security (IPSec) is a standard for security at the network or packet processing layer of network communication. Earlier security approaches have inserted security
at the application layer of the communications model. IPSec is
especially useful for implementing VPNs and for remote user
access through dial-up connection to private networks. A big
advantage of IPSec is that security arrangements can be handled without requiring additional software.

IPSec provides two choices of security service: Authentication Header (AH), which essentially allows authentication of
the sender of data, and Encapsulating Security Payload (ESP),
which supports both authentication of the sender and encryption of data as well. The specific information associated with
each of these services is inserted into the packet in a header
that follows the IP packet header.

Table 3.2. Definition of IPSec

ensures that authorized users have continual access to information and resources. Legitimate use means that resources cannot be used by unauthorized
persons or in an unauthorized way. Nonrepudiation means that customers
cannot claim that the transaction that was executed on their behalf was not
in their interest. Today many people refuse to pay for goods ordered over the
Internet because they have not ordered the goods themselves.

These five components may be weighted differently, depending on the particular application. A risk assessment must be performed to determine the
appropriate mix. A number of different technologies can be used to ensure
information security.

Confidentiality and integrity can be implemented through cryptography,
which offers a high degree of security. By encrypting the data, no one is able to
tell what the information is about. Through strong authentication, it is possible to ensure that nobody sees, copies, or deletes a certain piece of information.
With strong authentication and strong encryption in use, the only way to break
in is to have the necessary certificate for authentication and the key for the encryption. An authorization system is able to prevent access in an unauthorized
way by authenticated people. Nonrepudiation requires a trusted third party
that time-stamps the outgoing and incoming communication and is able to verify the validity of a digital signature. By time-stamping the communication, it
is easy to find out if a certain email had been sent out in time.

To ensure end-to-end security, this does not suffice, as it is also necessary to protect the customers' computers. First of all, customers need to be educated as well about the security issues on the Internet. While they normally do not need additional technology to secure the communication (the browser and the mail program are capable of doing this), a digital certificate will make life easier for customers and businesses to make deals over the Internet.

A digital certificate allows customers to identify the real identity of the business, and vice versa, making it possible to build a trusted relationship between the two. Digital certificates are issued by trustworthy third-party organizations that are able to verify the identity of the certificate holder. The certificate authorities issue the certificates and allow users to verify the certificates at any given time. The only problem in using digital certificates is the missing legal frameworks in some countries. Actually, the Internet requires a global legal framework. More information on the legal issues on Internet business can be found in Chapter 4, while an in depth review of the security issues can be found in Chapter 11.

3.3.4 Payment Solutions

As more and more companies conduct business over the Internet, electronic payment becomes more important than ever before. For many businesses, on-line payment is the bottleneck for the fast completion of transactions. Everything is digitized except for the payment. Offline payment is in most cases very slow and expensive compared to what is available on the Internet. Therefore, many companies have started to offer digital payment solutions.

In order to make electronic payment solutions accepted by a worldwide audience, certain requirements must be fulfilled. The most important issue with digital payment systems is acceptability. If a customer pays using an electronic payment solution, the company on the other end needs to be able to accept the payment via that particular solution. If this is not the case, customers may go off to another online business that supports their preferred online payment solution.

The electronic payment solution should be very flexible and open to the different requirements of the customers. If desired, their identity should be protected, just as it is with cash. Nobody knows where the money comes from or where it goes. Although this may sound a lot like criminal behavior, it reflects part of the privacy issue on the Internet. If money can be followed around, advertising agencies can get a detailed picture of a certain customer, such as his or her buying patterns, and many people understandably want to avoid this.

A successful online payment solution needs to be convertible, meaning one form of currency can be exchanged for another form of the same currency or another currency. In the real world it is possible to exchange a 10 euro bank note for some coins or for some dollar notes. This mechanism needs to be provided on the Internet as well. The transition between virtual funds and real money especially needs to be ensured.

In order to make the transaction appealing for customers, the cost per transaction should be zero or near zero. Payment via credit card or cash does not impose additional costs on the buyer. Another important point for efficiency is tight integration with existing applications. Only if payment can be tightly integrated into the business application can it reduce costs for the business and speed up the whole transaction.

To make customers feel good about using a certain payment solution, make sure any choice they make is a reliable one. As an analogy, imagine a customer goes into a shop to buy a book. At the register, the customer hands over the money to the cashier. But the money disappears before the cashier can grab it. Although this is highly unlikely in the real world, it can happen very easily on the Internet. Therefore, it needs to be ensured that at no point in time is the money neither with the client nor with the merchant.

Scalability of the payment solution allows you to add new users to the online business without bringing down the service. The security architecture allows financial transactions over open networks, such as the Internet. Digital payment systems are a prime target for criminals all over the world. In the real world, copying coins or bank notes is very difficult, but not impossible, if you have the right equipment. But replication takes time and money, and false bank notes are in most cases easy to detect, as they all have the same serial number. On the Internet, replication costs are near zero and changing the serial number is made easy. Therefore, one must ensure that the payment system is secure; otherwise, it will not be accepted by the customers. The Internet is an open network, which allows anybody to eavesdrop on the traffic, so modification of messages needs to be prevented by the use of digital signatures.

On the Internet three types of payment have been established: micropayments, consumer payments, and business payments. Micropayments are cash transactions with a value of less than approximately 5 euros or dollars. Suitable payment solutions are based on the electronic cash principle, as the transaction costs for these systems are nearly zero. Consumer payment solutions are based on the premise that transactions have a value between about 5 and 500 euros or dollars. Typical consumer payments are executed by credit card transactions. The business payment solutions are designed for a transaction with a value of more than 500 euros or dollars. Direct debit or invoices seem to be the most appropriate solutions. Each of these payment systems has different security and cost requirements, depending on the payment paradigm that is used. Please read Chapter 14 for in depth information on electronic payment solutions, products, and paradigms.

3.3.5 Database Management Systems

Although the majority of Web pages are still static, more and more companies are starting to use dynamic Web pages, which get their content from internal databases. Databases are also used on intranets for storing large portions of data in a structured way. Most applications today use or require a database in order to run fast and efficiently.

The database server is in most cases a separate box that contains the company's databases. If the company is large, then you can expect a whole data center equipped with database servers. By moving the data onto these dedicated servers, clients are able to send requests to that server and the server responds. This allows clients to work in a client/server or distributed environment, making the data independent of the creator or a special computer. Any device with a database connector is able to add, modify, or delete information in the database if the user of the device has the authorization to do so.

Other advantages of a distributed database environment is that the clients do not need to perform the database queries and that only the required traffic is going over the Internet. The clients' processing power can therefore be used more efficiently for other tasks. Today's database management systems (DBMSs) are highly sophisticated and are even able to take on part of the application's processing burden.

Databases are able to use stored procedures, triggers, and rules for better integration with applications. A stored procedure is a predefined sequence of SQL statements, which can be compiled and stored on the system as a database object. The enterprise applications access these stored procedures for functions they perform more often, reducing the load on the application server. The triggers are stored procedures used to perform automatic actions. They are activated automatically by events, such as *insert*, *delete*, and *update* that the database server runs across in the normal course of database processing. *Rules* are a special type of trigger, which are able to verify data before it is inserted into the database.

By running parts of the application on the DBMS, it is possible to balance the processing load in a typical three-tier Internet application. The three tiers are the database server, the Web/application server, and the client browser.

A simple trigger such as add a new set of data into the database automatically adds the data and the name of the user who entered the data to the database. A more complex trigger could do calculations on input, and so forth. DBMSs also support rules for data, making it easier to find false input in the database. Multiuser access is a must for all systems, as several clients will try to access the same data at the same moment. A locking mechanism prevents data from being overwritten by someone if someone else is already working on it. Although stored procedures, triggers, and rules are very powerful, the disadvantage is that they are not portable from one system to the other, as the capabilities vary greatly.

Another important feature is the two-phase commit, which ensures that a server crash will not result in a loss of data. The data is therefore stored in a redundant and recoverable process.

Just as when it comes to choosing the right platform, there is actually no way to tell which DBMS is the best one. Most DBMSs run on all major platforms, making them independent of the platform layer below. The most commonly used systems are the following: DB/2 by IBM,[37] Informix Online Dynamic Server by Informix Software,[38] Interbase by Inprise,[39] OpenIngres by Computer Associates Inc.,[40] Oracle Server by Oracle Corporation,[41] SQL Server by Microsoft,[42] and Sybase SQL Server by Sybase.[43] All of these systems are available on most UNIX platforms and Windows NT, with the exception of Microsoft's SQL Server, which is available for Windows NT only.

Depending on your needs and your applications, you should choose the DBMS in conjunction with the underlying platform in order to get the fastest combination possible. Depending on basic features of the operating system, such as caching and network services, the speed of the system will be high or low. But not only the underlying platform is important; the application layer, which is above it, more or less dictates the DBMS. It does not help to have the ultimate platform/DBMS configuration if your applications do not support it. Buying an additional server for the DBMS costs less than buying a new platform for the applications, in most cases.

High-end UNIX systems are predestined for database management systems, as they provide multitasking and multithreading capabilities. These can be exploited to offer a huge number of simultaneous connects from the clients. DBMS servers handle the connections from clients either by using a process per client, a thread per client, or a combination of both. The advantage of processes is that if one client connection dies because of an error, all other connections won't be affected, as each process runs independently on the system. In multiprocessor environments, the processes can be distributed evenly over the available set of processors without much overhead. The disadvantage of this system is that many concurrent processes will eat up your resources fast.

A thread, on the other hand, is a lightweight process running within a process. A process will spawn several threads that share the same address space on the system. Threads use up to 20 times less resources on the system and are faster because they share memory. Another advantage is that programming threads is more portable across platforms than is interprocess communication. The major disadvantage is that if all threads run in a single process, a crash

[37]http://www.ibm.com/

[38]http://www.informix.com/

[39]http://www.inprise.com/

[40]http://www.cai.com/

[41]http://www.oracle.com/

[42]http://www.microsoft.com/

[43]http://www.sybase.com/

within the process will kill all of the threads. Threads also do not scale as well over several processors, as processes do.

Most modern DBMSs use a combination of both paradigms to get the most out of the system. By running a small set of parallel processes that spawn threads, the above mentioned issues can be resolved. If a process crashes, it will take down a set of transactions, but not all of them. With some intelligence, it is also possible to reroute the threads to another process.

As more and more customers tend to get a low-end solution, such as Windows NT, which does not handle threading perfectly, the client connections are handled through a single thread, making it possible to get the most out of these systems. The reliability of such a system is, of course, much lower due to the nature of the low end operating systems.

The performance of most database management systems in the market is improved by bypassing the functionality of the operating systems. Instead of using the operating system to write to the hard disk, the DBMS is often able to write directly to the hard disk. This has the advantage that disk access is much faster, resulting in a faster query. The major disadvantage of this idea is that if something goes wrong, you cannot use standard disk tools to repair the disk and therefore need to rely on the DBMS vendor to provide the necessary tools. The same applies to backups. Standard backup tools won't be able to backup the database data.

Another way of increasing the speed of the DBMS is to pack it into the system at kernel level, meaning that it runs as part of the operating system. The advantage of this is that has a higher priority on the system and will result in a better performance. The disadvantage of this method is that if the database software crashes, it will also pull down the operating system. On UNIX, normal programs terminate without touching the operating system, making it possible to restart the application immediately after the crash. In the case of a crashed operating system, a reboot is often required, which may take a while.

Today most DBMSs are still based on the relational model. This model is rather simple to understand, as it uses only two-dimensional tables linked by a set of common fields. This makes the model perfect for most problems in the current client/server world of the Internet. As we are moving to the more distributed Internet world, multidimensional and object-oriented database management systems are becoming more important. This also has to do with the change in programming paradigm. Old style programming in C or Pascal is superseded by object-oriented programming languages such as C++ and Java. Using an object-oriented database makes programming easier for the newer languages, as everything is implemented using a consistent paradigm. This new breed of DBMS is able to store more complex data structures and therefore contain more intelligence, which is critical for the New Economy. They can also be used for online analytical processing (OLAP). Objectivity[44] and GemStone[45] are two of the software manufacturers. Although these new systems are slowly gaining market share, the traditional relational model won't become obsolete in the near future.

The most important standard in connection with DBMSs is SQL. At the moment, there are three flavors of it: SQL-89, SQL-92 and SQL3. These standards are defined by ANSI.[46] SQL-89 is supported by all DBMSs, but as you can see, it was developed in 1989 and is not uptodate anymore. It can be used to interchange data between different databases, as it can be seen as the lowest common denominator. Most of the functionality of modern systems is lost in the transit, though.

SQL-92 is the current standard for databases and supports features such as embedded SQL support for modern languages, dynamic SQL, and standardized error codes. SQL-92 supports intelligent agents, which can interact automatically with the database and generate output. More information on intelligent agents can be found in Chapter 6.

A third standard is currently being developed and is code-named SQL3. The most outstanding feature is the support for Object SQL capabilities, enhancing relational database systems in such a way that they can include features such as encapsulation, methods, user-defined data types, and inheritance. The gap between relational and object-oriented databases is getting smaller. We will probably see a merge between the two models in the future.

In order to decide which DBMS suits your needs best, you should also look at the additional software bundled with it. The administration and monitoring tools, for example, may be important for some companies, while others have only simple databases that are not mission-critical. Tools for backup and restore should be available, for the system that uses the operating system for accessing the hard disk as well as for the system that bypasses the operating system. For the latter case, special programs for administering the raw hard disk should also be included. As the requirements for every customer are different, tools for performance tuning should also be available in order to calibrate the database parameters for optimal performance.

Security is a major issue and should not be neglected. Users should be authenticated before letting them access the database, and authorization should provide the necessary means to allow or disallow access and modification to certain tables, columns, or rows within the database. The standard implementations of database management systems are not designed to be highly secure and therefore rely on other middleware components to secure the database. Packet filters, routers, firewalls, and application gateways help to ensure security for the databases. Refer to Chapter 11 for more details about information and Internet security.

---

[44]http://www.objectivity.com/

[45]http://www.gemstone.com/

[46]http://www.ansi.org/

If you want strong security built into the DBMS, you need to look out for special versions of the standard DBMS. These systems have additional audit features and intruder alarms. The disadvantage is that they are slower because of the added security. In any case, you should determine if it is necessary to have the security on the database level or on another level of the system, such as the operating system.

To find the right DBMS for your company, you should first find out what your business processes are like and how the DBMS is going to be integrated into them. Although the above-mentioned DBMSs have all the same core features, the additional features vary and will help you decide which DBMS is the right one. Don't start buying the database server first and then think about how you can solve your business problem. Companies that buy a DBMS because they have people slightly familiar with that particular DBMS end up having to buy a new DBMS and send the employees to expensive product training in order to implement the business process. This approach requires changes in your IT organization. A business-savvy person needs to work closely with IT or even work for IT. IT should not dictate the business solution, but should implement it by using the most appropriate platform and middleware.

3.3.6 High Availability

In the Internet age, business is everything but usual. It is powerful, explosive, and fast-changing. Every minute a company's site is down means a loss to the company. High-availability computing, once considered a strategic advantage, has now become a tactical necessity.

E*Trade,[47] for example, suffered heavily from an outage in October 1997 when the company experienced a subscriber growth rate of 175 percent per month and heavy market fluctuations caused several system overloads. Many investors were temporarily shut out from the site and couldn't execute trades. Angry investors who lost time and money because of the unavailability and reduced performance eventually filed a class-action suit against E*Trade. E*Trade systems also stalled in July 1999, leaving customers unable to trade for two hours.

E*Trade isn't alone. Many other e-commerce systems have gone down for extended periods of time. A July 18, 1999, article in the San Jose Mercury News,[48] "Reliability of E-stores Under Fire," explained that outages happen because of the sheer volume of customers, pressure to grow the business, and inadequate support and management of the e-commerce IT environment.

What are the true costs and consequences of downtime? Look beyond IT costs and assess the total cost and impact on your company's mission–now and into the future—from all sources. Downtime at the wrong time can cause a chain reaction.

---

[47]http://www.etrade.com/

[48]http://www.mercurycenter.com/

One way to mitigate downtime is through high availability. High availability involves hardware systems, software systems, IT support processes, and data center infrastructure to minimize downtime events and their associated recovery times. The key question: What is your threshold of pain—that is, the downtime, whether scheduled or unscheduled—that your business can tolerate? Check out Table 3.3 for the different levels of high availability.

It's difficult to convey precise meaning when the market uses terms like high availability, fault resilience, fault tolerance, and continuous availability almost interchangeably. Industry analysts measure availability in terms of impact on the user.

- **Level 1**—Work stops and the system shuts down. Data integrity remains intact.

- **Level 2**—Users are interrupted but can quickly log on again.

- **Level 3**—Users stay online. The current transaction might need restarting and performance might degrade.

- **Level 4**—Users don't notice a thing. The transaction immediately cuts over to a backup system without interruption.

Table 3.3. Which levels of high availability exist?

First, let's define downtime. This is the time a customer's system is unavailable to do useful work, usually measured in hours per year (or converted to a percentage of uptime). If a failure can be masked (the customer's system still runs during the entire failure event, including repair), the failure and its associated repair times don't count toward downtime. To measure downtime, you multiply the number of downtime events per year by the mean time to recover.

To resolve the problem, a company can increase system availability either by limiting the amount of downtime events per year or by reducing the impact to the customer by reducing mean time to repair (MTTR). Obviously, the best way to reduce downtime is to reduce downtime events. For each downtime event, you must pay for the time to recover from that event, which can get expensive.

Depending on your business model, high availability may play a more or less important role. If your target market is small and medium enterprises in the United States, a downtime on the weekends and during the night may be acceptable. If you're a consumer-driven company doing worldwide business, you had better have a system that's running every day, every hour, and every minute.

High availability is like security. You can't really see the value of it as long as everything runs smoothly. During normal operations, high availability may seem like a waste of money, but when there are problems, it's invaluable.

Building a highly available environment means building a redundant environment. Instead of having one network connection, you have at least two; instead of one server, you have two. If one component fails, the other one takes over, and the necessary repairs are done without any interruption of service. The price is much higher, but it also means a better and steadier revenue stream because you're meeting your customers' needs.

Before you implement a high-availability strategy, you need to understand the real demands on each system and application in your operation, and choose components accordingly. Weigh the cost of quality and reliability against scalability and performance. Simple questions need to be answered: Is one backup system enough to safeguard against outage? Is triple redundancy for some components overkill or simply prudence? These and many other questions need to be answered.

One major problem with high availability is that many software components are not easily duplicable. This means that some software parts cannot be made highly available because they do not support the concept of high availability. Therefore it is very important to ensure that software investments are made in components that support high-availability solutions.

3.4 Choosing the Right Enterprise Applications

3.4.1 Software Trends

New trends in software are targeted towards dynamic business environments with shifting competitive landscapes, evolving industry roles, and increasing customer demands. Technology is playing a more strategic role in every area from customer interaction to business processes integration. An increasingly mobile workforce and customer base requires companies to enable anytime, anywhere access.

Software companies therefore have to improve operational efficiencies, offer new services that build customer loyalty, and quickly produce profitable new revenue streams. The transition from a client-server business model to one defined by services is a challenge for many companies that are still learning about the business ramifications of the Internet. Meeting this challenge will reduce IT complexity and increase its flexibility to quickly deploy new solutions. Only if these factors are built into the software stack can companies trust their software vendors to stay with them for the next few years.

3.4.2   Imaging Technologies

The Internet is a huge library of mostly textual information, but reading on the screen is hard; therefore, most texts are rather short and images are used to present content in a very condensed way. Two types of images are used on the Internet: static and dynamic image formats. All Web browsers natively support the static image formats. Static, in this case, means that the image itself cannot change its colors, perspective, or resolution. All browsers understand the static file formats GIF, JPEG, and PNG.

The GIF and the JPEG formats have been in use since the introduction of the World Wide Web. The reason for the invention of PNG is simple: the other two formats have problems. The GIF was developed by CompuServe and has a bad reputation for being the format of choice for pornographic images exchanged on the CompuServe network. GIF uses the patented LZW compression algorithm from Unisys; Unisys could therefore charge licensing fees for the use of all GIF-supporting programs. While such fees have not been imposed, it is best not to rely on this format. GIF images support only up to 256 colors. This was fine until true color graphic cards became the standard in all computers.

JPEG, on the other hand, is a *lossy* image format. Depending on the strength of compression, the image loses information. The compression algorithm tries to remove data that cannot be distinguished by the human eye, making it a good format for viewing. But as soon as you try to change a JPEG image, you will notice that this hidden information is missing. When applied to photos, you won't notice the loss, but with clip art and text, you can see the difference immediately. The advantage of JPEG is that the files are compressed at a ratio of 1:10 or more, so that your 500 kilobyte images become less than 50 kilobytes to download.

When CompuServe announced at the end of 1994 that the GIF format uses a patented algorithm, the Internet community started developing a new format (after the obligatory inflammatory weeks on Usenet) that would be free of charge and better than GIF and JPEG together. The PNG project is a perfect example of Internet cooperation and efficiency (similar projects are Linux, Mozilla, and Apache; also see Chapter 15 for more information on open source projects). Using mainly email and newsgroups, developers from all over the world have designed and implemented this new standard.

Static images are the best choice for images that do not contain content, for Web page design purposes only, and for low-quality images or noninteractive pictures. Static image formats are not designed to deliver high-quality and interactive imaging. A simple example would be to offer a small thumbnail of an image on a Web page, and then by clicking on the image, you could get a higher resolution image of the same picture. Many people think that this may be a good solution, but it becomes highly complicated when there are thousands of images on the Web site. The use of interactive image formats can simplify the administration. From a business point of view, static image formats will be important to your Web designers, but won't help increase sales over the Internet. The future of static image formats is PNG. It provides the best solution quality with the smallest image size. Other formats may be in development, but none that would revolutionize the area of static images.

If we look now at dynamic image formats, we can see that there is a whole range of different products on the market. Dynamic image formats are able to change resolution, perspective, light, color, and so on. In the context of Internet imaging, dynamic does not mean Java applications, Director movies, or Active X controls that can also deliver dynamic and interactive image formats. They need additional programming. Dynamic image formats do not require programming, though they do require design.

A dynamic image contains meta-information about the picture itself, allowing you to modify its appearance without having to create a new picture. Think, for example, of an apple that can be viewed from all sides without having to reload the Web page. Looking at an apple in GIF format, you cannot change the perspective of the apple, meaning you cannot view the apple from the other side because the GIF format hasn't stored any information on what the other side may look like. Adding meta-information to the data is crucial for processing it and for creating added value to the customer. See Chapter 6 for an in depth discussion on this topic.

FlashPix, QuickTime VR, and VRML are three breakthrough technologies that provide a profound basis for dynamic Internet imaging. There are many other formats out there, but none of them fit as well into the requirements of today's online businesses. Chapter 13 discusses the static and dynamic formats in depth.

3.4.3 Content Preparation

Content preparation has become more complex over the last few years, not only because customers expect more from online businesses, but also because technologies change the face of the Web site every so often. Although many sites are still pure HTML and treat all customers in the same way, some Web sites do not care about the average customer. Look at kimble.org.[49] This site requires a T1 connection to the Internet and a high-end PC with the latest release of a browser and the Flash plug-in installed. Kimble, the "0wn3r" of the Web site, prefers a few cool visitors with the right equipment on his Web site.

But even businesses that create HTML Web sites only will no longer do this with Notepad or a similar tool. The good old days of simple, static HTML pages are over. The problem is less the missing HTML knowledge of the Web designers and more the dynamic management of HTML pages, which makes it impractical to work with simple tools for large sites. Today's Web sites con-

---

[49]http://www.kimble.org/

tain not only HTML text, but also graphics, animation, interaction, and sound. To manage these multimedia sites, it is necessary to have four basic types of software: Web page editors, graphics software packages, multimedia tools, and sound software.

Web Page Editors

As we have learned, increasingly sophisticated Internet technology and Web pages require more sophisticated tools. One of the goals is to make coding pages unnecessary for novices and easier for more experienced programmers. But more important is maintaining the consistent look of all Web pages and control over changes and links. As Web pages need to be updated from time to time, it is necessary to have a change history to make sure that you know exactly when what appeared on your Web site.

Two types of Web page editors are available. Pure text editors give HTML a rich set of code entry, manipulation, and management tools (such as Sausage Software's[50] HotDog). On the other hand there are pure WYSIWYG (What You See Is What You Get) editors that look and behave much like modern word processors (such as Mozilla Composer), the difference being that the output is saved as HTML. Some editors are a combination of text and WYSIWYG editors, such as NetObjects' Fusion.[51] These products make it possible to design an entire Web site without even a superficial acquaintance with HTML.

At the time of writing, there are more Web page editors than HTML commands available, making the decision about which editor to use very difficult. The availability on your preferred platform should be considered. Your graphic design department will most likely use Macintosh computers for the artwork, so expect them to do the Web design as well. As the graphic design department is not an IT department, the software should be user-friendly and easy to set up.

Even more important are the site management features. The content and the design should be kept in separate places in a database in order to make it easy to add new pages and to change the design of the complete site in one attempt. Therefore, the content should be saved in the database and the design should be stored in templates. Most sites will manage with fewer than 10 templates for the whole Web site. In order to make publishing the site as easy as possible, it should be possible to upload the content to a staging site first, where the changes can be tested before they are put online and made visible to the public.

As many pages appear and disappear over time, it is necessary to ensure that all links that point to obsolete pages can be removed with a single mouse click. If new pages appear, it is also necessary to ensure that they are linked into the rest of the Web site.

---

[50]http://www.sausage.com/
[51]http://www.netobjects.com/

A good Web page editor offers a set of standard client-side scripting programs that can be included on the Web page to make it more interactive. In addition to the predesigned pages, the Web page editor should support the inclusion of self-written scripts, syntax-checking on the script, and syntax-checking for the HTML code. The HTML code should be checked against HTML 3.2 and HTML 4.0, and in addition, the syntax check should provide a check to ensure that the output will look good in every browser, as not all browsers are 100 percent HTML-compliant.

Another important issue is code efficiency. If you work in WYSIWYG mode, you lose control over the underlying HTML code; many software packages produce very overblown code. Instead of real HTML output of 1 kilobyte, some programs deliver the same Web page with 10 kilobytes or more. Although this may not seem like a lot, it will add up to a large sum if your Web site is well visited. Customers will not be happy if visiting your site takes longer than visiting others. Even worse, it will congest your connection and the cost for the transaction will be higher, as most ISP contracts are based on either time (minutes) or volume (megabytes). A spellchecker is also a very useful feature that finds typos that occurred during the text input.

One of the best Web page editors is DreamWeaver,[52] which has some appealing features, such as dynamic HTML. This allows you to create animations and transitions on a Web site without much trouble. Word.com[53] is one site that features some nice JavaScript animations, called JavaScript Sprites, developed in DreamWeaver.

Content Management

The significance of content on the Web is rapidly increasing. With the growing number of available documents on the Web, traditional methods of maintenance have become more and more inadequate. The only alternative that guarantees a structured Web site and a properly administered process of information is a content management system. Therefore, content management solutions need to offer processes to coordinate users as well as to automate the publishing of documents. This ensures sound and up-to-date publications on the Internet, though many people unfortunately underestimate the amount of work involved.

Traditional Web page editors are not able to handle the automatic generation, control, and organization of content. Content management systems need to handle large quantities of documents. Over time, every company collects more and more information, and often the information cannot be removed, because customers and partners rely on it. Another important factor is workflow management for the coordination of the course of business. This allows the content management to become part of the day-to-day business for every

---

[52]http://www.dreamweaver.com/
[53]http://www.word.com/

employee. The import of external documents should be supported, allowing documents from word processors, for example, to be converted and included on the Web publication. The process of versioning documents makes it possible to track changes over time.

While general document repositories such as Documentum[54] offer the above-mentioned features, they are not designed for the Web. But there are dedicated content management packages, such as NPS from Infopark,[55] which offer a tight integration of content into Web servers, electronic business applications, and other online services. A more detailed view on content management systems can be found in Chapter 8.

Graphics Software

There are many graphics software packages on the market, but two programs have become the most popular graphic solutions, and not only for the Internet. They are Adobe's Photoshop[56] and Paint Shop Pro.[57] The major difference between these software tools is the fact that Photoshop is a commercial tool, while Paint Shop Pro is distributed as shareware, meaning that you can get a free evaluation copy of it for a certain period of time, and then register. This difference is also reflected in the price of each package. Another very popular tool on Unix is The Gimp[58], which has many features of Photoshop and even looks similar.

Photoshop is the standard tool for graphic designers and offers a rich set of features, such as layers that make it easy to compose images and move single elements around on a page. This also makes it a viable tool for designing Web pages. It is easy to precisely position elements on a page, even though this requires cascading style sheets on the browser.

Photoshop will not output HTML directly, but if you are only interested in making HTML mock-up pages, then it is a good tool for evaluating different designs. The typographic control of Photoshop is not as good as in Adobe Illustrator, but good enough for most Web pages, as the typographic control on Web pages is also restricted through the underlying HTML code.

Photoshop can also be used to create single elements on a Web page. Selected items can be rotated, flipped, and scaled. This allows designers to easily create beveled buttons, for example, which are used on many Web sites. This can be done by making a circle on one layer, then copying that layer and scaling the circle down—then the beveled box is ready. In addition to creating elements, Photoshop can also be used to define patterns that can be used as background graphics.

---

[54]http://www.documentum.com/

[55]http://www.infopark.de/

[56]http://www.adobe.com/

[57]http://www.jasc.com/

[58]http://www.gimp.org/

For newcomers, Photoshop has a relatively steep learning curve, but as your graphic design department will probably have worked with it, there should be no major issues or surprises. The program itself is also relatively small (18 megabytes), so that enough memory on a computer should be available.

Paint Shop Pro, on the other hand, has evolved from being a graphic converter to a full-blown design and paint program. Therefore, it offers some conversion features that are not available in Photoshop, making it an ideal tool for converting images from TIFF to JPEG, for example. As a result, it also offers a nice picture browser, allowing you to preview large sets of images through a rather simple interface.

Although Paint Shop Pro has some built-in filters, it does not offer the wealth of filters Photoshop does, which can be used to create special effects for the Web. If you look closely at the features, you can see that these two programs actually do not compete with each other, but rather enhance each other, as each has invaluable features the other application is missing.

But deciding on the graphical toolbox should not be part of your business problem. The imagination of your artists is far more important than the tools they use. A simple-to-use tool will increase the efficiency, but it won't make a bad designer create superb Web design elements. While it may make sense to define a standard for word processors and spreadsheets throughout an enterprise to reduce work and promote consistency with these documents, it does not make sense to impose restrictions on the graphics design department. They should be free to use any tools they need. The files they create need to be converted to a Web-compatible format before they leave the department anyway.

Besides these two applications—which are the most commonly used applications for graphics and design—there are many others, such as MetaCreations' Painter[59] or Corel PhotoPaint,[60] that offer similar functionality and are in the same price range.

Multimedia Tools

Defining multimedia tools for the Web is very difficult. Actually, every Web browser provides the functionality required to create multimedia applications through the use of HTML, JavaScript, and cascading style sheets (CSS), often referred to as DHTML, or Dynamic HTML.

Although this is very powerful, it requires Web designers to learn how to program in a traditional way. Many Web designers have little or no knowledge in this area. Therefore, many designers will want to use traditional multimedia tools, such as MacroMedia's Director[61] or Flash,[62] which are used for CD-ROM productions.

---

[59] http://www.metacreations.com/

[60] http://www.corel.com/

[61] http://www.macromedia.com/software/director/

[62] http://www.macromedia.com/software/flash/

While Director is the ultimate tool used to develop complex applications for the Web, Flash is used to create beautiful, resizable, and extremely small and compact navigation interfaces, technical illustrations, long-form animations, and other dazzling effects for Web sites and other Web-enabled devices (such as WebTV[63]). Flash is far easier to learn for Web developers of all skill levels. Flash graphics and animations are created using the drawing tools in Flash or by importing artwork from your favorite vector illustration tool.

Director has been extended to become the premium software package for the World Wide Web. The software has been enhanced to understand all the Internet formats, including MP3 and JPEG. The software's intuitive visual development metaphor makes it easy to create, import, animate, and control media. When you need sophisticated interactivity, leverage Director's easy-to-use drag-and-drop behaviors or powerful object-oriented scripting language. The final multimedia application is then saved in the Shockwave for Director file format, which requires the appropriate free plug-in from MacroMedia to be installed to view the content.

Sound Software

If you look at the file formats on the Web, you will find some that are commonly used. While .wav, .aiff, .au are standard audio sample formats that have been used in the past on Microsoft, Apple, and Sun Microsystems platforms respectively, they have become over time the standard formats for exchanging high quality snippets of audio over the Internet. If you have a short piece of audio that you want to make available, then you would choose one of those three, as they are all understood by the browsers, and a click on a button will cause a sound to be played. This can be done easily through a JavaScript program that controls the sound associated with a certain Web page.

Besides the sample formats, MIDI is very common on the Internet. Many Web sites start MIDI files in the background. This can be very irritating when you look at a Web page that makes a lot of noise without your having asked for it. The MIDI format was actually used by musicians to exchange tunes and control music hardware that understands the MIDI format. It allows you to save a complete song in very little memory. MIDI files are between 10 and 100 kilobytes for songs up to 10 minutes, making it a very convenient way to transport files. The downside of MIDI is that you will hear only the electronic representation of the original song, and there is no voice that really sings the song. In order to get the real audio, you would need to have the real-audio hardware. Still, for many areas, MIDI output is sufficient. MIDI provides only instrumental versions of music. There is no singing in MIDI.

Gallery-Net[64] offers its customers classical music while they are browsing through the Web site. Unlike other sites, the customers are not forced to hear

---

[63]http://www.webtv.com/
[64]http://www.gallery-net.com/

the music (they have to select it actively) and they have the ability to choose the music they like.

The Beatnik Player,[65] another very common player, offers a mixture between the sampled format of AIFF and WAV and the MIDI format, where the song is already structured. David Bowie[66] has used the Beatnik technology to allow his fans to remix his song "Fame" on the Internet. RealPlayer[67] offers the possibility to hear streaming audio via the Web. *Streaming audio* means that audio content is created at the time it is heard and is transmitted in real time to the customer. It can also be used to transport content that is not live, but its real strength lies in transmitting live audio. Radio utilizes RealPlayer on the Web, making it an indispensable tool for the many people who enjoy live radio on the Internet.

For recorded content that does not need to be played in real time, MP3 has become the format to use. It compresses audio files with a compression ratio that is on average about 1:10 and allows everyone with an MP3 player to replay the recorded content. It can be compared to the standard sample formats, such as AIFF, but does not require as much space on your hard disk.

Depending on the needs of your application and your customers, first decide on which type of delivery you require and then decide on the format. Since today's sound applications are all able to convert sounds into each of these formats, this should not be a cause for concern. Business is the only critical issue here.

3.4.4   Data Warehousing

Data warehousing is becoming a popular business application and is already used in many companies. A data warehouse is a copy of the business transaction data specifically structured for query and analysis. The operational system cannot hold its data for infinite times; therefore, data is moved to the data warehouse. With widespread use of the Internet, the amount of transaction data is increasing rapidly. Data warehouses are used in two areas: They can support decision-makers in the process of deciding, and they can be used to verify the results of a decision. Using live data for these applications would bring down the application server. The computations required for the decision-making process are very heavy and require a dedicated system, where data can be shifted around, depending on what results are required. In most cases it is not acceptable to have business analysis interfere with the operational systems and decrease their performance.

Vivek Gupta, a senior software consultant, in his book *An Introduction to Data Warehousing*,[68] defines a data warehouse as "a structured extensible en-

---

[65]http://www.beatnik.com/

[66]http://www.davidbowie.com/fame/

[67]http://www.real.com/

[68]*An Introduction to Data Warehousing*, Vivek R. Gupta, Chicago, 1997,

vironment designed for the analysis of nonvolatile data, logically and physically transformed from multiple source applications to align with the business structure, which is updated and maintained for a long time period, expressed in simple business terms, and summarized for quick analysis."

Decision support or executive information systems, which are widely seen as the precursors of data warehouse systems, have the following characteristics:

- **Consolidated views**—Consolidated views are available for products, customers, and markets, which also allows for more details.

- **Descriptive terms**—The systems convert the names of the data fields from cryptic computer terms to descriptive standard business terms to make it easier for managers to understand.

- **Preprocessed data**—The available data is preprocessed in order to match the standard rules better.

Table 3.4. Decision Support Systems

Gupta offers a historical view on how data warehouse systems evolved. In the past the functionality of the data warehouse was buried in legacy systems that offered some tools for the graphical representation and analysis of the data. With the emergence of the personal computer, data moved from legacy systems to personal computers, making it easy to analyze the local data, but difficult to get the whole picture. As networks were not very common, data could not be shared with other systems. Before the introduction of data warehouse systems, decision-support systems and executive information systems were used, which partly provided the functionality of data warehouse systems.

While decision-support systems tended to focus on details—useful for lower level to midlevel managers for their particular decision problems—the executive information systems provide a high-level view of the data. The basic data for this group of systems is normally the same, but is processed in different ways. This group of systems can be viewed as a precursor to the data warehouse systems. The reason these systems never became really popular was because they were very expensive. Table 3.4 gives a short summary on the functions of these systems.

http://www.system-services.com/

The data warehouse systems that evolved from these applications provide analytical tools that are able to satisfy more general requirements. The system targets not only analysts, managers, and executives, but also personnel who may use the system to analyze portions of data based on specific requirements. It is far easier to buy a standard product and integrate it with the overall business structure.

In order to make the data warehouse system a useful and successful tool for business analysis, data from more than one operational system needs to be combined. In order to integrate the data from different sources, the data needs to be transformed into a single data format that makes it possible to analyze the combined data in a consistent way. This, of course, cannot be done to the real production data. A copy is used, transformed, and analyzed. Data warehouse systems can combine data from sales, marketing, finance, and production applications. Once the data is combined, it is possible to cross-reference data and generate comprehensive information.

Data in the data warehouse is organized around time, as this dimension is often used as the primary search-filter criterion. Most people will want reports based on a given week, month, or quarter, and will compare the results with other weeks, months, or quarters. The time attribute is also used to cross-reference data between different operational data sources. This allows users to establish and understand the correlation between activities of different groups within a company. This unique feature makes data warehouse systems powerful and precious to their users.

Data warehouse systems not only integrate data from multiple sources, but can also analyze multiple versions of the same source. This allows users to verify if an upgrade of an existing application has improved the performance or if new employees are able to generate more revenue than other employees. By changing application software, the data warehouse can be used to combine software from the old and new applications to maintain a single business view of the whole company.

Once the data has been imported into the data warehouse, it becomes non-volatile, meaning that no modifications are made afterward to the information. Data that comes from operational systems is triggered to go to the data warehouse in its final state. Orders or production data are completed before going into the data warehouse. By moving this data to the data warehouse, you free up resources on the operational system and create an archive that can be used for multiple purposes. Keeping the data in the data warehouse for a long time does not cost a lot of money. Once the data is in the data warehouse, it keeps the operational system from filling up, thus saving costs on downtimes. In addition to viewing data in their final state, data warehouses can be used to compare snapshots of data that change all the time. Data warehouse systems are not designed to host dynamic data.

As you can imagine, every application provides different types and different formats of data. In order to make the data warehouse a success, the source data needs to be logically transformed to match the data formats coming in from other sources. Therefore, the architecture of the data warehouse is crucial. It needs to consider all lines of business in a company. The data warehouse architecture outlines the logical and physical structure of the data. The architect needs to structure the data independent of any relational model of any of the operational systems that are used as sources.

Before data modelers denormalize the relations for performance or other reasons, they try to achieve the Third Normal Form. The following three levels of normalization exist:

- **First Normal Form**—This relation describes a single entity and contains no arrays or repeating attributes.

- **Second Normal Form**—This is a relation with additional properties to the First Normal Form, meaning that all attributes are fully dependent on the primary key.

- **Third Normal Form**—This is a relation with additional properties to the Second Normal Form, meaning that all attributes are fully dependent on the primary key.

Table 3.5. Normalization of Data

In many companies, information is available from different resources. Information on prices and product numbers, for example, is stored in different types of operational systems that use different databases and formats. In order to make the data warehouse system work effectively, these items need to be consolidated. There are two ways to consolidate the data: Either at the source or at the destination. If you consolidate the data at the data warehouse, you save a lot of cost and time in the beginning, but will need to repeat the exercise for every change on the source system. If you consolidate at the source system, it will take longer, but will bring all your systems in line over time and reduce costs in the long run. The model of the data warehouse needs to be extensible so that data from different applications can be added. It is unlikely that you will be able to incorporate all data right from the beginning, but over time more and more data can be introduced.

The logical model of the database is aligned with the lines of business in the company. The entities in the warehouse model are based on actual business entities, such as customers and orders. This allows the person who is analyzing the data to get exactly the business view required, making the data warehouse independent of the source application data models.

In order to improve performance of the system, the database model needs to be denormalized. The maximum performance gain can be achieved when the data has been normalized first in order to achieve the maximum flexibility (see Table 3.5). Denormalization reduces the need for database table joins in the queries. Another reason is that the relationship between many attributes does not change in this historical data.

When entering new data into the data warehouse, it is necessary to scrub and to stage the data. *Data scrubbing* is a very tedious process and means that the data needs to be homogenized and purified before being entered into the data warehouse. *Data staging* means that the data is put into a staging area before it ends up in the data warehouse. This reduces the risk of putting the wrong data in the data warehouse.

The summary of the business views are, in most cases, simple aggregations based on predefined parameters, such as the sales figures of a certain product that can be viewed for a week, month, or quarter. In order to reduce the processing drain on the data warehouse server, the results of the most common summary views are stored on the server and updated on a regular basis.

The simplicity of the data warehouse system makes it a valuable tool for everyone and reduces the cost significantly for the analysis of business decisions. A lot of care has to be taken with the data entered into the data warehouse, as invalid data will falsify the results. A well-implemented data warehouse system is the key for understanding the business decisions of yesterday and making the right decisions for tomorrow. These features are highly important, because fast decisions are required in the Internet business world.

3.4.5   Enterprise Resource Planning

The introduction of the Internet has made the world appear very small indeed. The global village is already an electronic reality. As many organizations confront new markets, new competition, and increasing customer expectations, manufacturers needed to find new ways of reacting to these business challenges.

Business process reengineering (BPR) and information technology helped these companies to resolve the problems. In the 1960s, digital manufacturing systems were already available, but since they were only able to handle inventory control, a manufacturer had a very limited view of the production process. Ten years later, the focus shifted from inventory control to material requirement planning (MRP). These systems allowed manufacturers to control the flow of components and raw materials and offered ways of planning in advance.

Around 1990 the MRP was evolving into a system that allowed it to cover all business activities within a company, including human resources, projects management, and finance. These highly complex systems were called Enterprise Resource Planning (ERP)

Today ERP is used to manage all major business processes, including product planning, parts purchasing, inventory management, interaction with suppliers, customer service, and order tracking, which all provide information that can be very useful for the online business and automatic exchange.

By digitizing all these business processes, the manufacturers were able to lower the total cost in the supply chain and shorten the throughput times. The stock could be reduced to a minimum by implementing a just-in-time process, and the product assortment could be enlarged. Through digitization, manufacturers were able to improve product quality and provide more reliable delivery dates without raising prices. ERP allowed them to coordinate global demand, supply, and production very efficiently.

The efficiency of an enterprise depends on the quick flow of information across the complete supply chain (i.e., from the customer to manufacturer to supplier). ERP systems therefore need to have a rich functionality in all areas of business. In the past, large companies used electronic data interchange (EDI) to speed up communication with trading partners. Parts could be ordered automatically or customers could order goods from the manufacturer. Although EDI was a good system, it meant a large investment for every participating company, making it unavailable to smaller businesses. The costs for EDI were high because there were repeated costs for every installation. A company trading with 50 partners had to install 50 EDI interfaces. Each of the companies involved did too, making it 100 installations. EDI is a two-way protocol, which was fine in the client-server area, but in the emerging pervasive computing area, EDI in its traditional form will not survive. XML is replacing the functionality of EDI in more and more businesses (see Chapter 10 for more information on XML).

As many manufacturers are working on a global scale, they will have a lot of different suppliers around the world, and the ERP system needs to take this into account. The system also needs to have multisite management capabilities for companies that are organized in a decentralized manner. An ERP system should be able to address all the requirements of the financial accounting and management accounting of the organization. The ERP system should contain an enterprise information system in order to analyze the performance in key areas quickly and correctly.

The deployment of an ERP system typically requires a business process analysis and employee retraining, and then the development of new work procedures. Some people say that the company needs to adapt to the ERP system, as the software is so complex that it cannot be adapted directly to the needs of the company.

Selecting the right ERP software is difficult and requires a lot of planning. Some of the most important criteria for the selection can be found in Table 3.6. Remember that rapid implementation will lead to a shortened ROI period. Many companies start with a BPR cycle before starting to implement the ERP system. As a result, the BPR cycle does not always match the changing processes within the company and a decoupled BPR and ERP implementation will take far longer to integrate. The consequence is that additional customizations are required and higher costs are incurred.

When selecting ERP software for your company, you should consider the following topics:

- **Business processes**—The software should support all the business processes of your company.

- **Component integration**—The software should have a high degree of integration between the various components.

- **Flexibility**—The ERP system should be adjustable to the changing needs of your company.

- **Internet connectivity**—A component should be available to integrate the ERP system with your online business, making it secure and feasible.

- **Multisite support**—Global and local planning and control facilities need to be supported.

- **Quick implementation**—A short implementation period will reduce the wait for the ROI.

- **User friendliness**—The ERP system should be usable and manageable by nontechnical people.

Table 3.6. Evaluation of ERP Software

In order to reduce the time for implementation, two strategies can be used. The first strategy is to make the technical implementation based on the current business processes and enhance the processes after the first phase. This requires a very flexible ERP system, but makes it easy to start with. In order to keep the implementation simple, only a single site should be considered at a time. This can be achieved if improvements of the business processes are not required immediately.

The second strategy is to implement the ERP system with business improvement in mind. In this scenario, only certain parts of the business are considered, but they are improved and implemented over all manufacturing sites, and then the whole process is repeated for other parts of the business.

The Internet has changed the way ERP systems operate and interoperate with other ERP systems. It allows rapid supply-chain management between multiple operations and trading partners. An ERP system that does not support Internet connectivity is not acceptable by most companies anymore. By linking multiple ERP systems, it is possible to create virtual supply chains and therefore enable the end customer to monitor the production of a particular product.

The Internet has introduced a secure and direct self-service model for accessing the ERP system that allows customers and suppliers to interact with a company without contacting a sales representative. This requires a highly secure connection to the system, as the ERP is the heart of the company. Once it is in place, hackers are able to intrude and change order values or bring the ERP system to a halt. (More on security can be found in Chapter 11.) Only if the security can be guaranteed will the business partners have trust and confidence in the system.

Three groups of users will benefit from a fully installed ERP system: the customers, the suppliers, and the employees. Customers are able to place and trace. In addition to ordering products, they can also get additional product information. The Internet offers a unique platform for all these services. It allows users to incorporate workflow components easily to create real business transactions on the Web. Shipping information, inventory balances, and engineering specifications become available in an instant, making the production faster and easier.

The ERP system also offers some advantages for the supplier. Sharing manufacturing data with the suppliers allows suppliers to anticipate services and products required by the manufacturer without adding costs to the components. Changes in manufacturing will automatically be broadcast to all suppliers in order to change order volumes and products. Contracts can be put online and included into the workflow and revised whenever appropriate.

ERP is also useful for internal work, as it enables companies to expand their internal automation. Standard paperwork from human resources, expense reporting, approval processes, and purchase requisitions can be automated and stored in a single system. This reduces the resources your company expends to support employees while offering them automated methods for performing tasks that might otherwise take hours or days to complete. Employees can update their personal human resources information automatically by using a simple Web browser. Self-service has become a standard for many enterprise business applications.

Access to the business systems of your own company or those of your trading partners has been unified through the Internet, allowing for information retrieval on a self-service basis. This has helped to improve the service, reduce the operating costs, compress the cycle times, open new sales channels, and make it dramatically easier for people to do business with you and your company.

The best-known software providers of ERP solutions are Baan,[69] Oracle,[70] PeopleSoft,[71] and SAP.[72] Which solution best fits your company needs to be decided by your business needs. Again, the hardware and software platform should not dictate the solution. The ERP system that you implement should offer interfaces to the ERP systems of your partners, no matter what solution they are using. Otherwise, you will have a big problem. Having the same system will help a lot, but you can't choose your partners because of their ERP systems or your ERP system because of your partners. To be on the safe side, find common data formats—for example, XML—for the exchange of information.

3.4.6 Call Center Solutions

More and more companies are under constant pressure to provide new services for their customers. The Internet adds even more pressure. Every service that is put online requires a call center so that in case problems arise, people can call for assistance. While the Internet offers many possibilities, the telephone should not be forgotten. It offers a direct way of communication, and people are used to it.

As companies move toward digital customer contact, customers often feel like they get less personalized service, are put on hold too long, or are transferred from agent to agent and department to department. At each step along the way, they need to repeat information, resulting in a dissatisfied and frustrated customer. Your customers have several options today at the click of a mouse button. If they do not have a positive experience and their problems are not solved, you're at a competitive disadvantage. The service provider needs to improve the image, while at the same time, reduce costs and run a more efficient operation.

Regardless of what "customer care" is called in your company, it is the process that occurs when your customer contacts you with a particular problem. Typically, it's a question about his or her bill, a repair problem, or a need for information about a new service. What your customers want is a single point of contact providing convenience and satisfaction. They want the person whom they contact to be able to handle their needs without a lot of hand-offs and call-backs. This requires a call center solution.

The financial industry, for example, sees a major change occurring. Customers do not want to go to a branch to be served, but expect that wishes can be executed from anywhere. They also want more direct access to their assets. This means they want to pay their regular household bills, order travelers checks, buy and sell stocks and shares, arrange insurance, and order and

---

[69]http://www.baan.com/

[70]http://www.oracle.com/

[71]http://www.peoplesoft.com/

[72]http://www.sap.com/

pay for goods all through direct electronic services accessed from the home or office.

This change brings benefits to the financial industry. The cost per transaction is lowered since part of the labor is executed by the customer instead of an employee. Therefore, financial services are moving away from branches to very specialized call centers, which are cheaper to operate, more efficient, and can offer the full range of services desired.

Customers want to be able to manage all aspects of their accounts through a single, consistent, and efficient service process. This process could be handled over a phone, a pager, or an Internet terminal. This means the customer maintains a single point of contact, whether they are moving money from one account to another one, reporting a problem with the current account balance, or are interested in new services.

If we stay with the example of the financial industry, you will see that although a bank is able to handle the above-mentioned processes, they are all handled through different business units. A bank clerk who is responsible for your bank account will not be able to handle your stocks. These two processes are handled internally by two different lines of business. But as a customer, you are not interested in how the processes are handled internally. A bank that offers several types of services should also be able to serve you from a single point of access.

The Internet can hide these departmental issues quite well. When accessing a bank's Web site, the customer will not see which line of business is responsible for which part of the Web site. But once a problem occurs and the customer needs to get in touch with the company, the call center needs to aggregate all the information in order to be of service.

This will not only assist customers and give them a higher level of service, but will also help to identify cross-selling opportunities. This information can be brought back to the Web site to let the customers help themselves. The same systems can be used to offer customer-service representatives a simple and intuitive interface to access information across the organization.

In order for a call center to be effective, it needs to access multiple data sources within the company and carry out concurrent processing in different applications, without delaying the customer (who may be waiting online for a response). These customer-service functions also require powerful client processing characteristics at the desktop, if implemented in a traditional telephone call center.

A successful call center needs to be highly integrated and must create a single customer view through the integration of all relevant databases. The call center becomes the unique point for marketing, sales, customer management, distribution, and solutions.

Hewlett-Packard offers an integrated customer call center, named Smart Contact, that is divided into five focus areas: Contact Management Services, Enterprise Data Integration, Business Applications, Integrated Desktop, and

Integration Services. Smart Contact is able to integrate not only multiple databases, but also several channels, such as telephone, the Web, fax, and email. The solution is suitable not only for in-bound calls, but also for out-bound calls, such as telemarketing efforts, which can be integrated into all the key business applications that manage a sales campaign.

There are many other solutions on the market today. One other solution, called Remedy,[73] allows companies to build up a centrally managed telephony-based call center with the integration of other communication channels, in a way similar to Smart Contact.

While it may be appropriate for large companies to build up their own call centers using solutions mentioned here, many smaller companies will out-source this activity to a call center provider who will be able to manage the whole infrastructure in a very cost-efficient way. The Internet is able to reduce these costs even further, as it has a large impact on telephone costs, and the introduction of new technologies has reduced the need for a standard telephone-based solution. The Internet reduces the need for telephones in general and traditional call centers in particular. This does not mean that the Internet makes the telephone superfluous; as your business grows, you will encounter more people who prefer to have some form of personal contact.

LiveAssistance[74] offers a Web-based call center solution that allows customers to click on a button on a Web site that connects the customer with a person in the customer care center via the Internet. A new window pops up, where the customer is able to enter a text-based online chat. This allows the customer and the employee to communicate very efficiently. The call center is able to push URLs to the customer, which may be of help. This chat-based solution offers a very convenient but inexpensive way to build up a customer care center. Other companies add Internet telephony to their offering to increase various communication methods. The Internet telephony solution does require the customer to have speakers and a microphone to communicate with the call center, but does not require expensive add-ons for the call center architecture.

3.5 Building the E-Business Applications

3.5.1 Putting the Building Blocks Together

Now that you have an overview of the building blocks for an Internet business, you need to find the right blocks that fit together. Legacy systems are sometimes a problem when their standards are not available to the public. There are still enough companies who are not willing to share their standards with other companies, requiring you to select a certain piece of software in conjunction with another piece of software to make it work on a certain platform. Legacy systems are those that have been inherited from languages, platforms, and

---

[73]http://www.remedy.com/
[74]http://www.liveassistance.com/

techniques earlier than current technology. Most enterprise who use computers have legacy applications and databases that serve critical business needs. Typically, the challenge is to keep the legacy application running while converting it to newer, more efficient code that makes use of new technology and programmer skills. In the past, much programming has been written for specific manufacturers' operating systems. Currently, many companies are migrating their legacy applications to new programming languages and operating systems that follow open or standard programming interfaces.

It is expected that this will change over the next few years. As more and more technology is built on Internet technologies, it will become easier to integrate these building blocks into a seamless working solution. Before choosing your building blocks, look at the rest of the book for more in depth information on available formats and protocols that have become standards on the Internet, and then choose the applications—with your business model in mind—that support the appropriate standards.

As the computing paradigm shifts toward pervasive computing, the single application becomes less important and the service behind the application becomes what really matters. While today people think application-centric, in the future, people will think service-centric. They won't care anymore about the application that provided a service, but will specify the service they require. Instead of ordering Star Office, a business software similar to Microsoft Office, they will order a text input, layout, and printout service. These three services may come from different sources, and the customer will decide on the features and the pricing for the usage of that particular service. Applications will most likely not be sold anymore, but rented or leased for a certain period of time.

3.5.2   Integrating the Enterprise

In order to improve customer satisfaction and increase the speed of product delivery, many companies have started to link disparate applications within their enterprises. By integrating strategic business applications—such as e-business applications, virtual supply chains, and customer care centers—they are also able to cut costs drastically and simplify the business integration with customers and partners.

By tying together all enterprise applications, you can create an environment that is able to withstand the changing electronic world. It makes it easier to exchange or add applications, as the basic messaging system linking these business-critical applications does not change. This makes the architecture very flexible and allows it to adapt rapidly to the changing needs of the customers. The developers are able to focus on the business logic rather than on the architecture.

The integrated enterprise is able to support the flow of information across multiple business units, IT systems, and companies. An online order starts at a certain company, goes into the Web server, then on Web application servers and into a database. This system then often interacts with an accounting system, an inventory management system, and a shipping application. All these systems live on different platforms and often do not speak the same language. The applications often have different APIs and file formats and can't exchange information directly with applications from other manufacturers.

While many companies have tried to integrate these applications in the past, it was mostly an expensive project that required them to write some integration code between each application. It required a lot of programming and system knowledge. Although these complex architectures have become business-critical systems, they are difficult to maintain.

Three types of application integration software are being used to make the manual integration of these business applications simpler. The first type is the messaging middleware, which allows applications to exchange data in real time. This type of integration software is used in traditional mainframe and transactional environments, such as MQ Series, developed by IBM.

A second type of business process integration tool has been introduced that links the business-critical application on a business process level. Business-Ware, developed by Vitria,[75] allows developers to design business processes graphically, which may require several applications to complete. The software generates the underlying application logic and middleware needed to link the applications and allow the exchange of data in real time.

On the top level, a third set of tools allows the integration of a company into a virtual supply chain. They allow the automated connection of a company to its partners' systems over the Internet. Extricity has developed such a product.[76]

The integration of business-critical applications is needed to link existing systems within the company, and with partners, especially when mergers or acquisitions occur. Two companies that merge often have totally different IT infrastructures, but the same or similar business processes. In order to complete the merger, the integration of these two infrastructures is a key point, as it reduces the duplicate processes and costs. Through the layers of integration, this can be achieved very quickly and efficiently.

As a result of the business application, manual and batch processes can be replaced by automated processes. This dynamic business requires a tight but flexible integration among inhouse enterprise applications and between partner and customer applications. A more in-depth view on the integration of enterprise applications can be found in Chapter 10, where Web application servers are discussed. Web application servers offer not only integration, but also a unified Web front end, allowing clients to access the enterprise applications through a Web browser.

---

[75]http://www.vitria.com/
[76]http://www.extricity.com/

3.5.3   Enterprise Application Integration

Enterprise application integration, or EAI, has been a new buzzword for some time now, but hasn't really meant anything new. EAI is the integration of applications so they can freely share information, processes, and services. But EAI goes beyond classical system integration by rethinking technologies and approaches to make it a cost-effective reality. EAI focuses on the business issues at hand, which requires systems both inside and outside an enterprise to freely share information and logic in previously impossible ways.

EAI applies to almost any technology that links one system to another, including technologies over 25 years old. EAI is also much more than a middleware component that acts as a monolithic block between systems. In today's networked environments, it has to be much more flexible. Therefore, EAI provides a solution that could be described as many-to-many middleware technology. Products like message brokers allow enterprises to connect many diverse systems, typically without changing the source and target systems. This brings a big relief to many companies that do not have the money to develop new systems. They can continue using their old hardware and software and can provide flexible links in between.

This EAI hub might also provide centralized management of information moving between systems, with the flexibility to reconfigure the integration solution at any time, as business needs change. It may also provide the opportunity to share business logic, which is EAI's holy grail and make a company more efficient as it is suddenly able to access all information stored in various systems across the corporation.

3.5.4   Solutions to Integration

EAI is a concept, not a technology. EAI can be achieved through various means. This subsection explores the most common solutions in place. One of the simplest solutions in technology is the point-to-point solution, which basically connects systems in a company with each other. Point-to-point solutions are using traditional middleware software stacks that contain message queuing or connection-oriented services, such as remote procedure calls (RPC). One of the major issues with this approach is that the applications that need to be interconnected need to be changed in order to support RPC or any other transaction-handling code to communicate with the other systems. This typically happens by placing messages on one queue and receiving messages from another queue.

Point-to-point solutions work well for the integration of two applications. In the early years of the Internet, this was often the case, but nowadays EAI requires the integration of many different systems. Therefore, point-to-point solutions are no longer suitable. There are some advantages in point-to-point solutions, of course. It is easy to keep track of application-specific information such as application semantics, process descriptions, metadata, and interfaces. But once connections have been created between more than just a handful of systems, they don't adjust quickly to new business requirements. Changing just one of your systems can also involve changing a large number of connections.

A better way of integrating systems is through database-to-database connections. This means information is shared at the database level. The exchange of information on the database level can be achieved through two different mechanisms. First, the basic replication solution leverages replication features built into many databases to move information between databases as long as they maintain the same basic schema information on all sources and targets. The second approach is database replication and transformation software, sold by vendors like Constellar.[77] These types of products move information between different schemas on many different types of databases, including various brands and models, by transforming the data on the fly. That way, it is represented correctly to the target database.

There are several advantages over point-to-point solutions. First of all, since they are dealing with application information at the data level, companies do not need to change the source or target applications. This lowers the risk and cost of integration applications throughout the enterprise. Although this approach is promising, it does not work for all applications. SAP R/3,[78] for example, does not provide access to databases directly. In order to access data, you must go through the business logic components. If you try to go to the database directly, the whole SAP installation may become corrupt, as data can be inconsistent through direct access to the database layer.

A step further than just connecting databases and replicating data across various databases, federated database software presents any number of physical databases (which can be of various brands, models, and schemas) through a virtual database model. Once this virtual database has been put in place, the applications using databases should be redirected through the virtual database. This virtual database becomes the single point of application integration, accessing data from any number of systems through the same single database interface.

The advantage of this approach is that it merges metadata nicely among applications and hides the differences in integrated databases from the other applications using the integrated view. But it will not resolve all problems with the integration, the logic for integrating the applications with the databases still must be created.

Brokering mechanisms can also be used to integrate enterprise applications. Brokered EAI is built on existing asynchronous message-oriented middleware technology. This means that some type of middleware can connect to multiple systems, moving information in and out of those systems. The middleware component extracts information from one system, converts it (if required),

---

[77]http://www.constellar.com/
[78]http://www.sap.com/

There are many different ways of integrating applications within an enterprise. The following list shows some of the most common integration methods.

- **Point-to-Point**—Simple integration for two systems.

- **Database-to-Database**—Connection of database to exchange information.

- **Federated Databases**—Connection of all databases with a single view on the information through a new interface.

- **Brokering**—Integration via an asynchronous message-oriented middleware technology.

- **Composite Application**—Integration by sharing services.

- **Process Automation**—Flow of information from one processing point to the next in a chain.

Table 3.7. Types of EAI

and pushes it into another system. The conversion is done in a middleware hub that may split, reformat, combine, or change parts of the content so that the target application can understand it.

These hubs are also known as message brokers. To support the need for conversion, message brokers leverage rules engines, intelligent routing mechanisms, and transformation engines, but usually leave the messaging to some existing messaging infrastructure. This flexible mechanism allows the tight integration of all applications. The most used message brokers include NEON,[79] MQIntegrator,[80] ActiveWorks,[81] and STC Datagate.[82]

The major advantage of this approach is that neither the source nor the target systems need to be modified when using the brokered approach. Instead of modifying the existing systems, the message broker needs to be adapted. Therefore, most message brokers offer adapters to connect into common pack-

---

[79]http://www.neon.com/
[80]http://www.mqseries.com/
[81]http://www.activesoftware.com/
[82]http://www.stc.com/

aged applications such as PeopleSoft, SAP, and Baan, as well as common relational databases.

The message broker determines what events will drive the information migration, be it an update to a source or target database or invocation of a transaction. This creates an advantage over point-to-point systems, as in this approach the trigger events can be determined unobtrusively by reading the message envelope. The disadvantage of message brokers are the relatively high startup costs. But for companies with several systems that need to be integrated, the costs are relatively low per system.

The idea of composite applications is another way of integration that can be used in EAI. Instead of creating separate applications that need to be connected, the composite approach works the other way around. A company needs to create a single, centralized application (either logical or physical) that can provide a common set of services to any number of other remote applications. It means integrating the enterprise by sharing services. This is also known as method-level EAI, or integrating the enterprise by sharing application methods. This integration can be achieved only by using two technologies: application servers and distributed objects, which will be discussed later in the book.

To create a composite application, a set of shared transactions within the application server environment needs to be created. Many remote applications invoke shared transactions to share business logic and interact with resources, such as databases, ERP systems, and queues. The integration occurs through the sharing of business logic as well as through the back-end integration of many different applications and resources. Distributed objects let you wrap existing applications so they appear as distributed objects, thus providing the infrastructure for sharing data and methods. Distributed objects also let you reengineer applications so that they share a new set of objects in a distributed architecture.

There are several advantages to this paradigm. Applications are tightly integrated by sharing methods, and applications are bound to the business logic provided by these methods. From the outside, all integrated applications appear to be one. But in order to achieve this goal, all applications need to be modified to support distributed objects and an application server.

Last but not least, process automation can be used to integrate applications. Process automation means information is passed between participating systems while applying appropriate rules in order to achieve a business objective. Process automation lives on top of technology and describes a predefined set of steps that make up a business process. The process flow logic does not involve traditional programming logic, such as user interface processing, database updates, or the execution of transactions. Rather, it is concerned with the flow of information from one processing point to the next in a value chain.

This means that the process logic is separate from the application logic. The process logic coordinates or manages the information flow between the many source and target applications. Hewlett-Packard[83] has created a solution called HP Process Manager; IBM[84] provides FlowMart; and Vitria[85] provides a solution with its Vitria product line.

3.5.5   Selecting the Right EAI Technology

There is no simple answer to the question of which is the right EAI technology. It is a matter of understanding where your company is, and what your business drivers are, and then selecting the architecture that satisfies both. The decision depends also on the need for integration. How much information needs to be moved, what type of information needs to be moved between systems (e.g., pure data or events and state of process), and probably most important, how many systems need to be integrated?

As discussed, three different approaches can be considered: data-level, method-level, and process automation. The data-level approach, using database-to-database and database federation EAI (or the simplest level of brokering), works best for those domains, either at the department or enterprise levels, that can get by with simple information sharing. Systems that only need to share customer information from system to system, and do not need to share methods or entire accounting records, are good candidates for data-level integration. It is inexpensive, low risk, and reliable.

The method-level approach, using brokering or composite application EAI, provides a more tightly coupled solution. Applications are bound at the method or program level. This allows companies to share data as well as business rules, integrity restraints, and the process automation that exists within the applications. It is a good fit for organizations that need to share information and processes in real time. But it is an expensive approach to EAI. A logistics company requires real-time data from various sources to track shipments and therefore would be a good example for a company requiring this kind of integration.

The brokering approach works best for companies that need to share data as well as process information in a loosely coupled sense. Methods are invoked on the source and/or target systems, but they aren't shared. The composite application approach works best when a company requires a seamless, closely coupled solution. This approach really tries to bind the applications together in order to view them as a single application. A company that has sales people in the field could use this approach, as the sales people are "loosely coupled" to the corporate network.

For companies that appear to have workflow problems, such as automating tasks handled in a chain of separate systems, often involving relatively unstructured information and human interaction, the process-automation ap-

---

[83]http://www.ice.hp.com/

[84]http://www.ibm.com/

[85]http://www.vitria.com/

proach makes the most sense. Typically, no program code needs to be changed. Often, the lack of a simple mapping between the output of one system and the input of the next is handled by the intervention of human intelligence. This can be, for example, interpreting information coming out of the source system and entering the results into the target system or making a decision based on information. This works best if the applications are discrete, so that only little information or business processes need to be moved between systems.

As with most things, a mixed approach is the most suitable approach. The mixed approach enables you to select the best EAI solution for the problem at hand. This individual solution is also the most costly, because multiple types of technology need to be integrated. Large systems integrators have started to offer integrated solutions that better fit the needs of enterprises than just providing a software stack.

EAI is a very good concept, but unfortunately the major ERP vendors have not developed very good solutions yet. If your company has an ERP solution, you require some additional EAI software from a third-party vendor.

This subsection provides some ideas on how to integrate SAP R/3 with other systems. Oracle,[86] for example, has developed APIs for some portions of its ERP applications; other parts are inaccessible. The same applies to PeopleSoft, Baan, and SAP. In the old world order, these systems were not meant to be integrated with partners, suppliers, and customers. In today's Internet world, this is a necessity. Therefore, many companies have been forced to improvise interfaces, communicating directly with their ERP packages.

Things are slowly getting better. PeopleSoft has released its Open Integration Framework (OIF), which contains a set of mechanisms built around XML that allows other applications or middleware to link with PeopleSoft data and processes.

SAP R/3 also provides a set of well-defined interfaces for sharing data and processes, but unfortunately these interfaces are rather complex and overlapping. The architecture is not easy to understand; some technical issues make the integration difficult. Just like most ERP packages, SAP has been built as a monolithic application, which was not designed for communicating with the rest of the world. SAP enhanced this by adding interfaces allowing the communication with other SAP instances, but these interfaces are not really suitable for other applications.

3.6   Speeding up the Internet

3.6.1   Introduction

Many people get frustrated because certain Web sites are really slow. There are many reasons for slow Web sites, and even more excuses when something goes

---

[86]http://www.oracle.com/

wrong. But instead of complaining when something goes wrong, companies should invest in technologies to prevent problems in the first place. Content delivery management services run networks that can reroute Internet users to the server closest to them that stores the requested data. Through bandwidth conservation technologies it is possible to reduce the amount of data transmitted over the Internet. QoS technologies make sure that a certain bandwidth is guaranteed, and caching algorithms reduce the time to create new data. The following subsections describe the solutions in more detail.

Today the challenge on the Internet is to create Web sites capable of serving millions of users simultaneously. This can only be achieved by using an approach that tries to centralize when necessary and store locally whenever possible. Therefore, mirroring is a technology that has become increasingly important.

First of all, the company needs to evaluate the economics of international bandwidth versus local delivery. In many cases, the price of local processing power and storage is less expensive than bandwidth, making it more affordable to deliver content locally than move it over international telecommunications circuits. Depending on the type of content, the benefits differ. Many Web sites have a large amount of static content. Rather than send this static content between countries, it can be much more efficient to keep it in a local market. Other criteria for locally stored content could be determined by language, complexity of the content, and traffic.

Mirroring and caching provide additional redundancy in the unlikely event of a network failure, so the end user is always routed to the closest geographic location. Likewise, there is a correlation between the distance a transmission has to travel and response time.

Current models for deploying IP applications on a global scale necessitate the use, management, and monitoring of multiple, widely dispersed servers and hosting facilities. These complexities make it extremely difficult for multinational corporations to deploy and manage applications across the existing infrastructure. This complexity can be reduced through a highly advanced network architecture and integrated outsourcing service.

3.6.2 Content Delivery Management

One of the most promising solutions to reduce the lag on the Internet is called content delivery management. Content delivery management refers to running networks that can reroute Internet users to the server closest to them that stores the requested data.

As companies migrate key business processes to the Internet, they face a common challenge. Today's centralized Internet infrastructure solutions force users to traverse multiple congested networks to interact with a Web site. This approach prevents companies from attaining the scalability, reliability, and performance levels that are mission-critical for business-class Web sites today.

Akamai[87] is one of the leading providers of distributed application and content delivery services, enabling companies to reduce the complexities and costs of deploying and operating a uniform Web infrastructure, while providing businesses an advantage for offering users an unparalleled Internet experience. Akamai's EdgeSuite is an integrated suite of services for mission-critical e-business.

The Akamai platform is the foundation for the Akamai services that eliminate these traditional impediments, providing companies with the foundation for delivering limitless scalability, unmatched performance, and 100 percent reliability—regardless of traffic load, application, or content type.

Simply put, the Akamai platform is the integrated set of Akamai's patent-pending core technologies and expansive network infrastructure—the thousands of Akamai servers deployed across hundreds of access networks worldwide. This future-proof Internet infrastructure platform supports multiple Akamai services that place content and Web applications close to requesting users, thereby avoiding congestion points on the Internet.

Thousands of companies worldwide leverage the Akamai platform and corresponding services to create a uniform Web infrastructure that reduces ownership costs while improving end-user experience.

Digital Island's[88] Content Delivery Services move content closer to the end user and ensure a fast, guaranteed, and locally relevant customer experience. The services combine new technologies with a global infrastructure to improve a company's ability to conduct e-business more effectively.

An important component of Digital Island's Content Delivery Services is Footprint, a Content Delivery Network capable of distributing all major content types, including streaming media, authenticated content, and dynamic content. This service can increase Web site performance up to 10 times and ensures customers receive fast access to content, regardless of demand. Peaks can be circumvented easily.

Footprint improves the speed, performance, and profitability of Web sites through three simple processes: preparation, routing, and delivery. A company first chooses which content they want Footprint to serve, such as images, streaming media, HTML, authenticated content, or dynamic content. Then, some publishing tools change the appropriate URLs so the content can be served from the Footprint network. These modifications do not affect branding in any way.

Once the Web pages have been modified, the customer will be transparently directed to the closest and fastest server, based on network and load conditions. Once customers have been sent to the Footprint network, they stay there, greatly reducing the pressure on the originating server. At the same time, Footprint continually delivers only the freshest content.

---

[87]http://www.akamai.com/
[88]http://www.digitalisland.com/

Through content delivery management, many companies can have offer positive download experiences without having to invest heavily in their own infrastructure.

3.6.3   Bandwidth Conservation

The need for speed is a key factor on the Internet. Whether users are on a high-speed connection or a low-baud rate dial-up modem, everyone on the Internet expects speed. Furthermore, recent studies show that if a Web page hasn't loaded within eight seconds of a request, users most likely will leave. It does not matter what the reason is. Whether the site is down or too much content is loading, the average user does not care—if they can't access your information within seconds, they'll find it elsewhere.

Web designers need to ensure that Web pages can load rapidly, regardless of connection type. Although there is no tangible means to measure what is acceptable for file size, anywhere between 30 and 40 kb (including all images, content, and other media elements) is a suitable target size. This range covers a majority of dial-up users and all high-speed connections in a reasonable time frame, under eight seconds.

If your Web pages are taking too long to load, try some of the following suggestions to cut load time.

- **Reduce HTML Code**—Cut out unnecessary HTML, such as comments, font changes, and table elements that are not needed.

- **Use CSS**—Use CSS to control appearance rather than changing fonts and appearance on every page.

- **Define Images**—Define the dimensions of every image you use; this way, the browser can continue displaying content even if the image hasn't loaded yet.

- **Reduce File Sizes**—Reduce image file sizes by reducing JPEG quality or number of colors.

- **Split Content**—Split content into more pages to reduce load times.

Table 3.8. Speeding Up Load Time

Many Web designers use images to depict words and phrases. However, simply using font manipulation with special effects is often enough to deliver the same impact as using a graphic, while using significantly fewer resources. As a result, download times drop significantly.

Using fonts not only eliminates the need for using an image, but also permits the ability to perform special effects with great ease. Web designers can easily add underlining, bold, italics, strikethrough, and different colors in a flash.

Bandwidth savings can also be achieved by caching any Javascripts and CSS that are repeated often on a Web site. For example, most Web designers will repeat the same Javascript/CSS code from page to page throughout a Web site. Designers can move commonly used functions, code, and style sheets into an external file and refer to the file with one line from each page that requires it. This technique will enforce the external file to be cached and will only be retrieved once until the cache is emptied or expired.

Another advantage of outsourcing Javascript code to external files is the provision for search engine indexing. Often, search engines that read your pages will misinterpret your Javascript code as content and will index some of your code rather than useful content. Using this technique will not reveal to search engines your Javascript code and could possibly improve your search engine rankings.

An easy way to cut out bandwidth is simply to cut out unnecessary HTML code, Javascript, and any other components which you simply don't need.

Any client-side error checking that is done in VBScript or Javascript should be pushed to the server side. These error-checking scripts often take too much bandwidth and have loopholes, which can be more rigorously enforced if error checking is done on the server. For example, users who have Javascript and/or VBScript disabled will not go through error checking.

Graphic applications commonly save GIF files with more colors than needed. Commonly, GIF files will use the maximum number of graphics allowable (256 colors) and these excess colors get saved throughout your GIF files. By simply editing your image preferences to reduce the number of colors used from 256 down to the bare minimums (usually multiples of 16 are acceptable, such as 16, 32, or 64 colors), Web designers can usually cut out anywhere between 15 to 60 percent of the image file size. When these savings are tallied up for each image used, the bandwidth savings can become quite large.

In addition to color reduction, the actual palette size is reduced. For example, a 256 color image consists of an 8-bit palette. Being able to reduce the palette from 8 to 6 bits will cut the number of colors from 256 down to 64 and strip up to 25 percent of the file size. As a general rule, the less colors used, the smaller file size that can be accomplished.

This color reduction technique will not work with JPEGs since JPEGs use the full color spectrum for each image. As a result, use only JPEGs for high-resolution images (over 256 colors) and GIFs for lower definition images.

One of the most common tricks to shortening wait time is to change the order in which content loads. Instead of slashing out file size or bandwidth, many Web designers can use additional HTML code to predefine sizes of images and tables and cut out valuable wait time.

Tables can be used to easily align and position elements on a Web page; however, they cannot display any content embedded within the table until the close table tag is found. This means that each cell, each row, each subtable cannot be viewed until the </table> tag has been found. This being the case, a lot of Web designers may find it convenient to separate each row in a table into a separate table.

For example, let's assume a web page we are viewing has a large table that consists of 5 rows, each having 2 cells. Rather than having one large table, Webmasters can cut valuable load time by slicing the table into five independent tables, each having one row (which consists of 2 cells each). This way, each table can load and be displayed rather than forcing users to wait until the entire page has loaded.

3.6.4 Quality of Service

A successful e-business infrastructure makes it quick and easy for authorized users to access the appropriate information and services while it remains well protected from intruders or unauthorized personnel. Businesses that fail to bolster their infrastructure to handle rising IP traffic can count on big problems, such as frustrated customers and business partners. Building an IT infrastructure that can handle current and future e-business demands has become a strategic initiative.

Building a stable infrastructure, however, is one of the greatest challenges IT managers face. Reconstructing the enterprise to meet demands of e-business will also be important over the next few years. Investments will go toward building combined voice/data networks that use high-bandwidth technologies such as Gigabit Ethernet, and integrating network management platforms, storage area networking, and wireless communications. Once these high-bandwidth networks are in place, businesses will focus on finding ways to make them perform better.

To ensure that the most critical e-business applications receive the infrastructure services they need, companies increasingly are looking to two emerging technologies: QoS and policy management. These tools are designed to work around the "best-effort" performance that is an inherent quality of IP networks such as the Internet.

Without QoS, all data on the Internet are treated as equal—there is no way to allocate bandwidth or guarantee high performance for specific applications. This results in an Internet that is unpredictable and unreliable for certain applications, which could severely limit its growth and use, not to mention the development of future networked applications. Thankfully, QoS on the Internet and IP networks enables all sorts of new multimedia and real-time applications to run over them.

When a network and an application both incorporate QoS protocols, the application is able to request and receive predictable bandwidth or priority service. Policy management describes the use of rules, or policies, set by the enterprise to establish the level of service that will be granted to particular users or types of traffic. Companies that offer policy management technology include Lucent,[89] Cisco,[90] and Orchestream.[91]

These infrastructure technologies use different methods to meet the same goal: getting the best-possible performance out of an increasingly crowded Internet. And while content management—an additional technology—-doesn't directly affect network performance, it is being integrated with caching, load balancing, and policy management systems with increasing frequency because it is a critical piece of the e-business infrastructure puzzle.

Content-management systems are used to oversee the way an enterprise generates, compiles, publishes, updates, and ultimately removes Web content from its site. Leading content-management system vendors include BroadVision,[92] Interwoven,[93] Macromedia,[94] Mortice Kern Systems,[95] and Vignette[96].

Microsoft[97] is collaborating with Cisco[98] to develop new QoS technologies that will let companies better define and enforce policy management decisions. The QoS technology will let applications communicate their transaction type to a network, allowing the network to grant priority delivery to certain applications based on set policy management procedures.

Hewlett-Packard provides a tool called WebQoS.[99] HP WebQoS is an enhancement to the Web server, providing an advanced platform for assuring high service quality for e-services on mission critical Web sites. WebQoS stabilizes service delivery, assuring fast and consistent service quality to customers even under the extreme operating conditions found on the Internet. It optimizes resources and permits administrators to build more cost-effective solutions. And WebQoS enables businesses to prioritize service-levels, allowing higher service quality for the most important users and applications. The software transforms the Web server from a passive work engine to an active one. WebQoS proactively monitors service-levels, capacity, and demand, and adjusts workloads via policies configured by the administrator. It operates transpar-

---

[89]http://www.lucent.com/

[90]http://www.cisco

[91]http://www.orchestream.com/

[92]http://www.broadvision.com/

[93]http://www.interwoven.com/

[94]http://www.macromedia.com/

[95]http://www.mks.com/

[96]http://www.vignette.com/

[97]http://www.microsoft.com/

[98]http://www.cisco.com/

[99]http://www.hp.com/go/WebQoS

ently to Web servers and to application software. WebQoS performs admission control on new sessions and optionally prioritizes admission to a site.

Incorporating tools such as caches, load balancers, and policy management, QoS and content management can strengthen the enterprise infrastructure and contribute to a successful e-business launch. Companies in the midst of planning an e-business strategy would do well to keep this in mind, because an infrastructure failure in this environment means a large, public failure in business.

3.6.5 Caching

Caching is a logical response to the requirement for faster and more differentiated services on the Internet. The simplest form of this is content caching, which brings static information such as documents out of centralized systems and closer to users. Inktomi's[100] success has been the result of providing static document caching technology to all of the major Web portals, such as Yahoo!, Excite, and InfoSeek. Since these portals provide generic content to large numbers of users, caching popular HTML pages makes searches on those sites as fast as possible.

Neither caching nor load balancing are new concepts, but equipment manufacturers and software developers are applying them to the Internet in new ways. Caching, which stores most recently used Web pages in order to speed retrieval, reduces network traffic by moving data closer to the users who are accessing it. Since the data does not have as far to travel across the public Internet or across an enterprise network to reach the person who needs it, caching reduces network congestion.

Before caching was possible on the Internet, enterprise and service providers exhausted their resources by adding additional bandwidth and hardware to match the demands of the expanding Internet. However, bigger pipes alone don't meet the requirements for today's and tomorrow's content demands. New types of content such as streaming media and web-enabled applications, have pushed existing networks far past their limits, limiting innovation, and growth. Solving this problem requires a more intelligent infrastructure.

CacheFlow,[101] for example, provides a suite of Internet appliances called CacheFlow Server Accelerator series. The products reduce WAN bandwidth utilization up to 60 percent and enable users to deliver 5 to 10 times more content over the same infrastructure. The Accelerator series can offload as much as 95 percent of a site's content delivery from Web servers, which are then free to handle database queries or run applications.

CacheFlow is spearheading a vendor-partnership initiative called Adaptive Content Exchange (ACE) to create multipurpose solutions that enhance network performance. CacheFlow is working with the switching company Top

---

[100]http://www.inktomi.com/

[101]http://www.cacheflow.com/

Layer Networks[102] on solutions that incorporate traffic management, policy management, and QoS with caching and load balancing. CacheFlow is also working with F5 Networks,[103] which delivered the first load-balancing products for the Web, to develop a similar multitechnology approach to e-business infrastructures.

There is strong demand for caching products, particularly when it comes to streaming media, because so many companies are concerned about what would happen to them if a Webcast caused a major network slowdown, as during the 1999 Victoria's Secret fashion show. Streaming applications can break or come close to breaking a network. There is the fear that this could happen at any time.

It's increasingly common for Internet caching tools to include load-balancing capabilities. Server load balancing is a traffic management function used to distribute traffic evenly throughout a network, avoiding bottlenecks and overloading servers.

E-commerce caching does for transactions what content caching does for HTML documents—it moves dynamic data and processing forward in the network, providing better user response, richer delivery of personalization services, and greater system reliability. Persistence[104] combines e-commerce caching in its PowerTier EJB Application Server with PowerSync replication between application servers. This allows shared information in the PowerTier cache to change with the same integrity that databases have traditionally provided. These changes are also synchronized across multiple PowerTier caches.

Without e-commerce caching, every transaction request must be referred back to a centralized system for processing, making the centralized system both a bottleneck and a single point of failure. The analogy would be trying to build a phone network by having a single switch in New York City and switching every call through that switch. Instead, phone companies provide decentralized local switches that are used to handle local calls. For any scalable Internet e-commerce application, the same decentralization at the application server level must occur.

E-commerce caching is most useful for applications in which the number of information reads exceeds the number of writes. E-commerce caching allows extremely efficient transaction processing for applications geared towards providing information to help external customers make decisions. Internet users access information differently than corporate internal clients. Internet users are more interested in browsing, learning about, and comparing products rather than buying products.

If users are not buying, what are they doing? They are evaluating products, gaining information, and doing research. However, their research is costing companies money and stressing the centralized back-end data. By eliminat-

---

[102]http://www.toplayer.com/

[103]http://www.f5networks.com/

[104]http://www.persistence.com/

ing trips to the back-end system, e-commerce caching improves system performance. Multiple transaction processing points allow e-commerce caching to provide almost unlimited scalability at a much lower cost than centralized systems. By distributing the transaction processing load, e-commerce caching also eliminates the single point of failure common to all centralized processing systems, which is a downtime in the transaction engine.

E-commerce caching provides a straightforward technical solution that eliminates the centralized bottleneck for Internet services. The same broad approach has been used to eliminate bottlenecks in technologies as diverse as disk drives and databases.

Chapter 4

AVOIDING LEGAL ISSUES

4.1 Global Contracts

4.1.1 Legal Preface

Due to the uncertain state of a global legal framework for the Internet, the information in this chapter should be not construed as legal advice or opinion on any specific facts or circumstances. There is a lot of movement on regulations regarding the Internet, both on a national and international basis; therefore, you are advised to contact a qualified lawyer for specific advice. The contents are intended for general information purposes only and will most likely change.

4.1.2 Doing Business over the Internet

The Internet drove the trend to global business and global business enforced the trend towards e-business. But the greatest obstacle to truly global e-business is the myriad legal restrictions. Italy, for example, bans online auctions that sell used goods. In Singapore, it's illegal to post ads for Viagra. Germany bars retailers from offering unlimited guarantees. China does not allow sites to carry telephone traffic over an IP network, so a company with a call center as a part of its Web could be locked out of doing business in China. And so on. Many other laws are in place, which are not compatible with globalized companies.

Paper contracts, for example, are not the ideal document form in the global village. I found out myself the hard way. I got the contract for this book from Prentice Hall and had to sign it and send it on to Hewlett-Packard Press. Unfortunately, HP Press moved on the day I sent out the contract, so it never got to the destination. I waited for two weeks and sent out a new set of contracts to HP Press. The day the new contracts arrived at HP Press, the old ones arrived there as well. You can imagine that this is not how it should have happened. And believe it or not, the same happened to the contract of the second edition. I sent it out and it got lost again.

Disputes on the Internet in an online shopping scenario often occur because of one of the following reasons:

- The customer pays, but the merchant does not deliver.

- The customer pays, but the merchant delivers the wrong goods, the wrong quantity or broken goods.

- The customers pays, but the money does not arrive at the merchant.

- The merchant delivers, but the customer refuses to pay.

- The merchant delivers, but the customer has not ordered anything.

Table 4.1. Legal Disputes on the Internet

Although all information regarding the book was transmitted electronically from southern Germany to northern California, the contract could not be signed electronically. It was technically possible to sign the document electronically, but legally there was no way at the time that such a signature could be validated and authenticated, in the event of a problem.

As the Internet is available worldwide, business does not stop at national borders. An online offering in a Web store can be seen from any country, and usually, anybody is able to buy the goods. If everything goes well, nobody has to bother about laws and regulations. But what needs to be done if something goes wrong? If we look at our simple example of the Web store, we can identify several possible issues between a merchant and a customer in this e-commerce online shopping scenario, which you can find in Table 4.1.

These are the most common issues between buyer and seller. In order to resolve them, laws are in place to support both the buyer and the seller. The problem that arises with the Internet is that, unlike in a local shop, the buyer and the seller may be in two different countries, and the Web server could be in a third country.

The important thing for the courts to decide is *where* the business transaction has taken place. Laws are enforced depending on the country where the transaction has taken place. In most cases, the country in which the Web server is placed is not taken into consideration. (It is not always clear where a server is located.) The top-level domains (TLDs)—such as .de, .uk or .com—can be bought by anyone who is willing to spend money. There are no legal restrictions on where such a TLD can or cannot be used. What counts is the country where the *seller* is located.

In many countries, casinos need to follow special regulations to open and conduct business. The same applies to online casinos, so many entrepreneurs have decided to move their business venture to a country where gambling is allowed with little regulation. Many Caribbean countries have an excellent connection to the Internet, and many online casinos are hosted there. Just putting the Web server there is not enough, however, in order to make this a legal offering for American entrepreneurs. An American company needs to establish a subsidiary in the Caribbean in order to legally pursue this venture. The same applies to many other countries. Some countries in Europe, for example, have high taxes on gambling; the casinos have to pay more than 90 percent of their income to the state. Moving the digital business to another country may help them circumvent these tax issues.

The European Union published some guidelines for online business in May 2000 that need to be implemented in national law by the end of 2001 (see Table 4.2). These guidelines ensure that at least within the European Union, a common legal framework is in place.

The following summarizes the guidelines of the European Union on E-Business.

- **Terms and Conditions**—Terms and Conditions must be presented before anything can be bought over the Internet.

- **Equalization**—Electronic contracts are now equal to paper contracts. Together with the guidelines on the digital signature, digital contracts can be used in court.

- **Establishment**—The location where a company is established is independent of the location of the web server.

- **Single Market**—The dealer can sell in the whole of the EU, if this is in line with the laws and regulations of the country where the dealer is established.

Table 4.2. EU guidelines for E-Business

These guidelines enhance already existing guidelines for the electronic signature and telesales. Further projects are already in progress to unite national laws and simplifying the use of intellectual property. This will make cross-border business easier for all parties involved. By harmonizing laws and taxes cross-border business becomes more transparent to the businesses and to the customers.

4.1.3 Jurisdiction on the Internet

As the Internet creates a global village without global laws, jurisdiction on the Internet is a very important topic. When business is done over the Internet, it is important to know if it is covered by the jurisdictions of other countries. The concept of *extra territoriality* is critical for any type of business on the Web.

If the electronic business is located in France and the customers are in Italy and Spain, it is necessary to know which jurisdictions are in control. In the real world, there are many regulations that support customers by making the laws of their countries take precedence.

Most businesses in the real world have terms and conditions that fit the country the customers and the business are in. On the Internet, customers from all over the world are suddenly able to deal with a particular company. The electronic business needs to create online terms and conditions that will comply with the laws of every country.

Putting up a Web page and starting an online business without any limitations regarding terms and conditions will most probably infringe on the laws in most countries around the world. As there is no way to restrict a Web page to a certain country, a global solution is required. Global terms and conditions may not be available; therefore, it is necessary to look into all countries where you expect to do business.

For all other countries, it is important to draw the attention of a customer to the terms and conditions of your country of origin, including information on how to enter a contract or reject it and which law will be applied in the event of a dispute. This text should be presented on the home page and a link should be provided from each Web page on the site.

In August 1999, Amazon.com was accused by the Simon Wiesenthal Center[1] of selling banned books in Germany. In Germany, Adolf Hitler's *Mein Kampf* and other hateful literature is banned by law. While Amazon.com offers these books on its Web site, its German subsidiary Amazon.de does not. Other online booksellers, such as Barnes & Noble,[2] also offer these books on their Web sites, which is a problem for German law. Although these companies are based in the United States, they are suddenly liable in Germany.

Amazon.com is of the opinion that international customers who order books at their site are treated like tourists who are responsible for the import of books into their country. Amazon.com has no program or person looking into each sale to check if the book is banned in the buyer's country. But Amazon.com is risking the loss of the German market. Amazon.com is exposed to German laws

---

[1]http://www.wiesenthal.com/
[2]http://www.barnesandnoble.com/

because it has a German subsidiary. It is not clear who is violating the law—Amazon.com for offering the book to German customers, DHL for delivering it to Germany, or the German customer for ordering it.

4.2 The Web Site

4.2.1 The Domain Name Battle

Once a company decides to conduct electronic business, it needs to register a domain name. This translates the numeric IP address into a more friendly form of text. Instead of typing a series of numbers, most people prefer to type meaningful words, such as www.wired.com, which is much easier to remember and less error prone. Registering a domain name is not difficult, but getting one that fits your business name, logo, or trademark can be difficult.

On the Internet, every domain name needs to be unique to avoid communication errors. But they are assigned on a first-come, first-served basis, meaning that *anybody* can register the domain name that you would like to use for your company or product.

Internet domain names are composed of two distinct elements: the TLD, and the second-level domain (SLD). The TLD contains information on the origin of the Web site, such as .it for Italy, .jp for Japan, and .za for South Africa. The SLD completes the domain name by adding a company name, trademark, acronym, abbreviation, noun, or any other word to the TLD.

The problem with domain names is that they are not trademarks. Anyone can register a domain name for an already-established trademark, and many people have registered domain names with trademarks, without any relationship to the trademark owners. In some cases people have been using the trademark without knowing about the trademark, and in most of these cases, a court battle was not necessary. One example is altavista.com. A small company called Altavista Technologies used to own the trademark to represent its company. A company named Digital[3] started to offer a highly successful search engine with the name Altavista, but as the domain name was already registered, Digital used altavista.digital.com for the search engine. In 1998, shortly after Compaq acquired Digital, it paid more than three million dollars to the owners of the altavista.com domain in order to expand its search engine business.

Other companies buy domain names with trademarks in order to sell them to their rightful owners. Prices for these registered domains have ranged from a few hundred dollars to a few million dollars, compared to the approximately one hundred dollar biyearly fee paid for purchasing a domain name in the first place. At the time, there was no court interested in a legal battle over domain names, so it was quite easy for these companies to get the money they were requesting.

---

[3]http://www.digital.com/

In order to prevent domain name issues, you should consider the following steps:

1. **Check for existing trademarks**—Conduct a trademark search prior to applying for a domain name to determine whether the proposed domain name would infringe on an existing trademark used in connection with goods or services similar to those that you propose to offer.

2. **Check for famous marks**—A name or trademark that is famous can't be used in any other product or service. Offering "Coca-Cola translations" would be a violation of this law.

3. **Register trademark**—In order to make sure that your domain name is secured, register the domain name as a trademark and start using the domain name at the same time.

4. **Check foreign countries**—Register the trademark and the domain name in all countries that are relevant to your business now and in the future.

Table 4.3. Preventing Domain Name Issues

The domain name for MTV,[4] for example, was acquired by a former employee of the company at a time when MTV had no plans to go online, and it even supported the use of MTV.com by the employee. Soon after, the company wanted to go online and was not able to use the domain name. Hasbro[5] attempted to register the domain name "candyland.com" for use in connection with its popular children's game, but the name had already been registered by a company to identify a sexually explicit adult Web site. In the early years, there was no way to get these domain names back.

But since then, things have changed. An individual who had registered panavision.com had to hand over the domain name to Panavision,[6] because the defendant was violating the U.S. Federal Trademark Dilution Act. Many similar cases have happened in the U.S. and all over the world. Although a domain name is still not a trademark, it has become much easier for trademark

---

[4]http://www.mtv.com/

[5]http://www.hasbro.com/

[6]http://www.panavision.com/

owners to reregister the domain names that contain their trademark names. See Table 4.3 for a short introduction to acquiring domain names.

New regulations for the registration of domain names have also helped resolve court battles. Depending on what has been registered first, the priority will be given to the owner. If a trademark, such as Panavision, has been registered before the domain name, the trademark owner will also be granted the domain name. On the other hand, if the trademark has been established after the domain name has been registered, as in the case of Altavista, the owner of the trademark has no rights to obtain the domain name.

In May 2000, a discussion on generic-terms domains began and another judge in Hamburg decided that it was unfair to use generic terms in domain names. The judge decided that a generic term would provide an unfair advantage over the competition.

In order to prevent legal issues for your company, check both the availability of domain names and registered trademarks before applying for your domain name. If you want to be on the safe side, register the trademark if you have a domain name, and vice versa.

Besides the legal issues on a particular domain name, it often happens that unhappy customers of a particular Web site get a domain name that puts a negative light on the company. Chase Manhattan Bank, for example, preemptively bought the domains Chasesucks.com, IhateChase.com, and ChaseStinks.com, while Walker Digital, a company founded by Priceline.com chief executive Jay Walker, registered Priceline-sucks.com and Pricelinesucks.com, to prevent customers from using these domains to express their views on these companies.

It is not possible to ban people from using these domains, especially in the United States, where citizens are protected under the laws of free speech. It is also not possible to register all domains that contain a certain keyword; therefore, randomly buying domain names is not very effective and only costs money. The better way is to understand the needs of your customers and try to resolve their issues. There will always be some customers who are never satisfied.

4.2.2   Linking and Framing Issues

The hypertext format allows the interlinking of documents on the Web. The links are not restricted to a particular part of the Web. Any Web page can be linked to any other Web page without restrictions. Links are provided as a service to other information resources with similar content or as a means to link advertising into a Web page.

As there are no legal restrictions for the Web, everybody is interlinking with other sites, and this is common practice. The problem arises as soon as links are used to pretend to provide pieces of information that have been created by others. It is very simple to create a news service by providing headlines to the latest news on other servers. People will come to your site because you have the latest news headlines, but all you did was provide links to the work of others.

Although there are no rules regarding linking, over the past few years it has become clear that so-called *deep linking* (i.e., direct linking of a particular Web page) is considered pirating a Web site if done in large scale. But providing a single link to a particular document is no problem.

In 1997, Microsoft was sued by Ticketmaster[7] because it was providing direct links to the ticket sales portion on the Web site. Through the direct link, it was bypassing the Ticketmaster home page, its associated advertising, and the disclaimer. Many customers were not aware that they were moving on to another site and to another company. Hewlett-Packard also links to other companies from its home page,[8] but displays a disclaimer before leaving the Hewlett-Packard home page. This ensures that the customers understand that they are leaving a certain site and that the owner of that particular site is not responsible for the content, services, or products of the sites that are outside of its realm.

Many others should have used this same technique to prevent damage to its image. The ministry for family affairs in Germany[9] should have provided information when visitors left its page. The opposition in Germany started a campaign against the government, because it was possible to get from the home page of the ministry "directly" to a pornographic home page. By clicking only six times, a visitor could get from the ministry's home page to the pornographic home page. What was not mentioned on the site was that the home page of the ministry linked to a Web directory, which in return linked to some other sites before getting to the undesired home page. This created some hysteria in Germany. By providing a short text making clear that by pressing the link, the user leaves the home page, this ambiguity would not have occurred.

Framing is considered to be an even worse problem. Frames have been invented to partition a Web page into several parts that can be loaded individually. With frames, it is possible to separate the navigation bar from the content. It also makes it easy to place a different banner ad every 30 seconds on the screen without the need to reload the complete window. Although the idea itself is not bad, frames create more problems than they are able to resolve. With frames, it is also very easy to create a navigational bar with your company logo and then link to other sites. As people see your logo, they will think that the document in the other frame is also part of the site. Web site owners will object in most cases if they find their content being framed at another site, particularly if their content is surrounded by paid banner advertising.

Some students in Germany tried to circumvent paid advertising on the *Spiegel* homepage.[10] The site consists of three frames: the upper frame contains advertising, the left frame is used for navigational purposes, and the lower right frame contains the content. The students created a no-advertising

---

[7] http://www.ticketmaster.com/

[8] http://www.hp.com/

[9] http://www.bmfsfj.de/

[10] http://www.spiegel.de/

Spiegel Web page that allowed anyone to navigate through the *Spiegel* site without looking at the advertising. This reduced download times and increased the number of visits to the Web site. The *Spiegel* advocates brought this case to court and tried to remove the other site from cyberspace, which eventually was ordered by the court, as *Spiegel* was losing money on banner advertising. In order to prevent "attacks" from other sites, a small JavaScript now checks if the site is being framed or if frames are missing, and resets the browser windows to the original URL of the *Spiegel* company.

Fortunately, search engines such as HotBot[11] are able to search not only for content, but also for sites that link to your site. Check these sites on a regular basis to see if they are linking to or framing your site in a manner that is not appropriate.

4.2.3 Online Disclaimers

A problem with having a Web site is that everyone could become an adversary in the event that a difficulty arises with the information, services, or products that you have provided. In order to prevent financial loss and damage, every Web site needs a properly worded disclaimer. It needs to be written in a clear and unequivocal manner in order to be understood by anyone in the world. But because of differing national laws, a disclaimer or parts of it may not be valid in all countries.

If your Web site contains only some contact information, then a simple disclaimer will be enough, but as soon as you provide information, products, or services that businesses rely or act on, the disclaimer on your Web page needs to be as watertight as possible. If your company deals a lot with French-speaking and German-speaking countries, it is advisable to translate the disclaimer, as it may not be understood correctly by nonnative English speakers. A simple translation will not do it. It is necessary to check the local law and see if the disclaimer applies or if it needs to be adapted.

Once the wording of the disclaimer has been completed, it is necessary to find a good location for it on the Web page in order to make it easily accessible. On some sites the disclaimer is almost hidden, which renders it very ineffective. In some countries, such as Germany, it may even be illegal if the disclaimer is not presented in a highly visible manner. Putting the full disclaimer on the homepage, on the other hand, would be overkill. Typically, a link from all pages should be provided to the disclaimer, and in the case of accepting a business transaction of any kind, the customer should be notified about the disclaimer. The text could be presented in a text box on the Web page, as done, for example, by Lufthansa Cargo when customers order the SameDay online service.[12]

---

[11] http://www.hotbot.com/
[12] http://www.sameday.de/

4.2.4   Content Liability

The liability for content will vary in different countries. If your Web site contains only information about your company, it is necessary to create a process for the automatic verification of the content. Other than a magazine, for example, which is published periodically, Internet content is updated constantly. Therefore, the publishing processes need to be adapted to support the Internet presence. If you have to wait a week until you can publish anything on the Internet, you will eventually lose out, and since your company is liable for the content, you can be easily sued for publishing inaccurate information.

If you are an Internet provider, things become more complicated, since you are hosting other companies' services, information, and products. In order to prevent your company from damage, it is necessary to create a disclaimer and rules that explicitly forbid certain material on your servers. Although most countries consider Internet providers to be in a similar position as telephone companies, in some cases they are considered to be responsible for the content of the servers.

In 1998, Felix Somm, who headed the CompuServe[13] operations in Germany until he was indicted in 1997, was convicted in Germany of violating local pornography laws. Somm had been accused of trafficking pornography and neo-Nazi propaganda, which are both prohibited by German law, and was blamed for not blocking access to pornographic pictures that were available on the Internet. By convicting Somm, the court appears to be saying that Internet service providers in Germany are responsible for Internet content and must take affirmative steps to block access to objectionable material. This verdict fortunately is based on the German legal system and does not affect the laws in the United States.

Although a judge who apparently did not understand how the Internet works made the decision, it is an indication that illegal content can be a problem for every party involved in providing the information.

The situation has changed dramatically in Germany, though. New regulations make it quite clear who is responsible for content. It is the person that uploads the content to a Web site, and not the ISP.

This does not mean that all judges now know what to do. In March 2000 a new case was brought against CompuServe. AOL provided a forum where people started to trade MIDI files. A court ruled that CompuServe was responsible for the forum and therefore for the copyright violations.

4.2.5   Intellectual Property on the Web

Copyright protection on the Internet has several fundamental limits, defined by international agreements. In many countries, an expression can be pro-

---

[13]http://www.compuserve.com/

tected, but ideas or facts cannot be. A work that is very similar to another work does not infringe copyright either. Before the Internet arrived, these rules were easy to handle, as copying in many cases was at least as much work as rewriting in one's own words. On the Internet, information is copied very easily and very fast. Just copy the information from a site and paste it into your Web page. This can be done in seconds—and even automatically by specialized programs.

Brad Templeton has written a very interesting article about intellectual property on the Web.[14] His article, titled "The Biggest Myths About Copyright," gives a good overview on the issues of copyright. Today, almost every piece of information is copyrighted, whether a copyright statement is visible or not. Using that material is a violation of the copyright, regardless of whether you charge money for it or not. This applies especially to the Internet. Although information is freely accessible, it does not mean that the information can be reused for commercial purposes.

Many companies have started suing people who are running fan sites on the Web if they use copyrighted material. In the beginning, everyone was setting up fan pages without thinking about copyright issues, as these fan pages were created mostly for fun, and not for making money. But as trading banner advertising became more popular, many fan pages started to make money, which was not in the interest of the copyright owners. One example is *Star Trek*.[15] The owner of the *Star Trek* logos and images asked all fan page owners to remove the copyrighted information from their pages, leaving most pages blank. The number of *Star Trek* fan pages has decreased since then. This has angered many of the fan groups, who started to protest against this decision on the Web.

Other copyright owners try to bundle the fan pages into a single site. Look at ACMEcity,[16] which allows fans of various comic figures to create their own Web pages on that particular server. The fans are able to use a set of a few thousand images, sound, and other media as long as the pages remain on that particular server.

In May 2000, the producers of the television show Big Brother[17] tried to admonish anyone who tried to set up an unofficial fan page. In this case it is questionable if intellectual property is involved since the whole concept was without content.

The awareness of copyright issues has increased over the last few years, but people still want information on the Web to be free. Web technology enables the free transfer of information, and restricting it is difficult. The major advantage of the Web is that copyright owners can use search engines to discover copyright breaches easily.

---

[14]http://www.templetons.com/brad/copymyths.html

[15]http://www.startrek.com/

[16]http://www.acmecity.com/

[17]http://www.bigbrother.de/

Interestingly, the biggest problem on the Web does not come from text-based content, but from copied images, sounds, and programs. Images are easily scanned in and put onto a Web site. Many images come from books or magazines. The JPEG image format allows images to be presented on every screen of any type. The images are compressed so they do not take a long time to download. The music business fears the MP3 format, which compresses in a manner similar to the JPEG format, with a ratio of 1:10 or even higher. It allows complete compact discs to be copied over the Internet in a reasonable time. The files can be downloaded onto a computer and from there copied onto a cassette or another compact disc. And now the movie industry fears the Dvix standard that made available all movies online in a highly compressed format.

Distributing pirated versions of software has been made much easier with the Internet, and many sites offer pirated software for download. This is also one of the reasons why more and more companies offer free software, as protecting the software would cost more than distributing it for free. Until a few years ago, copying software was not protected by law, and only very recently have laws been introduced to protect databases (in Germany, for example, in 1998). Many countries still do not have copyright laws.

Most Web sites today consist of a database that contains travel information, email directories, or product information. Copying databases over the Internet is just as easy as copying information or software. Copying the database of Yahoo! is easy (as it is publicly available on the Internet), and without the copyright protection of the database, we would see many replicate sites popping up on the Internet.

The law does not apply for all types of databases. In some countries, databases that contain all information about a certain topic without sorting them systematically and methodically are not included, as they do not contain any added value. But this again is not true for all countries; therefore, do not assume that you have the right to copy the database from a Web server. If you use only small parts of a database, this is considered fair use. Copying the complete database onto a private system is not allowed without the permission of the database owner.

4.2.6 Online Auctions

One of the most disputed areas in online business is the online auctions. Not only are they the most publicized cases, but also the most spectacular ones. And most surprising is the fact that different judges have ruled differently for the same matter. Although online auctions are described in more detail in Chapter 7, let's explore some very interesting cases of the past. Remember, almost anything is sold through the Internet. In online auctions houses, property on the moon, dead dogs, marijuana, human kidneys, and even undelivered babies have been on sale. While many items on sale seem illegal, the situation is not that clear. Although e-business has now been growing over the last few years, online auctions have a very difficult status, as they are not really well defined. In most cases an online auction is a flea market or a promotional tool. But many fear those auctions that feature low prices and bad quality.

Let's look at some recent problems with online auctions. Hardware.de,[18] an online auction site in Germany, for example, was dragged into a lawsuit because a company tried to sell HP[19] toner cartridges to customers through an online auction. In one case the auction stopped at 15 dollar/euro and the seller refused to ship the cartridges as the street price for these particular cartridges was at about 25 dollar/euro. The seller tried to pull out of the auction after it finished, due to the low price. They claimed that offering a product online does not mean that they are willing to sell it. The court ruled against the seller and decided that it had to sell the cartridges at the cost of the highest bid. This sounds quite reasonable, but unfortunately other judges have other opinions.

In Münster, not far from Hamburg, a judge decided just the opposite. A Volkswagen dealer tried to sell a car in an online auction, but was disappointed with the low price it generated for a new car. The highest bid was only just above 10,000 dollar/euro. The dealer decided not to ship it to the customer, and refused to sell it at that price. The judges decided that the dealer was right, because no legal contract was signed over the Internet. In this case the dealer was lucky, as there had been no minimum price set.

In Italy all auctions online are forbidden by law, but it seems that nobody really cares. All big players in online auctions have an Italian Web site, and business seems to do quite well. In Germany several organization tried to prohibit online auctions, but failed.

There are many other cases around the world, where similar problems have occurred. The major inhibitor to online business is the changing interpretation of the laws in different countries.

4.3   Encryption Algorithms

4.3.1   Key Escrow

Discussions in many countries are going on about encryption algorithms and privacy issues. Encryption algorithms allow transmitting information using code that cannot be read by people who do not have the right key or password. Law enforcement agencies and governments all over the world discuss the possibility of disallowing encryption in order to keep up public safety. Many politicians think that criminals are the only ones using encryption technologies. But this is not true.

Encryption algorithms are essential for e-business. See Table 4.4 for a simple encryption algorithm. Without privacy protocols, every business transaction over the Internet could be made public and used against the participants in

---

[18]http://www.hardware.de/

[19]http://www.hp.com/

the transaction. Would you want to show your competitors how much business you are doing with your customers, or even let them know who your customers are? Of course not, but still many politicians think that it is better to ban encryption.

Some countries, like France, already allow the use of encryption only if a copy of the keys that are used for the encryption have been sent to a governmental agency. This concept, called key escrow, allows the government and the police to decipher encrypted messages. The idea behind it may be good, but it won't work. People and businesses won't trust encryption algorithms if they know that the government is able to read their information. And it won't keep criminals and terrorists from using it.

In most countries the possession of weapons is illegal, but criminals still use them. Making encryption illegal will be an even worse scenario. All business transactions over the Internet would become public, and this information would be used by other companies to ruin businesses. Even if encryption were to become illegal all over the world, it is likely criminals would still use it, since they clearly don't care about what politicians or the laws say. A detailed description of encryption technologies can be found in Chapter 11.

One of the simplest encryption algorithms is ROT13. With this algorithm, every letter is assigned a number. A becomes 1, B becomes 2, and so on. If you now write "HELLO," you assign each letter a number and add 13 to it, then replace the number with a letter again. If the number is larger than 26, subtract 26 in order to stay within the range of the alphabet. "HELLO" becomes 8, 5, 12, 12, and 15. Now add 13 to each of the numbers and you get 21, 18, 25, 25, and 28. Since 28 is larger than 26, we subtract 26 from 28 and get the following: 21, 18, 25, 25, 2. This becomes eventually "URYYB," which has no resemblance to "HELLO." This is an example of a very simple encryption algorithm. It is sufficient, if you are afraid that someone is scanning your mail in transit for keywords. Using this simple encryption, they won't find the keywords anymore. But even this won't be really secure; adding a little decryption algorithm to the scanner can be done without too much trouble.

Table 4.4. A Simple Encryption Algorithm—ROT13

4.3.2 Legal Issues on Export

Governments all over the world fear strong encryption. Originally developed for the military, it uses complex mathematical algorithms to encode text and binary code. In 1991, Phil Zimmermann wrote a 128-bit encryption program called PGP[20] (Pretty Good Privacy). The program was distributed over the Internet and suddenly people from all over the world were able to encrypt and protect their data.

In the United States, ammunition is treated as such and requires a special export license. As Zimmermann did not request such a license before releasing PGP over the Internet, he was arrested, as publishing on the Internet is the same as exporting it to other countries. Anybody throughout the world is able to download the application. After three difficult years in court, the government relaxed the restrictions on encryption algorithms.

In 1996 encryption algorithms were dropped off the list of controlled ammunition. Still, it is illegal to export any technology that uses encryption algorithms that are stronger than 40 bits without the written consent of the U.S. government. In order to export strong encryption algorithms, you need to leave the keys with the government. The only exception is the banking sector, which has a special regulation that allows exporting 128-bit keys for banking applications. But the laws on exporting encryption algorithms in the U.S. are not very logical at the moment.

In 1994, Phil Karn requested permission to export his book *Applied Cryptography*. The book discussed encryption algorithms and had a floppy disk that contained all of the source code. The book was approved for export, but the floppy disks were not. The export of encryption algorithms in digital form is forbidden, but exporting it in book form is not. Karn sued in order to find out what the difference was. Although the case is still pending, others are using this hole in export restrictions to get algorithms outside of the U.S.

For example, PGP was developed in the U.S. In order to ship it to international customers, the source code has been printed out. The resulting book of more than 5,000 pages has been exported to Finland, where some people scan in the source code and put the program back together. PGP supports key lengths of up to 4,096 bits in version 5.5. It is actually no problem to extend the number of bits to a higher number, but with each additional bit, encryption and decryption take longer to complete. Although 1,048,576 bits may be really safe, it is impractical, as it takes too long to encrypt. Not even your grandchildren would see the result of the encryption and decryption.

There are two types of encryption: symmetric and asymmetric. With symmetric encryption, it is legitimate to export 40-bit keys, and with asymmetric, it is possible to export 512-bit keys. Browsers use symmetric encryption and PGP uses asymmetric encryption algorithms. A more detailed discussion on

---

[20]http://www.pgp.com/

Using the brute force method, it is now possible to hack a 40-bit encrypted code in very little time. There are even screensavers that use the free time when a user is not working at a certain computer to hack 40-bit encryption algorithms. Just recently a text with 56-bit encryption was cracked in three days.

By adding a bit to the key, the strength of the key is doubled. If it takes three days to crack a 56-bit key, then it will take approximately six days for a 57-bit key. A key with 64-bits can be cracked in 768 days. Faster computers will eventually decrease the time to crack these keys; therefore, it is important to use keys with more bits. At the time of writing 128-bit keys are safe, but soon you will have to switch to 256-bit keys in order to be sure that nobody can break into your information.

Table 4.5. Breaking Encryption Algorithms

encryption algorithms can be found in Chapter 11.

As exporting encryption technologies in book form is very time-consuming and error-prone, encryption algorithms developed in other countries become more important for e-business transactions. Some of the most important companies are Baltimore Technologies[21] in Ireland, which develops public key infrastructure software; Brokat[22] in Germany, which creates online banking software; Softwinter[23] in Israel, which programs encryption software for Windows NT; and C2Net[24] in Australia, which develops the Stronghold Web server that allows SSL-enabled transactions at 128 bits. These companies offer encryption algorithms that use any bit rate your application requires, without any restrictions on export. They can also be imported into the U.S., as there is only a restriction on export.

The U.S. Congress is under pressure from the software industry to change this policy, as it destroys the encryption technology market for American companies. It hinders free trade and the development of new technology in the U.S. While American companies try to find a compromise with the government, companies in other countries move on to develop and introduce new technologies, giving them the leading edge over their competitors in the U.S.

---

[21] http://www.baltimore.ie/
[22] http://www.brokat.de/
[23] http://www.softwinter.com/
[24] http://www.c2.net/

4.3.3   National Encryption Laws

This subsection provides a brief overview on the national laws in different countries around the world. Governments have only recently realized that laws and regulations are needed. As knowledge and awareness are still being built up, laws are changing constantly and quickly. Just remember the former chancellor of Germany, Helmut Kohl, who, when asked a few years ago what he thought about the information highway, thought the questioner was talking about the German Autobahn. Since then, awareness has increased significantly within governments. But due to the global nature of the Internet, it is difficult for single governments to be able to solve legal issues on their own. National governments view the Internet as a threat to their power.

Remember that you should not count on the information given here as being valid at the time of reading, and policies and laws are changing rapidly. France, for example, has just recently abandoned its policy of disallowing the use of encryption. Great Britain, on the other hand, has been talking for a while about introducing regulations on encryption technologies. On this book's Web page[25] you will find up-to-date information on national encryption laws.

Table 4.6 has a list of some of the larger countries around the world with national regulations on the use of encryption, and how import and export are handled by these countries.

4.3.4   Digital Signatures

Not only can encryption technologies be used to ensure that nobody other than the authorized persons are able to read a certain message, it is also possible to ensure the authenticity of any given message through a digital signature. Internet services offering public key infrastructures (PKI) offer both functionalities as part of their service.

Contrary to public belief, it is possible to sign digital documents in a way similar to how traditional documents are signed. A digital signature is not a scanned image of a handwritten signature or a typed signature. The digital signature is an electronic substitute for a manual signature. Technically speaking, it is an identifier composed of a certain sequence of bits that is created through a hash function, and the result is encrypted with the sender's private key (which can be decrypted by anyone who is in possession of the public key). By adding the digital signature to the digital document, it can be easily verified who signed it, when it was sent off, and whether the document was altered during transit.

Once the encrypted message has been sent out, the recipients are able to decrypt the message using their private key. If a signature is found, the same hash function that the sender was using is invoked, and the message digest of the recipient is compared automatically with the result of the sender. If the two results match, the message was really sent by the sender. And it can be

---

[25]http://www.ebusinessrevolution.com/

Country	Use of Strong Encryption	Export of Strong Encryption
Australia	No restrictions on use.	Some restrictions on export.
China	Not allowed.	No information.
European Union	No restrictions on use.	No restrictions on import and export.
India	No restrictions on use.	No restrictions on export. License for import is required.
Israel	License is required, but almost always granted.	Regulations for import/export exist and are handled case-by-case.
Japan	No restrictions on use.	License for export is required. No export of encryption software is allowed.
Russia	A license to use encryption is required.	No restrictions on export. License for import is required.
Singapore	No restrictions on use.	No restrictions on import and export.
South Africa	No restrictions on use.	No restrictions on import and export.
South Korea	Not allowed.	Import/export of encryption is prohibited.
United States	No restrictions on use.	License for export is required for encryption software of more than 56 bits.

Table 4.6. National Encryption Regulations

verified that nothing has been changed in transit by checking the integrity of the message.

As digital certificates are difficult to forge, nonrepudiation has become possible on the Internet. If a person has sent out a certain message, it can be traced back easily through a PKI and the signatures. The PKI is used to store the time when a certain message has been sent out, which can be very important in some business cases.

Digital signatures form the basis for legally binding contracts in the course of electronic business, since they electronically provide the same forensic effect that a traditional paper document and a handwritten signature would. In order to use digital signatures legally, a framework needs to be created in all countries that defines exactly what a signature is and how it can be created. In the European Union, several initiatives have been started, both on a Union-wide level and on a nationwide level, such as the "Signaturgesetz" in Germany. But it is unlikely that national legislative initiatives can be used on the global Internet.

A prospective directive for establishing a legal framework for the use of electronic signatures[26] was presented in 1998 by the European Commission. By defining the minimum rules for security and liability, the proposal ensures that digital signatures are legally accepted throughout the European Union. It creates a framework for secure online transactions.

4.4 Developing a Dark Site

4.4.1 Reasons for Crisis Management

Products or services sold online may possibly be defective or have some sort of a problem. If there is more than a single incident, the manufacturer or retailer will get in trouble. If such a disaster happens to your company, you have two possibilities. Either cover it up and hope that nobody will notice or go public with all the information you have, warning people and giving them advice on how to resolve the problem.

The first choice is no longer an option with the wide use of the Internet. You just cannot keep something secret—normally, too many people are involved and someone will leak it to the Internet. So the only thing you can do is go public and let everybody know that you are aware of the problem and take the responsibility for that particular issue.

In order to be prepared for such a situation, you need to create a *dark site* that can go online in case of a problem or an emergency. A dark site is not a sort of voodoo site, but a site that is kept secret until it is necessary to use it. The dark site contains information on your product you would not have released, but may be helpful in case of defects.

---

[26]http://europa.eu.int/comm/dg15/en/media/infso/com297en.pdf

Product defects are not the only issues that can cause problems. Unhappy or angry online users are able to put up Web sites with negative information about your company, your product, or both. Due to its infrastructure, every Web page has the same priority on the Internet. If someone puts something up against you, you had better take it seriously. It takes only a few people with a Web site to set back the whole production of a company. But even worse than Web sites are emails, which are sent out to other Internet users at the speed of light. In the real world, one bad experience is relayed to fewer than 50 people in most cases. Bad experiences on the Internet are sent out to thousands of people with a single mouse-click.

4.4.2 Disaster Recovery

Ulrike Brandt, a financial journalist, has written a very informative article on Internet crisis management in the German financial magazine *Wirtschafts-woche*,[27] where she discusses the topic of disaster recovery and where you can get additional information. The topic is very important, but unfortunately, not many managers are aware of it.

Just look at the case of Intel.[28] In 1994, Thomas Koenig, a mathematician, found out that the newly released Pentium chip did not calculate correctly. Under certain conditions, divisions, remainders, and tangent and arctangent floating-point instructions produced results with reduced precision. He reported this error to the chip manufacturing company, but Intel put him off. First, it denied the existence of the bug, then stated that the problem affected only very few users. Then Intel wanted the users to prove that they needed that special calculation to certify for a replacement.

All this created a huge outcry on the Internet; Web sites were put up and heated discussion threads started in the Internet newsgroups. The result was a huge avalanche that landed on Intel. The media talked about the problem, users sent angry emails to Intel, wanting their chips replaced, and the chip sales dropped. As a result, Intel gave up in December 1994 and offered to replace all faulty Pentium chips[29] and had to stop the complete production of that particular chip, even though it was right that only very few were affected. But giving up production of that particular chip was not so difficult, as faster chips were already in the pipeline. The next generation of Pentium chips, without the error, was already designed and the roll-out phase began soon after.

Since then, Intel has changed its strategy. Even though it still cannot guarantee that their chips are error-free, it is now more open to customer issues and maintains an online database with known errors in the chips. With the introduction of the Pentium II, Intel also invented a way to update some parts of the microcode on their chips so bugs can be removed without replacing them.

---

[27]http://www.wirtschaftswoche.de/ "In Sekunden zerstört," *Wirtschaftswoche* 45/29.10.1998, pp. 157–160.

[28]http://www.intel.com/

[29]http://www.intel.com/procs/support/pentium/fdiv/

The first release of the Pentium did contain a bug in its floating point processor that returned a faulty result when performing a floating point division (FDIV). To see if your Pentium has the FDIV bug, enter the following formula in the Windows calculator:

$$x = \frac{4195835}{3145727} \times 3145727 - 4195835$$

The result should be $x = 0$. On faulty Pentiums, you will get $x = 256$ instead. In this case you are entitled to receive a free replacement for your faulty Pentium chip.

Table 4.7. The Pentium FDIV Bug

Its newer chip, the Pentium III, on the other hand, seems to be a marketing disaster. The Pentium III chip contains a digital ID that is unique for every processor. The reason for it was to provide a means to check the identity of a particular user for online transactions. Intel's serial number is appealing to corporate customers, because they can more easily track technology assets through the identifying serial code.

Although many online companies like the idea of identifying customers, privacy groups have called for consumer boycotts and legal action and created a Web site called "Big Brother Inside"[30] that resembles the Intel motto of "Intel Inside." Many people (hackers and software company employees) have started to crack the safeguards imposed by Intel to make the serial number secure. Although at the time of writing nobody was able to crack the highly secure ID number, the message that gets out to the customers is the wrong one, at least from Intel's point of view.

Other companies do not seem to be affected by angry users. Microsoft,[31] for example, does not seem to have this problem. Although there are many anti-Microsoft sites on the Internet, Microsoft is not losing market share because of them. Ford[32] had problems in 1995 similar to Intel's. Due to a technical problem, some Ford drivers claimed the car could go up in flames. The online activists, calling themselves the "Association of Flaming Ford Owners," decided to put up a Web page[33] with the image of a burnt-out Ford on the main page and flames in the background (see figure 4.1).

---

[30]http://www.privacy.org/bigbrotherinside/
[31]http://www.microsoft.com/
[32]http://www.ford.com/
[33]http://www.flamingfords.com/

Figure 4.1. Flaming Ford Owners' Homepage

In April 1996, Ford had to recall more than 8.7 million cars and trucks in the United States and Canada to have the ignition switches replaced (with potentially up to 26 million cars and trucks that may need a replacement). The action cost Ford more than 1.5 billion dollars. In this case it is not known if their claims were right or not, but that is not the point. The incident happened in 1995, but the Flaming Fords Web site is still up and running in 2001. Today more than 20,000 links exist to that particular Web site. People may stumble over it and decide not to buy a Ford.

In December 1998, Ford issued a short press release that it had to recall more than three million cars because of a possible corrosion problem. I found this snippet on Yahoo!'s *dailynews* site[34] (search for "Ford Recall Issued," December 23, 1998) and went then directly to Ford's home page to check if they have a press release with more information on the incident, but was not able to find anything. Ford's search engine gave me no more information, nor was there a link from its home page as one might have expected. Maybe there was information online, but I couldn't find anything within 10 minutes of searching. It may also be that because of the holiday season, no Webmaster was around to update the information. But not being there during holidays may ruin your business even faster, as more people have time to surf on the Internet.

The Internet enables consumers to talk more freely about their experience with a certain product or service, so it becomes vital for all companies to keep

---

[34]http://dailynews.yahoo.com/

an eye on the Web to track down people who are not happy with their products. If you think you can just shut down the Web site of that particular consumer, you do not understand how the Internet works. Once information has been put online, it is virtually impossible to get rid of the information. If you cut off somebody's Web site, they will find 50 others who will replicate their content immediately. The more pressure you put on people, the less effective it becomes, as more and more people join in to support them.

There is no way you can stop people from publishing their opinions on the Web, no matter how right or wrong they are. The only thing you can do is set up a Web site that tells consumers that you are aware of the allegations. If the allegations are true, you had better put some additional information online about how to solve the problem. If the claims are false, put some evidence online to prove you are right. In any case, respond quickly or you will lose out, no matter if you are right or not.

4.4.3 Negative Campaigning

In addition to angry consumers, negative campaigning can spell bankruptcy for your company. Negative campaigning by your competitors can also ruin your image with the public. Instead of showing the advantages of their own products, they will start to find all the disadvantages of your products.

In December 1998, Sun[35] launched a Web page with information on Hewlett-Packard's newly introduced UNIX Server HP V2500.[36] Depending on your point of view, the information presented on that particular Web page is either positive for Sun or negative for Hewlett-Packard. In the European Union, law prohibits, for example, negative campaigning and comparative advertisement. But on the Internet, national laws are not always applicable. Putting up the information on a Web server in another country is fairly simple. Countries like Bulgaria just recently introduced laws against software pirates, but there are still enough countries where the Internet is beyond the scope of the law. But in our example, merely putting the desired page onto an American Web server would resolve all legal issues regarding the content.

Another problem is the media. Due to the amount of information a magazine or newspaper receives each day, it is virtually impossible to check if all of the data is correct or incorrect. Especially in the U.S., we can see a tendency to print information without double-checking it. Together with negative campaigning, this can have a negative impact on your products and/or your company. Therefore, always keep an eye on the Internet. Look out for these tendencies within your user groups, keep in touch with them, seek dialogue, and in the case of an emergency, react quickly. In our interconnected world there is no way to avoid a disaster if you are not open to your customers. This is one of the reasons political dictators fear the power of the Internet. They

---

[35]http://www.sun.com/

[36]http://www.sun.com/realitycheck/headsup981215.html

just can't control information anymore, which is their only real power over the people.

In the event of an emergency your company needs to act quickly. Therefore, you have to take some steps before, during and after the crisis:

- **Risk audit**—Do a risk audit of your company on a regular basis.

- **Documentation**—Develop plans for documenting tasks and responsibilities for the emergency.

- **Keyword monitoring**—Constantly monitor the Internet (especially Web sites, mailing lists, newsgroups and chat areas) for special keywords.

- **Crisis manual**—Develop a crisis manual and put it on your intranet.

- **Dark site**—Design a dark site with all the necessary information.

- **Simulations**—Do simulations of emergency situations on a regular basis.

- **Up-to-date**—In case of emergency, always keep the dark site up-to-date.

- **Information**—Inform your target group and the media via e-mail about the emergency.

Table 4.8. Risk Management

4.4.4 Online Experience

In October 1996, a 16-month-old baby died from an infection of E-coli bacteria. The baby had ingested apple juice made by Odwalla,[37] a California-based juice company. The apple juice was suspected of being the source of the bacteria. Within 12 hours, the management of Odwalla recalled the apple juice from more than 4,500 shops and set up a Web site with information on the incident.

---

[37] http://www.odwalla.com/

It contained a statement by the management, and a frequently asked questions (FAQ) page on E-coli bacteria written by doctors, to help the victims. A team of experts was online to calm down the frightened consumers. The site also provided links to the Web site of the Food & Drug Administration (FDA)[38] that contained additional information on emergency situations. Although another 66 cases of E-coli infections were registered, a survey showed afterward that almost 90 percent of the customers were willing to drink Odwalla apple juice in the future. The investment in releasing all information and creating the dark site had been spent wisely.

After the horrible crash of the MD-11 off the Canadian coast in September 1998, Swiss Air[39] set up a first press release on its Web site within hours. Important phone numbers, a condolence Web page, and some other statements were available on the Internet the same day. In the following days, more information was released, including the radio chats between the tower and the pilots and the names of the deceased. The very efficient Webmaster rescued Swiss Air from losing its highly successful business as a result of this single, though extremely tragic, incident. It also helped the relatives of the victims to find out more on the incident without having to search for information all over the place, as often happens.

Figure 4.2. Swiss Air's Homepage

---

[38]http://www.fda.gov/
[39]http://www.swissair.ch/

The Deutsche Bahn,[40] the German rail service company, lost a large amount of credibility after the derailing of one of its high-speed trains in May 1998. Information was not available on the incident immediately after the accident (neither online nor offline), nor was the Bahn responding to the families of the customers in a sensible way. A general letter was sent out to each of the families with advertisements for rail journeys. The company was not prepared for handling such an incident. It seemed that they thought that it could never happen. *Der Spiegel*,[41] the most-read German news magazine, compared this accident to the tragic incident of the *Titanic* in 1912.

You need to start thinking about a strategy long before an emergency occurs. You should conduct a risk audit for your company, analyzing what could go wrong with your products. Develop plans where the tasks and responsibilities are documented for the emergency situation. In order to learn about emergencies in advance, you need to monitor the Internet seven days a week, 24 hours a day. First you need to create a list of keywords and then check Web sites, newsgroups, search engines, and databases on a regular basis. Mailing lists and chat areas should also be visited if your target group is using these types of media. This is the only way to find out about dissatisfied customers and aggressive competitors. Your emergency plan should be available on your intranet so that people know what to do whenever they need to, and a printed copy should also be available in case of a technological breakdown.

4.4.5 Digital Complaint Services

Another factor that needs to be taken into account are online complaint services, which are hoping to make money by resolving consumer disputes with Internet retailers. These services are able to bundle complaints against companies and create class-action suits in a very simple and effective way. Consumers will get access to a brand name and experience in linking up with major companies to make sure the complaint goes to the right person quickly.

Complain.com,[42] Fightback,[43] (see Figure 4.3) and Complain To Us[44] are three service companies that specialize in this area. These companies charge a flat fee if they get involved in writing a letter and following up complaints. Fightback, for example, charges $25, while Complain.com charges $19.95 for any case that is pursued personally, while all other complaint resolutions are free of charge.

Consumers can fill out a form with information about the product or service they purchased, what went wrong, the actions they have taken to resolve the dispute, and the resolution they are seeking. In order to qualify for the online

---

[40] http://www.bahn.de/
[41] http://www.spiegel.de/
[42] http://www.complain.com/
[43] http://www.fightback.com/
[44] http://www.complaintous.com/

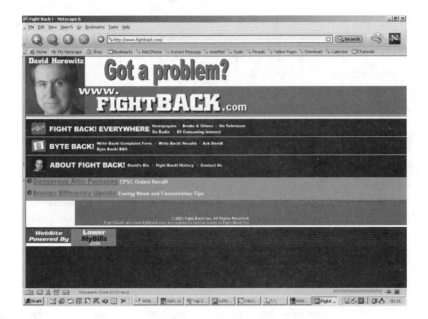

Figure 4.3. Fightback Homepage

complaint service, the customer must have tried to contact the customer care department themselves.

Complaint.com does send a letter of complaint to the company, and the consumer will receive a confirmation within four weeks if the issue has been resolved. If the problem persists, the letter will be sent once more to the company, but this time to the chief executive. If that does not help, consumers will be referred to partners such as law firms to pursue further action.

While single complaints won't be very effective, the aggregation of complaints and the publicity on the Web site will drive companies to respond to the issues of their customers. The above-mentioned companies also have plans to publish the contents of their complaint database on the Web, making it easy for customers to look up complaints from the past and find out how to resolve a particular issue.

4.4.6 Strategic Planning

As mentioned earlier, it is important to develop a dark site that contains basic information about your company and your products. It should inform your customers on security measures and should contain a list of experts they can contact in the case of an emergency. The dark site should replace your normal Web site within an hour, or better yet, within 30 minutes of a disaster. The management needs to be informed about the Internet presentation and to release statements as soon as possible. The Web site needs to be updated as soon as new information about the emergency is available.

The dark site should also be put on removable media, such as a CD-ROM or ZIP disk. Just in case your company gets cut off the Internet, you can send the information to an ISP that is able to quickly set up an emergency site. In this case, inform the public immediately via TV, radio, or newspapers about the incident and tell them about the emergency URL. Many of these steps need to be taken, even if your company is not presently on the Web. But with the Internet, you have to be even faster in your communication of the crisis. If you don't talk about it, then someone else will for sure. Remember, the competition on the Internet is extremely tough.

Doing all this is not cheap, but not doing anything is far more expensive, as we have learned from the examples presented here. Larger corporations have special task forces for emergency situations. While that would be overkill for small and medium-sized enterprises, they also need to keep an eye on the Internet.

Specialized search engines will monitor the Web for them. They only need to key in their desired keywords, and these search engines will monitor the Web day and night. As soon as something happens, an email will be sent off that triggers a beeper or other alarm to get the attention of the responsible person so that the company can react to the threat from the Internet. Two Web sites that offer this service are "The Informant"[45] and "Mind-It."[46]

Many small to medium-sized companies will most likely outsource the task of monitoring the Web. Specialized companies will take over the task. They will become the watchdogs over content, and they will also react in the case of a crisis. Investment in such a company is a good bet for Internet investors. These services are needed, and their revenues will increase quickly in the future.

Although dark sites and other means of prevention won't reduce the liability for an error in a product, these measures will certainly help to limit the financial damage that can ruin a company.

---

[45] http://informant.dartmouth.edu/
[46] http://minder.netmind.com/

Chapter 5

MARKETING STRATEGIES ON THE WEB

5.1 Internet Marketing Technologies

The Internet offers a wide range of new technologies to increase your marketing activities on a global, around-the-clock basis. The basis for your business should be the corporate Internet Web page, which may link to Internet and extranet applications. Your marketing initiative should focus on presenting your Web page, as this is what everyone can remember and access with a simple browser. From there, you need to guide your customers to the particular places they need to visit in order to carry out the transactions they require.

The Web, mail, newsgroups, and chat applications have established themselves to allow communication between companies and customers. These applications are highly available, robust, and simple to use. Therefore, it is very important to understand the way they work and to know what to look for in order to use these tools successfully within your organization.

Tracking customers' experiences is also very important, but also difficult and different online. Customers are not bound to a limited set of offerings, as with newspapers, magazines, or television channels. The Internet offers an unlimited number of channels, so measurement of the Internet as a whole does not make any sense. The Internet also offers a much higher degree of interaction than traditional channels. Your customers and partners also have different expectations; they expect that your offerings will be available 24 hours a day, without interruption, and that they can ask questions whenever they feel like it. The Internet allows customers to talk directly to the manufacturers of the products, and they can easily bypass the shop where they bought the goods. This means that a manufacturer needs to set up an online call center as soon as its Web site goes live. People expect to be able to ask questions directly. If you are not able to fulfill the expectations of your customers (and your customers' customers), then you should not go onto the Web. But this, too, might mean the death of your business.

A strategy for Internet marketing should follow these rules:

- **Brands**—Your Web site becomes your most important brand.

- **Change**—Be aware that the rules on the Internet are changing.

- **Conciseness**—Keep your pages short and spread information across several pages.

- **Content**—Content is king; don't bore your customers.

- **Dynamic sites**—Create dynamic sites that use new technologies to adapt information based on user profiles.

- **Finances**—Try new markets with low advertising pricing schemes.

- **Free giveaways**—Create "freebie" offerings for your loyal customers.

- **Global village**—Think global, but localize.

- **Live events**—Online events create fast awareness.

- **Niche markets**—The Internet is a series of niche markets and mass markets.

- **Promotion**—Promote your site everywhere.

- **Syndication**—Co-brand your services and products.

- **Technology**—Use Internet technology to maximize your marketing objectives.

Table 5.1. Marketing Strategy on the Web

Online advertising moves commercials into new dimensions, as you are now able to place your advertisement on the desktops of a particular target group in real time. Everything becomes more dynamic. Businesses that remain static will lose out. The companies that are prepared to change their Web sites and adapt their businesses and marketing strategies will have the best chances for being very successful in the Internet age.

In order to be successful on the Internet, your company needs to focus on the five P's:

- **Products**—Review your products and choose the products that are the most suitable for your online business—put these on your Web page first.

- **Promotion**—Promote your site through advertising and offer cross-selling on your Web site.

- **Presentation**—The presentation of your online business needs to have easy-to-use site navigation, and the look and feel should be based on corporate logos and standards.

- **Processes**—Customer support processes need to be integrated into your Web sites.

- **Personalization**—Prepare your order management, logistics, and technical infrastructure to cope with the orders from the Internet and personalize the Web site for every single customer.

A typical sales and marketing cycle for an online shop requires the business to look out for the target customers and their needs. The next step is to create awareness and start an advertising campaign to attract customers to your online business. Before doing so, be aware that you need to have the Web site up and running. "Under Construction" sites will lead your potential customer base to other online sites that actually offer what they promise. Merchandising is also an important task to complete. It is necessary to decide which products or services can be sold over the Internet and how they should be positioned. Promotions are very common, so they need to be taken into consideration as part of your marketing campaign. Promotions are used to help advertise merchandise and services and to give customers incentives to make purchases.

To make your customers return to your Web site, you need a sales service that is able to answer their questions quickly. In order to learn from your existing customers and orders, it is necessary to save marketing data and analyze it. To further enhance your service, you need to establish post-sales service, which allow your customers to find out about the order status after the sale has been made. We'll explore these topics later in the chapter.

Other important issues in the sales cycle are transaction processing, which defines the way orders, tax, shipping, and payment processing are handled and fulfillment, which defines how orders are passed to the fulfillment center. These topics will be discussed in detail in Chapter 7.

5.2   Web Design

5.2.1   The Power of the Internet

Your Web site is your basic marketing message on the Internet. From there, you and your company can start the marketing offensive. Be sure that your marketing group understands the full potential of the Web. The Web offers more possibilities, but also more dangers, than other media. The rewards for conducting marketing the right way on the Internet are immediate, just as failures may result in an instant loss of customers. From a marketing perspective, your Web site is like the business card of your company.

Therefore, it is important for everyone in your organization to comprehend the power of the Internet. As soon as a customer gains Internet access, everyone in your company becomes instantly involved in electronic marketing. Your customers may view every online activity as a company activity, even though it may be the result of the initiative of a single employee. If one of your employees writes an email to one of your customers, this email may be resent to anyone, anywhere in the world, with little effort. Even emails that are sent within the company reach noncorporate mailboxes very quickly. So remember to set up some guidelines for your company email. Chitchat mail from employees to their friends should not be a problem, and it keeps the employees happy. If you do not allow your employees to send and receive private email, they will start using Web-based emailing services, and these waste far more resources and time than a little email to a friend will ever do.

5.2.2   Content Is King

The most important thing on your Web page is content; never let users leave your Web page without giving them information. This increases the probability that they will return to look for new information. Fancy graphics that take ages to download may win a design prize, but functional Web pages with content in the foreground are more important, and in the end, more successful. Respect the wishes of the customer and remove irrelevant images or text. Offer the option to customize the appearance of the Web pages.

Pictures and illustrations can be worth thousands of words if used correctly. Many images on the Web were designed for print media and offer too much detailed information that cannot be seen on the Web. Use graphics where appropriate that add real value to your site. In order to present high-quality images on the Web, use technologies such as FlashPix or VRML, described in detail in Chapter 13.

In order to build up a Web site quickly, you should repurpose your existing materials. Many companies think they can just copy their existing paper documents to the Web server, but this way of thinking is inappropriate. You must adapt the material and make it suitable for online use. Unlike traditional documents, which are linear, documents on the Web are nonlinear. On the Web there is no predefined sequence of reading. Adding links within and across documents further simplifies navigation and is common practice on the Internet.

The design of your home page is very important, as it is the first thing your customers are going to see. In order to make it attractive, you should stick to the following rules: Although nice graphics and large buttons are good, well-produced content is what will bring people back. The Internet lives off the information it provides to the users. On any given Web page, the customers should be able to find a summary of the content in the title of the page and in the URL. This methodology is also used by search engines to classify a Web page according to these entries.

Don't put more than 10 links onto one page, except for link lists. Usually it is enough to provide only two or three links to other pages. The user wants to be guided, not confused by your offering. Information should always be instant, understandable, and accessible, for these are the characteristics a successful Web page. Try to create Web pages with less text but without reducing the amount of content.

Instant means that the Web pages should be downloaded very fast, even with older computers and slower modems. *Understandable* means that the information should be presented in a way that allows everyone to get the message within a short time and with very little effort. *Accessibility* is currently the largest problem on the Web. People with physical disabilities have a hard time on the Web, as the information is presented in a very visual way and not necessarily in a logical structure. Using tables on a Web page will create a nicely laid-out Web site, but will make it difficult for blind people to read the text properly. Before going online with a Web site, the site should be checked by Bobby,[1] an online and offline application that analyzes Web pages for their accessibility to people with disabilities. Bobby is the full implementation of the 1998 working draft of the W3C Web Accessibility Initiative.[2]

Have you ever created slides for a presentation? The same method of presenting information in a very dense way should also be applied to Web pages, the difference being that you do not follow a linear sequence as with presentations. Users should always have the ability to create their own sequences. To reduce information overload or data burnout, Web sites should give users the information they have requested and nothing more. If users require more in-depth information, then give them a way to download the information in a useful format, such as a spreadsheet format for a database. Offer your customers several alternatives for document download. Text, for example, should always be available in HTML *and* ASCII format. In addition to these two formats, you can offer PostScript, Acrobat, and Microsoft Word, for better viewing and printing.

---

[1] http://www.cast.org/bobby/
[2] http://www.w3.org/WAI/

If you offer other information, be sure to serve the customer first. Users should not be forced to scroll down an endless page of irrelevant information before reaching the information they are looking for. Give users more control over the way they view your site, and make it more of an interactive experience. Create a user-friendly place they will want to visit again.

Another common design problem is having too much company information and not enough product information on the Web site. Although company information is also very important, very few customers need detailed information. Most of the customers want to buy products and services, not the company. The information on your Web site needs to answer the potential questions of the customers and not the needs of the company. See Table 5.2 for an overview on design rules.

In order to have a successful business online, the visual presentation of your Web site needs to adhere to the following rules:

- **Content**—Focus your attention first on content and then on design.

- **Consistency**—Design your site consistently without varying the content.

- **Density**—Break up content into little pieces without tearing it apart.

- **Design**—Use few colors without designing a monotone Web site.

- **Size**—Use small graphics with large impact.

Table 5.2. Web Design Rules

5.2.3 Feedback and Online Surveys

Every Web site should offer the option of customer feedback. A feedback form should be provided on a separate page that enables the customer to choose the reason for the feedback and give his or her name, email address, and the feedback itself. By offering reasons for providing feedback, the information can be automatically directed to the appropriate department, reducing the size of the customer care center. Figure 5.1 shows EuroSeek's[3] feedback form, which

---

[3]http://webdir.euroseek.net/page.cfm?page=feedback

allows customers to enter a statement on the usefulness of the Web site.

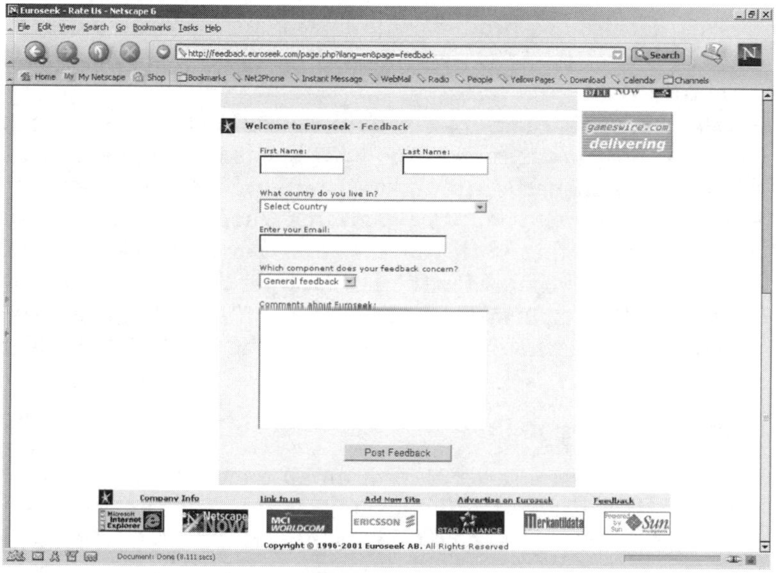

Figure 5.1. EuroSeek feedback form.

In addition to the simple feedback form, extended feedback in the form of a survey could help your customers better express their needs. In turn, your customer care center will be able to respond more quickly to the needs of the customers in general (in the form of an FAQ section). Typically, a single Web page is used to give feedback and fill in a general survey. Still, customers should not be forced to fill in the survey if they only want to give some feedback.

In addition to the general survey about the Web site, from time to time you should offer specialized surveys to learn more about your customers. These surveys should be combined with a prize in order to provide incentive to participate. Offering a book or a compact disc as a prize will make people more willing to give information such as their address. This kind of information may help the marketing department with promotions down the road.

5.2.4   Frequently Asked Questions

In order to build up an online service, it is necessary to have a customer care center in operation. Large sites such as eBay[4] receive more than 60,000 emails a week. Many of the senders ask the same questions. In order to reduce the workload of the response team and enhance the time of the reply, it is helpful to build up a database with frequently asked questions (FAQs).

---

[4]http://www.ebay.com/

An FAQ Web page consists of questions and their responses that may be interesting for most customers. On large sites, it makes sense to create separate FAQs for every service and product online. On the feedback page you should also provide the link to the FAQ page or database, and it needs to be presented very prominently.

You should ask your customers to consult the FAQs before sending an email to your customer care department. The FAQ needs to be updated regularly to include all questions that arise around a certain product or service. In addition to the FAQ, you could use a set of newsgroups where all questions are shown to other customers together with the answers. For example, I used Hewlett-Packard's "User Group Forum" for the HP Deskjet 340 to find out how to connect the printer to the Apple PowerBook. The question and the answer are still both on the Web and may help other customers who want to do the same.

5.2.5   Corporate Design Rules

Every company needs corporate rules for email, newsgroup postings, and Web design. This section will deal with corporate guide lines on Web design. The layout should be clearly defined so that people are able to recognize postings, email and Web pages from a certain company at a glance. All emails need to be responded to quickly, no matter to whom they are sent. If the person is out of office, an autoreply needs to be sent out to let people know that the mail has arrived at the destination. Employees should be informed about chain letters and virus hoax warnings on the Internet, as they can ruin the image of a company with a few mouse clicks. See Chapter 11 for more information on this topic. If your company has products for which special newsgroups exist, then some employees need to be "present" there, to read through the questions and answer as many as possible to help the customers with their problems. Spamming—the action of sending out information to people who did not ask for it—in newsgroups and on mailing lists is not an option for your company. These methods of direct marketing will ruin the image of your company.

5.2.6   Navigational Aids

The Web site should have a clear and simple-to-use interface that helps users contact the right people and find information and that offers the services customers require whenever they are needed. The more interactivity you offer, the better received the Web site will be. A search engine for the company Web site is a must. Enhance your existing Web site to become a portal (for more information on this, see Chapter 6).

The navigation and the graphics need to have a uniform look and feel throughout the whole Web site. Make it simple and clear. Have a navigation bar that every user can understand and replicate all graphical navigation bars in textual links, in order to support nongraphical browsers.

Design a simple navigation that is consistent throughout your Web page to guide your customers and give them control over the experience. Use labels for sets of Web pages so users know which area they are in. Define special logos for each of your areas (or channels), making it easy to identify them. Don't overuse graphical logos or icons; a simple label in the form of a word may be sufficient. As your site can be viewed globally, there are only very few icons that can be understood on a worldwide basis.

Provide site maps to help users find their way around. The user should always be able to jump directly back to the beginning of a channel or to the main home page. Don't make customers look for the navigation bar all over the page. Integrate it into your design, but make it clear that the navigation is separate from the content. Otherwise, your customers will waste time and may decide to go to your competitor.

About 80 percent of people read only 20 percent of a Web page. Most people never scroll down Web pages, but they like clicking on buttons. New Web pages also offer the chance to present new banner ads. But be sure that if you offer one chunk of information over several Web pages, the user always knows what is still to come; and remember, choose your page titles wisely.

5.2.7 File Size

Don't use large graphics for the design of the Web page. Many users still connect to the Web using a modem. The more seconds users have to wait, the more users will just go on to another site. Use larger graphics or videos only where you cannot offer the content in any other way. Always try to provide a low-bandwidth solution. All images on the Web should have an alternative text for people who switch off the automatic image loading option. This option is also very important for search engines, as they are able to index images as well by linking the text with the image.

The same applies to other types of documentation. If you offer a 10-MB presentation on your Web site, you should also allow the user to browse through it online. The conversion of large files to low-bandwidth versions is very important. Although the quality of the low-bandwidth document may not be as good, it allows the customer to get an impression of the content. In many cases there are more than two file sizes possible.

Real Media's RealPlayer,[5] for example, adapts its speed exactly to the speed of the modem. The quality of the sound depends on the modem speed but does not influence the content, which is always the same. As the RealPlayer has its own preferences, it is possible to set the speed of the connection. The hypertext protocol does not have the ability to adapt quality to the speed of the modem, so no matter how fast the connection is, the same data is transported. Therefore, other means of selecting the speed must be invented. Many sites ask the user to fill in a profile and try to match the entered data. If the user enters a certain

---

[5]http://www.real.com/

connection speed (such as 56K), the Web server will try to send data that best matches the requirements.

The major disadvantage is that every piece of information needs to be saved in a different quality, resolution, or density. RealPlayer for sound and Open-Pix[6] for images are two solutions that try to solve the problem by offering a quality-independent format that stores the content and is able to deliver the appropriate quality at any given time. OpenPix is described in more detail in the section "Dynamic Image Formats" in Chapter 13, and RealPlayer in the section "Streaming Media" in Chapter 10.

If you provide file formats that need additional components installed, such as plug-ins or help applications, then always provide a direct link to download the software component. Don't link to the site of the software provider; instead, link directly to the download page. Otherwise, people may get distracted and forget why they wanted to download a certain piece of software. Ask permission to host the software directly on your server; this will distract the customers the least.

All this is important for the image of your company. Brand names and corporate identity become more important on the Internet, as prices and services become nearly identical and access to the services becomes identical. Distance becomes irrelevant.

When introducing electronic marketing into your company, be sure to use the technology and the opportunities the Internet offers; otherwise, the Internet initiative of your company may fail.

5.2.8 Delivering Content to Network Appliances

In addition to the desktop computers and servers that are currently connected to the Internet, new network appliances will appear over the next few years. The difference is that these appliances have less memory, limited display, less storage, and lower transmission rates. In order to send information to these devices and to exchange data, these restrictions need to be taken into account. Keep in mind that the emergence of these appliances brings us ever closer to the reality of pervasive computing.

Jupiter Communications,[7] an online research specialist, has identified three different types of network appliances evolving from the already existing standalone products:

- **Personal-based**—Portable devices that customers carry around and use to connect to the Internet. Examples are mobile phones adhering to the GSM standard, such as the Nokia Communicator;[8] personal digital assistance devices, such as the Psion V;[9] and other wireless information de-

---

[6]http://image.hp.com/

[7]http://www.jup.com/

[8]http://www.nokia.com/

[9]http://www.psion.co.uk/

vices. Europe is leading in the introduction of personal devices, followed by Japan and North America.

- **Passenger-based**—These devices are built into transportation vehicles and provide services such as route planners and traffic or weather reports in personal vehicles, shopping networks for duty-free shopping on planes, and excursion programs on cruise ships. As more people tend to travel access to online services via passenger-based systems becomes more important.

- **Place-based**—These devices include a variety of non-PC terminals and Internet appliances that can be found in public. A set-top box in a hotel room or Web-based kiosks at a train station are typical examples of place-based and immobile solutions.

Depending on the type of Internet appliance, restrictions need to be considered. Mobile phones have a very small display, no colors or sound, and the communication speed is very low compared to traditional modems. Battery life is also an issue; the application should not use a lot of the battery that is required for the actual task of making and receiving calls. On mobile phones there is no space to put in a hard disk, so very little information can be stored on the phone itself. Information should be provided in textual form and should use very few black-and-white graphics.

A route planner in a car has other requirements. The information should be provided in an audio format and use very few graphical interactions, as these may distract the drivers from their task of driving the car. The connection speed is as low as with mobile phones, but the graphical display and processor speed will be much higher, as there is enough space in a car. Installing a hard disk into a car won't be an issue, so storing information in the car is possible.

A kiosk at the airport will most likely be a standard PC with a standard monitor and a modem or network connection, so restrictions are not expected, except that these devices will most likely have touch screens. Set-top boxes for TV sets have the restriction of low resolution, and small text will become illegible on the TV screen.

In a hotel, you will get Internet delivered over the TV set. As television has a much lower resolution than typical computer monitors, one thing that is a problem is white background, which can be found on many Web sites, combined with dark text. Although it appears perfectly on a computer monitor, this type of background can cause severe screen distortion on a television screen. A dark background with light-colored text is better for viewing on television.

These are just some of the restrictions on Internet appliances. These will become more and more important in the future, as this market will be growing very quickly. HTML in its current form is not able to cope with all these different devices. In the near future, XML will replace HTML, as XML separates information from layout.

5.3   Attracting Visitors to Your Site

5.3.1   Gaining Market Share through Content

Keep your content current so people come back regularly to check for news and updates. The Internet is changing; therefore, your company and your Web sites need to change as well, and adapt themselves to the new influences. If you do not invest in information, content, and intelligence, you will fail.

The Internet is used by many companies to offer real-time, up-to-date information. If you fail to offer the same, you will eventually lose out.

In order to keep customers coming back and to spread the word about your site, you need to offer something new each time they visit. All pages should contain the date when they were last changed. This puts some pressure on you to update them on a regular basis, and your customers have a simple way of checking how new certain information is. Using personalization and one-to-one marketing technologies, it is possible to show users what has changed since their last visit.

5.3.2   Offering Free Information

In order to get a loyal customer base, you need to offer free information, products, and services to everyone who comes to your Web site. Offer some form of incentive and discount to those who give you repeat business. Customers will not to go to a competitor if they are treated well by your company.

Most people come to a particular Web page because they have certain expectations of the service, content, or products. The number of surfers who look at Web pages just for fun is decreasing. The users with expectations want a piece of information, a service, or a product. Offer free giveaways, like screensavers or mouse pads, for customers who are willing to register on your site. Once users have registered, you need to offer some sort of personalization, such as greeting them by name when they return. Free white papers, product brochures, and other product or service information could be offered by the company.

5.3.3   Personalization

Once you know who your customers are, you can start to collect information on them. The more you learn about your visitors, the better you will be able to address their needs. Add information to your site that may interest your user group without having a direct relationship to your company (thus creating a portal). This will keep them coming back again and again. If you don't give away "freebies," in whatever form, you will surely lose customers to other companies.

Using data mining technologies, you can offer an effective marketing program to particular target markets. Once you understand the needs of your customers, you can create better products, content, and services. Online marketing can be used in a powerful, cost-efficient way to build up a very complex and efficient customer database.

At the same time, it is necessary to ensure the privacy of the customer's personal information. In the European Union and Canada, special privacy laws have been established. Don't forget to put up a privacy notice on your Web site, and keep the information confidential.

By recognizing the value of returning customers, your online offerings become more valuable, as the customers do not need to reenter information they were asked for in a previous session. Internet Explorer 6 and Netscape 6 offer a functionality that remembers input made in a Web form, making automatic form completion possible. Once you have entered your credit card information, the browser is able to add this information to other forms as well. Although this may reduce the typing for the user, it also increases privacy issues on the client. A well-protected server-based personalization system is therefore preferred.

5.3.4 Support Online and Offline Reading

As reading on the screen is more difficult than reading a newspaper or a brochure, you should condense the information to a much greater extent than you would do for printed media. The first paragraph of each Web page should contain a summary of the overall Web page. Use concise, straightforward language. Offer the user the option to download and print information. News.com[10] and Wired[11] offer news services that contain longer articles on a given topic, but they offer the opportunity to print out the text without a special Web layout. The information is offered in two versions, one specifically designed for the Web and one for printout.

5.3.5 Cross-Marketing and Cross-Selling

It is quite easy to follow users around on a Web site. The marketing department is able to create cross-references between products and services. This feature is used widely in online bookshops, for example. When buying a certain book, the customer is presented with five other books about the same topic or by the same author, or with books that other people have bought after buying that particular book.

This technology can be extended to virtually any business. It requires the marketing department to think about possible cross-references for the online products, and not only a few times a year, as with print catalogs. Cross-marketing on the Internet becomes highly dynamic. If one of your competitors decides to start a promotion for a certain product and displays the price

---

[10]http://www.news.com/
[11]http://www.wired.com/news/

reduction on the Web, you can counter the attack with a few mouse-clicks by adjusting your price or adding value to the article.

Although adding, changing, or removing cross-marketing initiatives has become very easy, the algorithms can be highly complex. If your software does not allow the automatic checking of your cross-selling, this may result in losses for your company.

5.3.6   Be Faster than Your Customers

When you design your Web site, remember that customers want to find what they are looking for *fast*. Don't hide information; offer a simple-to-use search engine. Help your customers go where they want as fast as possible. Using one-to-one marketing technologies makes it possible to anticipate the needs of the users. With every visit, it is easier to find the relevant information before the user has entered any request.

Your Web site needs to be designed in such a fashion that every single piece of information on your site can be reached with three clicks. People don't have time to click through all the pages on a given Web site. Once customers have reached the information (or products or services) they were looking for, you can add information on that page with links to related subjects. But be sure to give them the information first.

The most important rule on the Internet is that everything is subject to change. Be prepared that the rules for marketing will change with every new technology that is introduced. This means not only a passive preparation for change, but active contributions to change in order to stay ahead of the competition.

5.3.7   Event Marketing

Special events attract many new users and bind existing users to a certain Web site. Governmental Web sites in the UK[12] and in Germany,[13] for example, offer online chats and interviews with important politicians at regular intervals. These special events attract a lot of customers who would not have come otherwise to a particular site. *Infotainment* and *edutainment* are means to attract customers and present information in an informative and entertaining way. As people remain interested in what the government is doing, they are able to subscribe to mailing lists announcing new events, where the citizens are able to participate.

In February 1999, Victoria's Secret[14] broadcast its fashion show live on the Internet.[15] The event was a big success for the company, although many users

---

[12]http://www.number-10.gov.uk/

[13]http://www.bundesregierung.de/

[14]http://www.victoriassecret.com/

[15]http://webevents.broadcast.com/victoriassecret/fashionshow99/

were disappointed by the quality and availability of the streaming video. Victoria's Secret underestimated the interest of online surfers in seeing models in underwear—the server broke down. RealPlayer[16] was used to transport the streaming media. An estimated 250,000 copies of the software were downloaded per hour on the day of the event. This is at least 50 times more than on normal days. It meant a huge impact on the network of Real Networks and slowed down the whole system significantly.

The idea was good, but the technology was not ready. The Internet was not designed to be a real-time media, and new standards emerge slowly. The server crash could have been avoided by many different servers transmitting the event in many different locations.

President Bill Clinton's January 1999 State of the Union address could be seen without interruption as this event was transmitted by many different servers all around the world. Television stations around the world broadcast the event live on the Internet, including CNN[17] in the United States, the BBC[18] in the UK, and RTL[19] in Germany. The television pictures were transmitted via satellite to the television stations, so that intercontinental Internet traffic was not affected by the broadcast.

But still, the fashion show attracted more people. Not because Clinton was less interesting, but because people could see something that was not transmitted via television. Internet technology makes it easy to create video and audio items, but they won't have any impact if the customers do not view these items as special or useful.

5.4 Virtual Societies

5.4.1 Affiliate Networks

In order to market your online products, you need to syndicate your content or technologies to other sites or even to other media. A good starting point are portals, as they are a good place to offer your content, products, or services. The Internet is an infrastructure for many niche and mainstream markets; split up your marketing offensive into narrow target markets that correspond to zones or channels (see also Chapter 6).

Affiliate networks are a special form of customizing your online products, not for end customers but for resellers who want to extend their offerings by adding your services, products, or information. Your services, information, and goods need to be totally separate from the design of your Web pages. The resellers should be able to configure your offerings the way they need them, online and on-the-fly.

---

[16]http://www.real.com/

[17]http://www.cnn.com/

[18]http://www.bbc.co.uk/

[19]http://www.rtlnews.de/

Create a special reseller section where you offer not only customization of the digital products, but also marketing material that the resellers can use to promote your electronic goods.

Another good reason to create an affiliate network is to create brand awareness. The more Web sites you are able to recruit for your network, the more people will become aware of what you have to offer. Amazon.com's affiliate network is probably the best known. Thousands of Web sites have become resellers of Amazon.com's books, and the owners of these Web sites get up to 15 percent of each sale. Unlike in "real life," where manufacturers seek to build up a limited number of retailers that are geographically separated, entrepreneurs on the Web try to get as many affiliates as possible, as this increases profit and spreads the word about the service and the associated brand.

Amazon.com's affiliate network has created many niche bookshops on the Internet that focus on one or more topics. These niche bookshops have additional information on the books and concentrate more on the surrounding topics than Amazon.com could, but Amazon.com is still the big winner, since in the end the books are purchased from them.

Special online directories—e.g., Top Reseller[20] or Refer-It[21]—list affiliate networks, but be careful. Many companies try to appear as affiliate networks but are in reality companies based on the pyramid scheme. The pyramid scheme is forbidden in many countries, as it does not make money from selling goods, but by recruiting others. The pyramid scheme is a system based on multilevel marketing. Every person recruited for the pyramid scheme needs to provide another set of people in order to make money with the system. The scheme works only as long as more people participate. Once people understand how the scheme works and stop participating, the whole pyramid collapses. The only people that can make money this way are the initiators.

5.4.2 Internet Communities

The whatis.com[22] dictionary describes a virtual community as a community of people sharing common interests, ideas, and feelings over the Internet or other collaborative networks. Virtual communities can be defined as social aggregations that emerge from the Internet when enough people carry on public discussions long enough and with sufficient human feeling to form webs of personal relationships in cyberspace. Virtual communities might be thought of as subgroups of the "global village." Before the Web, virtual communities existed on bulletin board services (BBS) and many still do.

Try to map your target groups into Internet communities. Building up these communities on your Web site will not only enhance your one-to-one marketing strategy, but will also allow one-to-many and many-to-many communica-

---

[20]http://www.topreseller.com/
[21]http://www.refer-it.com/
[22]http://www.whatis.com/

tion within the user groups. It is also easier to customize products for certain communities and present them in a particular way.

The frog-lover community on your Web site should be able to get all the relevant information about frogs without having to click through a series of Web pages that contain no value to them. Saving your customers' profiles will make everybody happy, as they are treated in a very special way, and your company gets detailed information on the target group. But be careful about the information you gather; the customers should know what you are doing with the material. Ensure the security of the site in order to prevent break-ins from hackers. Your privacy regulations should be very clearly visible. Otherwise, you may have trouble with online privacy activists, who will try to shine a bad light on your company. Provide a link on every page to your privacy information, where you state what your intention is for the private information your customers provide.

One of the most famous communities on the Internet is the WebGrrls community.[23] The WebGrrls International community provides a forum for women interested in new media and technology. It is basically a network for exchanging job and business leads, and helps form strategic alliances. The mission is to mentor, teach, intern, and learn the skills to succeed in an increasingly technical workplace and world.

5.4.3 Bootstrapping an Internet Community

The biggest problem with building up an Internet community is getting the critical mass onto your site. The critical mass is the number of users, which ensures that when customers join the Web site, they will find people on there interested in communication. Without the critical mass, it is difficult to be successful. Until you reach the critical mass, every effort to demonstrate the community will inevitably fail, as new users coming into the system will not find enough peers to communicate with. Imagine a chat room that is empty most of the time. Anyone popping in for a chat will be disappointed. The same applies to newsgroups. If only a few postings are in the newsgroup and nobody cares to respond, people will not come back.

The more (inter)action you can provide to your target group, the more willing they are to come back and enjoy the services on your Web site. Therefore, some basic rules need to be observed. Communities should not be introduced on the first day of the introduction of the Web site. Let people get accustomed to the service, and feature some special chat events with interesting people. Only once you have established a routine for the target community can you expand the online chat to be open 24 hours a day.

The same rule applies to the newsgroups. It does not make any sense to open 20 newsgroups with a few messages in each. Start with a single newsgroup and see how the discussions develop. If there are strong trends towards a

---

[23]http://www.webgrrls.com/

single topic, open a new newsgroup or chat channel to accommodate the greater interest and create an even closer community feeling.

It is important to build a relationship before starting up a community. You need to step outside the confines of your Web site to do this, and the best way to do that is by launching a newsletter. By launching a newsletter, you can get a feeling about the interests of the people visiting your Web site and receive feedback on the contents. Through the newsletters, it is possible to refine the message of the Web site and the services on it. This feedback should not be provided only as a response to a newsletter. The visitors should also have the option to comment on the Web site. The first step would therefore be to post polls and surveys and create open comment areas, where people can leave their feedback without really talking to each other. This will get people in the habit of talking to the Web site owner. This requires a fast response time from the owner or Webmaster.

Once the newsletter has an established set of readers, start a conversation within the newsletter format. Each time you send out your newsletter, ask your readers questions and post their answers in the next newsletter. You might start by asking for simple opinions and tips and then expand into a deeper discussion by asking open questions on hot topics.

Before you launch your community, you need "stars" for your community— visitors to talk to, people whom community members recognize and whose opinions they value. You don't have to go out and hire expensive experts, though. You can do just as well by building the identities of people who regularly post to your newsletter. Once you've identified a few key participants, tap them to be experts in certain areas, have them field questions, and give them space on your site to talk about their areas of expertise. In short, make them stars on your site and get other people in the habit of talking to them. By following these steps, it becomes easier to set up a successful online community.

5.4.4   Interactive User Groups

Unlike traditional media, communication via the Internet is fast and offers interactive communication. Customers are able to talk directly to your employees, and vice versa. No matter who initiated the conversation, responding to is easy using email, chat, or newsgroups.

In order to attract customers, it is necessary to build up a dialogue between your company and the customers. The customer needs to experience interactivity in order to develop loyalty. Focus on the target group and try to convince them you can fulfill their needs. While Internet surfers who just browse through your pages "by accident" should not be ignored, they should get only general information about your company. If they are really interested in your organization, they will register with your site to access more information.

In order to offer your customers an interactive experience, put up links to contact email addresses. For every type of request, there should be a differ-

ent email address. If your visitors want to know abou
should send their mail to a different email address
wanted to comment on the Web site in general. Althou hey
by the same person, it makes it easier to classify the ey
or user requests. A real dialogue between your compa ad
will enhance the loyalty of your customers and the awar n
Your company, at the same time, gets valuable informs
base and is able to enhance products, services, and cont.
tomers even more.

Other simple measures to increase the interactivity of y
offering contests or sweepstakes. Giving away one of you
cost much compared to other methods of promotion. Not on
of users increase significantly, you also gather information c
And users love to take part in a contest. They will check ba
if they have won.

Customer service is also very important. Give them, for e>
information on product-order status. If you sell digital produ
offer demo or limited versions on your Web site that everyboc
helps the customers in their decision to buy a certain product.

5.5 Localization

5.5.1 Act Global, Think Local

Being online means that you compete on a worldwide basis and yc
target individuals from all over the world. The Internet has enforced u
globalization, which is the expression of deterritorialization and a bor
world. While globalization has become a fact, it is not true that a global c
has been established. The more that people get in touch with people from c
countries, the more they see their own culture as becoming more importance
is part of their identity, which they feel they would lose in a global cultu.
The effect can be seen quite clearly in Europe, where 15 countries have move
together to form the European Union.

While national boundaries have been lifted, the identity with the region
where the people live has risen to new levels. For many people it has become
less important to be German, French, or Italian. They see themselves as from
Bavaria, from Bourgogne, or from Tuscany. In the early years of computing, it
was thought that all programs need only be written in English, but the mistake was that in the early years, only well-educated people—who were native
English speakers or learned English at school—had access to these resources.
With the Internet, everybody is able to use it.

In order to cater to this change in society, be sure to have country-specific
or region-specific Web sites in the local languages. Customers from China or
Russia may not be able to speak English or another language, such as French or

ou target such markets, make sure you have translations online
the customs of doing business in these countries. Does your site
seball cards or fortune cookies? Countries in which these products
able wouldn't know what you are talking about. Localization is not
for-word translation activity. It is important to take into account
ral, and social differences.

s can be seen on a worldwide basis, you need to think about your
ups and your future target groups. Be sure not to offend other cul-
ligions with the content or the graphics on your Web pages. Although
not mean that you cannot display anything that may be viewed dif-
in other countries, you should be aware about possible issues when
with these countries.

decision to translate or not to translate depends on two basic consid-
s: business and legal. In order to make a product more attractive, it is
ary to localize a product or service in order to compete with a local man-
rer. In some countries there are laws that require all imported goods
ve the warnings, the safety instructions, and user installation informa-
translated into the local language. Even if translations are not required
ause the country you are exporting to shares your language, it may be nec-
ary to localize the product or service.

The format of dates, for example, is different in the UK and the U.S. And
rtain words that are shared among these two countries may have different
eanings. While the title "esquire" is still commonly used in the UK as a
synonym for "mister," it is not used in this sense in the U.S. anymore. And while
English-speaking countries do not expect to have a field in the address form for
the academic title, it is highly desired in Germany and Italy. A "Herr Professor"
wants to receive mail addressed to "Herr Professor" and a "dottore" in Italy will
expect a personalized Web page to greet her or him with the academic title.

Currency is different in Germany and Austria, although they share the
same language. Although the euro was introduced in both countries in 1999,
the people of Germany and Austria still have their own currencies until 2002.
Austria and Germany are in the European Union and share mostly the same
legal framework. The north of Switzerland, which also speaks German, is not
part of the European Union, and has different tax and law regulations.

Typical problems also involve symbols and gestures. Let's say your site
features a JavaScript graphic of a cartoon character waving at the reader. This
is not considered a friendly gesture in Greece or Nigeria, for example. In those
nations, the palm-forward wave is a nasty gesture indeed, as is the thumbs-up
signal in Iran—not to mention the thumb-and-index-finger "OK" sign, which is
most definitely not OK in Brazil.

Colors, too, carry different meanings in different places. A black site con-
notes hipness and sophistication in the United States. But in China black
means death—it is viewed as being unlucky and morbid. See Chapter 13 for
more information on the use of colors.

Another issue may be the form where customers fill in their postal address. Postal codes have different formats in different countries and the field "state" that is used in the U.S. is not needed in most European countries. This not only misleads some customers, but also results in bad records in your database. An address form that does not conform to the local usage may keep customers from using the offered service, meaning missed deliveries. There are many U.S. Web sites that offer their goods to European countries. These sites require you to fill in the "state" field. Obviously, a customer from a European company will not have any use for this field. But, if you leave it empty, the order cannot be processed, as the validation tool checks if all fields are complete. What makes this even worse is that many sites just output a general error message, leaving the customer in doubt whether the Web server failed or if the entry was wrong. This is definitely not the road to take toward becoming a successful global online competitor.

5.5.2 Local Adaptions of Websites

Localization is the process of adapting a product to meet the language, cultural, and other requirements of a specific target environment or market (a locale). This process often entails the use of special computer-based tools. Localization involves translation (e.g., of manuals and other documentation, screens, help texts, and error messages). With a properly localized Web site, a user can interact with it using his or her own language and cultural conventions. It also means that all user-visible text strings and all user documentation (printed and electronic) use the language and cultural conventions of the user. The properly localized site also needs to meet all regulatory and other requirements of the user's country/region.

Equally, product or Web site names may have to be changed to avoid unfortunate associations in the target language. However, the process also requires other nonlinguistic skills.

On the software programming side, screen dialog boxes and field lengths may have to be altered; date, time and currency formats changed; delimiters for figures replaced; and icons and colors adapted, to give only a few examples. What is more, in the case of so-called bidirectional languages (such as Arabic and Hebrew) and double-byte character sets (such as those for Chinese, Japanese, and Korean), more extensive reprogramming may be required to ensure that localized text and numerals are displayed correctly on the target platforms.

On the contents side, programs often have to be changed to conform to national and cultural norms. In multimedia applications, the color, size, and shape of objects such as coins and notes, taxis, telephones and mailboxes, buses and ambulances, traditionally vary from country to country. Vehicles may suddenly have to drive on the other side of the road, while dress codes will vary and symbols take on a new significance. Equally, mainstream business applications such as address databases and financial accounting packages have to be adapted to the procedures and conventions applicable in their new environments.

5.5.3 Cultural Differences

Although it may be hard to understand, other cultures will have difficulties with behaviors that are common in your own area/country. They will have totally different expectations that may lead to misunderstandings. A simple example would be the way people order drinks in a bar. In Germany you are served and pay when you leave; in Italy you have to pay first and then order; and in Ireland you order first and pay immediately. A German in Ireland or Italy would sit down at a table and wait until a waiter comes. But neither in Ireland nor in Italy would anything happen. The expectations are totally different. The German may think that the Irish and Italians don't like Germans and therefore get nothing to drink. The Irishman and Italian, on the other hand, may think that the German is not interested in anything to drink and will just ignore the person.

Although these countries are all in Europe, they have a lot of cultural differences and varying customs. It is therefore easy to imagine the differences in countries that are far more distant than Germany and Italy. The Asian countries, for example, have difficulties in using standard applications like a word processor from the United States, not because it has not been translated properly, but because the logic used is that of Americans and not of Asians. Therefore, programs such as RichWin[24] are very popular in China, because they modify standard applications on Windows to fit in with the way Asians think. English is written from left to right, some Asian languages are written from right to left; some from top to bottom. For the user to enter text, a completely new paradigm needs to be developed that easily allows the entry of information. And text input is just the tip of the iceberg on localization issues.

Disney[25] had large problems with cultural differences when it opened its theme park near Paris, France. Charles Hill, an important author on cultural differences, uses this example to describe the dilemma many companies get into when extending their business to other countries.[26] The American managers thought that they could use their existing business model and values and introduce them into the French market. It soon became quite clear that the company needed to adapt to the local market. Unexpectedly, EuroDisney customers were mostly Japanese tourists and Americans living in Europe. The Europeans who did come to the theme park were not staying as long as their American and Japanese counterparts. Instead of staying four days in the theme park, most Europeans came for one day, making it difficult for Disney

---

[24]http://www.richwinusa.com/
[25]http://www.disney.com/
[26]*International Business*, Charles W. Hill, Washington, 1998, pp. 64.

to fill all the hotels that they built around the theme park. These errors are often repeated by online businesses. Just because you know your local market does not mean that you are able to repeat the success in other markets or even create a global market for your products and services.

The following elements are core to any localization effort:

- **Languages**—Two aspects need to be taken into consideration: the software itself and its output.

- **Sorting Order**—Depending on the alphabet used, the sorting order varies.

- **Numbers**—The internal number could be 12345.67 and the external representation could be 12,345.67 or 12.345,67.

- **Date and Time**—The internal representation could be 19951231 and the external representation could be December 31th 1995, or 31-12-1995.

- **Quotations**—Different languages use different symbols for quotations.

Table 5.3. Elements of Localization

Not only will trying to provide a single business model that will work in every country fail in most cases, but also a single advertisement for several countries can easily fail if local laws are not taken into consideration. In an article in *The Economist*,[27] Kellogg's was cited as an example. Kellogg's[28] made a television commercial in the UK that was highly successful, but could not be used in any other European country. The commercial featured a child wearing a Kellogg's t-shirt promoting the iron and the vitamins in the product. The key line was "Kellogg's makes their cornflakes the best they have ever been." In France the commercial could not be shown, as it is against the law to show children in product endorsements. The Netherlands forbade the commercial because the reference to the vitamins and the iron were claims to health and medical benefits. In Germany the spot could not be shown because of prohibition against competitive claims.

---

[27] http://www.economist.co.uk/, "Advertising in a Single Market," *The Economist*, March 24, 1990, p. 64.

[28] http://www.kelloggs.com/

When localizing Internet applications, do not only translate the texts and adjust currencies, but think also about local habits. For example, if you have a French hotel on the Côte D'Azure, you could offer an online reservation service. French customers who want to book a hotel may want to take their pets with them, as this is very common in France. So there should be a check box they can click if they want to bring their dogs or cats along. If you now translate the pages into Japanese, then it would not make much sense to have the pet option, as it would be very unlikely that Japanese tourists would bring their pets to France. This option may confuse them, especially if the translations are not perfect, which happens quite often on the Internet. Badly translated texts destroy more business on the Internet than they generate.

Americans especially are not aware of the cultural differences and expect that their way of conducting business will be accepted throughout the world. Most non-Americans, though, will prefer to do business with people who are familiar with the local habits and rules. This is also reflected on the Web. Amazon.de[29] is a success in Germany because it uses a German top-level domain, the Web site is all in German, and it sells German books and is run by Germans who know how to conduct business in Germany. The success is not due to the Amazon.com logo or name.

In order to be successful in local markets, it is necessary to know how people react to your offerings. In southern Europe, for example, people are far more responsive to spoken words, while northern Europeans prefer a written order. A phone conversation with people from southern Europe is often more effective than sending an email.

When expanding your companies to cover other countries, get to know the local customs. The Internet offers the advantage of allowing you to visit foreign and local Web sites and see how they do business. In order to build up a subsidiary, get people from that particular country who know better than you what to do. If you are planning a major investment, then consider learning some phrases and visit the country. Otherwise, the investment may result in a failure and this can result in financial trouble for the whole company.

The National Forum on Cultural Differences[30] is also a good place to start investigations. The forum offers the opportunity to ask questions about cultural differences, and people who seem to know more about the other culture are able to respond. Although you may find some wrong answers there, in general, it is a good starting point for your worldwide expansion.

5.5.4 Translation Requirements

Depending on your budget, you should think about translating your Web pages into other languages. Many smaller companies use automated translation

---

[29]http://www.amazon.de/
[30]http://www.yforum.com/

services to produce foreign-language Web sites. Babelfish,[31] for example, allows automated translation on the Web into many different languages, such as Spanish, French, and German. Many people use this service to get a fast but rough translation of a certain Web page (which is precisely what the system was designed for). Some companies use the output as the basis for their localization efforts and are laughed at by the foreign-speaking online community. Offering automatically translated Web pages to serious customers is a good way of destroying business.

Figure 5.2 shows the Web page of MacNews.de, [32] which has been translated with Babelfish from German to English. Most of the text becomes unreadable after the translation, as Babelfish translates word by word, without understanding the meaning.

Figure 5.2. Automated translation of MacNews.de.

If you are serious about extending your business, then get professional translators and localizing experts. A professional translator tries to capture the exact meaning of the source text without compromising the integrity of the author's style of expressing ideas. A good translator will create culturally appropriate iconography and graphics and will modify the interface to suit the needs of the local culture.

This cannot be done by simple algorithms on a computer. A bad translation will reflect poorly on the image of your electronic business. The software

---

[31]http://babelfish.altavista.com/

[32]http://www.macnews.de/

that you are using should support localization; otherwise, it will become quite difficult to add new languages, currencies, and customs. Some additional information on internationalization of Web pages can be found in Appendix D.

5.5.5 National Boundaries

The Internet has removed national boundaries, meaning that anyone on the Internet can reach out for any type of information anywhere in the world. Unfortunately, the rest of the world is not yet organized in such a way. If we just look at the way digital broadcasting rights are handled, we can easily see what needs to be done. The most famous example is probably the Olympics[33] games.

The problem with broadcasting rights of the Olympic games is that they are typically sold regionally. So to win future rights, online businesses are looking to break the Net into regions, as they have trouble convincing the copyright owners to change their habits of selling rights.

Existing Internet addressing schemes allow Web sites to pinpoint a visitor's geographical location and thus block out surfers from certain countries. Although not 100 percent accurate, it will black out a large percentage of undesired viewers. This technology can be used not only to enforce digital media distribution, it can also mean that certain countries are able to ban all sorts of information that does not seem to be appropriate for their citizens. As nations assert their legal and cultural norms on their piece of the planet, efforts to divide the Net into separate sovereignties could become increasingly popular.

Yahoo!, for example, is not allowed to show Nazi objects on sale on its Web site to French users anymore. This effectively means that Yahoo! has to filter out all French users. China, meanwhile, has threatened to create a separate network of Chinese sites.

The free exchange of ideas could be inhibited by governments intent on blocking materials posted on foreign sites, or by Web sites trying to restrict distribution of specific content.

Erecting borders could turn the Internet into just another mainstream commodity. A small business in South America, for example, could lose a worldwide customer base by being forced to sell in South America only.

The easiest way to detect where a user comes from is through the IP address. Each IP address is assigned to an owner in a certain country. As most people access the Internet via an ISP, it is quite easy to determine where they come from. Realistically, the IP address is not a reliable source, as it can be easily changed, either by IP spoofing (see Chapter 11) or by calling in via a foreign ISP (which is expensive, but doable). A French user could make a phone call to Brazil to access a service provider there. From the Internet's point of view, that computer would appear to be in Brazil. In addition, anonymizing services, such as Anonymizer[34], allow users to hide their true geographic origins.

---

[33]http://www.olympia.org/
[34]http://www.anonymizer.com/

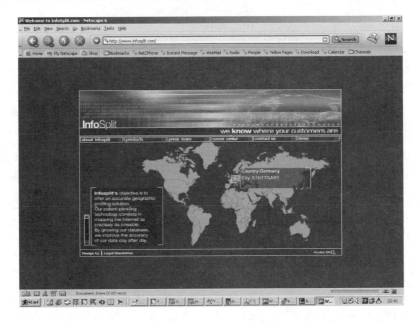

Figure 5.3. Geolocation works in many cases.

Companies like InfoSplit[35] (see Figure 5.3) and NetGeo[36] are developing ways to improve accuracy down to the ZIP code or city. Location detection will improve as more users use wireless devices that link with global-positioning satellites, and also as they connect through high-speed broadband networks that prohibit long-distance phoning.

Some Web sites already use location detection for targeting advertisements geographically—and to reduce Net congestion by steering visitors to servers closer to them that mirror the original site's content. In Chapter 3 you can find more detailed information on this topic from a technological point of view.

To improve accuracy of identifying the user's IP, many sites supplement IP techniques with credit-card registrations or other physical checks. In that case, someone would be permitted access only with prior authentication.

5.6 Promoting Your E-Business

5.6.1 Choosing the Right Domain Name

Before you can promote your Web site, you should choose a domain name that fits your business and needs. If you have a company that is well known, your company name should be the domain name. If you are offering services for a

---

[35]http://www.infosplit.com/

[36]http://www.netgeo.com/

particular target group, try to find a domain name that matches a keyword people would search for. Of course, two or more domain names would be the best solution.

Let's say your company is called Spaghetti, Inc., and produces Italian-style pasta. The most obvious domain names for the company would be spaghettiinc.com, spaghetti.com, or pasta.com. If your company has subsidiaries all over the world, the top-level domain (TLD) should be also bought for all target countries—i.e., for your subsidiary in Germany you would choose spaghetti-inc.de, spaghetti.de, and pasta.de, and for the subsidiary in Taiwan you would select spaghettiinc.tw, spaghetti.tw, and pasta.tw. The use of .com suggests that your site contains information in English. If you use other country codes, such as .se, you need to translate all information into Swedish; otherwise, you will not live up to the expectations of your customers. A complete list of the available TLDs can be found at many places on the Web[37] and can help to identify the number of TLDs you need to target.

If you are choosing more generic terms, such as "spaghetti" or "pasta," there is no need to create a new Web site for every domain name. You can easily link several domain names to one Web site. By using different TLDs, such as .de and .fr you could directly link to the German and French pages with the option of switching back to the English pages at any given time. Lufthansa, for example, is using multiple TLDs in this way. The .de domain[38] points to the German site and the .com domain[39] points to the English site. Ca5ino.com,[40] on the other hand, points to the same company and Web site as CasinoPlace.[41] Through the use of two different domain names, more customers are likely to be attracted by the content.

Of course, domain names are not always available; they may have been taken by some other companies. In this case you should check if these companies are infringing on your trademarks. If you have a company with a certain name and someone else is using the domain name, then you can get the domain name back without too much hassle.

A few years ago people bought domain names in order to sell them, which worked in the beginning, but nowadays almost all court rulings are in favor of the company that holds the trademark name.

To check the availability of domain names, you can go to InterNic[42] for American domains, Ripe[43] for European domains, and APNic[44] for Asia and the Pacific region. Your ISP is also a good place to check for domain name

---

[37] e.g. http://www.iana.org/top-level-domains.html

[38] http://www.lufthansa.de/

[39] http://www.lufthansa.com/

[40] http://www.ca5ino.com/

[41] http://www.casinoplace.com/

[42] http://www.internic.net/

[43] http://www.ripe.net/

[44] http://www.apnic.net/

availability—but compare prices with the domain name registries, as ordering a domain name is simple and can be done in about five minutes. You have to be especially careful if you order domain names through your ISP. Some ISPs register the domain in their name instead of your company's name. This makes it difficult to switch provider, as they, not you, have become the owners of the domain name.

In addition to the domain name, it is necessary to apply for an IP address, as all domain names need to be mapped to an IP address. In most cases a range of IP addresses is ordered, which enables a company to grow in the future more easily.[45]

Some people try to enjoy the success of certain Web sites, so they register domain names that are very similar to successful ones. The Web site whitehouse.com has nothing to do with the American White House Web site whitehouse.gov. The purpose of metacralwer.com is totally different than the meta search engine metacrawler.com. And finally the owners of office21.com have nothing to do with the German project office21.de, which tries to create "the" office for the 21st century.

Many companies are not bound to a country or region and use TLDs as part of their name. Even small countries in the Pacific region are participating in the domain name game. Tuvalu, owner of the .tv domain; Niue, owner of .nu; and Tonga, owner of .to have TLDs that are used very frequently. The TLD .tv is used by many sites centered around television. The TLD .nu is pronounced in the same way as "new" to suggest to people that you have a new site. The people of Tonga have become rich with the .to domain. Many sites have registered this domain, such as cryp.to,[46] go.to,[47] come.to.[48] Even Armenia (.am) is attracting foreign businesses, such as the i.am[49] Web site, which allows customers to build URLs such as http://www.i.am/danny/ (which is, by the way, not my site).

Such use of the TLD shows that the current system is no longer sufficient and needs to be replaced by a more sophisticated solution. Adding new TLDs won't help much. The whole system of domain names needs to be reviewed. Several new systems have already been proposed; Netscape's system is perhaps the best known. Netscape has a feature known as smart browsing, based on *keywords* that link to locations within Netcenter and on partners' sites. Netscape's idea is to replace the domain names with keywords or trademarked names. This would unify the concept of a search engine with the domain names.

---

[45]Due to an error in the IP address database, I was the owner of approximately one third of the Internet for a few days (the range from 195.125.0.156 to 255.255.255.255). This happened on June 20, 1998, and was corrected soon after, as it became impossible to chase hackers and spammers, and I did not want to take responsibility for them. But it felt good to "own" a large part of the Internet ;-). Unfortunately, I was not allowed to put the excerpt from the IP database into the book for copyright reasons.

[46]http://www.cryp.to/

[47]http://www.go.to/

[48]http://www.come.to/

[49]http://www.i.am/

The URL (Uniform Resource Locator) is a means to locate a resource on the Internet. Most common are URLs in the form of http://www.hp.com/. The http: is the type of protocol used for the connection. Commonly used protocol types are the following. You can try them out by typing them into a Web browser.

- **http**—Standard hypertext transfer protocol (HTTP), which provides a connection to any given Web server (example: http://www.realhamsters.com/).

- **https**—Encrypted HTTP connection to a Web server (example: https://banking.lbbw.de/).

- **ftp**—Standard file transfer protocol (FTP) connection (example: ftp://ftp.apple.com/).

- **telnet**—Telnet protocol to connect to a server (example: telnet://delos.lf.net/).

- **mailto**—Mail protocol to send out an email (example: mailto:president@whitehouse.gov).

Table 5.4. What is a URL?

Still, Netscape's model is of little use at the moment, as its proposal works only with the Netscape browser, and the company wants to host the name database. This would put all other browser producers at a disadvantage and would put all the control into Netscape's hands.

Another system that has been proposed is called RealNames.[50] The aim of the service is to simplify the Internet by replacing complex URLs with memorable words and phrases in any language. Instead of typing http://www.buecher.de/, one can simply type Bücher to be redirected to that Web site. The RealNames system is based on the Unicode code set, which not only contains the Latin character set, but all character sets in the world, including Russian, Chinese, Hebrew, and Arabic character sets. The advantage is that Arabic native speakers, for example, are able to enter an Arabic name in Arabic and will be redirected to the appropriate Web site. But RealNames has the same disadvantage as Netscape's smart browsing; the database is managed by only one group or company. They define the policies of use, and the policy of "appropriate use" on the RealNames Web site is not clearly defined. It cannot be ensured

---

[50] http://www.realnames.com/

that your names will be accepted, as RealNames decides on your submission. Another issue with RealNames is that it works on top of domain names. It means an additional layer of complexity.

A new system is still required, but it needs to be open and secure and should not depend on a certain vendor. Extending the current system with new TLDs, such as .info and .biz will not resolve the problem. An independent body such as the World Wide Web Consortium[51] will develop a solution that can be supported by the majority of Internet users. In any case, it should be browser-independent and replace the current solution of the domain name system. Such a solution needs to allow a smooth transition; otherwise, the chances are high that many customers will not be willing to switch.

5.6.2   Announcing the Web Site

Even the best site is useless if nobody knows how to get there. The domain name should be everywhere your company logo appears. Establish a presence in all search engines and online directories. Add metatags to your Web pages, giving general information on the content of a certain Web page, and use a set of keywords that increase the success of finding a particular Web page in a search engine. Additional information on search engines and metatags can be found in Chapter 10. Get the attention of the press and use traditional media to promote your Web site.

There are many strategies available to increase the visibility of your offerings. Find other sites that share a similar target audience and exchange banner advertising and links. Register your Web site with all search engines and directories. Some companies offer this service for money, but doing it yourself is easy and you retain control over your marketing initiative. Use the "Add URL" button that is provided on all search engines and directory Web sites, or use one of the free services that adds your URL to many search engines all at once, like SignPost[52] in the United Kingdom or MultiSubmit[53] in Austria.

Submit only the main page to Web directories. If you start submitting every single page to a directory, chances are high that all of your submissions will be ignored. Give precise information on the content of your Web site, its services, the information contained, and products offered. Submit to Web crawlers the most important pages, as the crawler is able to find the rest of the pages. If you have added a new subdirectory to your Web site, for example, then submit the first page of that subdirectory to Internet crawlers, and they will fetch all the other pages automatically. Metatags are important for them to collect the relevant data.

It is possible to post information about your new site to mailing lists, but be careful about this. There are some dedicated mailing lists for announcing new

---

[51]http://www.w3.org/
[52]http://signpost.merseyworld.com/
[53]http://www.multisubmit.at/

sites, but most general mailing lists will not accept this form of advertising and will ban you, if you do not adhere to their rules.

Your site should be promoted not only online, but also offline, using traditional media, and should appear in advertising, press releases, corporate literature, trade shows, letter heads, and business cards. As a rule of thumb, give out either the domain name, such as www.mycompany.com or the complete URL, such as http://www.mycompany.com/. Do not omit the slash at the end. Although Web browsers add the slash if you forget it, everybody should enter it. It requires two connections to the Web server, because the first request will return a request to the Web browser to add the slash. Although this may not seem important, it distinguishes companies that know what they are doing from the rest.

Tell everyone that you have a Web site up and running; tell your customers, clients, suppliers, partners, and competitors. And don't forget to mention what it offers and what it can do for them. But do not give out the information before your site is ready. Once you let users onto your site, you must be sure that nothing is missing and all links are "live" and lead to another Web page. A page that says "Under Construction" can mean the death of your online business. If you don't offer a service right away, don't tell people. If your customers are able to click on a link, then you set expectations. They expect to receive the service behind the link. If you fail to offer the service, they will go to another Web site. And who could blame them?

5.6.3 Managing Your Image

As the competition on the Internet gets more and more cluttered, consistency is one of the most important things to consider. A uniform image in the form of standard Web pages, emails, and newsgroup postings is essential. Your image should also be consistent with all your traditional communication methods, such as television, radio, magazines, newspapers, and direct mailings. The worldwide branding program of a company must be able to cross the boundaries of the traditional and new media and join them into one.

Not doing so may result in self-competition. Instead of selling more goods using all channels, the Internet may take away existing customers from newspapers, for example, and consequently not increase your profit. Customers may not recognize which Web sites, brands, and companies belong together. The Web sites may have little or no relationship to the rest of their marketing communications efforts. All types of media must be part of an integrated marketing strategy. New media should always try to attract new target groups or convince existing target groups to stay with a certain brand, but never should a target group be forced to change the media to stay in touch with a certain company.

Just as your letterheads adhere to the corporate or brand image in design elements and colors, so should your Web site. Anyone looking at your Web site should be able to associate it with your company or product in an instant. But remain innovative; don't just replicate your printed documents to the Web. Use Internet technologies to display your information in a new and exciting way—become more interactive! Use these options that would not have been possible without the Internet.

Some companies try to control the images of their brands online by banning their products from all other Web sites. Levi Strauss,[54] for example, has found out that it can better control its brands by operating its own stores. Instead of selling jeans to retailers, Levi Strauss sells them in its own shops, where it has greater control over the goods and the interior design. This, on the other hand, encouraged retailers to create their own brands. So the line between manufacturers and retailers has been blurred.

This behavior is typical of manufacturers who are not sure about their online strategy. While more and more digital companies spread their services over portal sites to create brand awareness and ultimately profits, traditional manufacturers try to protect their brands by banning the sale of their products on other Web sites. This does not really help sales, and this type of strategy will work only if the brand name is strong enough to make it in the highly competitive market. This helped Levis Strauss, because it was planning to introduce a new business strategy that included its own physical shops and its own Internet shop.

5.7 Banner Ad Campaigning

5.7.1 Basic Strategies

As many information providers have failed to make money selling the information directly to the customers, they use banner advertising as a revenue stream. The problem is that information is very easy to copy. A company that charges for information on a Web site will attract other sites to offer the same or similar information for free. The technologies required to sell content securely over the Internet, such as standard content encryption and authentication, are available, but too complex for everyday use.

While companies with specialized content, such as the *Encyclopaedia Britannica*,[55] make this payment model work, more companies are finding that the *netizens* (the citizens on the net) typically refuse to pay for general information they can find at other sites for free. Consequently, many site owners have begun to sell advertising to cover production costs.

Banner advertising is one of the easiest methods of advertising on the Web. Following some simple rules also makes banner ads an efficient and constant stream of revenue. Just putting some form of graphics onto some Web site won't be enough. You need to develop a strategy for your advertising projects.

---

[54]http://www.levis.com/

[55]http://www.eb.com/

You will find lots of Web sites that contain banner ads nobody will ever bother to click.

Users will be very upset if they have to wait for a banner ad. The ad never should slow down the speed of the content-related page. The users will go on to other sites where they can get all the relevant information in less time. This is bad not only for your banner advertising, but also for the content provider. In order to be safe with banner ads, use last year's technology to design them. The less bandwidth, color, and processor speed required to display the banner ad, the better it is.

An unattractive banner will reduce the chances of someone clicking on it. Not only does the Web page need to be designed appropriately, the banner ads need a clear design that fits into the design of the Web sites. You may have to engage a designer for the banner, but the payback will be immediate.

Complex animations may be cute, but most users won't appreciate them. They take too much time to download and do not help to attract people to click on the banner ad. If you use animations in your banner, use them wisely. Be sure that the message has the top priority.

In order to implement a successful online banner campaign, you should follow these rules:

- **Keep banners small**—The message must be visible within a few seconds, even on slow connections.

- **Invest in design**—Use a concise design to display your message.

- **Avoid complex animations**—Animations are cute, but take up a lot of time for downloading.

- **Make it readable**—Don't use ornamental fonts. Display your message in such a way that everyone is able to read it.

- **Make sure the link works**—The best banner ad is useless if the link leads to nowhere.

- **Design a compelling message**—Make a short, compelling statement about your product or service.

Table 5.5. Banner Advertising Rules

Many banner ads contain text and fonts that are illegible. Again, this will not get your message to the user, even though your designer may have thought that this particular design was cool. Remember to keep it simple, and your consumers will understand what you want to achieve.

Even the best banner will fail if the link it points to is not available. If you change the destination on your Web server, remember to tell all other sites that link to that particular page. To reduce the probability of a dead link, link the banner directly to the home page. Dead links are extremely bad for your company's image. Every few days, do an automatic check of all banner links pointing to your pages to be sure nobody has messed anything up. This way, you can be certain all customers get to see the information you have prepared for them.

If you want to encourage people to click on your banner ad, you need to create a catchy message. Remember that your ad is a representative of you and your company, containing a smattering of your personality and ability. Keep the message clear rather than clever. Never try to code a message. It does not help to have a good banner if nobody understands the message.

In order to put your banners onto other pages, use special agencies that are set up to provide the infrastructure to put banners onto a certain Web page at a specific time. Traditional advertising agencies missed the Internet opportunity, so new companies emerged. Two types of banner management agencies have been established on the Internet: banner exchange and banner selling.

5.7.2 Banner Management

A service known as banner exchange has been established on the Internet. Every Webmaster is able to sign up with a banner exchange service. How does it work? The Webmasters need to provide a banner promoting their own Web sites in a specific format and in turn need to allow other banners to appear on their Web sites. In exchange for a certain amount of views (just looking at the banner ad) or click-throughs (clicking on the banner ad) on the Webmasters' own Web page, either the Webmaster's banner is displayed on other Web pages or the Webmaster is rewarded with some money. Banner exchange sites can be divided into two different types: target market and general interest.

The first focuses on a very narrow target market; for example, Anthrotech,[56] exchanges banners on anthropology-related sites only; the Christian Banner Exchange,[57] as the name suggests, exchanges banners only between sites that are related to the Christian religion. The second type includes general-purpose banner exchange agencies, like 1-For-1[58] or Banner-Mania,[59] which both offer to put your banner on a wide array of sites, but also have the option of targeting

---

[56]http://www.anthrotech.com/banner/

[57]http://www.cbx2.com/

[58]http://www.1for1.com/

[59]http://www.banner-mania.com/

your banner to a certain type of Web site. The banner services also keep logs of the people who looked at the banner and clicked on it. An example can be seen in Figure 5.4 on the site of IndiaConnect.[60]

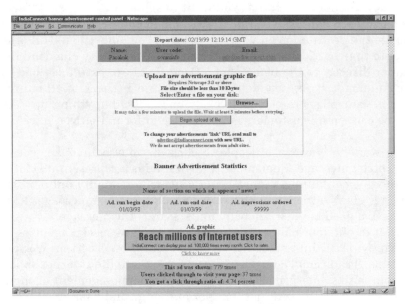

Figure 5.4. Banner administration on IndiaConnect.

Banner selling agencies, on the other hand, offer the more traditional approach of selling advertising to known publications. Instead of placing ads in a newspaper, you place ads on a certain Web site that many people go to each day (for example, the CNN[61] homepage). ClickThrough,[62] an intermediary that resells ad space, allows advertisers to place their banner ads on certain Web pages for a certain period of time. You have to decide in advance where you want to put which banner on which Web site. The solution is not very flexible.

Flycast,[63] on the other hand, allows you to buy and sell Web-advertising space in real time. Unlike "normal" agencies, where you can order 100,000 page views within a month, Flycast offers the option of putting banners onto a certain Web page at any given time. It allows you to watch the clickthroughs happen in real time. This allows you to make changes to your marketing campaign on the fly. If the clickthrough rate is dropping, you can move your banner ads to another Web site.

Using this innovative technology, it is also possible to try out banner ads on new sites with very low risk. Just place it onto a certain site and watch

---

[60]http://www.indiaconnect.com

[61]http://www.cnn.com/

[62]http://www.clickthrough.com/

[63]http://www.flycast.com/

the clickthrough rate. Your company does not need to pay the high prices for the "must have" sites, but still can reach its potential customer base. You can use this technology to put banner ads on 10 niche sites at a lower price than it would have cost to put it onto one major site.

If you have a consumer base that is online at a certain hour (e.g., office hours), you are able to increase the number of banner ads at a certain time. Using this method, it is also possible to reduce the costs during the time when your target market is offline (e.g., because they are asleep in a certain region).

5.8 Online Measurement

5.8.1 User Tracking

The Internet combines the tracking capabilities of direct mail and the instant gratification of TV and radio broadcasts with the addition of interactivity. But as mentioned in Chapter 1, measurement methods on the Web are still quite immature. It is not possible to take exact measurements on the Web. Still, some methods have been established that will be presented here, as accountability has become more important. Measurement services and Web sites use these methods to sell advertising space to their advertising customers.

The main tracking methods used on the Web today are counting, auditing, and rating. It is essential to understand the differences between them.

Counting is the process that is normally done by the Web site owners. It consists of monitoring and reporting user activity. The measurement is done on the basis of the Web server log files. The log files are then processed. The processed figures are then sent out to the advertisers. Because the figures are based on the log file of the Web site, advertisers can't be sure that the data is comparable across Web sites. Auditing is the method where a trusted third party takes over the control of the Web site log files and does the counting on behalf of the company. The information collected by the trusted third party is then made available on the Internet to interested parties. On the basis of audited numbers, advertisers can provide a good value proposition to buy space on certain Web sites. A rating system is based on the feedback of the users. Users can decide how they like a Web site, and based on this feedback, companies interested in offering space on their Web site can sell their ad space to companies.

5.8.2 Avoiding Problems

There is no clear definition of how to count one user. The problem is *spiders*— little robots sent out by search engines—and proxy servers—special servers that allow access to Web sites and save them in a cache in order to improve performance for other users that use the same proxy server. To speed up the browsing experience, ISPs and online services save copies of Web pages and images (including banner ads) on specialized servers and provide the data from *their* servers rather than yours. That means the banner ads are not counted in every case. The same goes for ads and pages stored locally in your browser cache file. The result is that you get inflated and deflated impressions. Depending on your user base, it could well be that twice as many people have seen your Web pages, but only half of them were actually connected to your site. Although this reduces the cost for the advertising (as you pay only for the impressions that reach the server), it does not give a complete picture of the online activity.

Spiders appear as users on the Web site and may take up to 25 percent of the online activity. Proxy servers relay requests from users so that the Web servers see only the address of the proxy, thus allowing 1,000 people to appear as one. In order to overcome both problems, it is possible to use cookies. But nobody can force the users to accept cookies from the Web server.

The measurement units used for online advertising are called *page views* and *visits*. Page views are all pages viewed by the online consumers, and a visit consists of all page views by a single customer.

5.8.3 Log File Analyzer

Every Web server is able to keep track of the users accessing its Web pages by saving the action in a log file. Analyzing log files on highly frequented sites is manually impossible; it is difficult and time-consuming, and the sheer volume can be overwhelming. Therefore, automatic log analyzer tools have been implemented that allow a graphical output of the data to make its analysis simple.

In order to analyze log files, it is necessary to import the data into the proprietary database of the analyzer. Filters can be used in most products that allow you to analyze traffic for a certain period of time or to analyze certain user groups or areas on the Web server. Once the data has been imported and the filters have been chosen, the data is processed and the analyzer creates graphical reports such as tables and charts. These reports make it easier to spot trends and patterns of the users on your Web site.

It is possible to see if people have trouble finding certain information, and it is possible to see where they were coming from (see Figure 5.5). The so-called referrer log tells you which site people have seen before coming to your site. Many analyzers have a database of search engines, making it easy to spot people who found your site on a certain search engine.

5.8.4 Online Rating Agencies

In order to gather even more information, advertisers are able to subscribe to online rating agencies. These agencies use special software that monitors the customers' activities. The software needs to be installed at the users' comput-

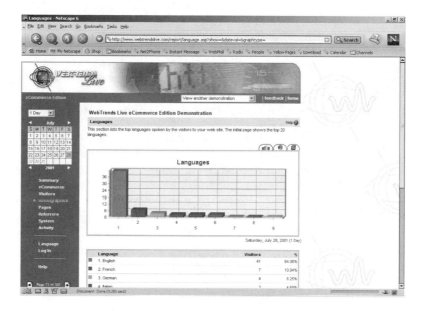

Figure 5.5. Sample report in WebTrends.

ers. The activities measured include Web site visits, online chats, and other Internet services. The advantage of this approach is that everything is recorded at the user level and not at the service level, allowing a better overview of the users' activities. The technology used is similar to the rating services on television. It is clearly not the best way of achieving demographic information, as the selected users cannot be representative, nor is there a limited number of available channels. It may well be that 1,000 users go to 1,000 different sites. You could, of course, choose a group of people who visit certain sites regularly and monitor the way they use the site. This may help you to organize the site in a way that makes it more usable for your customers.

Since the Internet is not a mass-medium, it is not possible to have a representative user group for the whole Internet. And while it is possible to select a niche group and monitor its activity, the results cannot be considered valid for the Internet as a whole.

Another drawback to these services is that most users that are monitored through these services are home-based, as corporate firewalls, other security measures, and corporate privacy policies do not allow the installation of the rating software on company computers. This blurs the results, as most companies today offer their employees the opportunity to connect to the Internet and to surf the Web.

Special software that monitors Web server log files and that cannot be tampered with has already been developed and helps to ensure that Webmasters

The most commonly used measurement units are the following. The results can be very different, so be careful. One visitor, for example, can be equivalent to 10 visits, 50 page views, and 200 hits. One ad click can be equivalent to 1,000 ad impressions. So get the Web server log files and verify the results yourself. This is not very difficult.

- **Page view**—An HTML page that has been successfully downloaded, including all embedded elements (such as graphics).

- **Hits**—Every access to the Web server, including HTML pages, graphics, sounds, and frames.

- **Visits**—A sequence of page views performed by a single visitor. If the user does not view a page for 15 minutes, then the visit is over.

- **Visitor**—A visitor is a user who can be identified by certain properties, such as email address or cookies.

- **Ad impression**—Number of banner views on a certain Web page.

- **Ad click**—Number of clicks on a banner for a certain Web page.

Table 5.6. Measurement Units

do not try to falsify the results of their own log files. These log files are authenticated by a third party and can enhance the predictability of the accounting. Advertisers who use all of the methods mentioned here can paint the most revealing picture of a certain Web site's activity.

5.8.5 Third-Party Auditing

As more advertisers and agencies go online, more money is spent on marketing. At the request of the advertisers, more and more Web sites—for example, Deja News[64] and Snap[65]—are now being audited through third parties. The

---

[64]http://www.dejanews.com/
[65]http://www.snap.com/

measurement needs to be as precise as possible, since it is used to help the advertisers make the right decisions.

As discussed, the problem is counting the users who sit behind firewalls and access Web sites through proxy servers. Some new software programs promise to solve this problem. I/Pro[66] and MatchLogic[67] are two companies that offer such programs. Both of their solutions are written in Java. You can gain greater control over your customers, but even those systems are not perfect, as they require a Java-enabled browser. Some customers still use older versions of a browser, others just switch off the Java functionality, and some firewalls just don't let Java applets through. These systems are better than nothing, but not good enough to really trust what they have counted.

5.9   One-to-One Marketing

5.9.1   Information Technology

Although we've discussed one-to-one marketing strategies throughout the chapter, this section goes into more detail. A Web site that does not use one-to-one marketing ignores the needs of the customers and won't be successful in the future. Information technology provides electronic businesses with the following possibilities: identification, interaction, differentiation, tracking, and customization. In order to develop a successful one-to-one marketing strategy, these possibilities need to be combined.

The Internet offers many ways to identify a customer, such as using a login and password to enter a certain Web server. Digital certificates can also be used to authenticate a customer; they can be stored in the browser or on a smart card. Browser cookies (personal information stored in the browser) and IP addresses are other means used to identify customers. Once a customer has been authenticated, the server should look up the personal record in the database to add new information about the customer. This helps the company to understand the buying patterns of the customer and to promote products that are of particular interest to specific individuals.

The Internet offers a wide range of communication possibilities, such as interactive chats, email, and newsgroups. These services allow customers to talk to digital businesses fairly easily, but the companies need to respond very quickly, as customers have higher expectations of exchanging ideas with the companies. Back in the Industrial Age, customers were not used to talking to businesses directly. Businesses used to talk to the customers through advertising, but communication between the business and customers was not as direct as the Internet now makes it.

To address the needs of the customers more directly, differentiation is very important, especially if you are a retailer and offer a set of products that you

---

[66]http://www.ipro.com/
[67]http://www.matchlogic.com/

have bought from various manufacturers. In order to differentiate your offerings from the other offerings on the Web, you need to add value to the goods, such as additional free services. You must treat all customers on a personal basis, addressing each customers' values and needs.

Digital business makes it easy to keep track of the customers. This tracking information can be stored in a database and can be used to create special offers on the Web site for a certain user, based on the previous visits to the site. The information that is collected on the Web site can also be used to understand the needs of customers when talking to them in person or via the telephone. Therefore, the information should be available not only to the application that sits on the Web server, but to everyone within the company who is in contact with the customer.

Information technology makes mass-customization easy. Instead of offering a product that appeals to the average customer, the offerings on the Web can be highly customized to the needs of the customer. This is especially easy if your company is offering digital goods such as online services, information, or products. Without computers, customization is impractical and far too expensive, and without the Internet, the customers cannot be reached automatically.

In the near future it will be possible to offer customized software packages to customers. Instead of buying a word processor that includes functions for every type of business, you will order a word processor that suits your needs. You will choose the 20 percent of functionality that is relevant to your business. This will not only reduce the cost for the customer, it will also increase the execution speed of the program and reduce the required memory. Modular design is the key to such products. It is not restricted to software but can be extended to any type of business. Componential design becomes more and more important.

5.9.2   Developing Customer Relationships

As briefly described in Chapter 2, the focus shifts from developing segments of information, products, or services to a target group to servicing individuals, whereby *individuals* may be end customers or businesses. The digital enterprise needs to focus on differentiating customers instead of creating differentiated products.

In the dynamic economy it is no longer possible to sell standard products. The products need to be built dynamically, based on the needs of the individual customer. Traditional companies focus on creating a highly sophisticated product that suits the needs of as many people as possible. The more additional functionality is built in, the larger the market potential may be for a certain product. But this also increases the complexity of the product, which in turn increases the price and the time it takes to understand it.

The one-to-one approach simplifies the use of the products, since only the basic functionality is built in. This reduces the amount of information to read,

In order to develop a successful one-to-one marketing strategy, you need to follow the principles of one-to-one marketing:

- **Identification**—Identify your customers in order to understand the buying patterns for every single customer.

- **Interaction**—Offer your customers automated assistance by preselecting goods, information, and services that may be valuable to a particular customer.

- **Differentiation**—Treat all customers on a personal basis. Address the values and needs of every single customer.

- **Tracking**—In order to understand your customers better, it is necessary to track down every transaction for every individual customer.

- **Customization**—Build product modules, information, parts, and service components that can be adapted to the needs of every single customer.

Table 5.7. One-to-One Marketing Strategies

as only the information that is required is presented; and it reduces the amount of time a service requires, as it only executes the services required by the customer. But this can only be achieved by fully understanding the needs of the customers.

Communication with the customer becomes more important and needs to be refined. Customers nowadays have many means of communicating with a certain company, only a few of which are fax, phone, and email. No matter how a customer contacts the company, the information needs to be brought together into a single database where special programs are able to extract exact customer profiles.

In traditional companies, for every product segment there have been different electronic databases (and other forms of data storage) where the information about customers is stored. Therefore, it was not possible to track the buyer profile throughout the company and offer the customer special offers based on that profile. There was no way to know if the customers tried to contact the company or to whom they talked. The companies were focused on the products and not on the customer relationship.

As Don Peppers and Martha Rogers, leaders in one-to-one marketing, explain it in their book *Enterprise One-To-One*:[68] "The customer base is the primary asset for the companies in the New Economy. The intelligence gathered about the customers enables your company to create the right offer for the right customer at the right time."

5.9.3 Customer-Centric Marketing

In order to provide customer-centric marketing, we need to shift the focus from the business to the customer. In order to be successful, business needs to view every product in the digital age from the customers' perspective. The judgment on the quality of service is shifted from the business to the individual customer. In the one-to-one society, the satisfaction of every single client needs to be measured.

Customer satisfaction is linked to the expectations of a particular customer; these are highly dynamic expectations. If your competitors offer a product at $200, then customers will expect a comparable product from your business in the same price range. If one of the other companies decides to half the price, then you will need to adapt fast; otherwise, you will lose your customers—unless you can convince them that your product quality is much higher.

In order to measure customer satisfaction, it is necessary to put service quality in the context of the competition. If you have the time and the financial resources, then you could even go forward and measure the customers' satisfaction with your competitors' products. The Internet has made it much easier to measure customer satisfaction. Every point along the way that a customer touches can be tracked and collected in a database. Every interaction is an opportunity to delight or disappoint a customer. Asking customers after each step about the satisfaction would be overkill and would annoy customers, but by tracking them quietly, it is possible to gather information on the success or failure of an online venture.

If you have a series of Web pages a customer needs to go through in order to do business with you, you can detect how much time a single customer has spent on every page. This information can be used to find out what is wrong with a certain Web page. Perhaps the purpose of the page is unclear or the design is difficult to understand. The gathered data will tell you which aspects of a given process work well and which ones need to be improved.

Damage control on the Internet is also very important, as we have seen in Chapter 4. A customer who is not satisfied is able to tell thousands of people with a few mouse-clicks. Obviously, keeping customers happy is extremely important and will ensure a steady revenue stream.

Traditionally, three types of customer-satisfaction measurements have been used: the relative importance of attributes, dimensions of customer satisfaction, and added customer value. Table 5.8 explains the types in more depth.

---

[68]Don Peppers and Martha Rogers, *Enterprise One-To-One*, Currency Book Publishers, 1997.

These reports have been issued periodically to keep business managers up-to-date. With the introduction of the Internet, these reports are not produced periodically anymore, but are updated in real time, offering the possibility of dynamically changing the marketing initiative.

Traditionally the following types of customer satisfaction measurement have been used:

- **Attribute importance**—Every service attribute contributes diversely to the overall satisfaction of the customer. Therefore, it is necessary to establish which attributes have which priority for a given customer and try to strengthen the most important attributes first. Every customer will have other priorities, so the system can become quite complicated.

- **Customer satisfaction**—Every dimension of satisfaction gets its own score, which then can be compared to evaluate the strengths and weaknesses of your electronic business. The results can be used to plan quality improvements and launch immediate updates of the service in case of problems. The data can be gathered by evaluating log files and by asking customers to fill in a survey either on the Web or via email.

- **Customer value added**—This index is generated by dividing your business's overall customer satisfaction by the scores of all businesses competing in a certain market segment. This will give you an idea of where your company is positioned in the market.

Table 5.8. Measuring Customer Satisfaction

The value of every business in the future will be twofold and will consist of intellectual property within the company and the customers of the company. The intellectual property will contain a lot of data about the customers; therefore, it is necessary to keep this information up-to-date. The information on the products and services the company offers is also extremely important, as it is needed to refine the manufacturing process for the products and to extend the range of services. Products will become less important in the future; services to the customer will become more important and will resolve the problems of the individual customer.

5.9.4   Advanced Personalization Technologies

In addition to the standard personalization technologies, there is technology known as rules-based filtering. Using this method, the customer needs to answer a set of questions to get the appropriate information presented. The rules can range from the country the users come from (to set up the correct language used) to the specific needs of each customer. A site may ask for a ZIP code or the name of your home town, for example, to find out which local news you may be interested in (or weather, or sports, etc.). It can also involve questions about personal preferences.

A new approach is becoming more popular. Known as *learning agent technologies and collaborative filtering*, it helps you refine the process of customizing a particular Web site to the customers. This technology tries to serve relevant material that may be of interest to customers by combining the preferences of the customer with the preferences of a group with similar interests. This way, customers automatically recommend products, services, and information to others with similar interests. Firefly,[69] for example, is using this technology to create automatic recommendations between users with similar interests. On this Web site, customers are able to rate music on a scale. If Customer One likes music from A and B, and Customer Two likes music from B and C, the system will recommend music from C to Customer One and music from A to Customer Two.

This system is also used by Amazon.com. Once you choose a book, it recommends a set of other books that have been bought by people who also bought that particular book. In order to maximize the one-to-one approach, a mix of several technologies rather than a single method should be used. Offering learning-agent technology in conjunction with rules-based filtering offers the option of guiding the customers while giving them the chance to adjust the guidance to fit their needs even better.

More and more products are becoming available. Some of the better known products can be found in Table 5.9. Some software solutions are able to simply play back data that the user entered, such as the first name of the customer (e.g., "Welcome back, Ralph"). The information collected on the user can also be used to calculate discounts or trigger special offers. The more advanced functionalities of one-to-one marketing include functions such as making suggestions. The idea behind making suggestions can be either up-selling (e.g., "Perhaps you would be more interested in this?") or cross-selling (e.g., "This T-shirt perfectly matches the trousers you've chosen").

One-to-one marketing can go even further by asking the customer a direct question. For example, after buying a car on the Web, the customers could be asked if they need insurance and/or a new license plate. Some companies keep track of all the items purchased and are able to check if new items fit together with the existing equipment. Imagine going back to the computer re-

---

[69]http://www.firefly.net/

More and more companies offer solutions that implement or include one-to-one technologies. A selection of software technologies can be found here.

Product	Description
BroadVision	The high-end tool recognizes customers and displays products and services relevant to that particular customer. **http://www.broadvision.com/**
Cold Fusion	Tool for rapid application development and site design. **http://www.allaire.com/**
Edify	Product specialized for electronic banking solutions. **http://www.edify.com/**
GroupLens	A collaborative filtering solution with rating services for content or products. **http://www.netperceptions.com/**
WebObjects	A framework for developing e-business applications that need to access legacy databases. Provides a strong one-to-one technology to serve data to visitors. **http://www.apple.com/webobjects/**

Table 5.9. One-to-One Technologies

tailer where you bought your Macintosh computer, since you now want to buy a Hewlett-Packard printer to work with the Mac. The online retailer knows what type of computer you have and will be able to show you a list of all Hewlett-Packard printers that are compatible with your computer.

In order to make one-to-one marketing work, business rules need to describe how the automated personalization works. A rules engine is used to solve problems by using facts (e.g., employees of Hewlett-Packard are first-class customers) and rules (e.g., first-class customers get a discount of 15 percent). Facts and rules are contained in a knowledge base. Rules engines and knowledge bases were first created for artificial intelligence systems. They are typically designed to seek out and acquire knowledge. Rules engines can work with information that is incomplete or appears incomplete. This is not usually the case with conventional transaction processing or database systems, so the addition of a rules engine makes the system appear to be more intelligent to the customers.

Even more advanced personalization features are built by a company called Savage Beast,[70] whose application allows consumers to find new music based on songs, albums, artists, and styles they already like—as well as moods, instruments, and more. For example, users can type in the name of a song and the system recommends a series of songs that are similar to that "source song," according to the proprietary matching algorithm and method of analyzing music. The user can then listen to any of these songs, buy a CD, download a song, and/or continue to discover new music.

In recommending songs, the system delivers related information, such as the artist name and album title, and educates the user about the music she or he likes by specifying the most prominent musical qualities of the songs (as determined by trained music analysts). These "focus traits" make the user's experience more engaging and make the music recommendations even more compelling.

Users can steer their search to emphasize one or more of these "focus traits" that are important to them. In response, the system conducts another matching process and delivers a new group of similar songs in which this particular musical quality is prominent. Users can continue this process indefinitely, discovering more and more music that fits their tastes.

As a user interacts with the system, searching for songs, utilizing the focus traits, and buying or downloading songs, the application adapts to the user's musical preferences, creating a unique "taste portrait" that deepens with each visit. Much like voice recognition learns speech patterns, the application learns what matters to each individual through passive or active music taste profiling and becomes a truly personal music guide.

Many companies are trying to provide similar services for products other than music that are based on "focus traits" rather than on technical product features. Setting up such a database is very complex and expensive. It isn't expected that many companies will succeed, but those that do well should do very well, indeed.

5.9.5 Beyond the Internet

The Internet was the first fully customizable medium. Other media, such as TV, radio, and newspapers, are not yet that advanced. TV programs are developed by TV stations and may or may not fit your needs. If you want to see or hear a certain program, you are forced to tune in at the time of broadcast, rather than at your own convenience.

With the imminent introduction of digital TV and radio, consumers will be able to customize programs. Instead of offering a 24-hour program, TV and radio stations will offer building blocks that can be accessed whenever the

---

[70]http://www.savagebeast.com/

customer wants. Instead of having the news update on the hour, the customer may choose to receive it at 20 minutes past the hour. Instead of presenting a program that tries to suit the majority, TV and radio stations will present personalized programs that suit the needs of the individual.

Newspapers will most likely become individualized in the near future. The first step will be to offer an updated version of the newspaper at any time of day. For example, in Germany, the newspapers on trains and planes are printed out onboard so that they are always up-to-date. Instead of issuing a newspaper daily, hourly updates will become possible. Individualizing the newspaper will be the next logical step. When subscribing to a newspaper, you will eventually choose which type of information is interesting to you. This is a novel idea, since few people have time to read through a complete newspaper.

It will be very difficult to customize books, but eventually it will become possible. One variable will be the type of book a person will buy. A book on e-business may become customizable—it will be 100 pages with high-level information for managers, or 600 pages with in-depth information for technical people. Some additional information from the customer would most likely be needed, but it would make one book customizable for very specific needs and reduce the time for people to find the right information.

5.10 Direct Marketing

5.10.1 Spam

Direct marketing on the Internet is powerful, but it is important you are careful not to misuse the power. Sending out an email to millions of people has become very simple, but although this brute force method may sometimes be effective, it is not good for legitimate businesses.

If you send out 5 million emails, you may reach 10,000 people who may be interested—which is perhaps more than you could reach with traditional methods—but you will have 4.99 million angry users. Unsolicited email can be compared to unsolicited faxes. Maybe just 5 percent of the 4.99 million users start to complain back to your company that they did not want to receive information from you, but this would result in 249,500 complaints, which is far too many to be able to detect the 10,000 who were really interested in your products or services.

The behavior of sending out millions of emails is called *spamming*. Spam is the term used to refer to any commercial mass email used to advertise or solicit business or participation in a multilevel marketing program. These emails are often anonymously mailed to thousands of recipients at a time. The senders usually ask the recipient to buy a product or service of some kind, or participate in a get-rich-quick scheme. The senders do not ask their recipients beforehand if they want to receive such mail. Spam mail is often referred to as bulk email, unsolicited email or junk email.

Spammers collect email addresses from various sources, such as newsgroup postings, Web pages, or mailing lists. Spam offering lists with up to 10 million email addresses are available for just $500. As these addresses are collected automatically by special programs, it's probably safe to assume that at least half of them are invalid.

Spammers also buy email addresses from Web sites that sell membership lists to anyone willing to pay. This is one way they keep their services free. Make sure you always check a site's privacy statement before submitting personal information. If they don't have one, don't sign up. Some other spammers use software that generates random and semi-random sequences of letters and numbers and pairs them with common email domain names. This generates even more traffic, since most emails are returned because the addresses are invalid.

The following rules help you with your direct marketing offensive:

- **Audience**—On the Internet, the audience targets you and not the other way around.

- **Clarification**—Question and confirm any message that appears to contain a critical mistake in typing.

- **Cross-borders**—The Internet is open to any culture and nation. Be sure not to offend your target audience.

- **Customers**—Use one-to-one marketing technologies to gain information on your customers.

- **Lists**—Don't rent or sell customer lists without written permission.

- **Log files**—Don't rely on Web server log files. Try to find more meaningful data.

- **Privacy**—Privacy is important. Treat any personal information as confidential.

- **Spam**—Never misuse email for spam; it provokes more anger than positive responses.

Table 5.10. Direct Marketing Rules

Most people consider spamming to be very rude. *Netiquette*, a set of behavior rules for the Internet, condemns the activities of spammers. Legislation in the U.S. and in Europe has not decided yet how to handle spam. There has been a lot of activity in the courts, but there is no clear guideline in sight. So far, most countries in Asia, Africa, and South America have no regulations on spam.

The true problem is the large majority of people do not know why they received a certain email. Many offers are cleverly written, as if they were sent to the wrong recipient. These emails normally contain tips for online or phone services that cost a lot of money. As a rule of thumb, don't reply to such email; it just confirms to the spammer that your email address is valid and someone is naive enough to respond. Never buy anything from spammers, no matter how good the offer seems to be. Spammers use false email addresses in most cases. They cannot be trusted; otherwise, they would have a Web page or a shop somewhere, where people could get more information on the products and services. And even if the spam contains a valid Web site, you should send an email to the ISP of the spammer, typically abuse@isp.com.

Most spammers use either completely false addresses or email addresses from free Web-based email services, which cannot be easily traced back to the sender. The worst thing that can happen is that the account of the user will be closed down, but it takes only minutes to set up a new one with the same or a similar service.

One of the most prominent spammers is Sanford "Spamford" Wallace, who also fought in court for his right to use spam for marketing activities. He was famous for sending out email to millions of people—so much that complete networks broke down. Spamming activities have decreased over the last few years, as more antispamming tools and new legislation have become available in the U.S. and across Europe.

Just before Christmas 1998, my father's account was put on hold because someone was using it to "promote" casinos on the Internet. During the holidays no one was available to explain to us why the account was put on hold. It took five days, several emails, and a phone call to reactivate his Internet connection. Spamming activities are monitored on the Internet, so the Internet accounts of people who do spam will be closed down immediately. In our case someone broke into the account and used it to appear as someone else (my father) on the Internet. This is sometimes called *spoofing*.

In order to get rid of spam, you need to inform your ISP about the spam you have received. You should also send a copy of the spam to the sender's domain.

A little example will demonstrate what needs to be done. Let's say your email is danny@danny.cn (sending e-mail to this address won't do much, as I haven't got an Internet account in China, and the domain name is not registered at the time of writing). You have received spam from spam@spam.org. You should forward the mail that you have received to postmaster@danny.cn and postmaster@spam.org; in addition, send mail to the user "abuse" at these domains. These two postmasters may be able to trace where the email origi-

```
Hello Folks,
Making Money Could Never Get Easier!
GET EXCITED!!  XXX launched 27 Feb.  Check out the
FASTEST growing Internet Marketing on the Internet.  If
YOU ever wished you were at the beginning of the other
successful online marketing ventures!
NOW is your chance to get in early.
XXX started promoting in the Major Magazine's and USA
Today!!
All spillovers, will go to your downlines.
DON"T GET LEFT BEHIND!!!!!
For more information, click on lower email address and
send itToday!!!
Committed to your Success!
```

Table 5.11. Typical Spam

nated and can then ban the user from the Internet. If the spam contains illegal activities—such as a pyramid scheme or phony investment offers—you should contact the appropriate law enforcement authorities.

The easiest route, however, is to just delete spam. Check your email program to see if it has spam-blocking or message filter capabilities so you can have it automatically delete the junk. This is probably easier than trying to stop it from coming in.

Have a look at Table 5.11 for an example of spam (it includes all the original misspellings). This example shows what type of unwanted messages arrive in mailboxes every day. Typical for spam are sentences written completely in uppercase to get the attention of the reader. Writing sentences in uppercase is like shouting at people and is considered rude in netiquette. References to well-known institutions such as *USA Today*[71] are added to lend credibility to the offering.

Email advertising is still possible using an opt-in mailing service. The opt-in email advertising distribution is a viable option to attain your target market. Unlike spam, an opt-in list sends email only to persons who asked to receive email about that particular subject.

---

[71]http://www.usatoday.com/

5.10.2   Mailing Lists and Newsletters

Fortunately, there are other ways of using direct marketing on the Internet. It is extremely important that you provide free information about your products and services to your customers. This can be done via mailing lists, newsletters, newsgroups and chat areas. Just remember, the customers must agree to have their email used for newsletters, and nobody should be forced to subscribe to a newsgroup or a mailing list.

Although email and chat rooms have been around for quite some time, they are still the most used applications on the Internet. They are trusted applications that are simple to use by virtually anyone who is online. Although many companies offer products that allow one-to-one marketing on the Web, email was always destined for that kind of business. Customizing emails is much easier than a complex Web site.

Email discussion lists and newsletters are explained easily. These emails are normally focused around one topic so people can read news, comments, and information provided by other participants of the discussion list. The main difference between the discussion lists and newsletters is that a discussion list has participation from its subscribers, while a newsletter is more of a one-way editorial product. There are discussion lists and newsletters for almost every imaginable business and consumer interest. One such mailing list is the Bugtraq[72] mailing list, which talks about bugs on UNIX systems.

Once you have signed up, you will receive email sent by subscribers to a special address then forwarded to all subscribers. Anybody who is signed up is able to send in a submission. Some lists also have a moderator who sifts through the incoming messages and sends them on to the subscribers only if appropriate. The email traffic created by mailing lists can vary from a few each day to hundreds each day. When Netscape put up its Mozilla[73] site, I subscribed to the Mozilla mailing list and received up to 500 emails a day. This was overkill. There were too many people who sent out emails without any value to me. So I signed off that particular list. The Mozilla people recognized the problem and split up the mailing list into several subtopics, which were more specific and produced less garbage. In addition to this, a gateway between mailing lists and newsgroups has been established in order to support push and pull from the users.

The push technology used in this case is the mailing list that sends all messages on to all subscribed users. The pull technology is the newsgroup where users can go, choose interesting topics, and read them. Asking a question works similarly; it can be either sent to the mailing list or posted in the newsgroup. The subscriber to the mailing list will receive all answers automatically, while the newsgroup reader must actively go back to the newsgroup and check for answers.

---

[72]http://www.bugtraq.com/
[73]http://www.mozilla.org/

Newsletters, on the other hand, are written by the maintainer of the mailing list or by several authors, and then are collected by the maintainer. The newsletter is sent out periodically: each day, each week, or each month. The topic of the newsletter is also very specific. Back issues of newsletters can normally be retrieved at their respective Web sites.

By setting up mailing lists and newsletters about a certain topic, you do appear as a person qualified in that particular topic. You may help your user group to better understand one of your products or services. If you offer a forum for your customers, make sure that a qualified person is on the list as a moderator to represent your company.

It is also useful to be on mailing lists created by others. By contributing helpful information, you can establish yourself and your company as qualified experts. This does not automatically increase your business, but maybe someone will remember your expertise and come back to you in the future.

Implementing such a discussion list or creating a newsletter is quite simple and does not cost anything, as you already have the infrastructure in place to serve it. All you need to invest is time and some ideas. Before starting up your own newsletter or mailing list, subscribe to some other mailing lists in order to learn how such a service works.

Mailing lists and newsletters do not have to be free, but keep in mind that if you send out information customers have to pay for, it is highly possible they will send it on to colleagues and friends without paying for another copy. The enforcement of copyright laws is too expensive if your document is sold at a very low price.

5.10.3 The Power of Email

Email can be used to promote your services and products. Just be sure not to create spam. Using more subtle methods will have a much greater effect. One of these methods is to use a signature file for every email that is sent out. Signatures are tolerated on all mailing lists, newsgroups, and ordinary email, if you stick to the conventions. The signature should be separated from the mail by adding a line with two dashes (i.e., --). The signature should not be longer than two lines. Put your name and your business into the signature, include your Web site address, and you can promote your business without harassing anybody. Table 5.12 contains a sample signature. By contributing useful answers in newsgroups, you can very effectively and gently plug your business. It may make sense to create different signature files for different media or target groups, such as different newsgroups or mailing lists. Avoid larger signatures, as they annoy many readers. Although adding graphics may be fun for you, it does not necessarily add value for the readers.

Autoresponders are also a very helpful application for your business. For example, if people need a price list for a certain service or information on a certain product, then they may choose to go to a Web site or send an email to

```
Dear Fred,

By holding the mouse button pressed over the back
button of your browser, you will see a list of the
previously visited sites, which makes it easier to jump
back more than one site.

I hope this helps,

Danny
--
Danny Amor, Kangaroo Management Centre Ltd.,
Visit http://www.kamacltd.cz/ or send mail to
info@kamacltd.cz.
```

Table 5.12. Example of newsgroup posting with signature.

a certain address and receive the information via email. Although this may not seem to be helpful, it actually is. Sometimes information on Web sites is divided up into several sections that make it difficult to grab the information and put it into a document. By offering autoresponders, it is possible for customers to request information in text format without formatting for the Web and graphics. If customers send queries in the form of email to your customer care department, an automated mail should respond and tell them that the email has arrived. And don't forget to put in the URL of your FAQ page, as it may help the customers in finding a response to their question before a human being from the customer care department is able to respond to their email.

You also have better control over your content by offering back issues of a newsletter via autoresponder. It is then possible to track down all users who are interested in it. You can use this information to offer them a subscription to the newsletter and other products or services you might offer. All these pieces of information must be in the same mail as the newsletter. Do not start sending dozens of emails to your customer base. If users request one piece of electronic mail, don't upset them with mail flooding.

Any email arriving in your inbox should be confirmed. If the mail appears to include a critical mistake in typing, it should be questioned by sending back a confirmation mail. Email messages do not convey voice tones, body postures, or other nontextual cues; therefore it is difficult to find out if the content should be taken literally.

Some email contains *emoticons*, such as :-), but they may be misunderstood if the other party involved does not know about the meaning of these symbols. An emoticon (or smiley face) is a sequence of ordinary characters that you can find on your keyboard arranged to express an emotion. Table 5.13 contains some of the more popular emoticons. For a very complete list, look at the Web site of Smilies Unlimited[74] or check with your favorite search engine for more information.

As it is difficult to express emotions on the Internet, emoticons have been invented. The following list shows some of the most common emoticons.

:-) Laughing. Joking. Being satisfied.

:) Laughing. Joking. Being satisfied. For lazy people without noses.

:-(Crying out loud. Sad. You aren't joking. You are not satisfied.

;-) Winking Smiley. You don't mean it; you are joking.

:-> Follows a really sarcastic remark.

(-: Left-handed Smiley.

:-* Kissing Smiley.

Table 5.13. Emoticons

5.10.4   Opt-in Mailing Lists

A special type of newsletter is the opt-in mailing list, already mentioned briefly. It provides consumers with specific product or service information on request. Unlike spam, the customers have expressed interest in receiving the information. Companies often ask for your email address before you are allowed to download a piece of information or a file. A small check box is usually provided that allows the request of additional information. In many cases it is already checked, meaning that without additional interaction, you will be put onto these opt-in mailing lists.

---

[74]http://www.czweb.com/smilies.htm

The major difference between opt-in and spam is that addresses that have been passed on to opt-in mailing list owners are used for only one purpose. Spam mailers reuse the same set of email addresses for any type of product or service, abusing the idea of email. Opt-in mailing lists have become the standard for customer-oriented mass mailings on the Internet. It is the only form of mass-mailing that is tolerated by customers and governments around the world.

5.10.5   Building an Email Address Database

In order to reach out to new customers, you need to know who is online and how they can be reached. A list of people who want to hear from you and your company needs to be built up. The problem is how to convince the people to give you their email addresses and to prove to them that you are not sending rubbish, but some useful information instead.

Getting people to your site is relatively easy, but convincing them to come back is the more difficult task. Sending a short email to the visitors as a little reminder may help. Customers who have used your services or bought your products are much more willing to buy another service or product from your company, because they already know you and trust your company and the products and services you manufacture, sell, or rent.

The trouble is getting hold of the email address and the permission of the recipient. One of the simplest ways of collecting email addresses is to have a link to an info mailer in your company (e.g., info@yourcompany.com). Invite people to send messages to this address.

Adding some type of interaction with your Web site makes it easier to convince people to leave their email addresses with you. The quicker the action and the simpler it is to use, the more people will use it. Offer the chance to receive updates on the Web site or offer a free catalog or sample of your product or service in exchange for the email address. Newsletters and mailing lists automatically show the email addresses of the participants. Be careful, though. Many people won't give out their addresses if you do not state clearly what you intend to do with them. Again, your privacy policy should be accessible from every page.

Another way to receive email from customers is to ask for their opinions. Either have a set of yes or no questions or request specific input. The customers can express their opinions on a given topic, such as a product or the Web site itself.

Surveys are another way to receive information on the users—and their addresses. As surveys tend to be more complex, offer something in return, like the results of the survey or a free sample of a product.

Once you have collected a certain number of email addresses, you need to decide what to do with them. You need to find a piece of software that allows you to manage the mailing list. Every time you send out a message to your subscribers, try to tell them something that is useful to them, in addition to asking for information that is useful to you.

5.11   Choosing the Right ISP

5.11.1   Direct Access to Your Company

Another important issue to consider for your online marketing activities is where your Web pages are hosted. Some companies have a direct connection to the Internet via a leased line; others use dial-up lines. Since dial-up lines create only temporary connections, most companies prefer to have an ISP host their Web pages.

No matter where your Web pages are hosted, you need to be sure that you have direct access to them 24 hours a day, seven days a week. As we learned in Chapter 4 in the section "Developing a Dark Site," changing the information whenever necessary is vital for your company. This applies not only to emergency situations, but also to new products to announce breaking news or changes within your company. The worst thing that can happen is that news about your company is discovered on your competitor's Web site before it is available on your own.

There are some minimum requirements that you should ask from your ISP, no matter if the ISP connects your existing or planned networking infrastructure to the Internet or hosts the Web pages and your email accounts only (see also 5.14). You need to ask your ISP to provide you with information on the reliability of the service. Your connection must be available 24 hours a day, seven days a week. In your contract you need to define how much downtime is acceptable for your company per year and what the ISP is willing to pay if the service is down for a longer period. If this is not defined, you and your company may run into financial trouble once your online business has become the portal to your company and something goes wrong with the Web site.

5.11.2   Dial-up Connections

A dial-up connection is suitable for companies that have outsourced their Web activities and require Internet connection for downloading mail and accessing some Web pages daily. With this style of connection, you use a modem and existing phone lines to reach an ISP. There are thousands of ISPs that provide dial-up access to the Internet. The cost for a dial-up connection ranges from $15 to $30, depending on the type of connection you want. Analog modems and ISDN connections do not differ in access cost. The List[75] contains a very large list of providers on a global basis. ISPs can be searched for by country, state, or area code.

---

[75]http://thelist.internet.com/

When choosing an ISP, check out the following:

- **Reliability**—An ISP should be up and running more than 99.9 percent of the time.

- **Performance**—Don't believe the marketing hype of the ISPs. Get performance data from third parties.

- **Tech support**—Establish the ISP as your partner. Create strong links between your company and the ISP.

- **Price**—Price is not everything. Look for an ISP that offers complete service.

Table 5.14. Choosing an ISP

Before picking an ISP in the United States, you should check if the ISP has a point of presence (POP) in your town or near enough to allow you to make a local phone call, so only the cost for the ISP would need to be paid. In Europe and most other parts of the world, the phone cost needs to be added.

Another important issue with dial-up is the availability of the service. It does not help if the service is very cheap but the line is busy all the time and you cannot get through. A good ISP will never have a busy line. Once you have decided on an ISP, pick up the phone and dial the phone number of the Internet access several times a day during the times when you hope to get online. This will help to ensure that you made the right decision.

Most ISPs offer additional services, such as additional email addresses and free Web hosting. Although useful, this is not really necessary, as you can get these services for free on the Internet. If you do not need your own domain name, then it will be sufficient to have access to the Internet; however, once your company Web site is up and running, all your employees will get an email address belonging to your domain. The Web site may not necessarily be hosted by the ISP that grants you access to the Internet. Often, local access and Web hosting are provided by two different companies. The Internet makes it easy to choose a company on the other side of the globe to provide Web hosting. This may be much cheaper than a local provider.

5.11.3 Leased Lines

Organizations with a significant number of employees requiring access to the Internet for their email and the Web will be more interested in a dedicated line.

This will give them constant access to the Internet, which may be cheaper in the end if a lot of traffic is generated throughout the day.

Many companies start with a dedicated line consisting of two ISDN b channels, giving your company a maximum of 128 kilobytes per second. Although this speed is good enough to handle email and some Web access, it will break down as soon as you get more than 20 people who are heavily browsing the Web. A local Web cache and proxy will help you to reduce the amount of traffic that is generated, but you won't get around the fact that you will need at least a T1 connection, which provides up to 1.5 Mb/sec of throughput. The ISP charges a flat monthly rate for the connection, which includes their fee and the cost of a dedicated line from your location to their nearest POP. The dedicated line will usually be provided by the local phone carrier. Most ISPs will be able to arrange this for you.

To be sure that your provider does not become the bottleneck in your Internet connection, you should only consider those ISPs that have significant backbone capacities and that are directly connected to the Internet's Network Access Points, or NAPs. Although there are many ISPs available, very few operate their own high-speed backbone networks. The other ISPs are connected to these backbones via larger ISPs. Choosing the right ISP will guarantee you the best speed possible. This can be done by examining their backbone network. It just does not make any sense to buy a dedicated line from an ISP that is not capable of passing through the traffic fast enough. Therefore, ask your ISP to provide you with a backbone diagram showing you how its POPs are connected to the backbone. This allows you to understand how your connection enters into the backbone and how your traffic will be routed to other parts of the Internet.

The ISP should provide you with the required hardware to set up the leased line, such as a preconfigured router that only needs to be switched on to enable Internet connectivity. The ISP should also offer you a selection of security products, such as firewalls to protect your company intranet, which you make vulnerable by a direct Internet connection. Although it costs less to operate a firewall yourself, you may not be in the position to do this because of missing knowledge or resources, just as with Web hosting. Because of the dedicated line, you would be able to handle the Web site yourself, except where resources are missing.

5.11.4   Performance Issues

The performance of your provider needs to be excellent for your services and for the connection of your customers. Don't be misled by ISPs offering 155 Mb/sec connections. 155 Mb/sec is very fast, but do you really know how many customers share the bandwidth of 155 Mb/sec at the same time? If there are 10,000 customers hooked up to the line, the average speed will drop to 0.0155 Mb/sec (or 16 Kb/sec). If you have 10 concurrent visitors, each of them will get an average of 1.6 Kb/sec (normal modems did 56 Kb/sec at the time of this writing). In most cases some people will get higher connection rates and others won't get through to the server at all. This can disrupt your service and will anger your customers.

The ISP should also be connected directly to an Internet backbone, which allows much higher transfer rates. Remember, the more computers in between the ISP and the backbone, the slower the connection will be.

The ISP should also offer good tech support, via both telephone and Internet. In your company you need someone who understands the issues of connecting to the Internet, and this person needs a counterpart on the ISP side. Select one from your staff and one from the ISP staff to act as a team. Most problems with your Internet connectivity can be resolved only if both parties involved solve the problem together.

5.11.5   Keeping Internet Costs Low

There are numerous cheap offerings, but in most cases, some extra money for higher quality services is well invested. ISPs should also be able to help you implement your business strategy. Check out if your ISP offers more than just pure hosting and connectivity. Some ISPs offer to increase traffic to your site by submitting it to search engines or directories. If you have to pay for it, stay away from these offers. Good ISPs submit your URL to at least some of the most popular search engines for free.

If you are not able to calculate the monthly costs for your Internet connection because an ISP has a very complicated pricing structure, then there may be many hidden costs involved. Always ask for flat-rate fees. These prices may seem to be higher, but in many cases they turn out to be cheaper in the end. Many companies forget to add the costs for the telephone company. Although this may not be an issue in the U.S., it is certainly one in other countries where telephone is a business on a pay-per-use basis, not only for long-distance calls, but for all calls, except for emergency calls.

Dial-up connections are not useful in most cases. A leased line will have higher initial costs, but the monthly costs are much lower and are fixed. The costs for dial-up connections cannot be calculated in advance, so expect the highest price possible. If your dial-up connections costs 5 cents a minute, the maximum costs are $5 \times 60 \times 24 \times 30 = 216,000$ cents (or \$2,160). Of course, you would not expect to use the line 24 hours a day, but don't be surprised if your costs are in this range every month.

While this chapter is mainly on marketing topics, this section provided a very brief overview of base technologies of the Internet, which are of use for the marketing group. The next chapters focus more on the application levels of Internet technologies. This quickly leads to business models, which should be the basis for every technology decision. Today, many decisions about e-business are made based on technologies without evaluating the value for the business.

This can create large problems later on. E-business is not possible without the technologies presented in this chapter, but should not be driven by these factors. The technology is merely the vehicle, not the driver.

Part II

E-Business Applications

Chapter 6

SEARCH ENGINES
AND PORTALS

6.1 Searching the Internet

6.1.1 Finding Something on the Net

Searching for information on the Internet is difficult for many people, so this section explains how search engines work and how to find the item that you are looking for. For your online business, it is very important to understand how search engines search and how people try to look for certain things on the Internet.

Some people who use a Web browser just enter a keyword where the URL is normally entered. Sometimes this leads to good results. The reasons are explained easily. If you enter a word into a newer Web browser, the browser first adds http:// to it and tries to find a Web page. If that does not work, it adds .com at the end and then www. after the http://. So entering "motorcycles" will lead you eventually to http://www.motorcycles.com/, which leads to the Honda Web site in the U.S. If you're searching for Harley Davidson motorcycles, then you could enter "Harley-Davidson" and the browser would expand the name to http://www.harley-davidson.com/, which leads you to the Web site of the Harley Davidson manufacturer. Some older browsers do not support the expansion of keywords, so people need to add these attributes manually, but adding http://www. and .com to the keyword is not that difficult. That was the reason why, in the early years, so many people registered domain names without using them; they had recognized the value they would have in the future.

Web browsers have a built-in feature that tries to guess what you are trying to achieve if you enter an incorrect URL. This feature is used by a new service called HTTP2.[1] It seems to have invented a new protocol for transferring information between a Web server and a Web browser, but in reality it does something completely different. You can go to the HTTP2 Web site and

---

[1]http://www.http2.com/

register a domain name that uses http2// instead of http://. The trick is that HTTP2 omits the colon. So if you have a site registered at HTTP2, the URL may look like this: http2//ebusiness. The idea of HTTP2 is exploiting a feature of most browsers: if it does not find an address http://http2//ebusiness, it expands it to http://www.http2.com//ebusiness, which is then redirected to the site you have registered at HTTP2.

If you are looking for a specific item, just type in the name and see if there is a Web site with the corresponding information. If there is no such Web site, then try out brand names associated with your search. If you are living in Germany and require information on ties (Krawatte is a tie in German), you could try http://www.krawatte.de/ and you will go to an online shop that sells ties and gives information on how to use ties properly. If you are interested in getting more information on Philips products in the Netherlands, you could try http://www.philips.nl/ and you will land on the Web site of Philips consumer products. Ferrari fans in Italy go to http://www.ferrari.it/ in order to buy merchandise or become a member in the Ferrari fan or owners clubs. Depending on the country you live in, you will have other ideas how to find your information. Some companies, especially smaller-to-medium enterprises, prefer to use the top-level domain (TLD) of the country of origin. As a rule of thumb, American companies use mainly .com; all others may use it, but not necessarily. If you search for a company in France, first try .fr as the suffix.

Most search engines on the Web have a basic search form and also a more complex search functionality that allows more in-depth search. Most search engines allow Boolean operations by combining terms using AND, OR, or NOT. If you want all words to be present in a document you are looking for, you can link the keywords with the AND command. If you use OR, any one of the keywords can be present in the document you are looking for. By using NOT, you are able to exclude words that you do not want to appear in the search results. If you do not give any Boolean expression, most search engines will default to OR.

Some search engines allow the use of + and -, which basically allow you to perform the same actions as the Boolean expressions. A + preceding a term means that it must be present in the search result. A - means that you do not want it to be present.

In addition to these standard search features, it is possible to truncate words and use an asterisk (*) as a wildcard to complete the word and find multiple forms of a given word. Using quotes around several words, it is possible to specify that words must appear next to each other in retrieved items. These advanced search tips vary from search engine to search engine. Before using any search engine, it is helpful to read the FAQ of the search engine you are going to use. The search results are much more exact, and the amount of time required for searching is reduced significantly.

6.1.2   Different Types of Search Engines

If you do not find the required information using the search tips from the previous section, then you need to consult an online service to find the piece of information you are looking for. Three different types of services have been established over the years: crawlers, directories, and metasearch engines.

The first crawler was created back in 1993. It was called the World Wide Worm. It crawled from one site to the next and indexed all pages by saving the content of the Web pages into a huge database. Crawlers (or spiders) visit a Web page, read it, and then follow links to other pages within the site and even follow links to other sites. Web crawlers return to each site on a regular basis, such as every month or two, to look for changes. Everything a crawler finds goes into a database that people are able to query.

The advantage of the Web crawlers is that they have an extensive database with almost the complete Internet indexed in it. The disadvantage is that you get thousands of Web pages as a response for almost any request.

Web directories work a little differently. First of all, they contain a structured tree of information. All information entered into this tree is either entered by a Webmaster who wants to announce his new Web page or by the directory maintainer who reviews the Web pages submitted. The directories where Webmasters can submit both the URL and the description often contain misleading information, as the information is not checked by anyone.

If the directory is screened by the maintainer, getting listed in most Web directories is a combination of luck and quality. Although anyone is able to submit a Web site, there is no guarantee that it will be included, as the maintainer decides what is suitable and what is not. For the webmaster, this decision is difficult to understand, as no explanation is provided about why a site has been accepted or not. Some directories charge for submission, which is basically a rip off.

Some crawlers maintain an associated directory. If your site is in the directory, the ranking of your Web site normally will be higher, as it is already preclassified. Many directories work together with crawlers in order to deliver results when nothing can be found in the directory.

Metasearch engines do not have a database with URLs and descriptions. Instead, they have a database of search engines. If you enter your keywords into a metasearch engine, it will send out requests to all the directories and crawlers it has stored in its database. The metasearch engines, with more sophisticated applications in the background, are able to detect double URLs that come back from the various search engines, and present only a single URL to the customer.

6.1.3   Net Robots

In the early stages of the Internet, Web surfing was a nice hobby, and you could choose from a handful of useful Web addresses. But with the growth of the Internet, it has become more difficult to find the right information through simple browsing. Programs that behave like Web browsers are far more efficient; they browse through the information and store the content at the same time in a form that makes it easy to retrieve afterward. These programs are called crawlers, robots, or spiders.

A robot retrieves a document and then retrieves recursively all documents linked to that particular document. While traversing the document, the robot indexes the information according to predefined criteria. The information goes into searchable databases. Internet users are then able to query these databases to retrieve certain information. The robots crawl the Internet 24 hours a day and try to index as much information as possible.

In order to keep the databases up-to-date, the robots revisit links in order to verify they are still up and running. Dead links happen when users move information or give up their online presence. In this case the information in the database needs to be removed.

Some specialized robots wander around and collect information for statistical analysis, such as the NetCraft[2] (see Figure 6.1) robot that collects information on the Web servers used on the Internet.

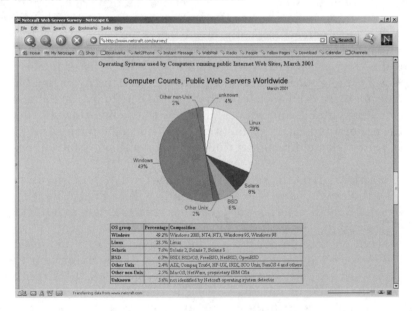

Figure 6.1. Result of the NetCraft robot.

Other robots perform site mirroring activities. Software archives, for example, are mirrored on a daily basis to reduce the load on a single server and spread it out to many servers on the Internet. Another reason to use software

---

[2]http://www.netcraft.co.uk/

archives is that it is easier to copy the new information once and then make it available to customers in a special country, instead of letting them download the information from a far more distant server. Tucows,[3] a software archive, uses this technology to mirror shareware and freeware programs throughout the world in order to guarantee fast download times for every user.

The Robots Exclusion Standard defines how robots should behave on the Web and how you can prevent robots from visiting your site. Although these rules cannot be enforced, most Internet robots do adhere to this standard. If you want robots to ignore some of the documents on your Web server (or even all documents on the Web server), you need to create a file called `robots.txt`, placed in the root directory of the Web site. You can go to any Web site and try to see if there is a `robots.txt` available (just try http://www.gallery-net.com/robots.txt, for example). A sample `robots.txt` could look like this:

```
User-agent:  *
Disallow:  /cgi-bin/
```

This simple file disallows access to the `/cgi-bin/` directory for all (marked by the asterisk) robots scanning the site. By protecting the `/cgi-bin/` directory, you make sure that no documents from that directory are read by robots and prevent these documents from appearing in search engine results.

Table 6.1. The Robots Exclusion Standard

Crawlers perform a very useful task, but they consume a lot of bandwidth, which can create frustration for the end user. Crawlers with programming errors can also create unwanted *denial of service* attacks on certain Web servers, as they are trying to retrieve information at a rate of speed that is far too high for that server. But the major problem is the lack of intelligence. A crawler can't really decide which information is relevant and which isn't. Therefore, combining Web crawler results with results from online directories will give the end customers the best search results.

There are also some problems with robot technology on the Internet. Certain implementations of robots have willingly or unwillingly overloaded networks and servers in the past. Some robots had bugs and started to flood servers with requests; other robots have been tuned intentionally to behave like this. Human interaction can also be a problem, as a human may miscon-

---

[3]http://www.tucows.com/

figure a robot or not understand what impact the configuration will have for contacted servers.

Although there are several problems, you can protect your site by implementing the Robots Exclusion Standard on your Web page (see Table 6.1). Still, most robots are managed well, cause no problems, and offer a valuable service to the Internet community.

6.1.4   Using a Search Engine

The use of search engines is actually very simple. You are normally provided with a text field, where you enter your keywords. These are extremely important. Get your keywords right and they'll bring you the information you need. It is best to start with general keywords and then add details.

For example, if you are looking for camp sites in Italy, try using the keywords "Camping Italy." Then, if this does not produce a useful response, add some more details like the region—"Camping Italy Tuscany Pisa Beach." The more keywords you add, the fewer results you will get (in some cases you won't get any results, so retry with some other keywords or fewer keywords). Also try keywords in different languages (e.g., Toskana, Toscana instead of Tuscany, or Italien, Italia instead of Italy). This is often very useful, but has the disadvantage that you may need to speak that particular language to understand the Web page.

Determining which search engine suits your needs best depends on your requirements. It also depends on the quality of the material you want to gather. If you need a large number of Web pages with many different aspects of the desired topic, then go for the crawlers. You can collect the information and use data mining procedures to evaluate the content. If you prefer only a few quality pages, then go for the directories, and if you need a mixture of both, then go for the metasearches. Use local search machines instead of global ones if you are searching for country-specific or language-specific information.

Finding the Web pages of relatives and friends is easy. Just use any of the above-described search engines and enter the first and last name as keywords. Provide additional information like the names of the kids, the street address, or anything else you connect to the person. If a person has a home page, you normally will find the email address on that page. If the person does not have a homepage, you can look up email addresses on email search engines.

In order to find a telephone number, check first on the home page. If the person has an email address, send an email and ask. Otherwise, have a look in the telephone directories on the Internet.

Finding all different types of files is easy. If you know the producer or distributor, then go to the appropriate home page. For example, patches for Photoshop can be found at Adobe's Web site. New levels of the game "Worms" can be downloaded from the Web site of Team17.[4] If you are looking for shareware,

---

[4]http://www.team17.com/

freeware, or public domain programs, then go to one of the program search engines.

6.1.5 Adding Information to Search Engines

Web sites need to be announced in order to appear in the search engine results. Therefore, the Webmaster has to go to the search engine and submit the URL. Depending on the type of search engine, either a human being or a computer will look at your Web page and decide if it will be added to the database. It takes a few seconds for a crawler to look at all your pages and store the relevant information into the database. A directory will need up to a month to check out your Web pages. Submitting the URL to every single search engine will take up too much time, so some people started developing submission tools. Most of them want a lot of money for submission, but some are free, such as the Broadcaster[5] service in the UK.

Chapter 5 contains more information on submitting URLs to search engines. In this section, we will concentrate on the way search engines classify a Web page. Most search engines first look at the number of appearances of a certain keyword on a given Web page. The next thing they look for is if the keyword appears in the domain name (such as www.keyword.com) or in the URL (such as http://www.blahblah.com/keyword/bla.html). Then, the search engine checks the title of Web page and looks to see if it can spot the keyword there. The important thing is the metadata that you can add to every Web page (see next section). If the search engine is able to find a particular keyword in every field mentioned here, the page will be classified as very useful to the customer.

Professor Attardi[6] at the University of Pisa[7] developed a methodology for search engines to weigh the relevance of Web pages. The first search engine to implement this methodology was Arianna[8] in Italy. In addition to the above-mentioned requirements, it counts the number of links pointing to a given Web page. The more people link to a certain Web page, the more important and relevant it is. This helps in presenting the most relevant pages first.

Having an affiliate network that points back to your company, therefore, will result in much higher relevance for your company compared to all your affiliates, as there is no link between each of the affiliates.

6.1.6 Adding Value through Metadata

By adding metadata to every single HTML document on your Web site, you enhance the probability that a search engine shows your page for a given request. The metadata is stored in metatags. Metatags contain information that

---

[5] http://www.broadcaster.co.uk/

[6] http://www.di.unipi.it/~attardi/

[7] http://www.unipi.it/

[8] http://www.arianna.it/

is not rendered visible by the browser, but that contains additional information on the document, such as information on the content, the author, the software that was used to create the document, or the keywords that are relevant on that particular page. The <meta> tag is used within the <head> tag to embed document metainformation not defined by other HTML elements. The META element is used to identify properties of a document (e.g., author, expiration date, a list of key words, etc.) and assign values to those properties. At least two metatags should be present on all pages: description and keywords (see also 6.2).

The following example shows how metatags could be used on a Web page about FlashPix. Four metatags are used:

- **Author**—The author of the content.

- **Generator**—The program used to create the Web page.

- **Description**—A short description of the content.

- **Keywords**—Keywords related to the content.

```
<HEAD>
<META HTTP-EQUIV="Content-Type" CONTENT="text/html; charset=iso-8859-1">
<META NAME="Author" CONTENT="Daniel Amor: daniel_amor@hp.com">
<META NAME="Generator" CONTENT="BBEdit 4.5">
<META NAME="Description" CONTENT="This page explains the usage of Flashpix.  There is a demo and links to other
Flashpix pages.">
<META NAME="Keywords" CONTENT="FlashPix, Java, JavaScript, Demo, Usage">
<TITLE>Flashpix</TITLE>
</HEAD>
```

Table 6.2. Using Metatags

The description tag contains one or more sentences briefly describing the content of the Web page. The summary, instead of the first few sentences on the page, is shown as the search result, resulting in a much faster understanding of what the page is about. The keywords tag helps search engines to decide on the relevance of a certain Web page for a given keyword. If you add the right keywords to the search, the search engines will show your page much earlier in the listing. Add keywords in all languages that are relevant to you. Other useful metainformation is listing the author of the Web page. Add the author tag and enter the name and email of the responsible person for a certain Web page, and people will know who to contact if they have questions. It can also be used by bots to index the authors of Web sites. This should be in addition to a Web-based feedback form on the Web page.

Infoseek,[9] for example, is able to search for metatags. It is possible to look for all Web pages that have been written by a certain person. By entering "author:amor" you will get a list of Web pages that have been created by people with the name of "amor," such as me. Programmers of Web utilities are able to see how many Web pages have been created with their tool. Bare Bones Software,[10] the maker of BBEdit, may count the Web pages by using "generator:bbedit," for example.

Metatags should also be multilingual. Add keywords in all languages you or your friends, family, or employees know. Look up keywords in dictionaries in order to extend the reach of your information, especially if your information is of value to many customers around the world, as multilingual and crosslingual search engines are not the standard yet.

6.1.7 Specialized Searches

In addition to general Web searches, many specialized search engines have established themselves. These search engines focus on a special file type and produce far better results than general search engines ever could. Before the invention of the World Wide Web, FTP sites had been very popular. These sites contained lots of files that could be downloaded. At that time a program called Archie was very popular. Archie allowed a search for file names. Today nobody knows Archie anymore, but file search engines are still very popular. Sites such as shareware.com,[11] filez.com,[12] and Aminet[13] allow the search for computer programs and data (images, sounds, fonts, etc.). Every file that is uploaded to one of these sites is accompanied by a short summary of the function and some keywords, which make the search simple.

One of the most popular file formats is MP3, which contains music. The music is stored in a highly compressed format and has almost CD-like quality. Although distributing copyrighted music over the Internet is illegal, many sites offer complete sets of CDs that can be downloaded. No matter what you are looking for, it is possible to find just about any CD on the Internet. You can download the music and put it onto your hard disk or burn it onto a CD. The music industry opposes the creation of these search engines, but can't do much about them. One of the most popular MP3 search engines can be found at Lycos.[14] A metasearch engine for MP3 is also available at 123mp3.com,[15] which

---

[9]http://www.infoseek.com/

[10]http://www.barebones.com/

[11]http://www.shareware.com/

[12]http://www.filez.com/

[13]http://www.aminet.org/

[14]http://mp3.lycos.com/

[15]http://www.123get.com/

allows not only a search over several dedicated MP3 search engines, but also a search for videos, lyrics, and Web sites.

Newsgroups are very popular, but without a search engine, it is not possible to find a certain thread on a given subject. Every day tens of thousands of messages are posted on the newsgroups; therefore, high-quality, full-text search engines are needed to retrieve the relevant data. Deja[16] is one example of a newsgroup that not only allows you to search for online postings, but also enables the users to post new messages.

6.1.8 People Search Engines

Private investigators are able to use the Internet to research personal information on people. Finding postal addresses, telephone numbers, and email addresses has become very easy through the use of specialized search engines. Generic search engines will find this information only if it is stored on Web pages, but most databases use dynamic Web page creation to present data, which cannot be crawled by Web spiders. Four11[17] allows the entry of a first and last name to retrieve the email address of a person, and TeleAuskunft[18] allows customers to search for telephone numbers and postal addresses in Germany. So far, no telephone book has been established on the Internet that has phone numbers from all countries around the world. A metasearch engine on phone books will be able to resolve this problem rather quickly, but nobody has thought about that yet.

While at present none of the databases compromise a person's privacy, the sum of the results can present a very detailed picture of an individual. In Europe, restrictive privacy legislation dictates that only telephone numbers are available on the Internet. This is very different from the lax privacy legislation found in the United States, which allows extremely private investigations to be conducted.

Infospace,[19] for example, allows the retrieval of phone numbers, postal addresses, financial data such as credit card limits, whether a person has been in court, driving license information, and even the names of neighbors. Although the service is not free of charge, it enables anyone with a credit card to become a private investigator without leaving the house. By using chat groups, it is possible to talk to friends, neighbors, or even the target person directly, using masquerading techniques. Masquerading means to hide behind a virtual identity that does not reveal your real identity.

Tracking people around the Internet has also become possible through new technologies. Using a social security number, it is even possible to go to other databases that are restricted to the person with the number. Just enter the number and you will be presented with some personal data. The Internet

---

[16]http://www.deja.com/

[17]http://www.four11.com/

[18]http://www.teleauskunft.de/

[19]http://www.infospace.com/

enables individuals and companies to track the behavior of people using the Internet, but also their behavior in the real world.

The DigDirt[20] Web site goes even further. It researches even more private details, such as visits to the doctor and credit card invoices, which make the person even more transparent. How often a person has been to the doctor tells something about their state of health, and a credit card invoice shows quite clearly where the person has been over the last few months, for example, and how much money has been spent.

Additional information can be found in local newspapers. Most newspapers offer an online search functionality where you can access the complete database of the newspaper—there you may find more information on a certain person. The person may play in a soccer team and may have scored a goal, for example.

This information could be used by an employer to evaluate if a candidate is suitable for a certain job. An online retailer could do some background checking on a customer before sending out the ordered goods. Many privacy organizations are worried by this latest technological development. More information on privacy issues on the Internet and how to resolve them can be found in Chapter 11.

6.1.9 Tracking Search Result Positions

As every search engine returns a whole set of Web pages for every query, it is important to appear within the first 10 results. Therefore, it is important from time to time to verify the position of your Web site in every major search engine. In order to move up in the ranking of the search engine, check out the Web pages that are ranked higher than yours. Download the Web site and look through the HTML code and content, and write down the URL. All these pieces of information influence the position of a Web site, as we have learned.

If you are interested in raising your position on various search engines, then you need to keep track of what you have submitted. Every time you change your Web site, you should resubmit the URL to every search engine. Web crawlers will automatically come back to your site at regular intervals, but by resubmitting the URL, it will be updated in that particular instant.

This, of course, can also be done automatically. Several Internet applications allow the automatic tracking of positions in search engines. One is called WebPosition.[21] This program allows you to find the exact position of each of your pages in every major search engine. In addition to this, it gives advice on how to improve the current position by comparing your page with the search engine's rules for an exact match.

Reports are generated automatically and search engine positions can be compared between the reports. WebPosition has a special built-in function called "Mission Creation." With this feature, it is possible to create Web pages

---

[20]http://www.digdirt.com/
[21]http://www.webposition.de/

that are ranked very high on a given search engine for certain keywords. If
you want to move a certain Web page into the top 10 of Altavista, the program
will help you through a simple process of changing your current Web page to
become the top address for that keyword.

In combination with a submission tool, you are able to increase traffic on
your Web page and direct more relevant people to your Web site. One such tool
is Submit-It,[22] which enables online and offline submission. All the relevant
information is entered into a form, which is then sent out to a large number of
search engines. The program does nothing more than you could do by manual
submission, but the automatic submission is much faster.

6.2 The Future of Searching

6.2.1 Issues with Search Engines

Searching by keyword is the most common method of using a search engine,
but the problems with keywords are the relatively imprecise results and the
return of too much irrelevant information. Keywords may have more than one
meaning and proper search results may only be found by using a synonym of
the keyword. Simple browsing, on the other hand, takes too much time to
find the relevant information. Directories like Yahoo! try to circumvent the
problem, but the manual process of classifying material on the Web also takes
up too much time, resulting in very few search results, since not everything on
the Web can be classified. Therefore, new paradigms of searching are needed,
as is new software that is able to categorize Web sites automatically.

The majority of search engines come from the United States and specialize
in English resources and information reflecting the American culture. People
who do not speak English or who are nonnative speakers have many disadvantages on the Web.

The centralized approach to information retrieval has made it extremely
difficult to cope with the multilingual and multicultural nature of the Information society (which consists of the part of the population that has online
access). The Internet has become a success throughout the world, but the
American search engines operate with a U.S.-centric company structure and
tend to concentrate on the English language. Although many search engines
have subsidiaries in other countries—like Japan or Italy—the way the information is presented is the American way and may not reflect the logic of the
people who are using it.

National search engines in Russia or France, for example, have to deal with
far smaller sets of information and specialize in the cultural and linguistic
environments they know best. Their disadvantage is that the queries are in
Russian or French, and the search results contain only a small subset of pos-

---

[22]http://www.submit-it.com/

sible results on the Web, as they are restricted to the language. This greatly reduces the possibility of using the Web as a source for the worldwide diffusion of information.

Larger search engines, such as Altavista, are able to perform multilingual searches that present search results in multiple languages. This is good if the searcher knows all the languages, but if, for example, a person from India finds a Japanese Web site on the search topic, this may not be helpful.

Text documents that are in special formats (such as PostScript or Star Office documents) are unreachable for many search engines, as the textual information is embedded into the binary structure of the particular file format. The same applies to scanned documents, Java applets, and video/audio clips. The content of these file formats is hidden from search engines today. Only if the description of the file format is known and included in the search engine is it possible to add the content for certain document types. This is relatively easy; it is just a matter of extra work. Infoseek,[23] for example, is able to index the content of Word documents. More difficult is the inclusion of content that is hidden in applications, as there is no way to tell where the information may be hidden. Consider writing a Java applet or a Flash program that is used as an educational tool for kids. Although it may contain a complete dictionary, the information is not visible to the search engines, as it is embedded into the application.

The research and development in information and data retrieval is aimed at improving the effectiveness and efficiency of retrieval. Individual and parallel development for database management systems has left this sector without a centralized vision and coordination between the different types of search engines. Search engines on the Internet are very specific and not able to cope with multiple database formats and file types. In order to make searches complete, a search engine needs to search over text, documents, images, sounds, and all other media formats. Therefore, database integration will be the single most important objective for the future of intelligent search engines.

In order to receive better search results, it is not only necessary to improve the search engine technology, but also the user interfaces, depending on the type of user (such as casual, researcher, business people, users with special requirements).

Neural networks will be used more commonly in the future to organize large, unstructured collections of information. Autonomy[24] is a search engine that uses the model of the adaptive probabilistic concept to understand large documents. The system is able to learn from each piece of information it has discovered. By putting together a set of not-so-relevant resources, the set should get the large picture by reading through all the documents. Therefore, it is necessary to rank information by importance.

---

[23]http://www.infoseek.com/
[24]http://www.autonomy.com/

This allows zones in a portal to be created automatically (an explanation of *zone* appears later in this chapter) or with a minimum of manual intervention, instead of manually creating the zones in the way Yahoo! does. In order to achieve this goal, such systems need to employ technologies for concept clustering and concept profiling.

Neural networks are also referred to as connectionist architectures, parallel distributed processing, and neuromorphic systems. It is an information-processing paradigm inspired by the way the densely interconnected, parallel structure of the mammalian brain processes information. Artificial neural networks are collections of mathematical models that emulate some of the observed properties of biological nervous systems and draw on the analogies of adaptive biological learning. The key element of the neural network paradigm is the novel structure of the information processing system. It is composed of a large number of highly interconnected processing elements that are analogous to neurons and are tied together with weighted connections that are analogous to synapses.

Learning in biological systems involves adjustments to the synaptic connections that exist between the neurons. This is true of neural networks as well. Learning typically occurs by example through training or exposure to a truthed set of input/output data where the training algorithm iteratively adjusts the connection weights (synapses). These connection weights store the knowledge necessary to solve specific problems.

Although neural networks have been around since the late 1950s, it wasn't until the mid-1980s that algorithms became sophisticated enough for general applications. Today neural networks are being applied to an increasing number of real-world problems of considerable complexity. They are good pattern recognition engines and robust classifiers, with the ability to generalize in making decisions about imprecise input data. They offer ideal solutions to a variety of classification problems such as speech, character, and signal recognition, as well as functional prediction and system modeling where the physical processes are not understood or are highly complex. Neural networks may also be applied to control problems, where the input variables are measurements used to drive an output actuator, and the network learns the control function. The advantage of neural networks lies in their resilience against distortions in the input data and their capability of learning. They are often good at solving problems that are too complex for conventional technologies (e.g., problems that do not have an algorithmic solution or for which an algorithmic solution is too complex to be found) and are often well suited to problems that people are good at solving, but for which traditional methods are not.

6.2.2 EuroSearch

One project to overcome the above-mentioned limitations of search engines is the EuroSearch project. EuroSearch is a federation of national search engines that gives much better results and is more suited to the challenges of the multi-lingual and multicultural global Internet. The founding members are national search engines from Italy, Spain, and Switzerland. The multilingual approach allows a query to be entered in the preferred language of the researcher, and the search engine takes care of the search on the search engines in the other languages.

Every national site that is part of the federation remains in the country of origin and is maintained by a native speaker who will ensure that the search works in his or her own language. At the same time, the EuroSearch[25] frame-work tries to remain open to other countries and services that would like to become part of the initiative.

The framework allows access and retrieval of documents that are not only in English, but also in a variety of other European languages. This makes it easier to find information provided in languages other than English that may contain the information the searcher was looking for. It enables people who do not speak English to retrieve information and information providers to present their information in their native tongue.

Unlike search engines that retrieve information only in one language, cross-language search results need to be presented in a form that the searcher under-stands. The description of the documents should be presented in the language of the query. Cross-language retrieval is not the same as multilingual. The multilingual systems support many different languages, but cross-language retrieval systems provide the increased functionality of retrieving relevant in-formation written in a language different than the user's query. The query is translated to the target language, and then the search engine is queried. In order to broaden the search, a thesaurus for every language needs to be incor-porated into every search engine, and automatic classification procedures need to be implemented.

The EuroSearch project wants to develop techniques and resources to im-plement a cross-language search engine and to improve retrieval and classifica-tion technologies. The ultimate goal is to create a federation of national search engines that work together in order to deliver better search results. A proto-type is currently being built that provides an interface to formulate queries and present understandable results in the users' preferred languages. This re-quires the system not only to translate the queries into a metalanguage, but also to translate the results and the resulting Web pages into the query lan-guage to make it accessible to the user. This approach makes the whole Web more accessible to non-English speakers.

EuroSearch will simplify access to information on the Internet, in and across different languages. A simplified and multilingual access to the wide variety of information on the Web will improve cultural exchanges and knowl-edge integration between European countries. This means a significant im-

---

[25]http://eurosearch.iol.it/

provement in the quality of the available information for every user. This will have an impact on the acceptance of the Internet not only in Europe, which is the main target market for EuroSearch, but in all non-English-speaking countries, as English is not spoken by all people that have access to the Internet today.

6.2.3 Natural-Language Searches

The idea of natural-language access to a database is not new, but still hasn't been achieved. Most search engines are not able to handle questions such as "Where can I get light bulbs?" or "How many legs does a horse have?" The answers to these questions can be found on the Web, but search engines are not able to understand the questions. If a page exists that lists a question and an answer on it, then you may succeed, but this is rare. Instead of receiving the answer "At shop XY in Z" or "four," you would receive a long list of search results, as the search engines split up the question into keywords. The search engine then searches for every word in the question.

The difference between conventional and natural-language search engines is the way pages get indexed. Unlike a conventional database, the symbolic approach to natural-language processing involves treating words as nodes in a semantic network. The emphasis is then placed on the meaning of the words instead of on the single words made of single characters. Only this will guarantee a correct search.

Figure 6.2. Natural-language search on Altavista.

A natural-language processor (NLP) for an Internet search engine needs a large and concise dictionary. Words are then represented by the way they are used (this approach is called case-based reasoning). Each occurrence of a word is treated individually, resulting in extremely large databases, as every word can have up to a few thousand individual meanings. The strength of case-based reasoning is in its flexibility. Since databases are based on semantics, imprecise querying may still retrieve information that is close to the answer but does not exactly match the question. A query for "information about football in the UK" could retrieve a structured extract from the database that can be navigated to select the correct question and answer.

The second approach is to add a thesaurus to the database. A query on "plant" will also look up "factory" and "flower," as both of them are related to "plant," even though they have totally different meanings. This entails a significant improvement in precision and recall rates over current search methods. Improving the syntax analysis is also very useful. By analyzing the syntax of a given query, it is possible to compare it with stored patterns in the database. Altavista supports natural-language queries, and the results get better every day. Figure 6.2 shows the results for the question "Where can I find information on natural language?" Only simple questions are supported, but it is already the next step towards complex natural-language search engines.

6.2.4 Image Search Engines

There are many images on the Internet, but unfortunately, it is not possible to search for them as you can for Web pages or music files. Unlike Web pages, where you can use text to describe what you are searching for, and music, where you can name the musician or song title, images on the Web are in most cases not of artistic value; otherwise, it would be possible to search for the painter or the picture title.

In many cases, people search for a boat, a house, or a dog to illustrate a text, for example. Image search engines on the Internet today are using the information that accompanies a picture, such as the file name (e.g., href='cat.jpg'), the alternative text (e.g., alt='this is a picture of a cat'), or the text that is next to the image ("the following image displays a cat"). This information is displayed if you move the mouse over the image.

As long as your search is very generic, the existing image search engines work very well. More and more people add the HTML alt tag to provide additional information on the image, which helps in finding the right information. But, unfortunately, most people do not care much about the alternative text (i.e., using the alt tag), which for textual Web images in most cases is wrong, incomplete, or nonexistent.

The problem arises as soon as you search for more specific images. "A red cat with a little ball" could be a very common request. Although it is highly unlikely that the filename will contain all this information, the alt text may contain it and the accompanying text as well, but don't be too sure. Another issue may be that the cat with the red ball is on a picture among many other things. It could well be that the Web page is talking about balls and will not mention the cat, or talk about a table on which the cat and the ball are placed. In these cases, image search engines that rely on textual information will fail miserably. Many images contain text that could help to index the image correctly; the problem is extracting the textual information from an image. The logo of Tucows,[26] for example, contains the alt tag "Moooo...." This information does not help anyone. Extracting the text from the logo would help in indexing the image correctly.

Apostolos Antonacopoulos[27] of the University of Liverpool in the UK started a project in 1998 to extract textual information from images on the Web. Although it is possible to extract the information from images very easily, there is no way to automate the analysis on such text at present.

In order to index and validate the information in an image, the characters embedded in the image need to be extracted, and then they need to be recognized. The task of identifying the text appears to be similar to the traditional techniques in optical character recognition (OCR). But there are several significant differences. The text in images has the advantage over scanned text because it contains no distortions from digitization. But other than scanned documents, the backgrounds on images tend to be complex (compared to plain white paper) and the characters are very small in order to keep the resolution low. A Web image is presented in 72 dpi, while scanned documents are at a resolution of 300 dpi. When using a lossy compression algorithm—such as the JPEG format—compression and quantization artifacts appear, making it more difficult to extract a character and then recognize it properly. The human eye is a very complex device, which cannot easily be replicated by a computer program.

Previous efforts to analyze text in images restricted themselves to single color text and ignored very small characters. As researchers and application designers were globally analyzing the image file, the performance was bad, and it took a long time to complete. As only very few characters use a single color, and many text fonts are small, this approach was not resolving the problem. Antonacopoulos' approach is different. The algorithms he used allow the identification of text with gradient color or textures on complex background textures. This allows the retrieval of textual information from images.

The results are achieved through several steps. First, the number of colors needs to be reduced. Although GIF images use only 256 colors, JPEGs use up to 16 million colors. By reducing the number of colors, it is easier to detect text within the image. By dropping bits, the number of colors is reduced to 512 colors. After the number of colors is reduced, a color histogram is created

---

[26]http://www.tucows.com/

[27]http://www.csc.liv.ac.uk/~aa/

that shows which color is used in the image and how often. By identifying the differently colored parts of the image, the colors present in the image have to be grouped in clusters according to their similarity.

After the algorithm has determined the main colors, the regions that share the same color are extracted, and a special technique is used to identify the connected components. This allows the contours of particular image regions that form closed shapes to be identified. By examining the relationships between regions, potential character components are extracted. The proposed system is working very well—so good, actually, that it has found its way into a commercial software package.

The next step will be to implement a search engine that recognizes objects in an image, but this is highly difficult and requires a lot of computing power, as a cat may be painted, photographed or drawn. The cat can run, sit, and jump, and the perspective can be varied. Although we can detect a cat very easily, expressing the looks of a cat mathematically is very difficult, so don't expect anything on the Internet soon. But then again, the first rule of the Internet is still valid: Expect the unexpected.

6.3   Intelligent Network Agents

6.3.1   Little Helpers on the Web

Intelligent agents are widely used in computer science and are part of the research in the area of artificial intelligence. Areas of agent research include user-interface agents, such as personal assistants and information filters, which perform networking tasks for a user. Another area of agent research is multiagent systems, such as agent communication languages and systems for coordination/cooperation strategies. Autonomous agents are programs that travel between sites and decide themselves when to move and what to do. At the moment, this type of agent is not very common, as it requires a special type of server where the agent can navigate. This section focuses on network agents, which are also known as *knowbots*, little robots that gather information on a network.

As we've discussed, search engines can help us find information, but the challenge is to remember where this information was when we looked at it last and to know if something has changed since we last visited the site. It sounds easy to save every interesting page in the bookmarks of your browser, but soon you will have hundreds of bookmarks on your computer, and many of those links will be dead.

The major disadvantage of search engines is that they require human interaction, which leads to incomplete sets of information. Even with good search strategies, it may take some time to locate the information desired, and time is money. In many cases, people are not able to locate content they need, although it is available on the Internet.

In order to reduce the amount of time needed, intelligent agents have been developed that are able to search on the Internet without continued user interaction. Let's look at an example. You look for information on Shakespeare's literature. No matter how hard you search on the Internet, you always miss some information, as there are far too many sites, newsgroups, portals, and chats to check out.

The idea of intelligent agents is to search for a set of given keywords (in our example, Shakespeare and literature) not only once, but repeatedly every hour, day, or month in order to always be informed of the latest developments about your topic. Simply putting together a query for a given set of databases would not resolve the problem, as the set of databases changes on the Internet all the time. New sites appear and existing sites disappear. The agent will keep you always up-to-date.

Intelligent agents should not only collect data, they should also be able to classify the data. This can be achieved by counting the times a certain word or its synonyms appear, or by analyzing the structure of the document. The difficulty is to characterize the importance and relevance of keywords that were found in a certain document.

6.3.2 Email Agents

One of the first applications for intelligent agents was to sort out unwanted email from the inbox. Although it is possible to automatically delete mail from certain email addresses, this does not help anymore, as spammers use fake addresses that change every time they send out email. Therefore, it is necessary to develop agents that are able to detect spam automatically by looking for certain keywords or a certain structure.

Another application in the area of email agent software is to prioritize email by importance. This type of agent moves the most important mail to the top of your mail folder so that you can read it first. The priority can be defined by sender, content, or structure.

In the first case, it is rather simple to build out-of-the-box products to prevent spam, as spam is seen negatively by most people. In the second case, it is necessary to customize the agent in order to support personal needs. This is much harder, as it requires the person who uses the agent to think about his or her email priorities. Although this exercise is helpful and will save a lot of time (especially if you receive a lot of email every day), you may not take the time to think about your email priorities.

6.3.3 News Agents

Over the past few years, more and more news agents have established themselves. These news agents are able to create a sort of customized online newspaper that displays only news that is interesting to the customer. The agents therefore need to visit all news sites and decide which of the offered news may be interesting to the particular customer. It then collects the information and passes it on via email or Web front end.

In Germany, two companies are competing in the business of news agents: Paperball[28] and Paperboy.[29] The competition between these services is getting them to add more online newspaper resources to their databases to create an even more detailed personalized newspaper, which can be viewed either on a Web page or via email.

In the past there have been some disputes between the newspapers and the digital news agents on how the information should be presented on the news agents' Web sites. Originally, the digital news agents collected the raw information and incorporated it into their own layouts, adding their own advertising. This is no longer possible; the news agents can only produce the headlines and some lines of text, and then they need to link to the original newspaper site in order to avoid legal problems.

There are still many privately owned sites that offer collections of news links that strip away the advertising. Depending on the popularity of these sites, online news services may sue the owners and try to stop these sites from operating. Still, for every site that is shut down, 10 new ones appear, making it difficult for Internet news providers to stop them. It is part of the Internet culture to make information available for free, even without advertising, but there is no technical way to stop it and only limited legal power available. See Chapter 4 for the legal aspects of this issue.

6.3.4 Personal Shopping Agents

The most interesting agent is the personal shopping agent, which scans the Internet for the lowest price for a given product. The shopping agent consists of a database containing merchants on the Web and information on how to access their databases. Once customers decide on a product, they are able to key in the product name, part number, ISBN number, or a keyword that relates to the product, and the shopping agent starts checking all the merchants for the product. If the search word is too generic, the customers will be presented with a selection of possible products. If the customers then decide on a certain product, the shopping agent will query all databases for the prices and availability. The prices displayed normally contain not only the price for the product, but also for shipping, so the total price as well as estimated delivery time are displayed.

DealTime,[30] developed by German students, has become highly successful. It specializes in searching for books on the Web. By entering the title, the au-

---

[28]http://www.paperball.de/
[29]http://www.paperboy.de/
[30]http://www.dealtime.com/

thor, or the ISBN number, the shopping agent looks for the book and presents the results in a list. The books are sorted by price, including postage and packaging. Final results list estimated time of delivery, too. The site provides not only the prices, but also delivery times and methods, making a comparison very easy. Sometimes it is cheaper to buy a book in Australia than in Germany. If the price is low enough, the shipping time of several weeks can be taken into account.

The following list contains a selection of shopping agents that were available at the time of writing. For a complete and updated list, please go to http://www.smartbots.com/.

Name	Description and URL
Auction Watchers	This specialized agent allows you to scan prices on Internet auctions for computer equipment. **http://www.auctionwatchers.com/**
Bargain Finder	Specialized in finding compact discs. Uses nine online shops for comparing products. **http://www.bargainfinder.com/**
DealPilot	The ultimate shopping agent for online bookstores. **http://www.dealpilot.com/**
E-Smarts	Complex Internet guide with shopping agents for bargain shopping on the Web. **http://www.esmarts.com/**
Jango	Offers price comparison of computer products. **http://www.jango.com/**
MySimon	MySimon can be taught to shop in new online shops with the guidance of the customer. **http://www.mysimon.com/**
Shopper.com	Compares 1,000,000 prices on 100,000 products available online. **http://www.shopper.com/**

Table 6.3. Overview of Shopping Agents

Jango,[31] a shopping agent developed by the American company Netbot, allows price comparison of computer products. As with DealPilot, the price list

---

[31]http://www.jango.com/

is not stored at the site of the agent but is retrieved at the moment of the customer's interest, therefore providing the actual price. The difference between Jango and DealPilot is the way payment is handled. DealPilot sends the customers to the book store, where they can pay using the store's own payment system. Jango, on the other hand, offers the option of paying at its site without direct access to the Internet shop that provides the product.

As more and more shopping agents have become available, a special portal for shopping agents has been set up. SmartBots.com[32] is a directory offering information on shopping agents from all over the world. See Table 6.3 for an overview on some of the most-used shopping agents that can also be found on SmartBots.com.

Shopping agents work for mass products, such as software, compact discs, and books, as they require no customization to the individual customer. Other products, such as cars or complete computer systems, won't be targeted initially by these agents, as the offerings differ too much on every Web site, as do the requirements of the customers. Cross-promotion and service are other points that cannot be dealt with by the shopping agents, as they cannot be expressed simply by value.

In order to allow these advanced features, the shopping agents themselves need to become highly complex configuration systems. Then a shopping agent could be implemented that is able to find a complete computer system at the lowest price possible by comparing all the components individually and looking for cross-promotions (e.g., a hard disk becomes cheaper if bought with a certain type of memory). This will require a large investment on the shopping agent site, as it needs to know which components work together and which of them do not. This information is different for every product. The shopping agents eventually become true brokers.

6.4   Portal Sites

6.4.1   Growing Together

A portal is a World Wide Web site that is or proposes to be a major starting site for users when they connect to the Web or that users tend to visit as an anchor site (as defined by the *whatis* online dictionary[33]). Portals contain lots of content in the form of news, information, links, and services, including ordering flowers, books, and CDs, or free email and Web space. As locating desired material on the Internet becomes more difficult, the value of fast, reliable, and simple-to-use portals increases.

"Portal" is now almost as abused a term as client/server was. Many are now confusing a portal with a website itself. This is not correct. A portal is a specific experience that a website provides. That view can be personalized. Thus, what

---

[32]http://www.smartbots.com/

[33]http://www.whatis.com/

happens at a certain URL will be different for each consumer, depending on their role, authorization, needs, profile, etc. Note that the layering in of portal functionality almost represents second generation activity for a website.

The experience for a business manager, for example, may entail seeing results from the latest cross-sell campaign run for a particular product line, getting the latest overall sales results for the product, comparing to a historical view of the product over the last year and therefore making a dynamic pricing decision. The experience for an IT manager may include seeing runtime statistics for an overall website, the number of downloads for a set of documents, the number of live connections, etc. and then shutting down a particular server because it is not meeting current SLAs for performance. The view for an end-user may include last orders placed, a tailored set of pulldown menus based on recent transactions, etc.

Portals are actually nothing new to the Web. These entry sites have been here right from the beginning. AOL[34] and CompuServe[35] in the United States, T-Online[36] in Germany, and Ireland Online[37] in Ireland, for example, have offered something similar for years. All online services have had a private Web site with special services for their customers, such as online banking, free email, search engines, chat forums, and online shopping malls. The difference between these first-generation portals and the current wave of portals is the target audience. With the first generation, only subscribers to AOL could see the AOL portal pages. The second generation, which is already online, is not restricted to availability for subscribers of a certain online service only, but can be accessed by anyone with a Web browser.

The reason online services have opened up their private portal sites is that search engines like Excite,[38] and directories like Yahoo![39] have started to offer services in addition to directory and search engine services. These services are accessible via a Web browser and do not require the user to be a subscriber to a certain online service. Digital's search engine AltaVista,[40] for example, added instant online translation to its search engine, whereby any Web page can be translated on the fly while being downloaded from its respective server. Yahoo! offers free email and a news service. You can even download a program from Yahoo!'s Web site that displays a ticker in your task bar on Windows computers, where you can see the latest developments in politics, finance, and sports.

The search engines and directories had to add new services to distinguish themselves from the vast number of similar services (there are more than 100

---

[34]http://www.aol.com/
[35]http://www.compuserve.com/
[36]http://www.t-online.de/
[37]http://www.iol.ie/
[38]http://www.excite.com/
[39]http://www.yahoo.com/
[40]http://www.altavista.com/

international search engines and 15 to 20 search engines per country, ranging from Germany's web.de[41] and the UK's GOD[42], to Fiji-Online[43]). The result was that they entered the domain of the portal Web sites. The search engines were already the most attractive sites on the Web, but with the addition of new services, they were able to enhance their customer loyalty.

By offering additional services through free registration, portals know quite well who their customers are and are able to respond to their wishes fast, which is very important if you live off banner advertisements. One-to-one marketing is the key to customer loyalty.

The third large group that became portals is software distribution sites, like Netscape's NetCenter[44] and Tucows.[45] The former is the largest portal in the world, worth more than $4.3 billion (this was the price AOL paid Netscape for NetCenter in November 1998), and the latter is one of the largest archives for shareware and public domain software on the Web. They were facing the same problems. They needed to distinguish themselves from their competitors. On the Internet there are only a few ways to distinguish yourself from the competition: price, speed, and service. If you do it right, you are cheaper, faster, and offer a better service.

The fourth large group of Web sites that became portals were the original sites offering free services such as email (such as Global Message Exchange[46]) and Web space (such as Xoom[47]). As users tend to come to these sites on a regular basis to check their email or to change their Web sites, these sites have a high potential for becoming a portal.

Jim Sease, a Web designer, offers a "metaportal" on his Web site.[48] He links to all sorts of portals, where users can get additional information. This may be useful for selecting a portal, but once you have found *your* portal, you will most probably stay with it and ignore the others.

Converting traditional shopping malls to digital shopping malls failed in most cases because only the environment, and not the information, was replicated. Having 20 shops within one domain is no help to the customer; a link to a page within the domain is just as far away as a link to another country. Portals combine shopping and information and pass the relevant information on. Users enter their requirements once and are guided through the possibilities of the portal. Most portals save user profiles in order to personalize the user's next visit. They remember what particular users did last time and use that information to guess what they may want to do this time by presenting them

---

[41] http://www.web.de/
[42] http://www.god.co.uk/
[43] http://www.fiji-online.com.fj/
[44] http://www.netscape.com/
[45] http://www.tucows.com/
[46] http://www.gmx.net/
[47] http://www.xoom.com/
[48] http://www.sease.com/

information and products that they are most likely interested in. By checking, if the user follow the provided links, the system can improve its predictability over time.

6.4.2 Digital Neighborhoods

Free Web space providers such as GeoCities offer a wide range of "neighborhoods," where customers can find other people with similar interests. Adding services, information, and product offerings to these neighborhoods will create a zone with added value for every participant. The zones create a virtual market space that is highly specialized. The zone on a certain portal can act as an umbrella for many companies of all sizes. These virtual marketplaces also make it easier to sell advertising space to potential advertisers, as the viewers are most likely to be of a certain target group.

If you look at various portals, you will find services there that you have already seen in other places. Portals tend to buy existing services and incorporate them into their Web sites. This is called *cobranding*. Netscape, for example, uses the Florists Transworld Delivery service[49] on its home page, so it is now possible to buy flowers through Netscape. At first glance, you will not even notice that you are using a third-party service, as FTD uses a special cobranded site with the design of Netscape's Web page. Snap uses the mapping service of Vicinity,[50] and Excite uses the email address book from WhoWhere.com.[51] Building up such services would break the financial neck of most portals, so they cooperate with existing service providers. For users, there is no big difference if they click on AltaVista's news section (which is provided by ABC News) or on the ABC News Web site.[52] The real advantage is the tight integration of different services. Read a news story on AltaVista and search for sites related to that topic with one click, or search for a certain keyword on Yahoo! and get a list of reference books from them (with support from Amazon.com).

Another startup service provider is ConSors,[53] an online brokering service company. They do not offer business support to their direct customers who come to their Web site. They want only the "intelligent customers" who are able to help themselves. But at the same time, they are offering brokering services to online banks, who can include the raw service into their product portfolio and offer consulting and other options around this raw service. This new paradigm of providing core services to portals has been taken onboard by Hewlett-Packard's E-Services[54] campaign. An in-depth review of the paradigm can be found in Chapter 16.

---

[49] http://www.ftd.com/
[50] http://www.vicinity.com/
[51] http://www.whowhere.com/
[52] http://www.abcnews.com/
[53] http://www.consors.de/
[54] http://www.hp.com/e-services/

6.4.3 Becoming a Portal Player

Becoming a portal player is not difficult. All you need to start is interesting, unique content and a good search engine. With some HTML knowledge, you can build a simple portal by adding your favorite links, a search mechanism, and links to free email, chat, and news feeds, thus creating a home page of your favorite bookmarks. Your browser bookmark file is a form of private portal. As every page on the Web has the same priority, there is no reason why five million people should not access your home page instead of AOL's. All you need is good marketing and a solution for these five million people.

In order to become a successful portal, you need to add services that are tightly integrated into your online offering. Integration is the main reason so many people choose portals over individual sites. Once you have registered with a portal, the information can be reused for all services within the portal. Although some may not like the idea of cross-selling personal information, most people do like the idea of their own personalized portal site. Once you have entered your credit card information for buying a book via a portal, this information can be reused to pay for something else within the portal or offer the same customers other products to complete the last purchase. The user does not need to reenter information. Being a major browser producer will help in establishing your portal. Netscape and Microsoft have highly successful portals because their home pages are the default home page of their browsers.

The GO Network,[55] for example, invites its customers to use a Web directory search for Web pages. News headlines and financial data are on the page, and it is possible to get a free email account. It is possible to sign in and customize the page to the needs of the individual subscriber. In Figure 6.3 you can see my customized page on the GO portal site.

While building up your portal, it is helpful to offer free services like Web space, free email, chat rooms, newsgroups, and free software for download. This will get the users' attention in the first place. They will come to your portal and try it out. In order to keep the customers attracted to your Web site, you need up-to-date news feeds, games, online help, and some online shopping opportunities. It does not matter if you build up your own service or if you buy it from someone else. Customers won't notice in most cases, but they will notice how easy (or difficult) it is to navigate within your portal and find information on a certain topic. Although portal owners have services directly included in their system, they should never exclude other services from their search engine. The customers should never have the feeling that the search engine only shows the preferred suppliers. If customers want to get in touch with another company, the search engine must be able to provide the information; otherwise, they will go on to the next portal where they feel that their requirements are better met. The services that are offered on the portal site should always be available as a suggestion and not as a "must-have."

---

[55]http://www.go.com/

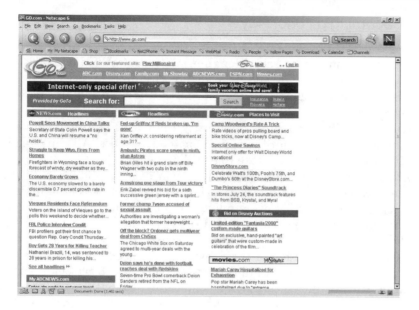

Figure 6.3. The portal site of GO network.

Search capabilities must have the top priority for your portal. This is the most frequently used service on the Internet. Information on the site needs to be organized in zones (sometimes called channels or guides) on general topics, such as computer, travel, arts, and cars.

Each zone combines all offered service for that particular topic. If, for example, you select the Entertainment section on Yahoo!, you will get not only the directory entries for that particular topic, but also links to related news and current events. You are able to join a virtual community using online chats, clubs, or message boards, and you get a list of online services that are related to entertainment, like online auctions, a classified section, yellow pages, and online shopping (with a direct link to CDNow[56]). It is even possible to see a listing of cinemas with timetables. All these services are offered by clicking on one simple link that says "Entertainment." Two or three years ago you would have found only a long list of Web sites where you could find more information on the topic, but no service at all.

6.4.4   Portal Owners and Service Providers

Portals have two major players: the actual portal owners—who integrates content and services—and the service providers—who add functionality and services to a portal. Depending on the structure of your company and your plans

---

[56]http://www.cdnow.com/

for the future, you should become one or the other, but ideally, both—building up a portal and provide dedicated services to other portals.

There are two different types of portals on the Internet: *horizontal* portals, which cover a lot of topics, and *vertical* portals, which have a tightly focused content area geared toward a particular audience. Gallery-Net,[57] for example, offers a directory for artists, art-related sites, online galleries, and virtual museums. In addition, it offers free email and chat, Web space, and a shopping area. It appeals mainly to art lovers and artists, but still offers a wide range of other activities from this one site, thus being the portal for many people around the world.

Another example is the Web site of Gravis[58] in Germany. Although it is the biggest retailer of Apple Macintosh products in Germany, its Web site consisted in 1998 mainly of scanned images of the printed brochure. There is no way to get any additional information on the products or on prices. It is not even possible to buy anything online. There are no online chats, no newsgroups, no FAQs—just a few 100 to 200 KB images, and that's it. Gravis has an extremely high potential of becoming a major Mac portal for Germany, but unfortunately, it did not see the potential of the Internet. When I asked about G3 accelerator boards, it took three emails to explain what I was looking for on the Web site. Finally, Gravis thought that it had understood and sent me the URL of the producer Phase5.[59] Obviously, the people in the customer care center have to learn how the Internet works. In the mean time their web site has changed radically, but it took quite a while for them to recognize the value of the Internet.

If you and your company have an interest in only one specific topic, it is quite easy to build up a portal using your knowledge and your products. If, for example, a company is selling dog food, creating a vertical portal Web site would consist of adding a search functionality not only for that particular site, but Internet-wide. It would need to offer online chats, email, Web space, newsgroups, and all the other things that we have discussed above, tailored to meet the needs of dog owners. Create a portal that would be the kind of service all dog owners would come back for. The vertical portal could be a zone in a horizontal portal, but with more detailed information and services than a general portal like Yahoo! or NetCenter could offer. A dog food company could ask Excite, for example, to include its services for dog owners on their portal, or even offer to outsource the dog zone on Excite's portal Web site.

As you can see, becoming a small portal is easy and can be a threat to the large ones, if done well. Be careful about offering services that are not related to your company. If these services fail, your company will be held responsible. Remember to choose your partners carefully.

---

[57]http://www.gallery-net.com/

[58]http://www.gravis.de/

[59]http://www.phase5.de/

6.4.5   Personalizing the Online Experience

To return to personalization and one-to-one marketing (personalization is typically driven by the customer, and one-to-one marketing is driven by the business), portals use these techniques to deliver precisely the information the customer needs in the way the customer wants it to be presented. The user profile, which consists of information the customers have entered and information they supplied while browsing the site, is used to organize the portal in the most convenient way for them. The simplest form of personalization is described in the previous section. All services that are available are focused on the customer's search topic. The next level would be to provide local weather reports and other local news of interest (e.g., movie listings). This would require that the users enter their home town or the ZIP code and the country they live in. This information about the user allows the portal to become even more personal. The more information the customer is willing to give, the better the portal adapts to the needs of the customer.

Most portals have personalized home pages for their customers, where they are greeted with their names, get the latest information on their stocks, see the latest news headlines on certain topics, see if they have received new email, and get a weather forecast for the next few days. Birthdays within the next five days of all relatives appear, and users can see if their chat partners are online as well.

All this pops up automatically each time customers enter their portal. From that point on, they are able to search for topics and use online services. Most likely, they will use the search engine offered by the portal and use the online services proposed by the portal as well. Tracking the movement of the users gives feedback on the usability of the Web site. Some pieces of information, for example, need to be put onto the home page, because 80 percent of the users want to know about it, but only 20 percent are able to find it. It also gives feedback on the preferences of the users (for example, if all users go to the "Cars" zone). This, in turn, helps the portal owner to enhance the services and help the information flow. The major obstacle is to persuade the users to provide the required information to deliver the services onto their personalized home page. See Chapter 11 for more information on the topic of privacy. Privacy concerns can destroy the best business case, if not dealt with properly.

6.4.6   Must-Have Features for a Portal

Search engines, email, and online chats are the services most popular with Internet users. Offering free email may seem to be superfluous, as everybody gets a free email account with his or her online access, but there are several reasons why they would need additional email accounts.

First, it could well be that several family members share one account and want to send and receive private email without paying for an extra account from their online service provider.

The second important reason to have email accounts available through a Web browser that does not require a special email program is that they are a very attractive offering for people who travel a lot. Just walk into the nearest Internet café or ask someone in an office with an Internet connection, and within seconds, you can read your mail and respond. Although Web-based emailing is far from being comfortable and fast, it offers a way to stay in touch while traveling and it is very simple to use. More advanced users may prefer to telnet to their accounts and use old-fashioned UNIX programs, such as Pine or Elm to check their email (or even telnet to the mail server on port 110, which opens the standard POP3 connection).

Third, people who are moving from one location to another may not be able to move their email account with them, because their online service provider is not available in the new location. Having a virtual email address gives them one address that is valid for any location.

A fourth reason is to have fun accounts. MOE,[60] for example, offers a wide range of different domain names, ranging from for-president.com to tweety-bird.com (my email address could look like this: danny@for-president.com or danny@tweety-bird.com). They are now in the process of becoming a portal as well, by adding new services such as Web space (I could receive the following URL: http://danny.for-president.com/) and weather reports.

Giving away free Web space was what GeoCities[61] offered in the first place. Now it is one of the largest portals on the Internet, offering everything from virtual communities, online shopping, and a search engine to stock quotes and many other things.

Online chats are a wonderful alternative to telephone companies and online services that charge per minute or per hour. Once you have started a chat, it takes quite a while until you really get engaged in a conversation (unless you know the people already), and once you have started, it is difficult to stop. Every portal offers online chats, ranging from Java-based chats to CGI chats. In-depth information on online chats can be found in Chapter 9.

6.4.7 Overview on Portal Solutions

This section provides a short market overview on the most popular software solutions in the portal area. The solutions offer different types of functionality, but all provide the basic functionality described previously. Again, it is difficult to say which solution best fits your needs. This depends on the existing infrastructure and on the required functionality. Open systems that are built on top of application servers should be preferred, though, as they can be easily extended. The disadvantage of application servers is that they require additional programming in most cases, while standalone applications can be set up by simple configuration.

---

[60] http://www.myownemail.com/
[61] http://www.geocities.com/

When selecting a portal solution, consider the existing knowledge within a company in order to reduce the implementation and maintenance costs. If knowledge is not readily available with the organization, ensure that the knowledge will be built up during the implementation or that the company has a long-term contract with a third-party that will act on behalf of the company. It is difficult to find a reliable partner, so it is best to do so immediately.

Brio.Portal

Brio Technology[62] enables companies to collect data and information in a heterogenic environment and organize it. A flexible and secure infrastructure allows access to personalized information, that can consist of many sources of structured and unstructured data.

BroadVision InfoExchange Portal

The BroadVision InfoExchange Portal[63] is based on the well-known BroadVision One-to-One server solution and expands the software stack with components that are required for an e-commerce and e-marketing solution. The InfoExchange solution is one of many Web applications that are available from Broadvision. Additional components from Broadvision can be introduced to extend the portal solution with billing, finance, or marketplace functionality, for example. This makes it possible to extend the portal while the business grows. Through the built-in one-to-one marketing components, the portal can be extended without large investments to satisfy the needs of the individuals.

getAccess

The product getAccess by enCommerce, Inc.[64] changes existing portals in such a way that it is possible to build up individual e-business relationships. Customers can be targeted individually through this solution, which provides information and services that are of interest to the customer. The customers see what they expect to see. In addition, the software stack provides adaptors to enterprise resources. This is done in a secure way that protects the internal network of a company.

Hyperwave Information Portal

Hyperwave[65] provides an enterprise information portal, which is based on the Hyperwave Information Servers. This makes it possible to create B2B applications in a central location that can be securely accessed from anywhere in the world. It provides the ability to exchange structured and unstructured data.

---

[62]http://www.brio.com/

[63]http://www.broadvision.com/

[64]http://www.encommerce.com/

[65]http://www.hyperwave.de/

One organization using Hyperwave is DLR[66] in Germany. DLR seems to be happy with the functionality it provides, but unfortunately, the Web site is not always reachable, indicating problems with the platform.

IONA iPortal Suite

The IONA iPortal Suite by IONA Technologies[67] enables you to create a multiplatform solution that combines various existing enterprise components during development, operation, and management. Through the combination of these existing components and the iPortal Suite, it is possible to create an enterprise portal solution with a single front end for all pieces of information and applications.

iPlanet

The iPlanet portal, a result of the Sun-Netscape alliance,[68] is one of the most stable and well known platforms in the portal industry. Because it is well known, it is easy to find people that know how to program it. With this portal, it is possible to administer users, personalize content and services, and aggregate information. The security and integration services provide the required infrastructure to create a portal in a short period of time. Although robust and well known, it lacks the functionality of other portal solutions that go beyond simple service and content aggregation.

Plumtree Corporate

Plumtree Software[69] provides personalized information displayed on an internal enterprise portal. It does not provide any special functionality for e-commerce, but remains a good solution for content aggregation on an internal portal.

Portal-in-a-Box

Autonomy Systems Ltd.[70] offers Portal-in-a-Box, which is a solution that offers some very specific features for the automatic processing and display of information. This solution makes it easy to aggregate content from various sources and structure them automatically in a way users may require. This enables companies to create automatic and personalized portal sites without editors, as far as the categorization, tagging, and linking of information is required.

---

[66] http://www.dlr.de/

[67] http://www.iona.com/

[68] http://www.iplanet.com/

[69] http://www.plumtree.com/

[70] http://www.autonomy.com/

Portalmanager

The Portalmanager by Infopark[71] is an add-on to the content management system NPS 4. Information created and managed in NPS 4 can be displayed online using the Portalmanager. This product can be used in content-rich portals that do not depend on e-business functionality (which is missing in Portalmanager), but can be incorporated by using products such as Intershop. See Chapter 7 for more information on Intershop.

Sequoia XML-Portal-Server

The Sequoia XML-Portal-Server by Sequoia Software[72] enables companies to categorize all information of an enterprise and allow personalized access to relevant data. The software is based on the XML standard and provides a good basis for the integration of external information providers.

TopTier

The TopTier portal solution by TopTier Software[73] provides complete control over enterprise applications and data. The view on data and services can be personalized. Using a version control service, it is possible not only for administrators, but also for users, to change or add content to the portal. This can be as easy as dragging and dropping information onto the portal site with a mouse.

Viador E-Portal Suite

The Viador E-Portal Suite developed by Viador[74] is a portal solution that targets the intranet enterprise market. Using this solution, it is possible to search for information, display the results, and distribute the information among co-workers. The solution also provides the ability to create new information and knowledge by combining existing pieces of information. The sources of information can be databases, unstructured documents, or even Web sites.

VIP'PortalManager

The VIP'PortalManager of Gauss Interprise AG[75] provides the creation of enterprise portals on the Internet. The solution contains functions required for the different users of the portal, such as customers, employees, managers, and business partners. It allows the creation of dynamic Web sites with personalized content and navigation.

---

[71]http://www.infopark.de/

[72]http://www.sequoia.com/

[73]http://www.toptier.com/

[74]http://www.viador.com/

[75]http://www.gauss-interprise.com/

6.4.8 Summary

Portals have become a standard on the Internet, and it is difficult for companies to ignore them. If a company wants to become sucessful on the Internet, it needs to take into account the functionality of a portal for its Web site; otherwise, it will not be attractive enough for the visitors. Visitors can be partners, employees, suppliers, or customers. Therefore, different types of portals have been established over the last few years. Following the drop-out of the dot-com, a strong trend towards implementation of B2E portals can be observed. Business-to-employee portals have a great advantage. They are not as visible as the other portals, but have an immediate effect on cost reduction within the company, and are therefore of interest to all companies around the world. A portal is no longer just a Web site; it becomes the digital entry point to a company. With more companies on the Internet, company portals become increasingly more important.

Chapter 7

SHOPPING AND ORM SOLUTIONS

7.1 Online Shopping

7.1.1 Reasons for Online Shops

In order to sell products through the Internet, it is necessary to *think* about the means needed to bring your products, services, or information to the customers. The Internet does not enable you to present these goods in a show room, and in most cases no sales assistants are available to answer customer inquiries.

Online shopping solutions are more adequate for selling products than services. Products require a catalog through which customers can browse and order products. The products can then be shipped to the customer or directly downloaded from the Internet (in the case of products such as software). The major difference between products and services is that products are mass-produced and may be mass-customized. Services in most cases require individual work by the service provider. Services may be completely different for every customer. A translation service does translate texts for customers, but every text is different. These services cannot be easily replicated or even stolen. A strongly personalized service helps the customer and the merchant, as the service is not useful for other customers in other situations. It is not even useful for the same customer in a different situation.

Before deciding which shopping solution is the right one, it is necessary to determine which products you want to sell on the Internet. Are you planning to offer standard products or highly customized services? The number of products you are planning to place on your Web site is also important.

If your company offers only a few products and has very low order volume, there is no need for a complex shopping system. A few Web pages with a description of the products will satisfy the needs of the shop owner and the customers. Each of the pages will contain a link to an HTML form that can be used to process the order. This approach does not cost very much and enables everyone to go online. Small art galleries are offering their pictures to customers over the Internet. If the order volume or the number of products increases, it is fairly easy to extend the system to process the orders automatically if the Web site is implemented in a modular fashion.

Once you begin to offer a wide range of articles, this system becomes difficult for both the shop owner and customers to handle. The shop owner will have difficulties keeping the Web pages up-to-date and consistent, and the customers will have trouble finding a certain product fast. Therefore, a shopping solution is required to handle the increased flow of information that is the basis for the online transaction. It should automate the process of selling goods over the Internet.

Shopping solution software should be easy for the customer to use, for example, it should save the preferences and personal data of the customer. This simplifies the order process for repeat customers and creates customer satisfaction. Customers should have different options for finding a certain product, either by browsing or by searching.

An important question to answer is, When can the return on investment (ROI) be achieved? Ask yourself what your goals are. Are you planning to be profitable in the short term, or are you planning more strategically and accept that the ROI will take years to pay back? Amazon.com needed five years to become profitable, but now it is the largest bookstore on the Internet.

7.1.2 Setting Up the Shop

Choosing the right shopping solution is not easy, as there are hundreds of different software solutions available on the market, and every day more and more appear. In order to select the right solution, three areas need to be examined.

It is necessary to know how difficult the setup of the shop is in order to determine whether or not your current staff is able to handle the setup or if external partners or new employees are needed. You have to find out how easy it is to process orders through the shopping solution. Then you must determine how difficult or easy the administration of the system is.

Depending on the skills of the shop designer, it is possible to find shopping solutions that are able to create complete online shops via wizards and templates. This is appropriate for people who do not have much experience with creating HTML pages or writing CGI applications. The disadvantage is that the shops are not as flexible as the more complex solutions, which use HTML templates that can be easily extended by the shop designer.

But more important than the skills of the Webmaster are the basic technical features. A good online shopping solution will have the ability to connect to existing product databases or at least allow the import of data into a new database. Electronic commerce cannot be conducted if data needs to be replicated manually all the time. In the electronic world it is important to be fast, and fast means that most steps, except for the decision-making ones, need to be automatic.

In order to create a successful online shopping experience, it is important to track users. Tracking users is necessary in order to know which goods a certain customer has chosen and to determine what preferences a certain user has stored.

There are several ways of doing this. Most Web sites use cookies to store information about the user. A cookie is a string of text that contains a user ID and maybe some user preferences, such as preferred language and the preferred layout of the Web site—but this information can also be stored on the server. A cookie needs to contain only the user ID to help identify and track the user. A cookie is created by a Web server and is then saved in a file on the customer's computer. The cookie can only be read by the Web server that put it onto the customer's computer, so there is no way that other sites can gain information on your shopping and browsing. Customers need to have installed the latest browser versions, as earlier versions had bugs that allowed cookies to be read from other Web servers. Some companies do not allow their employees to accept cookies, for privacy reasons, so there should be another way to authenticate a user.

Using basic authentication, users can log in to a site using a login name and password, which allows the Web server to identify that user. If cookies cannot be used to track the user, the login name can be added to the URL to identify a customer. Another way to track customers is to log their domain name or IP address and save this information in a log file.

Amazon.com, for example, uses cookies, basic authentication, and user-based URLs in order to make sure that everyone is able to use its Web pages. The cookie contains a user identification number that is read when the customer logs onto a Web page. The customer then is passed onto a URL that contains this identification number. In case a customer has switched off the cookies or is logging onto the Web site from another computer, customers can alternatively use basic authentication to identify themselves. If the login and password match the data in the database, the customer is passed on to the personalized URL. During setup, it should be possible to determine the way tracking should occur.

One of the most important issues for e-commerce software is internationalization. Internationalization should not be mistaken for localization. Internationalized software allows the shop owner and the customers to be anywhere in the world. It should allow the conversion of currencies to display the payable amount in the local currency, and sales taxes and shipping charges need to be adapted to every country and state. The simpler solutions use tables in the database, with predefined values for shipping, taxes, and currency conversion, but the more advanced systems allow the integration of shipping companies like UPS. The logistics partner will determine how much it will cost to ship a certain good to a given destination and how long it will take, and an interface

Several technologies can be used to track customers. In order to be tracked, customers need to be identified first. Identification can be achieved through

- **Basic authentication**—Customers identify themselves through a login and password procedure.

- **Cookies**—A Web server stores personal information on the customer's computer and retrieves this information whenever the customer returns to the server.

- **Domain name**—Customers are identified through their domain name.

- **IP address**—Customers are identified through their IP address.

- **Personalized URLs**—Customers access a Web server by using personalized URLs; i.e., every customer gets a unique URL.

- **Strong authentication**—Digital certificates are used to identify a customer. These reside either on the hard disk or on a smart card.

Once a customer has been identified, tracking occurs through the same means.

Table 7.1. Tracking Customers

to a bank provides up-to-date currency information. Some service providers may also keep a current tax database which can be accessed automatically through the shopping system. The setup process should help in choosing the right logistics partner and the right bank.

Localization, on the other hand, means that a certain site is converted to the needs of a certain country not only by translating a text, but by adapting processes, modifying navigation, and changing content.

There are many additional features an online offering needs to include, such as autoresponders, chat rooms, and newsgroups. Automatic search engine submission should also be an option in the setup process.

7.1.3 Processing the Order

Once the online shop has been set up, several features for processing the order are required, the most basic being a shopping basket functionality, which "collects" all the items a customer has chosen. The shopping basket should allow the customer to add items, remove items, and change the number of items selected. When the shopping process has been completed, the customer is presented with a list of all products and can do last-minute changes and proceed to checkout, where they need to pay. A shopping solution should support several payment methods, such as credit card payment through Secure Sockets Layer (SSL) and Secure Electronic Transaction (SET), paper and electronic checks, invoice, and cash on demand (COD). See Chapter 14 for further information on payment models.

Accepting only one payment method will not be sufficient, especially if your price range is very broad. In order to maximize sales in your Web shop, you should accept not only several payment methods, but also several order methods, such as ordering via Web page, email, fax, telephone, and "snail" mail. Companies who already sell through traditional channels will require these payment and order models, and for digital startup companies, these features will enable entrance into traditional channels. This also leaves flexibility to cope with future growth. Depending on the company culture, it may be necessary to check if the customers' addresses are valid and if their credit card limit has been reached.

Automation of the order and payment process is also a very important feature of online shopping solutions. Automatic acknowledgments via email or fax should be delivered after the customer has ordered an item from your shop. The acknowledgment should contain all information that is relevant to the order, such as shipping address, all ordered items, date and time of the order, and contact addresses for your company.

The online shopping software should ensure that the customer's privacy is guaranteed by storing all customer-related information in a secure place that cannot be accessed by hackers. When sending out an email acknowledgment, the credit card information should not be included—or only the last few or first few digits should be included for the verification of the customer—as hijacking email is very simple on the Internet.

Cross-selling and cross-promotion should also be standard features of your shopping solution. These features present merchandise that is related to the items a customer already has chosen. A customer may decide to buy a dining table. The online shop should then propose chairs, plates, forks, and knives that go well with the dining table, and offer a discount if the customer buys all the goods together.

Repeat or high-volume customers should receive automatic or negotiated discounts for certain products, and online order tracking is also a feature your online solution needs to include right from the beginning. Customers should be able to check the status of their orders at any time. The tracking feature and a customer feedback feature reduce the load on the customer care center and reduce costs, as more customers use the self-service.

In order to further automate the process of restocking, an inventory management module should be implemented to automatically reorder goods that drop below a predetermined level.

7.1.4   Administration of the Shop

In order to make the online shop successful, it is necessary to adapt to change very quickly. Therefore the administration tools of the online shop need to support all required features for fast change and should be easy to use as well.

Some products allow changes to be made offline, first testing and then uploading them to the server. This method restricts changing information to a certain computer that has the required software and the data installed. Avoid solutions that require all changes to be made offline and the whole database to be reloaded to the server. An alternate method would be to use an online administration interface and update the information in real time. Please note, this is also not the optimal solution, as changes cannot be tested before showing them online. A wrong price can affect your sales, as it did in the unfortunate case of buy.com.[1]

Buy.com claims to have the lowest prices on the Web. In February 1999, they offered a Hitachi 19-inch monitor for $164, which is more than $400 below the correct price of $588. Customers called in to verify that this price was correct. As the wrong price was in the database, the customer care center confirmed the price and within very little time, hundreds of orders were made as the word spread very fast on the Internet. Buy.com first refused to honor the orders, but then decided to sell the remaining monitors in stock (about 150) at the low price. They cancelled all other orders and offered those customers a different monitor already in the $164 price range. Immediately after the event, buy.com changed its sales policy, adding a section about typographical errors, which basically stated that wrong prices on the Web site do not have to be honored by the company. As a result, a group of customers filed a class-action lawsuit against the company.

In a similar incident, ShopNow.com[2] lost an estimated $50,000 when it accidentally sold a number of Palm V organizers for $79, which was $300 below the regular asking price. The company received about 250 orders for the Palm V at $79. In the interest of customer relations, ShopNow sold one Palm V at the discounted price to each of the customers who placed orders.

Although pricing errors on retail Web sites are not a trend in online commerce, they can damage the business of single online merchants. They are an indication that online companies are under more scrutiny than their tradi-

---

[1]http://www.buy.com/
[2]http://www.shopnow.com/

tional counterparts, where such mistakes could go unnoticed except by a handful of customers. A wrong online price is communicated within an instant into chat groups, newsgroups, and mailing lists, flooding the online shops with orders.

Therefore, database quality assurance and a staging area for a Web site are critical for the success of an online shop. These two points are important prerequisites for any type of electronic business. Database quality assurance includes automatic procedures to verify the content of a database by defining a set of rules, such as the minimum prices for a set of products and the maximum range of allowed changes. In addition to this, a person needs to verify the changes made before going into production. A staging area should be available that is an exact copy of the online shop and that can be used to test changes. Moving the new online shop from the staging area to the production area should be done automatically.

A shopping solution should not force the company to invest in new database technology but should use the existing database infrastructure for the online shop. If only one database for the products is used, errors in replication are minimized. The shopping solution should contain interfaces to other applications that are necessary for the buying process, such as a backend ordering system and a payment process. Direct links to other inhouse systems enable additional services to the customers, such as order tracking and availability of products. In order to minimize investment in new technology, the shopping solution should be available for your preferred operating system and hardware platform.

The existing inventory system should be tightly integrated in order to allow your customers to check on stock availability before ordering. Even if you do not want to offer it to your customers, you still need this functionality internally to organize reorders of goods. Certainly, it is essential to check out the costs of integrating your Internet ordering system with your inventory control system before committing to it.

The HTML presentation of the online shop should be done through templates that contain variables that will be replaced by product names and prices stored in the database. This allows the layout to be changed for the whole shop by changing only a few templates instead of thousands of Web pages.

Marketing staff should be able to add, delete, and change product information. Changing data in order to create a special price promotion, for example, needs to be easy enough that the marketing department is able to do it without technical training. Other marketing instruments, such as customer buying history, Web server log files, user preferences, direct mail, and affiliate program management need to be standard in the product you are choosing.

Some companies prefer to divide their merchandise into several online departments to make it easier for customers to find products. Quelle,[3] for ex-

---

[3]http://www.quelle.de/

ample, does not have one shop on its Web site, but a "row" of smaller shops. One shop is for fashion, one is for technology, and one is for books. Although a central catalog and one shopping solution is used, Quelle's approach shows competency in every field by having an extra shop.

Reporting is also a very important feature. Customer behavior and buying patterns need to be presented in a visual way so that managers are able to base decisions on these reports. The reports can show how many customers visit the shop every day, how effectively the shop works, how easily customers can find the products, and how satisfied they are. The reports should be customizable and need to show results from different perspectives, such as time, product, and person.

7.1.5   Quality of Service

To support the growing businesses of the Internet the selected solution needs to be scalable, offering your company growth over time without having to replace the underlying solution. The solution you choose should be able to handle 50 products and 5 orders per day just as well as it could handle 5 million products and 50 thousand orders a day. Additional hardware and a better Internet connection will be necessary, just as other pieces of the architecture will need to be updated, but the basic business process should not be changed and the shopping experience of the customer should not be affected. This leads us to another important issue, which is performance. Although you are online 24 hours a day, seven days a week, you won't experience the same number of customers every day and every hour. You will certainly have peak times, when more customers flow into your online shop, and quiet times, when almost no customers visit your shop.

Quality of service (QoS) on the Internet becomes even more important. In the real world customers have only a limited selection of shops they can visit; in many cases there is only one shop nearby selling a certain product. So service is sometimes a problem, but the shop owner just doesn't care, as people are still buying the products. On the Internet, dissatisfied customers will always have a choice. Therefore, do something about your QoS. A customer who is looking for a certain item and is slowed down by your Web site will eventually find another site that is faster. A customer in the process of paying will not come back if the Web server crashes at that particular moment.

Today many Web sites overprovision the hardware in order to ensure availability at peak times. This is expensive, so alternative techniques are discussed here to solve the problem. First of all, analyze why your server is experiencing problems at peak time. Are there paying customers who are locked out at this time? What pages are most frequently visited during this time? Do you offer large files for download?

Once you have answered these questions, it becomes quite apparent what needs to be done. If there are customers who lose their connection while paying, it is necessary to implement a sort of service prioritization, meaning that the payment service on your Web server will have more dedicated resources than other services running on the same server, such as browsing the catalog or searching for items. During the peak time, this won't resolve the overload of the server, but it will prevent customers who are in the process of doing business with you from being disconnected. If you have Web pages that are visited frequently, or if you offer large files for download, then think about mirroring these parts to other servers around the world. Either use one of the thousands of free Web space services or ask one of your business partners to exchange not only banners, but also Web space, making the download more local for the customers. This way, a customer from the United States does not have to go to a European Web site for the download of a particular program, but can download it from a mirror in the United States.

The second step to ensure QoS is to prioritize certain user groups. It often makes sense to give known customers a higher priority on the Web server than passersby. When you have a successful Web site up and running with lots of return customers, you especially want to make the shopping experience as comfortable as possible. By providing a better QoS for registered customers, you are able to attract new customers to your site.

Better management of resources on the Web server now makes it possible to prioritize services and user groups. This ensures that registered and known customers would experience a better service on your Web site, but it still does not solve the problem at peak times, as an overload may lead to a server crash. In order to prevent a server crash, the connection to the Web server needs to be restricted. The restriction can be implemented through different mechanisms. The simplest method is to display a Web page saying that the server is overloaded and to ask the client to come back later. This is, in fact, not much better than letting the server crash. In addition to telling the customer to come back later, it is possible to reserve a time slot in the near future, where some resources will be dedicated to that customer. The Web site would still say that the server is "too busy right now," but it would ask the client to wait for thirty seconds. A little JavaScript would then automatically reconnect to the site after thirty seconds and the customer would be able to buy something. Another way of restricting access would be to redirect all new customers to another server that contains the same content. This requires you to mirror the complete server to another location or create a local cluster where several servers contain the same solution. This is only justified if the online shop is large enough. Another means of restricting the access to the site is to disallow access for all unknown customers during peak times and invite them to register in order to continue shopping on that site.

Although it seems quite complicated to implement the above-mentioned measures to enhance the QoS, it actually requires only a small program called

WebQoS[4] to be installed on the Web server and to feed it with the rules. The program has been developed by Hewlett-Packard and can be downloaded for free from its Web site. It works on HP-UX, Linux, and Windows NT platforms. In many cases, it does help to increase the level of service while reducing the required hardware.

This little piece of free software was first used during the Soccer World Championships in France in 1998 and helped the Web page[5] to enter the *Guinness Book of World Records* for the most visited Web site in history.

7.2   Shopping Solutions

7.2.1   Business Requirements

Not every shopping solution includes every feature mentioned above. Depending on your requirements, one or the other solution will fit well, but in most cases some additional programming is required to implement special processes that are not supported by the software.

The minimum requirements are the components that can be found in Table 7.2. A customer entering an online shop should immediately grasp what type of shop it is, just like in a real shop. In order to make shopping easy, a shopping basket is required; otherwise, the customer needs to go to a checkout page for every single item. The order and payment process should be comparable to the real-world process in order to make it simple to use and understandable for everyone.

In many countries, selling goods is illegal if the customer does not know what the terms and conditions are. Therefore, it is necessary to display the terms and conditions on the screen, before the customer accepts the order. Although this may not be valid for all countries, offering the terms and conditions will ensure that you do not get into trouble if people from other countries purchase goods or services in your online shop. An example can be seen in Figure 7.1, which displays the terms and conditions page of Lufthansa Cargo's Same-Day[6] service.

The shopping solution needs to provide interfaces to enterprise and legacy applications in order to reduce costs significantly. Most important are the interfaces to existing databases, as your company does not want to handle product sales for every channel in a completely different way.

7.2.2   Technical Requirements

Aside from the business requirements the shopping solution should provide, you must also look at the technical requirements in order to make an informed

---

[4]http://www.hp.com/go/webqos/
[5]http://www.france98.com/
[6]http://www.sameday.de/

Online shopping solutions should include at least the following features. Many products offer additional features, but the following are essential:

- **Database**—Product information needs to be stored in a database, separate from the layout.

- **Interface to applications**—The shopping solutions need to provide interfaces to other applications, such as a payment processor and the ordering system.

- **Payment**—The shop should support several payment models, for supporting different business models and user preferences.

- **Reporting**—Through reports it should be possible to determine what customers really want.

- **Search engine**—Customers should find a particular item with one mouse click.

- **Shopping basket**—The customers' tool for collecting the products they want to order.

- **Terms and conditions**—In order to make contracts legal, it is necessary to display the terms and conditions.

- **Web design templates**—Use of templates to simplify the design process.

Table 7.2. Features of an Online Shopping Solution

decision. One of the most important questions to ask is if the solution is based on an application platform. Chapter 10 provides an overview of application servers. The important questions to ask are

1. Does the application server have a sound foundation?

2. Does the company building the application server have a good business background?

3. Does the application server support Internet standards, such as J2EE, LDAP, CORBA, and XML?

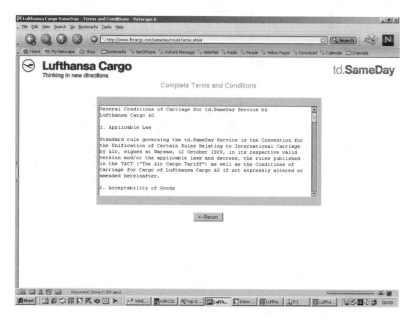

Figure 7.1. Terms and conditions at Lufthansa Cargo.

Only then can you be sure that the shopping solution can be used for a few years without having to be replaced.

Another very important issue linked closely to the application server platform is the readiness for integration with databases, ERP systems, payment providers, and other systems and processes, regardless of who owns them and what operating system and platform they are based on. It is crucial to determine if the integration is done in a point-to-point manner, whereby each service is connected directly, or via a messaging layer in between. This middleware layer is preferable, as the number of integrations and the complexity is largely reduced.

Another important question to ask is if the shopping solution allows the replacement of parts of the application with some "inhouse" programming or if it needs to be done by the software vendor. To make things more practial, the user interface should be easily modifiable to allow the marketing department and the graphics artists to change the visuals whenever they need to.

7.2.3   Taxation of Internet Products

Adding taxes to the online order can become quite complicated if you try to sell services and products on a worldwide basis. Just knowing how to apply taxes in the United States alone is very complicated. In California there are hundreds of different sales tax rates. Different counties in the state also have different rates, and on top of this, some cities add a percent or two! For example, the sales tax in San Francisco is 8.5 percent. In Marin, which is just next to San Francisco, it is 7.25 percent. Berkeley, which is also near San Francisco, has a sales tax of 8.25 percent.

In one part of Canada, even tax is taxed, making tax calculations even more complicated. In Europe, sales taxes depend on the type of goods or service being sold. Trying to keep up with the latest tax regulations manually is not possible.

Besides dealing with varying tax rates all over the world, you also have to deal with *Nexus*. Nexus is a legal term meaning "where you have a presence doing business." In the United States, for example, you are obligated to collect, report, and pay sales tax in states where you have a nexus. The important thing is that nexus is a legal term, so you should seek the advice of your tax attorney on this issue. You need to find out if having a Web server in the United States requires you to pay sales tax or not. Many companies have Web servers in the U.S. without being physically present there, as the servers are cheaper and connection is better in general.

Many online businesses don't calculate the sales tax online, but put a sign on their Web page stating that the sales tax will be added to the order. The fulfillment center then has the task of figuring out the correct sales tax. Although this may work for a while, many customers will turn away and go to other sites where they get the full price and don't encounter hidden costs. It is particularly important to provide your customers with the total amount of their orders if you want your customers to pay online. You cannot expect them to pay twice, once for the product and once for the tax. In many European countries, it is illegal to show prices without taxes included.

Therefore, it is necessary to introduce software that automatically calculates the correct tax. ClearCommerce[7] offers a tax calculator as part of its hosting solution. The Intershop[8] shopping software allows taxes to be added manually for every country and every product. Another good software solution is Taxware,[9] which offers tax calculations for U.S. and international jurisdictions, either over the Internet or as an independent software module. CyberSource,[10] on the other hand, integrates tax and other transaction features through its online service; you tap into its software via the Internet rather than installing the software on your own system.

7.2.4 Shopping Products

There are literally thousands of different online shopping solutions available. Describing every available solution in detail is not possible, so we'll explore some products that have proven themselves in the market.

---

[7]http://www.clearcommerce.com/

[8]http://www.intershop.com/

[9]http://www.taxware.com/

[10]http://www.cybersource.com/

Basically, you have three options for choosing the right shopping solution: Buy a ready-made solution, rent space in an e-hosting solution, or build the system from scratch with components and parts designed to your specifications.

It can be difficult to find the right solution for your business. A ready-made solution is best for companies who have the money and the know-how to install a complete solution on their own and to maintain it. It requires not only HTML knowledge, but also some programming knowledge to set up the shop and maintain it. These solutions have all the required e-commerce features with a few additional business rules built in as a bonus. If your business needs closely match what the package offers, buy it, as this will save you money and a good deal of time. The appropriate IT infrastructure needs to be set up, but as a reward you have total control over the availability and the content, making it a good solution for live transactions, which require up-to-date information and an order tracking system. The costs for setting up and maintaining the system are not to be ignored, but a company with an online shopping strategy will have to invest. If the system is lacking some of your business's critical features, you may need to rethink your choice. The solution may be a good fit right now, but will likely become obsolete as more and more features become necessary later on in development. Adding nonstandard features to a software solution can become difficult if not supported by the software vendor. Make sure that you choose an extensible solution. While the initial costs are pretty high, the customization is easy enough so that hidden charges won't be a problem for your site later.

Since smaller companies will often not have the financial backing to implement and maintain a complex shopping solution, they should look for electronic hosting solutions. This means that they rent an online shop from an ISP, which has paid for the software and hardware and has the infrastructure to operate the online shop. The company would only provide the layout and the products for the online shop. Setting up the shop is easy, because the whole store is administered through a Web frontend. Aside from the Web browser, no additional software needs to be installed. It is possible to configure some settings, and you're ready to go. This makes it more difficult to integrate with an existing fulfillment system, but small companies won't have an automated fulfillment system in most cases and the number of orders will be low, so they can be processed manually or semimanually. A hosting solution can also be appropriate for larger companies who do not see the Internet as their key strategy for the moment, but need to start using the Internet in order to learn more about the medium and its possibilities.

When evaluating the available solutions, you should consider not only the cost of the package but how much it will cost to customize it to suit your individual needs. Often, what looks like an inexpensive setup at the outset can end up eating away at your budget as you try to add new features or redo the design. E-hosting services in general are fairly cheap to get started, but there's a pretty steep cost for configuring them to work and look the way you want.

The third option can be divided into two suboptions. Hewlett-Packard calls them *Chapter One* and *Chapter Two*. Chapter One shops can be built from scratch using tools such as Allaire's Cold Fusion[11] or Pandesic,[12] which offer building blocks for setting up online businesses. These tools make it easy to create complex sites, if the appropriate programming knowledge is available. Through these products, the complete solution does not need to be coded in Perl, Java, or C++, but only the missing parts must be added. Still, it requires a lot of hard work. The next generation, called Chapter Two businesses, do not require these services to be built from scratch. Instead of using components from a single vendor, these e-services can come from any source on the Internet and be built into a complex online shopping solution with very little programming. The advantage of this approach is that if one of the components from another vendor provides more functionality or has become cheaper, it is possible to exchange the building block on the fly without disrupting the service.

Once this new class of online businesses starts to appear, the options will fade away. Companies will start to offer very special services, such as tax calculation, shipping, or product presentation on the Internet, and anybody who uses the same standards will be able to use these services. The following solutions offer the options mentioned in this section.

Beans Industry Cappuccino

Cappucino is a shopping solution developed by the German company Beans Industry.[13] The company offers an innovative solution based on Java. Unlike most other shopping software, Cappuccino cannot be bought—it can only be rented. Depending on the size of the online shop (in this case the number of products), a rental price is paid each month. The pricing is very moderate, allowing small companies to go online very fast.

The concept of Cappuccino is to download the complete shopping solution at once, using a Java applet (see Chapter 12 for more information on Java). Instead of having to reconnect to the server for every single page, all product information is downloaded immediately. This is useful if the product catalog is small, but otherwise the initial download time would be too great.

The advantage is the speed of the navigation once the applet has been loaded. The disadvantage is that the applet is not as customizable as a Web page is. It is possible to add elements, such as the company logo, but it still always looks like a very technical shop, which may not be appealing to everyone.

---

[11] http://www.allaire.com/products/ColdFusion/

[12] http://www.pandesic.com/

[13] http://www.beansindustry.de/

BroadVision One-to-One Commerce

BroadVision One-to-One Commerce[14] is an extensible and flexible electronic commerce application that helps you sell more efficiently to your online customers, whether they are consumers, businesses, or channel partners. With its instant personalization feature, it enables fast-moving, high-transaction companies to instantly change the products, prices, promotions, and other content to better meet user needs, as demand changes. The software is scalable, offering a high throughput in transactions without sacrificing personalization.

The shopping engine allows you to create a good shopping experience for your customers. The system enables the full integration of enterprise, payment, and shipping systems to leverage your existing investments and service relationships. The site management tool is easy to use and allows business managers to change incentives, ads, products, and other content without having to know much about the underlying technology. The content and catalog management tools enable business managers to add, change, stage, and publish content from wherever they are through a simple-to-use visual interface.

HP Emporium

HP Emporium[15] offers a cheap online shopping solution. It is totally managed and hosted by Hewlett-Packard, meaning that the customers do not have to worry about the operation and maintenance for the first phase. The fixed price is a low risk for the customer, while offering the company growth over time.

HP Emporium allows companies to explore, experience, and evaluate the power of the Web for six months while the shop is hosted by Hewlett-Packard. Several workshops are held to allow a company to expand its business after the six months. With Emporium, companies are able to go online almost immediately and gain the required knowledge in the meantime. This allows a timely entry into e-commerce.

The online store consists of the shopping solution in the frontend and payment processing, shipment, and marketing management modules in the backend. The six months online are accompanied by five workshops. The first workshop is the kickoff workshop, which is set up to develop the project plan and the teams required within the company and Hewlett-Packard to support the shopping initiative.

Once the resources and the project plan are decided on, a marketing workshop is used to develop the marketing plan. Immediately afterwards, a workshop explains the e-commerce solution to the company. After the completion of these three workshops, the digital shop is ready to go online.

After three months, an intermediate workshop is planned, where the interim results are discussed and analyzed. And after six months, the analysis

---

[14]http://www.broadvision.com/
[15]http://www.hpemporium.com/

of the final experience is performed and the next steps are discussed. Then the company is prepared to deal with online shopping. It can let Hewlett-Packard host the solution, move on to an ISP, or host the solution in its own environment.

IBM Net.Commerce

Net.Commerce,[16] developed by IBM, is a complex shopping system complete with shopping basket and full search functionality. It is fully localized, making it a good solution for shops with many products.

It provides a set of integrated software components to sell goods and services through an electronic catalog on the Internet. This out-of-the-box solution gives companies the ability to start simple and grow fast. It comes complete with catalog templates, setup wizards, and advanced catalog tools to easily build effective and attractive electronic commerce sites. Net.Commerce can be used both in B2B and B2C applications.

The product comes in three flavors: START, which is suitable for small-to-medium enterprises; the PRO edition, for large online retailers; and a version for hosting servers for ISPs. The software supports both single and multiple storefronts and is scalable over single or multiple machines. Net.Commerce is available for many different platforms and offers a good system integration with databases and legacy systems. Both static and dynamic Web pages are supported, to enable multilanguages, for example.

In addition to the storefront, it contains a payment module suitable for accepting credit card payments using the SET and SSL standards. A wizard makes it easy to set up shops. A module for order tracking and personalization support is integrated as well.

i-Cat Electronic Commerce Suite

The e-commerce suite by i-Cat[17] is a complete solution that consists of ready-to-use templates that can be used to create the layouts for the shop. The standard search functionality and an index are available. Customers are able to register and the information is saved for returning customers. The standard shopping basket is also available, and resellers are able to register and get special prices.

Promotions can be created through the simple-to-use administration interface. It is also easy to change the pricing of the products. In addition to the typical shopping functionalities, i-Cat has built-in security features that allow secure payment over the Internet. CyberCash, CheckFree, First Virtual, Open Market, OM-Secure Link, SET, and SSL payments are allowed (see Chapter 14 for more information on payment solutions). In addition to these preinstalled payment solutions, it is possible to create new ones using a standard-

---

[16]http://www.software.ibm.com/commerce/net.commerce/
[17]http://www.icat.com/

ized API. i-Cat runs on all major operating systems and works together with the most common Web servers. User identification is done by password and not by cookie.

Intershop Online

The Intershop[18] solution offers another complete, open shopping software package. Like i-Cat, it uses templates to create the Web shop frontend. Search and index functionalities are also available. Customers are able to register their address and preferred payment method. Promotions and pricing can be configured easily through the Web administration interface.

Payment methods are preintegrated and include SET and SSL credit card payments, invoice, and cash on delivery. The payment methods can be easily extended, as our team at Hewlett-Packard has proven. A smart card identification and payment solution can be integrated into the existing software without too much trouble, making it an easy-to-use software package that can be easily extended with some programming.

Internet Factory Merchant Builder

Merchant Builder by the Internet Factory[19] is a flexible, easy to administer solution that uses templates. It is cheaper than Intershop and offers a good starting point for startups that do not want to sell thousands of products online.

Access to network databases with open database connecitvity (ODBC) is possible, and CyberCash, ICVerify, and First Virtual payment solutions are included. It is possible to create financial reports, and additional tools for developing merchant applications are included. Merchant Builder is a truly open solution, as the full source code is included.

Microsoft Commerce Server

Microsoft Site Server 3.0 Commerce Edition[20] is Microsoft's solution to e-commerce problems. The solution is highly integrated into Microsoft BackOffice and its development tools. Simple sites can be designed by modifying some basic templates, while complex sites can be designed and customized through Visual InterDev.

SQL Server is bundled with it, giving you a complete database package. Built into the software are *pipelines*, which are visual models that let you manipulate the order of the business processes. Two types of pipelines are available: one for the e-commerce online shopping solution and one for the operational resources management (ORM) type B2B solution.

---

[18]http://www.intershop.de/
[19]http://www.ifact.com/
[20]http://www.microsoft.com/

As all server features can be scripted and programmed through COM objects, the pipelines can be extended to adapt to any scenario. This requires in-depth knowledge of the Windows platform and the product itself. Using the GUI pipeline editor, users can tweak or add code to various steps along the way, once the whole business pipeline has been implemented.

Cross-promotions are supported natively by the system. Any combination of rules and database fields can be used to create special sales, cross promotions, and customer-based promotions. It also offers Web site analysis tools that give you feedback on how many customers are using the site and what their preferred products are.

ElMedia NetSell

NetSell, developed by ElMedia,[21] is a product that is simple to use. The administration is done through a Web browser, and updates are made directly to the production data, making it suitable for smaller shops with only a few products. Larger shops won't want live updates; they will need a staging area where they can test the changes first. A shopping basket and a customer database for registered customers is available.

The NetSell software is designed to work at an ISP site, which hosts the Web server and the shopping software.

Open Market LiveCommerce

LiveCommerce by Open Market[22] is an Internet application that uses an embedded object-oriented database technology to generate a very flexible enterprise-scale catalog system. LiveCommerce is designed for very large catalogs with up to 100,000 items. It offers a fast and flexible navigation capability and offers customized searches according to the customers' requirements by generating the desired catalog page for the browser.

It is possible to use LiveCommerce as a standalone Internet catalog system, just like many others, but its strength lies in the integration with other systems, such as transaction and inventory systems. The latest release incorporates a new store setup wizard, making it even easier for small- to medium-sized merchants to take advantage of the features. Dual currency support has been integrated to present prices in two currencies at the same time, such as Deutsche Mark (DM) and Euro, which is a legal requirement for Euro participants.

---

[21]http://www.elmedia.de/

[22]http://www.openmarket.com/

Yahoo! Store

The Yahoo! Store[23] is another product that cannot be bought, only rented. The software resides on the Yahoo! server and merchants are able to administer their shop via a Web browser. It uses an intuitive interface, has a built-in search engine, and offers peerless statistical tools. The pricing options are very powerful and flexible, meaning that it is easy to customize the prices to the needs of the seller and the buyer.

The rental price per month depends on the number of items you want to sell via the Web. Depending on your focus, it may make sense to outsource the hosting of the Web server and the shopping software. In general, a company will outsource all parts that are not strategic for it. If shopping is just an add-on to your core business, then this can be a good solution.

7.2.5 Comparison of Online Shopping Solutions

Table 7.3 presents a short summary of the features and the types of solutions we have explored. It is difficult to say which solution best fits your requirements. Price, type, and platform will be the first things you need to consider. Then look at the Web sites of the independent software vendors for detailed information on the functionality of their solutions. The better the functionality matches your business requirements, the better positioned you will be to make money through the online shop. The price normally gives an indication of the complexity of the product.

While all of these products are interesting to companies that want to go on-line and to ISPs that want to offer these services to their customers, a new type of selling-shopping solution has come up. In 1999 Hewlett-Packard introduced its Commerce for the Millennium,[24] a complete shopping solution designed for ISPs. Instead of selling a piece of software to the ISP, Hewlett-Packard sells a black-box to the ISP that contains not only a shopping solution, but also the required backend infrastructure, including a link to a bank for online payment and a billing system. Hewlett-Packard has preintegrated all the necessary components for this solution, making sure that all components are interconnected and allow the required flow of information between the store front and the business backend. In addition to the business infrastructure, Hewlett-Packard also provides Internet architecture consisting of hardware, such as servers and routers, that make it easy to add it the to existing equipment of an ISP.

What makes this solution unique is that ISPs do not have to pay up front for the hardware, software, and installation, but instead, pay on a transactional basis. Every time a business transaction takes place in one of the shops the ISP hosts, Hewlett-Packard receives a small fee. This makes it easy for ISPs to expand their business rapidly without having to put together single components

---

[23]http://store.yahoo.com/
[24]http://www.hp.com/

Product	Type	Platforms	Price
Beans Industry	Hosting	Java	low
Broadvision	Product	AIX, HP-UX, Solaris	high
HP Emporium	Hosting	HTML	low
IBM Net.Commerce	Product	Windows, AIX, HP-UX, Solaris	high
iCat ECS	Product	Windows, AIX, HP-UX, Solaris	medium
InterShop ePages	Hosting	HTML	low
InterShop Enterprise	Product	Perl	high
Internet Factory	Product	Unknown	low
Microsoft	Product	Windows	medium
ElMedia NetSell	Hosting	HTML	low
OpenMarket LiveCommerce	Product	Unknown	medium
Yahoo! Store	Hosting	HTML	low

Table 7.3. Comparison of Shopping Solutions

and enables businesses to go online at a lower price, as the cost is recouped over time.

7.3   Implications of the New Economy

7.3.1   Generating Revenues

Using standard software solutions, it is now easy to set up and operate an online shop. This is not enough to be successful, but by paying attention to some basic rules, you can create an online shop that will thrive!

As product prices become more and more irrelevant due to the enormous amount of competition, it is necessary to create unique selling positions. This means that you must offer more than what everyone else offers. As more and more shops offer the same products, it is necessary to distinguish yourself by offering value-added services.

Creating a new bookshop may seem silly with such heavyweights like Amazon.com and Barnes & Noble already enjoying a strong presence on the Web.

But it may make sense if instead of trying to compete with these giants, you find a niche market where you have more expertise than a general bookseller. Creating a vertical portal site where you also offer books will help generate sales in your book shop and at the same time generate hits on the rest of your site. The books offered deal only with the vertical industry you are targeting. By providing additional services and information, your vertical portal can become a central hub for the industry. A good domain name is also important; if people cannot remember how to access your service, they can't come back.

7.3.2   Pricing on the Internet

While the production price is going down, the actual final price for the end customer is not decreasing that much anymore. If we look at the prices, we can see that whenever a technology drops below a certain price, it is replaced by a newer technology. This is especially true for computer hardware. Although the speed of computers is increasing rapidly, the prices are going down only moderately, and older equipment is not available anymore.

As more and more services become digital, it is possible to customize them in such a way that they exactly fit the needs of the customer without necessarily increasing the price. Instead of reducing the price, the price seems to approach the maximum a buyer is willing to pay.

Many think that services and digital products in the information era should be free. The major reason is that many people cannot distinguish between the value of the product and the cost for replicating it. A film may cost $200 million in production, but through Internet replication, costs are nearly zero. Does this mean the film should be given away for free?

The Internet is built on the premise of free information distribution, which was fine while it was solely an academic network. With the introduction of the World Wide Web, more and more commercial companies have become involved and they want to receive money for their products. The problem is that once a product has been digitized, it can be copied without a problem. This can be one disadvantage of the open standards for commercial organizations.

On the Internet we will see three new ways that prices will be set (see also Table 7.4). The first pricing scheme is built on the premise that the price is not based on the production costs anymore, but tends more and more to be determined by the buyer's willingness to pay. The market force behind this fact is the market power obtained by product differentiation. Even then, prices can be set at the consumer's value. Therefore, its price will not be zero unless the product is truly valueless.

The challenge for companies deploying a dynamic pricing application will be to make sure customers feel they have received a fair price. Customers may feel cheated if they discover lower prices after they placed their orders.

In order to determine these new prices, it is necessary to have more information on customers' preferences. Sellers who can gather information on their

The Internet offers new ways of creating revenues for a company, other than pricing the goods and services above the cost of production.

- **Advertising pays the product**—By adding advertising to the core product or service, it can be sold under production cost.

- **Buyer's willingness to pay**—The price is floating depending on demand and offers in the market. The Internet becomes a large auction.

- **Transaction-costs based billing**—The basic service or product is free and the customer needs to pay a low fee for every subsequent transaction.

Table 7.4. New Paradigms on Pricing

customers will have an advantage, as they can present the right products to the right customers at the right time, and will be able to charge the highest prices. If we refer to the example of the film in section 7.4.2, this will mean that in the beginning, the price for a copy of the film will be very high, as many more people will be interested in viewing it. As time goes by, the price will drop to zero, as fewer people are interested in the movie.

This can be done because digital media has very low costs associated with digital replication. The viewer will not see a difference between the original file and the copied file, and what is even more important, the viewer will not care. Artwork, on the other hand, cannot be copied in such a way. The older the artwork gets, the higher the prices become. A copy of a Picasso[25] can be downloaded at no cost, without having impact on the price of the original, as the original picture is more than the frame, the canvas, and the colors used to form the artwork.

The second pricing scheme is based on the premise that it is possible to sell prices under cost of production and make money out of other revenue streams. The British magazine *The Economist*[26] asked an interesting question: Is it possible to sell dollar notes for 90 cents on the Web? The short answer is yes, of course. While companies in the past calculated their prices on the cost of pro-

---

[25] http://www.compulink.co.uk/~phreak/picasso/
[26] http://www.economist.co.uk/

duction, more and more companies have additional revenue streams for making money. Actually, all newspapers and magazines work this way. Have a look at your favorite newspaper. It may cost 25 cents. The real production costs are likely to be higher. Traditional television and radio content are free to the consumer and are financed entirely through advertising. The same applies to most Web sites that offer content. But more and more Web sites that offer goods and services use this paradigm to offer unbeatably low prices.

Free PC[27] is such a company. Free PC, as the name suggests, gives computers away for free. In order to qualify for a free computer, it is necessary to answer a list of questions. If the customer meets certain demographically attractive requirements, the customer will receive one of the computers for free. In order to qualify, you need to be part of one of the target groups of the advertising, which you have agreed to view whenever the computer is switched on. Half of the hard disk's space is reserved for advertising information, updated every time the customer goes online.

Other companies offer similar packages, which are good enough for the occasional computer user. Professional users will be hindered by this type of bombardment and will not be as productive as they could be.

Another way of pricing is based on the transaction costs. Instead of paying a one-time price for a product, you are forced to pay for it every time you use it. The good old telephone service works this way in most European countries, and more and more digital services require transaction payments instead of one-time fees. In Finland, Nokia[28] has started a Web site where customers are able to compose new dial tones for free. They can use the composing software for free, but once they have decided on a new dial tone for their cellular phone, they need to call a special number and enter an ID. This will transfer the dial tone from the Web site to the cellular phone and a transaction fee of approximately 40 cents is charged.

The same could be applied to online word processors, for example, which could be used for free, but the user would be charged a small transaction fee every time a document is saved. The same could apply to loading, printing, and spellchecking. By removing the initial cost, the product, service or piece of information becomes more pervasive. And if the transaction fees are low enough, more customers are willing to spend some money on the product. Instead of having 1,000 customers who each pay $100 for a product, you can have 1,000,000 customers who pay 10 cents per transaction. This generates a higher and more constant revenue stream for the company.

Due to the moves on prices for digital products, nondigital products are now moving, too. IBM, Compaq, and Hewlett-Packard, for example, are actively investigating dynamic pricing models for their online retail sites as a way to reduce inventories and optimize profits.

---

[27] http://www.free-pc.com/
[28] http://www.nokia.com/

IBM is able to automatically adjust pricing on its server line in real time based on metrics such as customer demand and product life cycle. As a result, customers will find that pricing will dynamically change when they visit IBM's Web site on any given day.

Compaq, meanwhile, has been conducting limited testing of dynamic pricing at its Factory Outlet Web site, which offers excess and refurbished products. But Compaq plans to extend dynamic pricing to its main Web site in the near future.

HP calls its dynamic pricing strategy "contextual pricing." Pricing changes as customers add multiple items on certain promotions. HP is currently applying the strategy across its entire product line.

7.3.3   Implications on Price

The Internet enables the free exchange of information, which also means that pricing information flows more freely. The cost of exploring alternative offerings and substitute products is nearly zero. In market segments where products and services are not differentiated sufficiently, a price war will take place. Tickets, for example, are such products. Many airlines offer online auctions for empty seats on airplanes. Based on the last minute model, customers are able to bid for the seat. The core business of travel agencies, checking for flights and booking tickets and hotels, becomes more and more self-service on the Internet. Online banking makes life difficult for many bank clerks. As the cost for the business transaction drops, the price for the customer drops as well.

Although many customers still prefer known brands, the low-entry cost to the New Economy will drive down prices for established brands to the level of no-name products or services. Known brands are subject to greater scrutiny in the realm of overwhelming information availability. The Internet offers a huge opportunity for newcomers to pose a threat to known brands; the cost for establishing a new brand is high, however. Amazon.com spends most of its money on the marketing campaigns to market its brand. The costs for the operation of the business are almost negligible.

7.3.4   Implications on Cost

By digitizing processes—such as moving distribution from physical products to digital products or using Internet-based inventory tracking services—costs can be cut dramatically. The shortened duration of the time spent in the value chain provides both benefits and operational challenges. The technical challenges can be resolved easily through advanced hardware and software, but in order to stay in front of the competition, the operational challenges need to be resolved.

Companies need to handle all of their processes in parallel through real-time transactions. The Internet enables companies to drive down costs by introducing new processes, which either enhance existing processes or replace them. This requires resources to be redeployed, particularly in the back office, as the front end is represented by a Web application. Only very few online systems are self-funding at the time of writing, but costs can be saved in the backend by changing the processes and adapting them to the needs of the New Economy.

7.4   Electronic Software Distribution

7.4.1   Benefits of ESD

Electronic software distribution (ESD) is a particular way of selling products via the Internet. The key feature is that it is not necessary to ship out products to the customers via traditional logistics companies. Shipping costs drop to nearly zero. The product and the manual are downloaded by the customer from the Internet.

The only shipping fee that occurs is the online time of the customers, if they are connected via a provider or telephone company that charges on a minute or hourly basis. I remember one incident in 1997 when I downloaded the Visual Café Java compiler package from Symantec[29] for the Macintosh, which at that time was already over 20 MB in size. I had ordered it directly from the Web site and downloaded it from the United States to my Mac in Europe, taking about six hours to download the complete package. My biggest fear was that the download would be interrupted and I would have to try again. Worse than trying again was the fact that I was allowed only one retry. I was lucky; the software was downloaded the first time. ESD has evolved over time to overcome these problems. Faster modems and new concepts have made ESD a secure and inexpensive solution for the distribution of software. Not only can software be distributed through ESD, but so can music, videos, and books.

Customers, publishers, and channel partners can all benefit from ESD. Customers, for example, experience a new shopping convenience as they can expect instant gratification. No matter what time of the day customers access a Web site, they will be able to download the product immediately. This also allows quicker access to updates and new releases for registered customers. ESD allows new pricing alternatives, such as try-and-buy and pay-per-use.

The benefits for the publisher include lower cost of goods sold compared to a physical distribution. The publisher does not need to replicate the product or the packaging, which also makes returns simple. There can be more efficient sales of niche and low-volume products, and ESD also offers a more efficient channel for updates and selling upgrades. It also allows a faster time to market for new or replacement products. The paradigm of ESD improves the inventory management by avoiding stock-outs in the channel.

---

[29]http://www.symantec.com/

The advantage for channel partners is that they do not need to carry a physical inventory, and therefore do not have any inventory-carrying costs. The sales environment is much more scalable without the traditional cost increases. Flexible and timely pricing and special offers with immediate feedback help the channel partners develop new target markets and get returning customers to the Web site by offering free upgrades, additional information, and bug fixes. The channel partners also do not have to deal with geographical boundaries. The products can be sold all over the world, with a faster time to market. The digital distribution chain makes it easier and more flexible to bundle and un-bundle products.

7.4.2 Problems with ESD

Although ESD offers a lot of advantages, it also has some disadvantages, which can be overcome if the traps are known and appropriate security mechanisms are implemented. Downloading software without special protection will allow the customer to copy the software to anyone and destroy the legal revenue stream of the software distributor. Forrester Research[30] calls it the "Digital Distribution Wars."[31]

The problem is not new. Software pirates have been illegally copying software for years, but the Internet offers new ways to spread the illegal software. In order to make ESD a success for a company, it is necessary to protect the software in such a way that copying becomes impossible or infeasible. The faster the Internet connection, the more easily large software packages can be downloaded from the Internet. So far, university students and business people have the best connection to the Internet, but more and more households are getting high-speed access, making it easier for anyone to get direct access to software. Just as pirated software has helped the explosive growth of the personal computer, it now helps the explosive growth of the Internet, even though the content industry does not want to acknowledge this. In 1985, the FTP tool enabled pirates to exchange software over the Internet, and today's search engines make it even easier to find pirated software.

Another problem with ESD involves new devices that are especially designed for pirated content. Diamond Multimedia[32] upset the music industry when it released the Rio portable MP3 player in October 1998. Although there is some legal MP3 music available on the Internet, at sites such as mp3.com[33] or orbos.de,[34] most of the music available in the MP3 format on the Internet is illegal—for that reason the Rio portable is successful. It also makes the copying of music much easier than it used to be.

---

[30] http://www.forrester.com/

[31] *The Forrester Report*, "Digital Distribution Wars," Michael Putnam, April 1999.

[32] http://www.diamondmm.com/

[33] http://www.mp3.com/

[34] http://www.orbos.de/

Although most software or content is available digitally, so far very few companies have put up their digital content for sale directly on the Web. All the premium material has been held back. Media and software firms have extensive libraries of desirable content, but they will not distribute it digitally without a way to protect their revenue. Some companies are not able to cope with the quick change in technology. Instead of getting into digital distribution, they sue the startup companies, which use the new paradigms and technologies to sell their content over the Internet. The recording industry, for example, tried to stop Diamond Multimedia from releasing the Rio portable. Diamond Multimedia and the record industry together could have introduced a new standard for online music that would help stop piracy, but instead the music industry chose to see Diamond Multimedia as a competitor.

7.4.3 Making ESD Profitable

The content industry is pursuing new digital formats that make it possible to copy-protect the content. Threatened content owners are developing new secure publishing formats. To make the digital distribution business successful, technology firms and content owners must agree on protection principles and build a new digital infrastructure. To achieve robustness and flexibility, this framework surrounds content with compression formats, copy prevention methods, devices, media players, and licensing systems.

Agfa,[35] Hewlett-Packard, Kodak,[36] and others responded to digital imaging piracy by creating the Digital Imaging Group[37] in September 1997. Their FlashPix format, together with copy prevention technology from cSafe and fingerprinting from ImageLock, forms a secure infrastructure for image commerce on the Web. More information on FlashPix and other image formats can be found in Chapter 13.

The music industry responded to the threat of MP3 with the Secure Digital Music Initiative (SDMI) in February 1999. While the music industry backs the SDMI effort with the goal of settling protection and developing devices for the customers, it is also battling the efforts of IBM[38] and Liquid Audio,[39] which are proposing their own secure formats.

It is just a matter of time until people download videos from the Internet. In May 1999 the first pirated copies of the new *Star Wars* films appeared on the Internet. The file was 1.3 GB, too large for most people to download in reasonable time, and too costly. But it can be expected that within a few years bandwidth will be good enough for anyone to download the file within a few minutes or watch the movie in real time over the Internet. In 2001 this has

---

[35]http://www.agfa.com/

[36]http://www.kodak.com/

[37]http://www.digitalimaging.org/

[38]http://www.ibm.com/

[39]http://www.liquidaudio.com/

become reality. Every blockbuster is available on the Internet even before you can see it at the cinema. A new format called Divx and general availability of DSL have made this possible.

The software for real-time movie-watching is already available. Realplayer from RealNetworks[40] and QuickTime by Apple[41] already enable viewing of films and TV programs in low quality. Increased bandwidth will increase the quality of service.

The Internet and other digital media have eroded the distinction between music, video, games, and images. All these media merge into a new type, which is basically digital content. The newly formed content industry will have to create a multimedia rights clearinghouse to prevent unauthorized copying of the content. The existing clearinghouses, such as ASCAP and BMI, will most probably merge into this new multimedia rights clearinghouse, as these single industries merge. Imagine a racing simulation where the player is able to choose any type of music for the background music. The game and the music are merged into a group of digital content. This can be done only if the clearinghouse can track the copyright owner of the game and the music and charge the consumer a small sum for the usage of it. It will become possible to download films, games, music, and images from different Web sites, with the licenses stored in a single location in the backend.

Commerce Direct International[42] (CDI) is a clearinghouse that runs its service on centralized servers and works directly with software publishers rather than retailers. McAfee Associates, Inc.[43] and Corel Corp.[44] are using CDI's encryption, wrapper, and transport technology to sell their security and photo library products through their own Web sites.

Cable companies and broadband Internet access providers will merge into the single space of content providers, being able to charge for downloads and put it onto the invoice of the ISP or cable provider. This will mean that content providers will use new technologies and formats, as the current content formats are far too easy to copy. One problem with these new technologies is the encryption that is used. This will put the United States in a bad position, as the export of encryption devices is very restricted. Other countries that are producing encryption software and content devices, such as Israel and Japan, will benefit.

7.4.4 New Licensing Models

ESD allows for new licensing models that are slowly being adopted by the software publishing industry. This change has been inspired by advances in license

---

[40] http://www.real.com/
[41] http://www.apple.com/
[42] http://www.cdi.net/
[43] http://www.mcafee.com/
[44] http://www.corel.com/

management systems, which allow billing for the actual usage of a certain digital product instead of having a fixed price for the software. Depending on business rules, the price can be adapted easily for different occasions.

These license management systems have additional functionality, allowing developers the ability to monitor and track the usage of their products. With these technologies embedded into their products, developers can negotiate almost any license model shaped by various criteria, ranging from length of term and number of invocations to number of concurrent users. Software leasing may become viable for many companies.

These new license management systems not only allow software companies to monitor the use of their applications and content providers to monitor the use of their audio or video data, but also local network administrators working for a certain company to create a software inventory of all connected computers that reside on a company intranet. Employees will have the ability to install software from anywhere, with a centralized license management system in place. This also helps to reduce the amount of pirated software on company computers.

Software manufacturers and content providers are now able to provide new forms of licenses, and three types will become important in the future: concurrent licenses, licensed periods, and licensed sessions. The concurrent licenses term allows a maximum number of users who are allowed to access a service or software at the same time. This type of license is often used for Web software, as it allows the control of the number of users accessing a certain piece of software at a given time. Database management systems are also often sold on a concurrent use model, as their value increases with increased numbers of concurrent users.

The licensed periods model allows software manufacturers to operate a subscription business. The products are given out to the customers and can be used for a specific period of time, such as a month or a year. Shareware or tryware are typical pieces of software that are given out to customers for free for a certain period of time for testing purposes. Customers are able to test the software for 30 days and are then required to pay for the license or delete the software from their hard disk (see Chapter 15 for more information). Digital certificates are also often based on the licensed periods model. They expire after one or two years and require the owner of the certificate to go back to the certification authority to get a new one. The reason is twofold. It allows the certification authority to make money from the renewals and the certificate is rechecked every two years for security reasons, just as you have to renew your passport every few years.

Licensed sessions mean that a certain piece of software or content can be used or viewed. This form of license gives customers a fixed number of sessions or a fixed amount of time. This is especially interesting for content providers. Most hotels around the world allow the viewing of pay television. Once you have paid for a film, you are able to view the film for a certain period of time (normally one day) or a certain amount of times (normally twice). A similar license could be applied to content that is distributed over the Internet.

7.4.5 ESD Products

Products that allow ESD need to adhere to some rules that will be accepted by the people who use them. Trying to invent bullet-proof protection is a waste of time. Every protection can be cracked, no matter how good it is; therefore the balance between ease-of-use and copy protection should be maintained. The copy-protection should be transparent to customers and should limit abuse to determined attackers. They are the real threat to your company—not the otherwise honest people who might make a copy for a friend from time to time.

The content industry needs to wrap content into a format that protects itself. This means that even if you are able to copy the content, the source is always encoded into the content so that pirates can be located easily. Watermarks are a good way to simply protect content. Companies like Channelware[45] have developed technologies that can decrypt files on the fly while a game or application is being run. As soon as you exit the game or application, the decrypted program is removed. In conjunction with digital watermarks and online registration, it protects the content even after the distribution.

To make ESD products more secure, it is necessary to separate the license from the content. This means that someone needs special software or devices to unlock the content. Just passing on the content will not enable anyone to use it. The license is personalized, meaning that it is very easy to trace its origin. To unlock protected content, the encryption key needs to be sent to customers, via email, for example. The advantage is that if a download could not be completed, it can be resumed based on the license records.

A good ESD product must be able to handle the complex tasks of delivering software and data to all systems dispersed on the Internet or on a company intranet. It needs to be able to verify that the software was installed successfully and is ready to run. Problematic software should be deinstalled and older versions restored if a problem occurs. A good ESD program also will help keep track of the versions of software and data that are currently installed. This will help to create an effective marketing initiative for Internet customers, as they can be informed about updates and bug fixes. On company intranets, automatic updates can be executed and it can be verified that all users have the same version running on their systems, making user support easier. A good ESD program should be able to distribute software to as few as one or two computers or as many as thousands of systems at various geographic locations.

It should be ensured that the ESD products do not require additional hardware for the customers. Dongles (hardware keys)and other types of hardware protection have not been accepted by customers in the past, and this is not likely to change in the future. As the software is updated, new hardware would

---

[45]http://www.channelware.com/

be required on a regular basis. A content-independent protection may be acceptable.

Companies like Reciprocal,[46] Digital Delivery,[47] InterTrust,[48] GLOBEtrotter,[49] Release Software,[50] and Digital River[51] have already created ESD solutions for immediate use. It is expected that they will adopt new international standards that are currently in the process of being defined.

7.5 Configurator Tools

7.5.1 Reasons for Configurators

In order to create a product, collaboration is essential. Designers and engineers need to work together to create a product to particular specifications. Through computer-aided design (CAD) software, this has been possible for quite some time. Using Web-based configurator tools, the collaboration can be easily extended to the customers so that they can create and buy unique products over the Internet.

Through a product configurator, customers are able to assemble product components into a finished product. The customers are elevated to a level of technical abstraction where they do not need to know which components fit together or how. These pieces of information are programmed into the configuration application. Through the Internet, customers from all over the world are able to assemble complex products themselves, directly at the site of the manufacturer, without needing the technical background required for every single piece, thus resolving the need for a technical expert as an intermediary.

The use of configurators reduces the number of technical people in presales and sales, as the customers are able to answer all questions regarding the configuration themselves. All major computer vendors, such as Dell[52] and Hewlett-Packard,[53] offer online configurators for their computers. Since computers today consist of many components, it is important to know which soundcard works with which main board and graphics accelerator. There are also many types of memory chips, processor upgrade cards, and other hardware, which won't work together in every combination. Instead of ordering the hardware products one by one, customers can now order through the configurator in a context. This context allows customers to select the appropriate hardware components. The number of returns is reduced through configurator tools, and the customers are more willing to buy a product, as they are sure it will work

---

[46]http://www.reciprocal.com/
[47]http://www.digitaldelivery.com/
[48]http://www.intertrust.com/
[49]http://www.globetrotter.com/
[50]http://www.releasesoft.com/
[51]http://www.digitalriver.com/
[52]http://www.dell.com/
[53]http://www.hp.com/

with their existing configuration.

All major car manufacturers have been using configurators for quite a while on their Web sites. See Figure 7.2 for the online configurator on Alfa Romeo's homepage.[54] Originally, they were used by the salespeople when talking to customers. Now that more and more cars are sold over the Internet, these tools are also accessible directly by the customer. Based on the component selections, a price is dynamically returned to the user, which makes the product configurator a good tool for Web-based sales as well.

Figure 7.2. Alfa Romeo's online configurator.

By using Internet-based configurator tools, companies are able to collaborate with a much broader audience and extend their business. In many cases intermediaries were used to create configurations for the end customer. With the new generation of configurator tools, these intermediaries can focus their business on other services. Product-oriented companies need to look into Internet product configurators in order to survive.

By using configurators, customers are able to create customized solutions and receive pricing quotes in an instant. This also helps the manufacturer to reduce the time for producing the solution, as the orders can't be inaccurate or incomplete anymore. This also eliminates the order entry rework, necessary if no configurator is used. All of this results in increased customer satisfaction related to a higher quality quote to delivery process. Configurators align solutions to the needs of the customers.

---

[54]http://www.financealfaromeo.co.uk/

7.5.2   Configurator Products

Many configurator products are available and offer varying degrees of functionality on the Internet. The following list of products gives an overview of the best configurator solutions available at the time of writing. The Internet enables customers to perform a number of "what-if" scenarios, without the need to understand every component of the product in detail.

Primus

Primus[55] offers a packaged software application suite called 2Order Interactive Selling System. The software is designed for client/server configurations and for standalone computers such as laptops, and offers Internet connectivity. Besides product and pricing configuration, the suite offers solutions for interactive negotiation, quote and order management, proposal generation, a marketing encyclopedia, and data synchronization. Through 2Order, manufacturers are able to analyze the requirements of the customer more accurately. Once the customer inputs the requirements, the system is able to configure, price, quote, and sell the products and services. The software is available for the Windows platform, which makes it a good choice for salespeople and their laptops, but a less stable solution for the general public on the Internet.

Cincom

Cincom[56] offers a whole suite of products, called iC Solutions, for configuration. They allow you to generate complete, accurate configurations. Cincom streamlines the configuration process by offering a complete suite of products for the sales force.

   The iC Configurator Developer is the core product, offering easy management of information about customer requirements, products, and services. It is possible to define attributes and features and add alternative configurations in case the original configuration is not available. It is also possible to convert unique customer requirements into customer solutions.

   Through iC Connect, the salespeople do not have to connect to a server, but have all information stored locally, making it a good solution for customer visits. The data is copied from the server before going offline. Once the computer gets back online, all orders and updates for the configurator are exchanged.

Firepond

FirePond[57] offers a comprehensive set of tools for sales and marketing, called SalesPerformer. One part of the solution is called SalesPerformer Configuration and offers one of the best configuration engines available today. It allows

---

[55]http://www.primus.com/

[56]http://www.cincom.com/

[57]http://www.firepond.com/

salespeople, partners, and customers to create accurate product configurations. Through a mix of representation, it is possible to create simple to complex product configuration models. This is achieved through optimized solvers that address Boolean logic, conditional logic, fuzzy logic, spatial placement, and many other deployment-proven modes of configuration. SalesPerformer Configuration is the only solution to represent configurations in all of the modes at the same time. In addition to this, it is even possible to use several solvers to mix inference engines to solve very demanding problems.

The configurator can be used, for example, first to determine which type of product fits the business needs of the customers, and then the same configuration logic can be applied to further narrow the usage criteria, such as a specific model, options, and engineering specifications. The final outcome is a highly customized product that has been designed interactively by the customer but is buildable by the manufacturer.

Through the GUI, customers are even able to participate in complex configuration processes. This reduces the need for training and speeds up the time for a deal to complete. The user interface is highly customizable depending on the output device and sales situation, such as a salesperson talking to the customer or the end customer using the Internet to configure a system.

Friedman Corporation

The Friedman Corporation[58] offers an integrated configurator for three key industries: building and home products, capital equipment, and consumer products. The multiplatform software is highly modularized. Specializing in ERP solutions for discrete to-order manufacturers, it offers a good solution in high-volume and complex order-entry manufacturing environments.

Gedys

Gedys[59] offers a suite of products to implement product and service configurators. The suite consists of the products net.select, web.select, and Web-ROM. Depending on the size of the company, you can choose either net.select or web.select. Both of these allow you to start with a small core product and then add new modules as your needs grow. The third product, Web-ROM, enables the functionality of the Internet-based solution to be extended to salespeople traveling with a laptop and to kiosk-based terminals without permanent connection to the Internet.

---

[58]http://www.friedmancorp.com/
[59]http://www.gedys.com/

Planware

The Konfex configurator by the German software house Planware DV-System GmbH[60] offers a lightweight product, used by many small-to-medium enterprises in German speaking countries. The system is able to create an online configuration system for companies that offer highly customizable products. Konfex is subdivided into four pieces of functionality. The actual configuration tool provides tools for checking the technical feasibility, and for price calculation, and a template feature for Web pages. One customer is Erwin Junker Maschinenfabrik,[61] which uses it for the configuration of spare parts.

Trilogy

Trilogy[62] is the maker of the Selling Chain Suite, which is a comprehensive, integrated sales and marketing solution. One of the most famous configurator tools, which is used on the PC Order[63] Web site, for example, is able to manage the flow of information between a company and its customers. It provides a company with appropriate customer information needed to price, market, and sell its solutions, while giving the sales channel and end customer access to sales information needed to make an informed buying decision.

SC Config, Selling Chain's configurator, delivers accurate solutions and quotes by incorporating the preferences of the customers and the choices made during the product selection. The user-friendly administration system allows nontechnical staff to define product relationships.

7.6   Auctioning on the Internet

7.6.1   Reasons for Online Auctions

In the past few years the first generation of online enterprises has started to use the Internet for communication, representation, and in some cases a limited amount of transactions. The next generation of online businesses has started to emerge and does not provide the above-mentioned services but takes them a step further by dynamizing transactions. Dynamizing transactions are transactions with dynamic pricing. New applications and business processes are being developed to grasp more of the potential of the Internet.

Interactivity is the key to dynamic transactions, where prices are adjusted in real time to the offerings on the market and the demand for these offerings. This means that technologies and processes used for the stock market, with its real time price adjustments, are used in other industries and segments to adjust prices immediately. One of the most important instruments for dynamiz-

---

[60]http://www.planware.de/

[61]http://www.junker.de/

[62]http://www.trilogy.com/

[63]http://www.pcorder.com/

ing prices is the business model of online auctions. Online auctions can help reduce the costs and increase the revenues for companies, if used intelligently. Although auctions may not be suitable for every transaction over the Internet, they help to get rid of inventory that is obsolete or superfluous or does not sell very well.

Dynamizing prices also means that there is no longer a need for partnerships or long-term contracts,but that companies can instantly buy goods and services from anyone offering a solution to their problem. This enables companies to buy cheaper and sell more expensively. The advantage is easy to see, since it maximizes the revenues of a company. But there are also some inherent disadvantage in dynamizing prices. In some cases a company is not able to buy any products or services, either because nothing is available on the market or prices are too high—this means a major risk for the company. By strategically buying all goods of a certain brand, it would be possible to control that brand. The company that bought the goods would be able to increase the price, if there is high demand, and the manufacturer would not be able to do much about it, since the result of the auction is not predetermined.

A study conducted by Forrester Research[64] suggests that the market will more than double from the year 2000 to 2003. Other researchers have similar figures. The most important thing to notice is that while growth is linear, the revenues grow exponentially. META Group[65] predicted a market of about 8.5 billion dollar/euro in 2000, but expects that the transaction volume will increase to about a 100 billion dollar/euro in 2004.

When thinking about the introduction of online auctions, consider the reasons for doing this in advance. Again, many companies have jumped on the bandwagon, holding auctions without really knowing what it means for their companies. There are three different groups that are interested in providing online auctions. Traditional auction houses, such as Christie's[66] or Sotheby's,[67] want to expand their existing business onto the Internet. Businesses want to use online auctions as marketing tools to attract new customers and sell off goods quickly. Online startups see auctioning as a basic module for their online marketplace.

Depending into which category you fall, you will have different requirements and needs. Auction houses can use the Internet along with their brand names to establish a new channel. These traditional auction houses also provide a lot of trust with their brand. So buying a Rembrandt at Christie's is probably a good idea, while it may not be on eBay, as you probably would not really trust the authenticity of such a high-priced item offered on eBay.

Businesses of all sorts are trying to use online auctions to sell off old models. In Germany alone, the market for this type of auction is about 30 billion

---

[64] http://www.forrester.com/

[65] http://www.metagroup.de/

[66] http://www.christies.com/

[67] http://www.sothebys.com

dollar/euro. Many companies want to get rid of old inventory but have not been able to sell off these goods in time to interested companies or end consumers. Through the Internet, they can sell these goods within minutes for favorable prices instead of having to dump them. Companies that produce goods with a very short lifecycle can use this business model to make sure that they make profit on every single item they produce.

Online auctions can also be used as a marketing tool to attract new customers and provide a bargain momentum for existing customers. While sales through auctions are not really much lower than normal sales, the marketing effect is huge. Typical auction sales are about 8 percent below normal street price.

Online startups have different ideas about auctions. They act as an intermediary, either by buying goods and selling them afterwards or by providing a platform where buyers and sellers can meet. A study developed by Kevin Chui and Rami Zwick at the University of Hong Kong sees antiquities, computers, and consumer electronics as the most important product categories on the Internet. In Table 7.5 you can see a complete survey of products that are sold in online auctions.

The table shows two trends. In earlier times, antiquities have played an important role, and this hasn't changed. But a second large market has been established: the market for computer equipment. It is only a matter of time until all the other product categories become as powerful as these two.

Another very interesting observation can be made, though. Some auction sites have begun to offer services, such as IT and marketing services, and others offer cattle auctions, property auctions, land auctions, pet auctions, airplane auctions, wine auctions, flower and tobacco auctions, and more. Any type of product or service will soon be auctionable.

7.6.2 Types of Auctions

Following is a short overview on the different types of auctions used on the Internet. In auction theory, there are four standard auction types: English auction, Dutch auction, first-price sealed-bid auction and vickrey auction. These auctions are the most common types of auction on the Internet.

The most common is the English auction. The English format can be used for an auction containing either a single item or multiple items. In an English auction, the price is raised successively until the auction closes. The high bidders at that time are declared the winners and each bidder is required to pay the seller the amount of their winning bid.

The bids are sorted in order of price, quantity, and then time. If bids are for the same price, the bid for the larger quantity wins. If the bids are for the same price and quantity, then the earlier bid wins. The sort order applies only when there is a tie. You can increase your bid to tie an amount, but you win on a tie if you win in the sort order. You must use the next highest bid increment.

The following table provides the most popular products on auction web sites.

Product Category	Percent of Websites
Antiquities	62%
Computer hardware & peripherals	55%
Computer software	46%
Consumer electronics	29%
Toys	26%
Sport and fitness	25%
Jewelery	25%
Books, music, films	22%
Office supplies	21%
Household	18%
Other	11%
Instruments	10%
Photography	10%
Autos	10%
Clothing	9%
Airplane/train tickets	6%
Travel	6%
Services	5%

Table 7.5. Most Common Products

If an auction is for more than one of an item, you may have to accept a partial win on your bid.

Automatic (or proxy) bidding is a common technology used for online auctions. Under this system, you bid the maximum amount you are willing to pay and the software places your bid at the minimum level required for you to win. If another bidder outbids you, the system will keep bidding for you until it reaches the maximum you specified. eBay[68] is using this technique to make it easier for bidders to stay in the race.

A quick-win auction can be considered a subtype of the English auction and is only valid for an auction of a single item. In this type of auction, the seller declares a threshold price. If a bidder matches the threshold price, the auction

---

[68]http://www.ebay.com/

closes immediately and that bidder is declared the winner. The advantage for the bidders is that the maximum price is guaranteed, and this makes it easier to plan for the future. In this case the maximum price is fixed, but the first that accepts that price will receive the goods. In certain areas, where not many people are interested in buying the goods, the price may even stay below and the highest bidder wins after the auction is terminated.

Another very popular form of online auctions are Dutch auctions. They have been used in flower auctions in the Netherlands for the past several hundred years. In a Dutch auction, the price of the item falls rather than rises as the auction progresses. Merchants place listings offering a group of products at an opening price, which then drops after regular intervals of time have passed. You can see when the price will drop and how far on the listing page it has fallen. A bid on these listings guarantees you the item you agree to purchase at the specified price.

Sixt,[69] a rental car company, for example, provides a Dutch auction every week, where they offer used cars on their Web site. The car configuration is presented online and the auction starts with the highest possible price. Every few seconds, the price goes down several hundred dollars/euros. There is only a single car per auction, which means that the first one to bid wins. This auction is the most difficult to control for a bidder, since there is no way to see what the other bidders are doing. So no one knows how long someone has to wait in order to make a good bid. For Sixt, this model works very well, because many people buy at a high price to make sure that they get the car.

The first-price sealed-bid auction is the third type of auction that is of interest here. Every bidder provides a single bid, which is sealed and cannot be changed. All bids are then collected by the auctioneer and published at the same time. This means that the bidders do not know what the others have bid. The offer with the highest or lowest price wins the auction (depending on who the initiator of the auction is). This auction is not dynamic, as it does not give the other bidders a chance to overbid the highest bid.

This type of auction is used for large proposals but is only useful if the target price for the object or service is more or less known. As there is only a single chance of bidding, the bidder needs to have a good knowledge about the other bidders and their bids. Otherwise, the bid could be too high or too low compared to the others. Therefore, the first-price sealed-bid auction is not really usable in all situations.

The Vickrey auction, which is the least used on the Internet, uses a bidding process very similar to the first-price sealed-bid auction, but with one difference. Instead of paying the highest bid, the winner has to pay only the price of the second highest bid. The advantage of this auction type is that bidders are more likely to increase their bid, because they know that if they win, they will not have to pay that price, but will actually end up paying less.

---

[69]http://www.e-sixt.com/

7.6.3   Auction Software

Following is a short summary on the most common auction software products currently on the market. The software packages and vendors are most likely to change, so please use this list just as a guide, just like all other software reviews within this book.

Auctioneer 4

Auctioneer 4 by NetMerchants[70] is a software solution with some special features that make the auction process easier for the customer. Customers, for example, can register for email catalogs with their preferred products. This means that a customer or prospective bidder can select from a list of product categories and will be notified if a certain product or group of products is on sale. Through this system, a customer does not need to be online all the time to look out for good opportunities to bid on items of interest. This is especially useful for collectors.

This technology is also used when a known customer enters the site. All offerings are personalized to the requirement of the customer to make it easy to navigate the site. Auctioneer 4 provides various payment methods and an open interface to connect to others. It can be administrated through a Web interface and provides a simple-to-use installation guide.

Some Web sites that use Auctioneer include erock.net[71] and Boxlot.[72] It is a suitable choice if you already have a Web site and want to extend this option with C2C (consumer-to-consumer) auctions.

Moai LiveExchange

Moai Technologies[73] provides an auction solution based on Java technology. The LiveExchange exists in three different versions. The first version, called LiveExchange Enterprise, provides the ability to receive several bids from multiple bidders. The second version, called LiveExchange Marketplace, provides the option to create a marketplace or exchange that can be used by multiple buyers and sellers. The third version is the LiveExchange ASP software, which can be used by ISPs on an infrastructure level and can be redistributed towards their clients.

The software is able to deal with English, Dutch, and reverse auctions and is able to support B2C, C2C, and B2B auctions, depending on the version you want to buy. The software enables companies to create rather complicated rules for their auctions, based not only on prices, but for example, on geography or other features.

---

[70]http://www.netmerchants.com/

[71]http://www.erock.net/

[72]http://www.boxlot.com/

[73]http://www.moai.com/

A company that is using LiveExchange is Homeauctioneer.com, which enables people and companies to offer their houses and apartments online. In order to bid on that site, every bidder needs to go through a credit check first, reducing the number of fraudulent bids significantly.

The solution provides a good control over enterprise-critical real-time transactions and provides an open interface towards ERP and other backend systems. All three versions are available on Windows NT, Sun Solaris, and Hewlett-Packards HP-UX.

OpenSite Auction

A complex auction Web site can be built with OpenSite Auction by OpenSite Technologies.[74] The software supports various auction models and complex marketing campaigning. Besides the B2C auctions, OpenSite has a focus on B2B auctions, which play a more important role.

The software is available in three different options: OpenSite Auction Professional, OpenSite Auction Merchant, and OpenSite Auction Corporate. The professional version is for smaller companies with a limited budget who want to hold only a limited set of auctions per year. The software consists of a set of Web pages that are built into an existing Web site. In addition to the web pages, there is a search engine, a credit card check, and a billing mechanism also built in to the program.

The Merchant edition is suited for those who want to build more complex auction sites. Besides the functionality, the professional version also allows banner advertising and normal online shopping transactions.

The corporate edition of OpenSite is a turnkey solution for Web sites dealing with auctions only. The software can be extended easily through the integration of Oracle databases and through the use of the ISAPI interface of Microsoft. The corporate edition also allows for private auction and credit card transactions. A private auction has restricted access, meaning that only people with an invitation are allowed to participate in the auction.

MM Enterprise Auction Server

The MM Enterprise Auction Server (EASe) developed by Market Makers[75] provides companies with a simple mechanism for real-time auctions. With MM EASe, companies can provide their own auctions over the Internet and are able to create their own marketplaces. MM EASe is a powerful and flexible system that is easy to use and not too expensive.

The software consists of a powerful server, which is scalable and therefore able to handle any number of auctions at the same time. It supports all important auction models and provides a flexible structure of the database. The soft-

---

[74]http://www.opensite.com/

[75]http://www.marketmakers.de/

ware enables companies to create auctions automatically. The system provides interfaces to credit checks and online payment systems. The site is managed through a Web interface.

MM EASe provides three different use models: licensing, leasing, or hosting. If you license the software, you receive the software and can install it on your system. If you lease it, you don't have to have a dedicated server; it will be handled by Market Makers. Hosting goes a step further by including the auction solution into an existing Web site.

WEBtropolis AUCTIONnet

The software solution WEBtropolis AUCTIONnet von WebVision[76] provides a complete online sales solution for real-time auctioning and online shopping. The software is based on the WEBtropolis software framework, which can be easily adapted to the needs of the customer.

The software supports all auction models and provides online credit card checking functionality, which allows you to check if a given credit card number is valid. The software is able to conduct several auctions at the same time and provides an administration interface to control all parts of the system. The Web site is generated dynamically, as it is using templates. This means that it is easy to change the layout because it needs to be done only once (in the template) for the whole Web site. The built-in search engine is based on the AltaVista technology and provides a powerful mechanism to search for items on the Web site.

7.7 Operational Resources Management

7.7.1 Reasons for ORM

Every company requires operational resources in addition to the goods that are required for production. These resources are the nonproduction goods and services that are required and managed on a daily basis to run the business. The areas for operational resources include capital equipment (such as computer equipment); maintenance, repair and operating (MRO) supplies (such as office supplies); and travel and entertainment (such as travel services).

In many companies the buying process for operational resources is managed by many different organizations, and hundreds of different suppliers provide services, goods, and information. Although the operating resources do account for a large amount of company spending, typically the buying process is not well organized and managed. In many cases a paper-based process is used for ordering new pencils and phone lines. Today many companies operate their buying process via telephone and fax.

---

[76]http://www.webvision.com/

Because of its decentralized approach in many companies, every department is able to handle the operational resources on an individual basis, which results in higher prices than through a central buying organization. Another cost factor is the maintenance of the relationships with the suppliers and the missing real-time features, such as order status.

Once a central buying organization has been put in place, the paper-based process needs to be digitized in order to automate, control, and leverage it. As long as the process is not digitized, the company is not able to control the spending or the suppliers involved in the process.

ORM solutions put catalogs online and automate the purchases and the approvals. Beyond saving paper costs, the goal is to stop renegade spending and instead channel purchasing to selected vendors at prenegotiated prices. ORM allows operational resources to be managed more strategically by using the Internet and its connectivity to provide a communication infrastructure, where buyers and suppliers can work together on a direct basis without losing control over the spending. Actually, the company gets more control over the spending through the electronic management system. Introducing ORM does not necessarily require additional hardware or software to be installed, as many systems run on standard Web servers and browsers, which can be run on any computer platform. Through the use of electronic communication, the cost per transaction can be lowered significantly and the process can be highly automated.

Decision support tools enable the buyer to identify supplier discounts that have been introduced through a central buying process and are able to build strong relationships. ORM is not only reducing the cost per transaction, in most cases it also reduces the number of suppliers. In many cases different departments order their operational resources from different suppliers. Through central buying and ORM, the number of suppliers can be reduced dramatically. The supplier consolidation will reduce costs even further.

ORM is one of the online services in the business-to-business arena that will be implemented first, as it presents a huge opportunity to cut down costs. Driving down the operational costs automatically increases the profit for the company. In order to deliver the expected benefits, a complete solution must exist that provides a B2B connection between users, processes, and systems.

By implementing an ORM solution, companies are able to easily compare several suppliers of a certain product and track the orders on a buyer basis. An authorization of the buyer can be easily implemented and a workflow process can be implemented to replace the manual authorization steps. The ORM solution is able to provide an order status and an integration with the installed business systems.

The infrastructures on intranet and extranets enable companies to implement ORM solutions very efficiently. The purchasing catalog of a company can be easily created by extracting the negotiated products and prices from the various catalogs of the suppliers. Thus, suppliers are able to offer one catalog, which can be used for many purchasing departments of various companies. The purchasers are able to integrate all suppliers that offer their catalogs in the same standard without any trouble. A scalable connection between buyers and suppliers needs to be implemented in order to allow large and small partners to do business with each other. Purchasers and buyers need to agree on a price for every product or group of products. Price negotiation will take up most of the time.

ORM systems are moving business from proprietary EDI networks, which are mostly run over secure private networks, to the public Internet. These EDI networks are very costly to maintain and even more expensive to set up. Companies that already have them may want to stick with them to recoup their investment, but most companies are more than happy to give up these networks to eliminate the costs of maintenance. Those companies who haven't started yet won't go into the risk of building up a private network if the same business can be conducted securely over the Internet at a fraction of the cost.

7.7.2   Business Requirements

As discussed, ORM can only be implemented successfully if the company already owns a central buying department. In addition, a company-wide intranet and direct links to the Internet are required to make the system work for everyone in the company. Therefore larger corporations are the most likely target market for ORM applications. Manufacturers are less likely to require an ORM system, since they have a lot of production goods that need to be bought on a daily basis—therefore they already use a sort of ORM system. Manufacturers are ideal sellers in a digital ORM system. As we saw in Chapter 2, they are typically at the beginning of the value chain. Large corporations offering services and information are more likely to be willing to invest in ORM systems, as they do not buy operational goods on a daily basis.

In order to make the ORM even more successful, the supplier base needs to be consolidated. This process is being executed in many companies, since maintaining a large set of suppliers costs a lot of money. These companies are the ideal implementers for ORM solutions. Instead of sending out orders to many suppliers, the ORM system is taking the place of a virtual supplier, where all orders are sent. The ORM system then separates the orders and sends them out to the real suppliers. In batch mode, the ORM system is able to collect many small orders for a single product and then send out a larger order at the end of the day, receiving additional discounts.

A good ORM system should fulfill certain requirements in order to make sense in larger companies. Smaller companies may not need the complexity of large-scale ORM systems, but having all features will make the system more powerful and extensible. Table 7.6 contains a short summary of the required functionality.

The administration of the ORM system is very important and should be done through a Web browser. The purchasing department should be able to administer the users and the system. The design of the ORM system should be possible through the administration, and by using HTML templates new pages should be easily set up within minutes. The ORM system should be customizable in such a way that it can look and feel like all other enterprise Web applications.

ORM systems should include at least the following functions to be a useful and extensible solution:

- **Administration**—Although this may seem trivial, a good ORM system needs an administration tool that can be used by nontechnical persons.

- **Catalog support**—The ORM system should support multiple catalogs from different suppliers.

- **Enterprise integration**—A good ORM system needs to integrate tightly into existing enterprise processes.

- **Localization**—Multinational companies need multilingual purchaser catalogs with local prices and products.

- **Reporting**—Tools for generating reports are a must.

- **Workflow**—Automated workflow should be possible directly through the ORM system.

Table 7.6. Basic Features of ORM Systems

An important point to focus on is the administration of the users. Different roles should be assigned to people with different powers. Authorizers, requisitioners, and buyers have different rights in the ORM system. Buyers, for example, should only see the necessary products. Therefore, it should be possible to assign product groups per user and assign spending limits for every single user as well. In most cases the users will be linked to group rights, as managing the rights of every single user will involve too much manual administration. Each buyer should also be assigned to a cost location so that transactions from various departments can be expedited.

The ORM system needs to support multiple suppliers and their catalogs. The buyer front-end should integrate all the different suppliers and should allow a search over the consolidated catalog and compare prices between different suppliers of the same or similar products. The ORM system should automatically show the lowest price first. Ideally, the system allows the import of different catalog formats, making it easier for suppliers to become part of the system. In addition to an import feature, a connect feature is also useful. Instead of uploading catalogs, the ORM system connects to the original database, thus guaranteeing the most accurate and up-to-date data possible.

In order to automate all processes around purchasing, it is necessary for ORM to be integrated into existing enterprise solutions. Legacy systems should also be integrated, as they often contain the business logic for processes such as accounting.

Localization is very important, even if you have only a small regional company. If the catalogs and the ORM system are localized in your preferred language, you are able to choose from a far wider range of suppliers. If your company sits in the Czech Republic and you have a supplier in Taiwan, then it would help if the catalog appeared in Czech in order to compare it better to a supplier from the Czech Republic. Automatic price and currency conversions are also very important. In Europe, support for multiple currencies is essential. Many companies operate on a European-wide basis. In the European Union the transition phase for the euro requires every product to have prices in euro and the local currency until 2002.

A report generator is also a crucial component of the system. In order to work effectively, it is necessary to be able to track how the system is used. Reporting also helps the administrator to see if everything works flawlessly, and helps the management to see how effectively the work completed. The report generator should typically have a set of standard reports and the ability to create customized reports.

In order to integrate well with the existing enterprise applications, a workflow environment is very important. Typically, ORM solutions do not contain a workflow component, but allow the connection to existing workflow applications. This makes it easier to integrate the ORM solution into the existing enterprise process environment.

7.7.3 Succeeding in the ORM Market

Although ORM systems have been available for some years, very few companies are using them until now. The problem lies not in the technology. The software vendors have concentrated on the purchasing companies, as they will profit most from the ORM system. In order to convince the purchasing side to use ORM, it is necessary to have many suppliers using the system—and that is the problem. As long as the purchasers are not actively using the ORM systems in large quantity, it does not make a lot of sense for a purchaser to use the system.

Understandably, software vendors have started to change their business model and started to pay more attention to the suppliers. In March 1999, Ariba announced a partnership with Hewlett-Packard whereby Ariba would host the catalog of Hewlett-Packard on its Web server and keep it up to date. Although Hewlett-Packard still has to buy the software license, Ariba is taking over the costs for maintenance, which are much higher. By outsourcing the catalog management, more organizations are able to participate in ORM.

Shortly after the implementation of Ariba.com, Commerce One started its own purchasing site.[77] Unlike Ariba, Commerce One opened up its site to rival makers of ORM software. Commerce One is offering standard API, which allows other software solutions to tie into the site. Instead of trying to push their own standard to the Web, the ORM software manufacturers try to offer bridges between the solutions in order to create a larger market, thus offering a valuable service for more companies.

The ORM vendors are moving from a product price to a transaction price. Instead of licenses, transactions are becoming more important. Companies who want to use the service of one of the companies are required to pay per transaction, which will be around $1 per purchase order.

Although it will still be possible to buy the software and install it, the transaction model will enable smaller companies to enter the ORM space, making them tough competition for the larger companies who can afford to install their own ORM systems.

7.7.4   ORM Solutions

Many ORM solutions are available today and offer varying degrees of functionality on the Internet. The following list of products gives an overview of the best and most commonly used ORM solutions available at the time of writing.

Ariba ORMS

Ariba ORMS[78] is a Java-based solution that runs on all platforms supporting Java. The system consists of several components that talk to each other over the Network Application Architecture (NAA). Ariba ORMS contains a set of preconfigured business applications, which allow the automation of processes, such as capital equipment and MRO.

Over the NAA, these business applications are able to talk to each other and link to legacy systems and databases using adapters. Ariba ORMS comes with a wide range of adapters, such as connections to Oracle,[79] PeopleSoft,[80] and SAP.[81] If the adapter is not available, it is possible to write a new adapter that suits the needs of the company.

Through the use of Java, the user interface adapts nicely to the varying output devices, such as browser clients and enterprise servers. Finance departments, purchasing agents, and suppliers can be integrated into a single system, where everyone is able to communicate with the necessary partner.

---

[77]http://www.marketsite.net/

[78]http://www.ariba.com/

[79]http://www.oracle.com/

[80]http://www.peoplesoft.com/

[81]http://www.sap.com/

Ariba ORMS is able to subscribe to supplier catalogs on the Internet and aggregate the information into a single buyer catalog. This is done automatically and requires no action on the buyer side, once a supplier catalog has been subscribed. The internal workflow engine is able to manage most of the processes required for the purchasing department.

But there is a major disadvantage for companies outside of the United States. The software is not localizable in the current version, nor is a localized version available. This means that it is not possible to use other languages for the user interface, nor is it possible to have catalogs in several languages, using multiple currencies.

Commerce One Commerce Chain

The Commerce Chain solution by Commerce One[82] consists of two products, BuySite and MarketSite, which together form a complete ORM solution. BuySite provides a solution for internal processes ranging from requisition to order. MarketSite starts to work from order through payment—the typical supplier tasks. Commerce Chain builds a bridge between these two solutions and offers a complete ORM solution.

The advantage is that this integration works perfectly. The problem is to get other supplier systems integrated. The connection uses proprietary protocols, making it difficult for other supplier systems. BuySite offers all the tools to implement the most common processes required, while MarketSite offers the option to present the catalogs from various suppliers and allows comparison of the offered goods and services.

The reporting feature is one of the best in the field. It is highly configurable and allows even buyers to create reports that suit their needs. Besides the configurable reporting, many standard reports are included.

Although there are no standard interfaces to legacy or enterprise applications, Commerce One offers a service where existing applications will be integrated into the Commerce Chain solution. Although this may seem like a good service, a standardized set of interfaces would be more useful, as customized interfaces will cost a lot of money.

Just as with Ariba, the major problem with Commerce Chain is missing localization. Without this feature, the software becomes unusable outside of the United States. International companies that want to implement ORM on a worldwide basis require this feature; therefore, the localization needs to be added to the product either by individual application development or by introducing it into a product.

---

[82]http://www.commerceone.com/

Infobank InTrade

InTrade, developed by the British company Infobank,[83] is a newcomer to the ORM arena. Their software has been set on top of some standard Microsoft products, such as the Internet Information Server, the Site Server, the SQL Server, and the Commerce Server. This approach does not require large investments in hardware, but restricts the use to Windows NT. A porting to another platform is very unlikely, as none of the underlying middleware components are available for other platforms.

InTrade is an open solution. Suppliers connect over the Internet to the purchasing server. If suppliers wish, they can use the InTrade supplier for offering the catalog over the Internet. If they have another system already installed, InTrade Purchaser allows the import of data from other systems. In this case the purchasing system acts also as a supplier system. The advantage of this is that the supplier does not need to install software from Infobank; the disadvantage is that the supplier needs to create different catalogs for every purchaser and needs to upload them individually to the purchasing server.

With the supplier server installed, all purchasers can be served at once. The data on the supplier server is replicated to the purchasing server through the standard replication methods, making the system faster for the purchaser, as all data is locally available and only updates need to be replicated. The data between supplier and buyer can be exchanged through a proprietary protocol or via XML over the Internet.

The Web-based administration tool allows total control over the functionality of the system. InTrade is the only system that is fully localized, including language and currency. A German and a French version are already available; other languages are expected soon.

Netscape CommerceXpert

The Netscape CommerceXpert suite of products consists of several modules for both suppliers and purchasers. ECXpert, the basic module, provides all the required functionality and infrastructure to set up a B2B ORM system. It provides interfaces to exchange information over existing EDI networks and the Internet and for the integration into the ERP system.

On top of this module, the purchaser needs to get BuyerXpert and the supplier SellerXpert, which provide the required functionality for the purchaser and the supplier respectively. BuyerXpert contains an order management system, a workflow engine, and an online catalog presentation system. SellerXpert, on the other hand, provides the same functionality as BuyerXpert, with the addition of the payment functionality.

CommerceXpert is compatible with OBI (Open Buying over the Internet; see Chapter 14) and allows the exchange of data via XML. The major advantage

---

[83]http://www.infobank.co.uk/

of Netscape's solution is that by adding new modules such as MerchantXpert and PublishingXpert, the B2B system can be easily extended to become a B2C online shop at the same time.

CommerceXpert supports multiple currencies, date formats, and languages, making it suitable for large companies that have subsidiaries around the world. It is also useful for nonnative English-speaking companies who can easily localize the application to suit their needs.

7.7.5 Comparison of the Procurement Solutions

From the comparison chart shown in Table 7.7, you can see where the ORM solutions have come from. All five solutions have their advantages, and if you look at the row with the roots, you can see where each of the solutions was originally positioned. That does not mean that you cannot mix the solutions or even choose a technology from one sector to deliver a solution in another. We have seen enough examples to prove this, but people tend to stay in the sector they feel comfortable with already.

	Ariba	Commerce One	Infobank	Netscape
Administration	Java	HTML	HTML	HTML
Catalog	Import	Import	Replication, Import	Connect
Integration	High	Good	Good	High
Localization	None	None	Full	Some
Platform	Java	Windows	Windows	Solaris, Windows
Reporting	Full	Full	Some	Full
Roots	Buyer, Purchaser	Value-Added Network	Buyer, Purchaser	Buyer, Purchaser
Workflow	Built In	Connect	Basic, Connect	Connect

Table 7.7. Comparison of the Procurement Solutions

7.8 Joining the Shopping and ORM Solutions

As we have seen in this chapter, shopping and ORM solutions have a very similar functionality, but different target groups. While the typical shopping solution targets many end customers by offering the products of a single shop, the ORM solution tries to integrate as many shops as possible for a single buying organization. The shopping solution is a one-to-many relationship while ORM solutions target the many-to-one relationships.

This means that suppliers need to offer two catalogs, two databases, and so on, in order to provide a service for both markets. In order to further reduce the overhead on the supplier side, shopping and ORM solutions will eventually migrate to offer many-to-many relations serving both the enterprise and the end customer market with a single database and a single, highly customizable catalog.

This can be achieved quite easily using ORM solutions with little modification by creating a new instance of the catalog for a new company. How? By placing it on the public Web site, allowing end customers to access it. For this catalog, the various roles for the ORM solution become less important and cost locations have to be replaced with credit card payment systems. The actual buying process is similar.

Typical shopping solutions will need stronger modification, as many components required for ORM solutions are missing—such as workflow. In order to migrate to a unified solution, the software manufacturer needs to invest far more. But this investment will guarantee the survival of the software company if it wants to remain a major player. Netscape is one of the first companies to offer a complete solution, and CommerceXpert is able to deal with both scenarios. In the near future we will see shopping portals that will enable end customers and companies to buy products through a unified interface, but with differentiated services.

ORM solutions have become a strong value proposition for most companies, as it helps to reduce costs significantly, and this is a major economic driver, especially in an economic downturn, as we experience it in 2001. Companies are more than willing to spend on these systems, making them very attractive.

Chapter 8

SUPPORTING E-BUSINESS COMPONENTS

8.1 Content Management Systems

8.1.1 Introduction

Although content management systems (CMS), customer relationship management (CRM), and knowledge management systems (KMS) are essential in order to properly conduct e-business, these three components are not visible in the front end. Still, they are essential in having an up-to-date Web site (CMS), knowledge about the customer (CRM), and organizing information in such a manner that knowledge is created (KMS).

CMS, CRM, and KMS are essential in order to have a complete business up and running. There are more components, such as a logistics and enterprise resource planning, but to cover these component as well would go beyond the scope of the book. CMS, CRM and KMS are very closely related to the e-business front-end system. Content and customers are the basis for every e-business—and content and customers create the biggest problems in running an e-business.

Developing an effective KMS has become necessary for most e-business companies. For instance, in the investment banking industry, in which bankers (the "sell side") underwrite and market securities to institutional clients and individuals (the "buy side"), the sell side marketed its proprietary research only to the buy side. However, with technology advancements supporting easy availability of equity research and other investment information, investment bankers had to open their research to the public, feeling pressure not only from traditional businesses but from upstarts that are taking advantages of the new technologies.

Content is the substance of every e-business. Content comprises the sum total of a site visitor's experience. How effectively a company manages its content has a direct impact on bottom line cost, top line revenue, and customer retention. As such, content is the currency for competing in the digital age.

Managing content across the enterprise is no simple task. Content is grow-ing exponentially, in both volume and variety, and it is virtually impossible for webmasters to keep up. In order for a company to satisfy its constituents, busi-ness users throughout the organization must become content managers and contributors.

Businesses still feel the pain of not managing their content and the busi-ness processes around it effectively, but they are often hard-pressed to know where to turn for solutions and how to sort through the barrage of homoge-nized marketing pronouncements from so many vendors.

CMS provides many standard workflow components that include content scheduling. You can schedule not just a single page for publishing, but an entire package of updates. A CMS can simultaneously update multiple pages or even do conditional updates. It also gives you the benefit of a real approval process, rather than the haphazard approach that often passes for a process. The end result is content that's less likely to include "junk," such as broken links or related-content links that are not really related to the content at all.

8.1.2 Definition of Content

As we already have learnt, content is the currency of the digital age, as it is the substance of every e-business. Content comprises the sum total of a site visitor's experience, and how effectively a company manages its content has a direct impact on bottom line cost, top line revenue and customer retention.

During the e-business projects I have been involved in, content was the biggest issue. The major reason for that was that most people do not really understand what content is or where it comes from. In some cases the whole project was ready to run, but had to be delayed because the necessary content could not be found. This may sound strange, but finding digital assets is one of the most complex tasks in e-commerce projects.

The reasons are manifold. The first problem is that most companies have not used a CMS for the management of their digital assets in the past. Product data is stored in the production system, price data in the pricing system, and marketing data perhaps in a QuarkXPress file. A Web site requires access to all data, as the web site represents all areas of a company. So getting all the data into the Web site is difficult, even if you know where to find it. In most cases you need to convert the data in order to make it compatible for your e-business solution. But where the information is, most companies do not know. Small companies do not have to contend with that issue, but imagine a large manufacturer that produces more than 400 different products. All the prices, marketing texts, technical texts, manuals, product-related information, configurations, and so on converted to an Internet-ready format. This can be a very difficult task if no company-wide CMS exists. The problem becomes even more complex if one of the products becomes obsolete or its specifications change. Everything needs to be updated on a regular basis. Without a CMS, it quickly becomes a nightmare. If the information needs to be differentiated by country and language, the task is complicated even further.

Therefore, many people first need to understand what content really is (see also 8.1). Most people think of Web content as page elements such as text, graphics, controls, multimedia, banner advertising, and scripts. In other words, if it is on a Web page, then it qualifies as Web content and therefore needs to be managed. This narrow definition works in many cases and is sometimes referred to as the creative content of the Web site. Some CMS vendors prefer this limited definition of content because it allows them to more easily offer end-to-end do-all content management solutions.

However, this limited scope of content does not take into account many other items that need to be created, gathered, and maintained on an e-commerce Web site. For instance, applications and other software components are of fundamental importance to e-commerce sites. Without the programming logic contained in these applications, it is not possible to take orders, track customers, personalize the visitor's experience, or communicate with fulfillment partners. It is critical to coordinate and fully test the interactions between creative content, such as text, images, and page elements and application content.

Content is much more than most people think. It can be roughly put into the following categories:

- **Pages**—Web pages and page elements such as text, graphics, controls, multimedia, advertisements, and scripts.

- **Programming Logic**—Applications, middle-tier components, database procedures, and other programming logic that enables and supports e-commerce.

- **Transactional Data**—Database information that directly supports the creation of dynamic Web pages or enables the customer to execute business transactions.

- **Downloads**—Downloadable or online viewable files of all types.

- **Support**—Content on ancillary support sites in addition to the primary public site

---

Table 8.1. What is content?

Another type of content on Web sites is sometimes referred to as transactional content. This information is usually maintained within databases that Web pages or middle-tier applications access on a regular basis. Examples of transactional content include information about products, orders, accounts, shipments, and promotions. Often, this transactional content is used to generate dynamic Web pages after being transformed into HTML text elements, images, tables, or graphs and then delivered to the customer.

Many sites create their own CRM systems so that their representatives can manage customer issues promptly and in a satisfactory manner. These support Web sites access the same customer and order information that the public site uses, or they access at least a replicated version of that data. Supplementary sites, such as customer support sites, require careful design and updates that need to be carefully coordinated with developments on the public Web site. In addition to everything else, this kind of content needs to be managed.

Another form of content available at most e-business sites consists of downloadable files. These file objects can be Microsoft Word documents, PDF files, archives, images, or any other type of file.

8.1.3 Definition of CMS

A CMS is a database that organizes and provides access to all types of digital content—files containing images, graphics, animation, sound, video, or text. The database contains metadata about the digital assets and may also contain links to the files themselves in order to allow them to be located or accessed individually. A CMS is usually used to manage digital assets during the development of a digital resource, such as a Web site or multimedia production.

It might be used by authors, editors, or those responsible for the management of the content development process (content managers). CMS range from very basic databases to sophisticated, tailor-made applications. These more complex systems can be integrated with the eventual digital resource in order to enable access to digital assets and to allow regular updating.

In order to better understand what a CMS is, it is important to know what it is not. A CMS is not a library, archive, museum management, or cataloging system. It does not provide the functions of a picture library system. It cannot be used to do word processing or manage other text files containing lists of digital resources. A CMS does not contain information about the presentation of the digital content (e.g., end-user interface, navigation, design, or layout). Content work should not be related to layout work. Unfortunately, many Web sites mix content and layout, making it difficult to change the layout or change content, as both are somewhat interwoven. CMSs are not aimed at ordinary users. Using these systems requires training and may have different interfaces depending on the type of user (e.g., editor, system manager, image manager).

Building a Web site today without a CMS is almost impossible, as visitors expect dynamic content and improvements on the user interface all the time.

A CMS makes it possible for a news editor, without knowledge about HTML or the Web, to write a story and publish it on a Web site within minutes.

Content management procedures enable the design, authoring, review, approval, conversion, storage, testing, and deployment of all Web site content. Once in service, content needs to be maintained, monitored, upgraded, and eventually, retired and archived. Comprehensive end-to-end content management also consists of sophisticated reporting and analysis components.

Effective content management requires clearly defined roles and documented workflow for all forms of content. This includes review and approval processes and clear interdepartmental hand-offs.

The overall process of managing Web site content may or may not be supported by specific commercial or inhouse tools. The important point to keep in mind is that the process needs to be well defined and supported by the organization. Once the process is analyzed and fully understood, it is much easier to determine the tools and third-party packages, if any, that can add value to the content management process.

Managing the capture or creation of digital images requires metadata to be recorded—this documents the capture, ownership, location, and licensing conditions relating to each image. Even for a few dozen images, this may add up to hundreds of different pieces of information, so managing them would not be possible without some automated assistance.

Similarly, managing a Web site with even a few pages is a time-consuming task when updates are required—perhaps when a page is added, which requires the navigation menu to be updated on other pages, or when a logo changes, which then needs to be reflected on all pages. For this reason, the use of templates, which draw on content held in a database, is a vital management tool. Without this type of application, the Web site would either fall out of date very quickly or would require ever greater staff resources to retain its currency.

8.1.4 Selecting a CMS

By now you should understand that a CMS is necessary, not only for Web development, but for the management of digital assets that can be used for anything from Web sites to printed brochures. Using a single source for all publications reduces costs significantly and increases the speed of the publications.

The process of selecting a CMS is similar to choosing any other computer system components. First, it is necessary to develop a profound business case. Based on the size and complexity of the planned project, you need to decide from the outset the scale and scope of the system required to support the development and delivery of the project. Existing systems and skills need to be taken into account, as they can contribute to the complexity of the solution, but also reduce the cost of the proposed architecture. The existing content and how it is stored currently needs to be taken into account. A CMS should not be for the Web only. It should be able to store and manage all other content that is processed within the enterprise, for printed brochures, for example.

Based on the business case, a company should create a list of the functions and the recording capabilities the system will require. If the business case and the knowledge of the market suggest that a simple, off-the-shelf, inexpensive package is required, then it may simply be necessary to follow your organization's internal rules for purchasing software and demonstrating value for money. However, larger projects will almost certainly require more complex systems, which require the project to go out to tender and invite responses from vendors and developers.

8.1.5   The Role of XML in CMS

Content management software solutions are turning to eXtensibe Markup Langauge (XML) and eXtensible Stylesheet Language (XSL) (more information on XML and XSL can be found in Chapter 10). With XML, the content can be given a structure through clearly defined sets of tags that are easily understandable and therefore easily reusable. Viewing the content is handled through XSL. XSL examines the XML file and applies appropriate formatting to specific tags according to predefined rules.

For content management purposes, XSL lets you set up your formatting templates, and the content for the templates will be structured according to the XML rules. XSL makes it easy to create content for different front ends. For example, it is easy to create content for a Web browser, a mobile phone and a television set. All these devices require different settings, but could display the same content. Using three different XSL structures, the content will always be displayed in an optimal way. XSL also makes it possible to create PDF files or Word documents automatically, because these file formats are seen as just another front end by the CMS.

Most CMS solutions have built-in XML support. Unfortunately, the support is not always the same. In some solutions the import and export of XML is possible; in other solutions XML is the basis for all processes. Rhythmyx Content Manager by Percussion Software,[1] for example, provides native support for XML. It sends all data through an XML filtering process. This filtering process assembles the content from various sources and flows to the XSL module to be converted into a displayable format, such as HTML or PDF.

The Tridion DialogServer,[2] for example, lets you perform all your content authoring and management tasks through a browser interface and stores all content in XML format. Eclipse by Chrystal Software[3] provides support for XML documents and XML design tools. BroadVision[4] provides a new content

---

[1] http://www.percussionsoftware.com/
[2] http://www.tridion.com/
[3] http://www.chrystalsoftware.com/
[4] http://www.broadvision.com/

creation and interactive publishing tool called BV One-to-One Publishing that lets you design your content structure in XML, and content is stored as XML in a repository that checks for XML validity. Through an XML pump, BroadVision allows you to publish in various formats, such as HTML, WML, and PDF. Adding new XSL stylesheets is easy and makes it possible to create content for any type of device or usage.

Vignette,[5] on the other hand, does rely on XML only. It supports data stored in a variety of database formats, including XML. The company also provides an XML-specific server called XML Connect, and XML is fast becoming the standard throughout its product line. Last, but not least, eBusiness Technologies' engenda[6] is fully built around XML, including XML templates and the conversion of Word documents into XML.

8.1.6   ICE

As a result of using XML, several new tools and solutions have been developed. One of the most important solutions in the content management area based on XML is the Information and Content Exchange (ICE) protocol that will enable the automated exchange between business partners. It has been developed by more than 70 companies that first got together in June 1998. Among those companies are Adobe,[7] CNet,[8] Microsoft,[9] Sun Microsystems,[10] and Vignette.[11] In October 1998 ICE was proposed to the W3C[12] as a standard.

ICE allows the easy syndication of content. It will not only automate, but also regulate and control the flow of information. ICE is defined as an XML standard. It is a bidirectional protocol, which exchanges XML-based messages between systems in order to control the transaction. The format of the actual data is of no importance. Everything can be used, including ASCII text, RTF, PDF, HTML, and XML, just to name a few.

In order to establish the basis for the information exchange, it is necessary to install certain tools on the two systems that want to exchange the information. On the one side, the information needs to be converted into ICE packets and transmitted. The other side needs to receive the packets and move them into the appropriate CMS.

The system architecture contains an ICE-compatible syndication server that acts as a syndicator, which can access a CMS. The CMS then controls the integration and distribution of content. By using this protocol and architecture, it is possible to reduce the cost for integrating external content. ICE enables

---

[5]http://www.vignette.com/

[6]http://www.ebt.com/

[7]http://www.adobe.com/

[8]http://www.cnet.com/

[9]http://www.microsoft.com/

[10]http://www.sun.com/

[11]http://www.vignette.com/

[12]http://www.w3c.org/

the creation of content offerings that can be redistributed and enables a large network of content providers to work together.

The protocol supports four types of operations: subscription management, data transfer, logfile generation, and administration. The management of subscriptions allows you to limit times and set the number of content packages sent per day, the mode of transmission, and additional metadata. The metadata contains copyright and other information on top of the actual files. The data is transferred in packets. The protocol can check the correct and complete transfer via internal routines. If data is lost on the way to the receiver, the data is resent automatically. For diagnostic purposes, and to make sure no error is omitted from the log, all activities are stored in logfiles. The administrator has the ability to remove bugs and check for problems.

ICE is also able to restrict itself to only certain types of content. It can be defined, for example, which graphical formats will be accepted when exchanging files via ICE and which will be rejected. There are plans in the works to introduce a constraint language into ICE in order to make the definition easier.

The transmission of data via ICE is done through the HTTP-Post protocol. This makes it possible to secure the content via SSL, PGP, or S/MIME (a definition can be found in Chapter 11). Users can certify their data packets and make it easier to identify the sender of the data. Using standard Web-login mechanisms, it is possible to restrict the access to the data.

Vignette[13] is one of the frontrunners of the ICE protocol. Its Syndication Server allows the use of the ICE protocol in its CMS. Even sites that do not use the Vignette CMS can profit from the Syndication Server by using an ICE unpacker tool, which makes it possible to grab external content via ICE and unpack it.

Shiftkey Software[14] is another company that offers an ICE-compatible content syndication server. The software accesses HTML and XML files directly on a site and requires no CMS. One of the clients of Shiftkey is Reuters,[15] which uses the software to distribute multimedia news packets to other Web sites.

8.1.7   Product Overview

DynaBase

The DynaBase Web Content Management[16] and Dynamic Delivery Solution provide all the capabilities a company needs to build a thriving e-business, as well as the flexibility an e-business team needs to effectively serve e-business and e-commerce content and to manage its lifecycle online.

In addition to offering powerful and versatile packaged content management and delivery functions, DynaBase is XML-enabled. This permits you

---

[13]http://www.vignette.com/

[14]http://www.shiftkey.com/

[15]http://www.reuters.com/

[16]http://www.dynabase.com/

to separate content, format, and business logic, and provides a solid foundation for DynaBase's powerful search and dynamic page assembly capabilities. As a result, you can create, index, maintain, and deliver e-business content with great flexibility while streamlining the management and communication of many different types of business data.

DynaBase can be integrated with existing authoring systems. Authors can continue to use their preferred editing tools by launching them directly from within DynaBase. Moreover, many different kinds of content contributors, such as graphic designers, script developers, and HTML authors can easily add files as necessary.

To keep content flowing smoothly, DynaBase lets an e-business team develop new content at the same time existing content is being served to the site, and then permits a rapid switch to this new content as quickly as it is needed.

DynaBase is also designed to integrate easily with other applications and tools. Because it is client-aware, DynaBase also supports a variety of delivery media, such as Web browsers, palm-held devices, and print. DynaBase lets companies deliver up-to-date, high-quality content dependably, in a structured format, scaled and personalized to suit the various audiences. And even as DynaBase delivers content, it gathers and manages new content continuously, so it can be delivered upon the next site update.

With DynaBase, companies can automatically gather both new and legacy content and e-business-based applications from multiple sources. These include content contributors using remote authoring systems, as well as backend systems, such as the databases where vital corporate information resides. Only the combination makes a successful solution.

eGrail

eGrail Enterprise Content Server (ECS)[17] includes a core set of content management services that allow for site preparation, configuration, and management functionalities and for content/document preparation, creation, management, and rendering functionalities. This core set of services includes the ability to manipulate fundamental eGrail entities such as objects, pages, articles, and multimedia assets along with their multichannel instantiations.

The content management core is surrounded by another layer of services that includes environment deployment engines, workflow, full content production management, and intelligent rendering and caching. Finally, an outer layer of functionalities provides content applications such as e-commerce, personalization, and calendar tools.

eGrail's open architecture supports functions and models that comprise enterprise content management processes. All entities, such as objects, formats, and content are stored in the backend repository. eGrail can manage many sites on the same repository or distribute sites across several repositories, uti-

---

[17]http://www.egrail.com/

lizing the most popular relational database management systems and XML-native repositories.

The major component of the backend is the eGrail ECS. This system provides the essential content management services such as intelligent rendering and caching, environment deployment control, security, archiving, and XML import/export utilities, with APIs for J2EE, rendering, and the front-end administration server.

Content creators, editors, and Web developers interact with eGrail through a browser-based administration server. This capability makes access to eGrail location-independent and platform-independent. Manual content creation and control is complemented by backend services that include an aggregation engine capable of handling syndicated content as well as content delivered by other applications within the enterprise.

Objects are the building blocks of a Web site created with eGrail, and objects give eGrail its ability to manage content at a highly granular level. Objects may contain text, script, HTML, XML, graphics, and other Web and application technologies.

Objects can be nested to describe very complex pages or grouped into composite objects called content layouts. Content layouts and other objects can be embedded in templates. Using this content decomposition approach, any document or template, however complex or detailed, can easily be captured and decomposed into simpler elements. This is not possible with the more common file-based systems.

eGrail objects, as well as entities like pages, articles, and templates, have multiview capabilities. There can be several views (dimensions based on language, format, site, template, and page) to this feature, enabling any object to be instantiated with respect to one or many dimensions.

eGrail's deployment engine controls the flow of documents to any environment, including staging or production environments that support J2EE, .NET, or any other technology. These environments can also integrate Java application servers. eGrail collaborates with any application server or any server-side scripting language.

During rendering, all elements in a page—including static content and snippets of code forming interactive applications—are collected to form a document. The rendering algorithm is akin to a compiler. The rendering engine is agnostic to the specific format. It can create documents in any format, including XML, HTML, and WML. The rendering engine can form an entire document or selected parts of a document.

eGrail's new Advanced Workflow Engine supports the simple specification of tasks through wizards and the presentation of "in-basket" GUIs to editors, writers, and testers. It lets writers and editors collaborate on content creation, from task assignment through publication. Easy-to-use wizards allow precise task-tracking (such as page or article creation) for a defined set of content contributors and editors.

The eGrail front end and backend architectures are capable of managing sites with hundreds of thousands of pages in multiple formats and multiple languages.

Support of a rich set of interfaces allows an organization to completely and seamlessly integrate eGrail with any third-party or homegrown application out-of-the-box. It is this seamless interfacing with best-of-breed applications for syndication, application servers, middleware, e-commerce, and personalization that future-proofs organizations to be ready for new technologies.

Infopark NPS

The content management software NPS from Infopark[18] provides Web based business processes to control the publication of content. Data for the product information come together from a variety of internal and external sources. The information is frequently available in a variety of formats. The data are consolidated by the content management system. Attributes supplement the content and contain information for the target platform. The product information can thus be found in the Internet shop as well as on a CD-ROM for the sales division or stored as supplementary information in the data warehouse. The NPS Enterprise Affiliate Server supports the ICE interfaces of shop systems such as Intershop Enfinity.

Multiple Web servers are often used for large e-business sites. Thus, bandwidth can be saved and load balancing is possible. Geographic distribution, in branch offices or worldwide subsidiaries, for example, can often only be realized effectively with multiple Web servers. NPS can distribute identical content to multiple Web servers. All Web servers are supported, regardless of their operating system platform.

Here, the benefit of the enterprise digital asset stream concept becomes apparent, in which the creation, administration, and delivery components are seen separately but within the shared context of the Web-based business process. In addition, NPS has full multi-customer processing capabilities. In other words, a single NPS server software installation can be used for the administration of multiple Web presences. Multi-customer processing capabilities are also a prerequisite for the deployment of NPS as a classical application service.

Application service providers who generally also offer Web hosting solutions can thus use a single NPS installation to manage the Web servers of a large number of customers.

NPS operates on the basis of transactions. With the concept of microtransactions, individual work steps of the various users are processed with high performance in the server. Competing attempts to access the same content are recognized immediately, and write attempts are rejected. The transaction principle also accommodates a large number of editors working simultaneously, and thus provides excellent scalability.

---

[18]http://www.infopark.de/

With NPS, an intelligent and flexible information system for Web-based business processes is available. Content is contributed by the departments, while the content management technology is provided by the enterprise IT. With NPS's system-independent operability, individual staff members can provide and interlink information throughout the corporate environment. Subject-related content screening determines the various content classes as the starting point for the CMS, making NPS a good solution for your business needs.

Interwoven TeamSite

Interwoven's TeamSite software is designed as an open and scalable platform, letting companies leverage their existing investment and harness best-of-breed application servers and e-business engines. Based on a completely open, XML-based platform, TeamSite software offers a flexible, scalable, standards-based platform for creating, managing, and deploying the large-scale and business-critical Web content needed to maintain an advantage. TeamSite is composed of several modules, which are described here in a bit more detail.

TeamSite's Casual Contributor interface provides URL-based access to tasks and Web assets, enabling all contributors, regardless of technical expertise, to directly access TeamSite tasks just by pointing and clicking on a URL. With TeamSite, all users, such as authors, editors, administrators, and masters, can embed links to tasks, workflow, or any content file for editing or modification in email messages. The Casual Contributor Interface also enables external users to work securely from remote locations.

TeamSite WebDesk provides a GUI that allows non-technical business users to use TeamSite with minimal training. Features such as Favorites, Recent Folders, Task List, Preview Panel, and In-line Asset Management Command allow users to easily navigate to files and assigned tasks from within a single window. TeamSite also provides SSL-encrypted connection over HTTP for remote editing and uploading of Web content.

TeamSite provides administrators with a powerful, easy-to-use browser-based GUI for user and system management functions, such as configuration management for performance tuning, UI (user interface) options, and proxy server mappings. This UI also allows users to look up system information and logfiles, configure the TeamSite server and perform server operations from a remote location without requiring root access to the server. It also provides a centralized framework for administering most Interwoven products.

The SmartContext Editor is configurable at the user level. Users can access their tasks directly from the SmartContext tab, which allows editors and above to assign individual or multiple pages for editing to designated contributors.

TeamSite WorkflowBuilder allows users to design complex workflows visually and generates TeamSite-specific workflow XML files. TeamSite Workflow-Builder allows the authentication against any TeamSite server. It can add a workflow template to the list of available templates and automatic validation of submitted workflow templates is easily accomplished using this tool.

TeamSite offers the following simple yet powerful user interfaces:

- **Browser Based GUI**—provides point-and-click access to all Web components in an intuitive, cross-platform user interface.

- **SmartContext QA**—allows users to stage and test changes in the context of the entire site, avoiding the Web manager bottleneck.

- **SmartContext Editing**—enables collaboration, staging, and virtualization though a very easy-to-use and intuitive interface.

- **Interwoven Merge**—a Java-based, 3-way visual file merging application, providing detailed source comparison and conflict resolution.

- **Visual and Source Differencing**—enables users to view two version of a file side-by-side in their fully functioning form.

- **Global Report Center**—allows administrators to query TeamSite and generate custom reports on system and user activities.

Table 8.2. TeamSite Interfaces

TeamSite manages the access and versioning of all types of content, including HTML, graphics, downloads, source code, server-side executables, scripts, and more. TeamSite also allows developers to use their preferred tools and client platforms, leveraging existing investments in content, systems, and expertise as a result of the open file system architecture.

The solution integrates with any combination of backend systems, application servers, and production servers, including legacy systems, business-critical databases, content delivery, and personalization systems.

TeamSite provides a robust environment for managing the content contributors' work with a concurrent development capability that enables parallel site development. Content contributors can work individually or in teams, from either local or remote work locations in their own private work area. Once they are satisfied with their efforts, their work can be sent to a staging area, where it can be combined with the work of others and tested prior to being sent to the live Web site. At every step of the way, users can check their work in the context of a fully operational "virtualized view" of the entire Web site.

TeamSite respects the native operating system file and directory permissions necessary to provide strict access control for enterprise-level security. Authentication to the TeamSite system can be controlled via LDAPv3, integrating TeamSite with corporate security policy, which is on Solaris only. TeamSite provides support for content entry and display of both single-byte and multibyte content. This includes the ability to manage metadata in local languages, allowing content to be more easily searched and shared across multiple initiatives. In addition, TeamSite supports the use of multibyte comments for all workflow events, which enables the entire content lifecycle to be managed in local languages.

Web managers can capture, categorize, and version any set of metadata, organizing files into logical categories and subcategories. These metadata can be searched to locate Web properties based on data types, categories, language, and specific keywords. The solution enables improved access to FrontPage Webs and Visual InterDev projects directly from within TeamSite.

TeamSite offers robust versioning and rollback capabilities. It is possible to use file and database versioning, so each contributor's individual update can be tagged. Through "the whole site archiving" feature, it is possible to backup and restore the site in cases of problems. A site rollback is also possible without problems.

The TeamSite workflow engine provides an advanced task-based environment for controlling complex, multistage Web site development. With the new WorkflowBuilder, users can easily design complex workflows. This ensures a shorter development cycle and greater control over the development process. TeamSite's robust workflow engine enables organizations to manage content, improve project management, and ensure content integrity.

TeamSite enables more users to contribute content with significant performance improvements for common end-user file-system related operations. Through efficient datastore management capabilities, TeamSite reduces the disk space needed to maintain large Web sites and significantly optimizes resource utilization. With a built-in striping capability, TeamSite enables large-scale Web operations to span the TeamSite datastore across multiple file systems, resulting in significantly lower IT management costs.

NCompass

NCompass Resolution,[19] a Web CMS for the Microsoft platform, enables enterprises to deploy dynamic Internet, intranet, and extranet applications. It enables business users to communicate directly with prospects, customers, part-

---

[19]http://www.ncompass.com/

ners, and coworkers by publishing rich, targeted content directly to the Web. This enables companies to streamline Web communication with automated publishing tools.

NCompass Resolution gives business users powerful content creation and workflow tools and offers a complete set of tools enabling business users to create effective Web content. Resolution's centrally controlled templates, built by your own Web designers, ensure site consistency, usability, and layout.

Resolution's support for multibyte character sets for languages such as Japanese, Chinese or Korean means authors can publish content in the language of their audience.

The software manages content for diverse Web applications, including Internet, intranet, and extranet sites. These sites are supporting e-business initiatives like CRM, employee portals, and e-commerce.

NCompass Resolution provides a tight integration into Microsoft Commerce Server 2000. The Resolution Content Connector enables enterprises to use the full functionality of NCompass Resolution to manage content for e-commerce sites built using Microsoft Commerce Server 2000.

Resolution's template-based system and separation of content from format makes site-wide changes fast and easy. Dynamic server clustering means you can scale your Web deployment to match the size of your audience. Resolution stores content as reusable objects in an SQL database, and not as static pages in a file system, enabling content sharing across your enterprise Web applications.

RedDot

RedDot[20] is a complete package for content management. It does not require additional client software. In fact, a Web browser is all an administrator or editor requires. RedDot supports Microsoft Internet Explorer 5.0 (or later) and Netscape Navigator 4.0 (or later). Either a local network or the Internet can serve as connection. Since RedDot is very intuitive, it requires very little training.

RedDot also provides powerful features for the administrator. Workflow operations can be easily created, managed, and altered through a simple-to-use interface, as HTML pages combine content, navigation, and design instructions. These operations makes management of pages difficult and requires HTML knowledge on part of the user. Through RedDot, it is easy to keep the site design consistent.

Through RedDot's Administration interface, it is easy to maintain a decentralized approach to content, which requires a more sophisticated user and group authorization. Administrators, subadministrators, chief editors, power users and authors—all need suitable applications to fulfill their tasks. With RedDot, it is easy to set up new roles and users.

---

[20]http://www.reddot.com/

One very important task is the simple migration of existing projects. This allows the easy switchover from other content management systems and static web sites without any CMS. To migrate existing projects, existing HTML code is used to create the templates. These automatically created templates can then be grouped together to reduce the number of templates.

RedDot enables companies to make editors out of users. Employee, service partner, vendor, or customer—anyone will be able to contribute to the Web site. The RedDot server runs on a Windows NT or 2000 server, which is typically set behind a firewall. With the data entered by an editor, RedDot server creates logical links from which the pages are created. This includes the created or edited page, the related template, data objects used to fill the placemarkers (i.e., texts, graphics), elements of other pages calling this page, and links to other pages. Data objects are stored in a file system or an ODBC database.

Information on the current state of editorial work can be obtained by using RedDot's dynamic preview. The preview temporarily creates the selected page by using the Internet Information Server and related ASP (Active Server Pages) interface that is integrated in Windows NT IIS.

Following the authorization process, the page is generated and uploaded to the live server via FTP or HTTP. The process can be triggered by either the editor or a timer. When a page is created, all links will be automatically verified and updated if necessary. Server-based scripts will be executed when the page is called up.

Roxen Platform

The Roxen Platform[21] contains not only a comprehensive production, distribution, delivery, and management system, but also enables the necessary Internet structure, such as Web serving, Web application, and integration capabilities as well as Web auditing and information retrieval.

Roxen Platform provides the ability to distribute content authoring to the information owners themselves in a very hands-on and easy manner. The Roxen Platform addresses the five roles involved in the Web site; the information owner, the designer, the web developer, the administrator, and the visitor. The platform has a 100 percent Web-based interface for simple handling and management regardless of the user's intent.

Roxen Platform is a suite of tightly integrated tools for collaborative Web site building, publishing, administration, application development, and integration. This enables the customer to run one core package for all Web-related work. Using a Web content management (WCM) system will thus minimize the need for external consultants.

The utilization areas are, for example, public Web sites, corporate intranets, and enterprise portals—wherever correct and updated information is business-critical. These sites are often maintained by a large number of users, and

---

[21]http://www.roxen.com/

in order to handle this complex situation today and tomorrow, a professional WCM system is needed.

The Roxen Platform addresses the four most common roles in a Web site organization:

- **Information owner**—Keeping the Web site updated.

- **Administrator**—Keeping the Web site available.

- **Web designer**—Keeping the Web site attractive.

- **Web developer**—Keeping the Web site dynamic.

Table 8.3. The Roxen Platform

Regardless of the roles, working with the Web should be easy for the entire organization. In general, individuals do not have to know everything about the Internet as long as they can use familiar tools when working with the Web. Roxen Platform provides the means to erase technology thresholds.

The open and modular approach of Roxen Platform provides great flexibility in terms of personalization, scalability, and integration as well as migration possibilities. All content (text, images, etc.) is separated from the layout (navigation, design, etc.) through the use of templates.

Using a template-based Web site enables swift and immediate content editing and makes site-wide changes very easy to perform. Depending on the visitors' origin, the whole Web site, with its content and navigation mode, can be personalized, increasing the experience and security.

SiteStation

SiteStation[22] provides distributed WCM, Web-based document management and knowledge management features.

Distributed WCM puts Web publishing content control into the hands of nontechnical users who are the originators of the content. It provides faster updates, dynamic control of timed content (through timed publishing controls), and searchability for fast access.

SiteStation document management enables the use of a browser to simplify the task of selectively sharing documents and files over the Internet, with check-in/check-out and edit control. SiteStation creates a secure, online searchable knowledge base that is similar to a library card catalog system, except that

---

[22]http://www.sitestation.com/

in this library, you see only those index cards or volumes that are permitted, based upon your password access level.

Dynamic Publishing means your Web site can easily display different content depending on today's date and the viewing rights of the user. SiteStation lets you post articles with start and expiration dates and associate images with your content. Because all content is managed, it lets you control who can edit and who can read it. If you do not have rights to the content (or if you do not log in as a valid user) you will not see links to managed content unless it is intended for public viewing.

All content is maintained in the SiteStation database, and links between managed documents are controlled so you cannot have dead links in the system, even when pages are deleted or expire.

The SiteStation card catalog manages content just like a library card catalog. The card catalog contains metainformation for searching your documents and information to control how and where a document is displayed.

Content is organized into folders, which are containers for pages and other folders. A single document or folder can appear in more than one parent folder. This enables content to be selectively targeted and shared, while allowing documents or collections of documents to be maintained in only one place but visible in multiple sections of a site. Thus, a logical site hierarchy and structure is maintained, and the site is easy to navigate.

Anonymous users may view unrestricted content, but based upon user login, the user may see more links to additional content based upon permissions. A user must have at least read-access rights to a specific page of content, or its existence is hidden and no links to it will be visible to that user.

User security is set at the user group level, and a user can be a member of more than one group. If a user does not have at least read-only access to a particular document, links to it will not appear in pages or searches. Users who are authorized to create content are able to control who has access to view or edit that content.

Content security is set at the folder level. All documents created or displayed in a folder inherit the security restrictions of that folder, and subfolders inherit the security properties of the parent folder, which can be overridden.

8.2   Customer Relationship Management

8.2.1   Introduction

While CRM has been widely discussed in the past, still many people do not completely understand what it means. Therefore, a short introduction is in order. Recall what it is you like about shopping at your local grocery store. The shop owners probably know you, maybe even your name and possibly what you bought the last few times. They can help you with your shopping because they are familiar with what you like, and they may even tell you about offerings that may interest you. But since the introduction of supermarkets and mass consumption, the personal shopping experience has been exchanged for lower prices.

The Internet now offers the unique possibility of combining mass consumption with a personalized shopping experience. Although you still may prefer going down to the local market to buy fruit, vegetables, flowers, and other things, the idea of having a personalized service is appealing. In order to make this idea a reality, a CRM strategy needs to be implemented.

Nowadays, companies can use the Internet combine mass consumption with personalized shopping, only for millions of users, in every conceivable region of the world. They can store information about the customer on databases and then use it to tailor their services to the customer individual needs. Promotions become more effective through the ability to target the audiences most likely to respond. Referrals respond to data gained on the customers preferences. Purchases are quicker and easier due to prior input of information.

CRM is a business strategy that aims to understand, anticipate, and manage the needs of an organization's current and potential customers. It is a journey of strategic, process, organizational, and technical change, whereby a company seeks to better manage its own enterprise around customer behaviors. It entails acquiring and deploying knowledge about customers and using this information across the various touchpoints to balance revenue and profits with maximum customer satisfaction.

However, CRM is a strategy that must be tailored to each market segment, and therein lies the challenge and the opportunity. To be effective in managing the customer relationship, an organization needs to define its customer strategy. To do that, there must be an understanding of customer segments and their needs. This is a mandatory requirement if one is to understand which products and services to offer and if that offering will be identical for each segment.

The company needs to create a channel and product strategy. This defines how the organization will deliver its products and services efficiently and effectively, ensuring sales productivity and effective channel management. Last, but not least, it is very important to understand what a robust and integrated infrastructure strategy means. This entails creating an environment to enable a relationship with the customer that satisfies the customer's needs. It requires an ability to achieve proactive customer management and reactive customer care.

To be successful, it is important to better understand the customer and provide the intelligence required for more effective strategies aimed at customer retention. Therefore it is necessary to target and serve customers on an individual basis (one-to-one rather than mass marketing) and establish long-term relationships with them (relationship rather than transaction marketing). Companies need to remove all barriers and distortions created by the non-value adding intermediaries placed between the supplier and the customer.

The reason for implementing a CRM system is easily explained. Loyal customers spend more with particular companies. Customer loyalty, measured in repeat purchases and referrals, is the key driver of profitability for online businesses, even more so than for offline companies, according to a series of joint studies in online retail by Bain & Company[23] and Mainspring, which was conducted in 2000. For example, the average repeat customer spent 67 percent more overall in the third year of his or her shopping relationship with an online retail vendor than in the first six months. And, over three years, customers referred by online grocery shoppers spent an additional 75 percent of what the original shopper spent. According to industry analysts, retaining a customer costs about one-tenth as much as acquiring a new one. The study also found that the average online apparel shopper was not profitable for the retailer until he or she had shopped at the site four times. This implies that the retailer has to retain the customer for 12 months in order to break even.

However, you should be aware of potential pitfalls that might trip you up. CRM networks take an inordinate amount of time, money, and work to set up if they are to be effective. They cannot be part of an e-business project. They are their own projects, which may run in parallel to an e-business project, but don't need to. The importance of using CRM must permeate the entirety of your company; it is not simply an extension to your online presence. Otherwise, your employees won't use it, and the system might as well not exist. You must integrate the CRM network into every aspect of your operations, online and offline, to maximize efficiency. Finally, and foremost, you must remain focused on your customer's needs. Many companies focus on what they can do rather than on what needs to be done. This leads to waste, as the best system on the market may not be the best for your customers.

8.2.2 Selecting a CRM

As you may have noticed by now, CRM is the key to creating a successful business, an not just e-business. Therefore, CRM requires a comprehensive strategy, carefully designed business practices, and integration with existing applications and contact channels. Selecting the right CRM software has to be part of an enterprise-wide strategy. The software selected will be the foundation of the company's customer service strategy and the means by which they can take that service to the next level. An effective CRM strategy may require a dramatic shift in organizational focus, from a departmental-centered or product-centered view to one that places the customer at the center.

Remember, a successful online business is centered around the customer. Developing this strategy requires participation and buy-in at all levels, especially senior management.

When selecting a CRM solution, you should look out for the following features that need to be present. In today's world, a CRM solution must be Web-

---

[23]http://www.bain.com/

enabled, meaning that information can be exchanged with the online business. It needs to be an integral part of your online offerings, adding functionality to your offline strategy by placing the customer information on a Web-front, making it easy for all employees to access the customer information easily and reliably. All channels of a company need to be integrated into the CRM system; this means that all enterprise applications need to be connected to the CRM solution—not only to feed data into it, but also to get information from it. The CRM solution should be the only repository of customer-related data. Not all channels, applications and services should have their own databases; they should be connected to this central system. Naturally, this includes the call center.

In order to be open for future growth or change of business strategy, the CRM solution should provide a flexible workflow engine that can be adapted to changes in the future. The system should not depend on a certain search engine to make it easy to upgrade or move to another search engine in the future. The solution should have the ability to service multiple types and skill levels of users and allow support of all facets of the operation. And the solution should provide integration into the Web application server and allow knowledge capture in real time. An advanced user interface should be provided for more experienced customers.

To avoid problems when implementing a CRM solution, you should consider the same issues as with a standard e-business implementation. To avoid confusion, it is necessary to have clear goals, processes, and workflows, which include good communication between the members of the team. This can be done only if the customer needs are properly understood, the priorities are set accordingly, and the right resources have been identified. And of course, a lack of quantitative measurements will not help to make this project a success.

A successful CRM implementation enables an enterprise to use customer data to match enterprise resources to customer needs in an optimal manner. This requires that customer data, such as descriptive data (e.g., who, where, age, and income), transactional data (e.g., purchases, costs, and channels), and interactional data (e.g., service requests and sales offers), be collected throughout the enterprise and analyzed to turn it into meaningful information. Following that effort, a customer relationship strategy is developed to support high-quality interactions across several channel.

This will ensure that your service delivery will be consistent across all channels and will result in a holistic view of the customer. The level of service improves by performing real work rather than merely tracking and routing service requests, and it provides the highest degree of accuracy and reliability. As a result, effective self-service options can be done out-of-the-box, integrating front-office with back-office systems seamlessly.

To summarize, your CRM strategic objectives should be to maximize the effectiveness and productivity of all channels; deliver stellar service; increase selling time with each customer; enable better communication and information sharing between sales, service, and marketing; decrease sales cycles; and achieve higher call-to-sale ratios.

8.2.3 Product Overview

There are many different software solutions available in the CRM arena. Describing all of them in detail would be a book of its own; only a small selection of products is presented here. Selecting a CRM solution is very difficult because it needs to fit to the company, its processes, and existing infrastructure. Just as with every software category, there is no optimal solution for everyone. CRM is even more complicated, as it requires interaction with all systems and processes in a company once it is fully implemented.

One factor is the size of the company. The larger the company, the more complex issues the solution needs to handle. The following overview shows some examples in the SME (small to medium enterprise) area and some in the large corporations area. In the SME arena we find solutions such as ACT!, Applix, Epicor, GoldMine, Onyx, Remedy, Sales Logix, and Siebel Mid Market. On the enterprise market, the following solutions play a role: Clarify, Quintis, Siebel, and Vantive.

ACT!

ACT![24] 2000 lets you organize data in a way that's in line with the structure of each account or organization—by individual, group account, or company—while providing a clear overview of your contact information. Every activity, every note, every conversation, every email, fax, or proposal can be organized and strategized. And the ability to define your own group rules makes assigning new or existing leads and contacts a smoother process.

The solution also provides tools for complete calendar and schedule management, from printed calendars and address books to actual alarms for meeting reminders. To empower the salespeople on the road, ACT! provides bidirectional synchronization with a PalmPilot. Changes made on both the PalmPilot and in ACT! are supported, and each is updated with the most recent changes.

Using Paragon Software's FoneSync software, included on the ACT! CD, lets you bypass manual entry and transfer up to 250 names and numbers from an ACT! database to a digital phone with the click of a mouse.

ACT! 2000 supports the sales process with forecasting and sales tracking features. It generates informative graphs that illustrate the sales pipeline. It is possible to predefine a detailed series of activities. The result will be a pipeline management process that is highly effective from prospect to closing, and all set within the specified timeframe.

---

[24]http://www.actsoftware.com/

Applix

Applix iEnterprise[25] offers organizations the ability to manage and analyze customer data as well as provide a collaborative solution that extends access of this data to customers, employees, and partners. With Applix iEnterprise, companies can run their entire enterprise from a central site, enabling users around the globe to quickly and easily access corporate information. This means that critical customer data is available anytime, anywhere. This operational process is what truly enables a company to be customer driven.

Applix iSales helps marketing and sales force succeed in every phase of the sales cycle—from initial lead generation through qualification, close, and fulfillment. It connects disparate databases so the sales force can efficiently assemble, process, track, and use critical information. It empowers salespeople to make more profitable business decisions.

Superior customer satisfaction requires that the support team quickly and efficiently manage and resolve customer issues. Customers are demanding more from a service department than ever before, and iService tries to transform customer service into superior customer satisfaction. The ability to create customer loyalty, whether by offering callers appropriate incremental products or services, by periodically surveying the satisfaction level of the customers, or by passing product feedback on to a development staff, is what today's organizations demand from a service application.

Using Applix's unique QuickSolve resolution technologies to retrieve answers faster and easier, and iService's fully integrated quality assurance module to provide seamless integration to engineering and product development, iService also combines with iSales to form one of the leading CRM software solution for SMEs.

Clarify

Clarify's[26] eFrontOffice tries to integrate, consolidate, and route information from every customer interaction. It does not matter if it is Web-based, via email, over the phone, or face-to-face. The result is a complete view of the customers, which enables companies to provide them with personalized service. Clarify eFrontOffice can turn a call center into a profit center.

Clarify eFrontOffice allows the personalization of self-service and self-sales in customer-specific portals. It allows the inclusion of an email response management, and initiating and maintaining relationships with prospects through Internet marketing.

Clarify eFrontOffice integrates all interactions in a single routing and queuing system. This includes auto-response (email), self-service (Web), and live interaction with salespeople, field service professionals, or call center agents.

---

[25]http://www.applix.com/
[26]http://www.nortelnetworks.com/

It prioritizes requests based on customer value, not on the method they use to communicate with you. If a customer initiates contact via email, the message doesn't get lost. Instead, the solution allows the call center to handle email in exactly the same way as a telephone call, complete with prioritization by service level agreement, product, and expertise required.

Clarify eFrontOffice integrates self-service and self-sales into a single view, giving customers a rich online experience. Through dynamically created portals, customers can update their profiles, initiate customer service cases, view tailored promotions, manage new sales orders, and undertake a variety of other tasks. The solution allows them to customize and control the information they see—for example, to view only open support cases or active purchase orders. "Call me" and click-stream monitoring are two technologies to speed up the customer care process. The solution supports XML and can be integrated with IBM's Net.Commerce Server and Microsoft's Commerce Server platforms.

Epicor

Epicor eFrontOffice[27] is a set of integrated sales, marketing, and customer support tools for SMEs. eFrontOffice is an integrated CRM solution running on Windows that enables companies to manage the entire customer lifecycle.

Part of Epicor eFrontOffice suite is Epicor eSales, which empowers a company with contact, lead, opportunity, and account management, all in one package. Sales teams can be formed and managed, milestones set and measured, literature sent, competitor information accessed, correspondence generated, and potential revenue forecasted.

This eCRM tool increases sales efficiency by supporting structured sales methodologies and by freeing salespeople from administrative overhead, enabling them to concentrate on selling. Sales representatives are empowered to focus on the right opportunities with the most current and accurate information at their fingertips. eSales can make sales teams more knowledgeable, responsive and proactive in communicating with prospects and customers.

With Epicor eMarketing, companies can manage marketing campaigns, pinpoint their targets, and capture qualified leads. Additionally, they can measure the costs and benefits and analyze ROI on their marketing activities.

Epicor eSupport is a tool for managing the support needs of the customers. It enables the efficient management of the entire workload, from handling calls to requesting customer shipments. Companies can track all products their customers purchase, as well as any products that are returned for service or replacement. eSupport's AnswerBook feature, an online store of answers to the customers most frequently asked questions, makes it easy for anyone in the company to give fast and accurate answers.

The Epicor eFrontOffice Connector is designed to connect remote sites and laptop users to centralized information. Data can be synchronized and ex-

---

[27]http://www.epicor.com/

changed bidirectionally between sites, as well as between individual sites and a central database. Through a sophisticated "data slicing" process, it is possible to ensure that locations or individuals receive only the information they need. Access to timely information results in more efficient service calls, faster sales cycles, and satisfied customers.

GoldMine

GoldMine[28] provides the tools businesses need to gather, store, and analyze customer information in order to retain customers. Designed for the workgroup, GoldMine collects and centralizes all information flowing through an organization; the result is an internal organizational structure that has every employee working at maximum effectiveness and efficiency.

Goldmine makes it possible to manage prospect and client information, so teams can spend less time on administrative tasks and more time realizing results. GoldMine bridges the gap between complex, expensive sales force automation software and lower end contact managers to give you high-end results.

Onyx

Onyx Software[29] provides products and services that enable all customer, prospect, and partner interactions to be managed via one enterprise-wide system. The solutions require skilled professional services for deployment. Simply put, Onyx software would be overkill for simple contact management.

The Onyx Enterprise Portal is a Web-based product that combines CRM functionality with third-party applications and rich contextual content from the Internet. It pulls all this together in one common interface so sales, marketing, and service people have a single interface for everything they do. It also gives companies a framework on which to build customer and partner portals.

The Onyx Customer Center is a Web-enabled client/server solution for managing customer information across sales, marketing, service, and support teams. By coordinating all customer interactions, Onyx Customer Center enables companies to provide their teams with a single, comprehensive tool for managing, sharing, and viewing all customer information. Customer Center enables companies to more effectively acquire, retain, and expand customer relationships.

The Onyx Customer Center – Unplugged provides Internet data synchronization of comprehensive customer information, giving remote employees a single tool to access and update all corporate customer information without being connected to a network or the Internet. Leveraging consolidated data between the field and headquarters, a company is better able to acquire, retain, and expand customer relationships.

---

[28] http://www.goldminesw.com
[29] http://www.onyx.com/

Onyx Enterprise DataMart provides a view into the performance of the front office operations through a prepackaged database. Since it is preconfigured to work with the Onyx Front Office database, it eliminates the need to build a custom database and can immediately generate trend reports to assist in making sound business decisions. Built-in extensibility can support the various customizations that are unique to your business, giving you fast and effective indicators of future performance.

Avaya

The Avaya eContact Suite[30] includes a set of media connectors that link to email systems, e-commerce software and tools, interactive voice response (IVR) units, automatic call distribution (ACD) switches, and imaging systems. This enables the call center to use existing equipment investments to work across different communications channels. The media connectors link to the eContact engine, which provides a single point of control for all forms of electronic interaction, allowing the call center to apply business rules across each channel and execute microcasting and mass personalization strategies via a common software platform and user interface.

The eContact Suite includes Avaya's computer telephony integration technology and desktop applications for consumer call centers, support departments, inside sales, consumer relations, and human resource call centers. And the eContact Suite works with applications from other companies, back-office systems, and legacy systems, giving you a complete system for handling customer transactions. One simple set of customization and administration tools works across the entire suite. Reporting software lets companies drill down to the information they need to make quick decisions, such as determining how many products you sold over the Web on any given day.

Remedy

Remedy CRM Solutions[31] help companies strengthening their customer relationships by automating sales, marketing, customer support, engineering, and quality assurance processes across the organization. The idea is to integrate as much as possible.

Remedy's workflow process automation technology ensures that nothing is lost or overlooked, from tracking leads to closing sales, from servicing customers to fixing product defects. As a result, Remedy CRM Solutions boost the productivity and effectiveness of marketing, sales, support, engineering, and quality assurance personnel.

Remedy is easily deployed, and through easy adaptability, it conforms to the company's way of doing business, protecting its investment in business

---

[30] http://www.avaya.com/
[31] http://www.remedy.com/

processes that work best. Built-in expandability and scalability supports the evolving and changing business.

Remedy applications are built on the innovative Action Request System technology. This multitier architecture has the power and scalability to support all sizes of business needs. Remedy CRM Solutions can be implemented individually or as an integrated suite. Integration enhances collaboration among sales, marketing, support, engineering, and quality assurance departments because they can share important and up-to-the-minute information.

Sales Logix

With SalesLogix2000,[32] sales, marketing, and support teams will get a tool to support them to target, close, and retain customers for life. SalesLogix2000 for Sales provides a high-end solution for large corporations. It allows companies to manage campaigns from start to finish, improve customer loyalty, and to learn the secrets of their success.

SalesLogix2000 for Marketing tracks all campaigns, including responses received. When a company associates a lead source with each contact, it will easily find out where the investment should go. It lets you send emails, faxes, and literature; schedule a phone call; or automatically trigger a Web-based marketing campaign. It can also improve communication.

The software provides data mining tools that let companies find buyers within their database and offer them additional or entirely new products. Through the built-in segmentation of the markets, companies know which customers are buying what products and can see the buying cycles and offer specials at the right times.

Through a Windows-based interface, SalesLogix2000 for Support lets the support representatives see call details, customer history, service contracts, and product returns. It also allows them to categorize, track, and prioritize requests by status, category, issue, customer, or date.

Siebel

Siebel eBusiness Applications[33] enable organizations to immediately leverage the Internet to acquire new customers and enhance each and every existing customer relationship. Siebel eBusiness is built on current and emerging Internet computing standards and provides comprehensive out-of-the-box functionality, a scalable Web-based product architecture, and flexible application customization capabilities. Siebel eBusiness Applications are built on the same Web-based architecture that other Siebel front office applications leverage, enabling organizations to deploy one integrated multichannel system to manage all customer touchpoints.

---

[32]http://www.saleslogix.com/
[33]http://www.siebel.com/

Siebel eBusiness enables companies to create and execute Internet-based marketing campaigns to identify and acquire new customers, develop customized product and service offerings that meet customer requirements and expectations, facilitate unassisted selling over the Web, provide 24/7 customer service and support, and manage channel relationships to ensure optimum effectiveness and efficiency.

Siebel eSales is a Web-based application that supports unassisted B2B and B2C selling over the Web. Siebel eSales includes a visual product catalog, Web-based quote generation, self-service solution and product configuration, and online ordering. Siebel customers quickly can set up shop on the Internet, leveraging product data, marketing collateral, and configurations across their multiple selling channels—the field, call center, indirect channels, and Web. Siebel eSales electronic product catalog allows Web users to view product information in an intuitive GUI. With Siebel eSales' eConfigurator, customers can verify that a configuration is valid, buildable, and orderable. Siebel eSales is fully customizable so that organizations can integrate it into their enterprise Web site and tailor it to meet their eBusiness needs.

Siebel eMarketing enables organizations to create, execute, and assess Web-based marketing campaigns. With Siebel eMarketing, enterprise can segment their customer and prospect bases, target them with a personalized, automatically generated Web-based or email-based communication or promotion, and view OLAP-based graphical reports that assess the effectiveness and return on investment of each campaign. Using Siebel eMarketing, organizations can extend their global reach by using the Internet as a cost-effective marketing channel.

Siebel eService allows organizations to provide world class customer service and support through the Internet. Siebel eService provides Web-based and email-based service automation to manage the entire service process, allowing customers to easily create new service requests, enter service details, locate and track progress of open service requests, and view a knowledge base of solutions. Siebel eService also proactively notifies customers of important events via email, both acknowledging receipt of the service request and informing the customer of updates or resolutions. Service centers that deploy Siebel eService can increase customer satisfaction and dramatically reduce their cost of providing high-quality, 24/7 service

Siebel eChannel enables companies to maximize the revenue-generating capacity of their multitiered, global distribution channels while lowering overall costs. It allows organizations to manage channel partners as extended virtual sales and service organizations. Siebel eChannel allows organizations to route leads, opportunities, accounts, and service requests to the appropriate channel using configurable business rules and to track their performance on all assigned items. Siebel eChannel enables channel partners to browse product and pricing information, configure solutions, and generate quotes and online orders, automating the entire partner/vendor relationship. Through all interactions, sophisticated security rules ensure that partners and vendors are able to keep sensitive information completely confidential.

Vantive

The Vantive[34] solution, recently bought by Peoplesoft,[35] consists of several modules: Sales and Marketing, FieldService, HelpDesk, Quality, Web Self-Service, Partner Desktop, and VanWeb. Vantive Sales and Marketing supports the entire sales and marketing process, providing tools that can help sales reps to sell more effectively. Tools bundled into Vantive Sales facilitate the sales process; these include knowledge tools, opportunity management software, quote and proposal software, forecasting and enterprise reporting software, and administrative tools. Tight integration with Microsoft Outlook gives reps a single screen for managing tasks, contacts, schedules, email, and calendars.

Vantive FieldService provides a set of capabilities to serve as the foundation of the entire service organization. Personnel throughout a company's service organization will be able to allocate, schedule, and dispatch the right people, with the right parts, at the right time.

Vantive HelpDesk enables internal help desk operations to improve productivity and reduce costs while enhancing the quality of service by effectively tracking and resolving employee requests for technical assistance.

Vantive Quality makes it easier to consistently deliver customer-aligned products and services by integrating product quality and enhancement processes across the business enterprise.

With Vantive Web Self-Service, customers can access support information over the Internet via a Web browser. This product enables companies to extend web-based support functionality to their customers, decreasing support and service costs while increasing customer satisfaction.

For organizations that sell through a multitier distribution model, the Vantive Partner Desktop is a Web-based application for increasing sales performance by shortening the sales cycle. With this product, channel partners can access Vantive Sales over the Internet through a browser interface without installing any additional software.

VanWeb is a development technology that Web-enables the Vantive Enterprise. By leveraging Java technology, VanWeb enables users to interact dynamically with a Vantive Enterprise application using any standard Web browser. The Vantive Web Self-Service application extends the reach of the call center by delivering a powerful and customizable ready-to-run support Web site.

---

[34]http://www.vantive.com/

[35]http://www.peoplesoft.com/

8.3   Knowledge Management Systems

8.3.1   Introduction

A KMS can be defined as a "flow of messages or meaning which may add to, restructure, or change knowledge." Information is raw material for production of knowledge. Knowledge can be defined as information in a certain context. KMSs have different characteristics compared to conventional information systems; for instance, users have more control over the attributes of, relationships between, and structure of information within the system. KMSs need to be closer to users' thought processes than typical business applications.

Technologies that serve knowledge management functions did not suddenly appear overnight. Artificial intelligence (AI) and expert systems are, in a sense, yesterday's knowledge technology. In spite of somewhat tarnished reputations, they will continue to contribute to today's KMSs.

Significant competitive advantage can be obtained when an organization's knowledge, stored as both structured and unstructured data, is captured, managed, and put to work in a meaningful and efficient way. Managing knowledge is a common sense approach for improving business results, supported by an advanced technology infrastructure. Cutting costs and improving efficiency are the business goals. The goal of knowledge management is to improve the creation, dissemination, and exploitation of knowledge for the purpose of building stakeholder value. Ultimately, knowledge management is the ability to get the right information to the right people at the right time and in the right context, so that a business can run more smoothly and efficiently.

Not all information is valuable. Therefore, it's up to individual companies to determine what information qualifies as intellectual and knowledge-based assets. In general, however, intellectual and knowledge-based assets fall into one of two categories: explicit or tacit. Included among the former are assets such as patents, trademarks, business plans, marketing research, and customer lists. As a rule of thumb, explicit knowledge consists of anything that can be documented, archived, and codified, often with the help of IT. Much harder to grasp is the concept of tacit knowledge, or the know-how contained in people's heads. The challenge inherent with tacit knowledge is figuring out how to recognize, generate, share, and manage it. While IT in the form of email, groupware, instant messaging, and related technologies can help facilitate the dissemination of tacit knowledge, identifying tacit knowledge in the first place is a major hurdle for most organizations.

Knowledge management includes capturing information and knowledge about a company, its practices, and its competition, and storing it in a place where other people can find and distribute it on demand to people who need it. The use of the Internet and corporate intranets has changed people's perception of the potential for sharing knowledge across the organization. In particular, it has focused attention on the role of unstructured information.

Management systems are very user-biased and can be quite unusual; this can cause severe difficulties (expense and time) in design and implementation. Therefore, traditional IT strategies are simply not suitable for building KMSs. A new paradigm is required to support knowledge management.

Using traditional information management systems results in the following scenario. Imagine a system where the users seem unable to define exactly what they want and keep changing their minds on what is agreed. Therefore, it is necessary to better understand what a KMS can do for you and your company before trying to "adapt" existing systems.

The following features are only the top levels of a taxonomy of knowledge management functions. They can be further subdivided into a nested hierarchy. As discrete functions, they are served in various combinations by a range of current software applications and by products increasingly integrated as components of corporate intranets.

- **Information Management**—Finding, mapping, gathering, and filtering information.

- **Knowledge Creation**—Developing new knowledge.

- **Sharing Knowledge**—Converting personal knowledge into shared knowledge resources.

- **Learning**—Understanding and learning by acquiring or extracting knowledge value.

- **Adding Value**—Adding value to information to create knowledge.

- **Action**—Enabling action through knowledge, such as performance and management.

- **Processing**—Information processing of shared knowledge resources.

- **Delivery**—Transferring explicit knowledge to coworkers.

- **Creation**—Building a technical infrastructure.

Table 8.4. Basic Features of KMS

A KMS does not have to be costly and elaborate; it can be very simple, very complex, or anywhere in between, depending on the requirement. Therefore, cost is not the key issue. The key issue is to organize information in such a way that people who contribute information and knowledge are rewarded. People who want to inform themselves can do it in the most efficient way, meaning that information and knowledge needs to be structured in their way of thinking. Therefore, a key necessity for a KMS is a personalized view of knowledge. A KMS must be tailored for each organization, not only for the individual within the company, because every system is different and even small requirements can have a big impact on the design.

Although a company should use only a single KMS, it is of utmost importance to tailor or personalize it in such a way that it looks very different to different types of user (e.g., end users, analysts, information experts, specialists). Every type of user should be able to get the most out of the system; it therefore needs to be highly personalized. As a result, the system's complexity will be hidden from most users.

To make the system more usable, you should apply entity relationship diagrams less rigorously than for database applications, as this fits the needs of the users. By developing the solution in a modular manner, it becomes easy to plug in new technology when it becomes available and makes it easier to adapt the solution if the company grows and acquires other companies.

To get extra functionality, a company should build on top of existing applications wherever possible, but should not try to stretch products, tools, or modules too far past their inherent capability, or the system will lose flexibility and become overly complex.

As a rule of thumb, you should assemble the final result as late as possible in order to guarantee the quality of the components of the process.

Expect severe design trade-offs in some areas (this does not mean the design is wrong, just that some requirements can be very stringent). Therefore, you should find ways to minimize the impact of the trade-offs by embedding them in machines, not in people processes. Be prepared for unusual conclusions about how costs are allocated (e.g., development vs. training vs. support), and about how project risk can be minimized.

In an ideal world, a KMS could retrieve, organize, and deliver only the information a user requested. But systems aren't intelligent enough to do that, at least not yet. For example, although they can be query structured (e.g., databases) and unstructured (e.g., documents) data sources, they can't decipher the content of an image. That job falls to a human. Smaller companies can get by with ad hoc cataloging of information accumulated by managers and staff as part of their regular duties. Larger companies employ specialists to acquire and manage the data and so relieve the company's decision makers from the role of data gatherers. Given such titles as subject matter experts, domain experts, or competitive intelligence professionals, these handlers care for and feed the system.

An effective knowledge management program can help a company do one or more of the following:

- **Innovation**—Foster innovation by encouraging the free flow of ideas.

- **Customer Service**—Improve customer service by streamlining response time.

- **Revenues**—Boost revenues by getting products and services to market faster.

- **Employee Retention**—Enhance employee retention rates by recognizing the value of employees' knowledge and rewarding them for it.

- **Operations Streamlining**— Streamline operations and reduce costs by eliminating redundant or unnecessary processes.

Table 8.5. Benefits of knowledge management

Most KMSs convert data into knowledge by cross-referencing internal documents. For example, the system might index data sources according to a competitor's type of business, by a customer's history, and by a person's name. Multiple cross references, backed by a system that rates the information, enhance its ultimate usefulness. Using this technique, one business discovered that several managers of a primary client formerly worked for Microsoft. Digging deeper, they discovered that the company was financed by Microsoft, which prompted them to modify some of the rules governing their professional relationship.

Most organizations today consider it a strategic imperative that their IT infrastructure extends the enterprise's information, resources, and business processes to employees, partners, and customers in a unified and collaborative manner. The Delphi Group[36] found out that in a typical Global 2000 enterprise, 64 core applications, 8 office automation packages, 14 middleware service providers, 17 database products, 9 network protocols, 15 OS, and 11 hardware platforms all must be somehow integrated and rendered accessible through multiple Web interfaces, including B2C, B2B, and B2E Web sites.

---

[36]http://www.delphi.com/

Achieving this ambitious goal, however, means that the enterprise will quickly realize a number of compelling benefits: Unifying Web infrastructure reduces total cost of ownership; personalized self-service access to applications and information improves productivity; collaboration and interaction enhances relationships across the enterprise; the enterprise begins to speak with one consistent voice; and the enterprise is effectively extended to key stakeholders. Initial attempts at building such an environment, though, will likely be plagued by the problems of multiple Web site maintenance, legacy system silos, hard-to-find, outdated content, and inconsistent messages and content.

8.3.2   Difficulties with KMS

Although KMS sounds quite straightforward, creating one is quite a difficult task. Even if you could cover all the required functions with technologies, you're going to face intractable challenges you most likely have no authority to overcome. Today's technologies and software solutions have the answer to most problems related to KMS, but there are still some problems that cannot be solved with these technologies.

One major problem is the missing loyalty of knowledge workers towards the organization they are working for. Many people do not share information voluntarily and take the knowledge with them when leaving the company. Another big problem is that people within an organization are not always willing to enter their knowledge into a KMS, as knowledge means power and giving away their knowledge means also that they lose some of their power. People who share their knowledge can also be laid off more easily once their knowledge is within the company and no longer within a single person.

In businesses where evaluation, promotion, or compensation is based on relative numbers, individuals sharing their knowledge reduce their chances of success, and those holding back have a relative advantage. This discourages cooperative behavior.

Since the knowledge management concept requires cooperation to work, it will succeed only if employees trust that their donations don't undermine their job security or, more commonly, their job competitiveness. This can be achieved if the usage of knowledge-management concepts is personalized in every way possible. Contributors need the feeling that their work of adding knowledge is valued. Employees researching information and knowledge should have the freedom to email to someone for further questions, if the system is at its limits.

If this sounds like a lot of problems to be solved, there are even more problems for contributors. Typically, employees are so busy with their daily work that they are not able or willing to spend even more time on filling a knowledge management database with content. The problem is that even if companies provide rewards for this additional tasks, employees will see them only in mid-term to long-term range. There is no obvious instant reward in sharing knowledge with others.

Therefore, it is very important to free up some time for employees to update the knowledge database and to create rewards for those who contribute. A reward could be simply based on the number of contributions, but this would probably create many submissions at a low quality. A better reward would be a ranking system, where coworkers rate the quality of a contribution. Ideally, a combination of both would be used.

There is no knowledge management solution out there that can be bought completely as a product and that needs only configuration. Knowledge management is too complex; it is not a technology-based concept. Don't be duped by software vendors touting their all-inclusive KMS. Companies that implement a centralized database system, electronic message board, Web portal or any other collaborative tool in the hope that they've established a knowledge management program are wasting both their time and money. While technology can support knowledge management, it's not the starting point of a knowledge management program. Make knowledge management decisions based on who (people), what (knowledge), and why (business objectives). Save the how (technology) for last.

If a company is not going to treat the knowledge management initiative as a strategic and high-priority effort (just like any strategic e-business initiative), a company should not waste time trying to deploy it. Even if the deployment is purely departmental, the management team may need to make some strategic changes to address issues such as financial compensation based on contribution of knowledge to the corporate information store. This may occur because a knowledge management implementation requires a shift in philosophy for most organizations, not only in how people work, but more importantly, in how they interact with each other.

8.3.3   Selecting a KMS

Before selecting a KMS, a company should define its corporate goals in trying to implement the knowledge management concept and outline a set of supporting objectives.

Although technology should not be neglected, it is important to understand the processes behind the technology. The rush to implement intranets is one of the forces driving serious interest in knowledge management. An intranet is a good means of making an organization's knowledge accessible and reusable for all employees.

Many vendors of information-oriented products have rushed to introduce Internet-compatible products in an effort to grab the market opportunity. But computer applications already addressed aspects of knowledge management for years before intranets were hailed as the next magic bullet for business productivity.

No single technology defines knowledge management. In fact, knowledge management is not about technology. It is basically a multi-disciplinary concern encompassing important aspects of cognitive science, information design, interpersonal communication, organizational dynamics, library science, motivation, training, heuristics, publishing, and business analysis.

However, it is as big a mistake to assume that technology has no answers for us as it is to assume that technology has all the answers. Why? Because the many brilliant minds behind the technologies have been concerned with specific information aspects of knowledge management for many years. What's more, lessons learned and best practices within these existing technologies will be enormously instructive.

Depending on the current needs, the existing strategy and vision, and the existing infrastructure, you should try to select a KMS rather carefully. Do not expect to make a decision within days. It is a complex issue that requires time to find the proper solution.

8.3.4   Product Overview

Broadvision InfoExchange

Broadvision's[37] approach does not specifically mention knowledge management as core competence. Instead, it provides an enterprise portals as the strategic platform for personalized self-service and collaborative e-business. The centerpiece is the introduction of BroadVision InfoExchange Portal 6.0. It provides personalized access to information along with a powerful, collaborative business process environment.

Designed for simple integration with other e-business applications from BroadVision and third parties, and for easy extensibility via open standards (including J2EE technologies), BroadVision InfoExchange Portal 6.0 is an open, secure, and scalable e-business platform available to rapidly deploy and cost-effectively operate secure e-business and knowledge management applications.

Through BroadVision's competencies in the areas of personalization, enterprise-class scalability, and content management, BroadVision InfoExchange Portal 6.0 presents a portal platform that helps the growing number of enterprises seeking a single solution to connect otherwise disparate B2C, B2B, and B2E initiatives. The Portal extends an enterprise's information, resources, and business processes to employees, partners, suppliers, and customers in a unified and collaborative manner.

This solution allows companies to unify the way in which organizations interact with their key constituents. It offers a common architecture and platform for creating robust, scalable and secure B2E, B2B, and B2C portals.

Through the personalized self-service features of BroadVision InfoExchange Portal, enterprises can improve the productivity of all of their constituents, providing them with exactly the right information they need—when they need it, where they need it—to work together more effectively and efficiently.

---

[37]http://www.broadvision.com/

The software provides role-based, context-based, and navigational personalization capabilities, which ensure that users can find the exact information they need, quickly and easily. It also delivers collaboration and process management capabilities for productivity and content management capabilities. This enables enterprises to maintain consistent content while reducing the associated time and expense of creating and managing that content.

Through J2EE and Enterprise Application Integration (EAI), it is easier to access multiple information sources and applications. It enables end users to get quick and easy access to databases, applications, other Web sites, and external data feeds such as stock quotes and news. This access can be provided in an intelligent way by connecting various sources of information, creating additional value and knowledge. The solution also incorporates a wide range of access and delivery devices as part of its infrastructure, including pagers, fax, email, and mobile devices.

BroadVision enables enterprises to consolidate the myriad Web sites existing in organizational silos into a handful of enterprise portals supported by a centrally managed, highly scalable environment with distributed administration and content management capabilities. The portal brings together structured and unstructured data, organizational knowledge, and transactions from the multiple information systems that exist in the organization. Through its personalization technology, BroadVision InfoExchange Portal delivers the right information to the right people, at the right time, without creating information overload, and it empowers users to build community through collaboration.

Cogito

Cogito[38] represents organizational knowledge as an internal network of concepts and relationships that is highly flexible and intuitive. This means that not documents, but a database of unique ideas (and relationships among those ideas) from which documents can be generated are the basis for the knowledge. One way to use the Cogito approach is as a compound document management system.

Cogito's storage model is a network database. Ideas correspond to records, or nodes, in the database. Relationships are pointers to related ideas. Information about a concept exists in only one place, even though it may be included in many different documents. A document, then, is simply a view of the knowledge base. Concepts may also be linked to external files so that you know which files contain those concepts.

Cogito's "sentient technology" is patented, but its node/relationship model for representing and storing knowledge is similar to that of "semantic networks." Semantic networks have been used not only in such academic pursuits as fine-grained textual analysis, but in large-scale medical informatics products as well.

---

[38]http://www.cogito.com/

At least three important principles of managing explicit knowledge resources are at work in semantic networks: deconstruction, unique identity, and explicit typing. Information resources can be deconstructed into a database of ideas and relationships among those ideas. Every identity of information elements is unique, which means that there is only one correct solution to a given problem. Relationships of meaning require explicit typing in order to make semantic networks work.

With meaning borne by relationships as well as by content, semantic networks provide not only rapid access to, but also understanding of information, because knowledge is represented by the conjunction of relationships and content. And Cogito's solution provides the basis for this.

grapeVine

grapeVine[39] is a KMS that is especially of interest to companies that have already invested heavily in Lotus Notes. grapeVine will provide a way to use the existing Notes infrastructure to store, organize, and send information through the Notes messaging system.

grapeVine provides all of the groupware capabilities one would expect from Notes, as well as strong security and administration features. Unfortunately, grapeVine does not provide sophisticated reporting and analysis tools. If an organization already uses Notes databases to store information, grapeVine will be easy to get up and running, because much of the knowledge base will already be in place.

First, a Knowledge Chart—a Notes database containing categories and subcategories of keywords, which is the outline of the knowledge base—must be built. This task is usually done by the knowledge manager or person closest to the information. As with the other solutions, you need to plan ahead to determine what resources will be monitored before you build a Knowledge Chart. grapeVine comes with a few predefined Knowledge Charts to help you build a knowledge base and a wizard to help smooth the road. Users can suggest new keywords, but the Knowledge Chart is generally maintained by a single person to ensure the quality of the chart.

Once this task has been completed, an administrator defines an Information Resource, which is a description of the type of information you need to find and where to look for it. Based on keywords in the Knowledge Chart, the Information Resource searches the company's document repositories and sends a copy of the found information to grapeVine's Eureka database.

Typically, the data will come from a Notes database, but it can also be pieces of HTML files or office files, such as Microsoft's PowerPoint presentations or Corel's WordPerfect documents, converted into ASCII format. The solution unfortunately does not support all file formats natively. Once the Eureka database is populated, grapeVine users can browse it just as they would any

---

[39]http://www.grapevine.com/

other Notes database or search for critical information using standard Notes searching techniques.

Users can also automatically receive alerts via Notes email. grapeVine users set up profiles that define their individual search parameters. grapeVine searches for information in the Eureka database and delivers it through the Notes email system. By defining a user profile and requesting to receive alerts, the user no longer needs to search the Eureka database. As users receive information, they can see who else is receiving the same information by checking the names of the other recipients listed on the document, or they can select a topic from the Knowledge Chart to see who else is interested in that topic.

This solution uses a grapevine metaphor to disseminate information. By commenting on information received through an alert, you trigger other user profiles and add more people to the grapevine. This procedure lets you avoid sending email to a list of people who may not be interested in the information. You can also send documents as message attachments directly to the Eureka database.

Hummingbird Fulcrum KnowledgeServer

Fulcrum KnowledgeServer, which was bought by Hummingbird,[40] is an integrated suite of software that can improve the way organizations manage information resources. Knowledge workers can conduct single, unified searches across multiple information sources no matter where the information is stored.

The solution analyzes the content of items to find the information that matters and puts that information into a context. The unique Knowledge Activators create links to information sources, ensuring a seamless searching process for information users.

Fulcrum KnowledgeServer gives users the tools to quickly search for information in thousands of folders from any accessible information source that has been indexed, no matter where it is located. The client applications offer techniques such as Similarity Searching, item summarization, fuzzy searching, and multilingual stemming. A search can be based on a word, a phrase, or the full text of the item. Alternatively, users can choose to search by structured properties, either standard or custom.

To provide searching in many different environments, Fulcrum Knowledge-Server uses server-based indexes. When users search for information, it is the index that is searched, not the information sources. Users can process the items they retrieve using the same options, regardless of the information source or item format. The majority of the items found can be viewed with search-term highlighting, even if the native authoring application isn't installed on the computer.

The item-viewing technology supports over 200 office item formats, including Adobe Acrobat PDF, HTML, Lotus Notes database notes, and Microsoft

---

[40]http://www.hummingbird.com/

Exchange messages. Knowledge is an increasingly critical business asset. The business problem is how to take information, put it in context, and make it useful knowledge.

In most cases 80 percent of an organization's electronic information is un-structured: information in files, messages, memos, reports, and proposals created in different formats and stored in many locations. This flood of information begs for structure to put it in context—to filter through what is available and find what matters—and so deliver its value to you.

This solution takes the traditional network view and ties the elements together in the Knowledge Map. Knowledge Folders extend the Knowledge Map to give a business an intuitive view of an organization's information.

Intraspective

Intraspect 4 provides the platform on which to build, deploy, and manage collaborative applications. The core attributes are Web-based workspaces that enable community-scale collaboration and a dynamic knowledge base that captures the results of online work for learning and reuse.

Intraspect integrates with the tools people use today: email, desktop and enterprise applications, and the Web browser. Users will find Intraspective is easy to use.

The result is a knowledge base of how people use information to do their work and manage their relationships. As people use the system, they are adding to the growing knowledge base without doing anything other than their own work. Intraspect captures the results of this knowledge work with its business context, including authorship, history, metadata, and relationships to other information.

Access is provided through any standard Web browser, email program, or Web folders. No special client software is required. A robust access control system insures the security of information in the group memory.

Intraspect provides three packaged applications: Customer Collaboration, Services Collaboration, and Product Collaboration. Each application solves a particular business problem and can be deployed independently or together and integrated into existing enterprise applications.

Good knowledge management is a foundation of enterprise collaboration management and Intraspect creates a "group memory" that captures information created and used by people as they do their work. The more they use it, the more valuable it is to everyone.

The ability to easily customize the user interface, build workflow-specific business applications, and integrate with enterprise applications drives rapid adoption, use, and ROI within an organization.

Expertise can be leveraged across employees, customers, partners, and suppliers by working in virtual communities that cut across organizational and geographic boundaries.

KnowledgeX

The KnowledgeX solution has been bought by IBM[41] to create an even more compelling knowledge management strategy. The key objective is to identify relationships between distinct pieces of information, such as how changes in your competitor's product line relate to its current stock price. Although this may sound good, achieving this goal is not easy. Before getting the information, a complex project must be set up. Months of in-depth planning and manual labor by a trained IT administrator (or someone who is responsible for tracking competitive information) are required up front.

Large companies can use KnowledgeX to track key information about their competitors. SAP,[42] for example, uses the system on a global scale to look at all of the key people employed by its competitors and to track statistics such as where the employees have worked and attended school and how they've been quoted in the press.

KnowledgeX provides a graphical front end to information stored in an SQL database. In the KnowledgeX world, objects are people, places, and things, and roles are titles. The software creates an SQL table for each object and role and finds the relationships between them. A knowledge base, or collection, consists of data pulled from multiple sources, such as ASCII data, HTML files, video, or audio. KnowledgeX accepts as many as 250 unstructured file formats.

You can use predefined objects or add objects to the collection manually. Each object can then be related to other objects, which is a time-consuming job when placing massive amounts of information into your collection at once. However, the analyst or administrator developing the collection must verify each object, find and create relationships, and make corrections. You can choose to validate everything automatically, but this is obviously not very smart.

Once the database is populated, users can look for information and relationships by dragging and dropping items on the graphical workspace. The system displays a palette of icons representing objects and a palette of questions. You can create new questions by dragging and dropping objects to the question palette.

Some predefined questions come with the product, but if these relationships have not been defined in advance, no results will be returned. The system responds to your question by drawing a map of the relationship between objects.

This graphical drag-and-drop interface takes a while to get used to, so it pays to learn the product properly. As with other solutions, KnowledgeX comes with a built-in viewer for viewing stored documents.

KnowledgeX does not support the searching within any of the documents in the database, though. The searching feature will only search objects in a collection or workspace based on the words placed in a description box when the object was added to the collection.

---

[41] http://www.ibm.com/
[42] http://www.sap.com/

Sovereign Hill

This solution comprises three Sovereign Hill[43] components: InQuery, WebAccess, and InFinder. The InQuery portion is a fairly standard search engine. Besides just being able to perform a straight search, InFinder allows you to refine your search by names or concepts. For example, if you are trying to retrieve information about Microsoft, InFinder can prompt you with a list of the related names or concepts it found in its first search pass. In this scenario, InFinder might discover, and allow you to explore, the relationship between Microsoft and Steve Jobs, and you might learn something that you didn't otherwise know.

The WebAccess toolkit enables companies to build a browser-based front end. This layer, along with the HTML code that must be developed, is the glue that binds everything together and defines most of the product's capabilities. The Web front end makes for an easy user experience that does not require any custom software on the desktop.

Lastly, the InFinder component is a special database that understands names, nouns, and concepts. This portion of the Sovereign Hill solution is what holds the promise of exploring relationships within your knowledge base.

KnowledgeX is able to discover hidden relationships buried within the many discrete pieces of information that you enter. But populating KnowledgeX can become tedious. There also is a delicate balance between the databases you set up and their content. The database engine is capable of understanding Microsoft Word, Corel WordPerfect, text, SGML, and HTML documents.

The Sovereign Hill solution is a database with a Web-browser front end that you can query. It is unfortunately far from finished. First, the administration utilities are crude and command-line based, which does not make the system very accessible. Second, it requires a good deal of HTML coding. A good solution should have little or no HTML coding and a good administration tool.

Wincite

Wincite[44] provides a solution that requires in-depth customization to define the content you want to track, design the data entry screens, and set up the "briefing books". Wincite's solution does not find any magical relationships hidden within data. It organizes the information that analysts feed into the knowledge base and distributes it throughout the organization. The knowledge base is easily built by linking Wincite to external files or inserting data directly into the system. Findings are consolidated into tailored reports that you can post to a Web site or send via email.

The solution is primarily a tool for the analysts in your organization who already are responsible for tracking your markets and competitors, filled with

---

[43]http://www.sovereinhill.com/

[44]http://www.wincite.com/

the company's analysis, expertise, and insight. The product stores and organizes intelligence and allows it to be easily distributed to the employees who need it. The end result and value is as good as the quality of analysis you put into the system. It amplifies the good old rule of thumb: garbage in, garbage out. In many ways, the product looks and acts like a database: It stores, organizes, and facilitates the distribution of data.

Wincite uses a multidimensional database model squeezed into a relational database. The stored information is organized into what the interface calls "notebooks," "topics," and "subjects." The naming convention can fool you. Subjects aren't hierarchically underneath topics; instead, they are really "subject companies" or "subject people." So, for example, a notebook could have the title Knowledge Management and topics might include "customers" and "products," while subjects might be companies that make products and have customers. This structure replaces a fully hierarchical approach in which you could create multiple levels of subfolders to break information down into finer subcategories.

Although information can be manually entered, it doesn't have to be. Data fields can dynamically draw their content from linked files, documents, and worksheets. It actually imports this information each and every time you view, print, or distribute the contents, so you don't have to worry about the data not being current or synchronized.

It allows a company to leverage existing infrastructure and processes to track competitors without having to do double entries in Wincite. It works with a variety of office applications, but if your users need to publish content to the Web, they should be running Microsoft Office in order to maintain most of the formatting.

Wincite distributes information through what the company calls briefing books, but you can think of them as more of a collection of reports. Wincite uses Microsoft Access as the backend database, which probably is adequate for most workgroups, although you can scale up to any ODBC-compliant backend, such as Oracle or Microsoft SQL Server.

Chapter 9

INTERACTIVE COMMUNICATION EXPERIENCES

9.1 The Basics

9.1.1 Communication Experience

As you know by now, the Internet started as a communications medium between people and businesses. Every business requires at least a minimum of communication between the involved parties. Even though this communication may be automated and between computers only, without it the business cannot be executed.

The basic communications features of the Internet—mail, news, and chat—are still the most used applications and will remain so in the future. For this reason, an entire chapter has been dedicated to interactive communications. There is no need to discuss how email or news postings work, as everyone is able to grasp their functionality within seconds—they are the digital replica of normal mail and bulletin boards. Online chat is nothing new compared to normal chit-chat, but the Internet offers new ways of communication, and here we will focus on the new possibilities.

Although all technologies that are presented in this chapter can be used for private communication, the focus is on how to add value to your business by using new and innovative communication technologies. These technologies do not offer radical new solutions, but try to integrate existing technologies to increase the effectiveness of the communication.

Although they have been around for years, peer-to-peer (P2P) technologies have taken off recently with companies like Napster[1] and Gnutella,[2] making news headlines around the globe for their service in music file distribution.

---

[1]http://www.napster.com/
[2]http://www.gnutella.com/

P2P technologies enable many different ways of communication between two parties and is not restricted to swapping music files only. Later in this chapter, we'll explore this promising technology that has become a mainstream phenomenon.

9.1.2 Talking to Your Customers

Typical communication between a company and its customer is done either via normal mail, a phone call, or email. Although in theory this is very effective, it is possible to offer customers even better service by offering direct communication through online chats, for example. The advantage of online chat is that customers are able to help each other without contacting the company, just as in newsgroups. Mail, email and phone are direct communication methods, but require a lot of work in the customer care center.

As many customers are likely to have the same questions, it is a good idea to offer FAQ pages, where most simple questions can be answered. But since more complicated questions cannot be answered through a static Web page, it is often necessary to walk through situations, such as installation, with the customer.

By offering the customers a dedicated chat group, it is possible to deal with more customer requests at the same time. Online chat offers written communication in real time, but in order for it to succeed, it is necessary to obey some rules and to implement them in a standard way. This reduces the overhead for learning how to use these new technologies and does not require any additional software installations on the computer of the customer. A Web browser should be able to handle the requests of the customer.

If other software is required, it is necessary to give a detailed description of where to download and how to install the software. The easier it becomes for the customer to access this form of direct communication, the more success it will have. Implementing a bad solution (e.g., one that it is too complicated or takes too long to download) will increase the number of unsatisfied customers.

Direct communication via chat or newsgroups requires the company to think about new communication standards. As the responses are very direct, it is necessary to ensure that only qualified people are answering the questions. If they can't, a standardized process is implemented, which allows end customers to track questions being passed from one department to the other. If the customers are not able to track the query, they will most likely submit the same query by another means. This creates additional work for the customer care center and can skew the statistics used to track problems.

9.1.3 Interacting with Partners

Interaction with partners can be done over the same channels as contact with the customers, but due to security reasons and traffic, more complex methods of communication are involved. As information shared between partners needs to be treated confidentially, the communication channels need to be secured by encryption. Also, documents are often shared among the partners, so lightweight online text services, such as online chat or newsgroups, are no longer ideal solutions.

As documents and applications are exchanged it is necessary to keep track of each version number and the person who made the last changes. This is also important from a legal point of view. Contracts, for example, could be created interactively through an advanced online forum, enabling both parties to revise the proposal and add comments from their legal departments.

Currently, people are used to talking to partners over the phone, via email, or face-to-face. You may find, especially among older employees, a resistance to the use of these new forms of communication. In some cases the employees prefer to send voice mail instead of email, making it harder for the recipient to grasp the content. While communication costs are important for end customers, some employees are less willing to save money by using advanced technical communication methods. The training of your employees will replace their fears with knowledge, providing a more productive environment for everyone.

9.2   Moderating Online Meetings

The Internet and its technologies offer a great set of solutions for creating effective meetings. Solutions on the Internet include newsgroups where people can take part in a meeting on a certain topic in an asynchronous way. Instead of responding immediately to a question or request, the other members of the meeting are able to respond whenever they have time. The same paradigm is used for mailing lists, which have the same functionality but are based on the push methodology, while newsgroups use pull mechanisms. *Push* means that the content is brought to the computer of the participant actively, while *pull* requires the participant to look up the newsgroup to see if new information is available.

While both technologies have proved to be very effective on the Internet, they do not truly represent an actual meeting, where decisions have to be made within a certain period of time. Online chats are getting closer to a virtual meeting, where all participants meet in a chat room to discuss a certain topic in real time. The advantage over a real meeting is the fact that everything that is said is captured digitally, making it easy to follow up on or create a summary of the meeting. But online chats do not replicate the complexity of a real meeting. There is no whiteboard to write down certain points or to create drawings on the fly.

These missing features are included in newer versions of online chatting software. They allow participants to draw pictures online during the meeting, distribute documents during the conference, and guide the other participants through a set of Web pages, similar to a slide show.

These products are good enough for day-to-day meetings where the participants know each other very well and do not require nonverbal expressions to understand the others. In business meetings with partners or customers who do not know each other, it makes meaningful communication easier when people can hear the voice or see the picture of the other participants. For example, "I'm not sure" can be interpreted in different ways. It could be "maybe," or "no," or actually "I'm not sure," depending on the individual's culture and the nonverbal expression accompanying the words.

Voice-over-IP and video-over-IP have become more common over the last few years and and are gaining acceptance as a replacement for the business conference, where you speak for 30 minutes to someone on a certain topic. Using webcams, online voice, textual chats, and Web sites has made it possible to reduce costly and time-consuming travel to a minimum.

9.2.1 Problems with Real-Time Applications

As connection speed increases, more and more people are able to redirect phone calls to the Internet. The obvious reason for Internet telephony is to significantly reduce the cost of long distance voice communication. In addition, Internet telephony introduces entirely new and enhanced ways of communicating. Video conferencing, application sharing, and whiteboarding are just a few of the applications that are already accompanying real-time voice communication over the Internet. More advanced systems hook up the telephone with the computer, which in turn is connected to the Internet. More simple solutions require some speakers and a microphone for the communication.

The Internet was not designed with real-time capabilities in mind. Its basic idea was to maintain service, even when some of the servers dropped out; therefore, stability was more important. In order to make phone calls over the Internet successful, a certain bandwidth needs to be guaranteed; otherwise, the call will be interrupted. Email does not require a guaranteed bandwidth; the connection can even break down. The email server will just send out the email whenever the connection is back up again. The same is true for Web pages. If connections slow down, it will take longer for the Web page to be loaded—but if you are in the middle of a conversation, this is not desirable.

The Internet is a packet-switched network, which has been used for applications where a variable QoS is tolerable, such as for email and file transfers. It does not matter if a file is a bit slower or if the transport of an email takes five seconds longer. During the transmission, it is possible to do something else. A phone call, for example, requires a dedicated line (or path). Packet-switched networks do not dedicate a path between sender and receiver and therefore cannot guarantee QoS. Unlike telephone networks, the Internet allows many people to share a single line. In order to serve all people at the same time, the transmitted information is divided into packets, which contain a sequence number and a destination address. On the Internet there is no way to prioritize users or applications, as all packets are treated exactly the same way, no matter what they contain.

It is also not important in which sequence the packets arrive at the destination; since they are labeled, the destination host is able to recompose the packets into the file or email that it was sent to. You will get notified once the whole message has been transmitted. But a telephone call is more like a stream with constant transmission. It is easy to imagine it would be difficult to understand if the words in a sentence arrive in the wrong order.

QoS becomes more important with real-time applications. Text-based chats work quite well on the Internet, as they require only very limited bandwidth. QoS products guarantee bandwidth over a network, enabling real-time applications.

The telephone network, on the other hand, is a circuit-switched network, which means that QoS is guaranteed. When a number is dialed, a connection is built that is exclusively used for the two participants connected. No matter how much traffic (in this case, speech) is going over the line, a dedicated circuit is ready to transport all voice data that is spoken during the telephone conversation. The same applies to television and radio transmission, where one channel is dedicated to one transmission. On the Internet many people share one circuit, which reduces the speed for every single person, though it is impossible to predict how fast a connection will be at any given time.

IP-based networks need additional hardware and software that is able to communicate the bandwidth with other network devices. ATM networks offer QoS abilities in the protocol, making it easy to define minimum bandwidth requirements, but ATM networks are not 100 percent compatible with IP networks.

So far very little software is able to talk to network devices and request a minimum bandwidth. Most applications just hope that there is enough bandwidth available to accommodate all transmissions.

9.2.2   Internet Telephony

The most popular application on the Internet that requires QoS is Internet telephony. Although the quality is not as perfect as normal phone services, it is good enough for many to use. The human brain is able to overcome transmission problems and the resulting reduced voice quality. Often, it is even tolerable if single words are omitted, as the listener is able to get the word from the context. These are drawbacks of the current packet-switched Internet, which are more than compensated for in exchange for the possibility of making long-distance calls for the price of a local call.

The quality of Internet telephony depends on two characteristics. The first is the quality of the connection. Typical Internet connections have some communication failures, which require the application to resend certain packets until all arrive at the destination. This does not work with real-time applications. The packets need to arrive in the right order. Every packet that is delayed or lost will mean a decrease in quality, as the system will interpolate the missing packet. Interpolating means that the software makes a guess at what the missing packet may have contained by analyzing the packets next to the missing one. The more packets that are missing, the more distortion will be audible and the fewer words understood.

The Resource Reservation Protocol (RSVP) seems to be the most prominent signaling protocol on the Internet. It reserves resources on the communication path as determined by the corresponding routing protocols. Since IP is a connectionless protocol, different routes are possible, of course.

RSVP is not involved in data transfer, as it currently operates over UDP and IP. It operates on *flows*, which define connections for IP diagrams. It is the flow label that provides association of IP diagrams to RSVP reservations. The very important aspect is that RSVP supports multicast; that is, it allows receivers out of a multicast group to issue their service requirements. It is based on a receiver-oriented approach, where the receiving node indicates to the network and the transmitting node the nature of the traffic flow that the node is willing and able to receive.

This enables support of heterogeneous QoS within a multicast group. The big advantage can be seen in the RSVP flexibility on the type of resource reservation that is signaled. There are two principal disadvantages—RSVP cannot provide hard service guarantees (because of the possibility of dynamic route changes during an established RSVP flow) and the flow state information that needs to be held inside the routers leads to a rather complex router design and implementation.

Table 9.1. The Resource Reservation Protocol

The other characteristic on the Internet that will determine the quality of the voice transmission is the connection speed of the parties involved in the conversation and the connection speed on the network segments in between. Depending on the speed, a latency may occur. This latency can sometimes also be noticed when calling over a satellite, where the arrival of information has a slight delay. The slower the connection speed is, the more delay there will be. Although latency can be annoying, it will only slow down the conversation. It won't break it up in most cases.

Depending on how much each of these characteristics influence the conversation, it is possible to have good quality conversations that are very similar to telephone chats or to have very bad connections that more resemble alien transmissions from outer space. In order to keep the latency factor low and the quality of the connection high, use Internet telephony when you know that less people are on the Internet, like at night. And for intercontinental calls, look for times where either your continent or the other one is at sleep. As a rule of thumb, the overall connection speed on the Internet is best when corporate America is asleep.

With the introduction of IPv6 (see Chapter 3) and other schemes like the Resource Reservation Protocol (RSVP, see Table 9.1), you are allowed to reserve certain amounts of bandwidth for Internet applications requiring real-time communication. Also, available bandwidth is increasing all the time, making the need for QoS less urgent.

One Internet telephony application is Netscape Conference, which is built into the Netscape Communicator Suite. If you have Netscape 4 or higher installed and a sound card, speakers, and a microphone, you can start using this application immediately.

By entering the IP address of the other people taking part in the conference, a connection is set up and the people can speak. The disadvantage with the IP address is that many people who dialup a provider get assigned a dynamic IP address that changes with every dialup. Finding out the IP address is not easy for a nontechnical person, so before the Internet phone call starts, this issue needs to be resolved. Most software products propose a solution whereby the customer connects to a central repository and sends the current IP address to it. People who know that particular person will get to know that she or he is online and what the correct IP address is.

Unlike traditional voice conferences, Netscape Conference offers additional features worth noting. A conference "whiteboard" offers the option of drawing and sketching, adding visual information to the voice conference. Another important feature is "collaborative browsing." This feature allows one participant to take the others through a series of Web sites while talking. The Web pages may contain additional information about the topic of the phone conference. While talking, it is possible to exchange files, and textual chat is also available in case the sound transmission is so bad that people cannot understand each other. Although this product is very basic, it offers many features that make phone conferences easier to manage. Within corporate networks, the software can also be used if employees from different locations need to get in touch with each other.

A competing product is Microsoft NetMeeting, which can be downloaded from Microsoft's home page for free. It allows Internet telephony and application sharing. Application sharing is similar to the collaborative browsing feature of Netscape, but extends the sharing feature to other applications of the Microsoft suite. It allows several Internet users to view and edit information simultaneously. This enables users to view the same Excel spreadsheet, talk about it, and modify it during the conversation. Although this feature is good on a company intranet, it also offers many ways for hackers on the Internet to steal information or interrupt the session.

Besides Internet telephony, NetMeeting also offers textual chat, file transfer, a whiteboard that can be used by all participants, and the option for transmitting video.

The VocalTec Internet Phone[3] is another application strictly focusing on Internet telephony. It is one of the oldest applications for Internet telephony on the market. Besides the usual features, such as textual chat, file transfer, whiteboard and video transmission, VocalTec offers a direct integration with telephony gateways. The reason is that many companies use the VocalTec gateway software. A list of gateways can be found on the Web site of VocalTec.[4] VocalTec has become one of the largest infrastructure providers for IP telephony.

No matter which Internet telephony software you choose, the software will most probably be able to communicate with other software that provides the same functionality. This is because of the H.323 standard, which was developed by the International Telecommunications Union (ITU).[5] The H.323 standard provides a means for transporting voice, data, and video over packet-switched networks. This standard is supported by all of the above-mentioned software packages. See Table 9.2 for more in-depth information on the H.323 standard.

Most of the products mentioned here do not require additional hardware besides a sound card, speakers, and a microphone, which are all part of any standard multimedia PC. It is even possible to enhance the experience by adding extra hardware.

One such product is the Internet PhoneJACK by Quicknet Technologies.[6] This hardware product offers a telephone socket that allows normal telephones to connect to the computer and to the Internet. Any standard phone can be used to make phone calls over the Internet, so you do not have to have a microphone and speakers. The phone call over the Internet becomes more like a real phone call. In addition, a special digital signal processor (DSP) is able to reduce echo effects and provide real-time compression facilities. Compression reduces the size of the information that needs to be transmitted over the Internet, therefore reducing the possible latency and improving the quality.

---

[3]http://www.vocaltec.com/
[4]http://www.gold.vocaltec.com/iphone5/services/itsp_list.htm
[5]http://www.itu.int/
[6]http://www.quicknet.com/

The H.323 standard provides a foundation for audio, video, and data communications across IP-based networks, including the Internet. The following list shows some of the highlights.

- **Bandwidth management**—Special network managers are able to limit the bandwidth available to H.323 applications.

- **Codec standards**—The compression and decompression of audio and video streams is highly standardized.

- **Flexibility**—Offers devices with different capabilities to take part in one conference.

- **Interoperability**—By adhering to the H.323 standard, interoperability between applications is achieved.

- **Multicast support**—Reduces bandwidth by sending out a single packet to many destinations at the same time without replication.

- **Multipoint support**—Offers high quality support for conferences with more than two people.

- **Network independence**—H.323 does not depend on a certain type of network, making it future-proof.

- **Platform and application independence**—H.323 is not bound to a certain type of hardware or operating system.

Table 9.2. The H.323 Standard

9.2.3 Internet Telephony Gateways

Through special gateways, it is possible to extend the possibilities of Internet telephony to those who do not own a computer or do not have an Internet connection. Instead of routing a phone call through traditional phone lines, a telephone company may decide to route it through the Internet. Therefore, voice needs to be moved from the circuit-switched network to the Internet. This requires a digitization of the data at one end and a digital-to-analog converter at the other end. In order to work efficiently and be cost effective, the gateways need to be installed in every town that is connected to the Internet telephony system. This allows customers to make phone calls to every location at the cost of a local phone call.

The caller connects to the Internet telephony gateway by dialing a special prefix to the actual phone number. The telephony gateway takes the incoming call, identifies the country and area code where the recipient is located, and looks for the nearest Internet telephony gateway. The second gateway makes a local connection to the recipient.

In 1995, Jeff Pulver introduced his Free World Dialup project,[7] which consisted of Internet telephony gateways to the public phone system in 42 countries around the world. The gateways were operated by almost 500 individuals that installed these gateways on their computers, allowing people to use them for noncommercial phone calls. Unfortunately, the Free World Dialup service has been abandoned, as it was not profitable and involved too much work for a single person to keep up with.

These forward-thinking individuals were the first Internet telephony service providers (ITSP). After a short test period, the traffic increased so much that an individual was not able to handle it on a free-of-charge basis. Now, ISPs have started to become ITSPs.

There are a number of commercial ITSP, such as Internet Telephony Exchange Carriers (ITXC)[8] and TransNexus,[9] that find Internet telephony gateway service providers around the world who will cooperate with one another. Another interesting example is in Germany: the Deutsche Provider Network (DPN),[10] one of the largest backbone ISPs, which has started a cooperation with Interoute Telecom, a telecom company, to install an Internet telephony gateway for end customers.

In addition to standard telephone-to-telephone conversations, it is also possible to talk from or to a computer-based user. In this case, only one gateway is required, either at the caller's or recipient's site, depending on who is using a standard phone and who is using a computer.

More organizations are starting to allow Web surfers with Internet telephony software to connect directly to agents in their call center by using an Internet telephony gateway. The Internet telephony gateway feeds calls from the Internet directly into their system. Some well-known providers of Internet telephony gateway products are VocalTec,[11] MICOM,[12] and Vienna Systems.[13]

Another interesting product is Net2Phone,[14] which is operated by the telephone company IDT.[15] It is the most popular telephony gateway, and requires a

---

[7] http://www.pulver.com/fwd/

[8] http://www.itxc.com/

[9] http://www.transnexus.com/

[10] http://www.dpn.de/

[11] http://www.vocaltec.com/

[12] http://www.micom.com/

[13] http://www.viennasystems.com/

[14] http://www.net2phone.com/

[15] http://www.idt.com/

special piece of software installed on the computer. In order to use Net2Phone, it is necessary to get an account with IDT, which is debited whenever you call someone through its software. The account needs to be prepaid before calls can be placed. Before every call, the caller is notified about the account balance and how long the maximum phone call can be, based on this account balance.

Net2Phone is very good if used for calls to or within the United States, but lacks quality when calling other countries. Everyone is able to test this piece of software for free by calling toll-free numbers in the U.S., which are free of charge. The complete list of toll-free numbers can be found on the Internet at inter800.com,[16] one of many telephone directories.

Internet telephony can be used to build up call centers very easily. Many Web sites operate under the premise of "do-it-yourself." It is not uncommon that problems or questions arise during a Web transaction and the customer needs to talk to someone directly to resolve the issues. Using Internet telephony, it is easy to incorporate a "call-me" button into the Web site that automatically sends out a request to the customer care center and initiates an Internet phone session. By pressing the button, the actual IP address together with the name of the customer is sent to the customer care center, which then is able to call the customer and go through the Web pages to answer questions.

Today, small call centers need to buy their own hardware. With the introduction of Internet telephony, it is possible to create enterprise call centers (ECC), where multiple small call centers can share a single piece of hardware. This also makes it easy to move from traditional call centers to a multimedia call center where email and faxes can be processed like any other call.

The advantage of such a solution is the tight integration and the resulting interactivity that becomes possible. Banking solutions have already integrated Web and phone into a single backend. Edify,[17] for example, offers the option of changing between phone and Web in a single session. It is, for example, possible to type in the account number on the keyboard and use the phone to enter the password. In this case, a real phone that has a gateway on the bank server is used.

9.2.4 Internet Fax Gateways

Internet fax gateways are simply a natural extension of normal fax machines. They are slowly replacing fax machines in many locations. Although the importance of the fax itself is slowly decreasing, it still has one major advantage over the Internet. Documents that are signed and transmitted over a fax are regarded as legal documents. Another important point is that a fax machine costs much less than a computer and does not require any interaction in order to see an incoming document. It is printed and visible as soon as it has arrived. Some provide an audio confirmation to announce the arrival of the fax.

---

[16]http://www.inter800.com/

[17]http://www.edify.com/

With fax gateways, it is possible to exchange documents with people who do not own a computer and useful when content is more important than clear printouts. The legal status is lost in the transition through the gateway, but the major advantage of having printouts wherever needed is still valid.

Fax gateways serve two purposes. You can send faxes to people without a fax, but with an Internet connection—and the other way round—send email to people without Internet connection. Sending email through a fax gateway if both participants have email is not good, but using two fax gateways to send faxes can reduce the cost of the transmission. Many fax gateways allow you to transmit faxes at the cost of a local phone call to any place in the world. If both parties have email, sending it through fax gateways will not provide any convenience, except for the automatic printout of the email on the fax machine. This reduces the quality of the communication and makes it harder to keep a consistent documentation.

9.2.5   Video Conferences

Video conferencing software has the same problem over the Internet as telephones: quality of service. Video transmission requires a lot more bandwidth than pure audio transmissions but is based on the same standards, making it easy to integrate Video over IP into existing networks. In order to make video conferencing possible, it is necessary to install a camera and a microphone on the desk of every participant.

Today all computers are equipped with a soundcard, making it easy to add the microphone, but the camera requires additional hardware and software. This combined with the additional cost have been show-stoppers in many cases. Although a webcam starts at about $99, many companies have not been willing to spend money on this equipment because they fear that it will congest their networks.

One of the best selling webcams is the Connectix QuickCam,[18] which is designed for video conferencing over the Internet and can capture 24-bit still images at up to 640 × 480 resolution.

The camera itself is a golfball-sized black sphere with a lens that can be manually focused from one inch to infinity. There is no microphone or speaker built into the camera, so the video software automatically interacts with the audio card and any microphone and computer speakers. The camera is able to automatically adjust brightness, although there is a slider on the side for setting it manually. Clicking on the appropriate icon changes from still capture to motion.

The camera produces a maximum frame rate exceeding 15 frames per second at a CIF (Common Interchange Format) resolution of 352 × 288 pixels. This frame rate is just fast enough to avoid obvious jittery, jerky, and flickering animation. Videos are saved as AVI files, while still images can be saved

---

[18]http://www.connectix.com/

in BMP, JPEG, or TIFF formats. The camera is bundled with Videophone 3.0, Netmeeting 2.0, and VIVO Active Video Now, making it easy to do the first steps in video conferencing.

The most commonly used software for video conferencing is CU-SeeMe. It is a freeware product available for all major platforms, making it the current standard for video conferencing. White Pine,[19] the developer of the software, has recently released an enhanced version of CU-SeeMe.

Enhanced CU-SeeMe supports video connections of 28.8 Kbps or faster and offers color video, a phone book, and a whiteboard. The software is easy to use. You simply log on to the Internet, call up Enhanced CU-SeeMe, and enter the IP address for the person or server you want to reach. The software supports three kinds of conferencing: point-to-point, in which you communicate with one other person via the Internet or a private network; group, in which you join an existing conference by connecting to that group's server; and one-way, in which you receive broadcast data from a server (similar to a TV or radio program). You can open up to eight video windows at once, access numerous public CU-SeeMe videoconferences, and store your favorite IP addresses in the phone book.

The whiteboard module enables users to type and insert colored lines into an online conference without a hitch. While the module supports many common graphics formats, you have to export your word processor and spreadsheet documents as plain ASCII before they can be imported into the whiteboard.

Besides White Pine, other companies have started to use CU-SeeMe as the basis for their products. One of these products is called CU-SeeMe Pro, which has powerful applications such as collaboration on virtually any Windows-based application, full-color video and audio support, exchange information on an electronic whiteboard, files transfer, and much more.

The software is able to tap into the NetMeeting directory to find people and allows connections to people with NetMeeting, ProShare, or other clients that adhere to the H.323 standard.

9.3   Internet Chat Solutions

9.3.1   Internet Relay Chat

The most popular open standard for real-time chats on the Internet is the Internet Relay Chat (IRC).[20] AOL Instant Messenger[21] and ICQ[22] may be more popular with Internet newcomers, but these applications are based on proprietary standards and the protocols used are not supported by other companies or applications.

---

[19]http://www.whitepine.com/

[20]http://www.irc.org/

[21]http://www.aol.com/

[22]http://www.icq.com/

IRC has been available for many years and was intended to be a replacement for the program "talk," which allowed two people to type in real time to each other. IRC is a multiuser, multichannel chat network that allows people to "talk" to each other in real time, no matter where they are located.

In order to go onto the IRC network, you need to install an IRC client, such as ircII,[23] ircle,[24] or mIRC,[25] or connect to one of the dozens of Web sites that allow access to the IRC network. IRC is based on the client-server model. Clients connect to a particular server and the server distributes the message sent in by a client back to all recipients that are on a particular channel. Most IRC networks consist of more than one server, so there is also a lot of server-to-server communication involved.

To get online, you need to choose an IRC server, a nickname, and a channel where you want to meet other people. Everyone on the IRC network is able to open up a new channel just by entering a name. If the channel name exists, the user will enter the channel and meet the other people there; otherwise, a new channel will be created. Some channels are focused on one topic, other channels offer a more generic platform for people with the same interests.

Channels with names like #Germany or #Italia have been designed for Germans and Italians or people who want to visit these countries. As the topic is too general, these channels are crowded; often more than 300 people are on the channel and communication is almost impossible (see also Figure 9.1). Most successful channels range from 2 to 30 people, which makes it possible to participate in an ongoing discussion.

Topics may vary from time to time and are influenced mainly by technical and political news. It often happens that technically focused groups start to discuss politics in the event of a crisis. IRC was very crowded during the Persian Gulf War and during the war in Kosovo. Since the IRC enables anyone who has an Internet connection to participate, it was possible to get firsthand reports from people living in those areas.

On other occasions, such as during large trade shows—Comdex[26] and Ce-Bit[27]—information is distributed rapidly throughout a community. People at the trade show are able to diffuse technological news to many people in one shot by being present at the show and on the IRC network. Over the years, computer companies have held press conferences on IRC, where end customers could ask questions directly.

Unlike the Web, where most people are forced to understand English, the IRC offers enough space for people who do not speak English. There are discussion groups for every language, country and culture, and if one is missing, it is easy to open up a new discussion channel where that language and opinion are

---

[23] http://www.irchelp.org/
[24] http://www.ircle.com/
[25] http://www.mirc.co.uk/
[26] http://www.comdex.com/
[27] http://www.cebit.de/

Figure 9.1. A day in IRC.

expressed freely. This is, in fact, much easier than developing a new Web site. A simple command is needed to set up the channel and inviting people to this channel can be done via e-mail, fax, telephone a web site or any other means.

The person who opens up a new channel has special powers, which allow her or him to throw out other people or ban them completely from that particular channel. These powers should be used to organize communication in the channel. If someone starts to insult other people without reason on the channel, the *operator* is able to throw the person out, and if the person returns to the channel to continue insulting people, then it is possible to completely disallow access to that particular channel. These powers can be passed on to anyone else on the channel, in case the initiator is not available.

The operators set the standards on the channel. The way people should behave can be enforced by them, and in many cases there are Web documents explaining how to behave properly on a certain channel. One such example is my home channel #amigager. It was originally the home of Amiga[28] fans in Germany, but now has evolved into a group of Internet experts who are either working for large companies—such as Hewlett-Packard, IBM, Peacock, or the Deutsche Provider Network—or are studying or teaching at a university. They use the forum on a daily basis for the exchange of information, opinions, and programming tips.

---

[28]http://www.amiga.de/

The netiquette for the channel is available online,[29] of course, and if people do not behave accordingly, they are warned once and asked to read the channel FAQ. Although the channel itself is fun and everybody would survive the death of the channel, it does simplify work. Instead of looking up some programming constructs in a book or searching for information on a new standard on the Web, the question is thrown into the channel and a highly qualified answer can be expected within a few seconds, thus reducing the time spent programming and writing documentation. Just one warning: The channel has a reputation for ignoring beginner (or so-called *newbie*) requests. The channel lives off the exchange of information, and it is highly unlikely that you can ask one thousand questions and get a response to every single question. In order to receive information, you need to show competence in some area and a desire to contribute in the future.

Many channels are up and running 24 hours a day. Virtual communities have been created, where people not only meet every so often on the same channel, but also start to see each other in real life.

Although IRC has been around for a very long time, very few companies have used it professionally and no company is using it as part of its customer care center. But there is a huge potential in IRC, as customers want a fast response, just as fast as when calling in or sending an e-mail. Another great feature is the transcript of the channel can always be used to update an existing FAQ.

Communication over standard IRC servers is not secure. The text you transmit to the IRC network is communicated in clear text to the server, which may pass it on to another server and then to the clients. It is very easy to eavesdrop on the IRC network, but this should not worry you. If you do not have anything to hide, then nobody will get to you.

Criminals, for example, have used IRC in the past for trading pornographic images of children, which is forbidden in most countries. Identifying these people over the IRC network is very easy and gets them arrested within a very short time. Although some people you encounter on these servers may be rude, the IRC is a good place for communication.

9.3.2 Java Chat Rooms

As IRC requires the downloading of a special piece of software that needs to be installed and configured, it is not accessible to everyone, especially if the software is not available in your mother tongue. Luckily, a new chat software has been developed that is accessible to anyone who is able to use a Web browser. Although there are some HTML-based chat rooms available, the large majority of chat systems on the Internet are Java-based.

Java applets are downloaded at the same time as the HTML page. This may contain advertising or instructions on how to use the applet. Once it has

---

[29]http://faq.amigager.de/

been started, it connects back to the server, which then passes the text input from the user to other users who are also connected to the same server and have chosen to chat within a certain channel.

Gallery-Net,[30] for example, is using a Java chat applet to allow its users to chat away while they are visiting the Web site. This allows them to exchange ideas, email addresses, and news about art or anything they wish to talk about. The Java chat in this case is not moderated.

Another company that uses Java chats is Audible.com,[31] which uses the online chat for customer support. Customers cannot talk to each other in this chat, but can ask the help desk of the company, if they have a problem, for example, with the Web site. In Figure 9.2 you can see the chat solution run in a separate window.

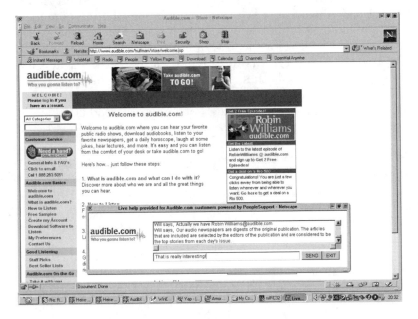

Figure 9.2. Java chat on Audible.com.

Two types of channels are used: moderated and nonmoderated. In moderated channels the participants cannot talk freely, but need to get permission from an operator to talk. In nonmoderated channels people are able to express themselves freely without restrictions. Nonmoderated channels are much more common and more accepted by users. Moderated channels are normally used for interviews or press conferences, where you do not want everybody to chat at the same time. These two types are not exclusive to Java chats, but are a general feature for most chat technologies.

---

[30]http://www.gallery-net.com/
[31]http://www.audible.com/

9.3.3 Virtual Worlds

As computers get faster it has become easier to create virtual worlds on the Internet where a three-dimensional person represents "yourself" while chatting, looking at images, or buying goods on the Internet. Virtual worlds make the experience more personal on the Web. Instead of being only an IP address connected to a server, you are able to style yourself and appear onscreen as a human being (or as an alien, if you prefer).

These virtual representations also make things easier for people who are not as knowledgeable about the Internet and its technologies. They can use the same paradigms they are applying to the real world in a one-to-one manner on the Internet. A chat room suddenly becomes a living room where cakes and coffee are served, while an online shop has a real shop assistant that is able to answer questions, if necessary. While most shopping sites offer email addresses and FAQs to resolve most questions, this does not reflect the real world. Would you go into a shop and look for the FAQ or email address to send off a question?

One of the simpler programs for virtual worlds is Microsoft Chat, which allows people to select a body that everybody sees while they are chatting. The chat software uses the IRC protocol to connect to standard servers, but it adds a graphical interface on top of the text-based chat. Instead of seeing pure text, you have comic figures that can walk around in a chat room and exchange their opinions.

Besides this rather simple chat solution, there are more sophisticated online shopping solutions that are implemented in a virtual world in order to make the shopping experience as comfortable as possible. We will discuss them in further detail Chapter 13. One of them is Virtual Reality Online Shopping,[32] which creates an integrated environment for e-commerce using virtual reality and virtual communities.

Their virtual reality consists of several virtual-reality shops into which you can go and choose from a wide range of products. The mall consists not only of the shops, but also of a whole environment around the shopping mall, where you can engage in chats and watch artists. The project tries to emulate a real shopping experience, and it is quite intriguing to enter this virtual world.

Instead of getting the users to find certain goods immediately, they are left to wander around, just as in a real shopping mall, where the experience is more important than the shopping. Still, customers are able to use short cuts through a search engine.

Another very interesting online shopping experience is Activeworlds.com,[33] which is a virtual world featuring an online shopping mall called @Mart. More than 100 online businesses like Amazon.com and Beyond.com[34] have already opened shops in @Mart.

---

[32]http://www.vr-shop.iao.fhg.de/
[33]http://www.activeworlds.com/
[34]http://www.beyond.com/

Shoppers walk around the @Mart virtual mall by pointing their mouse or using the arrow keys on their keyboard to proceed. Although the environment is 3D, the merchandise is displayed in 2D. A detailed description of the products is displayed when clicking on one of the graphics. The actual purchase and payment process is then done on the merchant's Web site and not in the cybermall, so that companies can add a fancy virtual shop, but do not need to replicate their existing infrastructure.

Both shopping solutions allow customers to meet other customers in the shops and exchange opinions on the quality of the merchandise. Shop owners are also able to interact with customers and answer questions or discuss the price of the goods.

When the technologies get even better, so that it is possible to recreate the real look of people in a three-dimensional world, it can be envisioned that business meetings can take place on the Internet. It will also become possible to conduct events such as presentations directly on the Internet, without anyone having to travel around the globe to attend. In many cases it is not necessary to physically be at a certain location in the business world, but participation is still desired. Through advanced Internet technologies, this will become reality.

9.3.4   Internet Newsgroups

Internet newsgroups support the efforts of virtual organizations or teams that must work together even though they may not actually be together in either time or space. Newsgroups are a very old and proven technology and maximizes human interaction while minimizing the interference of the technology.

Newsgroups allow asynchronous meetings and discussions on the Internet, unlike the real world where meetings and discussions are mostly synchronous (see also Figure 9.3). The advantage of newsgroups is that it is possible to answer questions whenever someone has time to do so, no matter where the person is located. This works only if the answer to the question does not inhibit your continuing with your work. It means that work in the New Economy is far more diversified and a single person is handling more than one task at a time. While computers in the early years were able to execute only one task at a time, they are now able to handle several tasks at the same time. This paradigm is taking over the working world as well.

Factory workers that execute a single task all day long are becoming slowly but surely the exception. The workforce is moving to a more diversified workplace, meaning that several tasks are executed at the same time, even if this requires a change in the mindset of many companies. Jobs can be executed much faster this way. If an employee has only one job to do, he or she will stop when there is a problem and the answer to a question is needed before work can continue. If the employee is working on several tasks, she or he can put the task on hold and continue with others, resulting in much less wasted productivity time.

This also requires that employees be more knowledgeable, able to execute more than one task at a given time. Lifelong learning is the only way to compensate for the changes in technology and business processes. Internet newsgroups are a good way to support the paradigms of the New Economy.

The virtualization of supply chains and teams makes the development and execution of processes more efficient, but cannot be managed without the use of new technologies, such as Internet newsgroups. Virtualization means that a supply chain or team can be put together on a case-by-case decision instead of having to be put together for all cases.

Figure 9.3. A response to a newsgroup posting.

The traditional newsgroups were not part of the Web, but more and more companies are bringing traditional newsgroups to the Web. Deja[35] and Supernews[36] are the most prominent examples of this trend. This makes it easier for people to access and use them. Although the technology is very basic, newsgroups are second only to email in importance.

9.3.5   Digital Communities

Companies that provide a completely new service on the Web are really quite intriguing. One of these companies is eCircle,[37] which enables members to create so-called *eCircles* on the Web. eCircles are mailing lists or newsletters that

---

[35] http://www.deja.com/

[36] http://www.supernews.com/

[37] http://www.ecircle.de/

allow anyone on the Web to become an editor of an online magazine. eCircle publishes and circulates the online magazine, so the editor needs no special technical skills beyond his or her own area of expertise.

Every member in an eCircle automatically receives all messages sent to the mailing list via email or can read the postings on the Web, whichever a member prefers. Messages can be either forwarded automatically or approved first by the eCircle manager.

The creation and maintenance of an eCircle is free of charge, enabling any type of business or group of people to add value to their Web sites. This concept allows any type of group to stay in contact with subscribers and issue a newsletter on a regular basis via email. Through the Web interface, members are also able to look through an archive of previously posted newsletters and postings. The eCircle concept brings together the idea of mailing lists, newsgroups, and newsletters to form a powerful platform for online chatting.

9.4 Peer-to-Peer Technologies

9.4.1 Introduction

Napster[38] has epitomized the use of peer-to-peer (P2P) networking in ways no other implementation can begin to match. P2P technology is the term used to describe a gamut of services that once more promise to revolutionize how we live and do business. In this case Shawn Fanning, the founder of Napster, harnessed the distributed power of the Internet very effectively. While most companies and users have been moving from fat-client to thin-client, Napster has shown to the world that both can peacefully coexist to take full advantage of all the computing resources available (see also Table 9.3).

P2P computing allows users to swap information between computers without reliance on a central server to facilitate the transfer. P2P is a term used to describe any software that makes direct communication between a group of computers over the Internet possible. It fundamentally differs from the Web in that no single computer, technically speaking, is more important than another. P2P networks are perhaps the most "democratic" of all the architectures. With no central server, everyone on the network becomes both a content supplier and a content consumer.

As Clay Shirky, an independent e-business consultant and author, put it: "P2P is a class of applications that takes advantage of resources, storage, cycles, content, human presence, which are available at the edges of the Internet."

This is obviously different from the Web model in which many people have become content suppliers. P2P networking offers the network architecture to exploit this mostly untapped resource. A P2P architecture is also inherently more robust, since there is no central point of slowdown or failure.

---

[38]http://www.napster.com/

Using the Napster model, users searching for a particular MP3 file log on to the Napster server, using the Internet to conduct a search. Napster then searches for the files through the PCs of the other users connected to Napster at that time. When it locates the file, Napster redirects the requesting computer, to the responding computer and the transfer is performed between the peers. Napster maintains the databases that help it determine where the file may be located and to complete the connection between users—while getting out of the middle of it. User PCs download software from the Napster site to help connect to the service and to manage the requests for downloads and outgoing connections.

Napster has solved a seemingly complex problem with both elegance and style. The Napster software and the Napster site are easy to use, friendly, but most important, effective, even as the public debate on shutting down the service continues.

There are some inherent advantages of P2P technologies that are the reason for the current hype.

- **Cost savings**—Content distributors can save a lot of costs.

- **Swarm distribution**—Aggregate low-bandwidth peers by breaking the task of delivering content into lots of smaller data delivery tasks.

- **Distributed load-balancing**—Resolves issues around bottlenecks and temporary shortages of bandwidth or storage space.

Table 9.3. Advantages of P2P

In some P2P networks, such as Napster, information on the location of files is stored in a central directory, but the files themselves remain on users' hard drives. In others, like Gnutella's, there is no center at all. Even the directory is disbursed among the users. In techie terms, the distinction between "client" and "server" evaporates; each computer on the network plays both roles simultaneously. This commanded the attention of several bright individuals and a range of companies who hope to bring some of the advantages of this architecture to new markets, especially to business users.

In the future, P2P business is going to move away from sharing files on a broad public scale to sharing personal information in small groups online.

People will use P2P networks to share their family photo albums, chat and work together, or come together to interact online in other multimedia-rich ways.

Once consumers create more of their own content, there will be a market for P2P software that allows them to manipulate and exchange it online. Businesses that provide useful services to online communities will also find a niche, especially those that can be used as a branding opportunity for real-world products like clothes and other goods.

Hotline,[39] a system developed by Hotline Communications in Toronto, Canada, is widely regarded as the first popular P2P network. Hotline was renowned for being an Aladdin's cave for pirated software, and for most of its early years was dominated by hardcore Internet users and computer geeks.

In Hotline's network, people and businesses meet as equals with the intention to interact and share information rather than passively consume it—as they do on a Web site. That means sharing anything from pictures and music to other software programs and video clips. The key in these virtual communities is that they can collaborate and communicate with each other in real time without having to rely on a central server.

The effect is similar to having an open-ended conference call on your telephone, with the added bonus of being able to share and jointly manipulate any information that can be communicated in digital form. P2P networks like Hotline will provide opportunities to have deeper relationships with the user.

Many companies now have jumped on the marketing bandwagon and promise products in the near future to support the new paradigm of P2P computing. Intel,[40] for example, is convinced that P2P computing will be central to the future of the computing industry and is thus determined to provide products for this market, including P2P applications. Intel is looking into setting up an industry-wide forum to ensure that a communication foundation for P2P exists which is secure, open, and adaptable.

Sun Microsystem[41] is trying to promote the Jxta programming language it wants to develop with partners. Sun will release Jxta under the Apache license, making it open to others for modification on an open-source model of development. Many other companies have come up with similar products and services to support the needs of the people better in the future.

Dial-up and other low-bandwidth users still make up 80 percent of the systems connected to the Internet. Simple file-sharing architectures move complete files, each transfer involves the exchange of an entire image, mp3, or video file. While this works reasonably well for sharing small files among broadband users, the delay of trying to push a large file down a narrow dial-up connection is too big for most users to tolerate. This means that most P2P solutions ac-

---

[39]http://www.bigredh.com/
[40]http://www.intel.com/
[41]http://www.sun.com/

tively discourage dial-up users from providing resources. Mojo Nation[42] uses a system called swarm distribution to resolve this issue. The Mojo Nation architecture takes each piece of content published, breaks it up into hundreds or thousands of small fragments, and then scatters these fragments among the peers. This data is retrieved by downloading the fragments in parallel and finding a replica of the original fragment if a peer is overloaded or disconnects.

While no one wants to wait around for a user connected to the Internet via a 56 Kbps dial-up line to deliver a 15-minute video clip, it is trivial for that user to provide a 64KB fragment of the original file within a reasonable amount of time. The bottleneck moves from the upload speed of the slowest member of the network to being the download speed of the user requesting the content. This allows the Mojo Nation architecture to take advantage of the asymmetric nature of most user connections to the Internet. Instead of trying to force the entire file down a small pipe, Mojo Nation uses a swarm of agents, running in parallel, to deliver fragments of the original file, which are then reconstructed locally for delivery. This approach increases the speed of the single download and reduces the load on the network.

9.4.2 Consumer-to-Consumer

Napster was designed to combine swapping MP3 music files with an online chat system. It was launched in January 1999 and word-of-mouth among American university students spread like wildfire. Enthusiasts worldwide soon knew about Napster and were swapping recordings from musicians, from Abba to the Spice Girls to ZZ Top, without paying a penny.

By late 1999, record labels got wind of the revenue they were losing and filed for an injunction to close Napster. The legal wranglings have continued, but in November 2000 a landmark event took place. German media group Bertelsmann,[43] the owner of BMG,[44] one of the record labels suing Napster, announced it was going to break from the pack; it signed a deal with the renegade company to use Napster technology to its advantage.

Bertelsmann has injected $50 million into Napster to develop technology that will let the company charge a subscription fee for the service and keep track of what files are being traded and by whom. The company is trying to persuade the other major labels to follow suit.

The problem for copyright holders is that in pure P2P networks, no one controls the content transmitted across the network and there's nothing anyone can do to stop it. It's like blaming car manufacturers for bank robbery because cars are used for getaways or suing the telephone companies for enabling industry espionage. On P2P networks there is no single person responsible for all content or services.

---

[42]http://www.mojonation.net/

[43]http://www.bertelsmann.com/

[44]http://www.bmg.com/

Although Napster is the most famous P2P solution on the Internet, there are many other P2P service providers. The following list is just a short excerpt from the ever growing list.

- **Aimster**—http://www.aimster.com/, AOL's version of Napster that incorporates Instant Messaging and closed-group file sharing.

- **Freenet**—http://freenet.sourceforge.net/, an anonymous, decentralized file-sharing network.

- **Gnutella**—http://www.gnutella.com/, the most widely used decentralized, file-sharing network.

- **Swapoo**—http://www.swapoo.com/, the Napster equivalent for video games fans.

- **MojoNation**—http://www.mojonation.net/, trades files in exchange for "Mojo", the currency gained from donating computer resources like hard disk space and processor time.

Table 9.4. Free P2P Services

9.4.3 Business-to-Consumer

One of the most prominent problems on the Internet is the lack of reliable download servers. Through P2P technologies, companies can provide high-availability download services. A P2P model can help to solve the problem of distributing patches, upgrades, and even new copies of software via networked computer. This approach to distribution would require only a fraction of the time it takes to otherwise distribute the software or software patches, as every copy multiplies the parallel download capabilities of the network. While security around this process is a concern, as it could be misused to distribute viruses, the problems are surmountable.

Online auctions is also an area of great expansion through P2P technologies. Rather than maintaining specific auction-item details by updating the eBay[45] or Amazon[46] auctions databases, why not use those services only for the metadata on the items, but keep item details locally and under user control.

---

[45] http://www.ebay.com/
[46] http://auctions.amazon.com/

The auction site could then concentrate on running the auctions and keeping the user feedback areas up-to-date without dealing with huge amounts of auction item details and graphics. Under this approach, updates on items offered for sale would be instantaneous, data integrity would improve, and the overall auction shopping and buying experiences would be vastly improved. It would be much easier for end users to sell goods through various auctions through a single interface. A local program could be used to store information about the items, and the user could decide which auction Web site would suit its needs best. Bidders could have an easier time browsing through all auction service providers if the interface were the same for all of them.

Manufacturers can also profit from P2P networks by using locally stored copies of catalog information that would serve as a single source or single point of information. This would greatly improve information flows throughout the supply chain. Again, data integrity would be improved, and inventory records might actually begin to reflect reality, instead of what happened yesterday. Through the P2P network, an update of the catalog would replicate quickly and easily so that all online vendors of a certain product would receive their copy of the catalog without the manufacturer having to redistribute it to all resellers individually. Further, new online shops would be able to sell a product instantly if the catalog were available in a commonly used XML format.

9.4.4 Business-to-Business

In the prevailing model of B2B commerce on the Internet transactions flow through large, centralized exchanges. These exchanges play two valuable roles: aggregation and facilitation.

As aggregators, they bring a group of dispersed trading partners together into a virtual marketplace. As facilitators, they provide software tools and protocols that enable the traders to do business electronically, exchanging information, processing offers and bids, coming to terms on deals, and following through on them.

The exchange-based B2B model has been a compelling one. It has attracted vast investment, intense corporate interest, and reams of press coverage. But, unfortunately for the exchanges and fortunately for pretty much everyone else, its days may be numbered. A new and better B2B model—P2P networking—is emerging. It will enable all companies everywhere to locate trading partners on the fly and complete transactions swiftly, securely, and efficiently, without the need for a central aggregator or facilitator.

P2P networks offer important advantages over the exchange-based model. First, and most obviously, they allow companies to avoid the fees charged by exchanges. Second, they reduce the complexity and expense of networking. It is much easier for a company to integrate its internal information systems with a single P2P program, or "peering portal," than with a bunch of different exchanges. Finally, while membership in exchanges is limited, often determined along industry lines, P2P networks have no bounds. A company can search as widely as it wants for new partners and products or for lower prices or better terms. More of the power of the open, ubiquitous Internet is harnessed in a business-to-peer (B2P) model than in an exchange-based one.

This does not mean the end of digital intermediaries in B2B markets. Third parties will still be needed to provide services that companies do not want to do themselves or do not trust one another to do. Running an auction is a great example of a function requiring an unbiased provider. Internet auctioneers such as FreeMarkets[47] should continue to thrive in a B2P world, even as the auctions become more efficient. The auctioneer's system will tie in to the B2P networks, automatically collecting data from company peering portals and hosting auctions in which people and machines place bids.

All technical requirements to shift B2B on to P2P networks are in place or will be soon. The only real question is timing; how quickly will companies realize the advantages that unbounded direct connections hold over centrally controlled exchanges? Judging by the speed of previous Internet advances, it probably will not take long.

Some companies believe they can take advantage of this model to generate an even larger repository of knowledge within an enterprise by making certain that everything generated on every company computer is somehow accessible, according to established security policies of course.

P2P networking also encourages the idea of something called edge services. Currently, the Internet is great at hiding the location of important services. For example, your video-based news service may be "centrally" located half a continent away.

P2P offers the opportunity to replicate important information throughout the network, encouraging data to migrate to locations closer to where it is most likely to be used on *"edge"* computers.

One company already making a living on P2P technologies is Net Market Makers,[48] who act as peers to manage the activities of procurement, fulfillment, and inventory controls. The supply chain engine is the glue that ties together a private e-commerce environment for all manufacturing resources planning (MRP) data and activities.

Another tool is IMaestro,[49] which is being used to expand on the distributed auctions idea. It offers a plug-in to enable the core applications of messaging, data exchange, chat, email, building of communities, and other real-time messaging features. It also provides a framework for developers to exploit these features in their own applications for peer users of the system. IMaestro is used for auctions where auction metadata is centrally stored, and interested bidders can search for items of interest. When a search is successful, bidders are then redirected to the peer system where they can chat with the item owner,

---

[47]http://www.freemarkets.com/

[48]http://www.netmarketmakers.com/

[49]http://www.imaestro.com/

The following areas can be easily be enhanced through the use of P2P technologies. They can replace existing technologies and be added on to existing processes, solutions and technologies.

- **Supply Chain Automation**
- **Collaboration**
- **Message Exchange**
- **Knowledge Share**
- **Distributed Caching**

Table 9.5. P2P usage in the B2B Area

exchange data and images, and place their bids. Furthermore, peers can upsell other peer auctions to help move goods faster.

Collaboration can also be made more efficient through P2P technology. Consilient[50] has designed a software to eliminate the barriers to collaborative partnering by aggregating data and automating common business processes.

Two new P2P systems hope to reshape the investment management community: Liquidnet[51] and WorldStreet.[52] Liquidnet aims to build the largest liquidity pool exclusively for buy-side traders, thereby redefining buy-side trader workflow and potentially the market for block orders. WorldStreet focuses on building peer network solutions that will allow financial institutions to share information on a targeted basis. Combining a new concept called "package routing" with traditional customer relationship management (CRM) capabilities, WorldStreet intends to become the "control panel" for the buy side by enabling users to access peer network capabilities within their existing workflow applications. WorldStreet Net is planned as the platform that will be behind Wall Street's biggest deals.

Many other solutions are about to appear as P2P becomes more important throughout the world. Although many think it is just useful for copying MP3 files, it actually can be used in all sorts of businesses, as you have seen here.

---

[50] http://www.consilient.com/

[51] http://www.liquidnet.com/

[52] http://www.worldstreet.com/

9.4.5   Distributed Computing

People excited about P2P networking also often talk about a related topic known as distributed computing. The idea behind distributed computing is to take advantage not only of the underused storage capabilities of machines on the network, but also the processing power.

Since most estimates suggest that companies use as little as 25 percent of their existing computing and storage capabilities, tying these systems together in a large company can often approximate the power of a large supercomputer.

Distributed object technology fundamentally changes all this. Coupled with a powerful communications infrastructure, distributed objects divide today's still monolithic client/server applications into self-managing components, or objects, that can interoperate across disparate networks and operating systems.

The component-based, distributed-object computing model enables IT organizations to build an infrastructure that is adaptive to ongoing change and responsive to market opportunities. In the age of global competition and increasingly narrow market windows, companies that can initiate rapid change—not just respond to it—are better prepared to capitalize on opportunity and are more likely to succeed.

Distributed applications provide an opportunity to establish and maintain a competitive advantage by creating a flexible IT infrastructure. However, they also bring new requirements. To operate in today's heterogeneous computing environments, distributed business applications must work on a variety of hardware and software platforms. They must integrate old technology with new and make use of existing infrastructure. Furthermore, suitability for enterprise-class applications calls for capabilities beyond conventional Web-based computing: scalability, high availability, ease of administration, high performance, and data integrity.

In fact, research efforts such as SETI@Home[53] are already using this untapped power spread across tens of thousands of computers on the Internet to filter through signals from space in search of aliens. The potential for other efforts, both inside and outside of corporations, is mind-boggling.

To this end, two major industry groups have already formed to help foster these developments. The Peer-to-Peer Working Group, backed by Hewlett-Packard,[54] IBM,[55] and Intel,[56] is hoping to promote P2P computing for business applications.

Likewise, the New Productivity Initiative, backed by companies such as HP, Compaq, and SGI, are working to create a programming model that would make it easier for developers to create distributed applications.

---

[53]http://www.seti-inst.edu/

[54]http://www.hp.com

[55]http://www.ibm.com/

[56]http://www.intel.com/

9.5   Internet-Based Trainings

9.5.1   Reasons for Internet-Based Trainings

As lifelong learning becomes part of working life, new technologies are needed to transport the information to the interested parties. In many cases it is not possible to conduct courses, as too few trainers know about a certain topic and are restricted by their location. Internet-based training (IBT), which evolved from computer-based training (CBT), offers a way to quickly move knowledge to the people who need to know about a certain topic. It offers 24-hour availability and a strong personalization that adapts to the knowledge and the needs of every single learner.

Providing learning facilities is more than just a necessity for a company. It needs to be part of the strategy of every company, as the results of the training have direct impact on the business results of your company. In order to make training more effective, a new paradigm needs to be introduced and the training efforts need to be consolidated. It is very important for the training department to understand the company's business goals. A successful company needs to ensure that the majority of employees have knowledge of the company's overall strategy and their roles in achieving the company's goals.

A problem for many companies is that some business units are setting their own directions, creating a misalignment with company goals. By having different goals and directions coming from different levels within the company, the employees will be confused and not know what the "right" direction is. This results in a waste of training investments.

Besides the bad business performance caused by the misalignment, training efforts will be less effective. Training will be held in parallel, multiplying the costs, as every course needs to be designed individually and resources are wasted. While this is bad, it does keep the employees on track with company goals. Much worse is the business unit that creates trainings that have nothing to do with company goals and cannot be used for future projects.

In order to overcome problems with the rapidly changing business environment, new training models are required. The new paradigm needs to be based on a company-wide training department, which coordinates and develops training programs for the complete enterprise. This eliminates multiple efforts in developing training. As many companies have offices in several countries, the training needs to be adapted to the needs of the country, as not all goals of the entire corporation may be of interest for all countries; some countries may not sell a certain product or service.

It is not just the products or services a company offers that influence the training offered by the training department. Many training programs are designed around the products and services used within the company, such as software products like a word processor and a presentation designer. In order to simplify the exchange of information between departments and business units, computer software should be standardized. This also helps to reduce the amount of training required. If only one word processor is officially supported by the company, it is only necessary to offer one type of training for it. It also reduces the amount of training required, as employees are able to help each other.

Through the coordination of a centralized training department, not only can new training programs be introduced far more quickly, but also the costs for training programs can be reduced significantly. Licenses that need to bought, rented, or leased from other companies tend to get cheaper if ordered in larger volume.

In order to build up a centralized training department, it is necessary to find out why so many departments and units are developing their own training programs. There are many reasons why departments choose to design them and these reasons need to be investigated in order to create a successful corporate training department. One reason may be that the central training department is not responding to the needs of the business units. The ever-faster changing business rules need to be reflected in the training department. New methodologies need to be created that allow the training department to create new courses more quickly.

These courses need to be accessible before they are completed. If the training department finishes creating the first unit, it needs to be made available digitally so that employees can start to learn while the training department prepares the next unit.

If companies merge, an important metric is how many products from the acquired company are sold in a certain timeframe by the salesforce of the acquiring company after an e-learning project brings them up to speed on the acquired company's products. E-learning is perfectly suited for such situations because a curriculum can be distributed to each individual's desktop, and the logistics of classroom learning—accomodating multiple schedules, planning a time and place, and gathering a group—are avoided.

Another problem with many traditional learning programs is that they are measured by the wrong units. Instead of measuring the number of days of training per employee, for example, new measurement methods need to be developed that reflect how the training helped to achieve the goals of the corporation, unit, or employee.

E-learning will only grow in importance once companies view this method of training as a way to foster enterprise transformation. Transformation includes gaining new competencies and launching new products and services while evolving into an e-business.

Manufacturers need to train strategic audiences other than their own employees. Auto manufacturers could provide technical product information and updates to dealer salespeople and even mechanics. There is incredible pressure to deliver this content very succinctly because most car salespeople would rather be selling cars. So the dominant metric might be how conveniently a manufacturer can get the information to the audience. For example, is the curriculum packaged and delivered in a way that minimizes the time a salesperson must spend in accessing and utilizing the information?

9.5.2 The New Paradigm

The new training paradigm ties the training and learning activities to the goals of the company, group, and individual, and its success is measured by achieving the goals in all three cases. This also requires a change in the view of the managers. Training should not be considered as a cost that cannot be avoided. Lifelong learning of all employees needs to become part of the business plan and to be seen as a key contributor to the success of the company.

The new learning can be successful only if the business goals are clearly defined and training is an integral part of these goals. This requires new thinking by the business managers, as well as by the training organization. Instead of only supporting the goals, the training department should now help to define them. It should help to recognize the directions and communicate these goals to all employees in the company. This ensures that everyone knows about the goals and works together to achieve the company vision. Only if this can be ensured will the company be successful, as it does not waste resources and money on courses that lead in the wrong direction.

This requires not only the adjustment of business goals, but also the review of business processes and adjustment of them accordingly. Once the goals and processes have been aligned and the training department has started with the new form of training, the training department should be measured on how accurately each individual employee, team, department, and the whole company meet the expected goals. They should not be measured on the amount of training they have executed.

In industries with constant innovation, like pharmaceuticals and financial services—where new products are rolled out many times during the year—time to market with sales of new products based upon the new competencies of the salesforce becomes an important e-learning measure. The sooner employees grasp the new knowledge, the sooner the new expertise can be applied to a revenue growth strategy. This "time-to-understanding" metric is important for capturing the downtime and opportunity costs incurred during training, especially as more companies consider constant learning an integral part of an employee's job.

9.5.3 Just-Enough Training

The cost for training can be reduced by developing training courses that teach exactly what the employees need to fulfill their work. This requires companies to create more dynamic training programs, which can be adapted to the needs of the single employee. An employee that needs to know how to print over the network does not need to know how to install a printer. Training, therefore, should not consist of massive blocks of knowledge, but of small modules, which can be assembled on the fly.

When training programs are assembled this way, it is also easier to provide just-in-time (JIT) training. Whenever employees require specific training, it will be available in an instant. The employees will be able to go to the intranet training Web site and choose the appropriate modules themselves. All courses should be available online for self-learners, though it still makes sense to offer training with a live instructor.

Learning should not be dictated by the training department. In many cases employees are able to learn from each other much faster than through the training department. The training department should offer courses for informal learning so that knowledge can be passed on to employees. In smaller companies this will happen on a daily basis between employees while they talk about problems, but larger companies are too large to let everyone speak with everyone. Therefore, mailing lists, newsgroups, and chat groups can be very effective instant-learning tools.

Chat groups offer the most immediate reaction to a query. A question posed in a chat room will get you answers within minutes, or even seconds. Mailing lists are a bit slower, with response time of about one to five hours. Newsgroups are the slowest alternative (with typical response times up to 24 hours), but they have the big advantage that the question and answer are available at any time after the question has arisen. Many newsgroups also carry FAQs to reduce the load of repeated questions.

The major problem with these technologies is that the employees do not get training certificates. Do-it-yourself training also does not make visible to managers how much employees learned in the past year, yet it seems these self-paced training programs are far more effective. Perhaps someone should come up with some statistical tools that count how many questions one has posed in newsgroups and mailing lists and how many answers one has provided (being effectively a trainer for that moment). This could make the use of newsgroups and mailing lists more accepted within companies who see these technologies as just a waste of time.

Although we explored lifelong learning in a company, the same rules are valid on the Internet. The Internet could be seen as a large company with a lot of free knowledge, where no one possess the same knowledge but everyone can exchange it freely! Lifelong learning is not only a matter for business, but also for society. In order to ensure that people have access to new information technologies, they need to learn how to use them. Otherwise, society will be split into two parts: those who have the knowledge, money, and technology to further their knowledge and wealth, and those who have no access to these resources and are therefore at a disadvantage.

9.5.4   Training Management Software

To achieve the above-mentioned goals, it is necessary to have the right software in place that is able to administer the whole process of training on a company-wide or Internet-wide basis. This means that all training programs need to be developed by a single organization within a company in order to reduce duplicate training sessions that cost money to develop and maintain. Many companies employ other organizations in addition to training departments, but this leads to many overlapping training courses. Organizational managers should try to encourage the development of training courses, but only if they are coordinated together with the training department. This is sure to please everyone, as the departments can ensure high-quality content, and the training department can ensure high-quality training management.

One software solution that is designed to manage and operate the training department is the solution from Saba Software.[57] The training management software provided by Saba has been written entirely in Java, making it easy to deploy. It allows for the continuous assessment of how each learner learns best, as well as his or her competency, certification, and content needs. This feature is often used by managers to see how their employees have performed in the past and how this has changed since they last visited a training program. The software allows users to plan the best mix of online and traditional educational offerings, and online content purchase, conversion, or development based on global-demand forecasts.

Education can be delivered using personalized mixes of traditional and online offerings available in any and all content delivery tools. It tracks the learning and financial results you deliver on a global basis. Customer satisfaction, education effectiveness, profitability, return on investment, and bottom line business results can be measured and improved instantly.

Saba provides enterprise applications that help you accelerate the transition to online learning. The Saba Education Management System, for example, allows major enterprises around the world to create competency-driven, Web-enabled learning environments that deliver personalized, cost- and time-effective online learning to employees, channel partners, and customers. It provides a Web-based solution for all learning needs.

It also supports all learning technologies. Because learning is driven by content availability, Saba can integrate with all open content delivery tools, including CBT, WBT, IBT, distance learning, electronic performance support systems (EPSS),[58] multimedia, CD-ROM, and synchronous and asynchronous delivery tools. At the same time, Saba supports open industry standards such as AICC.[59]

While Saba provides the whole infrastructure to set up a complete training management solution for a large corporation, many smaller companies would

---

[57] http://www.saba.com/

[58] http://www.epss.com/

[59] http://www.aicc.org/

be happy to use existing infrastructures to save money and time for the implementation. Several companies have started to provide this infrastructure to allow small-to-medium sized companies to develop their own training programs or select from existing programs on the Internet.

One such company is Internet University,[60] which offers customizable courseware programs and a participant management platform that enables any type of organization or individual to extend its educational programs worldwide. Internet University has formed alliances with academic institutions that plan to launch or expand online distance learning programs. Clients and allies of Internet University receive a complete solution to their online distance education challenges.

The main features include a virtual campus, which features the online learning platform and a comprehensive student and online course management system. The management system enrolls students, handles secure online credit card transactions, tracks student progress, automatically grades and submits results to an online student record, and provides feedback to students and reports to faculty and administration. Internet University's administration system allows you to add and delete class sections, and edit and revise courses remotely.

The second module, the Internet University Instructor, consists of the course development tools, which can be used by faculty and instructional designers to create their own online courses. The third module, the Internet University Platform, takes care of the servers, communications lines, software, and staff to set up and maintain the Internet server system for each individual organization that wants to offer courses for its employees or for all who are interested.

This and similar offerings enable companies and individuals to start a life-long learning initiative that matches the needs of the individual while accommodating the needs of the company.

---

[60]http://www.internetuniversity.com/

Part III

Internet Technologies

Chapter 10

COMPARING WEB
TECHNOLOGIES

10.1   Finding the Right Browser

10.1.1   The Browser Market

Although I promised not to use any statistics in this book, I will borrow a series of statistics to find out which browser is the preferred tool by users on the Web. Actually, I want to show that this "knowledge" is not relevant at all.

In the German online magazine *Telepolis*,[1] Armin Medosch tried to find out which browser is the preferred browser: Netscape or Internet Explorer (IE). The background of this story was a news flash with the statement from Websidestory[2] that about two-thirds of Internet users use Internet Explorer and only about one-third use Netscape. This headline brought a reaction from many Netscape users who could not believe that so many users were using IE. Medosch found out that these figures were based on a set of customers that used a certain program called HitBox, which is available to Microsoft platforms only and requires customers to apply for it. Therefore, the data was not representative of the Internet as a whole. Table 10.1 shows some Web sites and how much share the browsers Netscape and Internet Explorer have. This data was compiled in January 1999 and should not be used for generalization.

As you can see, the results vary and depend on the Web site. You will get different results for different content on the Web. There is no way to check if the data in the table is correct, but even if we assume that it is correct, it is not really helpful. If you look, for example, at the home page of Heise and compare it to the Heise newsticker page on the same server, you already get different results. It all depends on the customers of the site. Microsoft customers will more likely use Internet Explorer while Heise customers—more likely in the UNIX market—will attract more Netscape users. This example makes it quite

---

[1]http://www.heise.de/tp/, Armin Medosch, 28 January 1999, "Zahlenspiele update: IE zieht doch nicht davon."

[2]http://www.websidestory.com/

The following shows several Web sites and the percentage of users that use Netscape (NS) or Internet Explorer (IE) to access them. The missing percentages account for users who use other browsers.

Web Site	NS	IE
http://www.heise.de/newsticker/	75%	22%
http://www.gallery-net.com/	71%	18%
http://www.nmr.de/	70%	24%
http://www.heise.de/	67%	30%
http://meta.rrzn.uni-hannover.de/	65%	33%
http://www.spiegel.de/	62%	35%
http://www.casinoplace.com/	61%	36%
http://www.rp-online.de/	57%	39%
http://www.mediatechbooks.de/	55%	20%
http://browserwatch.internet.com/	48%	38%
http://www.websidestory.com/	33%	64%
http://www.microsoft.com/	34%	62%

Table 10.1. Browser Usage

clear that the Internet is not a mass medium; it is the infrastructure for many mass markets and even more niche markets.

If you look at the statistics and count together the numbers of Netscape and Microsoft, there is on average a gap of about 10 percent on every Web site. This percentage represents other browsers on the market and this number is increasing. As a rule of thumb, no matter what business you do, do not expect users to have a certain type of browser. Textual information should be provided in such a form that it can be read by any browser. Web applications are something different. If you support the latest standards for your online banking solution, this is just fine, as this requires reprogramming for every version of the browser.

Although the statistic is from 1999 and figures have since changed, the basic proposition is still true. The world has changed dramatically; standard Web browsers are not the only application accessing web-based information. Mobile phones, PDAs, and other devices, such as televisions and refrigerators, connect to the Internet and use browsing applications that have different requirements than standard desktop computers with monitors.

10.1.2 Sticking to the Web Standards

Many Web sites do not comply to the Web standards defined by public bodies such as the W3C or the IETF. Some people try to take advantage of proprietary standards or extensions to the Web standards on their Web pages to create a special layout, content, or application. But many Web pages do not adhere to the standards simply because the programmer does not care or does not know the exact standard. With a little work, it is possible to create Web pages that conform to the Web standards.

A standard is composed of elements and structures. In many cases some elements are used in the wrong context or structures have been extended without regard to the restrictions of the particular standard. Although the source code may be very similar, it won't be understood by all applications. Depending on the application, it will either accept or ignore the extended standard—or will fail. Unlike humans, who are able to get 100 percent of the meaning with only ninety percent of the information, a computer needs 100 percent correct input to give out a fully functional output. Computers are not good at guessing what they need to know. By adhering to the standards, it is possible to maximize the accessibility to the widest range of applications.

Many people think that checking the input against a certain application verifies that the source is correct. In most cases, the input will fail in another application. A programmer should always test the source code against the standard, and not against an application that tries to adhere to the standard (and most likely will either have bugs or an incomplete implementation).

A Java programmer, for example, could develop a special Java applet for every browser. But this is not desirable, as it requires a lot of extra work for the programmer. The programmer is forced to create workarounds and wastes time maintaining several revisions of a single program version.

Web standards are designed to be both backward compatible and forward compatible at the same time. Older source code should always look good in new applications, and new source code should also look good in older applications. Using extensions that are not part of the standard will break this compatibility and the interoperability between a set of applications that use the same input (e.g., HTML files).

10.1.3 Global Browser Player

A Web browser works by using a protocol called HyperText Transport Protocol (HTTP) to request a specially encoded text document from a Web server such as Apache.[3] This text document contains special markup written in the Hyper-Text Markup Language (HTML). This markup is interpreted by the browser, which renders the document's content in an appropriate manner for the user's convenience. Until last year, this was mainly done on a desktop computer, but

---

[3]http://www.apache.org/

today browsers exist on all sorts of devices.

The HTML may include such things as references to other Web documents using hyperlinks, suggestions for text color and position, and other content such as images and audio and visual content. Web pages may employ a technique called cascading style sheets (CSS), which is becoming more widely implemented by user agent developers to make layout suggestions for various media. More details on these technologies can be found throughout this chapter.

The idea behind the Web was developed by the British researcher Tim Berners-Lee, while at CERN in Switzerland. CERN is the European Organization for Nuclear Research, the world's largest particle physics centre. Founded in 1954, the laboratory was one of Europe's first joint ventures and has become a shining example of international collaboration. From the original 12 signatories of the CERN convention, membership has grown to 20 members. The first Web browser to capture the public's imagination was Mosaic, which was written by Marc Andreesen and other undergraduate students at the National Center for Supercomputing Applications (NCSA)[4] in the United States. Most of that group went on to form the core of Netscape Communications Corporation. Since then many other browsers emerged, but most base their ideas on the Mosaic browser. Following is an overview of the most frequently used browser software solutions and their main features. The four competitors are Netscape's Communicator, Microsoft's IE, the text-based Lynx browser, and the newcomer, Opera, from Norway.

Netscape Communicator 6.2

Netscape Communicator[5] is probably the best-known browser in the world. The browser is available for many platforms, and unlike Internet Explorer, the non-Windows versions are as available as the Windows version, making Communicator the browser of choice if the user is working in a mixed operating system environment.

Based on Gecko, the open-source browser engine developed through the independent Mozilla Project,[6] Netscape 6 provides all features that are required today, but is slimmer than its Microsoft counterpart.

The first thing you notice when you start up Netscape 6 is the new, simpler, slicker look of its modern theme. Themes (or skins in Web parlance) are switched easily from the view menu, with Netscape's classic look still available. With themes, third parties can create custom looks that let a user express his or her own style in the browser, giving clubs, radio stations, sports teams, or magazines a great way to build user loyalty through branded themes available at their Web sites.

---

[4]http://www.ncsa.uiuc.edu/SDG/Software/Mosaic/NCSAMosaicHome.html

[5]http://www.netscape.com/

[6]http://www.mozilla.org/

My Sidebar, is a resizable window that displays a collection of customizable tabs and can keep you connected to what's important to you on the Web, with tabs that are great for dynamic data like news feeds and stock prices. The tabs are actually skinny Web pages that are continuously updated and can contain almost anything. My Sidebar supports the same standards as the main browser, so tabs can be mini-applications as well as just HTML pages. To add tabs, just click on the More Tabs button. If the basic list doesn't thrill you, click on the Find More Tabs button and get a page with hundreds of tabs from all over the Web. In Figure 10.1 you can see the sidebar functionality on the left.

Figure 10.1. Netscape 6.2.

Netscape Instant Messenger is now integrated through a tab on My Sidebar. The integrated messenger client provides basic messaging and text formatting from within your browser, mail, and address book. So far, it does not provide voice chat, sending images, and file transfer. It does import your buddy list from AIM and display it in the tab, and the integration with Netscape Mail and the online address book lets you store your buddy list online.

Netscape 6 now lets you do a search directly from the URL line by just entering your keywords and clicking the search button. If you have the search tab loaded on My Sidebar, it opens with your results and displays a Web page with the collected results in the main browser window. When you surf to a page, the What's Related sidebar tab shows a listing of similar sites.

Bringing desktop and Web closer together, and hoping you'll spend a little cash, Netscape 6 now puts the print page button on the tool bar. While convenient for knocking out a hard copy, it also links to the HP-sponsored Print Central on Netscape's site, where you can purchase printing supplies and services. The Calendar tab is actually a logon for Netscape.com's WebCalendar, the online calendar to keep your dates available from anywhere you need to access them.

With the enhanced Cookie Manager, users now can control who can and can't set cookies, and can read what information is being stored. Netscape lets you save passwords for sites that require login when you enter your username and password. You can also specify that you don't want to save a password for a site, and Netscape won't ask again on that site. Using the Password Manager, you can view and remove the URL and usernames you stored.

When you fill out forms on the Web, Netscape 6 can also store your information. If you go to fill out another similar form, you can recall the saved information and use it to fill in the form automatically. The Form Manager lets you control whether Netscape saves the data, as well as view, delete, and modify the data you stored.

Netscape 6 is based on open source and Web standards, and developers have a vast range of options for customizing and developing for Netscape 6. With support for themes in Netscape, developers and companies can create personalized or branded looks with the Theme Builder, a free downloadable utility. Developers who want to dig in deeper can program their own themes and interfaces from scratch using XUL (pronounced Zool), an XML-based user interface language. XUL was developed by Netscape to allow user interfaces to be created that work across all supported platforms. For developers, this means they can create application UIs that run on multiple platforms or devices without writing specific code on each.

ISPs and consultants can create their own branded versions of the Netscape 6 browser using the Netscape Client Customization Kit, or CCK.[7] The CCK lets the developer customize logos, colors, and splash screens, as well as create the installation files through a series of wizard screens. Vendors can also get a free license from Netscape to distribute their custom browsers.

With close support of industry Web standards, Netscape 6 allows corporate developers to create powerful Web applications rivaling standalone programs. Companies can deploy an application across multiple platforms without having to write special versions for each OS. Updates need only be done once and loaded on the company intranet, cutting cross-platform support headaches without compromising functionality.

Because Netscape 6 is built on the Mozilla project's Gecko engine, developers can leverage the community that supports it. Hundreds of developers have contributed to the project, creating a wide range of sites and resources for information and support.

With its full Web-standards support, open-source development platform,

---

[7]http://home.netscape.com/download/cck.html

and innovative features, Netscape packs a lot of punch into its browser. If you are looking for a browser that is available on a vast majority of platforms and that supports newer releases of Java and JavaScript, then Netscape is the best choice (or Mozilla, if you do not need the plugins that come with Netscape and which is even better).

Internet Explorer 6

IE,[8] which comes with every version of Windows sold and is freely download-able for other platforms (MacOS, HP-UX, Solaris), is one of the most popular Internet platforms. Similar to Netscape's Communicator, its functionality goes far beyond the scope of a simple browser. Besides the browser feature, Web-casting and a basic collaboration feature are built in. Just as with Netscape solutions, IE offers the possibility of actively pushing information to the desk-top of the user.

IE 6 is similar to Netscape 6 in many other ways. IE 6 has adopted some of Netscape 6's new tools. For example, IE's Personal Bars (which are similar to Netscape 6's Sidebars) load small Web pages that reside on the left side of the browser window and deliver content from specialized Web sites.

The Media Bar plays streaming media, but also makes it much easier to find the content itself. The Media Bar now features tons of links and tabs that point to everything from Internet radio stations to movie preview clips. There's a catch, of course: All this streaming content comes straight from Microsoft-owned WindowsMedia.com.[9]

IE 6 now supports the new, but not yet finalized, P3P privacy standard, a standard that lets you control how Web sites use your personal data. You can turn on the feature in IE's Privacy tab, and a little icon at the bottom of the browser window appears whenever you encounter a page without P3P rules attached. Double-click the icon, and up pops a dialog box listing the content that failed to pass the privacy check.

IE 6 also includes a new, sophisticated cookie manager that lets you, among other things, reject third-party cookies. Sites such as Amazon.com use first-person cookies to present you with customized recommendations whenever you shop there. A third-party cookie comes from a different (or third-party) Web site, usually an advertising network such as DoubleClick. Third-party cookies let ad networks track you across multiple Web sites, which raises privacy con-cerns for some. IE 6 offers a check box in its Privacy tab that lets you always reject third-party cookies, making you untrackable by ad networks.

IE 6's Image toolbar makes it easy to copy pictures from the Web. Hover your mouse over a picture, and a small floating toolbar automatically pops up. Click an icon on the toolbar, and you can easily email the image to a friend or save the picture to your hard drive.

---

[8]http://www.microsoft.com/ie/

[9]http://www.windowsmedia.com/

When running IE on Windows, IE can be highly integrated into the operating system. As this feature is not cross-platform compliant, not many applications have appeared so far. Although the basic concept is good, the idea of supporting only Windows is not good. Still, it is possible to create local applications, written in HTML and JavaScript, that can easily interact with resources on the Internet.

In addition to support for JavaScript and Java, IE 6 supports Active X components, media controllers, and VBScript, which are all Microsoft developments, available only on Microsoft platforms. Although these technologies provide some very good features, they are not designed for the Web, which contains not only Microsoft-powered computers, but others as well. No doubt Microsoft would like to see this change in the future.

A ratings service in the browser can be used to protect your family or business from inappropriate content. Web sites that are members of the PICS rating system[10] (see Chapter 11 for more information on PICS) are automatically detected and displayed when appropriate.

When installing IE, a scaled-down edition of Outlook is installed, called Outlook Express. This is Microsoft's email and news client, and it allows users to send and receive email and news postings. In addition to Outlook Express, a scaled-down version of FrontPage is installed, which allows the creation of simple Web pages.

IE 6 isn't as radical a departure from the previous IE as Netscape 6 was over Netscape 4.x. Some attempts to integrate tools, such as MSN Messenger, are still only half-baked, and the upgrade consists mainly of a bunch of little tweaks, from the Image toolbar to Outlook Express's antivirus features.

All these features make IE a complete solution, especially for users of Windows. There are some disadvantages. Microsoft removed Java completely and the JavaScript implementation is always one version behind Netscape's browser releases. The JavaScript problem will disappear as soon as Microsoft take the ECMAScript standard on board, which is no longer a Netscape standard (see later in this chapter for more information on ECMAScript). A Java plug-in can be downloaded at Sun's[11] Web site to solve the Java problem.

Opera 5.12

Opera[12] is number three on the browser market. Although it has only a very low market share, it is fast becoming very popular, as it has some features that the two major browsers lack. While Netscape and IE are becoming dinosaurs that require users to download software packages exceeding 15 MB, Opera is just over 1 MB. Opera is fast and functional, but lacks some features such as Java and Active X support. It also has only limited support for plug-ins.

---

[10] http://www.w3.org/PICS/
[11] http://java.sun.com/
[12] http://www.operasoftware.com/

Opera is a new product and is much faster than Netscape and IE, as it has not been built on older versions where typically code is added instead of completely replaced. Opera does not try to enforce new standards, but is built on the actual standards recommended by the Internet bodies, such as the World Wide Web Consortium.[13] Forms, frames, tables, and fonts are displayed correctly and videos are displayed in-line without additional plug-ins. JavaScript and SSL are also supported, making this browser ideal for people who have little memory and slower systems.

Following the trend of Microsoft's Explorer Bar and Netscape 6's Sidebar, Opera includes the dockable Hot List, a tabbed window to access your bookmarks, contacts, and Opera Mail. The new integrated search field lets you choose search engines and conduct your search from the URL line. Since your search is plugged into the URL automatically, you can also save searches as bookmarks. While previous versions required a special plug-in to run Java applets, Opera 5 now lets you install the JRE (Java Runtime Environment) in a single package.

The new built-in email client lets you have multiple accounts, import from Eudora and Outlook Express, create folders, and search your email. As an interesting extra, Opera 5 lets you access WAP (Wireless Access Protocol) sites that previously could only be accessed with WAP phones or a development emulator.

Opera uses a multiple document interface (MDI), which opens multiple pages in a single window, rather than in separate browser windows like Netscape and IE (see Figure 10.2). To navigate between windows, you click on tabs on the window bar, similar to Win 9.x's start menu bar. By default, Opera also gives you the option to save open windows when you exit.

Some of the most popular Netscape plug-ins, such as Platinum's Cosmo-Player and Adobe's Acrobat reader, are supported but it cannot be guaranteed that all plug-ins will work. Since the software is produced in Norway, the software has been localized right from the beginning. French, Norwegian, and German versions of Opera are already available, and many other languages are to come.

The software is also being ported to platforms other than Windows including Linux,[14] Amiga OS,[15] and Mac OS.[16]

Opera was developed by a small software company that cannot afford to give the browser away for free. Users can either pay 39 Dollar/Euro or get a banner-sponsored version that shows banner ads while browsing. If you are not in need of the latest hype, then Opera is a good choice.

---

[13] http://www.w3.org/

[14] http://www.linux.org/

[15] http://www.amiga.de/

[16] http://www.apple.com/macos/

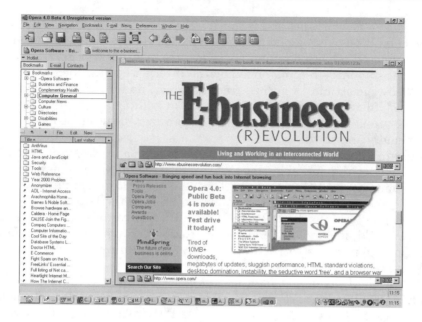

Figure 10.2. The Opera browser.

Lynx

The smallest browser on the market, Lynx, is only about 500 kilobytes large. Lynx[17] is a text-based browser; therefore, it does not support images, Java-Script, Java, Active X, or sounds. It does not even support a mouse. It is only capable of displaying textual information. Although this may seem strange to many people, it actually displays what usually matters—the textual content. It is by far the fastest browser on the market.

Although it does not support the latest hype, it is important for online businesses to be aware of this browser. It provides a very restricted view to your online offerings, similar to the view of embedded devices and search engines. If you can view your Web site through Lynx and still understand what it is all about, you can expect that people using mobile phones or other embedded devices will be able to get the information provided on your Web page. Have a look at Figure 10.3.

Even if customers are not able to execute a Web-based transaction, such as ordering stocks, they may want to see the actual stock price and then call their broker to place the order. Information therefore needs to be readable from any type of device. The same applies to search engines; if you are able to view your Web page through Lynx, you can be sure that a search engine will be able to index your site properly so that it can be easily found by customers and

---

[17]http://www.lynx.org/

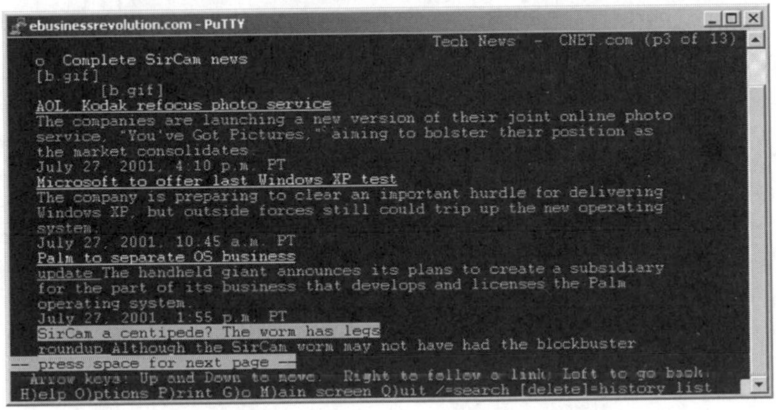

Figure 10.3. News.com using Lynx.

visitors. Information that is hidden in Java applications, plug-ins, or images cannot be accessed by search engines; therefore, it is necessary to add some text to explain the image or the application so that search engines know what their purpose is.

Customers who are in need of information and have only limited resources—such as a very old computer (e.g., a Commodore 64 or MS-DOS computer), a bad connection to the Internet because of a slow modem, or limited access to the Internet, such as a telnet account on a UNIX server—will use this browser.

By checking your Web site with Lynx, you will also ensure that physically impaired people will be able to use the site. The information in textual form can be processed in a speech browser and can guide them through the Web site. Images without additional information, for example, are like black spots on a Web page, and you will be able to detect them easily with Lynx.

Lynx cannot be used to do secure electronic business over the Internet, as it does not support SSL-encrypted connections. Lynx can be downloaded for free, and every Web designer should have a copy. Only if a Web page is usable with Lynx should you release it to the general public. Lynx can be used to verify if a Web site is usable on network-enabled devices, such as mobile phones and palmtops.

Many sites need JavaScript or SSL encryption to implement processing logic and security. But these technologies should really be used when there is a need for them, and not just because they are available. A Java ticker may be cute, but the same information can be presented in nonmoving text. In any case, textual metainformation should be provided to explain the content of the Web page and the reasons for using these advanced technologies.

10.1.4   Comparing Browser Technologies

Table 10.2 compares the four major browsers. As you can see, there is no major difference in functionality; the differences are mostly in the implementation of the functionality. Every browser has a slightly different implementation, making it almost impossible to use the more advanced features of the browsers without running into trouble. IE 6 and Netscape 6 are more standards-based, but it is highly unlikely that both browsers will become truly interchangeable. Part of the marketing strategy of both companies is to provide something more valuable than the other, and this is mainly achieved by adding new functionality. Therefore, they have included functionality that is not part of any official standard.

	Netscape 6.2	IE 6.0	Opera 5.12	Lynx 2.7
Frames	Yes	Yes	Yes	Partly
Form	Yes	Yes	Yes	Yes
Tables	Yes	Yes	Yes	Partly
Fonts	Yes	Yes	Yes	No
CSS	Yes	Yes	Yes	No
JavaScript	Yes, 1.4	Yes, 1.3	Yes, 1.2	No
Java	Yes, 1.4	Plugin, 1.4	Yes, 2.0	No
Plug-ins	Yes	Yes	Yes	No
News	Yes	Yes	Yes	No
Mail	Yes	Yes	Yes	No
HTML Editor	Yes	Yes	Yes	No

Table 10.2. Comparison of Browser Technology (1)

With a delay of one or two releases, the new functionality is becoming part of a standard. Therefore, it can be expected that all major browsers will soon be able to understand HTML 4.0 correctly, without any browser-specific additions. The problem lies more in upcoming standards, such as XML, RDF, and DOM. The Resource Description Framework (RDF) is a general framework for how to describe any Internet resource such as a Web site and its content. The Document Object Model (DOM), a programming interface specification being developed by the World Wide Web Consortium (W3C), lets a programmer create and modify HTML pages and XML documents as full-fledged program objects.

As these standards are still in early development, all companies will try to add some gimmicks, which break in other browsers. While JavaScript has become standardized in the 6.0 releases of the major browsers, we will see the introduction of XML in the 7.0 releases. There will not be much hassle with them, but it can be expected that new standards will be defined that are unclear today and therefore will force different implementations across the browsers.

10.1.5   Other Browsers

Besides the four big players in the browser market, many other browser applications have been developed, which for one reason or another have failed to become more popular. Some of the niche market browsers are presented here. Table 10.3 compares the runners-up.

	Amaya	Arachne	iBrowse	iCab
Frames	No	Yes	Yes	Yes
Forms	Yes	Yes	Yes	Yes
Tables	Yes	Yes	Yes	Yes
Fonts	Yes	Yes	Yes	Yes
CSS	Yes	No	No	Yes
JavaScript	No	No	Yes	Yes
Java	No	No	No	Yes
Plug-ins	No	No	Yes	Yes
News	No	No	No	Yes
Mail	No	Yes	No	Yes
HTML Editor	Yes	No	No	No

Table 10.3. Comparison of Browser Technology (2)

Amaya

Amaya[18] was developed by the World Wide Web Consortium (W3C), which is maintaining and developing the HTML standard. It can be used to verify if your HTML pages are sticking to the standard. It supports HTML 4.0 and CSS, making it a good verification platform for Web developers. Many Web sites use features that are Netscape or IE-specific and are not displayed correctly in Amaya. There is no support for JavaScript and cookies, which is used on many Web sites nowadays, rendering these sites unreadable.

---

[18]http://www.w3.org/amaya/

The major problem with Amaya is stability, rendering the browser unusable for daily browsing. It is a useful tool for developers, as it includes an integrated HTML editor and sticks to the HTML standards. Together with Lynx, it should be installed on every Web developer's computer. Amaya is freeware and available for several platforms besides Windows.

Arachne

Arachne[19] was developed by some Czech programmers for DOS-based computers. It uses less then a megabyte of RAM and fits on a floppy disk. Arachne supports HTML 4.0 and has a built-in mail client. Unlike most DOS-based applications, Arachne has a nice GUI that allows the user to browse through Web sites using a mouse, if available.

Since Arachne was for people who do not have any software for connecting to the Internet, it includes software for dial-up accounts. This makes it a bit difficult to use with Windows-based computers, as the drivers of Arachne interfere with the drivers of Windows, but with some configuration, it is possible to use both.

Because it is using a DOS interface, it is much faster than a Windows-based system. In addition to the browser and the email client, there is a Telnet and FTP application included. For people with very old DOS-based systems, it is the only possibility for getting onto the Internet with modest costs (for the software and the modem).

As it has been developed in the Czech Republic, it is fully localized and supports many different languages. At the time of writing, a Linux version is being developed that can be used to port it to other UNIX flavors.

HotJava

HotJava[20] was developed by Sun Microsystems using the Java programming language. Its design is modular through JavaBeans technology and is platform-neutral. Sun wanted to develop a browser that would run on all network-enabled devices, ranging from appliances such as a mobile phone to a large network server.

HotJava is the only browser that has 100 percent support for Java, as it is written in Java. But this is also its disadvantage: It is really slow. Both HTML pages and Java applets are slow compared to all other browsers, and no JavaScript is supported. HTML is fully supported up to version 4.0; the browser accepts cookies and is able to encrypt communication through the SSL protocol.

It is possible to download either the source code or the binary version. The HotJava browser is available in two versions, either as a full-featured Web

---

[19]http://home.arachne.cz/
[20]http://www.sun.com/software/htmlcomponent/

browser or as a JavaBeans component that allows the display of HTML in any application that includes this JavaBeans component.

Although the browser supports all major standards, it is not really an alternative to the major browsers; the latest version was far too slow for complex pages and Java applets.

iBrowse

iBrowse[21] is another browser that is, at the time of writing, only available for the Amiga[22] line of computers. Although many believe that the Amiga is dead, Amiga supporters are even more fanatical than the supporters of Macintosh computers. The Amiga hardware has stood still since 1991, but software is being developed, just as if the platform were still fully supported.

The Amiga platform has several Web browsers, but iBrowse is the market leader. The browser supports JavaScript and supports HTML 3.2, just as Netscape and IE do. But as Java is not fully supported in the Amiga OS, no Java applets are supported. It allows the inclusion of plug-ins, but they need to be written especially for the Amiga platform, so very few are available.

The browser does support most of the Netscape and IE extensions and has a built-in mail client. It is one of the few browsers that supported the HTTP/1.1 extensions right from the beginning.

One nice feature is the netstat window, which shows all files that are currently downloaded. This allows you to see how fast each file gets downloaded and allows you to abort the download of files. This is useful for Web pages with a lot of elements. If there are many images, it is possible to abort images that you are not interested in or that are too large.

The program is very compact compared to other browsers on the market, and runs with only 2 MB of RAM. This features makes the Internet accessible to people with older hardware.

iCab

Created by German developers, the Web browser iCab[23] may be able to compete with the two big browsers, Netscape and IE. Although iCab is currently available for MacOS only, it immediately had a large impact on the relatively small market. The iCab download is a minuscule 1.3 MB making it a real differentiator, but it has to make a sacrifice for its diminutive size: it doesn't come with any extras, such as plug-ins or Java support. But it supports all popular Netscape plug-ins and lets you include Apple's Mac OS Runtime for Java for Java support.

Highlights of iCab include a very user-friendly interface, a download manager for offline reading (which automatically creates a ZIP file for larger sites),

---

[21] http://cgi.www.hisoft.co.uk/amiga/ibrowse/

[22] http://www.amiga.de/

[23] http://www.icab.de/

and a special search tool that can be configured to use any search engine on the
Web. The browser requires only 4 MB of RAM and supports not only HTML
4.0 and CSS2, but also all common extensions of the Netscape and Microsoft
browsers. It has a special feature to bookmark frames in the state of display.
No other browser is able to correctly bookmark pages with frames.

iCab lacks an email program, though it does support sending mail by clicking on a mail link. To receive email, you need a third-party client such as
Eudora or Netscape Messenger, unless you use Web-based mail. Another very
important feature of iCab is its ability to mimic another browser. Unfortunately, many Web sites check for specific versions of Netscape or IE and disallow access to content, even though iCab would be capable of it. Therefore, you
can configure iCab to mimic a Netscape-compatible browser.

iCab's strength is its configurability. By default, everything is switched off
(this is the opposite approach of Microsoft). For example, you have to turn on
InScript, which is iCab's partial implementation of JavaScript. Another very
interesting feature is iCab's image filtering. Most browsers let you turn images
off, which can speed up browsing if you have a slow modem connection. iCab
goes a step further and actually filters specific images—for example, the most
popular banner ad sizes.

If iCab becomes available for other platforms as well, it has the potential to
become highly successful and a rival of Opera at the very least.

10.1.6   Offline Browsers

In addition to the online browsers, many offline browsers have begun to establish themselves. Why would you need an offline browser? Once you have
decided which Web site is interesting to you, you can simply download the complete site and read the content offline. All you need to do is enter the starting
URL and the program will download the Web page and all elements on the Web
page, such as style sheets, images, and sounds. Most programs offer the option
of recursively downloading all links from that Web page, eventually downloading the complete site.

Once you have downloaded the site, the normal Web browser can be used
to view the files on your hard disk. This works only with static HTML pages.
If you come across a Web site that builds dynamic Web pages or uses CGI applications or Java applets that connect back to the server, then offline reading
won't work properly.

The major advantage is that you can view the pages whenever you need
to and do not have to go online; but of course it may well be that you are
downloading pages in which you are not interested.

Most programs that are available work similarly to Web spiders that index
the content of Web pages for search engines. Offline Explorer,[24] developed by

---

[24]http://www.metaproducts.com/OE.html

MetaProducts, and WebZIP,[25] developed by Spidersoft, are programs that allow the retrieval of complete or partial Web sites.

Cli-Mate,[26] on the other hand, is highly specialized. It retrieves the weather forecast and installs it in the form of an image on the desktop of the computer. The information is updated automatically every time the user goes online. InfoNout[27] downloads the most recent movie listings automatically. This push technology is discussed later in this chapter.

The third type of offline browsers are applications that scan through the cache directory of the installed browser. Browsers use the cache to store the most recently viewed Web pages in a special directory in order to save download time for the last few Web pages. The files in the cache directory are not using the original file names, but use the date and time as a filename; therefore, it is difficult to recognize which HTML page contains what. The cache browser reads the <title> tag and presents this information to the user instead of presenting the cryptic filename.

10.1.7 The Impact on Business

The browser application has a huge impact on Internet business. It is the preferred piece of software to access online services, such as shopping and banking. The browser enables customers to service themselves via the Web. Although there are differences between the browser products, each of them is capable of understanding and processing HTML, the building block for all Web pages.

Browsers display the information found on Web pages, allowing customers to search for certain information within the page and to print out the information for reference. Browsers can also be used by digital companies to display and market products, information, and services to customers around the world, no matter which language they speak or which type of computer they own. All the customer needs is the Web browser, which allows the user to connect to the company's Web site. Although there are other means of conducting business over the Internet, the browser has enabled almost anyone to participate, as it is simple to use.

To expand your online business to a maximum number of customers, you should use Web technology such as HTML to design and implement a Web site that can be seen through a variety of browsers. The browser window is all the customers get to see of your company, so you need to make sure you do it right the first time.

---

[25] http://www.spidersoft.com/
[26] http://www.users.nac.net/splat/climate/
[27] http://www.boxoffice.com/download.html

10.1.8   Browsing into the Future

With the start of the new millennium (no matter if you think it starts in 2000 or 2001), the browser generation of today will soon be seen as prehistoric. Lately, the browser manufacturers have included more proprietary features, which increased the size and the complexity of the software. As a result, more and more bugs have crept into the software, making it more unreliable and more insecure.

But the biggest problem is that every browser manufacturer has bent the Web standards a little bit in its own direction making the browsers' advanced features incompatible. As a result, most Web pages still use a design based on very old HTML standards, just to be sure that everyone is able to read the page. This chapter is full of new and emerging standards that can enhance the Web dramatically, but only if all browsers support them in a consistent way.

Another important point for the millennium is the upcoming era of pervasive computing. This means that more and more devices that had nothing to do with the Internet will become Web-enabled. The first microwaves with Internet connection are already on the market, allowing users to surf the Web for recipes and order the required ingredients directly over the Internet at the local grocer. The microwave's function is to heat up food and not to connect to the Internet; therefore, the resources in the microwave will be very limited in order to maintain the price. Less memory, less colors, less speed will be most probable—or do you want 20 full-blown PCs all over your house? Most people would not—even if they could afford it.

If we look at the sizes of latest releases from Netscape with its Communicator 6.2 (just under 20 MB) and Microsoft with its IE 6 (just under 120 MB), we can see that these browsers were designed for the ever-increasing speed, memory, and hard disk space of personal computers.

It would be impossible to include these browsers in any device other than a computer. Browsers have become so complex that it is not possible to simply remove some of the features in order to make it fit into a device with 2 MB of memory.

Some of the other browsers mentioned previously are much smaller because they do not carry the burden of so much old code. But even Opera and the other browsers need to rethink the way they were written in order to fit into other devices. Making browser technology available for other types of devices requires manufacturers to make the source code very modular, as some devices have more capabilities than others.

By strictly modularizing the browser technologies, it is possible to create Web connectivity for almost any device, regardless of its features (e.g., limited memory, display). Netscape, for example, is working on two browser generations at the same time. The old one is based on Netscape 4 technology and on the old paradigm of creating software. New features are more important than

The next generation of Web browsers needs to adhere to the following features in order to meet customers' expectations.

- **Internet services**—Browsers need to tightly integrate services on the Internet, instead of offering them within the browser.

- **Open source code**—The source code needs to be available.

- **Real-time communication**—Live chats become more important.

- **Small size**—In order to support devices other than standard computers, the size needs to be reduced.

- **Speed**—Network-enabled devices are not as fast as full-blown computers; therefore, the browser needs to be very fast.

- **Standards compliance**—Web standards need to be implemented correctly.

Table 10.4. Features of Next Generation Browsers

speed and size, as computers get faster and equipped with more memory all the time. The new concept of connecting all devices to the Internet requires omitting features in order to make the application fast enough and to make it fit into the possibly limited memory of the device. Therefore, the new browser generation is modularized and completely rewritten using modern tools for optimizing size and speed. The first preview release of Netscape's new browser, called Gecko, has only 1.6 MB, yet maintains all features of the old Netscape 4.79 release. By reimplementing all features, the new browser is also much faster and the Web standards are enforced by better control over the single modules.

In order to reduce the size of the browser, some of the browser services offered need to be moved to the Internet. Instead of natively offering a functionality, the functionality will be delivered from a Web server. Your mobile phone won't have enough additional memory to add a full blown email application. But this is not really necessary, as there are enough possibilities on the Web to display, read, and send email. Web email is able to offer the same functionality as a standalone application, but does not require you to install a program on the client side.

All features except for the Web-browsing feature can be outsourced to the Web. Instead of opening up the news reader client, people can connect to Internet services offering all newsgroups. Instead of opening up a chat client, people can connect to a Web server that offers the same functionality. Every single service can be outsourced in this way.

The current generation of browsers offers the choice between built-in functionality and Web functionality. As connection speed to the Internet becomes faster, Web functionality becomes more accessible. Netscape offers a feature to look up stock quotes by entering "quote <symbol>," whereby <symbol> is the ticker symbol, such as AAPL for Apple or HWP for Hewlett-Packard. Simply try it, and the browser will return a Web page with all the financial information about the selected company.

The address book is normally outsourced together with the mail functionality, and companies have started to offer online calendar solutions. Online chats (sometimes called real-time messaging) are one of the favorite pastimes of the Internet community. They offer the ability to talk to people from all over the world at the cost of a local phone call. In many cases online chats have replaced phone calls and therefore are becoming more and more important. The next generation of browsers will have a much stronger integration with chat, and not only with text-based chat as we know it today. Consider that voice conferences and video conferencing will become standard functionality for many devices.

The next generation of browsers will need to be strictly standards-compliant in order to succeed. As Web browsers are given away for free, features that are not compliant won't be used, as Web developers need to be sure that everyone is able to access a certain feature. By supporting the W3C standards, new content and service sites can be implemented quickly and cost effectively. The most important move is the transition from HTML to XML as the base format for the Internet.

The W3C standards (such as XML, CSS2, DOM, RDF) enable the developers to create highly complex applications using the next generation of browsers. As current Web browsers do not fully support these new standards, documents in these new formats need to be translated on the server to standard HTML and passed on to the browser. Over time, these server translations can be removed. At the moment, the browser with the small feature set defines what Web sites are displaying. Only very few create advanced Web sites, as they can only be used by few people with a certain browser. Currently, the browser with the least standards support is the limit on standards adoption. By moving from HTML to XML, features can be added without needing to update the browser. This makes it even easier for developers to create applications and services.

Experience has shown that closed development leads to nonstandard implementations, limited hardware and software platform support, lower quality, and less interoperability. Open source, on the other hand, speeds up development and increases the quality. And because the source code is free, everyone is able to port the application to another platform. The software becomes available on not only more platforms, but also in more languages, as anyone is able to offer a translation for a specific language. More on open source and free software can be found in Chapter 15.

10.2   The Hypertext Markup Language

10.2.1   The Building Block

HTML is the fundamental building block of the World Wide Web. Hypertext is a form of text that contains links to other text, thereby connecting texts to each other in a nonlinear way. HTML is a nonproprietary format, developed by the W3C, based on SGML (standard generalized markup language). The hypertext documents are plain text files that contain embedded codes for logical markup. These documents can be created by simple text editors or highly sophisticated authoring tools.

HTML is not a programming language, but a *markup* language. It only describes a logical structure of a document, rather than document presentation. For example, it is not possible to alter the structure from within the document itself using only HTML.

HTML documents are stored on a Web server, which distributes the files to the Web browsers that connect to that particular server. The HTML files are then displayed to the viewer as they are, and also interpreted by the Web browser, which then creates the Web page according to the instructions that are part of the HTML code.

HTML was originally supposed to be device-independent. It was to be used on a variety of computer systems without change. The concept behind HTML was to provide a means to structure a document. It was left up to the browser on any specific system to take care of rendering the document in whatever way the browser author thought most suitable. Tim Berners-Lee, the inventor of the World Wide Web, was a researcher at CERN[28] and therefore more interested in structuring a document than creating a nice layout for it.

10.2.2   Web Page Layout

Over time, as HTML and the World Wide Web became more popular, commercial companies wanted to present information and goods on the Internet. The Web moved from being primarily a medium for exchanging scientific information to being a marketing medium. Companies wanted their Web documents to adhere to their corporate standards and needed to lay them out accordingly. But the original HTML specification offered very little support for layout and

---

[28]http://www.cern.ch/

presentation, so the demand grew for extensions. Various browser manufacturers introduced new HTML elements oriented toward presentation issues, which eventually became part of the HTML standard.

Most documents on the Web are described by HTML tags. These instructions are embedded within angle brackets ($<$ $>$) to distinguish the instructions from the text that you want to display. HTML tags are used to describe text elements and to define a layout. Therefore, each text element is surrounded by two HTML tags, the start tag and the end tag. The end tag is the same as the start tag, but a slash has been added. An example could look like this:

```
<title>this is the title of the web page</title>
```

Although the current release of HTML is case-insensitive, this cannot be guaranteed for future releases. If you use HTML through XML, for example, case-sensitivity is a basic requirement.

HTML tags can define not only formatting options, but also attributes. The <font> tag allows for different attributes, such as font size and color. Large red text can be created with <font size=5 color=red>. If attribute values use white spaces, then they need to be enclosed within quotes. The attribute information does not need to be repeated in the end tag. HTML is very powerful and simple at the same time. Anyone can create HTML documents within minutes.

Table 10.5. Introduction to HTML Tags

Therefore, HTML has also become a language for creating layout for a Web page. HTML uses tags to describe certain text elements. Originally, the tags were used exclusively to describe the structure of an element. For example, the tag <h1> was used to describe a heading. In order to make the heading distinct from the body text, the Web browser would display the heading using a font size of 36 points, while body text was 10 points. In later releases of HTML, under massive pressure from the major browser producers, the <font> tag was introduced, which allowed the HTML programmer to select a size for the font. Instead of <h1> this is a heading </h1>, it has become possible to use <font size=7> this is not a heading </font>. A short introduction to the use of HTML tags can be found in Table 10.5.

The problem with the <font> tag is that it does not explain what the text element represents. The text could be a heading, body text, a signature, a code segment, or any other type of text. Search engines have a very limited view of the world. Unlike humans, who are able to understand many things by context, search engines have to rely on the facts that are presented on certain Web page elements and do not have the ability to put it into context. Therefore, a correct classification within the page is very important. Automatic processing of documents is also very difficult, as there is no—or only little—structural information stored in the document.

By using standardized tags, the HTML code is independent of a particular Web browser or operating system. Any Web browser that understands HTML is able to read Web documents, interpret them, and create a layout for a Web page. Using logical tags, every browser is free to display a tag with a different style. While one browser displays emphasized text using bold text, another one may choose to display it in italic.

The main reason for introducing layout tags was that Web designers wanted to create Web pages that looked consistent in all browsers. Their job was not to describe content; they wanted to create a special design. The latest release of the HTML standard, version 4.0, tries to reverse this development by deprecating most tags that deal with presentation and not structure. These tags are moved into style sheets. An example are the attributes of the <body> tag. More on style sheets can be found later in this chapter.

A deprecated element, or attribute, is one that has been outdated by newer constructs and which may become obsolete in future versions of HTML. The browsers continue to support deprecated elements for reasons of backward compatibility.

10.2.3 HTML 4.0

In 1997, the W3C[29] released HTML 4.0. It builds on HTML 3.2, adding a host of new features. The new standard was developed by the HTML Working Group, which consists of many industry players, such as Adobe,[30] Hewlett-Packard, IBM, Netscape, Reuters,[31] Sun Microsystems, content specialists at HotWired[32] and PathFinder,[33] and experts in the fields of accessibility and internationalization.

The major news in HTML 4.0 is that is has been designed with embedded devices in mind. Unlike HTML 3.2, which was basically made for complex browser software only, the new recommendation allows access to Web content

---

[29]http://www.w3.org/

[30]http://www.adobe.com/

[31]http://www.reuters.com/

[32]http://www.hotwired.com/

[33]http://www.pathfinder.com/

from a broad range of devices, from smart televisions to cellular phones. The goal is to make HTML a fundamental building block for networked computers and mission-critical information systems in the business world.

Just like its predecessors, HTML 4.0 is an SGML application, which enables hypertext documents to be represented using text-based markup, providing interoperability across a wide range of platforms. It includes features for basic document idioms such as headings, lists, paragraphs, tables, and images, as well as hypertext links and electronic forms.

These basic features can be rendered on graphical displays, such as the Netscape browser; text-only displays, such as the Lynx browser; and speech-based browsers. These features were already present in HTML 3.2 and its Netscape and IE version cousins. There are special browsers for blind people that read out loudly the content of a Web page.

Some totally new features have been introduced into HTML 4.0 to make it more appealing for content providers and users. The new HTML standard provides a way for authors to embed objects and scripts and support style sheets in their documents. Although these features were already available in earlier versions, they have never been formally standardized, making it difficult to implement objects, scripts, and styles across a set of different browsers. This enables content providers to dynamically update pages and change the appearance on the fly.

Electronic forms have been updated to allow content providers to display rich HTML in any button. Until now, content providers could not control the design of the buttons in an electronic form. With the introduction of HTML 4.0, it is possible to create read-only controls and group form controls together. Another very important feature is that it is now possible to provide keyboard shortcuts on controls, making it easier for people who cannot use a mouse to control the complete form via voice control. Titles can now be added to any element, making the whole electronic form appear more like a standard desktop application.

Although frames can be considered one of the less useful inventions of HTML, there are substantial improvements in this new version. It now allows the creation of in-line frames in order to make compound documents by placing frames in HTML documents. This feature is very useful, and aside from this new architecture, the basic frame model could be discarded entirely.

The basic table functionality has been enhanced to allow row and column grouping. The improved border control delivers additional design control to improve the performance and the power of the tables. Although these features may be very useful for creating tables, they may again be misused to create complex Web page layouts. The layout should be controlled by the style sheets and not by tables.

Another very important feature update is the inclusion of new named entities, which now support important symbols and glyphs used in mathematics, markup, and internationalization.

In order to make HTML 4.0 a success, three flavors have been specified. By inserting a line at the beginning of the document stating which flavor you are using, the appropriate document type definition (DTD) will be used to validate the correctness of the document.

- **HTML 4.0 Frameset**—Should only be used if the documents use HTML frames to partition the browser window into two or more frames.

- **HTML 4.0 Transitional**—Should be used to support older browsers that do not understand style sheets correctly, while allowing all the possibilities HTML 4.0 offers.

- **HTML 4.0 Strict**—Should be used when you want clean structural markup, free of any tags associated with layout. Requires cascading style sheets to do the layout.

Table 10.6. Flavors of HTML

The new HTML standard has been developed with accessibility in mind. This means that embedded devices will be able to access the information, and people with disabilities will get additional information describing images, labels for form fields, and ways to associate table data with headers. This additional metainformation makes it easier to understand the content of an HTML page through a speech-based or Braille browser. Most Web pages today contain information that can be easily extracted through the human eye, as they contain many images that are self-explanatory, but are not accessible to these special browsers because of this missing metainformation.

The Web Accessibility Initiative (WAI) has developed authoring guidelines to support people with disabilities. For many Web pages, it will mean a major redesign, but it is hoped that when moving from HTML 3.2 to HTML 4.0, many Web page designers will include this additional information. It will open up the Web to millions of users who have been held back by pages designed only for people using graphical browsers. For online business, this can mean a lot of additional traffic to their Web sites.

Another important issue is internationalization of Web sites. In the past, HTML supported documents in other languages, but on any given Web page, only one language was supported. HTML 4.0 now provides the markup needed for any language and multilingual documents. The advantage is that authors can now make their documents more accessible to users, whatever their language is. This is achieved by supporting the international ISO 10646 character set and allowing authors to manage differences in language, text direction, and character encoding schemes. This makes it easier to create an English-Hebrew dictionary on the Web, for example. The English text will be written from left-to-right, and next to it the Hebrew text will be set right-to-left. The burden of internationalization is then passed on to the Web page editors, who now need to support this new paradigm to make text entry easy. With current Web page editors, to write correct HTML 4.0 Hebrew Web pages, it is necessary to write from back-to-front (from a Hebrew point of view). Japanese is written from top to bottom, and this cannot be easily implemented by HTML editors today.

10.2.4   Relevance to Online Businesses

HTML's impact on online business is very similar to the impact of the Web browser. In fact, both technologies are linked together very tightly. HTML is the underlying technology for displaying content in a Web browser. It allows customers to view product and service information easily and companies to develop such pages very easily. Although modern Web browsers require a lot of memory, most Web pages require only a little. The size of a typical Web site is between 20 and 50 KB, making the transport of information very efficient. Imagine if all the information on the Web were only available via word processor file formats. This would multiply the download by a factor of 10 to 20 without increasing the value for the customer or adding content. Actually, most word processors now allow the direct output of HTML, making it easy for nontechnical people to create Web pages.

HTML is easy to learn and implement, and therefore can be used by any company to present itself in a very interactive and multimedia way. Using HTML can also reduce costs significantly. Instead of sending out tons of material via traditional mailing services, customers are able to get the information on the Web themselves and print it out, if required. This also reduces the amount of paper used for printing.

10.3   The Dynamic Web

10.3.1   Moving from Static to Dynamic Web Sites

Most companies start out by using static pages to create Web sites. The major advantage of this system is that no programming knowledge is needed. Anyone with a Web page editor is able to get some pages up and online. Once the information is online, the only piece of software that needs to work is the Web server, which has become a very solid piece of software over the last few years. Static Web pages do not require as many resources as dynamic Web pages on a Web server, as the only action that the Web server has to perform is to locate the Web page on the hard disk and pass it on to the Web browser.

But many companies will eventually want to do more, and this requires them to tie Web pages to their databases. Using the database model allows for dynamic Web pages that let visitors add, insert, and delete data, while internal data is also available immediately on the Internet. Dynamic pages are more flexible and more useful than static pages, even though they may consume a little more resources on the Web server.

Consider an online shop with 10,000 articles. Using static Web pages, you would need to create a page for every single product, resulting in tens of thousands of Web pages, which are not manageable in any way. It becomes impossible to change the layout or add a link to every page. The same applies to online banking, ordering, or any other service that relies on data or information that changes over time. Using static Web pages, the whole Web page needs to be rebuilt, even if only a single line has changed. The overhead for creating static Web pages would consume more resources than dynamic Web pages allocate.

Static Web pages still exist, but are used only by individuals who have just a few Web pages online that they update infrequently. A company offering an online service needs to have its Web site always up to date, and therefore all the information presented needs to be up to date as well. Imagine a company selling printers via the Web, but not having its latest model online for sale because it took too long to add new static Web pages to the site. Using a dynamic Web site, the data on the new printer would be entered into the Web server's database and the information on the printer would become instantly available to anyone visiting the site.

Through the use of dynamic Web pages, companies are able to create standard layouts, saved in a separate location from the data. When a customer accesses your Web site, the layout and the content are combined on the fly to form a highly individual Web page, which answers the customer's query.

Almost all business sites use dynamic Web pages. They make it easy to make changes in the layout, as only very few layout templates need to be altered. This reduces the cost for the company and the time to market for a new Web page design. This paradigm allows design agencies to create the Web design without having to touch the content.

Through JavaScript, CSS, and DOM, it is possible to create dynamic Web pages on the client side. This reduces the load on the server and makes the Web application more responsive. Dynamic Web pages need not necessarily be prebuilt on the server, using CSS, DOM, or JavaScript. It is also possible to create client-side dynamic HTML.

10.3.2   Cascading Style Sheets

As discussed, HTML was developed to describe the logical structure of a document, but unfortunately, it no longer does so. In order to describe the layout of the document, the CSS was developed. They help HTML to become again what it was once designed for.

CSS allows you to control the rendering of elements on a Web page without compromising its structure. Fonts, colors, typefaces, and other aspects of style are defined in the CSS. Instead of using Web terminology CSS, uses desktop publishing terminology which addresses the needs of designers. The visual design can be addressed separately from the logical structure of the Web page, just as designers do. HTML does not offer the same possibilities that modern desktop publishing (DTP) systems do.

Style sheets are templates, very similar to templates in DTP applications, containing a set of rules specifying the rendering of various HTML elements. These templates describe how a document is presented on the screen or when printed out.

What designers always missed most was the typographic control. CSS allows Web elements to be positioned to control the layout on a Web page and allows the fonts to be downloaded dynamically. Images and text can be layered and overlapped and can be dynamically moved around the screen with scripts. CSS makes it possible to control the layout of any given document in a Web browser. Unlike HTML, CSS layout looks the same in all Web browsers.

10.3.3   The Document Object Model

The DOM is a model in which a document (such as a Web page) contains objects (text elements, images, links) that can be manipulated. DOM has been recommended by W3C. Using DOM, it is possible to remove, alter, or add an element to a given document. It is also possible to change the content of an element or remove, alter, or add an attribute. Through DOM, for example, it is possible to get a list of all H2 elements in a document or all elements with an attribute SIZE=4. This makes it possible to search for elements on a Web page and alter them on the fly. Through this mechanism, it would be possible to change the language of a Web site without reloading it.

Level 1 of the DOM specification allows navigation around an HTML or XML document and the manipulation of the content in that particular document. Level 2 allows the manipulation of CSS styles (used in an HTML or XML document) and includes an event model and richer queries on the objects specified in the DOM.

In order to modify the objects in the DOM model, a Web browser will most likely use JavaScript or ECMAScript (the standardization of JavaScript/JScript by the European Computer Manufacturer's Association [ECMA] defined by ECMA-262). This scripting language is embedded into the page itself and allows the manipulation of the objects on the page. An editor may also use a Java interface to manipulate the page in the editor. Java could also be used to create a DOM interface between a document and a database. But if not embedded into a Web page, the interface could be in any language, as the DOM is language neutral.

By providing a common syntax, DOM is more than just a broker between scripting languages and a document. Just as style sheets allow you to perform layout independent of content and structure, the DOM allows for interaction that is independent of content and structure. It uses the same paradigm but from another point of view. This allows you to create code (and therefore interaction) independently of Web pages, just as style sheets allow you to create layout independently of Web pages.

In order to make the DOM language neutral, it is necessary to define it in an interface definition language (IDL). Unlike the component object model (COM) or the Common Object Request Broker Architecture (CORBA), which provide language-independent ways to specify interfaces and objects, DOM is a set of interfaces and objects for managing HTML and XML documents that can be used on the Web, but also for applications.

10.3.4   Dynamic HTML

Although HTML is the best tool for publishing textual documents over the Internet, it is not designed to create interactive Web sites and multimedia-rich documents. Standard HTML is also limited regarding layout. But CSS allow pixel-level accuracy on the layout comparable to traditional DTP programs. This also makes the creation of online and offline documents from a single source easier.

Although it is possible to create dynamic Web pages on the server, meaning that the content is brought together at the time of loading, most Web pages are static once they are displayed in the browser, meaning that the content or layout cannot be changed without going back to the server. HTML, by definition, does not allow you to dynamically update content, change the appearance of content, or hide, show, and animate content.

To allow these features, Web pages need to become interactive. HTML cannot accomplish this, so scripting languages such as JavaScript or VBScript have been developed to take over this role (see also the section on JavaScript later in this chapter). These languages allow an increase in the interactivity of the Web page, but only in a limited fashion.

If we now put the three building blocks together, HTML, CSS, and JavaScript and/or VBScript, we are able to create highly functional, dynamic, and interactive Web pages that are similar to today's standalone multimedia applications. This is called DHTML, or dynamic HTML.

By exposing a DOM to the scripting languages, Web page designers get full control over the HTML document and its elements and are able to change the layout on the fly. The color of a heading can be changed, just as a block of text can be moved from the upper right corner into the lower left corner, or hidden completely. The event model that accompanies the DOM extends the scripting languages' awareness of user actions, allowing keystrokes and a larger variety of mouse actions to be interpreted by scripting languages.

DHTML makes it possible to create content dynamically on the client without having to reconnect to the server, which is often desired when working on a slow connection. Another very interesting feature is data binding—currently supported only by IE—which allows the server and client to be connected in such a way that data in the database can be bound to elements in an HTML document. This allows you to view database content on a single Web page. Most Web sites reconnect to the server and get a new HTML page with database content. This functionality allows you to keep the HTML page and the layout and refill the content of single elements with new data entries.

DHTML allows the creation of complex client-side applications that do not necessarily need to interact with a server. Many games, such as Tetris, have been created in DHTML, and word processors, HTML editors, and spreadsheets have been created in DHTML, too. DHTML offers a way to provide applications on the Web for a limited period of time. Similar to Java applets, they allow user interaction; in general, they are faster than applets, as they are directly implemented in the browser and do not require a JVM to run.

10.4   Dynamic Server Concepts

Although DHTML is a good choice for smaller databases and Web sites, creating dynamic Web pages on the server is more appropriate for larger companies with huge databases. In order to process input or data from the client and from other sources, such as databases, it is necessary to create interfaces for communication. The common gateway interface (CGI) is an established protocol for a Web server application to receive data from a browser and prepare data before sending it back to the client. HTML pages may be embedded into the CGI applications. Server-side includes (SSI), on the other hand, can only prepare data before sending it to the client. SSI embeds commands into HTML pages, making it easy to use for people with little programming knowledge.

10.4.1   The Common Gateway Interface

The Common Gateway Interface (CGI) enables interaction between a Web server and a browser using HTTP. HTML documents are static and served by the Web server on the client side without changing anything. A CGI program is executed, and the results, such as flight plan queries or news updates, are delivered to the customers.

CGI programs are able to handle information requests and return the appropriate document or generate a dynamic document. They can act as a gateway between databases and Web browsers that understand only HTML, but not SQL. Customers are able to express queries using HTML forms that allow the selection of items and the entry of free text, which then can be passed back to the server. The data a customer enters into the form is submitted to the Web server; the CGI picks up the information and passes it on to a program that processes the input and passes the results back to the Web browser.

CGI programs are scripts (or executables) that are invoked by the Web browser and then executed on the Web server. CGI specifies how the data is handled between Web page and executable, but does not limit this information to any specific language. C, C++, Python, Perl, and Java are the most commonly used languages for CGI applications, but any language can be used. CGI applications are able to handle any type of application, depending on the imagination and ability of the programmer.

Although any programming language can be used to create server-side HTML preprocessor applications, this section gives a short overview on the most commonly used languages. Using Java, JavaScript, Perl, and Python, it is fairly easy to build applications that accept and provide data through the CGI.

Java

Java[34] is a hardware-independent language that runs on all major platforms. Many people know Java in the form of applets in the Web browser. As there are some problems with implementations in Java within Web browsers, client-side Java is not always the best solution. Different browser manufacturers support different versions of Java, which are of course incompatible. Java on the server, on the other hand, has become one of the major drivers. Server-side Java has the advantage of being browser-independent, if done properly. In addition, the server can be replaced without needing to rewrite or recompile the software. Java is described in depth in Chapter 12.

JavaScript

Server-side JavaScript needs to be compiled and can then be used by the Netscape Enterprise Server, in a way similar to CGI programs. Server-side JavaScript is only accepted by the Netscape Web browsers, while the client-side scripting engine is supported and accepted by all major browsers.

Client and server-side JavaScript share the same basic functionality. Webmasters that know how to write JavaScript code for the browser will be able to write server-side JavaScript. The advantage of server-side JavaScript is that the script is processed on the server and requires no special browser to view the page. The downside is that for every interaction, a connection back to the server is required, just as with any other application that resides on the server.

Perl

Perl is the most popular programming language on the server side, as it allows fast prototyping. Although many people think Perl[35] (Practical Extraction and

---

[34]http://java.sun.com/
[35]http://www.perl.org/

Report Language) is just a CGI language, it is a regular programming language used not just for the Web. Perl is a scripting language that has been optimized for scanning text files, extracting information from files, processing information, and printing reports based on that information.

Larry Wall, the developer of Perl, had intended to create a language that is practical, and therefore easy to use; efficient and complete, rather than beautiful. Unlike Java, Perl is hard to read. Perl combines some of the most useful features of other programming languages, such as C and Pascal, with applications—such as "sh," "sed," and "awk."

Python

Python[36] is another good choice in the context of Web server programming. It is an interpreted, interactive programming language based on the paradigm of object orientation. It has many similarities with Tcl, Perl, Scheme, and Java.

The syntax of Python is very clear, without reducing the power of the programming language. Classes, dynamic typing, dynamic data types exceptions, and modules are the standard constructs of the language, and it offers many interfaces to system calls, libraries, and windowing systems, such as X11 UNIX front ends and Macintosh OS.

Python can also interact with C or C++ applications, making it a suitable alternative for creating an extension language for applications that need a programmable interface. Python is very portable and is available on all major platforms, making it a good language to use if you run a multiplatform environment. The source code is freely available, making it possible to compile it even for currently unsupported platforms.

10.4.2   Server-Side Includes

Server-side includes (SSI) are commands that are included in HTML pages and are executed before the Web page is sent to the client. The commands are a special kind of HTML tag interpreted by the Web server. The advantage for Web developers is that they do not need to learn any additional language, but need only add some more commands to the Web page. The use is limited to the SSI extensions developed by the software company whose extensions you are planning to use.

SSIs offer a simple way of customizing a Web page. For example, it is very easy to define a variable that is replaced with the name of the customer identified by IP address, basic authentication (login/password), strong authentication (digital certificate), or via cookie. This feature enables you to welcome every single customer without having different Web pages on the server. It can also be used to omit or add specific information that may be uninteresting or valuable to the customer through simple "if-else" statements. SSI makes

---

[36]http://www.python.org/

HTML highly dynamic, but the main problem is that marketing won't be able to change the layout with a simple HTML editor, as the Web pages contain a lot of programming information that they would need to understand. Two programming languages that use the concept of SSI are PHP and ASP.

ASP

Microsoft introduced Active Server Pages (ASP) in December 1996. ASP, are programs that are included in the HTML page and are processed by the Web server. It is a programming environment that provides the ability to combine HTML, scripting, and components to create powerful Internet applications that run on your server. Unfortunately, only one Web server is supported: the Internet Information Server (IIS) by Microsoft.

It is an open technology framework, comprised of several different commonly used programming disciplines. This makes it easy to integrate heavy programs and databases to Web pages. At the core of ASP, we find VBScript. It acts as a glue to combine all the power of ASP into your Web pages, and often when people speak of ASP and ASP code, they really mean VBScript code. VBScript is the default script language in ASP, but you can use Perl, JScript, and others. ASP is run server side, meaning that the script is run on the Web server so that the Web page functions regardless of browser.

PHP

PHP[37] has become one of the most popular scripting languages found on the Internet, as it lends a great many capabilities to the Web programmer. Many tasks accomplished with some degree of difficulty in many other languages can be swiftly executed with but a few lines of PHP code. The fact that PHP 3.0 code can be inserted into HTML makes the language all the more convenient.

PHP was created by Rasmus Lerdorf. In what began as a personal project, the language quickly gained popularity and was almost completely rewritten by a group of six developers. The language enjoys an extremely active developing environment, due in large part to the fact that the language is freely available for download on the Web.

Much of PHP is a combination of Perl, Java, and C concepts. The syntax structure borrows heavily from C, making it an easy language to learn for even the novice programmer. PHP performs sophisticated mathematical calculations, provides network information, offers mail and regular expression capabilities, and much more. PHP's strongest feature is its database interfacing capability. Connecting a database to the Internet has never been so easy. What's more, it supports many of the most popular database servers on the market, including MySQL, Oracle, Sybase, mSQL, Generic ODBC, and PostgreSQL, to name a few.

---

[37]http://www.php.net/

One of the factors that make PHP so powerful is that it is a goal-oriented language. It is written to accomplish tasks quickly and cleanly.

10.4.3   Net.Data

IBM Net.Data[38] is an application that allows Web developers to easily build dynamic Internet applications using "Web Macros." They offer the simplicity of HTML with the power of dynamic SQL. Net.Data provides database connectivity to a variety of data sources, including information stored in relational databases on a variety of platforms. The most prevalent databases can be data sources for your Web application, such as DB2, Oracle, Sybase, DRDA-enabled data sources, ODBC data sources, as well as flat file and Web registry data.

Net.Data provides high-performance Web applications with robust application development function. Net.Data exploits Web server interfaces (APIs), providing higher performance than CGI applications. Net.Data supports client-side processing as well as server-side processing with languages such as Java, REXX, Perl, and C++. Net.Data provides conditional logic and a rich macro language.

With Net.Data, you get full support for Java, the standard for Web application development. You can use a Java applet to create a graphical chart, such as a pie chart, from the results of a Net.Data application. With Net.Data's support for JavaScript, you can validate data entered at the client's Web browser and call a Java application for additional logic. The solution offers a tight integration into databases and Web programming languages to create an interactive environment on the Web.

10.4.4   JavaServer Pages

JavaServer Pages (JSP) technology provides an easy and powerful way to build Web pages with dynamically generated content. It enables rapid development of Web-based applications that are server- and platform-independent.

Web site owners can use the tools and interfaces they already know to create dynamic Web pages. The application logic resides in server-based resources that the page accesses with HTML-like tags. By separating the page design from its content generation and supporting a reusable component-based design, JSP technology makes it faster and easier than ever to build dynamic and interactive Web-based applications.

JSP simplifies the generation of HTML pages. HTML-like tags and scriptlets written in Java encapsulate the logic that generates the content for the page. Standard HTML or XML commands handle formatting and design. By separating the page design from the application logic that generates the data, JSP technology-enabled pages make it easier for organizations to reuse and

---

[38]http://www.ibm.com/

share application logic through JavaBeans technology-based components or customized JSP specification-based tags.

The tight integration with the Java platform allows companies to leverage existing Java platform expertise and create highly scalable enterprise applications. This makes it also platform-independent and server-independent.

10.5 Web Application Servers

10.5.1 Reasons for Web Application Servers

Traditional Web services are based on a two-tier architecture, meaning that two components are used to create the service, such as a Web server and a database server. To make it easier for developers to isolate the business logic, Web applications servers are put in place, thus effectively creating a three-tier architecture that has become the standard for network-based applications. In this schema, the browser is not considered part of the architecture.

Web application servers not only isolate the business logic from the program logic, but offer additional features that are hard to implement in a two-tier architecture. Functions such as transaction management, clustering, and load balancing are easily added to the three-tier architecture.

Another advantage of a three-tier architecture is that it becomes easier to access data and services that reside on legacy systems without direct connection to the Internet. The Web application server creates a unified messaging system, which allows each application that is connected to exchange information. Therefore, the support code, which is used to connect the different applications, is encapsulated in a standard component, which is typically CORBA or COM. COM can be deployed only on PC platforms, while CORBA can be used on any platform. The CORBA model is more open because of the platforms and languages supported. Today, most Web application servers allow developers to write this support code in Java, JavaScript, Perl or C++. The development language is important because it may determine the application server platform and it affects the choice for the appropriate distributed computing model. Unfortunately, they are not easily interchangable.

Through Web application servers, it is possible to consolidate functionality from all sorts of applications into a new user interface, the World Wide Web. Web application servers eliminate the need for the clients to connect directly all core subsystems in the backend, as this requires extra knowledge for each application for every single employee. Through a Web application server, the backend applications can be accessed through a browser.

By installing a Web application server and integrating the business-critical enterprise applications, it is possible to move away from mainframes, if desired, without putting the service at risk. A transition has become much easier, as the underlying messaging infrastructure does not change. The first key architectural mechanism you will need to define in your new integrated system is data synchronization. All of your enterprise applications need to share the same data among themselves.

This leads to the databases, the backbone of any enterprise application. Most database vendors offer Web application servers, which tightly integrate applications into their databases. Although this will guarantee the highest possible speed for applications that require that particular database, it may lock your company into using a certain database vendor, as these solutions use proprietary protocols to access data. This can become a problem if you later decide to integrate applications that use another database system or choose to expand beyond database-centric applications.

10.5.2   Web Application Products

If we look at the market of Web application products, we can see that there is a wide selection of available software. At the time of writing, more than 100 professional products were released and available on the market. Unlike most software decisions, where it is important to base your decision on the business idea, the decision of which Web application server to use depends mainly on the installed base of software and hardware. An up-to-date list of Web application server products and background information can be found on the Application Server Zone Web site.[39] The following is a selection of Web application servers.

Avenida Web Server

Avenida Web Server[40] provides a powerful server-side Java technology (called servlet), which is not only easy to use, but also has a very small footprint. It is built on top of Sun's Java servlet architecture and provides the same API and the same plug-in capability into the Web server. The standard edition comes with four servlets with the following functionality: file, proxy, redirect, and virtual hosting.

The file servlet provides the functionality of a standard Web server and is able to serve Web content to the browser client. The second servlet, called proxy servlet, allows the server to act as a proxy server for access from the intranet to the Internet. It also has a tunneling feature built in, allowing the transport of HTTP requests transparently and securely to any given machine without revealing the source and the destination. The redirect servlet enables the server to redirect the HTTP request to another server with the same functionality. Through this functionality, it is possible to introduce load-balancing, which distributes the incoming requests over several servers. The virtual hosting functionality allows one Web server to appear as a number of distinct hosts with their own domain names and IP addresses. This is a feature that ISPs often use for their clients.

---

[39] http://www.appserver-zone.com/
[40] http://www.avenida.co.uk/

Although this product is a very good Web server, especially for ISPs, it lacks the features required to build up an integrated virtual enterprise. Through the servlet architecture, it is possible to build connections to the legacy applications in the background, but it requires quite a bit of additional work, as no standard adaptors are provided.

Bea WebLogic Enterprise

The WebLogic Enterprise product,[41] developed by BEA Systems,[42] provides an extensible application server that provides functionality for assembling, deploying, and managing distributed Java applications. WebLogic is able to connect business components written in Java with heterogeneous databases, network information resources, such as online Web services, and other business components, which do not necessarily need to be written in Java.

WebLogic is built on top of the BEA engine, which is a set of core technologies that BEA has acquired, integrated, and enhanced to create a high performing, easy-to-use, and comprehensive object management and transaction processing technology. Via the BEA engine, WebLogic is also able to leverage BEA's family of connectivity products that facilitate connection to other applications and data in the enterprise.

Through the Transaction Processing Framework, companies are able to focus on their business logic instead of on infrastructure issues. It simplifies the programming of CORBA objects and automates many tasks that were previously the responsibility of the developer, such as management of transactions and object states.

To achieve high-availability WebLogic has implemented a function to define replicated server processes that can take over the load when a server process fails. These server processes can be on the same or on a different machine.

WebLogic also tries to restart server processes that abnormally fail. The operator can specify the number of times it tries.

The application components can be managed through a graphical Java console that ensures security, scalability, performance, and transaction integrity. BEA WebLogic Enterprise is one of the best Web application servers on the market, as it offers a complete framework for the integration and provides many modules for standard applications to make the integration stable and simple.

Cold Fusion

Cold Fusion[43] by Allaire is one of the most popular products on the market. It allows the user to build and deliver scalable applications that integrate browser, server, and database technologies. A special developer product called

---

[41]http://www.weblogic.com/
[42]http://www.beasys.com/
[43]http://www.allaire.com/

Cold Fusion Studio enables developers to program through a visual interface and includes database and debugging tools in an integrated development environment (IDE). The prebuilt building blocks in Cold Fusion Studio enable an open integration with email and directory services, and database and enterprise systems.

The speed of Cold Fusion is achieved through its just-in-time compilation and its caching features, which allow developers to write portable Java code. Pages that are often requested can be served from the cache to reduce the load on the server. Quality of service is a stronghold of the Cold Fusion system, as it natively supports multiserver clusters with built-in load-balancing features and a failover system, which passes on requests to another server when either a system is overloaded or fails. This makes the system ideal for high-volume and transaction-intensive applications.

Through open database connectivity (ODBC) and native database drivers, Cold Fusion is able to connect to most database systems, and through CORBA and COM, it is very easily extensible. To round out the picture of an excellent development and deployment platform, it has built-in security features that complement the security strategy of a company that wants to provide applications on the Internet that were available previously only in-house or via phone.

Enterprise Application Server

The Enterprise Application Server by Sybase[44] is a scalable enterprise integration platform. It consists of a component transaction server, the Jaguar CTS, and a dynamic Web server, the PowerDynamo.

The platform provides a single point of integration for heterogeneous back-office systems and helps customers to extend their businesses on to the Web. PowerDynamo allows developers to create dynamic content for browsers and for automated transactions in a B2B scenario. The system provides broad support for Internet standards, such as HTML, Java, C++, JavaBeans, ActiveX, and CORBA. The business logic can be stored in multiple component standards to ensure the availability to any type of client.

eXcelon

The application server eXcelon by Object Design[45] offers high performance and high availability. It is a highly scalable data server that caches and serves all information to enterprise applications and Web servers, using the new standard for data interchange XML.

The software provides adaptors for all major database systems, application servers, and client software, and is easily extensible through the use of XML. eXcelon can be used as an application cache for existing data sources, meaning

---

[44]http://www.sybase.com/
[45]http://www.objectdesign.com/

that it can relay database information to the Web, for example. This reduces the number of interfaces to one, making it easy for customers to access multiple data sources, and provides a security layer, as the database servers are not exposed to the Internet.

The eXcelon server can also be used to create a complete data management system for new XML-based applications. In this case, eXcelon automatically stores, caches, and delivers XML data across the middle tier of multitier applications. Through the use of XML, eXcelon provides a very good architecture and is well-prepared for the future. What is missing is the preintegration with standard business software to make it the preferred solution for large companies. Smaller companies that do not have much standard software installed will find eXcelon a very attractive offering.

Inprise Application Server

The application server by Inprise[46] has been designed to allow for rapid application development (RAD) of platform-independent applications, built on open industry standards such as Java, C++, HTML, and CORBA. Using these open standards, it is easy to build an integrated end-to-end solution, bringing your enterprise applications to the Internet. The development, integration, deployment, and management of the whole architecture can be done through the Inprise application server.

This new integrated enterprise platform allows support for multiple clients, the middle-tier business logic, and backend enterprise database management systems through a single interface. Access to legacy systems is added easily through a standard API.

The solution includes the Java Web Server by Sun, but supports all other standard Web servers as well. To complete the picture of the application server, Inprise has added the Integrated Transaction Service (ITS) by VisiBroker that provides a flexible distributed and object-based transaction service that is fully compliant with the Java Transaction Service (JTS) standard. Also included is AppCenter, which is a distributed applications-level management tool.

Lotus Domino Application Server

The Lotus Domino Application Server[47] is an open and secure platform used for developing and deploying Web applications in a collaborative environment. The server allows dynamic business processes to be integrated with enterprise application systems.

It provides an integration with enterprise systems by leveraging current information assets with built-in connection services for live access to relational

---

[46]http://www.inprise.com/
[47]http://www.lotus.com/

databases, transaction systems, and ERP applications. The solution is optimized for collaboration by providing comprehensive application services like workflow and messaging. The simplified deployment and maintenance allows the use of integrated development tools. Standards support and server-to-server replication simplify the rollout, maintenance, and rollback of enterprise applications. The billing services allow companies to track, report, and analyze system usage for billing, charge-back, and capacity planning purposes.

Netscape Application Server

The Netscape Application Server[48] is an Internet application server used to develop, deploy, and manage enterprise-class business applications. The Application Server product line includes the Netscape Application Builder, for development of Java and C/C++ applications, and Netscape Extension Builder, for development of server extensions that enable connectivity to enterprise applications and legacy systems.

It provides the infrastructure for transactional, business-critical applications through prebuilt system and application services. Netscape's solution includes optimized end-to-end performance features, such as connection caching and pooling, results caching—which stores often-used database results on the Web server—streaming, multithreading, and multiprocessing.

Scalability and high availability are services already built into the system. One very interesting feature is the Client-Independent Programming Model (CIPM), which reduces development time required to support multiple client types such as HTML clients, Java, and C/C++ clients.

SilverStream

SilverStream[49] is an enterprise application server that allows corporations to build and deploy complex Web applications (mainly HTML and Java) on which they can run their online businesses. It is designed and optimized for intranets, extranets, and the Internet. The solution delivers both client-side and server-side Java and client-side HTML.

SilverStream provides the services required to deliver complex Web applications. It connects to multiple data sources, including relational databases such as Oracle and Informix; host applications such as CICS and MQ Series; ERP systems, such as SAP and PeopleSoft; and other data sources, such as Lotus Notes document management systems.

SilverStream is a solution that provides support for large-scale applications that can be deployed to tens of thousands or even millions of users, with a scalable, reliable, secure and manageable platform. SilverStream enables companies to develop complex applications through an easy-to-use set of commands. The business logic is encapsulated in middle-tier objects that are handled in a

---

[48]http://www.netscape.com/
[49]http://www.silverstream.com/

distributed way. Using SilverStream applications, developers can create and connect to these objects using COM, EJB, and CORBA, making it a very comprehensive solution.

WebObjects

Apple's WebObjects[50] is an application server environment suitable for large-scale projects. It supports visual development of user interfaces and the direct connection to existing business applications and data resources. It comes with a palette of prebuilt, reusable components and provides a seamless integration with all kinds of enterprise information systems. WebObjects handles application server requirements, including load balancing, state management, HTML generation, and Java client interoperability. WebObjects is available on all major operating systems and works across applications, business systems, and existing business logic.

WebObjects provides a rich set of development tools, solid performance and scalability, and a good set of enterprise data connectors. By design, this solution requires more lines of code to achieve similar results as other packages, but third-party add-ons can reduce the development time to match the times of its competitors.

WebSphere Application Server

The WebSphere Application Server[51] by IBM combines a runtime environment for Java servlets with connectors to common database formats. It uses enterprise middleware, object request brokers (ORBs), and runs on most Web servers.

Three different editions of the WebSphere Application Server are available that use the same basic set of technologies, but offer different functionalities, depending on the requirements of the customer. The Standard edition, which is the basic package, combines the control and portability of server-side business applications with the performance and manageability of Java technologies to offer a comprehensive Java-based Web application platform. It enables powerful interactions with enterprise databases and transaction systems.

The Advanced edition introduces server capabilities for applications built to Sun's Enterprise JavaBean specifications. Deploying and managing JavaBean components provides a stronger CORBA implementation that maps to portable Java technologies. The Enterprise edition is IBM's flagship and offers a robust solution to growing e-business applications. It combines IBM's transactional application environment, TXSeries, with the full distributed object along with the business process integration capabilities of Component Broker.

---

[50]http://www.apple.com/webobjects/
[51]http://www.ibm.com/

Zope

Zope[52] is an open source application server and portal toolkit used for building high-performance, dynamic Web sites. It allows companies to easily develop dynamic Web applications. Zope is completely managed through the Web. Zope's framework provides a secure architecture that includes access control, the undo feature, and private versions (which are versions that are used internally). Zope is based on Python and offers support for CORBA, COM, XML, and leading databases. More detailed information on Zope can be found in Chapter 15.

10.6 The Extensible Markup Language

10.6.1 Common Problems of the Web

In order to move on to do *real* e-business on the Web, it is necessary to understand why this is not possible using current technologies. This especially refers to the HTML standard that hinders the development of new applications on the Internet, as it was not designed to do anything but present documents in a Web browser. E-business has requirements other than displaying documents. Just to name a few requirements, documents need to be displayed, processed, rearranged, stored, forwarded, exchanged, encrypted, and signed. Using HTML, it is difficult to express the hierarchical relationship of data values (known from database records and object hierarchies). HTML reflects structure and presentation, but conveys nothing about the meaning of the marked-up document.

The most commonly used version of HTML, 3.2, provides many ways of displaying content using Java applets, CGI scripts, JavaScript, and plug-ins. But none of these technologies enables you to do anything useful to process the data without introducing an additional layer with middleware solutions. Many problems could be resolved by introducing new HTML tags into the standard, but there are several obstacles.

The biggest problem is that the HTML standard is moving very slowly. For years HTML 3.2 has been the basis for the standard, although 4.0 was recommended in December 1997. Unfortunately, HTML 3.2 introduced many tags that have been introduced by the browser manufacturers and have become standard (mixing structure and layout, as discussed previously). Remember all the sites containing "best viewed with browser X"? Although 3.2 is a standard, very few sites adhere to it.

In order to enforce the use of HTML 4.0, it is necessary to create new browser versions that everybody needs to download and install. The DTD in all browsers is hard-coded, meaning that the introduction of a new standard won't change the behavior of the browser (other than not understanding new structures and elements).

---

[52]http://www.zope.org/

In order to resolve this, two things need to happen. The DTD needs to become more flexible to support the needs of e-businesses, and the browsers need to be flexible in such a way that the DTD needs to become part of the document and not be part of the browser anymore. Every document will be able to include its own DTD, which formulates the elements in XML used in the document itself.

Today, most applications are tied to the browsers, but many corporations have applications installed that are not able to display the information in HTML, yet need to exchange the information over the Internet. Many customers also want Internet applications to have the look and feel of their applications, and this can be achieved by launching external applications from within the browser. The best solution is to have Web applications that understand the Internet protocols, such as HTTP and TCP/IP, that do not require a Web browser. This allows existing applications to be extended to talk to other resources, such as databases and applications over the Internet. While the Internet protocols help to establish the communication, XML enables the exchange of data between applications that usually have totally different data formats.

In order to create intelligence on the Web, search engines need to understand the content of Web pages, but so far they are not able to. In searching for a certain piece of information, it is highly likely that you get one good result and at least 100 incorrect ones (some search engines are even worse by a factor of 10 to 100). The problem is that search engines normally only index a set of words, document titles, URLs, and metatags, but do not know anything about the structure of the document. A search engine cannot decide if a document is a news article or a thesis, for example. There is no way to markup the significant portions of a document to focus on the important parts and ignore the noise (such as copyright statements, navigational bars, design elements). This would allow a much finer granularity of control over search engines. By adding additional attributes to Web elements, this can be achieved. Let's say you are researching information on a singer who also acts and writes (such as Cher or Madonna). It would be good to have a classification of the function of the person on the Web site. If tags like <singer>, <actor>, <author> could be used in HTML, the number of direct hits would be much higher. With XML, these tags can be easily defined and used.

Another common problem on the Web is the collection of related pages and saving them to your hard disk or printing them out. The current method is to save or print them on a page-by-page basis, which can become really annoying if there are more than 10 pages. In many cases it is also difficult to identify the other parts of a particular collection, as the document that links all resources together is not known to the person who looks at a particular page (often a link is not provided, as the owner of the link is aware that the document is part of a larger collection). In order to express the interrelationship, special metadata should be attached to the documents, making it easier to find the other documents related to the topic of a particular search. Although adding metadata is possible in HTML, the information is restricted to the whole document, not only to parts of it, which may be of interest for a particular search. Using XML, it is possible to create metadata for all text elements.

The current linking provided by the Web is limiting, as it works only one-way. If you link to another document, the other document does not automatically link back to you. Links with multiple targets are also not possible, and there is no way to automatically update the set of links you provide. Imagine you link to a document on another Web server and the document moves from one location to another one; then you need to alter the link on your Web site manually. But other linking mechanisms that provide these features have been around for some time, such as the Hypermedia/Time-based Structuring Language (HyTime) and the Text Encoding Initiative (TEI).

10.6.2   Moving to XML

XML is an ISO-compliant subset of SGML. XML is extensible because it is a metalanguage, which enables someone to write a DTD like HTML 4.0 and define the rules of the language so the document can be interpreted by the document receiver. XML is like an alphabet for building new languages and gives companies a way to start with a common foundation and a common alphabet. Every industry is able to define the specific terms they use.

A DTD is essentially a context-free grammar like the Extended Backus Naur Form (EBNF), often used to describe computer languages. A DTD provides the rules that define the elements and the structure of the language. A regular markup language defines a way to describe information in a certain class of documents (e.g., HTML). XML, on the other hand, lets you define your own customized markup languages for any type of document classes.

An example could be an address markup language (AML), which I made up, where one defines an element <address> that consists of <name>, <street>, <town>, <zip>, and <country>. The element <name> consists of the elements <first> and <last>. Rules can indicate if an element is optional, repeatable, or has a default value. The advantage is that any application that is able to understand XML will understand a document using the address markup language, as the application is able to learn the rules by loading the DTD.

Table 10.7 displays a document in the AML notation. Unlike HTML, the layout is not defined, nor is the sequence of the text on the screen. The AML could be used to create a database of addresses. Searching for last names is very easy, as the information is correctly tagged. Presenting all sets of addresses beginning with the letter "A" in the last name, then presenting this piece of information in a browser, for example, is very easy. Other than that, the layout can be specified for different needs. In Germany, the postal code is normally displayed in front of the city, while in the UK the postal code is at the end. In HTML you have to create separate pages for the output of the data, while our AML is flexible and can detect in which country the address is and print it out in the required form. The layout is not defined in XML, but in a presentational language, such as XSL or CSS. Using JavaScript and the DOM, it is easy to extract information.

The semantics and the structure of the data is preserved. The data is organized as in an object-oriented database. XML is about creating, sharing, and processing information. The purpose of XML is to provide an easy-to-use subset of SGML that allows for custom tags to define, transmit, and interpret data structures between organizations. These tags look like HTML tags, but describe the meaning of the information in a format that is predictable and precisely defined.

The introduction of XML will change the way we experience the Web today and remove two constraints that are holding back Web development: its dependence on a single, inflexible document type (i.e., HTML) and the complexity of the full SGML, whose syntax is very powerful but extremely complex. XML reduces the complexity of SGML and enables the development of user-defined document types on the Web. Some say that XML provides 80 percent of the benefits of SGML with only 20 percent of the effort.

The following document is written in AML, which we have defined in XML.

```
<?xml version="1.0"?>
<address>
<name>
<first>Daniel</first>
<last>Amor</last>
</name>
<street>Kangaroo Lane 101</street>
<town>Yuppie Town</town>
<zip>12345</zip>
<country>Petrolistan</country>
</address>
</xml>
```

Table 10.7. Address Markup Language (AML)

HTML has reached its limit of usefulness, as it contains a predefined set of tags for describing documents. This has been extended by many manufacturers with new tags that mainly support the layout and not the structure. In order to represent a document in HTML, it is necessary to conform to the existing tags. XML, on the other hand, allows organizations to create their own customized markup languages (and tags) for exchanging information in their domain (e.g., linguistics, knitting, or dog-feeding).

Although it will continue to play an important role for the content it currently represents, many new applications require a more robust and flexible infrastructure. E-business on the Internet will only work if the information that is transported is not restricted to one make or model or manufacturer. Information can also not cede control of its data format to private hands. In order to save time and effort, the information needs to be provided in a form that allows it to be reused in many different ways.

The presentation of XML documents can be implemented by using the document style and semantics specification language (DSSSL), CSS specification, or XSL.

10.6.3 Business Requirements

In order to survive, most companies need to improve the quality of the products, accelerate time-to-market, and reduce costs at the same time. The Internet has increased the need for achieving these goals in short time.

This goal is true not only for the products, but also for the information associated with them. If information is the product, then this subsection is also intended for the information product. To resolve the goal, it is necessary to resolve the challenge of delivering information on paper, CD-ROM, and on the Internet quickly, efficiently, and accurately.

This requires processes to be streamlined when the information is created. Redundant work needs to be eliminated. This is easily achieved by basing the information publishing process on the XML standard. This is especially important for companies who distribute information of great value, such as medical, legal, and business organizations.

As XML is format-independent, it is possible to easily generate multiple outputs. A document written in XML is able to generate documents for formats such as CD-ROM distribution, Internet delivery, help systems, and printed documentation. If information is collected from multiple sources, the integration becomes much easier than if only one format is used.

Another important factor is that computer data gets lost due to the fast change in formats. Much computer data has become unreadable because nobody is able to decrypt the information anymore. Many organizations need to store information for several years or decades, and require a format that remains readable in the future. With XML, it is possible to create documents that are still useful, although the hardware and software that was used to create the data may no longer be available.

Information by itself is not always useful. By providing reviews of it, it is easier to classify the content and create intelligence. A review could be simply the reading, rated on a scale from 1 to 10 on how appropriate it was in

Information needs to adhere to the following requirements in order to reduce costs and enhance productivity:

- **Conditional information**—A means is required that is able to identify conditional information.

- **Durable documents**—The information needs to be stored in a software- and hardware-independent way.

- **Integrated reviews**—Reviews of information enhance the quality by adding metainformation.

- **Multiple destinations**—A single document needs to be distributed in various forms, such as print, CD-ROM, and Web pages.

- **Multiple sources**—Different documents need to be integrated efficiently into a single document.

Table 10.8. Business Requirements

a particular situation to a questionnaire that needs to be completed. The reviews become part of the information and enhance the value of the information. Therefore, means of storing and processing reviews are necessary.

In many documents, information varies due to external factors. These external factors change the content, and a system is required to present the resulting information correctly. In a simple case, a product consists of several components and the document sums up the production cost. As the cost for the components may vary, the document should always show the actual production cost. XML provides a means to identify information that is variable and to control the presentation of the information based on external conditions.

10.6.4 Reformulating HTML in XML

XML is on the verge of replacing HTML in the browser world. HTML won't vanish, but will become just another one of the many possibilities of XML documents. This will make the Web even more dynamic and will simplify business over the Internet.

In May 1998, the W3C held a workshop on the future of HTML and discussed ideas for the next generation of HTML.[53] The result was that the next

---

[53]http://www.w3.org/MarkUp/Activity.html

generation of HTML will be reformulated in XML. Under the name of XHTML (extensible hypertext markup language) it will include a core tag set that will be used to markup headings, paragraphs, lists, hypertext links, images, and other basic document idioms.

All other important tags defined in HTML will be grouped in a separate tags set, such as tag sets for forms, tables, graphics, and multimedia. These tag sets will all adopt the XML syntax and will be able to be combined as needed. This means that the development of new tables functionalities can be conducted at a different speed from the development for graphics, without interference. Today, all parts of the DTD need to be updated in order to support a new version of HTML. In the future, it will be much easier, as only partial updates of the feature set of HTML will be necessary.

XML has many advantages over HTML. This table presents some of the reasons why your company should switch from HTML-based documents to XML-based documents.

- **Browser presentation**—XML can provide more and better facilities for browser presentation and performance through the use of style sheets.

- **Information accessibility**—Information is more accessible and reusable due to the flexibility of XML.

- **Richer content**—Through the use of new markup elements, it is possible to create richer content that is easier to use.

- **SGML compatibility**—As XML files are compatible with the SGML standard, they can also be used outside the Web in an SGML environment.

- **Tailored document types**—Document providers and authors are able to create their own document types using XML and are not restricted to the set of markup elements in HTML. It is possible to invent new markup elements.

Table 10.9. Advantages of XML over HTML

With the introduction of XHTML, style sheets will become very important, as XHTML has no control over the layout. Style sheets will take on the role of transforming markup for the purpose of displaying documents on different kinds of devices. With the imminent introduction of pervasive computing, people will want to access the Web not only from their computer, but also from mobile phones, palmtops, and other network-enabled devices.

In order to make Web pages accessible to these types of information appliances, tools will help to provide the correct display on every device. Therefore, conformance profiles have been introduced, which specify, among other things, exactly which HTML tags a given device has to support. The idea is that two different devices will present things in the same way if they belong to the same conformance profile and the document is within that profile.

Conformance profiles should greatly simplify matters when it comes to tuning markup to match the needs of the different information appliances. If the set of HTML features supported by a given class of devices can be precisely anticipated, then the markup can be transformed in a simple and reliable fashion. The transformation can take place either on the Web site, at a proxy server, or in the browser itself, depending on where the information about the device is specified.

10.6.5   Location of XML Documents

XML can be processed either in the browser (or any other client application) or on a Web server (or any other type of server). Depending on the location of the XML document, it will be processed differently and have different requirements.

Server-side Processing

Processing XML documents on a server will occur for one of two reasons: for exchanging data between servers automatically without user interaction or for wrapping database data to create custom content (for a Web browser that is not capable of displaying XML, for example).

If sharing data between organizations, it is necessary to agree on the tags and their meaning. Unlike EDI, where the agreement needs to be sent to a third party for evaluation, XML is more direct by allowing two parties to agree on a DTD used for exchanging data. With XML, it is very easy to send EDI messages over the Internet, so many people are working on XML/EDI bridges.[54] The Open Applications Group[55] is working on a set of XML DTDs for many kinds of businesses. Although these general DTDs may not suit your requirements, they help to set up fast business relationships on the Internet.

Sharing data is one of the applications that can be done automatically. Using XML, it is possible to use the basic processing tools for any type of data and applications that are not dependent on the format and syntax used.

Syndication is one of the applications that can be easily implemented in

---

[54]http://www.xmledi.com/
[55]http://www.openapplications.org/

XML. An information provider can easily integrate its service into many different sites with different layouts. The information provider can also provide only parts of the information to portal sites.

Creating dynamic content on a Web server is also facilitated through the use of XML. The content can be stored in XML documents without the layout. Content contributors can write their content in specialized applications that suit their needs and create XML documents as output. These documents are then stored automatically in a database and can be accessed instantly over the Internet.

Client-side Processing

A disadvantage of server-side XML processing could be that the data is processed and presented in a form that may not be viewable for a certain type of client. Think about a browser that is not able to display a certain type of tag or a client application that is not able to display the information provided by the server. In order to overcome these problems, it is possible to transmit the "raw" XML document to the client and let the client decide what to do with it and how to display it.

All browser manufacturers are busily working on their next releases that will include support for displaying XML documents. This means that they are able to display XML documents without having a server to transform the document to HTML first. Through the use of the DOM, a standard for accessing and manipulating XML data, Web site authors are able to alter the content within a page through JavaScript.

Using XML, it is also possible to transform XML to HTML in the browser. This allows a complete address book to be downloaded and a scripting search functionality to be used for displaying only the results you need. This will create a more individualized browsing experience, which has a slightly increased download time. Then, some applications can be executed without any interaction with the server.

10.6.6   XML Applications

Although XML is only slowly finding its way into Internet applications, many standards have already been created, which simplifies the processing of documents.

XSL

Similar to CSS, XSL separates the content from representation. It specifies the formatting characteristics of XML documents on the Web, while CSS specifies the formatting characteristics of HTML documents.

While CSS has its own proprietary syntax, XSL itself has been written in XML and can be extended through JavaScript. The formatting model is the same as in CSS and the highly complex Document Style Semantics and Specification Language (DSSSL).

Although it is possible to use CSS for formatting HTML tags, it is not necessary, as all HTML tags have a predefined representation in a Web browser. XML tags are highly dynamic and none of them have a predefined representation in a Web browser. A designer may create the tag <box>, which is perfectly valid in XML, if defined in a DTD, but no browser will know how to format this tag. XSL is able to add the missing style information to the XML tag.

Although CSS can also format XML documents, it can only be used for rather simple documents. But XML has been invented to create highly structured and data-rich documents. Unlike CSS, XSL can also transform XML documents, moving an existing document in a form to another document in another form. XSL is able to dynamically render a page when elements need to be rearranged, while CSS can represent the data only in the form in which it was originally placed in the file. XSL can be used, for example, to rearrange Web content for printing to fit better on a printed page, without the need of downloading another version of the same document.

Although XSL is extensible through JavaScript, many developers feel that its features can be replaced by JavaScript and the DOM.

SMIL

Based on XML, the synchronized multimedia integration language (SMIL, pronounced "smile") has been created by the W3C[56] and is a powerful way to synchronize any type of media (e.g., audio, video, text, and graphics) and build time-based, streaming multimedia presentations without having to learn a complex programming language.

Until now, it was necessary to use either programming languages such as Java to implement complex TV-like content or multimedia applications such as MacroMedia's Director.[57] Using simple instructions that are similar to HTML, you can build complex animations. The major advantage of this approach is that by using this interpreted language, the time needed to download multimedia content decreases dramatically.

The major difference between SMIL and Director is that there is not one large file that needs to be downloaded. Instead, images, sounds, and animations are downloaded one after the other in the order of appearance in the presentation. If components are used in several multimedia presentations the browser may have some already in the cache, reducing the download time even further. The customer is able to see the beginning of the multimedia much earlier and is able to decide if it's worth waiting for the rest of it.

Just as with HTML pages, replacing components is easy and does not require you to rebuild the complete page. With SMIL, you can replace compo-

---

[56]http://www.w3.org/AudioVideo/

[57]http://www.macromedia.com/

nents and use the presentation in an instant, without interrupting the service for your customers. The authoring process can be simplified by using SMIL.

SMIL is an application of XML and therefore supports hyperlinks in order to offer interactivity. SMIL was recommended by the W3C in June 1998, but so far only Real Network's G2 Player supports the SMIL standard. As soon as Web browsers fully support XML, they will also support SMIL. In Figure 10.4 you can see how Radio Deejay[58] is using SMIL on its Web site.

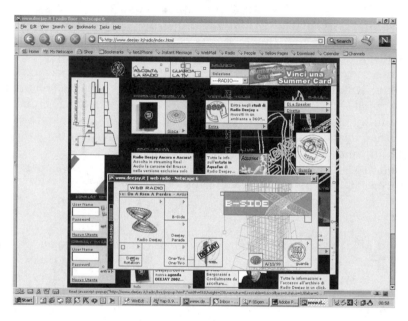

Figure 10.4. SMIL on Radio Deejay's home page.

SMIL was developed to complement other Web technologies, such as DHTML and DOM. Although Microsoft initially supported the SMIL initiative, the company now contends the technology is no longer compatible with its media player. Perhaps because they developed their media player at the same time, most other technology companies are jumping onto the SMIL bandwagon.

SMIL is not meant to be a replacement for existing multimedia technologies. It is possible to join the media formats and create an even richer experience.

RDF

Another very interesting application is the Resource Description Framework (RDF),[59] which has been developed by the W3C. RDF adds metadata to Inter-

---

[58]http://www.deejay.it/

[59]http://www.w3.org/RDF/

net resources, whereby a resource can be any object on the Web, such as a Web page, image, or sound. The metadata can be used to find a resource by adding a detailed description and keywords to the metadata, to rate the content, and to digitally sign an object on the Internet. Metadata is information about information and is an established standard for HTML pages using the tag <meta>.

The problem with the metadata of HTML pages is that computers are not able to understand the information. If the description of two Web pages is similar and points to the same type of information, such as "Germany is a country in Europe" and "Germany is a European country," while a human understands that these two statements mean the same thing, a computer will not be able to detect this without extensive programming. RDF associates unambiguous methods of expressing these statements so that a machine can understand that they have the same meaning.

Although RDF is able to improve search results on the Web, it is not restricted to this application. It is able to describe individual elements and the relationships between them.

Therefore, the W3C has developed a data model and a syntax for the RDF. The difference between RDF and similar frameworks is that RDF has been developed especially for the Web. The syntax for RDF is based on a special data model that defines the way properties are described. It represents the properties of a resource and the values of the properties.

Although RDF has been developed independently of XML, it can be easily represented in the extensible markup language. Therefore, the names of the properties and the values are not predefined, but can be chosen by those responsible for the Internet object. The creator of an RDF record can choose which particular properties or sets of properties will be used. In order to ensure the uniqueness of every RDF record, it uses the namespace mechanism, which is also used in XML and the Internet.

RDF is already used on the Internet. Netscape uses RDF to index site content in order to allow users to find information more quickly. The feature "What's Related" in Netscape Communicator 4.5 (and above) uses RDF to display related sites within the browser. Millions of users worldwide are using this feature and it is so far the most popular XML application.

10.6.7   Other Applications

XML applications are developed not only by the W3C, but also by companies and other organizations. The W3C is offering a standard set of applications, but every company is free to develop new and innovative applications based on XML, which can be for private, internal use only or can be made public for external review and use. For example, engineers at NASA[60] plan to use XML to develop an instrument control language for infrared devices on satellites and space telescopes. The XML syntax will be used to describe classes of infrared

---

[60]http://www.nasa.gov/

instruments, control procedures, communications protocols, and user documentation. Computers will parse the tagged data and generate instrument control code, most likely in Java.

Siemens[61] is using a system that allows employees to submit their timecards and lets managers approve them online. Each time card submission and approval is tied to basic human resource (HR) data such as name, serial number, and employee type. The timecard validation depends on pay code rules and frequency tables. Managers have the ability to temporarily delegate approval responsibilities, and the entire system interfaces to the corporate-wide directory service database as well as to the payroll system.

In order to achieve this goal, the data between the different systems needs to be interchanged. Therefore, a data format is required that can be shared among the applications. XML serves as the data interchange format in a time and attendance system and enables the integrators to reuse interface code, extend and modify data structures to accommodate personalization and internationalization, and design the system without worrying about limitations imposed by data sources. Data fields can be added without disrupting the existing structure and applications. Global development and the different holiday schedules of each country can be easily implemented with XML. The developer can use the same pay-period DTD, but just drop in a new holiday attribute. XML makes the localization of an application easy, maximizing code and data model reuse. Many other companies have started to use XML to integrate their existing applications and exchange data between different platforms and database systems.

10.6.8 Business via XML

XML has become the industry-neutral standard for information exchange. XML is used throughout the industry in a similar paradigm as EDI to exchange information in a very structured and predefined way. The difference between EDI and XML is that EDI had a limited set of structures that were accepted, and a new information structure needed months or even years to go through all instances to become a new industry standard. XML allows anyone to create new data structures on the fly. While this is great for communication between two parties, it poses a problem for industry-wide exchange of information. If every company develops its own XML standards, this could lead to incompatibilities and additional overhead for converting the data. The problem is less the different order of information and more that some companies may omit data or add information that other companies will not be able to process.

To automate the value chain and the intercompany business processes, it is necessary to define XML data structures that contain all information for a certain industry with the option of omitting or adding information for the exchange of data. Many fear that the independent software vendors will drive

---

[61]http://www.siemens.com/

incompatible versions of XML that best fit their own product strategies.

XML has been integrated by PeopleSoft, Oracle, and Baan into their enterprise resource planning (ERP) systems. SAP is integrating XML into its Business Application Programming Interfaces (BAPI), which give developers access to the internal workings of the company's R/3 software. If the manufacturers of ERP software agree on a common XML format, developers will gain a standardized, vendor-neutral way to access human resources, financial, and manufacturing data stored in these systems. But if the software manufacturers are not able to find a common standard, XML will not resolve the problem of proprietary APIs, which made life difficult in the past.

Today vertical XML vocabularies have already been implemented, which enable single industries to exchange information. So far, these vocabularies have been introduced for the financial sector, the content management industry, air traffic control, and the footwear business. Although this helps the single industry, it can create a problem in such a way that the number of industry-specific dialects of XML may get out of control unless cross-industry standards are implemented within the business software products.

XML proponents fear that the major software makers will use their financial clout to hijack the consensus-building process, leading to proprietary and incompatible versions of XML schemas that favor a particular vendor's software and architecture. In order to make XML a success, all companies need to agree on standards.

There should not be an XML schema for Hewlett-Packard and one for IBM, but instead, one for the whole industry, which can also be used by other industries to order computers, for example. Otherwise, the advantages of introducing XML cannot be exploited. Having several XML flavors accepted may still be valuable, but it would also be limited and would not achieve the actual goal of reducing costs and increasing automation.

While the independent software manufacturers need to adopt a generic XML standard, at the same time, each industry needs to develop an XML schema. For example, it is necessary to define data structures for types of computers, reseller locations, configurator restriction, and pricing models. These XML schemas are developed by standards bodies, such as the W3C, Commerce.Net,[62] RosettaNet,[63] and the Organization for the Advancement of Structured Information Standards (Oasis).[64] They are defining links within and between industries in a vendor-neutral way. E-business, supply chains, and other areas have already been addressed.

---

[62]http://www.commerce.net/
[63]http://www.rosetta.net/
[64]http://www.oasis-open.org/

10.6.9   Standard XML Schemas

The problem is that all the standards bodies are developing different standards for the same areas. For some time, it looked like the usual competitors would start a new standards battle over XML schemas just as we have seen battles over the right way to interpret HTML or the split in the industry over how Java should evolve.

Two portals have been set up that represent the two industry camps that want XML to follow their ways. The first is XML.org,[65] which has been developed by Oasis and is backed by software makers such as IBM, Sun, Novell, and Oracle. The portal has been established since 1998.

On the other side of the fence, Microsoft launched its BizTalk[66] initiative in May 1999, which has been established as an XML design clearinghouse, developer resource, and repository for XML schemas. To make BizTalk a success, Microsoft is backed up by ERP software manufacturers such as SAP, e-commerce software and service providers such as Ariba,[67] and partners in the industry such as Boeing.[68]

The XML portals provide a form for XML schemas that have been designed for specific industries, such as the financial sector, health care, and insurance companies. Microsoft's BizTalk portal has raised suspicion among competitors, which fear that Microsoft wants to take over the XML software application industry by defining its own standards without the consensus of the rest of the industry. Parts of the industry fear that this initiative could splinter the XML market.

Fortunately, Microsoft reconsidered its position regarding XML and joined Oasis in June 1999 to reduce the fears of the market. Companies have been stepping back from implementing XML, as they feared a standards war on XML schemas. Microsoft's decision to back Oasis has eased these fears and made it possible to develop a common framework for XML applications on the Internet.

10.7   Plug-ins

10.7.1   Advantages of Plug-ins

Plug-ins are add-in programs for Web browsers that are able to interact with the browser, Web pages, resources on the Internet, and local resources. Nowadays, most browsers support plug-ins. Plug-ins are normally used to add support for new file formats or to add interactivity. The reason plug-ins had become so popular (especially in the early years) is that they provide an easy way to extend the functionality of the Web browser without the need of downloading

---

[65]http://www.xml.org/

[66]http://www.biztalk.org/

[67]http://www.ariba.com/

[68]http://www.boeing.com/

a new browser. Now that browsers have more and more features already built in, the importance of the plug-ins is slowly vanishing, especially in the event of XML becoming the new basis for documents on the Internet. It will still take some years before browsers won't require any plug-ins. The trend is to move away from plug-ins and offer Java or Active X solutions instead.

Plug-ins are native applications, meaning that they are bound to a certain processor and operating system. This poses a huge restriction on their use on the Internet, as a plug-in needs to be rewritten for every computer platform. Only very few companies do (Adobe, for example, has ported its Acrobat plug-in onto 14 platforms), and it requires the user to install something onto the computer, which may be beyond the capabilities of some. Security is also a concern for plug-ins. As it has access to all your resources, a plug-in could easily format your hard disk or corrupt your data.

But there are some advantages that make plug-ins the best solution. Plug-ins are able to easily access any system resource, such as a printer, and allow high-quality printing of images and documents. Plug-ins are also much faster than a Java program could be.

10.7.2 Adobe Acrobat Reader

Besides HTML, the Acrobat portable document format (PDF)[69] is the most widely used format on the Internet. For textual documents that need layout and high-quality printing, many people use the PDF format, as the Acrobat plug-in is available for all major platforms.

Its integration with Web browsers displays PDF documents seamlessly and the high-quality printing is supported on standard and postscript printers. Most Web sites use PDF to distribute online brochures and technical documentation via the Internet. Motorola,[70] for example, uses the PDF format to give customers access to technical specifications of its computer chips. PDF offers some advantages over other text formats, such as Word's file format. It can be read on any platform and provides a high-quality output across all platforms and printers.

The Adobe Acrobat Distiller product (which is *not* available for free) is able to convert HTML pages and Postscript documents directly into PDF documents. A special printer driver can convert all types of documents to PDF on the fly while printing, making it easy for anyone to create PDF documents.

10.7.3 Apple Quicktime

QuickTime[71] was invented a few years back by Apple Computer and has become the most popular environment for multimedia CD-ROM and Internet

---

[69]http://www.adobe.com/acrobat/

[70]http://www.motorola.com/

[71]http://www.apple.com/quicktime/

productions. QuickTime was designed to simplify the task of working with and integrating the widest possible range of digital media types, not just sound and video. The QuickTime Movie format is actually so popular and good that it has become the basis for the MPEG-4 standard.[72]

QuickTime is able to play many sounds and movie formats, and the plug-in is able to communicate with JavaScript and Java applications, integrating the supported formats even better into the Web pages. QuickTime is available for Windows and Macintosh platforms only. More in-depth information can be found in Chapter 13.

Today, most filmmakers use the Internet as a marketing medium. In 1999, the first *Star Wars* prequel appeared and was heavily promoted on the Web. Many people went to theaters to see the trailer and left before the main film started. At the same time, the trailer was put in QuickTime format onto the World Wide Web.[73] The QuickTime format guaranteed the makers of the film the maximum exposure on the Web and the possibility of instant viewing through streaming technologies. The customer was already able to view the trailer while it was being downloaded to the desktop. With other formats, customers would have had to wait for the complete transfer of the file before the first picture appeared.

10.7.4 Platinum Cosmoplayer

Platinum's Cosmoplayer[74] is able to display documents in the virtual reality markup language (VRML). VRML is an interactive format with its own scripting language. The interfaces to Java and JavaScript enable you to create 3D worlds and to make them interactive as well. Using the fourth dimension of time, it is possible to move things around and change them. Using one of the above-mentioned languages allows us to kick "live" virtual people in a 3D world or to create virtual representations of people who wander through the VRML scene.

Cosmoplayer has been released as open source, and binaries are available for Macintosh and Windows. It is expected that the source code will be ported to other platforms in the near future.

The CosmoPlayer is used by many companies to display their products in three dimensions on the screen, allowing customers to turn them around and look at the products from all sides. Besides this more traditional approach to three-dimensional viewing, Platinum[75] uses VRML to display business data in three dimensions. Some people think that 3D business data views are not very useful, but in some cases they may offer some new insights on how to develop a business, which can be used to make the correct business decision. A car

---

[72]http://www.mpeg.org/

[73]http://www.starwars.com/

[74]http://www.cosmoworld.com/

[75]http://www.platinum.com/

manufacturer could use it to show off the cars in production or a realtor could show off a great house for sale. A more detailed description on VRML can be found in Chapter 13.

10.7.5 Macromedia Shockwave

Shockwave[76] has become the standard plug-in for multimedia on the Internet. It is already installed with Netscape Communicator, so no additional download is required for Netscape users. The plug-in is able to play back interactive Web content, such as entertainment software, business presentations, games, and advertising.

The files for the Shockwave plug-in are built exclusively with Macromedia Director, which is an authoring tool for creating rich multimedia applications. Shockwave is widely used and accepted on the Internet.

Casio,[77] for example, uses Shockwave to inform its customers about its G-Shock watches[78] and enables customers to watch episodes of G-Gurl, a cartoon character. Shockwave enabled Casio to develop a very interactive and futuristic Web site that matches the image of the watch.

10.8 JavaScript

10.8.1 Introduction to JavaScript

The JavaScript programming language is a very compact, object-based, platform-independent, event-driven, interpreted scripting language that can be used to develop Internet applications that can reside on the server or on the client. Without any network communication, an HTML page with embedded JavaScript can interpret the entered text and alert the user with a message dialogue if the input is invalid (see Table 10.10 for a simple example). JavaScript can also be used to perform an action such as playing an audio file, executing an applet, or communicating with a plug-in. JavaScripts are constrained to the client and cannot communicate with a server to exchange data with the server.

JavaScript allows cross-platform scripting of events (e.g., key press or mouse click), objects (e.g., form elements or style sheets), and actions. JavaScript is also able to create interaction between HTML, plug-ins, and Java. Contrary to popular belief, JavaScript was never meant to be a scaled-down version of Java or a replacement for CGI scripts. JavaScript was developed by Netscape and not by Sun (who invented Java), but uses a similar name for marketing purposes. JavaScript was originally called "Mocha," then renamed "LiveScript," and finally became JavaScript, as it is referred to in most publications. The actual JavaScript interpreter in most browsers is based on the ECMAScript

---

[76]http://www.macromedia.com/shockwave/

[77]http://www.casio.com/

[78]http://www.g-shock.com/

JavaScript can be easily integrated into HTML documents. A simple example is the following program, which checks if the first name of the user has been entered.

```
<html>
<head><title>The checkName JavaScript Example
Homepage</title></head>
<script language="JavaScript">
<!--
function checkName()
{
if (document.addressform.firstname.value=="")
{alert("Please enter a first name!");}
}
//-->
</script>

<body>
Hello.  Please enter your first name and press ok.
<form name=addressform>
<input type=text name=firstname>
<input type=button name=ok value=ok
onClick=checkName();>
</form>
</body></html>
```

Table 10.10. Integrating JavaScript into HTML

standard, which is the standardized version of JavaScript, supported by the European ECMA organization.[79]

Through JavaScript, even less-experienced developers are able to direct responses from a variety of events, objects, and actions. It provides anyone who can compose HTML with the ability to change images and play different sounds in response to specified events, such as a users' mouse click or screen exit and entry. It enables Web developers to verify customers' input before it is sent to the server, reducing the load and the required connections over the network. JavaScript also runs happily on very old and slow computers, as opposed to Java applets that may be far too slow to be of use on any older computers.

---

[79]http://www.ecma.ch/

10.8.2   Understanding the Value of JavaScript

JavaScript has many advantages over traditional programming languages. It integrates perfectly with the Web browser. It is able to access all objects on a Web page and manipulate them. This allows interaction without connecting back to the server.

JavaScript is a fairly universal extension to HTML that can enhance the user experience through event handling and client-side execution, while extending a Web developer's control over the client's browser. JavaScript programs can be used for verifying input from the user before sending it off to the client. This reduces the load on the network and increases the response time to the customer. Incorrect input is detected immediately and the user has a chance to correct the input without having to load a new page or reload the current page.

JavaScript can also be used for creating dynamic content. Depending on the type of browser, the JavaScript is able to display information in another format. Based on the user input, the display on the page can be altered.

Depending on the type of network application and bandwidth, the combination of client-side applications and server-side applications needs to be evaluated. JavaScript is able to create and read cookies, making it possible to preserve the state. A cookie is a piece of information that is stored in the browser and can be retrieved by the server that placed the information there. This piece of information can be used to identify a user, for example. Using JavaScript, cookies, and HTML pages, it is possible to create complex applications without the need of a server application, making it possible to offer complex services without investing in expensive hardware.

Minivend,[80] for example, is a shopping solution that does not require any server software besides the Web server. All information about the ordered products and information about the customer are stored in a cookie on the browser, and only when the customer decides to buy some goods is the information transmitted to the Internet shop. This can be done by sending an email to the owner with the order.

Although this example would not work with larger shops, it enables anyone to start up a business. This is true not only in the online retail business, but virtually any application can be implemented in such a manner.

In many cases JavaScript can replace client-side Java. It is a lightweight solution that users will be willing to tolerate.

10.8.3   VisualBasic Script

In Addition to JavaScript, VisualBasic Script (VBScript) has established itself as a scripting language for Web browsers. VBScript was developed by Microsoft and is only supported by IE. It is a subset of the Microsoft Visual Basic lan-

---

[80]http://www.minivend.com/

guage and is implemented as a fast, portable, lightweight interpreter for use in World Wide Web browsers and other applications that use Microsoft ActiveX Controls, automation servers, and Java applets.

Like JavaScript, VBScript is a pure interpreter that processes source code embedded directly in the HTML. VBScript code, like JavaScript, does not produce standalone applets but is used to add intelligence and interactivity to HTML documents. The VBScript engine provides the core runtime functionality and includes a minimal set of basic objects. The majority of objects used are provided by Microsoft IE. In general, anything that is specific to the Internet is provided by IE, and anything that is generally useful is provided directly in VBScript. The Web author can insert additional objects through the <OBJECT> HTML tag.

The major advantage of VBScript is the tight integration into the Microsoft operating system, enabling it to create highly sophisticated Web applications. Users that already have knowledge of Visual Basic will be able to create VBScripts without any additional training. It is possible to debug VBScripts using the standard Microsoft debugger, making it easy to trace down bugs in the script. Its tight integration into the Microsoft operating system is also a major disadvantage of VBScript. It does not run on other operating systems or on other browsers, restricting it to people who use IE and Windows. This goes against the rules of the Web, where everything should be accessible to everyone.

10.8.4   JavaScript versus JScript

As you now know, JavaScript was developed by Netscape and has become since then the client-side scripting language of choice. As the early specifications were developed by Netscape only, Microsoft developed JScript, which is very similar to JavaScript and is supposed to be compatible with it. Nevertheless, there are quite a few differences that are of interest, as online businesses want their applications to be compatible with all browsers.

Some of the differences stem from bugs in the implementation while others stem from the actual implementation. In the early versions, where Netscape developed the standard by itself, the JavaScript implementation was always ahead of the JScript implementation. Netscape 2.0 had a comparable implementation to Internet Explorer 3.0, for example.

Microsoft's approach to client-side scripting offers the developer a choice between the C-style syntax of Netscape's JavaScript language and the VB-style that many Microsoft applications developers are already familiar with.

The differences between JavaScript and JScript are very subtle, but large enough to make code break in one or the other case. While JavaScript is not case-sensitive for standard function names, JScript is. The function *onClick* can be written in JavaScript in any combination of capital letters (such as *OnClIcK*), but in JScript it needs to be written exactly as *onClick*. Another problem is the object hierarchy. The object hierarchies are different, requiring that code be written twice to accommodate both versions. This makes it more difficult to access objects on the Web page, but with some work on top of your original script, you can make it work in both browsers.

10.8.5 JavaScript Problems in Browsers

While JavaScript is now supported by all major browser manufacturers and even by the smaller ones, a problem remains, as the implementation is differing from browser to browser. This leads to Web pages that are not displayed correctly in your Web browsers and to applications that are not properly executed on the Web because you are using the wrong browser. It was bad enough to have several HTML implementations, but with differing JavaScript implementations, the Web designers were even more restricted when creating new Web sites. Either they would support only one version of HTML or one version of JavaScript; then programming was easy, but they would get many complaints from their customers.

There is an online bank in Germany that uses JavaScript, but only the version that is in Netscape 4.04. If you try to use any other browser, you will be stopped, as they do not support it. You can imagine how frustrated customers will be if they are limited to the exact browser version. They are not even able to update the browser in order to fix some bugs, as the server won't let them in anymore.

The other approach to supporting all versions can mean that you restrict yourself to the minimum that is supported by all browsers (but makes your Web site appear very dull) or else you create multiple scripts for every browser. Although it means some additional work in programming and maintaining, the extra work is a must nowadays to keep customers content and to implement the desired functionality.

10.8.6 Introduction to ECMAScript

In order to resolve the problem with the varying JavaScript implementations, ECMAScript was developed as the new standard for browser scripting. Named after the ECMA organization, ECMAScript[81] is based on several scripting technologies: JavaScript, developed by Netscape Communications, and JScript, developed by Microsoft. In late 1996, the development of the ECMAScript standard started and the first edition was published in June 1997. The ECMA standard was then submitted to the ISO organization, where it was approved in April 1998 as ISO/IEC 16262.

Manipulating computational objects and performing computations are the basic features of ECMAScript, which is a truly object-oriented programming language (as opposed to JavaScript). ECMAScript is not computationally self-sufficient, as there are no ways to input external data or output results to

---

[81]http://www.ecma.ch/ecma/ecma262.pdf

anything other than the host environment (in most cases a Web browser).

ECMAScript has been designed to manipulate, customize, and automate the facilities of an existing system. These systems have a user interface and ECMAScript provides a mechanism for exposing the functionality to a programmatic control. The host environment provides a set of objects, which can be addressed by ECMAScript.

The initial idea of ECMAScript was to provide a mechanism to enrich Web pages in the browsers and to perform programming tasks on the Web server. But now, more and more hosts, such as the KDE[82] project, are beginning to use the ECMAScript engine. The ECMAScript implementation will ensure that future versions of browsers will all understand the same scripting language without any variants.

In addition to the core language, the standardization process includes regular expressions and continues to support richer control statements and better string handling. Exception handling and internationalization and the features we've discussed are expected to find their way into the standard in the third edition, which was released in late 1999.

ECMAScript is able to provide scripting capabilities for different host environments, such as Web browsers or Web servers, but is not restricted to these host environments. Some of the ideas in ECMAScript are similar to other programming languages, in particular Java.

Web browsers allow ECMAScript access to objects, such as windows, menus, pop-ups, dialog boxes, and cookies. In addition, the Web browser provides a means to attach code to events, such as change of images and mouse clicks.

The scripting code used within a Web browser scenario is added to the HTML code. Most of the scripting is reactive and waits for the interaction of the user; therefore, it does not require a main program running in the background all of the time. The Web server, on the other hand, provides a host environment, allowing ECMAScript to process objects before sending them on to the Web browser. The Web server therefore provides a mechanism to lock and share data.

By using browser-side and server-side scripting together, it is possible to distribute computation between the client and server while providing a customized user interface for a Web-based application. Each Web browser and server that supports ECMAScript supplies its own host environment, completing the ECMAScript execution environment.

10.8.7 The Future of JavaScript

While many people still do not know what features the latest release (version 1.4) of JavaScript/ECMAScript really has, the developers at Netscape and other companies are already planning the next major release of JavaScript (or ECMAScript), which will be version 2.0.

---

[82]http://www.kde.org/

JavaScript was never designed to be a general-purpose programming language and this won't change in version 2.0. Its strengths lie in the quick execution from source, making it a viable language for being distributed embedded in Web pages. It can be used for fast prototyping by design. Its interfaces to Java and other environments and its dynamics are also strengths of JavaScript. The next major release will try to improve on these strengths, while adding new features such as JavaScript components and libraries, which can help in developing new applications and writing true object-oriented programs.

Also planned for JavaScript 2.0 are more security and robustness for the programs. Enhanced interfaces to existing languages and environments are planned, and additional ones will be introduced. It is planned to improve JavaScript's reflection and dynamic capabilities and to enhance the performance and add support for threads, allowing a single program to run several tasks in parallel. In addition, the language will be simplified where possible, reducing the possibility of errors.

These are the goals for the next release of JavaScript/ECMAScript, but the results may vary, as there is still a lot of discussion going on. All new features that will be implemented need to keep the language compact and flexible. JavaScript 2.0 is expected to be released in late 2001, with the full release of Netscape 6.5, Mozilla 1.0, and Internet Explorer 6.0.

Chapter 11

SECURITY ON THE INTERNET

11.1 Creating a Security Strategy

11.1.1 Information Security

Communication via the Internet is, by default, open and uncontrolled. This conflicts with the needs of digital businesses, which require privacy, confidentiality and integrity in their transactions. The growing demand for electronic business raises the awareness of security issues and concerns about conducting secure business via the Internet. News reports on Internet security are hypercritical and increase the fear that business on the Internet is dangerous. Network-based fraud is growing dramatically and has made Internet security a business issue, not just a technical issue, to be resolved in the IT departments of companies considering an Internet business strategy. Not surprisingly, as society becomes more dependent on network systems, information security will become even more of an issue.

To make a system secure, security software must be installed on a computer system. But to make the whole company secure, corporate security strategies must be developed and implemented to prevent human error as a factor in system security.

A major problem on the Internet is identifying other users. In a real shop, a customer is identified by his or her appearance, but on the Internet everyone looks the same. Although it is possible to pretend to be someone else in real life, on the Internet it is even simpler. On the Internet, nobody can be sure about the identity of the other person without deploying additional technologies. Governments are starting to provide legal frameworks to punish attackers and allow the creation of standardized digital signatures and certificates so that legitimate transactions can continue with no threats to security.

To enforce information security, unauthorized access to electronic data on the business-critical systems of the company must be prevented. Unauthorized access can result in the disclosure of information and the alteration, substitution or destruction of content. Individuals and organizations that use computers can describe their needs for information security and trust in terms of five major requirements: confidentiality, integrity, availability, legitimate use and nonrepudiation. Confidentiality is necessary to control who gets to read the information and to conceal the information for all others. Integrity assures that information and programs are changed only in a specified and authorized manner, and that the data presented is genuine and was not altered or deleted during transit. Availability ensures that authorized users have continued access to information and resources. Legitimate use means that resources cannot be used by nonauthorized persons or in a nonauthorized way. Repudiation is defined as "the rejection or refusal of a duty, relation, right or privilege". If an electronic transaction is viewed as a binding contract between two parties, a repudiation of the transaction means that one of the parties refuse to honor their obligation to the other as dictated by the contract. Thus, nonrepudiation can be defined as the ability to deny a false rejection or refusal of an obligation with irrefutable evidence.

These five requirements may be weighted differently depending on the particular application. In some cases, integrity is more important than legitimate use; in other cases, confidentiality is very important, while the availability of the system is not a problem. A risk assessment must be performed to determine the appropriate mix of requirements. A number of different technologies can be used to ensure information security.

Confidentiality and integrity can be implemented through cryptography, which offers a high degree of security. Encrypting data ensures that the information is interpreted only by the intended recipient. Strong authentication ensures that nobody sees, copies, or deletes a certain piece of information. Using strong authentication and strong encryption, the only way to break in is to have the necessary certificate for authentication and the key for the encryption. An authorization system prevents access in a nonauthorized way by authenticated people. Nonrepudiation requires a trusted third party that time-stamps the outgoing and incoming communication and verifies the validity of a digital signature. By putting a time stamp on every piece of information that moves between two parties, it becomes easy to know whether a certain e-mail was sent on time.

Security of the encryption key, assignment of liability, responsibility for the key, and audit of access to the key are all ongoing issues that must be addressed. There is no doubt that a cryptographic system, correctly managed and implemented, offers the highest security level for electronic information available today. But don't forget the education and security process reengineering, because they will decide on the level of security of the whole company. Maintaining security is an ongoing process of staying well-informed.

11.1.2 Information Policy

To ensure the security of its business-critical information, every company needs to develop an information policy that guarantees that processes are in place when something happens. The process for developing an information policy is circular because to increase safety, you must always return to the starting point. New technologies and ideas require you to continually update your information policy. Just as your Web page needs continual updates, your security process also requires continual updates. It isn't realistic to expect everything to work perfectly on the first try, so remember that education and updates will help you maintain a secure environment.

The first step of your information policy is to make a list of all resources that need to be protected. This includes not only computers but also printers, routers, firewalls on the technical level, buildings that contain the hardware, and those where backups are stored. You should specify who gets physical access to the hardware and logical access to the software. Physical access is often neglected; the best firewall software is useless if a hacker can walk into the building and copy the required files onto a disk.

After all resources have been listed, it is necessary to catalog the threats for every resource. This will be time consuming, but it is also the basis for a secure system. After the catalog is complete, you should perform a risk analysis that shows the probability of each threat. Because it is not possible to investigate every threat, the company will need to evaluate which threats can be ignored for the time being and which need to be addressed immediately.

To prevent the most probable threats, it is necessary to implement cost-effective security systems. Cost is very important in the security industry. Security cannot be measured by return on investment. By implementing a secure system, you add overhead and cost, and that money is not recoverable. It is highly likely that without the security system, your company would lose lots of money and business. Still, convincing upper-level management to invest in securing information can be difficult.

The processes need constant surveillance and updates to thwart new threats or security holes. This will guarantee that your system is always impenetrable. This is surely money well spent!

11.1.3 Threats and Challenges on the Internet

The Internet offers a wide range of possible attacks. Although most of them are very unlikely to occur, it is necessary to evaluate how dangerous such an attack can be. These threats can be divided into four basic categories: loss of data integrity, loss of data privacy, loss of service, and loss of control. See Table 11.1 for an overview on what these threats can mean to the company.

Computer hackers try to achieve one or more of these goals at any given time. An online bank in Germany, for example, registers about 1,000 attacks per day. It is not known how many of these attacks are really serious, but it shows that people are trying.

Many hackers try to break into the systems by looking for holes in the software or the configuration. Online banks are often the target, because the

Most threats on the Internet can be classified in these categories:

- **Loss of data integrity**—Information is created, modified or deleted by an intruder.

- **Loss of data privacy**—Information is made available to unauthorized persons.

- **Loss of service**—A service breaks down due to outside actions.

- **Loss of control**—Services are used by authorized persons in an uncontrolled way.

Table 11.1. Threats on the Internet

prospect of transferring money is a strong motivation for many people. Some hackers may be interested in disrupting banking services, but most of them would like to transfer money into their own bank accounts. In some cases, hackers do not want to gain access to the system, but instead implement malicious procedures that cause a so-called *denial of service* (DoS) attack. The goal of the DoS attack is to deny access to authorized users. This is achieved by attacking network components such as routers or computer systems, or by attacking applications or the operating system. This creates an inoperable condition, which may create a financial loss for the organization.

Modern security technologies have made attacks more difficult, but every day new vulnerabilities in application software and operating systems are published that offer new possibilities for attacks. To keep a system secure, the operating system and the application software must be updated on a regular basis.

There are many ways to attack a system. One way is to monitor the communication between two partners. Communication on the Internet is insecure by default. Information is transmitted in clear text. By monitoring communication, it is possible to retrieve private information that may be transmitted, including passwords. If you contact your mail server, for example, the login and password are sent to the server, and anyone on the Internet can intercept the transmission.

If hackers intercept the communication, they can also change the information before it arrives at the destination; it can be replaced or even deleted. The recipient won't notice the changes, without special software in place.

Another potential threat to a company's security is the theft of its software and hardware. Software, such as databases, may contain data such as private information and passwords; hardware may enable the hacker to understand how the internal network is built, or may contain hard-coded information and reveal how that information may be used—for example, smart cards containing information for opening doors.

Sniffing is a possibility to intercept traffic on a network. Using special software installed on a server within the network, it is possible to log all texts that are sent between the computers on the network. This requires a hacker that can install software on an internal network. Instead of sniffing network communication, it is possible to intercept the electromagnetic output of devices such as monitors. Devices are available that copy the content on a computer screen to another one at a distance of several hundred meters.

A denial of service attack can be executed by attacking known vulnerabilities of the operating system or application software or by exhausting the service, overloading it with too many requests. The system is then so busy dealing with these "requests" that responses to legitimate requests slow down and eventually fail.

Another method used to access a system is the Trojan horse. Hidden in harmless-looking software, the Trojan horse rears its head when the software is launched. The Trojan horse works in the background and collects information about the system and its users. These pieces of information are then sent out to the hacker, who can use the information to enter the system or control it remotely.

Another common type of attack is masquerading (also known as spoofing). By pretending to be someone else, a hacker is able to enter a computer system. IP spoofing is the way most attacks are conducted. Many systems are restricted to a certain set of IP addresses; by pretending to be a certain IP address, a hacker can get automatic access to certain resources. Many systems ignore requests from unauthorized IP addresses. Through IP spoofing, it is possible to appear as an authorized IP address. Although this will not automatically grant access to a certain system, it offers an entry point and may disclose information that can be valuable. If a hacker is using IP spoofing, the hacked system will start to respond and offer more points of attack.

Another way to receive information and to create intelligence about a target system is to look through the garbage bin in front of the office for old media, such as floppy disks, that may contain information that may be helpful to break into the system. This type of attack requires the attacker to be near the prey, which also makes it easier to find the hacker after the attack. This is actually quite common, because most attacks come from inside the company.

Another way to gain access to passwords and the internal architecture about the security system is to bribe the security personnel at the target site. If enough money is offered, some employees may be willing to disclose secret material. Although it may not be possible for a company to control every employee, the security system should never depend on a single employee. This is also important if an employee becomes ill, has an accident or decides to leave the company. Never leave the security of your organization in the hands of a single employee.

Physical intrusion is a more traditional way of acquiring information or breaking down a service. The attacker enters the building, bypasses the access controls, and gets the information. The attacker must be physically near the target to start the attack. This often helps to reveal the identity of the attacker, making this type of attack rather infeasible.

In connection with IP spoofing, many attackers not only present false information to users, but also collect information such as passwords. Imagine that your favorite bookshop on the Internet gets IP spoofed. When you enter the URL of the bookshop, the domain name is resolved to the wrong IP address, therefore presenting the wrong home page. Damage can be done by insulting the customers with a special Web page, but more professional hackers copy the content of the Web page to the new location and collect information from the customers. After the user has chosen books, existing accounts are accessed by login and password. If this information falls into the hands of the wrong person, imagine what damage can be done and how much time may pass before someone notices.

The fake Web site would probably redirect the information to the real Web site in order to prevent customers and the company from noticing the attack in the middle. In some cases, hackers do not care about this. The bookshop and the buyers would notice within a few days, because the number of sales would drop to nearly zero and the customers would not receive their ordered goods.

Another method of letting hackers into the system is (unintentionally) offering them information about the internal network. Many companies use domain names for computers that are enumerated, such as "system01.domain.org," "system02.domain.org," "system03.domain.org." This may make it easier for the internal staff to count how many systems are available, but it also makes it much easier for hackers to guess what machines are available and what their names are. Most companies use "www.domain.org" as their external Web server domain name, but the "www" is often an alias for the real system name. I have already come across systems that were called "xxx07.domain.org" and were at the same time the external Web server. By typing "telnet xxx01.domain.org," it is rather easy to find out whether other systems are connected directly to the Internet and which operating system they run. Another weakness of some companies is to open the internal DNS structure to the outside world. If nobody is supposed to see the internal network, then nobody needs to know which machines perform what function (such as mail servers).

Ideally, only a single machine is accessible from the Internet—the Web server. All other systems should be invisible, because there is no need to have direct access to them.

11.1.4 Social Engineering

The most sophisticated and successful attacks are not of a technical nature, but of a social one. Instead of using technology to break into technology, social engineering tries to get people to comply with the requests of the attacker. I do not mean hackers control their minds. Social engineering is about exploiting people's habits, so that they do not notice when someone has stolen information from them.

Most social engineering attacks involve the attacker's pretending to be someone else. Of course, this involves more than just calling the IT department of a certain company and asking for the passwords of the firewall computers. And although it seems unbelievable, it can end with this simple phone call (but lots of preparation).

Social engineering concentrates on the weakest link in Internet security—human beings. The only way to make a system secure in the Internet world is to take it off the Internet and switch it off, but this is impractical, of course. But even this does not guarantee that your system is really secure. In April 1999, some hackers were able to steal information from a nuclear research institution in the U.S. Their source was an insider who copied the relevant information onto a floppy disk.

Many businesses already rely on the Internet, and in the future almost all companies will require an Internet business link in order to be successful; therefore, every company is a possible target. Social hacking makes it easy to get into any computer system, because it is independent of the attacking system platform, operating system, and application software.

Social hacking works normally in a very indirect way. Anyone loosely connected to the people involved in securing the company network is a potential security risk. A quick call to the receptionist yields the names of people in certain organizations, who in turn are able to deliver additional information. After several phone calls—which cannot be traced as easily as email—the attacker has gathered enough information about the company and its procedures that s/he can call the responsible person at the security department and pretend to be someone else.

The pieces of information gathered may seem useless to those who provided the bits, like stray pieces of a puzzle. Only as a whole can the information be used to attack the company. To get the required information, it is necessary to adapt the internal processes of the company. Organizational charts and the company phone book are also very helpful in aiding one to appear as an employee. Unneeded internal documents should always be shredded to prevent anyone from stealing them from the dumpster. The use of floppies should be completely eliminated. It is too easy to get information from a discarded floppy. Hard drives and floppies that are no longer used should be completely destroyed. Social engineering does not require in-depth computer knowledge and enables anyone to become a hacker.

Another method of acquiring information is asking for it directly. A hacker may simply call the firewall administrators and ask for the password. To succeed, the hacker needs some knowledge of the company structure. The attacker may have read that the CEO of the target company is visiting another country in a time zone that is at least eight hours different and is giving a presentation there. If the attackers get the timing right, they will call the headquarters half an hour before the speech starts, pretend to be the CEO and ask for the password, complaining that the laptop that contains the presentation is not working. Due to the time difference, it will most likely be after regular work hours and only a few staff will be available. The hacker will request the information immediately in order to give the presentation on time. To make the employee really believe that the caller is the CEO, the hacker will most likely reference the boss of the employee.

Think about it. Would you give the password to the person calling? During the day, you might do some background checks, but at night, when you may be a little bit sleepy, you would probably just hand out the password. Social engineering works through information gathering and social pressure. "Give me the information before you get fired," is a typical strategy.

Attackers will use strong arguments when completing the final step in the information attack, because weak arguments will most likely generate counterarguments. Most people will just obey strong arguments. This will work especially well if the person you are attacking is less competent than you are.

No matter how well a system is protected, as long as people are involved in administration of the system, the system can be attacked indirectly. To make social engineering less likely to occur, it is necessary to educate everyone in the company. Every employee needs to understand the importance of security and what methods are available to eliminate the barriers.

In many cases, it is easier to hack the people in front of the computer than the computer itself. It is also true that preventing people from cracking is also much easier than securing the computer. Constant education is necessary.

11.1.5 Security through Obscurity

Many companies have been very restrictive with regard to releasing information about their security systems. Many companies believe that nothing will happen if they avoid talking about security. Other companies try to hide on their Web server information destined only for a few. Some have their extranets open to everyone and expect that if they release the URL to only a limited group of people, no one will be able to find the information. And other companies think that their security technology is so complex that no one will be able to penetrate it.

These principles have proven faulty, and most security experts consider open discussion and education about security concepts and technologies necessary. Open discussion on security standards is the key to successful technologies, just as open discussion on Internet technology has made the Internet a success.

Security through obscurity is a common strategy for companies trying to avoid coping with security holes. By ignoring security issues, the software vendors hope that no one will document the holes and find ways to exploit them.

The best security products are discussed openly—even the source code for the product is available for everyone to review. Although this may seem strange at first, because attackers can find out how the algorithm works, it enables third parties to review the code and make it even more secure. This requires the security software vendor to develop algorithms that provide strong encryption without making it possible to invert the algorithm. One fine example is Pretty Good Privacy (PGP), where the processes and algorithms are well documented without weakening the security.

11.1.6   Resolving Security Issues

Now that you are too scared to use the Internet because of the security issues, let's examine solutions to the most common attacks. The first type of attack is the denial of service attack. Most DoS attacks indirectly attack the service the hacker wants to hit. In many cases, another more vulnerable, service running on the system is attacked. A Web server, for example, should block all non-HTTP traffic. By ignoring traffic on all other ports than port 80 for HTTP, the server is far less vulnerable to DoS attacks and does not spend processing power on illegitimate service requests from Web clients.

Masquerading is another common threat to many digital businesses. By appearing as a legitimate user, an imposter is able to access private information and execute commands that are not publicly accessible. The problem here, in most cases is that the authentication is based on a single factor, such as a password or PIN. These pieces of information can be easily copied. To make authentication secure, a two-factor authentication is required, which involves not only the "something you know" factor, but also the "something you have" factor. If a company was smart cards together with a PIN, it becomes difficult for attackers to masquerade themselves as someone else. Why? Because two independent security barriers must be compromised before a successful attack can be made.

Although two-factor client authentication is far more secure, attacker may still to break into the system. The physical token, such as a smart card, contains a "secret," which is used to allow the customer into the system. This "secret" is unlocked by the PIN. To gain access, attackers must know the secret, or have the smart card and the PIN to authenticate themselves.

To prevent attackers from gaining knowledge about the "secret," the physical token must be made tamper resistant. Instead of reading the secret, an application can submit the secret to the smart card, and the card will determine whether the information is correct or incorrect. To avoid packet sniffing, the "secret" should never leave the token, and it should never be able to read the "secret" to prevent brute force methods of decrypting it. To make a physical token unique, it is necessary to map the holder of the token to the identity of its owner. This prevents several people from sharing one identity. To prevent sniffing of the PIN number, the validation should be done on the card. This also requires that the keyboard used to enter the PIN be attached directly to the token to ensure the privacy of the information.

A regular audit of the log files of the firewall, the Web servers, and the applications servers helps to prevent false authentication. A log file should log all failed attempts and should trigger a process. For example, if the number of attempts is getting too high, the log file should add mechanisms to control the life cycle of client authentication.

Another type of attack is DNS spoofing, which allows hackers to redirect customers to another server and capture sensitive client information. This is very similar to IP spoofing, but instead of redirecting a user based on the IP address, the user enters the correct domain name and is redirected. To ensure that the server a customer is contacting is the right one, it is necessary to add server-side authentication. This is done through a digital certificate on the server, which is unique for every domain name and IP address.

To prevent the alteration of information in transit, message integrity needs to be enforced. This is done by adding a message hash to the mail. The encryption of messages helps to prevent eavesdropping on confidential conversations, which makes it impossible for a private message between two parties to be intercepted and read by intermediaries.

One of the major problems on the Internet is the repudiation of messages, meaning falsely denying that a message has been sent or received. This is often done in business transactions, such as online ordering and payment. People often order goods and then repudiate. Online businesses must be able to ensure that nonrepudiation of orders can be enforced. This is done through the use of digital certificates, which identify a customer in a secure way.

11.1.7 Authorization

To move a business from a private network to the Internet, some security issues need to be resolved. First, a determination must be made as to who has access to which business applications and company-sensitive information. Many businesses have no clear policy on who has access and why, which makes it difficult after a breach in security to determine who leaked certain information. This authorization list should also include information on what each person is allowed to do with each of these business applications.

To enforce this authorization list, a company needs to develop and implement a consistent set of policies for all users of a particular system (e.g., employees, customers and partners) across multiple applications. A general authorization process needs to be implemented.

Authorization in general consists of a system architecture, which prevents unauthorized access to services and data by strictly enforcing rules on what a user is and is not allowed to do, based on his or her authenticated identity. The first step should be to move from a distributed administration of authorization to a centralized concept. Most applications have their own methods of implementing authorization. As more applications become available on the Internet, this distributed model creates additional security holes, because each application may have different bugs or holes that can be used to bypass the software. The costs for developing new software are also higher because new authorization modules must be incorporated. Centralizing administration and implementation lowers the costs for administration, implementation, and maintenance and allows a far more consistent view of security policies for security administrators.

A list should be maintained of each resource—such as a printer, file, database or application—and the users/groups who have access to that particular object. With the new concept of using a centralized directory for administration, each user or profile has a list of objects that he or she is allowed to access. The database contains information on who has access to which application, and the policies/rules for what users are allowed to do within each application.

11.2 Cryptographic Tools

11.2.1 Defining Cryptography

The prefix "crypto" comes from the Greek word "kryptó," meaning "hidden." *Cryptology*, from "kryptó" and "lógos," means "hidden word" and describes the fields of research in cryptography and cryptanalysis. The ancient Greeks used this discipline to hide information. Cryptography is the art of keeping information private in such a form that it is unreadable by another person without the right key. Cryptanalysis is the art of compromising algorithms developed in cryptography.

Encryption can be used for more than private communication. Encryption can transform data into a form that makes it almost impossible to read without the appropriate knowledge about the encryption schema. This knowledge is normally called a key. The key is used to allow controlled access to the information to selected people. The information can be passed to anyone, but only the people with the right key are able to see the information.

Cryptographic algorithms have been used throughout history mainly to keep communications private. During World War II, the first computers were built to decrypt messages sent by Germans over the radio. Nazi Germany was using the Enigma machine, a wooden box with dials and wheels, to send and receive encrypted messages. The box was so small that it could be used anywhere. U-boats, tanks and offices were equipped with the Enigma. The code changed on a daily basis so decryption using traditional methods was not possible. If a German officer was captured, his first directive would have been to destroy the Enigma because it was the most important device for the German military. British intelligence officers built a computer called Collosum, which could decrypt the information processed by the Enigma. Deciphering the Enigma codes helped to win the war.

After World War II, scientists turned away from cryptography and used computers for algorithm calculations. About 30 years ago, banks started to hook up networks of computers, because they connected all branches to a central mainframe. In order to secure electronic transfers, banks began using encryption algorithms like the Data Encryption Standard (DES), developed by IBM.

Encryption is often believed to be a component of security, but actually it is a mechanism used to achieve security.

11.2.2   Reasons for Encryption

In Chapter 4, we examined the legal issues of encryption technologies. Using encryption is important and will change the way businesses work. Strong encryption allows you to send confidential documents such as contracts or personal information by email. It also allows you to save confidential information on your mobile computer without fearing someone will steal it, making your data public knowledge. Without strong encryption, confidential information can be easily intercepted and possibly used against the owner of the information. Imagine a purchasing department of a company that wants to exchange information with its suppliers. The pricing sheets, product information, and contracts are specific to that purchasing department. Having this information available on the Internet to competitors could be problematic.

Businesses are exchanging more and more information over the Internet. In many cases, this information is of a financial nature, and in the wrong hands, it could possibly destroy the sender. To make electronic business feasible, information needs to be kept private. Without cryptography, privacy cannot be guaranteed.

The most important application that needs to be encrypted is email. Without cryptography, email would be the electronic equivalent of traditional postcards. Email does not have a physical form and can exist electronically in more than one place at one time. If you have encryption/decryption software installed, it will link to your mail program and encrypt/decrypt messages automatically without user interaction. All you have to do is indicate that you need a certain message encrypted. Encrypting email is like putting the email into an envelope, which is then put into a safe. Without the right key, no one can see the contents (although anyone could still take away the safe).

As computers and networks became a commodity for users, it became even more important to secure the information that was transmitted over the networks. After the computer world changed from mainframe systems to a server-client-based world, cryptography started to look like a fundamental business tool. The Internet, which is now the basis for most business transactions, is an insecure network; anyone can grab transmissions going from one place to the other. Because changing fundamental standards is a long and difficult process, security issues on the Internet are being resolved rather slowly.

Online banking and online payment are the most prominent Internet applications that rely on encryption. Internet customers are very sensitive about privacy issues. Therefore, all Web browsers support encryption of documents. There are some issues about browser encryption, because the standard key length is only 40 bits in the international version, which can be broken very easily. Additional encryption components are often necessary.

Access control can also be implemented through cryptography. Television subscription channels work this way. Because it is not possible to open or close channels to individual subscribers over a satellite, the information is encrypted and the key is distributed to the people who pay for it. This can be done either on a general basis or on a pay-per-view basis. Depending on the type of television channel, a key is valid for the whole day or the key changes for every program. In the latter case, the key for a certain program is distributed to the customers when they have paid for that particular program. The keys are stored in a receiver, which decodes the program. The receiver is connected to the television provider over a phone line, which is able to send the key or remove the key whenever necessary.

Business managers may believe that they do not need to consider cryptography, thinking it is just another new gadget for the technical people. It is crucial to realize that deciding whether or not to use encrypted communication has an enormous impact on the amount of business a company can expect to generate. With encrypted Web sites and email available, business managers are able to consider new business models that were not possible before.

11.2.3 Secret Key Cryptography

Secret key cryptography, also called symmetric cryptography, is the traditional form of cryptography. A single key is used for encryption and decryption. The two parties involved in the communication need to agree on the key before exchanging the information. The key should not be communicated over the same medium as the encrypted message. For example, if you send encrypted messages over the Internet, you should agree on the key over the phone.

The password (or key) is used to encrypt the outgoing messages, the so-called cipher-text is sent over the network, and the recipient decrypts incoming messages using the same key. Some of the algorithms are based on strong mathematical foundations. These systems cannot be cracked by another algorithm. The only way to crack them is to try out all possible keys. In January 1999, an encrypted message with 56 bits was cracked in 24 hours by the Electronic Frontier Foundation.[1] The time involved for cracking encrypted messages is dropping dramatically. Still, secret key cryptography has some ad-

---

[1]http://www.eff.org/

vantages over public key encryption. It is much faster and requires lower key length to get the same strength of encryption. The most common secret key techniques are stream ciphers and block ciphers.

Stream ciphers are known for their speed. The speed is achieved by operating on small units of the plain text. Normally, stream ciphers operate on the bit level. A so-called key stream, which consists of a sequence of bits, operates on the plain text using a bit-wise exclusive-OR operation. The encryption of a bit depends on the previous bits.

A block cipher, on the other hand, transforms a block of plain text with a predefined length (such as 64 bits) into a block of cipher text with the same length. The transformation is done by providing a secret key, which is used for the encryption. Decryption works the same way, by applying the same secret key to the cipher text.

Secret key cryptography is used in single user environments. If you want to encrypt your files on your hard disk, you would not use public key cryptography. Public key cryptography would be far too slow for this task. And storing public and private keys in a single environment does not give any advantages over having only one key. It would be useful only if you would keep the public and private key in separate locations, but you still need lots of processing power to encrypt and decrypt the hard disk.

11.2.4 Public Key Cryptography

Public key cryptography or asymmetric key cryptography has one major advantage over symmetric algorithms. It does not rely on a secure way to exchange the password. Symmetric key algorithms need the two parties to agree on a common key, which can be intercepted while transmitting the key information from one to the other. This would make encryption over the Internet useless, if the key is sent before the encrypted message. The key must be sent separately, although this prevents people or companies who do not know each other from doing business over the Internet.

In 1975, three researchers at MIT developed an algorithm to implement public key cryptography. Ron Rivest, Adi Shamir, and Leonard Adleman invented the RSA system,[2] which they named after themselves.

The RSA algorithm initially generates two distinct keys for every user. One of the keys is defined as the public key. The public key can be distributed freely to anyone via floppy disk, email, or hard copy. The public key cannot be used to decrypt any message; it can be used only to encrypt messages that can be sent to the owner of the public key. Only the person with the other key, called the private key, is able to decrypt messages that are encrypted with the public key.

In 1976, Whitfield Diffie and Martin Hellman, two professors at Stanford University, proposed a system that they called "public key encryption." Public key encryption uses two keys for every encryption and works well over insecure

---

[2]http://www.rsa.org/

networks. Every user generates a pair of keys. Each of the keys is a large integer, sometimes with more than five hundred digits. The two keys are related to each other in a way that, through special calculations, it is possible to encrypt a message using one of the keys and decrypt it with the other, but you cannot decrypt the message with the same key used to encrypt.

Of course, many mathematicians tried to find a way to break into the public key algorithm by doing some calculations, but so far nobody has found an algorithm that solves the mathematical problem. Decryption programs use brute force to break the key by trying out all combinations. Although not impossible, it is computationally infeasible, if the public key is long enough.

In most cases, RSA is not used to encrypt messages, because of the time-consuming computations it requires. For most messages it would not be infeasible, because it would take too long to encrypt and decrypt them. Instead, RSA is used to encrypt the symmetric key that encrypted the message. The SSL standard used to encrypt Web pages uses this feature. The URLs use https:// instead of http://. The key is generated on the Web browser and then sent to the Web server. Without public key cryptography, you would have to send the key over the Internet without protection.

To ensure that the key is transmitted securely, the Web server sends its public key to the Web browser. The browser decides on a symmetric key and encrypts the message with the public key of the Web server and sends it back. Only the Web server is able to decrypt the public key with its private key. The RSA key is used as an envelope for the symmetric key. Thereafter, the encryption is done by symmetric key, because it is much faster.

Through this system, it is possible to choose symmetric keys at random. If one is able to break into an encrypted message, it would not give any information about the keys used in the other messages.

If you choose to encrypt email, you can encrypt the symmetric key several times with different public keys. Each public key belongs to one of the recipients. So every recipient is able to decrypt the message. Every public key forms an envelope that contains the same key to decrypt the original message. This paradigm of secure messaging has been used in PGP and is used in a similar manner in SSL encryption on the Web.

11.2.5 Comparison of Secret and Public Key Cryptography

The most important advantage of public key over secret key cryptography is that the private keys are never sent out, making this type of cryptography more secure and convenient. In a secret key system, the keys must be transmitted, which poses a security risk. With secret keys, it is also difficult to implement an authentication mechanism. A digital signature using a public key infrastructure is very easy, but in a secret key infrastructure, secret information needs to be exchanged. To provide nonrepudiation, a third party is needed to verify the authenticity.

But there are also some disadvantages to public key encryption. Most secret key technologies are much faster than public key encryption algorithms. They are faster by at least a magnitude, which means that public key encryption is not appropriate for large files. To make a system secure and fast, both types of cryptography should be combined.

In mixed environments, messages will be encrypted with a secret key only, which reduces the load on the environment because the encryption and decryption algorithms work much faster. This ensures that security is enforced, but the environment is not out of business due to heavy load of the encryption algorithms.

In SSL encryption, which is used for the secure exchange of information over the Web, public key cryptography is used for exchanging the secret key. The Web server sends its public key to the Web browser. The browser creates a session key and encrypts the session key with the public key of the Web server. The session key is then transmitted back to the Web server, which decrypts the session key with its own secret key. This allows the session keys to be transmitted over an unsecured network. The session key is secure because it is valid only for that particular session and cannot be reused. After the session key has been transmitted, it is used for encrypting the connection, because it is fast! As long as computers are not at least 1,000 times faster than today, secret key algorithms will remain important.

11.2.6   Steganography

Messages that are encrypted using steganography look like harmless messages with attached images or sounds. A person who tries to intercept such a file receives only a message that appears to contain no secrets. Someone reading such an email, looking at such an image, or listening to such a sound would never detect any difference. In most cases, the hidden messages are also encrypted to make them even harder to detect. Only receivers who know that they will be receiving an encrypted message will be able to find it. Ideally, the receiver gets notified by the sender through another means, (by telephone, for example) about the hidden message.

Steganographic software tries to hide the information in the ordinary noise of digital systems of sounds and images. To remain undetectable, the hidden message must have the same statistics as the natural noise of computer images or digitized sounds. The problem is that encrypted messages usually look much more random than the ordinary "noise" they are trying to mimic. Computer-generated images are not a good place to hide information, because they are too regular. Scanned images offer enough places to hide information.

Some freely distributed software packages allow encryption via steganography. Unfortunately, the quality is not very high. If you analyze the data carefully, you will find the hidden message without much trouble. The emulation of natural noise often is not good enough.

The commercial steganographic software packages offer much better hiding options. Using this technique, it is possible to transmit data without anyone noticing it at all. In countries where encryption is not allowed, steganography is a way to avoid detection. Sending images over the Internet is nothing unusual, and checking them all for encrypted and hidden messages would be a very difficult, if not impossible, task.

11.3   Applications of Cryptology

11.3.1   Enforcing Privacy

Privacy is one of the major issues on the Internet. By default, the Internet is unsecured, allowing anyone to intercept messages going back and forth between two parties. To implement privacy, it is possible to encrypt the messages, making them unreadable to third parties. They are still able to intercept the messages; therefore, it is necessary to ensure that the keys are not transmitted in plain text over the Internet.

Privacy is an important issue not only on the Internet, but also on multiuser systems, such as servers where several people share one hard disk for private information. The files are protected by passwords, so it is necessary to ensure the security of these passwords. This can be done by storing the hash value of the password instead of the password. Decoding the password is possible, but hash values are irreversible. When a user enters a password, the hash value is calculated and compared to the hash value stored. This system makes it virtually impossible to steal data stored on that system without knowing the password.

Hashing is the transformation of a string of characters into a usually shorter fixed-length value or key that represents the original string. Hashing is used to index and retrieve items in a database because it is faster to find the item using the shorter hashed key than to find it using the original value. It is also used in many encryption algorithms.

In addition to faster data retrieval, hashing is also used to encrypt and decrypt digital signatures (used to authenticate message senders and receivers). The digital signature is transformed with the hash function, and then both the hash value (known as a message-digest) and the signature are sent in separate transmissions to the receiver. Using the same hash function as the sender, the receiver derives a message-digest from the signature and compares it with the message-digest it received separately. They should be the same.

11.3.2   Encrypting Email

The most commonly used application in cyberspace is email. It is simple to use and requires nothing special from your computer other than a connection to the Internet and a mail program. Email content is a plain text format that can be read by any computer system in the world. But the ease and friendliness of the application is also its problem. Any computer system in the world can intercept a message in transit and read the contents without any additional software. A simple text reader will do.

If you send email, the message is not being sent directly to the destination; instead, the mailer looks at the destination and then looks for some computers in between that can be used to relay the message. This significantly reduces the cost of transmitting the information, because every computer needs to transmit the information only to the next one. The path between source and destination is built up as the mail gets sent off. An email from Stuttgart, Germany, to Oxford, England, may even reach computers in between that are located in New York. Each of the computers in transit can easily check for certain senders and recipients and can save all the information in a file on the local hard disk.

Even if an attacker is not sitting at one of the computers in the path, there are ways to filter message streams and get the required information. The attacker would install a piece of software called a *sniffer* on the relaying computer. The sniffer then scans all email for certain keywords.

It takes only a few seconds to send an email to any destination in the world. No one would notice if someone picked up some information at a certain point; and no one would even notice that someone had altered information before sending it on, because there is no definite time limit for email delivery. Without nonrepudiation, email is insecure, and unfortunately in most cases this is the standard configuration, making the whole system insecure.

Unlike traditional mail (sometimes called snail mail), email does not have a physical envelope to hide the contents. And from a privacy perspective, email is even worse than postcards. Email on the Internet can be scanned for keywords easily and automatically.

There are several ways to encrypt email. PGP is the most secure system for email encryption on the market. If you use a version that was compiled by a trustworthy person and has proved to be secure, you are on the safe side. The encryption algorithm based on public key infrastructure is unbreakable. The source code has been open on the market for years and has resisted all attempts to break it. Others are able to decipher the message only if the recipient of the mail reveals the private key. PGP requires you to install a separate piece of software on your computer.

S/MIME (Secure Multipurpose Internet Mail Extension), on the other hand, is much easier to set up, because it is supported by both Netscape's Communicator and Microsoft's Internet Explorer natively. No extra software is required for using S/MIME. All you need is a digital certificate, which can be obtained from many sources, like TrustCenter[3] in Germany or GTE[4] in the U.S. S/MIME uses a method similar to PGP. It uses asymmetric encryption as

---

[3]http://www.trustcenter.de/
[4]http://www.gte.com/

an envelope to send a key to be used in the symmetric cipher that encrypts the message. S/MIME is far less secure than PGP because it uses a far lower bitrate for the key outside the United States. The source code was not made public until recently, when Netscape opened the Mozilla Web site and gave away the source code of its browser.

Another method of encrypting messages is the use of strong symmetric encryption algorithms that are not bound to the emailing software. Email is written with a text editor, encrypted with any strong encryption technology, and then sent off over the network. Blowfish, IDEA, and triple-DES are common choices. But the software to decrypt the files must be installed on all computers involved, and a channel must be established in order to exchange the keys securely. The procedure of installing, maintaining, and using this method is far too high to be of any value in a business environment, though it may be suitable for private use.

If you need to transmit information secretly in such a way that you send it to an account that can be read by more than one person, you can use programs like WinZip.[5] Almost everyone has the software, and it is very easy to use. The encryption technology used is quite good as well. The files are protected by passwords that can be cracked by brute force, but you can change the password each time data is transmitted, which requires the attacker to break in each time. The password can be easily transmitted via telephone.

11.3.3 Applying Encryption Technologies

If we look at encryption algorithms, we will find many different types and many different levels of security. Some, like ROT13, described in Chapter 4, are broken very easily, while others (like PGP[6]) cannot be broken by algorithm within a reasonable time frame (using a few thousand computers over a few thousand years is not really *reasonable*). You would need to have the password and the key to decrypt the information sent in PGP format.

This section tells you which encryption products suit which needs. Security and privacy are important issues for your company, so a tiny bug in the encryption software can create much larger problems than a bug in a word processor.

A bug in the encryption software (or hardware) may destroy your business, because your company secrets may become public. Most word processors offer the possibility to encrypt your documents, but these encryption algorithms are very weak and should never be relied on if you have confidential data on your laptop or intend to send it over an insecure network. They may be useful to keep colleagues from sniffing private data on a server, but they won't stop professional hackers. AccessData[7] has created a commercial software package that specializes in breaking the code of such programs. Its intended use is to

---

[5]http://www.winzip.com/

[6]http://www.pgp.com/

[7]http://www.accessdata.com/

Encryption technology can be divided into several encryption strengths, ranging from weak to unbreakable. If you want to check if your program uses strong encryption, check out the Web site http://www.password-crackers.com/ for an overview on programs that are not secure.

- **Weak**—Word-processing programs use very weak encryption, which can be broken with simple tools, so password-protected text are one of the least private kinds of transmissions.

- **Robust**—Using symmetric encryption technologies, one can create robust encryption, but the weakness lies in the transmission of the key, which cannot be sent over insecure networks.

- **Strong**—Using public key infrastructure, you can transmit the key over insecure networks.

- **Unbreakable**—One time pads are small systems that use a key that is as long as the message itself and can be decrypted only with the pad it has been encrypted on.

Table 11.2. Encryption Strengths

help someone access his files when he has forgotton his password, but it can be also used with the intention of breaking in.

Another popular method of securing documents is concealing them. Security through obscurity is a weak system. Actually, it is even worse than encrypting documents with a word processor. By placing documents in the wrong places, some people think that they can hide them from the rest, but unlike encrypted documents, all you have to do is look for that file. Using simple file search, you can retrieve most files. When weak encryption is used, you at least have the task of decrypting the information.

Because most people use a system or method to hide files and data (otherwise, you would not find your information anymore), it becomes easy to guess where other files may be hidden, after the first file has been found.

Strongly encrypted files can be put on public Web sites without having to fear that the information can be revealed, even though they may be stolen. Even the algorithms and the source code of the most popular encryption tech-

nologies are published, so that everybody is able to understand how the encryption works. The security comes from the algorithms, not from the system
used to implement the algorithms. If one keeps the key secret, no one else can
break the code.

11.3.4   Digital Signatures

Cryptography can be used for more than just encrypting and decrypting information. Authentication is one of the most important points in building a
trustworthy relationship. Often, authentication is achieved by signing a document. To make electronic documents legally usable, it is necessary to have a
mechanism that provides a means to authenticate the author of a document.
Just like in the real world.

To make the system feasible for digital business, only a small part of the
message is encrypted with the private key for signing. This part is called a
digital hash. The hash code is a function that reduces every possible message
to a fixed number of bits. No matter how long the file is, the hash will always be
the same length. The trick is that the hash code is different for every message.

The hash function is a one-way function. It is not possible to create a certain
hash code and find a message that would fit exactly that code. Think of a hash
code as a seal on an envelope. Sending along the hash code with an email will
guarantee that no one has altered the email while in transit, but it does not
allow you to prove who the sender was. Because the hash code uses a fixed
length, the time for encrypting the hash code is always the same.

Digital signatures use public key encryption technologies, such as RSA, but
not in the same way as standard encryption works. Instead of encrypting the
message with the public key of the recipient, the hash of the message is encrypted with the private key and then decrypted with the public key of the
sender, which is known to the recipient. Anyone would be able to decrypt the
hash of the message, because the public key is public (as the name implies) and
may be found on a public key directory server. But the fact that you are able
to decrypt the hash of the message with the public key of a certain person already proves that it does come from that person. Only the person who owns the
private key is able to create a message that can be decrypted using the public
key.

There are two reasons for using the hash code for the digital signature. One
is that it is takes too long to encrypt the whole message for signing purposes
only. The second reason is that not everyone wants to encrypt a signed message. In many cases, the message is meant to be public, but the author wants
to certify the authenticity of the message.

To encrypt the message safely and sign it at the same time, you would encrypt the mail with the private key to prove that the message is from you, and
then you would encrypt the message with the public key of the recipient to
make sure no one can view the contents.

A digital signature binds a document to the possessor of a particular key, but this is often not good enough, if the time when it was signed is unknown. A contract signed digitally is not valid if there is no date stamp or time stamp on it. An online purchase of an item at a reduced price, which is available only for a certain period of time, requires a time stamp to certify that the product was bought within the time frame.

A digital time stamp is required to validate the time of the signature. This is done by adding the exact time and date to a document by a third party and encrypting this information with the private key of the third party. This digital time stamp binds a document to its creation at a particular time. This system cannot be used on a worldwide basis because there is no legislation that guarantees a certain form of date stamp to be valid. As long as every country has a different legislation, it is not possible to ensure that a date stamp coming from one country will be considered legal in another country, even if it seems okay.

11.4   Privacy on the Internet

11.4.1   Footprints on the Net

Anonymity is switched off by default on the Internet. Every person online leaves clear footprints behind. This fact is not known to many users. Every Web site that is visited is able to create a personal profile of the user without special interaction with the customer. Marketing departments love the possibilities the Internet offers, allowing them to trace the preferences of customers with amazing accuracy.

Most companies today have privacy policies on their Web sites stating what they do with the information they receive from you, both voluntarily by filling in a form and involuntarily by clicking on a link. Online businesses are eager to collect information to sell products and services that suit the interests of the customers. Some of the online businesses that do not have privacy statements on their Web site collect information about customers and visitors, and offer the profiles to other organizations.

As you know, Internet browsing reveals lots about a customer. With every request for a new Web page, the name of the browser (e.g., Netscape Communicator 6.1), the operating system (e.g., MacOS 9.2), the preferred language (e.g., French), the Web site that has been last visited (e.g., http://www.yahoo.-com/) and the IP address (e.g., 194.100.177.194) and domain name (e.g., foo.bar.-org) of the computer are sent automatically to the server. JavaScript allows the server to get even more information about the computer of the client, such as screen resolution and number of colors.

These pieces of information are sent back automatically to the server, and most people have no way to stop it. It is possible to switch off JavaScript, but lots of information is still sent out. Although each single piece of information that is sent out does not harm your privacy, the sum of information may.

Knowing the language and the domain name may reveal the region in which you live, while the browser and the operating system may reveal what type of customer you are. All this information can be used to guide you more precisely through the online offerings, but they can also be used to guide you to reveal more information.

Cookies are a common tool to gather information about a customer. The cookie is a file that is saved on the customer's computer and contains site-specific information, which can be retrieved by the site owner. The cookie may contain information about the password required for a certain Web site, a user name, an email address, or purchasing information. The design of cookies prohibits the exposure of this information to other sites, but bad implementations in the past have shown that it is possible to extract information. Another problem is the general security issue of the operating system on the customer's computer, which enables hackers to steal the "cookies.txt" file without leaving a trace.

The popular ICQ program and its UNIX predecessor, Finger, allow you to retrieve personal information about the owner of a certain email address. These programs also let you see when the person has read email last and whether he or she is currently online. Although Finger has no centralized database, ICQ stores all user information in a central repository. To use ICQ, the user fills in a personal questionnaire, which is partly available to other visitors on the Internet.

Whenever customers use online services, they leave details about themselves, such as name, postal address, phone number, and email address. This information is used when the customers returns to the Web site. The problem is that the information must be stored in a secure place, so that no one else can see the information. Misconceptions and misconfigurations of the Web server have provided personal information to the public in the past, and more incidents can be expected in the future.

The customer base is becoming more and more the capital of the online business. Getting access to the customer base of a competitor will enable you to target new customers directly with special offers or direct mailing (or even spam). The customer base also helps you understand how the company works and which products are doing well.

Another means of gathering private information about a customer is to give away free software, free baseball caps, or free T-shirts in return for personal information. A special type of new free software shows advertising on the screen while the program is running. The advertising is personalized to the profile of the user. One such program is Copernic 99,[8] which allows the search of several Internet search engines at the same time. Before downloading the software, the customer fills in a questionnaire, which makes it easy to target advertising afterward.

---

[8]http://www.copernic.com/

Another way to collect information about a person is to look through news-groups. Persons who post messages into a certain newsgroup reveal their e-mail addresses and their personal preferences. People who read and post into a travel newsgroup for Spain are most likely interested in traveling into that region. Spammers use this information to target their messages in a very di-rect and efficient way.

Remember the Internet is, by default, an open system. It can trick you into revealing private information without being asked, if nothing is done about it. Although personalization of frequently visited Web sites is convenient, having your private information made public can have a negative impact.

Many privacy organizations are fighting to establish standards on the In-ternet, but because the Internet does not belong to anyone in particular, it is not possible to enforce standards. New standards evolve slowly and must offer advantages to the user in order to be accepted.

11.4.2   TRUSTe

The mission of TRUSTe,[9] an independent, nonprofit privacy organization, is to build customers' trust and confidence on the Internet. The goal is to acceler-ate growth of electronic business by certifying that a certain online business is trustworthy, and that business with that particular site is safe. TRUSTe is a renowned organization that gets support from established companies and indi-vidual experts, and was founded by the Electronic Frontier Foundation (EFF)[10] and the CommerceNet Consortium.[11]

TRUSTe issues a branded online seal, called a "trustmark," that bridges the gap between users' concerns over privacy and Web sites' desire for a standard on self-regulated information disclosure. The "trustmark" is awarded to Web sites that comply with the privacy principles established by TRUSTe and agree to allow third-party control over the enforcement of their privacy policy. A Web site with the "trustmark" symbol means that the business has provided a spe-cial facility where customers are able to check what information is gathered, how it is used, and whether it will be shared with others. Because this infor-mation provided in a standard way, customers are able to decide more easily if it is safe to give out additional information, such as postal address or credit card numbers.

The major advantage of TRUSTe over similar initiatives on the Internet is the fact that the Web site owners agree to let an independent third party check whether the privacy policy is enforced. These checks are performed pe-riodically, and if customers complain about the misuse of private information, additional checks are performed.

---

[9]http://www.truste.org/

[10]http://www.eff.org/

[11]http://www.commercenet.org/

11.4.3   The Platform for Privacy Preferences

One of the initiatives of the World Wide Web Consortium is the Platform for Privacy Preference Project (P3P).[12] The goal of the project is to create a standard for privacy practices. Although TRUSTe provides a very good service, the privacy information provided on each TRUSTe site is currently not machine-readable (machine-readable means that rules can be applied to the information). The wording of every site can be different, making it more complicated for the end user to understand what exactly will happen to the information provided. The P3P standard defines a way for Web sites to inform the users of the sites' practices on privacy, before the first page is presented. The information is presented in human- and machine-readable form, and should then be automatically compared to the privacy preferences of the browser. The information is presented in a textual description for the human readers.

Similar to the PICS (Platform for Internet Content Selection) standard,[13] the Web site owners must describe the policy. A Web service sends a machine-readable proposal in which the organization responsible for the service declares its identity and privacy practices. If a customer goes to a Web site that matches the preferences, the Web site is presented without delay. Otherwise, the customer is notified of the privacy practices of the site and must agree or disagree to these terms. While PICS provides a static description of the content of a Web page, P3P is able to respond to the wishes of the customer. If customers decide not to allow all information to be passed to the server, they have the option to choose which information is passed and then enter the site.

As a result of the "agreement," personal information may be transferred automatically from the customer to the site. This will help both the customer and the Internet business to speed up a possible transaction by providing basic data about the customer that would otherwise have to be entered repeatedly. In addition to the information to be transferred, a note explains how the data will be used.

Enforcing privacy standards on the Internet has become technically possible, but more important is informing the electronic customers of these issues. Most of them are unaware of privacy issues on the Internet. Although many people worry about security issues, they believe that their privacy is guaranteed. Especially in the U.S., companies freely trade information about people. People from Europe who visit these sites are not aware of this behavior because it is strictly forbidden in Europe.

11.4.4   Enforcing Anonymity on the Internet

Because your every move on the Internet can be traced by an application or server, it is rather easy to be identified. Enforcing anonymity is much more

---

[12] http://www.w3.org/P3P/

[13] http://www.w3.org/PICS/

difficult. Email leaves traces on the mail server and the transit server, making
it possible to trace the user of the email; Web servers log the IP address of the
Web client, making it also possible to identify the particular person. Although
an email address can be used by multiple persons, the identity of a person is
unique.

To resolve this problem, anonymous remailers have been set up on the Internet. These are free computer services that privatize email. A remailer lets
you send electronic mail to a newsgroup or to a person without letting the recipient know the name or email address of the sender. Messages sent to such a
service are processed in a way that all references to the original sender are removed. The header is completely stripped and replaced with the email address
of the remailer.

Any new user sending email through a remailer will get a new anonymous
email address, which makes it possible for others to respond to his or her email,
if desired. Replies to the remailer are then returned to the originator without
revealing the identity. To provide a successful remailing service, the system
must be easy to use and very secure. Neither a hacker nor a governmental
agency should be able to break into the system and get information on the
users. Additional security can be built in by randomly adding time before
sending the message. This means that you write a message and send it off.
The message will be stored on the system for a random amount of time and
will be then forwarded. This makes it impossible to trace the author of the
email, because she will have an alibi for the time of sending. This makes it
harder to connect mails that have been sent from your machine to mails that
arrive somewhere else. Remailers that encourage the use of encryption software are even more secure, because the administrator is not able to see which
messages are sent back and forth.

Anonymous remailers help to enforce privacy, but securing the remailer
will not resolve the problem because it is only part of the system. The mail
is sent from your computer to the remailer over a set of computers that can
all be used to intercept the message; therefore, it is important to encrypt the
message. Even if your mail is encrypted, it can create suspicion. Analyzing the
traffic going to and from the remailer can also be used to identify the origin of
anonymous messages.

The certainty of anonymity can be increased by sending a message not
through one remailer, but through a chain of remailers. Remember, not all
attacks are of a technical nature. Legal action can be used to reveal the author
of a mail. This has happened in the past and cannot be excluded in the future.
If a response is not required, it is possible to forward email without saving
the original in a log file. Legal action can require remailers to open their log
files. Using a chain of remailers would reduce the risk, because they may sit in
different countries, making it harder to get to the log files.

The Anonymizer[14] offers anonymous mail and Web browsing, which can freely previewed. Web browsing through the system is slower than direct surfing, but it ensures that no information about your system arrives at the target. All system information that your browser normally supplies is replaced with values provided by Anonymizer.com. This and similar services provide a valuable service for ensuring privacy on the Internet.

Another service specializing in email is the Nymserver,[15] which uses PGP and allows you to send email pseudonymously. To be secure that the services do what you expect them to do, visit your own Web pages so you can check the log files and send email to your own address to see whether you can trace it.

11.5   Fighting Virus and Hoax Virus Warnings

11.5.1   The False Authority Syndrome

Viruses are one of the most misunderstood concepts in the world of computers. Many people panic when they learn there is a virus on their system. They start to delete files, format the hard drive, yell at colleagues, or do other things that create more problems than the virus itself could create. The most important rule whenever you stumble upon a virus is to stay calm and take the time to get more information on the topic or, even better, follow the company rules for antivirus procedures, if any are available.

Be especially wary when people tell you about viruses. Rob Rosenberger, a security specialist, calls the problem "False Authority Syndrome" (FAS)[16] and the source "ultracrepidarians" (people who give opinions beyond their scope of knowledge). People suffering from FAS often assert conclusions from insufficient data and habitually label their assumptions as fact. FAS is common in the computer industry. For example, many people with PCs believe that they are able to do a good layout job for their documents just because they have the tools to do so (or at least they think Word is the ideal tool). But most of them have not received design training. In most cases, FAS does not do any harm (in our example, other people may just grumble about the design of the document), but with viruses, FAS does often create more harm than the actual virus does.

Researchers discovered a new virus in 1991. This virus supposedly would erase PC hard drives on March 6, the birthday of Michelangelo, the Italian Renaissance painter. Nothing spectacular happened until January 1992, when a computer manufacturer announced that it had shipped PCs with the virus by accident. The media got the press release and built up a story. "Hundreds of thousands of computers were already infected with the Michelangelo virus," they reported. Although many virus researchers dismissed the hysteria, the media would not stop the press coverage on Michelangelo. Self-made virus

---

[14]http://www.anonymizer.com/

[15]http://www.nymserver.com/

[16]http://kumite.com/myths/fas/

To save your company from losing information or being sued because of receiving or spreading a virus, you should consider the following preventive measures for your company:

- **Use anti-virus programs**—Install this software on each computer and at the firewall level. Provide updates on your intranet.

- **Have a backup strategy**—Develop a backup strategy for all important data. Be sure to perform virus checks on your backups as well.

- **Educate the employees**—Organize introductory courses and have a direct link from your intranet homepage to a frequently-asked-questions (FAQ) page.

Table 11.3. Developing a Strategy to Combat Viruses

experts gave interviews in the news and explained the danger of this particular virus.

On March 6, 1992, no more than 20,000 computers worldwide were infected and only a few were really unprepared. Five years later, in March 1997, antivirus experts could not confirm a single incident related to this particular virus.

Although this example is rather dated, it shows quite impressively how a virus, the media, and False Authority Syndrome can work together to create hysteria among computer users. One positive aspect has come from this event: All major computer manufacturers now include an antivirus program with their software. Laws have been established in various countries that forbid the distribution of viruses, and heavy penalties may result from such an activity.

As discussed in Chapter 4, in the section about dark sites, developing a strategy during an emergency won't help you. By then, it is too late. Be sure to develop the strategy to combat the virus in advance. In an emergency, everyone needs to know what to do. Most people know how to act when there is a fire, but how many know how to behave in case of an electronic emergency?

11.5.2   Understanding Viruses

Making the right decision in an electronic emergency requires that you understand what a virus is. In general, a virus is a computer program, just like any
other program you have used. A computer program is composed of a set of commands that are either interpreted at runtime by certain language interpreters
or are converted into machine-readable code that is executed at runtime. Computer programs by themselves are neither good nor bad; Netscape Communicator and Adobe PhotoShop, for example, have been programmed to be highly
useful applications. Viruses, on the other hand, have been programmed with
the intention to be harmful. The difference may not be clear to everyone. It is
not intention that counts, but the results.

Three fairly common types of viruses exist:

1. **Boot sector viruses**—A virus that resides in your boot sector is the
   worst thing that can happen. Each time you start up the computer, the
   virus is started as well. This could mean that the virus is infecting all
   files on your hard disk while booting. After you start up the computer,
   all files and removable media will become infected. In most cases, you
   must boot from another device, such as a CD-ROM, to bypass the virus
   startup. In the worst case, the virus recognizes antivirus programs and
   deletes them before you can run them.

2. **Executable viruses**—This type of virus works by infecting executable
   files such as programs and libraries. The executable virus must be loaded
   into the system to cause damage. After it has been started, it attaches
   itself to all executable files that are started. By attaching the malicious
   code, it is infecting the executable. Normally, it adds the virus code to
   the end of the program. After the infected file is executed, the virus executes and loads itself into the system, restarting the vicious circle. An
   executable virus remains in memory from the time it is executed until you
   turn off the computer, even if you exit the program it originally infected.
   If the virus infects Word, for example, every application that runs after
   Word will become infected as well, thus spreading the virus all over your
   system. Make sure that the antivirus program checks all applications
   before they are started by the system. The Michelangelo virus is such a
   virus. If your computer is infected with Michelangelo, just do not start
   your computer on March 6 and you will be safe.

3. **Macro viruses**—Macro languages are integrated languages within applications that allow the application to perform automated actions. Macro
   languages are often used to create automatic layouts or perform calculations based on the input of the user. They allow you to extend the functionality of the application. In most cases, macro programs are harmless
   and useful, but due to missing security restrictions in many applications,

it is also possible to create viruses. Macro viruses usually infect Microsoft Word and Excel, the most widespread applications of their genre. They use Visual Basic to run their macros, because VB is powerful and easy to learn. Unlike the executable virus, however, the macro virus does not exist in memory after you close the host application. Loading Word or Excel documents into other applications is harmless. Other programs do not understand the macros. So removing macro viruses is fairly easy. For example, if you load a Word document into Star Writer, you simply save it in Star Writer and the virus is gone because Star Writer is immune to Microsoft viruses.

Virus attacks are a major issue on Windows and Macintosh computers and common among users of standard applications with macro languages. But there hasn't been a virus around for years on UNIX platforms, primarily due to the security restrictions of UNIX systems and the open standards. Boot sector and executable viruses are less of a problem on intranets and company computers, but more of a problem with software pirates. Employees tend to get their software from a single source within the company, which makes it easy to verify that programs are virus-free.

"Catching" viruses from HTML pages is a popular myth. It is possible that certain Web pages will crash your browser, but this is normally because of badly written code within the browser and not because someone intentionally wanted to crash your computer.

Another important area of virus activities seems to be Java applets, but Java applet viruses do not exist. Through the sandbox principle of Java, it is not possible for Java applets to attack other resources. Java applets can't save to your hard disk, read from your hard disk, or format your hard disk, unless you enable the applet to do so. But would you ever click on a button that says, "Please click me, and then I will be able to erase your hard disk?"

Java applications, on the other hand, can be malicious, because they are executable on your computer. See Chapter 12 (Dealing with Java) for more information on the difference between a Java applet and a Java application.

Active X components can be malicious because they are ordinary executables that have all the rights of any program, thus they are able to delete files or format your hard disk. Internet Explorer can be configured to restrict these features, but not everybody understands the security levels in the browser. A sandbox model for Active X components would be nice to have, whereby the program is not able to see any resources on the computer.

Generally, if you find a boot sector or executable virus on a company computer, there is good reason to look for pirated software on that particular computer (and a good chance you will find some). Other sources for viruses are the "fun" programs that people share. They are not useful, but some people think they are so funny that everyone needs to see them. They often contain professional viruses, not simple macroviruses. But macro viruses are a big problem

The level of destruction differs from virus to virus. Even the most destructive virus won't be able to do any harm if you prepare yourself and your computer. With simple measures, you can protect yourself against them. Viruses can be classified in the following way:

- **Level 1: Annoying**—Displays messages on your screen, but does not cause any real harm.

- **Level 2: Harmless**—Displays messages on your screen and prevents programs from operating, but will cause no permanent damage.

- **Level 3: Harmful**—Destroys the data for the program it has infected, but all other data will remain intact.

- **Level 4: Destructive**—Destroys all data, prevents the computer from operating, etc.

Table 11.4. Levels of Virus Damage

on company computers, where people send their Word documents and Excel spreadsheets to their colleagues and partners. When one document gets infected, it spreads fairly fast throughout the company if no protective measures have been taken (and unfortunately there are still some companies). Large documents should always be zipped or, even better, put on a Web page where others can download the document. This prevents overloading the mail servers, and recipients who work on low-bandwidth networks (e.g., working from home via modem) especially will be grateful.

The most malicious macro virus, discovered in March 1999, was called "Melissa" and had a huge impact on the Internet. Melissa is a cross between a spam mail and a virus, making the results even worse. Within hours, the mail systems of many large corporations had to be shut down because of the virus. Although the code is rather simple, the virus spread with speed that astonished everyone. The email sent had a subject of "Important Message From" with the sender's name at the end, lending credibility to the message. The text of the message read: "Here is that document you asked for ... don't show anyone else ;-)." Attached was a Word document called list.doc, containing a list of URLs for pornographic sites.

The document contained a Word macro, which was executed when the document was opened. The macro, written in Visual Basic, connected to the email

Several viruses have made headlines. According to a research of *Der Spiegel*,[a] these received the media attention, but they probably were not the most dangerous. The dangerous ones are those that are not discovered by the media.

- **Melissa**—March 1999. The Melissa worm used Microsoft Word to send itself via attachment to fifty people in the Microsoft Outlook address book.

- **Chernobyl**—April 1999. A very aggressive program that invoked on the 13th anniversary of the Chernobyl disaster. It erases the hard disk and disables the booting of the computer.

- **Explore Zip**—June 1999. This virus destroys all Microsoft documents. Explore Zip combines the speed of Melissa with the nastiness of Chernobyl.

- **Babylonia**—-October 1999. This program was offered in chat rooms as the ultimate weapon against the Y2K bug. The program opened a connection to a server in Japan and mutated while destroying files on the computer.

- **Bubbleboy**—November 1999. The virus appeared with the announcement "Bubbleboy is back" in the email inbox. It is relatively harmless because it only replaces the user name with Bubbleboy.

---

[a]http://www.spiegel.de/

Table 11.5. Most Famous Viruses

client Outlook, and pulled 50 e-mail addresses from every directory it could find, and sent the document with your name as the sender to these people. If you were lucky and did not use Microsoft Exchange as your emailing backbone, the virus would get 50 addresses and stop working. If you relied on Exchange, it would go to the Enterprise directory and get 50 people from there as well. This would eventually lead to a collapse, because the virus replicated itself throughout your company without trouble. Microsoft, the maker of the mailing software, was forced to turn off its internal mailing services for a while to get rid of the virus.

This type of virus infects the normal.dot template, which is used for every new document in Word. The template contains the standard settings of the user. Every document that is created after the virus has hit your machine becomes infected, quickly spreading the virus over the Internet. Just a few days later, a cousin of Melissa—the Papa virus—appeared on the Internet. Instead of using Word, it was embedded into an Excel macro that sends out 60 e-mails from the address book. Unlike Melissa, which did this only once per computer, the new Papa virus sent out the virus every time you opened Excel. But since antivirus companies were already familiar with Melissa, Papa was not difficult to detect and destroy. Papa also contained a bug, which prevented worldwide distribution within a day.

The Papa virus infected only users of Outlook and Word. The virus could not spread itself to those using Netscape and Word, or Outlook and Ami Pro. Again, the intelligence of the virus was not in the code, but in the way the code was spread. Melissa was harmless compared to what damage the Papa virus could have caused.

In May 2000, a little more than a year after Melissa first surfaced, a new generation of virus appeared. The first of them was the "ILOVEYOU" virus. The virus came as a love letter and spread across the Internet at light speed, shutting down mail servers in many companies. Experts consider this the fastest spreading virus. According to the antivirus company, Trend Micro,[17] more than 500,000 computers were infected on the first day of the outbreak, with more than 350,000 in the United States. The virus itself was contained in an attachment called Love-Letter-For-You.txt.vbs. If you clicked on the attachment, the virus started up and sent itself to all email addresses in the user's address book. In this way, it was similar to the Melissa virus.

The ILOVEYOU virus modifies important system files on the computer and the network, and blocks the mail server through the large amount of emails. Throughout the world, companies had to take their mail servers off the net to rid them of the mail virus because they were so clogged with emails that nothing worked. Among these companies and institutions, you could find Microsoft itself, the Wall Street Journal Asia, the Financial Times Germany, the British House of Commons, and the German Ministry of State. The big problem with this virus was that the sender of the email was a friend, acquaintance, or business partner, meaning that the user trusted the source of the virus. The really dangerous part was that the virus connected to the Internet to look for updates, meaning it was possible to modify the virus on the fly, making it invisible to updates in the antivirus software packages.

Fortunately, the virus did not spread to all computers. Again, it was restricted to those computers running Microsoft operating systems and Outlook. Although the majority of people work on this platform, this demonstrates how important it is to diversify the platform strategy in order to be less vulnera-

---

[17]http://www.trendmicro.com/

Some simple procedures allow you to protect your computer from all sorts of email viruses. A complete guide can be found at http://www.axent.com/ or at the Web sites of other other antivirus research companies.

- **Reconfigure Outlook**—Switch off the automatic execution of applications in Outlook.

- **Deactivate Windows Scripting Host**—Average users do not require the Windows Scripting Host.

- **Remove .vbs File Extensions**—Remove the .vbs file extensions from the registries.

- **Install Updates**—Always install OS updates. MacOS does this automatically, for example.

- **Filter Attachments**—Filter scripts, executables, and batch file from your email attachments.

- **Be careful**—Do not open attachments if you do not know the sender.

Table 11.6. Protection against Viruses

ble to security issues. Of concern is that the virus was written in Visual Basic Script, meaning that any school kid could have written it. The ILOVEYOU virus was still relatively harmless, because it "only" deleted JPEG and MP3 files. But the hysteria around the virus created more damage. The German tabloid *Bild*[18] published the headline "Internet Terrorists Create Killer Virus," which obviously exaggerated what really happened. Similar headlines were published around the world, creating greater hysteria among the users of the Internet and doing nothing to solve the problem. The scap goats were the programmer of the virus and Microsoft. But neither of them was to blame. The real culprits were those who opened attachments without thinking about what they were doing. All people infected with the virus were to blame as well. Many companies explained to their employees how to send and receive emails but never invested time in explaining the risks of email viruses. And many people who use home computers never considered themselves vulnerable. Unfortunately, people tend to forget these lessons relatively quickly. Since the

---

[18]http://www.bild.de/

ILOVEYOU incident, many other similar viruses have appeared. While I was writing these lines, the Homepage virus struck the online community world-wide, and it doesn't appear people will be any more cautious about their emails in the near future.

Figure 11.1. Important emails get lost because of viruses.

It is actually quite easy to reduce the risk of being infected by a virus. Table 11.6 provides an overview of steps that end users can take. But companies and ISPs can do much to reduce the spreading of the viruses. The first step is installing an antivirus solution on the mail server. But even without this quite expensive solution, it is possible to reduce the risk by filtering all executable files in emails. By switching off the Windows Scripting Host, .vbs files cannot be executed if they arrive on a user's desktop. This requires many systems to be reconfigured. Therefore, mail-server-based filtering reduces the risk in general. It would be easier if Microsoft had switched on all security measures in the standard configuration, but Microsoft has never been famous for security. And people tend to place too much trust in the software they use. This is true not only for Microsoft, but for all operating systems and applications. It would be ideal if all Internet users would go through a security workshop before going online. This would reduce the virus threat. But this is not going to happen. Therefore, it seems likely there will be an increase in virus-related attacks in the future.

11.5.3 Deploying Antivirus Solutions

Many businesses have both an intranet and a direct connection to the Internet, so it is important to protect not only single computers but the network as a whole. It is not enough to install an antivirus program on every computer. In addition, standard measures should be applied to network-connected computers and standalone computers. This protects the computers from infiltration by viruses via floppy, zip disks and other removable media. Most antivirus solutions are able to scan incoming email as well, but this should not be necessary anymore. All mail should be checked at the firewall. This leads to the second part of the antivirus strategy. All inbound and outbound traffic of your company should be checked at the firewall. Incoming traffic needs to be checked to protect your data on the intranet and all computers. It is just as important to check outbound traffic in the form of Web pages and email. No program or email should leave your company without being checked for viruses. A virus in a mail or in a program on your Web page can destroy your company's reputation. Although checking for viruses at the firewall is very important, applying it to large installations is difficult because the antivirus software runs on Windows NT only and not on high-performance UNIX. Scalability is an issue. Checking email only is not such a big problem, because email is not a real-time application. But would you want to wait for 10 minutes when downloading a file from a Web server to have a virus check?

Suppose you have an important document and need to send it out to a few hundred people. If the document contained a virus, you would spread this virus to dozens of corporations all over the world. Tracing back to the origin will take some time and effort, but it is possible and has been done successfully in the past. The distribution of viruses is illegal in most countries. So spreading the virus could have legal consequences, which could either affect the sender directly or the company for which he or she works.

Regular backups are an important measure against computer viruses. This is true even if you are backing up the virus that eventually causes the damage. Even if the virus is in the backup, you can safely restore all your data, obtain one of the antivirus solutions, and remove the virus before continuing with your work.

11.5.4 Required Software

As mentioned above, it is important to install an antivirus solution on every computer within your company. There are many different solutions available on the market (see Table 11.7 for an overview). Most of them have the same basic functionality but vary in terms of pricing, speed, and support. Most important for any antivirus software is the availability of the virus definition files. Virus definition files contain information about viruses, and updates should be available on demand (via a Web site, for example) and via push technology (e.g., an update emailed to you every week) to keep the software up to date. The best solution is useless if the database is old.

No matter which solution you choose, the following components should be always be included as a minimum:

- **Scanner**—This part of the solution scans all files on local hard disks, floppies, and network drives for viruses. It does not work automatically in the background; it must be started by the user.

- **Shield**—This part of the solution is automated and works in the background. It looks out for viruses while downloading software from the

Internet or inserting a floppy into the disk drive.

- **Cleaner**—After a virus has been found, it must be removed. This is the role of the cleaner. It scans the database for remedies and tries to remove the virus. Often, it is easy enough to delete the virus, but some viruses destroy the actual data, making it impossible to restore the original state.

At the writing of the book some of the most used solutions are the following (sorted alphabetically):

Company	URL
Datafellows Company	http://www.datafellows.com/
Dr. Solomons	http://www.drsolomons.com/
IBM Antivirus	http://www.av.ibm.com/
McAfee Associates, Inc.	http://www.mcafee.com/
Norton Antivirus	http://www.norton.com/
Thunderbyte	http://www.thunderbyte.com/
ViruSafe Virus Center	http://www.eliashim.com/

Table 11.7. Antivirus Technology

After you have installed such a solution, viruses like Michelangelo or Melissa won't have a chance on your computer and your local network. Whenever you receive a new file, no matter how it is sent, the shield will start to check for a virus and an alarm will go off if something is found. Most antivirus solutions erase the virus immediately and do not require you to do anything about it. Just be sure to inform the sender of the file about the virus, so that the source of the virus is extinguished. In order to catch all incoming viruses, you need to update your virus definition file on a regular basis, as often as every week. Otherwise, the newest viruses will just slip through.

Even though firewall antivirus solutions may not be a viable solution, some additional measures for your Web and FTP servers should to be taken. If you cannot virus-check all files on the fly, then let scripts run over your Web server once a week to check for viruses to be sure that you are not spreading viruses all over the planet.

11.5.5   Ignoring Hoax Viruses and Chain Letters

Some viruses cannot be caught by software because of their implementation. They are not spread by computer code but by users (normally via email). Therefore, it is important to understand the threat.

In October 1998, the whole email system of the U.S. Postal Service broke down. It appeared that a well-meaning employee forwarded the "Win a Holiday" virus alert to every email account in the usps.gov domain. Other employees hit the "reply to all" button, causing servers to overload. The administrators at USPS had to perform emergency maintenance to get the email system back up.

```
VIRUS WARNING !!!!!!
If you receive an email titled "WIN A HOLIDAY" DO NOT
open it.
It will erase everything on your hard drive.  Forward
this letter out to as many people as you can.
This is a new, very malicious virus and not many
people know about it.  This information was announced
yesterday morning from Microsoft;
Please share it with everyone that might access the
Internet.  Once again, pass this along to EVERYONE in
your address book so that this may be stopped.
Also, do not open or even look at any mail that says
"RETURNED OR UNABLE TO DELIVER"
The virus will attach itself to your computer
components and render them useless.  Immediately delete
any mail items that say this.  AOL has said that this
is a very dangerous virus and that there is NO remedy.
Send this to all your online friends ASAP.
```

Table 11.8. The "Win a Holiday" hoax

The "Win a Holiday" virus alert is a simple email (see also Table 11.8). It tells the users not to open another e-mail titled "WIN A HOLIDAY." This simple email disrupted the whole communications network of USPS with a few lines of text. Viruses are not necessarily cleverly written programs, but may also be cleverly written emails (called virus hoaxes).

The virus hoax did not attack the mail servers directly, but targeted the employees, who (by default) are afraid of viruses. For many people, the Internet is a mystery; therefore, they believe whatever is written in email, especially if renowned companies like AOL or Microsoft are mentioned. It is a myth that opening email enables viruses to erase your hard disk (more myths can be found at Kumite's[19] Web site). This myth applies only to the email itself and

---

[19]http://www.kumite.com/myths/

not to its attachments that may be infected by viruses. And keep in mind, it is neither Microsoft's nor AOL's job to release virus alerts. If such an email mentions a company that releases virus alerts, go to that company's Web page and look in the news section to verify the email.

If you receive virus warnings or chain letters in your email, be careful! An Internet chain letter is a message that is forwarded to hundreds of people. The recipient is requested to send it to others. If each person sends the letter to only 10 other people, the ninth resending results in a billion email messages. When you get a virus warning or chain letter, either delete it or send a copy of the mail to your local system administrators or security officer. They will be able to tell you whether the threat is real or just another virus hoax. Do not send it to your friends and relatives because you will congest the network and lend the reputation of your company to the message (and your own as well), making it appear to be authentic even when it is not. Everybody in your company should understand what a virus hoax is. Have a direct link from your intranet home page to a FAQ section on viruses and virus hoaxes, where all employees can find the latest developments.

Also, be careful when receiving "updates" via email. If you have not requested an update for a certain program, do not install the application that is attached to the email, especially if the mail comes from a mass mailing or was posted in a newsgroup. In January 1999, a "bug fix" for Internet Explorer was distributed via email. It appeared to come from Microsoft Support, but instead of an update for the browser, it installed a Trojan horse on the victim's computer. The file "IE0199.exe" displays an error message after starting the application, so the user thinks that something went wrong during installation and doesn't bother about it afterward, but the Trojan horse remains in memory and tries to connect on various ports to a Bulgarian server[20] and exchanges information with the server. The virus actually replaces a file in the Windows environment, so that the virus launches each time you reboot.

The U.S. Postal Service example dramatically shows the harm that false virus warnings can do to your company. Though these e-mails do not pose any real risk, they may lead to significant productivity loss and disruption in the environment, which may mean a financial loss for your company.

Antivirus programs are not able to stop virus hoax emails because computer programs are not spreading the viruses—humans are. Therefore, it is very important to inform and educate all employees. An excellent resource for more information on urban legends and net hoaxes is the Urban Legends Web site of about.com,[21] which should be made available to employees.

---

[20]http://www1.infotel.bg/
[21]http://urbanlegends.about.com/

11.6   Conflicts in the Information Age

11.6.1   Information Attack

Although you may think that no one is interested in private information about your company, someone out there maybe. Your security experts may have a tendency to concentrate on just the threats they are trained to deal with, but attackers do what they are good at doing. Unfortunately, your security experts may be missing the necessary protective measures.

Most hackers are good at guessing passwords or at stealing them. Many people buy software that uses preinstalled passwords. These passwords must be changed after the system is up and running, but many users do not do this, enabling others to easily enter a system. Even if you change your password, there is a good chance of guessing it. Many people use the company name, the name of a spouse, a birthday or any other information that can be remembered easily. Many people use "hello" or the login name as a password. Do a test: Go to the computers of your colleagues or employees and try "hello" or the login name. You will probably find some computers that are easily unlocked.

Many programs on the market allow you to test whether a given login uses a password that can be guessed easily. These programs rely on multiple dictionaries with words from several languages. The program encrypts a word from the dictionary and compares it to the encrypted password until it finds a match. One of these programs is simply called "Crack," and is available as freeware.

Complex software packages most likely contain bugs. Bugs normally terminate a program or refuse to execute a certain function, but some of them may lead to weakening the security of the system. A bug in a word processor most probably won't open up your computer to the Internet, but if the Web server contains a bug, it may allow intruders to enter your computer by persuading the Web server to let them in. Sometimes, the reason for security holes is not buggy software but the configuration of software. Incorrectly configuring a firewall may open your intranet and allow hackers to read your corporate data without trouble or, even worse, to modify or delete the data.

In some cases, the system is not insecure, but data is still revealed to people who should not have access to it. A person who has been authorized to enter a system uses resources to modify the status of his or her authorization and is able to access data and applications that should not be accessible. This is often accomplished using documented and undocumented weaknesses of operating systems and programs to bypass the security system. A viable way of doing this would be for an intruder to walk up to a certain computer and reboot the machine. After a reboot, the intruder could install a virus or copy confidential data from the hard disk. With Windows-based systems, it is especially easy to get into the system. For example, if you protect Windows 95 with a password, pressing "Escape" will be enough to skip the password protection. On Windows

NT, you enter the system as guest and use the "getadmin" tool to receive superuser privileges. Stealing information from a Windows computer is even easier if unencrypted backup tapes are stolen.

11.6.2 Information Warfare

Officially, information warfare does not exist, yet all governments are developing mechanisms to protect themselves in the event of an attack. Information warriors try to capture or destroy the enemy's information, processes, and systems.

Information warfare can be conducted on three different levels: personal, corporate, and global. The methods are always the same in these attacks on the privacy of certain persons, companies, or countries. The attackers try to steal information from them. The information is saved in many different databases the attackers try to access. The bank has information on financial details, the doctors have health information, and the corporations, information on new products. All this information can be used against you. It can be falsified and published. The difference among the three types of warfare is the degree of damage they can cause.

Battles are fought every day in information warfare, as individuals, companies, and governments try to penetrate the computer systems of enemies and competitors. The more technologically advanced the organizations or persons are, the more vulnerable they become.

The weapons in the information war are most likely used by cyber terrorists; in the future, armed forces may use the weapons in a strike against the enemy in wartime.

The information society is extremely vulnerable to disruption. Because of the importance of electronic communication and data exchange, attacking the information backbones can cause much more damage than a bomb.

11.6.3 Cyber Terrorism

The Internet reflects the real world using new technologies. Therefore, it reflects the pleasant and the evil sides of life. Terrorism is a threat in the real world and in the cyber world. Cyber terrorism is a threat to everyone who is connected to the Internet: every single person, every club, every company and every governmental agency. Terrorists use force to coerce others to promote their political or social objectives. There is no difference in motivation between real-world and cyber terrorists except that cyber terrorists use computing resources to intimidate others.

Cyber terrorists can easily destroy the business of a large corporation, if the company has not taken preventative measures. Banks that connect their internal databases to the Internet are just as vulnerable as companies that do business-to-business transactions over the Internet. As soon as you open a

These weapons, among others, can be used in information wars:

- **Chipping**—Replace standard chips with Trojan horses.

- **EMP bombs**—Destroy the electronics of all computers through nuclear and nonnuclear detonation.

- **Human engineering**—Pretend to be someone else to gain information via phone, fax or email.

- **Jamming**—Use this to block communication of the enemy by emitting electronic noise.

- **Logic bombs**—This is a certain type of Trojan horse that can release a virus or worm.

- **Nano machines**—Tiny robots attack the hardware of the enemy.

- **Spoofing**—Faked email and TCP/IP packets by-pass the firewalls and other security measures.

- **Trap doors**—These mechanisms allow attackers to enter a system without being noticed by the security settings.

- **Trojan horses**—These code fragments hide inside programs and perform undesired functions.

- **Viruses**—These code fragments copy themselves into a program or modify it.

- **Worms**—These are independent programs that copy themselves from one computer to another.

Table 11.9. Weapons in Information Warfare

little hole into your firewall to let partners and customers participate in your processes and share your data, you create a potential security risk.

Terrorists have realized over the past few years that killing a president or CEO of a company just provokes anger among the employees and the public, but does not do any damage to the attacked institution. Although a murder is tragic, it does not stop a company or government from working. Cyber terrorists work like real ones, but without being even near the location of the deed.

Follow these simple rules to protect yourself and your company from cyber-terrorist attacks:

- **Passwords**—No corporate computer system may have passwords that can be guessed or found in a dictionary. A regular password audit is necessary to check for compliance.

- **Network**—Change the network configuration as soon as vulnerabilities become apparent. Network audits on a regular basis are also necessary.

- **Patches**—Assign a security officer the task of subscribing to the important security mailing lists and informing everybody about new security leaks.

- **Audits**—Every system needs to be checked in regular intervals and log files need to be analyzed on a regular basis.

Table 11.10. Protection from Cyber Terrorism

The Internet offers the terrorist many more options of damaging an institution. Shutting down a power plant via computer networks (by infiltrating private networks or by using security holes on the Internet), can be done from remote locations without having to fear being caught onsite. Finding the terrorists is more difficult because masquerading techniques and stolen accounts can hide terrorists quite well. And companies are not keen on publishing information about a threat, because they fear the bad publicity.

Cyber terrorists have different strategies for attacking, depending on the type of institution. These are the most common:

- **Virus attack**—A software company can be attacked by someone planting a virus into a software package. The software is sold to customers, and the virus destroys valuable information on their computers or opens a back door to their intranets.

- **Alteration of information**—A bank can be attacked by someone altering bank accounts. Money could be moved from one account to another, thus ruining the image of some of the customers and the bank.

- **Cutting off communication**—An airline can be attacked by someone cutting off communication between airplanes and the tower. In the worst case, the airplane is not able to land and subsequently crashes.

- **Killing from a distance**—A hospital can be attacked by somone changing patient information. The patient records could be altered in such a way that a kidney patient will get a liver transplant or the dose of a certain drug is altered to kill the patient.

- **Spreading misinformation**—A company can be attacked easily by someone spreading misinformation. The incorrect information is spread over the Internet and hundreds of thousands of customers are misled.

Terrorist attacks can have different effects, ranging from a simple denial of service all the way up to assassination. In 1996, the U.S. government created the Commission of Critical Infrastructure Protection. The commission consists of all important companies in the field of power generation, communications technology, and computer industry. The companies are united to develop solutions for an eventual cyber-terrorist attack against the United States. Another important goal is to create awareness of the problem in the private and public sectors, because many companies and agencies are relatively ignorant about this topic.

Aside from shutting down all connections to the outside world, there is no way to make your company 100 percent secure. Mission-critical systems should be disconnected from public networks. Apart from isolation, the most common method of protection is encryption. Another solution is to use the firewall to monitor all communication between the corporate network and the public Internet.

Cyber terrorists have nothing in common with hackers who try to break into systems. Most hackers try to break into systems just for the sake of breaking in. Cyber terrorists break into systems in order to harm the owner by stealing, deleting, or altering information, products and services.

A new type of online activism called *hacktivism* has begun to emerge. These are online activists who break into Web servers to demonstrate against something. In July 1998, protesters of the nuclear tests in India hacked more than 300 sites and replaced the content with an atomic mushroom. One of the sites was the official Wimbledon tennis tournament Web site.[22] Hacktivists want to create awareness for political reasons. They are not interested in destroying or stealing data. They claim that the use of the digital form of civil *ungehorsam* (or disobedience) and online sit-ins is a right for everyone. Their cyber demonstrations have nothing to do with cyber terrorism, but, as in real life, the protest for a "good thing" is always relative.

On September 9, 1998, the Web site of the Pentagon was under attack by members of the Electronic Disturbance Theater[23] (EDT). The EDT wanted to

---

[22]http://www.wimbledon.org/
[23]http://www.thing.net/r̃dom/ecd/ecd.html

protest against the treatment of the Zapatists in the Chiapas region in Mexico. By destroying the Pentagon Web service, they hoped to make a statement and urge the U.S. government to reconsider its position. Unfortunately for these cyber activists, the Pentagon was prepared for such an attack and responded by sending back the HTTP requests to the originating Web server. The server of the EDT broke down before it could do any harm to the Pentagon server. This event shows quite clearly that the U.S. government is prepared.

Another incident began in May 1999, when some hackers started an information war against the FBI,[24] putting the Web site out of service. Although the FBI was able to stop the attacks within a short time, they could not get their Web site up for days. While they were defending their Web site, the hackers broke into the Web site of the U.S. Senate[25] and replaced the home page with their own. AntiOnline[26] documents these incidents, making it possible for everyone to see which Web sites were and are under attack. Governments throughout the world have recognized the potential threats and have started to protect critical infrastructures, such as services in the telecommunication, finance, traffic, energy and water industries, and emergency and governmental services. Although there haven't been any serious attacks on these vital services, this could change in the future. Using the Internet, it is possible to destroy an entire country. High-tech countries, such as the United States, are especially vulnerable to these attacks. Single persons could try to attack the power network and create a national blackout that would destroy all electronic devices, if not properly protected.

11.6.4   Eternity Service

To prevent terrorist attacks on Internet services, Ross Anderson, a student from Cambridge University, has developed a methodology[27] to manage data. Anderson theorized that by using many interconnected servers all over the world, it is possible to achieve very high reliability of storage of data and services. He called it the Eternity service, providing new ways of creating, storing, and handling copies of data of high importance—with a high degree of reliability. The Eternity service is designed to be resistant not only to threats such as natural disasters and vandalism, but also to political or court decisions, religious leader orders, and activities of secret services.

The Internet was designed as a communication platform resistant to denial of service attacks; when parts of the Internet are destroyed, the Internet as a whole is not harmed. Some services may be destroyed, but if backups exist, it is possible to reinstall them in another area. The Internet is supposed to be able to survive a thermonuclear war.

---

[24] http://www.fbi.gov/
[25] http://www.senate.gov/
[26] http://www.antionline.com/
[27] http://www.cl.cam.ac.uk/users/rja14/eternity/eternity.html

The Eternity service proposes to construct a storage platform with similar properties using the Internet as the infrastructure. To replicate data across the Internet, you use redundancy and scattering techniques.

Availability is a very important goal in the private sector—actually far more important than confidentiality and integrity. There are many types of documents that need to be protected from destruction. Records of births and deaths, medical case notes, and real estate property documents are just a few examples of documents that are vital for society in general and for individuals in particular. Without certain documents (such as a birth certificate), a person can become a "nobody."

Another problem in our rapidly changing world is the longevity of documents. Computer formats appear and disappear quickly, so data can no longer be read and programs can no longer be executed. Through the use of Eternity servers all over the Internet, important data can be saved in a very secure way. Although an attacker may be able to destroy parts of the Internet, the stored information will be still available, and regular Internet services won't be disrupted.

All information from different customers is stored into the database and replicated all over the world. The data is encrypted to maintain the anonymity of the customers and the confidentiality of the documents. The information is buried in the vast amount of other information, so that even if the particular document can be found by hackers, they are not able to pass on the information.

11.6.5 FreeNet

FreeNet,[28] created by 23-year-old Ian Clarke in his final year at Edinburgh University, complicates matters still further for copyright holders because it guarantees anonymity to the publisher of a file on the network. It's also considered a very efficient system for distributing files over the Internet. However, it has yet to gather a mainstream userbase because of its poor interface.

Despite his anti-copyright leanings, Clarke recently moved to California to start up a company called Uprizer,[29] with the aim of making money from FreeNet. The first issue he'll be looking at is how to charge for content distribution on FreeNet without relying on copyright, making it possible to distribute copyrighted content without having issues with legislation, because copyright owners will be paid through their technology and business model.

---

[28]http://freenet.sourceforge.net/
[29]http://www.uprizer.com/

11.7 Client-based Security

11.7.1 Digital Certificates

A digital certificate is the most commonly used way to bind a cryptographic key with one or more attributes of a user. It allows the receiver of a message to verify the authenticity of the communication. Digital certificates have greatly helped to build up trust in electronic business on the Internet.

A digital certificate is a file that is encrypted and password-protected and includes personal information about the owner of the certificate, such as the name of the holder, the postal address, and the email address. Other personal information can be encoded as well, such as a credit card number, depending on the business requirements. A public key is included and used to verify the digital signature of a message sender previously signed with the matching private key. Also included is the name of the certification authority that issued the digital certificate and the validity period of the certificate.

A list of certificate authorities who issue digital certificates can be found in Table 11.11. To issue a certificate, the authority must verify the personal information of the holder. This can be done by different means, depending on the required security involved. The cheapest version of a digital certificate involves checking that the supplied email address is valid. More secure solutions require the holder of the certificate to validate it by appearing in person or sending in a copy of his or her passport or driving license.

Many sites offer a free digital certificate for private use. The following list contains some of the more popular certificate authorities (in alphabetical order):

Company	URL
Baltimore Technologies	http://www.baltimore.ie/
BelSign	http://www.belsign.be/
Thawte	http://www.thawte.com/
TrustCenter	http://www.trustcenter.de/
VeriSign	http://www.verisign.com/
Xcert	http://www.xcert.com/

Table 11.11. Free Digital Certificates

Digital certificates are used to secure the communication between browsers and servers (using SSL encryption), between customers and merchants (using credit card SET encryption), or between two email partners (using S/MIME).

Client-server authentication using SSL is achieved through the following process: A series of messages is exchanged before the first secure page is displayed. The browser connects to the server and the server sends its digital certificate to the browser. This is done for two reasons; first, it is used to identify the server, and second, the public key that is stored in the certificate is used to encrypt the session key. The identification of the server certificate is checked against the certification authority that issued it. If the identity is okay, then a session key is created, which is used for encrypting the following communication.

After this has been decided, a dialog box informs the user of the digital certificate on the server and asks the user to select the appropriate digital certificate. The certificate is then passed on to the server, which checks the validity of the certificate and the certification authority. Most Internet applications do not require the customer to have a digital certificate, because the process for distributing certificates in large numbers is still complex and expensive to handle. It is expected that the process will be simplified and standardized to make digital certificates feasible for more applications on the Internet.

United Parcel Service[30] started two services in mid-1999 that allow businesses to send signed legal documents instantly over the Internet. The shipping company has launched a digital-certificate-based confidential document exchange service and a service to exchange documents among disparate email systems. Both services cost customers less than the price of shipping an overnight letter.

11.7.2 Smart Cards

Smart cards have been heavily promoted in Europe and are slowly becoming popular throughout the rest of the world. In Europe, applications in commerce, public transport, and health care have been developed over the past few years and are highly successful.

Depending on the type of application, you will require different levels of memory on the smart card. If you want to put data or applications on the smart card only once, it is sufficient to put a little chip on the card that contains read-only memory (ROM). If your program needs to store temporary information on the card—for example, when exchanging data with a terminal—random-access memory (RAM) should be added. After the smart card has been removed from the terminal, the information is lost. Most applications require electronically erasable programmable read-only memory (EEPROM), which allows data and applications be stored permanently on the smart card. Unlike ROM smart cards, the applications and data can be loaded, executed and removed from the card at any time.

Actually, all smart cards on the market today use EEPROM chips. Some factors limit the size of EEPROM on the smart card. Although 256 or 512 MB

---

[30]http://www.ups.com/

Smart cards have an embedded microchip instead of a magnetic strip. The chip contains all the information that a magnetic strip contains, but it offers the possibility of manipulating the data and executing applications on the card. Three types of smart cards have been established:

- **Contact cards**—This type of smart cards must be inserted into a reader in order to work, such as a smart card reader or automatic teller machines.

- **Contactless cards**—Contactless smart cards don't need to be inserted into a reader. Just waving them near a reader is sufficient for the card to exchange data. This type of card is used for opening doors.

- **Combi-cards**—Combi-cards contain both technologies and allow a wider range of applications.

Table 11.12. Types of Smart Cards

are fairly common in today's computers, smart cards store only up to 16 KB. This is more than a 1,000 smaller, but still enough to hold complex applications. In the early 1980s, 16 KB actually was more than most applications needed, but as graphic user interfaces became popular and the complexity of the programs rose, the amount of memory a program requires increased dramatically. Smart cards have many restrictions that do not allow them to use much memory. Smart card chips have standardized dimensions and no power supply other than when introduced into a smart card reader. The price for EEPROM is still very high, because computers use mainly RAM. Factors that limit the size of the memory include battery life and size of the device.

The newer releases of smart cards can hold more than a single application. Multiple applications from multiple organizations can fit on one card. For example, the application of electronic cash provided by your bank can be on the same card as the access control to your office. Multifunctionality requires security for every application. If an application runs on the card, it should not be allowed to view data stored by other applications on the same card. Each application should have its own compartment on the smart card. The limitation to multifunctionality is the amount of memory on the smart card itself.

Information on smart cards can be accessed in four ways, depending on the type of application you want to provide and the type of memory you are using. With read-only smart cards, information is loaded once onto the card. Information stored on the card can only be read. It is not possible to add, modify or erase information. Suppose that an application allows access to a building. The smart card would contain some information on the user, such as the name and employee number. The information could be stored in ROM, because the information will not change for a given employee.

Some smart cards, such as telephone cards, allow you to add information only. Every time someone makes a phone call using a phone card, the application checks how many units have not been used and allows a phone call to be made. Every unit used during the phone call is added to the list of used units. The cards do not allow the modification or deletion of information, thus preventing the fraud of putting the cards back into their initial state.

Some smart cards do allow information to be deleted or modified, just like on a hard disk; these are often used for storing data, such as telephone book entries. Some data on the smart card is stored in such a way that it can never be accessed. The application is loaded onto the card and can be executed only without access to the source code or data associated to it. Key generation and password processing are two applications that should never be revealed to the outside world if you want to protect all other applications on the card. Table 11.13 contains a short overview of the different types of smart cards.

Information on smart cards can be accessed in these ways:

- **Read Only**—Information can only be read from the smart card.

- **Add Only**—Information can only be added to the smart card.

- **Modify or Delete**—Information can only be modified or deleted.

- **Execute Only**—Programs can be executed only without seeing any information.

Table 11.13. Information Access

Maintaining security is the major issue with smart cards. If a hacker is able to copy or manipulate the content of one card onto another one, it may destroy the business of the smart card application issuer. This means security functions must be at the core of all smart cards. However, different applications require different levels of security, and absolute security cannot be guaranteed.

The key to ensuring effective protection against manipulation or copying of smart cards requires secure hardware with which physical countermeasures are taken. A secure operating system is necessary, meaning the communication among all components involved in the security system is encrypted. The overall level of security is only as good as that of the weakest element in the chain.

Common threats to smart cards are loss of authenticity (the uniqueness of the card cannot be guaranteed), integrity (the completeness of information cannot be guaranteed), confidentiality (the privacy of the information cannot be guaranteed), and availability (the service on the card cannot be guaranteed).

Smart cards are protected by a PIN (personal identification number). The security issue is that the PIN needs to be entered via a keyboard. Technically, it would be possible to intercept the communication between the keyboard and the smart card reader. Therefore, newer smart card readers, such as the Gem-Plus GCR 410, are connected between computer and keyboard, thereby ensuring that the PIN is not transmitted to the computer.

Smart cards are widely used today. Typical applications include:

- **Health**—Some smart cards contain personal health information, allowing the transfer of patient information between doctors.

- **Finance**—Cash cards, such as the Mondex card in the UK and the Geld-Karte in Germany (see Chapter 14), allow financial transactions.

- **Mobile communications**—The GSM (Global System for Mobile Communications) network uses smart cards for user identification, allowing users to switch to different phones and keep the same phone numbers.

- **Stationary telecommunications**—Typically, prepaid phone cards are based on the smart card system. This reduces the cost for maintenance and handling and prevents fraud, theft, and credit loss.

- **Transportation**—Payments for subway tickets and toll bridges are common applications.

Smart card applications will become more popular because they enable customers to conveniently pay for goods and services. The number of smart card readers attached to computers is still very low, preventing the smart card from being a viable solution on the Internet presently. As more and more keyboard makers include smart card readers into their keyboards and the latest releases of operating systems include drivers for smart cards in the standard installation, it will be a matter of time until smart cards are the preferred method of authentication and payment on the Internet.

11.7.3 Biometric Identification

The most common way to identify a person is a password-based solution, such as with digital certificates or smart cards. But passwords are not perfect. To be secure, they must be difficult to guess. But this makes them also difficult to remember. This is acceptable as long as one has only very few devices to operate. But as more services become available electronically, more passwords and PINs must be remembered. Your mobile phone, your bank account, your email, your computer, your online shopping sites all require passwords or PINs in order to recognize you. Biometrics offers a solution to the password problem by replacing the authentication method so that no passwords have to be remembered.

Biometric identification is a means of automatically identifying persons based on their unique physical characteristics or behavioral traits. It is an upcoming alternative to digital certificates and smart cards, with the advantage that it is strictly based on the physics of the human and does not rely on any files that could be copied or any passwords that could be cracked. Instead of using a technology that is based on something you know or something you possess, biometrics is based on who people are or what they do.

Everyone has unique and stable features, such as fingerprints and eyes, and standard ways of doing things, such as speaking and writing. These features are much harder to forge and are almost always available. Only in a very few cases are the features not available, such as when you break your arm and are not able to write for a certain period of time.

Biometric technologies include fingerprint, iris, and retina scanning. The analysis of handwriting is also a common method of biometric identification. Voice and hand print recognition are also promising technologies.

Although the technologies have been available for several years, few companies are currently using biometric technologies. The technology is still immature and too expensive. The rate of false identification is often too high to be tolerated, and users resist some forms of biometric identification. The scan of the retina is a procedure most people are unwilling to support, for example, as long as they are skeptical that it will harm the retina.

Because the accuracy is lower than with digital technologies, trade-offs must be compensated. This is often done by using more than one technology to identify the user. A fingerprint scan in combination with voice recognition will be more reliable than one of the technologies alone. Biometric applications are CPU-intensive and require high-end computers to support a large user base.

Biometric authentication requires users to register fingerprints, voice prints, and faces. These features are digitized, and key features are extracted and converted to templates. These templates are then compared with the person in front of the identification device. Matches will never be exact, because the conversion from analog to digital always includes loss of information. To reduce the number of false rejections or acceptances, the sensitivity threshold must be adjusted very carefully. Unlike digital technologies, which either have a completely correct answer or a completely false answer, biometric technologies deliver answers like "most probably," "very likely," "probably" and "unlikely." Depending on the hardware and software used, the threshold must be set in such a way that wrong answers are eliminated.

> Identification via physical attributes has many advantages over passwords and digital certificates, but there are also some drawbacks:
>
> - **Acceptance**—Biometric identification is still not widely accepted.
>
> - **Accuracy**—By design, no biometric approach is 100 percent accurate.
>
> - **Cost**—The cost for implementing and maintaining biometric systems is higher than a password-based system.
>
> - **Privacy**—Personal information is required for biometrics to work. This information must be kept in a secure place; otherwise, it is possible to replicate it or otherwise misuse it.

Table 11.14. Issues with Biometric Identification

It is rather unlikely that every computer will be equipped with a biometric device in the near future. But manufacturers of embedded systems such as mobile phones may more easily embed such a functionality into their devices. To operate a mobile phone, a fingerprint could be used instead of the PIN, making the system more secure without the need for a larger infrastructure. The mobile phone would allow the caller to scan his fingerprint and store it in the device. Every time callers switch on the phone, they would need to identify themselves via fingerprint.

Another promising technology is voice recognition, because it can be used remotely, just like a password. It is possible to use voice recognition to deal with your bank and initiate money transfers, for example. The major disadvantage of voice recognition is the ability to record the human voice and have it replayed by another person.

Signatures have been used widely in the past, but they are easy to forge. To enhance the security of signatures, biometric sensors not only register what you have written, but also how you have written it. Such a device measures the speed and direction of your hand movements as you form your signature. Some devices also measure the force with which you press the pen against the paper and the angle at which you hold the pen, increasing security.

Besides the traditional biometric applications, companies have started to develop more unusual systems. Security systems that detect the body odor of the individual are planned. BTG,[31] a security company, has developed a technology that identifies individuals by the blood vessel patterns in the back of the hand. These are just two examples of what can be measured from the body. There are even more patterns that are unique and characteristic for every single person.

With the introduction of new, more powerful hardware and more intelligent software, biometrics will become the solution for personal identification.

11.8   Server-based Security

11.8.1   Introduction

The issues of Internet security and privacy capture the attention of virtually all who use computers. Internet vandals have made headlines recently by unleashing DDoS (Distributed Denial of Service) attacks on major Web sites. Most attacks on computer networks can be prevented if system administrators take the appropriate steps to secure and monitor their networks. Server-based or network-based security is a must for all e-business Web sites.

11.8.2   The Need for a Firewall

As more companies become Internet-enabled—by setting up public Web servers and internal networks—the necessity for security also rises. Network security can be implemented through different means, but most commonly through a firewall.

Firewalls are systems that protect trusted networks from untrusted networks, and vice versa. A firewall implements an access-control policy, which allows users from either network to access certain resources on the other network. Every owner of a network must determine what resources need protection. Companies will most likely need a firewall to protect their internal documents from the outside world.

Firewalls are designed to prevent access to certain company systems connected to the Internet. This access control protects the software and the data on that particular device. Firewalls help to protect systems against vandalism and theft, which are the main threats to every system.

A system connected directly to the Internet usually offers one or more services. To protect this service, a firewall can deny all other access to the computer. For example, a Web server should serve Web pages to customers. To maintain the server, additional services are running that are necessary for the administrator to add files or applications. These services should be open only to the administrator. Other users should not have any possibility of determining whether these services are running. A firewall can help to determine in advance where the user is coming from and offer the services the client is allowed

---

[31]http://www.btg.co.uk/

to see. Customers will then see the Web page, while the administration services (such as FTP or telnet) are restricted to a certain range of IP addresses.

Several strategies can be used to secure these services. The most conservative would be to place the Internet services on an isolated Web server that has no connection to the internal network. This offers the best security—but also the least value to the customers, because the information will never be up to date. The second strategy is to use application proxies that require no additional investment in software and hardware, but require a blind trust in the used proxy software and the proxy administrators. The third alternative is to use a multilayered firewall, which does not require additional investment in consulting, but does require lots of configuration.

Firewalls play a central role in any security strategy. They allow internal clients to access resources on the Internet without exposing the internal client to external threats. For the outside world, the whole company is accessing the Internet as one person through the use of proxies. This strategy does not reveal anything about the internal networking structure of the company.

More sophisticated firewall solutions use a multilayered approach, whereby an external firewall is followed by a "demilitarized zone" (DMZ), then a second firewall, which protects the internal network. A company would typically put all servers that are needed for customer interaction, such as Web server, FTP server and mail gateway, into the DMZ. Remember that every service you offer to your customer requires an additional hole through your firewall, which increases the possibility of a security breach. Therefore, a multilayered approach offers a good solution for adding functionality without decreasing security.

11.8.3   Server Protection

Companies that connect servers to the Internet should be concerned about hackers abusing the offered resources for illegal purposes. Suppose that a hacker added pirated software to a company's Web server and published the URL. People would look for that software and could slow down the server with lots of server requests. Other hackers could misuse existing servers for their own calculations or for the printout of pages.

The results of launched attacks against other companies using your computer resources are often false claims by law enforcement agencies and other Internet sites claiming that the owner has tried to break in. Even if the claims prove to be false, it can damage the business of a Web site. To help law enforcement to find hackers, companies should make regular backups of log files and ensure that all applications and services are producing log files correctly.

An alarming signal of a break-in should sound when you discover that a log file has been deleted or the history of the UNIX shell is empty. Hackers will try to attack the system by breaking the passwords of legitimate users. This makes it easier for the attacker to move around the system without arousing suspicion in other users.

Most attacks are successful because of configuration errors in the external systems or in the operating system. Some attackers try to find errors in the network devices or the applications that run on the external servers in super-user mode. Bugs in these programs can open the system to an attack by passing on the powers of the programs to the attacker.

Hackers can easily break into a system when that system has failed to protect important files, especially executable and password files. Many hackers have been able to break into a system because they managed to get the password file, which they could easily download via FTP or HTTP. The passwords are encrypted, but breaking the encryption can be done easily on the hacker's system, so no one notices a hacker trying to guess a password. The hacker decrypts the password file and enters the system as a legitimate user.

Although Web servers are common points of attack, newer releases of software offer good protection, and only configuration accidents allow attackers to bypass the software. The situation is far worse for application servers connected to the Internet. Often, the software was not designed to incorporate security, which makes the server vulnerable and the major point of attack.

By invading external servers, hackers can gain information about internal servers, which contain far more critical information about the company. Strong host security for external Web servers must be implemented, no matter which firewall you use. Only if the server itself is secured will a firewall be able to block unwanted traffic. A firewall is not able to enhance the security of a server platform.

This has major implications if your intranet is connected directly to the Internet at the same point where the Web server is placed. If hackers are able to break into the Web server, there is a good chance that they will also be able to get into the intranet. Strong host security can prevent this type of attack.

A secure system must be able to detect break-in attempts. New paradigms or newly found bugs in the software will always be a threat to security; therefore, several precautions should be taken. Hackers often change configurations to work in a familiar environment, lower security parameters, or add users to the system. By periodically performing a system integrity check, it is possible to verify changes in the configuration. The integrity check should be able to confirm that key files, such as the password file or the security settings of the system, haven't been tampered with. An unauthorized change in the configuration may indicate a security breach.

In addition to regular system integrity checks, it is necessary to implement an audit system that constantly monitors whether security has been compromised. This allows an administrator to intervene and limit the damage. See Table 11.15 for an functional overview of an audit system.

Automatic audit reports must be evaluated and analyzed. This is time-consuming but necessary to create an alarm mechanism that automatically detects certain patterns in the audit, which may be part of an attack. To work effectively, the alarms must be configured in such a way that only the relevant

An audit system must fulfill the following requirements to complement a security strategy:

- **Adaptable**—The audit logs should be provided in a standard format, which allows tools to create audit reports for management.

- **Automated**—In case of a resource problem, the auditing mechanism should be able to resolve it either by freeing up other resources or shutting down the system to prevent further damage.

- **Configurable**—Adding, editing, and removing subsets of system activities should be possible at any time.

- **Dynamic**—It should be possible to check out the session log files to free up hard disk space.

- **Flexible**—The consumption of system resources should be controlled in a flexible way.

- **Manageable**—Tools for managing the files of various sessions should be included.

- **System-wide**—The audit system should be able to monitor a wide range of system activities on the operating system and application level.

Table 11.15. The Audit System

attacks are displayed on the administrator's screen. The threshold should be fine-tuned so that threatening attacks are noted, without compiling thousands of unnecessary reports. A typical alarm pattern occurs when users log in from IP addresses unknown to the attacked system. If a user logs in from somewhere in Korea and then from Switzerland within 24 hours, the system should sound an alarm. It is possible that the user has moved from Korea to Switzerland, but this can be easily verified. Port scans from a certain IP should send up a red flag, because this signifies someone is trying to find out which services are available. Repetitive failed logins are also a reason to be concerned about a loss of security.

The alarm system should be flexible and allow either automated actions or manual interaction of the administrator. An automated action could be to deny access to a certain IP address if a port scan is identified. This can be used by a hacker to create a denial of service attack, by spoofing IP addresses. A manual interaction is necessary immediately afterward to verify that the automated action was appropriate. The alarm should be able to send email, trigger mobile phones, or alert applications.

11.8.4   The Honey Pot

A new paradigm has been invented to stop hackers from breaking into systems any further. In June 2000, suspected Pakistani hackers broke into a U.S.-based computer system and thought they had found a vulnerable network to use as an anonymous launching pad to attack Web sites across India. But this was not the case; instead they walked into a trap known as a honey pot—a specially equipped system deployed by security professionals to lure hackers and track their moves.

For a month, every keystroke they made, every tool they used, every word of their online chat sessions was recorded and studied. The honey pot administrators learned how the hackers chose their targets, what level of expertise they had, what their favorite kinds of attacks were, and how they went about trying to cover their tracks so that they could nest on compromised systems.

Clifford Stoll used the idea first in his book "Cuckoo's Egg." This concept was refined by Lance Spitzner, a former tank commander in the U.S. Army. Spitzner is actually applying the tactics and techniques he learned in the Army to the Internet. Unlike the honey pots invented by Stoll, which were baited with known vulnerabilities designed to mimic various computers, Spitzner and his team put unmodified production systems online—networks with the same specifications, operating systems, and security as those used by many companies. Another important distinction between the early honey pots and Spitzner's version is that he posts all findings[32] on the Internet for others to comment on and learn from.

In one of his first honey pot episodes, early last year, Spitzner spent four days following a so-called script kiddie around his honey pot, watching as the hacker used ready-made programs to cover his tracks and gain control of the system. Script kiddies are mostly children, teenagers, and students who use ready-made tools to break into other systems. They often don't know the consequences of their work. The hacker does not have deep knowledge about hacking, but relies on known bugs in operating systems and applications. Spitzner, wary of scaring away the hacker, had to tread carefully, making sure to leave no trace as he, in turn, explored the system's logs. Based on what he learned, Spitzner was able to arm common operating systems like Linux and Solaris against most script kiddie attacks.

Some tools for security consultants have already been developed based on the outcome of the work done with honey pots. One program, called Snort, allows the consultant to eavesdrop on network traffic into the honey pot. The

---

[32]http://project.honeynet.org/

next step is to extend the honey pot from a server system to a transactional e-business site. The idea behind this is to find out more about hackers going into e-business sites. The intent is to make the honey pot irresistible to the more skilled hackers, called blackhats, who are looking to steal credit card numbers, rather than just vandalize Web sites.

The long-term goal of the honey pot project is to create pre-emptive security countermeasures based on findings about the tools and psychology of these hackers. Companies can use the honey pot for training their consultants, but should not rely only on a honey pot. At the same time, it is of utmost importance to invest in an intrusion-detection system if the organization does not have a dedicated team of highly trained administrators. Although the honey pot cannot be the only security measure, it helps to detract the hacker from the real targets, and allows for the observation of current technologies used in hacking without having to become a hacker!

11.8.5 Intrusion Detection Systems

The process of preventing and detecting security breaches by monitoring user and application activity is known as intrusion detection. Intrusion detection is a proactive process that requires the constant attention of system administrators. To remain secure, network systems must continually be probed for new security weaknesses.

Intrusion detection is important because it is impossible to keep up with the rapid pace of potential threats of computer systems. The Internet is changing rapidly every day, and businesses are expanding exponentially using the Internet as a resource. Because of its quick evolution, system monitoring and administration are becoming endless tasks. Intrusion detection tools make it easier for administrators to keep a secure network environment.

Who is attacking our networks? The vandals probing networks for security vulnerabilities may be curious teenagers, disgruntled employees, or corporate criminals from rival companies. Network intrusion is a systematic process. Unauthorized access is usually gained by exploiting operating system vulnerabilities (flaws in installed software). This can be done a number of ways. After an attacker chooses a target, he executes software to determine the remote operating system, searches various underground Web sites for flaws in that particular operating system, and then executes scripts that exploit the victim system. Virtually all server attacks progress in this manner. Intrusion detection tools help system administrators stop network attacks and aid in tracking down the attackers.

Rather than taking standard security precautions, many administrators feel that installing intrusion detection software can lessen the burden of network analysis. Additional software can also help remove unnecessary modules, better apply file permissions, and implement cryptography.

An intrusion detection system can be divided into the following categories:

- **Network Intrusion Detection System**—Monitors packets on the network wire and attempts to discover whether a hacker/cracker is attempting to break into a system.

- **System Integrity Verifier**—Monitors system files to find when an intruder changes them.

- **Log File Monitor**—Monitors log files generated by network services.

- **Deception System**—Contains pseudo-services whose goal is to emulate known holes in order to trap hackers.

Table 11.16. Intrusion Detection Systems

LIDS (Linux Intrusion Detection/Defense System)[33] is a free software package for i386 Linux architecture with the primary goal of protecting against root account intrusions. For LIDS to properly secure the server operating system, it must restrict the use of modules and raw memory/disk access, protect boot files, and prevent access to I/O ports. LIDS also logs every denied access attempt, locks routing tables/firewall rules, and restricts mounting. Another interesting features is its ability to hide system processes. Users logged into the system will not be able to execute a simple command such as "ps aux" to reveal running daemons. After LIDS is installed, it is first executed as a boot image initiated by LILO (Linux Loader). This feature guarantees that the system will remain secure throughout the entire boot process. LIDS has proven to be an effective tool in both intrusion detection and prevention.

Intrusion detection is a process that must be executed by system administrators in order to maintain secure networks. An administrator must understand the importance of protecting his/her network, realize how exploited vulnerabilities can bring a system to its knees, and know how to react to security incidents. System administrators must stay informed of all system advisories, flaws, and software updates. Failing to take appropriate actions to fix known problems can prove to be fatal to network servers. Table 11.16 illustrates various methods of intrusion detection and how to react when a breach has oc-

---

[33]http://www.lids.org/

curred. If network administrators do not remain informed of software updates and fail to closely monitor their servers, network security will remain problematic. Intrusion detection is a necessary process that must be fully understood and executed to maintain network security.

11.8.6   Attacks from the Inside

Although securing the internal system from the outside world is very important, about 80 percent of all break-ins are done from within the company, by trusted users. Employees are able to get administrator or root passwords on a system rather easily by simply asking the responsible person. In many cases, access to the super-user account is granted because someone needs to install a new application or create a backup of some data. Although most employees will limit the use of the root password only to what they are asked for, some will use super-user power to explore the system and do direct damage. An indirect way to cause damage is to introduce security issues, either voluntarily (by lowering the security parameters) or involuntarily (by installing buggy software), which can be exploited afterward without having to know the root password (which was changed by the administrator, for example).

To reduce the risk of internal attacks, system-level authorization control must be implemented. By breaking up the super-user powers into single powers that can be attributed to single users, total control over the system by unauthorized people can be prevented. Each user on the system has a set of powers associated with the tasks that he or she is required to fulfill. A user adding software to the system, for example, does not need the power to add or remove users to or from the system, and a user who wants to back up data does not need access to the kernel configuration. Although this makes user administration more tedious, it makes it much easier to find out who modified what.

Authorizations should be altered whenever the administrator thinks it is necessary. Reduced authorization is also very helpful. A user who makes a backup every Friday should not have the authorization to do this on any other day, without the consensus of the administrators. The authorizations should be assigned at login time, after the user has been authenticated.

In addition to the system-level authorization, an application-level authorization system can provide additional security for every single application. This system prevents authenticated users from using a system in a way that they were not authorized to do so. Guest users in an application should not be able to perform administrative tasks, for example, and should not access services and data that they are not authorized to use. Otherwise, they could obtain services and data that they haven't paid for.

Making application-wide authorization secure requires that all attempts by a client to access unauthorized services and data be logged. Automatic alerts inform the administrators, who then can intervene and protect the system from further damage.

11.8.7   Protecting Digital Businesses

To ensure the availability and security of your digital business, you should not trust any networks to which your system connected. This encompasses internal networks, extranets, and the Internet. Use a firewall to allow controlled access to certain resources. Firewalls are normally placed on the boundary between the Internet and the intranet, but this is often not enough. It often makes sense to place firewalls *on* the intranet to protect resources that should not be available to every employee. Personnel information must be protected to ensure privacy, for example.

Firewalls are also used to control access within the company. Imagine a company distributed all over the world, forming a global intranet. Each company site should be protected via firewall to ensure that a break-in in one site does not affect the other subsidiaries.

But firewalls are not general-purpose access-control systems and are not able to detect an insider's abuse of authorized access. A firewall does not detect or prevent insider attacks. Remember that insider attacks comprise 80 percent of all attacks. Therefore, the firewall needs to be integrated into an overall security strategy that prevents attacks not only from the outside, but also from the inside.

Another security problem is tunneling by malicious programs. Tunneling uses application protocols to pass malicious applications or data. Firewalls cannot protect networks from malicious programs, such as viruses and Trojan horses. A firewall is not designed to scan the huge amount of data going in and out. Some firewall solutions offer APIs to integrate a virus scanner, but the problem is that virus scanners are far too slow for real-time applications and for high volumes of traffic.

Firewalls also cannot protect against the attacks that do not go through it. Although many companies are afraid that Internet connectivity may leak internal data to the outside world, leaks can be accomplished easily through social engineering and theft of media. Therefore, it cannot be said often enough that a firewall will not resolve all security issues that a company will have in the Information Age. For a firewall to work, it must be a part of a consistent overall organizational security architecture. Firewall policies must be realistic and must reflect the level of security in the entire network.

Just as it does not make sense to build a house, and then lock the doors but leave all the windows open, it doesn't make sense to set up a firewall if you do not also institute security policies for floppy disks, fax machines, or phone calls.

11.8.8   Trusted Operating Systems

A firewall serves a very specific function based on the premise that the Internet is used for browsing, content serving, and mediating access to internal servers such as mail, news, and FTP servers. It is placed in the data path between the external and internal clients and servers, and the configuration of the firewall tells who is allowed to talk to whom. Firewalls work on the TCP/IP protocol level allowing ports (i.e., services) to be opened or closed. If the data is not encrypted, it can even do some content filtering, which enables checking whether outgoing mail contains company internal documents or incoming mail is infected by a virus.

But this is no longer the standard function of the firewall. The goal of a firewall is to determine how to direct traffic and who is allowed to see what. Firewall manufacturers "harden" the operating system by applying the latest security-relevant patches and removing all unnecessary services from the firewall machine. A so-called "trusted computing base" is formed by the firewall software and the operating system, which works in a highly specialized and security-oriented way.

Firewalls are secure only as long as no other applications are executed on the firewall machine. If nontrusted applications are added to the firewall machine, it is possible to circumvent the firewall rules. Firewalls are highly specialized gateways that cannot perform any other tasks, such as application services.

To work efficiently, today's electronic business must run middle-tier applications that operate on the boundary between an intranet and the Internet (or extranet). This requires a new philosophy for security. This new philosophy won't eliminate the need for firewalls, but will add the need for trusted operating systems (TOS) for handling electronic business applications.

Real-time applications require this middle tier to access internal databases directly. In mission-critical applications, access to the original database is a must. In these cases, a solution with a traditional firewall will either be not secure enough or not fast enough. Fast access to critical resources allows companies to take advantage of current business opportunities.

To make the business available to as many people as possible, it is necessary to create a Web front-end. This poses new security issues, especially with browsers. With Web-enabled applications, companies expose the heart of their business to the whole world. Attacks on the companies' mission-critical applications and information are significantly more damaging than the shutdown of a single desktop.

As businesses move to phase four of their electronic business evolution, risks increase along with profits! Companies that once provided only information about their business are now addressing queries and updating information. This translates into greater value to the customers. In phase four, real business transactions are conducted over the Internet. This offers the highest value to the end customer, but also puts the company at risk if security cannot be guaranteed at least to 99 percent.

To ensure security for business transactions, mission-critical systems should not be placed on a standard computer, but on a system with a TOS. These systems have been certified to support the tough B1 and B2 level U.S. defense industry standards and E3 European standards.

The advantage of a TOS is that it uses data partitioning and is based on the least-privilege paradigm. Data partitioning means that operating systems place data on the machine in several partitions. Programs, files, communication resources, and network interfaces can be put into separate partitions. Unlike partitions on the file system level, these logical partitions allow only programs within a certain partition to see the data of exactly this partition. A special mechanism allows the exchange of information between partitions. Because only one tiny hole separates the partitions, it is easy to define rules for the exchange of information. In a traditional operating system, applications can protect their own files. If the application makes a mistake, the data in the file can be disclosed or damaged. It is up to the application to set file permissions properly. Segregating information into partitions reduces the probability of errors.

A typical trusted operating system consists of two partitions, one connected to the Internet (outside) and one connected to the intranet (inside). The only two applications running on the outside partition are a Web server and a daemon that allows connections to the inside partition. No data is placed on the outside. Requests from the Internet are accepted by the Web server and passed on to the daemon, which then decides whether the request is valid. The business logic is placed on the inside partition, and every application has its own set of privileges stored in a database. By default, an installed application is not allowed to do anything on the trusted system. Every application should be examined, and a determination should be made as to which privileges the application must run without compromising the security. This information must be stored in the database and attributed to the application. If the entry in the database and the attributes of the application do not match, the application is not launched, creating an additional layer of security.

Trusted operating systems also offer the ability to remove the root account from the kernel. Instead of checking against the root, the checks are made to a set of privileges, each of which grants a specific power. Instead of associating power with users, the powers are associated with programs. This allows the power to be given to the program only for the time it is running.

Hackers will have to hack into program accounts instead of user accounts. The rights they get when hacking a program account are available only for that particular application. A takeover of the system is then very unlikely. Privileges are not inherited, making it difficult to exploit the security flaws that applications may have. An error within an application will not bring down the whole system, as on traditional operating systems.

A trusted operating system can be used to allow real-time collaboration for research and development via the Web. When the necessary information is offered in real time to the researchers and developers, they can add information much faster. The product design teams need to protect their future designs from unwanted access, in order to stay ahead of their competition.

The same applies to financial institutions, which need to provide real-time services to their customers. At the same time, they must ensure that no unauthorized users gain access to account information. Financial services companies are showing individuals and businesses that the efficiencies gained from the Internet are extremely compelling.

Other industries are proving real-time information can benefit their customers as well. Health care companies are able to cut costs through the use of real-time information services on the Internet by transferring their policy management services to the Internet. Insurance companies are able to allow independent salespeople to shop for the best policies through special real-time access to the internal information.

These new strategic services create a critical gateway between users and the application resources on the intranet that support the online services. With traditional operating systems and application programming practices, the Web server becomes an extremely vulnerable point for security attacks that are difficult to stop.

11.8.9 Trusted Solutions

Two trusted operating systems mainly used for securing electronic business on the Internet are described here: Hewlett-Packard's Virtual Vault and Sun's Trusted Solaris.

Hewlett Packard—Virtual Vault

The Virtual Vault[34] trusted Web-server platform consists of a military-grade operating system based on HP-UX. The operating system complies with the U.S. Department of Defense Trusted Computer System Standards and is binary compatible to HP-UX, allowing it to run standard applications in a high-security environment. The additional security is built in to the operating system and network layers to protect sensitive information. To make the system Internet-ready, it is shipped with the Netscape Enterprise Server, which has been slightly modified to comply to the same standards.

A common problem with most operating systems is the super-user account, which allows total control over the computer to those with access. Virtual Vault has a special mechanism to address this. It breaks down the powers of the "root" into more than 50 distinct privileges. Each application is granted only the minimum privileges required to run properly. This makes it impossible for Trojan horses to attack a system, if they are able penetrate it.

The Web runtime environment is strictly partitioned, meaning that a security layer has been put in place to protect internal information from the outside. It had been originally developed to protect highly classified intelligence information in the Army, but it is now used by all installations of Virtual Vault to

---

[34]http://www.hp.com/security/products/virtualvault/

meet the security needs of companies on the Internet. See Table 11.17 for an overview of the standard partitions.

A program that needs access to data or to a program in another compartment needs special privileges to do so. The communication between "inside" and "outside" is secured by a so-called trusted gateway, which protects applications in the "inside" compartment from malicious attacks or bugs in middleware that might otherwise do damage to internal applications.

Four partitions are used with Virtual Vault in a standard configuration. The access between these partitions is very limited.

- **Inside**—Stores and executes databases, CGI programs, Java servlets, and middleware services.

- **Outside**—Contains the Web server and some middleware clients.

- **System**—Stores the external static Web pages.

- **System High**—Contains audit trails, for example.

Table 11.17. Data Partitioning with Virtual Vault

The static HTML files, for example, are stored in the "system" partition, which helps to protect their integrity. Because no programs are allowed to run in the "system," they are protected from being exploited by hackers looking for security flaws or misconfigurations. Programs can also be executed in another partition (also called a compartment), with no direct access to the "system" partition.

The trusted gateway provides the assurance that CGI programs installed on the Virtual Vault system do not contain malicious code. In many cases, hackers replace the actual CGI program to gain access to personal customer information and knowledge about the intranet. By using the trusted gateway, the administrator create checksums for all existing CGI applications and store the powers in a database. Every change within the CGI will stop the application from working.

Unfortunately, not all applications are Internet-ready. Many still consist of a single, monolithic component, which is the pre-Internet architecture. This architecture makes it difficult to protect the underlying server. To make the system secure, the monolithic application must be transformed into a more distributed component architecture. This requires a rewrite of major parts of the software, so an alternate means of getting online must be available. While the programmers work on the distributed solution, Virtual Vault offers the trusted gateway proxy, which allows access to monolithic applications without putting the server at risk. The trusted gateway proxy provides a proxy component that fields all Internet requests and forwards valid data securely to the middleware server that resides on the intranet.

Another core functionality of Virtual Vault has been implemented through the integration of Hewlett-Packard's free product Web Quality of Service (Web-QoS).[35] WebQoS adds so-called peak usage management, which prevents an overload of the server and minimizes the impact of unexpected surges in demand while maximizing the volume of completed transactions. This protects performance levels of active customers who are about to complete transactions.

As long as the resources are tied up with these customers, new transactions are not permitted on the site. The newly arriving customers will be redirected to another server in a defined cluster, making sure that the available resources are used up to a maximum.

As more businesses start to use Java on their business servers, it becomes necessary to take special precautions for the Java Virtual Machine (JVM). To make the business application secure, the JVM needs to run on the "inside" compartment, making it inaccessible to the Web server and to the attackers from the Web server.

Through the Web administration interface, it is possible to administer the system remotely from another intranet server. The interface uses standard Web pages, making it easy to understand with little training. Audit trails and alarms help administrators to ensure system security by providing valuable checks and balances. The audit reports reside in another secured partition, which is inaccessible to unauthorized applications.

Virtual Vault also offers tight integration into Hewlett-Packard's Open-View[36] software.

Sun—Trusted Solaris

Trusted Solaris[37] is a special release of Sun's operating system Solaris, which complies with the U.S. Department of Defense Trusted Computer System Standards. It includes CDE as the graphical desktop environment, and Solstice AdminSuite to control access to information and what users are permitted to do on the system.

Just like Virtual Vault, Trusted Solaris offers additional safeguards against internal and external threats, beyond the protection features of standard UNIX systems. While Virtual Vault is designed more to be the application firewall sitting between the Internet and the intranet, Trusted Solaris offers the pos-

---

[35] http://www.hp.com/go/domain/

[36] http://www.hp.com/go/openview/

[37] http://www.sun.com/products-n-solutions/government/trustedsolaris.html

sibility of connecting multiple servers and workstations to create a distributed system, whereby security can be implemented at multiple levels. Although this approach allows for more flexibility, it also offers more ways of attacking the system.

Trusted Solaris is binary compatible with the standard Solaris operating system, allowing most applications to run without modification on the secure system. Multilevel versions of some essential applications, including trusted databases, have also been developed to run on Trusted Solaris.

Trusted Solaris divides administrative tasks among a number of administrators, reducing the risk of a takeover from attack. Administrators entering the system must log on in the normal way and then assume a role. This enables all administrative activities to be traced back to a specific authenticated user. Three different types of administrators are available on the system: a security administrator, a system administrator, and an operator. A fourth root role is provided for software installation purposes.

The Solstice user and database manager enforce a "two-role control" for the configuration of user accounts, devices, hosts, and networks. This is achieved together with a new device allocation and profile manager. The profile manager allows the administrator to create execution profiles, which bundle sets of applications and actions with optional security attributes. Without an execution profile, a user cannot do anything on the system. Execution profiles are also used for configuring the powers of the administrators. It is possible to redistribute administrative responsibilities among administrators.

Trusted Solaris provides different types of labels that are assigned to files, windows, hosts, devices, networks, and other system objects, which users are able to access. These labels indicate the level of trust of anyone accessing the system by assigning a clearance, which defines the maximum and minimum sensitivity labels.

Mandatory Access Control (MAC) is used to compare the sensitivity label of the user with the object being accessed. If they do not match, the user is not allowed to access the object. This is similar to the data partitioning model of Virtual Vault. Discretionary Access Control (DAC), on the other hand, uses file permissions and optional access control lists to restrict access to information based on a user's identity or group membership. DAC is used along with MAC to control access to system files.

It is possible to set security attributes for each host and network, enabling communication. By default, no communication is allowed. The software can be tuned for communication between Trusted Solaris and other systems.

Trusted Solaris also uses the least-privilege paradigm, which removes the risk that occurs in standard operating systems because programs running as root are exempt from all policy controls. The root privileges are divided into almost 90 distinct privileges (compared to 50 in Virtual Vault). Trusted Solaris provides a tool that helps to identify which privileges are needed to run any given application properly.

11.8.10   Certification Authority

Digital certificates must be issued by a trusted third party called a certification authority (CA). The role of the CA is to issue a means of personal identification that is recognized on a national or worldwide level. A CA can issue different types of digital certificates required by individuals (e.g., in a Web browser) and organizations (e.g., on a Web server) wanting to identify themselves on the Internet. The certificates are available to any requesting party and can be obtained with different levels of assurance, such as Class 1, 2, or 3. Depending on the level of assurance, it can be verified whether the certificate really belongs to the person who has done a particular business transaction on the Internet. Class 1 certificates require only a valid email address to obtain the certificate, while Class 3 requires a higher level of personal identification, such as presenting your passport to the certification authority.

In addition to the general digital certificate, companies may decide to issue special digital certificates that can be used only for a special purpose, such as online banking or health care information. These special certificates are not available to everyone, but only to individuals who are eligible, as determined by the organization's membership or subscriber rules. These so-called private label digital certificates contain information specified by the organization to extend brands and end-user customer relationships into cyberspace.

To become a certification authority, it is necessary to invest significantly in technology, infrastructure, and practices. Because digital signatures and cryptography are both required for managing a CA, it is necessary to handle a high volume of computing-intensive traffic. To support the servers, special devices that handle only the encryption much be purchased. To manage high-volume deployments, it is necessary to combine the required cryptography and security protocols to support trusted applications with Web-based front-ends, scalable transaction engines, and secure databases. Because the database is the capital of the company, special physical security measures must be taken. The building needs special protection, the server room needs guards and ID checks, and the Internet connection needs a trusted operating system to monitor the activities.

To serve customers on a worldwide basis, the CA must have redundant communication links, automated backup, and recovery facilities that ensure the availability of the system at any given time. Trained customer service and help desk personnel are also required to ensure that customer problems can be resolved.

Most important are the practices that provide the core business values of the CA. The practice statement consists of a set of documents that establish the legal infrastructure and metrics for operating as a trusted third party on the Internet. It is a defined model of trust and a legally binding framework. The practice statement describes in detail the certification infrastructure, together with the foundation for the operations of the certification authority. The practice statement also describes how the application for a certificate works and what validation requirements are used for the application. The complete procedure of issuing is described in the statement, as well as when certificates are accepted and how they are used. Sections on the suspension, revocation, and expiration of the certificates are also required, as are the obligations of issuing authorities and the certification authority. All this information is necessary to ensure the proper working of the CA, for the sake of the customers and to meet legal requirements.

Security is a major issue for companies that want to connect to the Internet. Maintaining security requires good planning and execution. Technology can certainly help companies become more secure, but security cannot be guaranteed–especially if the necessary processes are not in place.

Chapter 12

DEALING WITH JAVA

12.1 Introducing Java

12.1.1 Definition of Java

Sun defines Java with the following two short sentences: "Java is a simple, object-oriented, distributed, interpreted, robust, secure, architecture-neutral, portable, high-performance, multithreaded, dynamic, buzzword-compliant, general-purpose programming language. Java supports programming for the Internet in the form of platform-independent Java applets."[1]

Although this is a concise definition of Java, understandable by a technical person, nontechnical people and especially business people will not have a clue why Java is such a success in the Internet world and what the above sentence implies for their online businesses. This chapter tries to explain the technical virtues of Java and how they can help to enhance the electronic service of the online business.

The sentence that is used most to describe Java's advantage is "Write once, run anywhere." It describes the unique feature of Java. It is totally hardware- and software-independent (or "architecture-neutral," as Sun describes it). There are no restrictions on which platform you use to develop Java items. If you develop your application on an Apple PowerMac, it will run on the Windows and UNIX families as well (the Sun buzzword here is "portable"). It does not matter whether you run MacOS,[2] BeOS,[3] or MKLinux[4] on the PowerMac.

You do not have to change anything within the program, nor do you have to recompile the source code. After the program has been written and compiled, it will run on all platforms that support Java. Today, all mainstream clients (Windows and Mac-OS-based, Intel and PowerPC-based) and servers (all UNIX flavors) support Java. Besides the original implementation by Sun and porting done by IBM, Hewlett-Packard, and others, there are several open

---

[1] http://java.sun.com/docs/white/langenv/Intro.doc2.html
[2] http://www.apple.com/macos/
[3] http://www.beos.com/
[4] http://www.mklinux.apple.com/

source communities that write runtime environments and compilers for Java (e.g., ElectricalFire,[5] Kaffe,[6] Japhar,[7] and Jikes[8]).

The promise of portability and architecture neutrality is delivered by the Java Virtual Machine (JVM), which provides a software environment and a translator between the Java applications and the system platform on which they are run. For example, system platforms could be Windows 2000 on an Intel Pentium processor or HP-UX 11i on the HP PA-RISC processor. As input, the Java compiler builds the application by generating an executable representation called byte-code. Byte-code is unique in that it is a set of execution instructions for the JVM rather than for the actual system hosting the execution. The JVM defines the execution engine for application logic written in Java. The Virtual Machine interprets byte-code to emulate the execution of applications on the host system. It is the actions performed by the JVM that represent application execution. This is unlike the traditional model in which the host system performs the actions representing application execution. This model allows the program to be resource-independent. Although it may be slower than a comparable C program, it fits perfectly into the Internet world, where you probably do not know what hardware and software platforms your customers use.

12.1.2 Validating the Business Case

One of the chief virtues of a Java environment is its ability to support real-time updates of information exchange across applications, across platforms, and even outside the enterprise to business partners. Another virtue is the ease of the application development. Querying databases on several platforms and locations becomes easy with Java, which has a standard way of conducting such transactions. In our information society, databases and information-driven applications become more important. Using the appropriate tools and programming language also becomes more important. The first area in which Java will succeed is in applications that benefit from enhanced information exchange.

Applications must be "Internet-enabled," so using programming languages that have integrated support for Internet features, such as opening ports on the lower level and transferring Web pages on a higher level, is helpful because it reduces time to implement. In Java, it is really easy, for example, to build a chat server. The chat server source code will have in its smallest form about 20 lines and the client, maybe 200 lines. Building applications that connect to databases or other services over the Internet is done fairly easily and consistently over all platforms.

---

[5] http://www.mozilla.org/projects/ef/
[6] http://www.kaffe.org/
[7] http://www.japhar.org/
[8] http://www.research.ibm.com/jikes/

Java offers unique features for the development of new services and products. The following are important features:

- **Ease of application development**—As a programming language, Java contributes to developer productivity by dramatically shortening software development time. Software that would take weeks to write with other tools can now be written in days with Java.

- **Application mobility**—This feature permits Java-based applications to run on any hardware platform that supports Java Virtual Machine.

- **Real-time information updates**—In a Java environment, information can be updated in real time across applications, across platforms, on the inside, and on the outside of a business enterprise. Many classes of applications are enhanced by this standardized flow of information.

- **Growth**—New ways of communication and collaboration have been created by the Internet. Java is able to support these services and enhance them through its language features. Your applications can grow at the same speed as your company.

Table 12.1. Java Business Value Proposition

Application development with Java becomes fairly easy as soon as you have to support more than one platform. Write it on a certain hardware platform and, if you stick to the Java specifications, it will run without changes on other platforms as well.

Java technology enables the exchange of information in real time throughout enterprises and beyond company boundaries, and so enables new classes of software technology for e-business, especially for electronic commerce, supply chain management, management repair operations (MRO), and customer interaction.

Java applets are not really of interest to enterprise-wide applications. They may be useful for certain applications in which users must interact with certain Java servers, but to save bandwidth, simple Web forms will often do. Java really makes a difference on the server, because Java technology for server-side applications permits more innovation and efficiency than ever before.

Java should be used in enterprise business solutions, server-side and infrastructure applications, and end-to-end application deployment. Server-side and infrastructure applications require information to be updated in real time throughout the enterprise, such as supply-chain management and enterprise resource planning applications.

Java applications have occasionally failed to provide real application mobility, because early versions of the Java environment were specified rather loosely. For example, a Java platform could be completely compliant, yet inconsistencies between implementations prevented true compatibility. Each version of Java code gets closer to delivering on the promise of true application mobility.

Consider an online shopping example. When ordering a product via the Internet, the Web application at the merchant accepts your credit card number and sends it to the bank to another application for a credit check. Another application at the supplier checks availability for the product you ordered, and if it is not in stock, places an order with an outside vendor for additional supply. That particular application must reply with availability, and all the information must be consolidated fairly quickly so that you, the consumer, will be informed that your order has been accepted and will be fulfilled by some specified date.

We now have a minimum of five applications involved. In the worst case scenario, each of the applications runs on a different platform with incompatible APIs. If all the parties involved had used Java instead, the exchange of information would have been very easy.

Java has attracted considerable media attention and industry hype. Realistically, businesses will incorporate Java technology because it enhances their own corporate goals, and not because they have read about it in a computer magazine.

12.1.3 Embedded Devices

We have discussed Java from an enterprise computing perspective but as it evolves, Java technology has implications for many classes of electronic devices: peripherals, instruments, measurement, and consumer electronics, which are also called embedded devices.

All large electronic producers recognize the growing importance of Java technology in the emerging market of embedded devices. Java is able to play a major role in embedded devices in two ways. With JavaOS, an operating system written in Java, it is possible to write complex applications on these devices with few memory resources and little processing power. The other option is to use the Java API to control these devices from another machine, such as a PC. On the embedded device, a real-time operating system (RTOS) receives the messages from the Java application and is able to respond in the appropriate way. If you look around your house, you will find many devices that already use chips—the washing machine and TV set, for example. These devices have their own hardware inside and operating systems. They are not able to talk to each other, nor can they be controlled remotely by a single device. If you have a TV and a VCR from two different brands, you probably use two different types of remote controls, because they cannot speak to each other. Using Java and standard APIs, would allow you to control all devices in your household from a single remote control or over the Internet. But this may not be the best thing to do. Without the necessary security infrastructure, hackers would be able to switch on your TV during the night and turn off your heat in winter.

Embedded devices are also network enabled, meaning that they are able to communicate with other devices or services. This communication is called pervasive computing, and it is about to become a reality. Based on this new paradigm, several companies have started to develop new technologies and strategies. Lucent Technologies,[9] for example, developed the Inferno technology to allow the connection of devices, and Hewlett-Packard[10] developed a complete new vision for the future of the Internet. Their E-Services initiative works at a higher level, not on the device level—but on the service level. See Chapter 16 for more detailed information on pervasive computing.

12.1.4 Java versus JavaScript

In December 1995, Netscape announced LiveScript, which then became Java-Script. It was developed independently of Sun's Java programming language. The first browser to support JavaScript was Netscape 2.0. The target user is the less experienced developer, who wants to add interactivity to his Web sites. Unlike Java, JavaScript is a scripting language, which allows the programming of events, objects, and actions. Java and JavaScript interoperate well but are technically, functionally, and behaviorally very different. JavaScript and Java are able to exchange variables and functions via a special API, called LiveWire, which was also developed by Netscape.

Java and JavaScript are distinct languages, with different purposes and features. JavaScript was designed to provide an easy way for Web authors to create interactive Web pages. Java is meant for experienced programmers; JavaScript is a simpler "scripting" language aimed at those with less programming experience. Like Java, JavaScript is a cross-platform language that can work with any compatible browser.

Table 12.2 provides a brief overview on the differences between JavaScript and Java applets. An in-depth analysis on JavaScript can be found in Chapter 10, because it is tightly integrated into Web browsers. Microsoft implemented its own version of JavaScript called JScript, which is partly compatible with JavaScript. As a rule, Internet Explorer is one version behind Netscape Navigator; i.e., IE's 4.0 JScript is compatible with Netscape's 3.0 JavaScript.

---

[9] http://www.lucent.com/
[10] http://www.hp.com/

Although Java and JavaScript have very similar names, they are quite different. This table shows the largest differences between Java applets and JavaScripts.

JavaScript	Java Applet
Interpreter—Interpreted by client—not compiled.	**Byte-code**—Compiled on server to byte-code format before interpreter execution on client.
Object-based—No classes or inheritance; built-in, extensible objects.	**Object-oriented**—Classes and inheritance; built-in, extensible objects.
Integration—It is integrated with and embedded into HTML.	**Attachment**—Applets distinct from HTML (accessed via HTML pages).
Loose typing—Does not require variables' data types to be declared.	**Strong typing**—Must declare variables' data types.
Dynamic binding—Checks object references at runtime.	**Static binding**—Requires references to objects at compile-time.
Secure—Cannot write to or read from hard disk.	**Secure**—Cannot read from or write to hard disk without explicit permission.

Table 12.2. Comparison of Java and JavaScript

JavaScript is an interpreted language, meaning that is not necessary to compile the code. People without in-depth programming knowledge find it easy to use. Only a browser and a text editor are required to write JavaScript applications. The language is not truly object-oriented, because it cannot create new classes or inheritances, but it has a built-in set of objects, that can be extended and accessed. JavaScript does not require the user to declare variables' data types, and objects are checked at runtime (as opposed to the compiler checks of Java). JavaScript does not allow access to system resources, such as printers or hard disks, but many bugs in the implementations have revealed holes that make it possible to read from a hard disk. Therefore, it is important to keep an eye on the browser manufacturer site and download updates or patches that resolve these security issues.

12.1.5 Example Business Cases

To make Java technology successful on the Internet, a sound business case must be behind it. If the new possibilities of the technology do not help increase profit, reduce costs, or help in other ways, most businesses will refuse to use them. This section describes four business cases that will be checked against the described technologies in the following sections. This will allow us to see that a particular Java technology will add value to the electronic business.

The Online Bank

A financial institution or bank operates in the conventional way by offering its services through its branches and the telephone. It wants to add online banking to its portfolio and create special Web pages for accessing information on customers' accounts and enable transactions through HTML forms. The interaction between Web browser and server is done through CGI programs, which talk to the back-end system, a legacy system, perhaps, that does not even understand TCP/IP. How can this process be simplified?

The Clothing Manufacturer

A clothing manufacturer designs and produces a collection every six months. The manufacturer organizes a show to present the products. Retailers are invited to participate and choose products appropriate for their shops. The show is organized in one location, where large retailers gather. Many smaller retailers do not attend, because it is too expensive. Instead, they go into larger shops to see what the larger retailers have ordered and order their goods on that basis. To reach the smaller retailers as well, the fashion manufacturer decides to create an online service so retailers can view the products, choose them, and combine them. The first step would be to install a shopping system from which the retailers can choose goods. But to make the system really valuable, it should be interactive. How can this be achieved?

The Cargo Service

A cargo service offers the transport of goods at short notice. To automate the process, the company offers a Web page with an HTML form, on which customers can enter the necessary data, and check flight availability and arrival times of the packet at the destination. Offering this service is not a great enhancement over ordering the pickup of the packet. To make the service really valuable, tracking and tracing should be implemented and payment should be possible directly over the Internet. How can this be achieved?

The Car Designer

A team of car designers needs to access the designs of a new automobile over the network. The information is stored in multiple databases throughout the company. To simplify the work of the designers, the information should be accessible through one interface. It should be able to combine resources to gather intelligence that is created by the wealth of information. How can such an interface be built and the information joined?

12.2   Java Foundation Classes

12.2.1   Technical Overview

When Java was introduced, the abstract window toolkit (AWT) was the graphical user interface (GUI) that was supplied with it. It provided a very simple library for building Java applications and applets. Java developers encountered many limitations when attempting to create a modern-looking application. Still, the AWT provided 100 percent portability from the source code and assumed a native look and feel on the deployment platforms.

The idea of the AWT is to provide a portable GUI library that works on all platforms. Instead of emulating the native look and feel of a single toolkit, the AWT uses a layered toolkit model, where each Java component creates a native component. Each Java component class wraps the native implementation, a rather complex issue because every native toolkit uses a different event model. This resulted in a somewhat limited use of a user interface.

In version 1.1 of the Java Development Kit (JDK), AWT became part of a comprehensive set of GUI classes called the Java Foundation Classes (JFC). This version provides a range of new features, such as a better event model, printing capabilities, a lightweight user interface framework, and JavaBeans compliance.

Using Swing, another component of the Java Framework, it has become possible to create applications with a professional-looking GUI, not only for the Web browsers, but also for standard applications. The AWT provided little integration into a desktop environment and limited functionality for creating larger applications.

The features of the JFC introduced in JDK 1.1 are presented in Table 12.3. The JFC is JavaBeans compliant, which means that an architecture- and platform-neutral API for creating and using dynamic Java components is used. The advantage of the JavaBeans approach is that Java programs are able to interoperate with legacy applications and can be easily distributed over the Internet.

The lightweight user interface framework used in the JFC allows components to be completely transparent. The components can be written completely in Java and do not carry overhead from the native system. The JFC com-

- **JavaBeans compliant**—Uses a consistent API to handle events.

- **Lightweight UI framework**—Enables components to be peerless and completely written in Java.

- **Delegation event model**—Supports visual development environments and development of distributed and multicast applications.

- **Printing**—Supports printers.

- **Data transfer/clipboard**—Allows clipboard functions not available in AWT, such as cut, copy, and paste.

- **Desktop colors integration**—Seamlessly integrates Java application into the desktop.

- **Graphics and image enhancements**—Provides extended support for rich graphical user interfaces.

- **Mouseless operation**—Allows every operation that can be done with the mouse to be executed via keyboard.

- **Popup menu**—Opens context-driven menus.

- **ScrollPane container**—Implementations of a highly configurable and resizable user interface.

Table 12.3. Features of the Java Foundation Classes

ponents have a consistent look and feel across all platforms. This means that GUI applications load and run faster. AWT was much more restrictive, because it did not allow developers to extend the components or change their look and feel. Converting existing AWT components to JFC is easy, making it easy to upgrade existing applications to the new paradigm.

The delegation event model used in the JFC is very different from the simple event model in the AWT. Using AWT, it was necessary to create complex if-then-else constructions to handle events, with the introduction of JFC events identified by class instead of by ID. The event listener communicated with the objects interested in a particular event, reducing the load on a system. With JFC, printing is possible. You can even send text or graphics to a printer using

Java code. With AWT, it was necessary to include native code, but then printing was restricted to a particular platform. JFC introduces printer support that can be easily integrated into applications.

One problem with AWT was its inability to cut and paste text to or from the Java program. The JFC introduces full clipboard support, which enables dynamic data types to be created, registered, and transferred. It is now possible to cut an image out of a Java application and paste it into Photoshop. Unlike the old AWT, the JFC is able to adhere to the system color scheme, which makes it easier for users to adapt colors to their preferred settings. The Java Foundation Classes enhance the graphical capabilities, by introducing functions to clip an image or flip it horizontally or vertically.

The JFC introduced mouseless operation, which enables users to use a Java program without a mouse. The advantage of this is that data entry and operational applications can be created and speed up the use of certain features. People who access computers through voice-control can access these applications more easily if there is a voice layer on top, which translates voice to letters. In addition to mouseless operation, popup menus have been introduced that open menus containing all the functions relative to the object to which the mouse points. These so-called context menus reduce the failure rate and increase the speed for using a program.

ScrollPane containers have been introduced to support automatic scrolling for a single component. It allows the content of a pane to be updated much faster than in AWT. The introduction of the ScrollPane container greatly simplifies the task of displaying information in a fixed area.

12.2.2 Checking the Business Cases

Looking at our four business cases, we can see that they can profit from the JFC. The Java Foundation Classes are able to create highly dynamic and modern graphical user interfaces for all types of applications. The online banking solution will profit from a Java interface that allows customers to choose all functions of the banking application. The application is able to change its look and appear as a standard application for corporate customers who have strict design rules for computer programs.

The clothing manufacturer can create an easy-to-use interface using Java and the JFC. Imagine a desktop for retailers on which they can order goods and create arrangements, which can be used as shop decorations. Instead of going to fashion shows, retailers are able to select skirts and blouses online, using virtual models. The Java Foundation Classes offer a wide range of functions that make it possible to create a virtual showroom without spending months on development. The Java applet is able to connect to the order system and automate much of the manual work that many retailers do regularly.

The cargo service will not profit as much from a Java graphical interface. The customers of the cargo service won't have additional functionality through the Java Foundation Classes. Instead of providing an extra graphical interface through a Web browser, cargo customers would prefer an integration of their existing ordering system. The integration is quite expensive and must be performed for every single customer, but the graphical interface could provide a first step toward integration with a reduced functional set.

Car designers can profit through an advanced graphical interface. The interface allows the designers to navigate through a design and describe the parts of the design in more detail. Using VRML scenes, the designers can check their designs in detail and give direct feedback on certain elements. Introducing an Internet-based design and review process enhances the collaboration between people who work in different locations.

12.2.3 Online Experience

Although the Java Foundation Classes are part of Java 1.1, Web browsers do not support the features natively. The features must be installed separately onto the computer, or install the latest Java plug-in from Sun, which supports all features of Java 1.1. Because it is not a standard component of Web browsers, few Internet solutions support the Java Foundation Class. It is to expected that new releases of Web browsers will support Java 2 and all its components, so it will only be a matter of time until JFC will be natively supported.

One of the largest banks in Switzerland, the Zürcher Kantonal Bank,[11] uses the Java Foundation Class to create an interactive banking experience. Using a Java applet for online banking outside of the U.S. was especially important, as encryption was not allowed to be exported. By special agreement, financial institutions outside of the United States were able to receive 128-bit keys for encryption (now any company can receive 128-bit keys in most areas of the world). But the standard 40-bit encryption was easier to use and adds a security level on top of the SSL encryption. This is easily done through Java, but the standard AWT interface is more than ugly. With the introduction of the Java Foundation Class, Internet Java applets are becoming modern applications.

12.2.4 Required Software

Until the release of the Java Development Kit 1.1, the Java Foundation Classes had to be added manually to the system. With the introduction of Java 2, the JFC has become part of the distribution and is the new standard GUI package used for all new applications. The AWT package is still available and will be used to maintain backward compatibility with older systems.

---

[11]http://www.zkb.ch/

12.3   Jini

12.3.1   Technical Overview

Jini[12] is the latest initiative by Sun Microsystems and allows all types of devices to be connected into so-called impromptu networks. Jini allows access to new network services and delivers those services in a simple way. Built on the Java standard, Jini technology creates a network consisting of all types of digital devices without extensive planning, installation, or human intervention. Each device broadcasts the services it offers to all other devices in the community.

An impromptu community is created when two or more devices create a network to share their services. They do not need prior knowledge of each other in order to participate. The communication is established dynamically and does not require that the devices exchange drivers to offer their services to the other devices in the community.

Unlike traditional networks, an impromptu community will consist not only of servers and clients, but all devices that create, modify, or receive information. The consumer appliance market—with products such as mobile phones, television sets, and personal digital assistants—can be easily included in a Jini network. Pervasive computing quickly becomes reality.

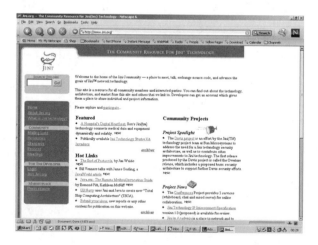

Figure 12.1. The Jini Community

Every electronic device today can handle information and contains a certain type of microprocessor. The devices are ready to communicate with the other devices, but today's networks are not prepared for the required pervasiveness. Jini is written in Java, so it can run on all devices that include a Java runtime

---

[12]http://www.sun.com/jini/

environment (JRE). It will also run on existing networks; no special network protocols are required.

Devices using the Jini technology use a process called "discovery" that searches for other devices using the Jini technology. When connecting a new device to the network, it tries to locate the look-up server and register its services. After the connection between the devices has been established, Java objects are sent to a look-up service, which represents the services as well as their characteristics and attributes. When a device in the impromptu community wants to use a service offered in that community such as applications, drivers, or interfaces, it can download the required data from the look-up server, which connects then to the desired object.

Jini-enabled devices need to update their registration periodically. If they fail to do so, the look-up service removes the services from the list. But removing a device does not interrupt the services offered by the other members of the impromptu network.

If a device has no Java installed, it still can become a participant in a Jini network. This is done by moving the objects to another device, which acts on behalf of the other system. The system talks to the look-up server and sends out the Java objects. The system acts as a proxy between the Jini network and the non-Jini-enabled device.

If there are enough resources (memory and hard disk) left on the device, it is also possible to install the Jini software to broadcast the services offered by the device to the Jini network.

Any Java application can use Jini software by creating a connection to the look-up server. The server will send back a list of services that can be retrieved by the application. If the application is interested in a certain service, the look-up server will send a Java object that handles all requests to the service. This object handles any device-specific details and the machine running the application does not need a driver for the device.

In the simplest case, Jini can be used to attach to a computer a device such as a printer, monitor, or hard disk, which all are Jini-enabled and work immediately without any driver installation. The paradigm of "write once, run anywhere" enters a new dimension. Jini software makes it easy to create distributed systems that share responsibility and resources.

Jini also enables you to associate devices, such as printers, to different people and places. Imagine that you need to print out a document from another office. You could simply click "print", and your document is sent to the printer that is next to you, no matter what type of printer it is.

12.3.2 Checking the Business Cases

The idea behind Jini is to improve productivity, save costs, and simplify the use of a network. The interaction among the network and the connected nodes (i.e., devices) becomes easier. It allows the simplified delivery of new products

and services over a network. Look back at our four business cases to explore
how Jini can make a difference.

Jini enables bank customers to deal with their bank from any Jini-enabled
device, if their online bank has a Jini connection network. A customer in a car
who has a Jini connection can make financial transactions without a normal
computer and Web browser. Depending on the functionality of the customer's
portable network device, the bank can offer certain operations. If the device
offers a graphical display, the bank can even send images that show the development of your portfolio. If the device contains a voice recognition feature,
online banking can be mixed with telephone banking to achieve the most convenient way for the driver to communicate with the bank.

The clothing manufacturer could network-enable its clothes. Although this
may seem far-fetched, first tests have already been conducted. A small chip
is woven into the label that identifies the type of clothing and how it needs to
be treated. When you put the clothes into a washing machine, the machine
automatically checks whether all clothes can be washed together. If not, the
washing machine reports exactly which piece does not fit.

The cargo company will be able to use Jini to facilitate the tracking of goods.
Every station needs a computer to communicate whether a packet has passed
through it. Stations include the pick-up from the customer, the airport check-
in, the boarding onto the plane, and the drop-off station at the destination.
The logistics partner picking up the packet at the customer site will not have a
computer to connect to the Internet. With Jini, a mobile phone can be used to
communicate the pick-up to the tracking system. The airport check-in probably
has access to the Internet and can communicate directly to the tracking system.
During boarding, a person with a bar-code scanner is not able to communicate
directly back to the tracking system, but adding a Jini interface to the scanner creates a hand-held networking appliance that immediately reports which
packets have been boarded. Through Jini, the devices in use can be used in the
future. This would make the transition easy, because the single stations would
not be required to learn a new technology. Jini would work transparently and
quietly in the background.

The car designers will benefit from Jini when they build the first prototypes. These prototypes can contain several Jini-enabled devices that allow
the designers to track the availability and functionality of their design components. An impromptu network can also be set up with other devices outside of
the car. Devices that measure traffic congestion can interact with the car, by
telling the GPS system in the car which route is the fastest, for example. Or,
as mentioned in the preface, the car can interact with gas stations and ask for
gas prices. This process could create highly dynamic gas prices, because gas
stations with low demand would try to become more attractive by lowering the
price for some minutes. Without the connectivity, there is no reason for gas
stations to lower prices for minutes, because only the cars that pass by would
notice. New cars often contain GPS satellite navigation systems and mobile

phones. In Dublin, Ireland, it is possible to get taxis with Internet connectivity, and in Helsinki, Finland, it is possible to pay for automatic car washing with a mobile phone. Device-independent interconnectivity becomes more important, and Jini is one possible way of implementing it.

12.3.3 Online Experience

Jini was introduced officially with Java 2. Although prerelease versions have been around for some time and tests have been conducted, there is no live system available yet. The major problem is not the software implementation, but the number of hardware devices that are able to understand Jini.

For simple tests, it is possible to install Jini on standard computers. Just remember that Jini's full strength lies in the interconnectivity of different types of devices.

12.3.4 Required Software

The Jini software can be downloaded from Sun[13] at no cost. The source code is also available and can be modified to the needs of the business case. Although there are some restrictions in the license, the software can be used freely.

The base software required for building a so-called Jini federation consists of the latest Java Virtual Machine, with extended remote method invocation (RMI), which has been enhanced to work with Jini. In addition, a look-up service is required, which consists of a database for services available in the federation. A discovery service is required to allow resources to register their services with the look-up service, and distributed security is required, which is a security framework built on top of Java's built-in security.

12.4 JavaBeans

12.4.1 Technical Overview

JavaBeans enables developers to write reusable components in Java. It is a portable, platform-independent component model written in Java. JavaBeans can be manipulated visually and combined to create traditional applications. The advantage of creating components rather than monolithic applications is that developers can create complex applications much faster and reuse some of the components for other projects as well.

JavaBeans also acts as a bridge between proprietary component models and provides a seamless and powerful means for developers to build components that run in ActiveX container applications. JavaBeans can be used to develop or assemble network-aware solutions for heterogeneous hardware and operating system environments, in which two different types of JavaBeans compo-

---

[13]http://java.sun.com/

nents will be in use. Either a JavaBeans component is used as a building block in which to compose a larger application or a JavaBeans component is used as a regular application, which can be embedded into Web pages, for example. These two aspects overlap programming. A calculator may live within a composite application as well as within a more normal compound document. There is no sharp cutoff between the so-called *composite applications* and *compound documents*.

A reusable software component is a piece of software that provides a well-defined functionality. The functionality is presented in such a way that other pieces of software are able to access this functionality. The functionality of a Bean (as Sun calls them) can be something very simple, such as a certain type of button or something very complex, such as an application. Imagine a company that wants to put a copyright statement into every program. Normally, the company would embed the code into the application. Although the code is not difficult to implement, it still can be responsible for bugs because it must be recompiled with the application. Moving the copyright statement into a Bean means that the code can be written only once and compiled only once. Then the functionality can be used by any application through the standardized JavaBeans API.

Although the functionality of every Bean is different, some features distinguish JavaBeans from other types of applications:

- **Customization**—Visual application builder tools are able to customize the appearance and the behavior of a Bean.

- **Events**—Events allow Beans to connect and communicate with each other.

- **Introspection**—Visual application builder tools are able to analyze how a Bean works.

- **Persistence**—After customization in a visual application builder, the Beans can be retrieved with customized features, for future use.

- **Properties**—Developers are able to customize and program with JavaBeans.

Table 12.4. Features of Java Beans

JavaBeans is a complete component architecture supporting properties for programming with Beans. A public interface defines the way a Bean interacts with other Beans. The interface consists of properties, methods, and events. Properties are named attributes of JavaBeans that can be read or set by other JavaBeans. Public methods can be triggered by other JavaBeans, and events are used to communicate with one another. JavaBeans can be automatically analyzed (called introspection) and their appearance is easily configurable (called customization) through a visual application builder tool. JavaBeans can be used to create both Java applications and applets. Applets can be designed to work as reusable JavaBeans. But applets are not automatically Beans, because they lack the features of a component.

The JavaBeans API tries to ensure portability. A Bean developed on a certain platform should behave in the same way on every other platform. To reduce the risk of having unsupported features, the API tries to remain simple and compact.

12.4.2 J2EE

Today, developers want to write distributed transactional applications for the enterprise and to leverage the speed, security, and reliability of server-side technology. If you are already working in this area, you know that in the fast-moving and demanding world of e-commerce and information technology, enterprise applications have to be designed, built, and produced for less money, with greater speed, and with fewer resources than ever before.

A natural extension to JavaBeans is the Java 2 Platform Enterprise Edition (J2EE)[14] architecture described here. Regular JavaBeans components are not considered J2EE components by the J2EE specification. JavaBeans components written for the J2EE platform have specific additions. First, they use instance variables and "get" and "set" methods for accessing the data in the instance variables. JavaBeans components used in this way are typically simple in design and implementation, but should conform to the naming and design conventions outlined in the JavaBeans component architecture.

To reduce costs and fast-track enterprise application design and development, the J2EE technology provides a component-based approach to the design, development, assembly, and deployment of enterprise applications. The J2EE platform gives you a multi-tiered distributed application model, the ability to reuse components, a unified security model, and flexible transaction control. Not only can you deliver innovative customer solutions to market faster than ever, but your platform-independent J2EE component-based solutions are not tied to the products and APIs of any one vendor.

J2EE applications typically use a thin client. A thin client is a lightweight interface to the application that does not do things like query databases, execute complex business rules, or connect to legacy applications. Heavyweight

---

[14]http://java.sun.com/j2ee/

The J2EE application parts are presented in J2EE Application Components.

- **Client**—Client tier components run on the client machine.

- **Web**—Web tier components run on the J2EE server.

- **Business**—Business tier components run on the J2EE server.

- **Enterprise**—Enterprise information system (EIS) tier software runs on the EIS server.

Table 12.5. J2EE Application Components

operations like these are off-loaded to Web or enterprise Beans executing on the J2EE server where they can leverage the security, speed, services, and reliability of J2EE server-side technologies. This makes J2EE very interesting for mobile or pervasive applications.

Business code, which is logic that solves or meets the needs of a particular business domain such as banking, retail, or finance, is handled by enterprise Beans running in the business tier. An enterprise Bean also retrieves data from storage, processes it (if necessary), and sends it back to the client program.

There are three kinds of enterprise Beans: session Beans, entity Beans, and message-driven Beans. A session Bean represents a transient conversation with a client. When the client finishes executing, the session Bean and its data are gone. In contrast, an entity Bean represents persistent data stored in one row of a database table. If the client terminates or if the server shuts down, the underlying services ensure that the entity Bean data is saved. A Message-driven Bean is an Enterprise JavaBean (EJB) component that may be considered a MessageListener, something that processes messages asynchronously.

The enterprise information system tier handles enterprise information system software, and includes enterprise infrastructure systems such as enterprise resource planning (ERP), mainframe transaction processing, database systems, and other legacy information systems. J2EE application components might need access to enterprise information systems for database connectivity, for example.

12.4.3 Checking the Business Cases

JavaBeans reduces the time it takes to develop applications, making development easier and less costly. You probably can see some advantages of reorganizing the way companies do business. And although JavaBeans does not directly influence each business case, it does influence the way the business' process of development is organized. Reusability is a an important factor. Instead of offering the same software package to all users, the JavaBeans model allows for highly configurable and dynamic application solutions. Look at the business cases again.

The online bank is able to create JavaBeans, which can provide a basic functionality for customers and employees. Depending on the type of user, additional Beans can be loaded. Using JavaBeans, it is also possible to start online banking simply, by offering the account balance at the beginning of the online session. Adding functionality then becomes very easy. Through the JavaBeans model, it is rather easy to add new JavaBeans when they become available, making the initial offering available very soon in the development phase. Because every JavaBean is separate, it is possible to update the functionality of each JavaBean individually. In monolithic applications, interdependencies are much higher in many cases, requiring at least a recompilation of the whole source code.

The clothing manufacturer can gain the same advantages as the online bank through the use of Java. By using JavaBeans, part of the development can be done in-house and some can be outsourced. For the online presentation, Web pages and JavaBeans can be intermixed, allowing the optimal presentation for the fashion. Standard HTML pages can be used for the textual description. The order form can be done using an HTML form, while the three-dimensional representation of the models can be written in VRML (see Chapter 13 for more information on VRML) and the interactivity can be written in Java. Using JavaBeans, features can be used in different applications, for different target groups.

The cargo company can write many components, which can be used not only for customer interaction, but also for internal processes. By recoding their internal business processes using JavaBeans, it becomes easy to extract the JavaBeans that are required for customer interaction.

Because cars already contain many electronic devices, and given the need for programming these devices, it may make sense to code the functionality into JavaBeans. This can reduce the time and cost for the availability of new devices and functionalities. New devices can be introduced into the next generation of cars much more easily if the functionality is coded into another JavaBean rather than the connection to the physical device.

12.4.4   Online Experience

Because JavaBeans has become part of the Java standard with version 1.1, it is still not supported by all browsers and only limited use has been made of it on the Internet. JavaBeans has been used mostly in application development offline.

Charles Schwab,[15] a Web-based securities trading company, uses JavaBeans to provide a common interface to its core systems for use by its business units via its intranet.

The application built in JavaBeans allows users to enter an account number and the system returns financial information from the core system. Two types of Beans have been used to create the application. Data access Beans allow access over the interface to the back-end system, and the viewer Beans display the data graphically on the desktop of the employee.

To achieve mission-critical application performance, the JavaBeans standard was enhanced by BeansExtender developed by IBM.[16] BeansExtender offers several enhancements over the JavaBeans standard including: the ManagedBean class, the instance-based aggregation model, "Bean Dipping," and the Assembly Surface builder tool. These features, together with the Java Active X bridge, provide a perfect solution for Charles Schwab, because existing Active X applications could be integrated into the JavaBeans model without modification.

Another application developed by IBM in its AlphaBeans programs is BeanMachine, which is an easy-to-use multimedia tool for enriching Web pages with special effects. BeanMachine consists of several JavaBeans components that can be used together to create applets in just a few mouse clicks. The Beans included offer sound effects, animations, text effects, and access to the database of your choice in JDBC. JDBC (Java Database Connectivity) is an application program interface (API) specification for connecting programs written in Java to the data in popular database.

An example for J2EE usage was created by Altura.[17] It provides a one-stop shopping solution called CatalogCity.com.[18] Through a combination of product syndication agreements with major Internet portals, as well as its own destination Web sites, Altura provides a one-stop business-to-consumer resource that provides consumers with easy access to more than 17,000 merchant catalogs and their products.

In 1999, they faced a major challenge. The traffic to Altura's Web site was growing rapidly, thanks in large part to the strategic relationships it forged with leading Internet portals. However, as traffic increased, Altura's IT managers began to experience some performance problems that they were unable

---

[15]http://www.schwab.com/

[16]http://www.alphaworks.ibm.com/

[17]http://www.altura.com/

[18]http://www.CatalogCity.com/

to overcome. Their existing solution offered no centralized services for managing multiple Web servers. The company also began to have frequent crashes in the web-application layer and had no way of being notified when these crashes took place.

To solve this problem, Altura chose to rearchitect its site around HP Bluestone's Total-e-Server,[19] the company's J2EE-based application-server foundation. Altura developers rewrote the multivendor, multilanguage, multicurrency shopping cart and other core business technology in the Java programming language and built a new production architecture around Total-e-Server.

As a result, Altura achieved an increased developer productivity. Sixteen application servers and eight Web servers now accomplish what previously required more than 120 servers to do. These changes simplified day-to-day management and maintenance. Now the company can support more users, more sessions, and more connections per server. Another important result is that syndication is much quicker. Through the reusablity and extensibility of the J2EE objects and the ability to deploy sites dynamically, it becomes easy for Altura to syndicate their content to other shopping malls rapidly or even to develop whole new sites for new customers in a short period of time.

12.4.5   Required Software

JavaBeans do not require extra software. Java 1.1 and above does support JavaBeans natively, and all major development tools for Java, such as Visual Café by Symantec[20] or VisualAge for Java by IBM,[21] make it easy to implement and use JavaBeans. Their visual interface allows the Beans to be clicked together and work together.

Many portals have been created that allow the download of freeware, shareware, and open source JavaBeans. These sites offer a wide range of JavaBeans, which make it easy for developers to create complex applications without needing to rewrite every single function. One such directory is Components.com.[22]

To support J2EE, it is necessary to have an application server that supports J2EE, such as Bluestone[23] or BEA WebLogic.[24] More information on application servers in general can be found in Chapter 10.

---

[19]http://www.bluestone.com/

[20]http://www.symantec.com/

[21]http://www.ibm.com/

[22]http://www.components.com/

[23]http://www.bluestone.com/

[24]http://www.bea.com/

12.5   InfoBus

12.5.1   Technical Overview

InfoBus is a compact Java API that allows the cooperation of applets or Java-Beans. The applets or JavaBeans can be on a Web page or in any other Java application and can exchange data through InfoBus. JavaBeans can become "data providers" and "data consumers," which are defined in the InfoBus architecture. A JavaBean that acts as a provider connects to a database and offers the data to the InfoBus. JavaBeans that act as data consumers can retrieve the data from the bus and process it. The advantage is that the processing JavaBean does not need to understand data formats and can concentrate on the implementation of the data processing. This segregation of provider from consumer is extremely powerful in that it enables applications to be independent of their data. JavaBeans are also able to act as consumer and provider at the same time.

The InfoBus specification extends JavaBeans by providing a set of enhanced interfaces to share and exchange dynamic data. The current release requires the JavaBeans to "live" within the same Java Virtual Machine. Although the design does not include provisions for connecting to other JVMs on different devices, it does provide facilities for writing a bridge between the JVMs. It can be said that all JavaBeans loaded from a single class loader are able to connect to each other.

The data exchange on the InfoBus consists of the following elements:

- **Membership**—By implementing the InfoBusMember interface, any Java class can join the InfoBus.

- **Rendezvous**—This protocol allows data producers and consumers to send out requests and accept requests.

- **Data access**—InfoBus has a set of standard interfaces for direct data transfer between a producer and a consumer.

- **Change notification**—After data has been transmitted, the consumer can be notified of modifications to the data.

Table 12.6. The InfoBus Process for Data Exchange

The InfoBus interfaces allow application designers to create "data flows" between cooperating components (see table 12.6). Unlike the traditional event/response mode, the InfoBus interfaces use few events and an invariant set of method calls for all applets. The semantics of the data flow are based on interpreting the contents of the data that flows across the InfoBus interfaces, as opposed to responding to names of parameters from events or names of callback parameters.

The standard communication between JavaBeans is based on the so-called introspection model, discussed earlier in this chapter. The InfoBus interface offers a tightly typed contract between cooperating Beans. The interface allows data flows to be created between cooperating Beans through direct procedure calls, which enables a Bean to share functionality with others easily.

12.5.2   Checking the Business Cases

Using device and format independent data solves most of the problems that programmers encounter in today's computer environments. Every application and device uses another format to encode data. InfoBus does not impose that applications use other formats of data, but converts data into a neutral format. This format can be used by any application connected to the InfoBus.

Think back to the four business cases we explored earlier. How will Infobus improve the business operations? The online bank can greatly enhance the data flow between the legacy system in the back-end and the front-end systems. Instead of converting the data to a format, the front-end application understands, and the data is offered to the InfoBus. The InfoBus is then able to deliver the information to any kind of device or application connected to the InfoBus. This enables the bank to switch front-end applications whenever a new version becomes available. The integration with the back-end system does not need to be considered. Security can be an issue if the InfoBus is used not only for communication between legacy and customer, but also for internal data exchange. Security measures would need to be implemented so that end customers are not able to see internal data.

The clothing manufacturer can present the data that he already has in many different ways through InfoBus. By offering the data to InfoBus, different applications can pick up the information and present it either graphically or textually to the customer. The information can then be presented visually to retailers, so that they can use the data for deciding which clothes fit into their shops. The same data can be presented textually for invoices and for automatic order processing.

The cargo company can create a highly sophisticated tracking and tracing solution by combining the strengths of Jini and InfoBus. Jini provides the networking infrastructure for all devices involved and the InfoBus protocol allows the exchange of information. This solution enables different types of devices to communicate with each other and pass on information.

The car manufacturer can create a virtual team using different hardware devices for the development. In addition, the InfoBus protocol could be incorporated into the design, allowing technical checks to be made more easily. Every device in the car is able to provide its information to a console that checks the availability and the quality of service of each.

12.5.3　Online Experience

The concept of InfoBus is quite new; so far no applications have been sighted on the Internet. But this is due to its nature. This type of information sharing will most likely happen first on company intranets, so it is invisible to the public. The next section that will benefit from InfoBus are information services, such as online banking, where Web applications serve as front-ends to legacy systems and databases.

Internet applications with interactive and dynamic features will be most likely using InfoBus, because the information used in the application can be updated in an instant. Normal HTML pages are very restricted. The current applet-servlet connections will be replaced with the InfoBus architecture in the near future. Instead of applets and servlets, JavaBeans will be used.

One offline application is Lotus eSuite,[25] which uses InfoBus for seamless application integration allowing programmers to write custom extensions using eSuite and other off-the-shelf Java applications.

12.5.4　Required Software

The InfoBus specification is also available free from Sun.[26] No special development tools are required for writing applications adhering to the InfoBus standard.

Distributed InfoBus (DI), developed by IBM,[27] extends the InfoBus standard in such a way that it can operate across devices and JVMs. This removes the restriction mentioned above, that only JavaBeans within a single JVM can communicate with each other. DI works like a bridge for JVMs and supports several network protocols, namely HTTP and IIOP. IIOP (Internet Inter-ORB Protocol) is a protocol that makes it possible for distributed programs written in different programming languages to communicate over the Internet.

12.6　Resolving Possible Java Issues

12.6.1　Speeding up Java

There are several ways of speeding up Java programs. Byte-code can be translated to native machine code. The JVM then directly executes, rather than

---

[25]http://www.lotus.com/

[26]http://java.sun.com/infobus/

[27]http://www.alphaworks.ibm.com/

abstractly emulates, the code according to the actual processor architecture of the system hosting execution. This performance improvement can be either done by just-in-time (JIT) compilation (i.e., when running the program, it will be compiled) or by using a native compiler like TurboJ[28] that translates the Java program to native code and saves it in this format to the hard disk. The disadvantage of the second approach is that after you have compiled the Java program using TurboJ, it is no longer hardware independent. You would have to recompile it for another platform, which is still easier than rewriting the whole application for the other platform. If performance is an issue, this may be the best way to go. The native compiler will appeal to large customers with known configurations who are willing to give up mobility for better performance.

The latest invention from Sun is their HotSpot[29] technology. Most people will prefer this so-called optimized dynamic compiler to native compilers for the good performance that maintains application mobility.

There are some problems with JIT compilation. Because the JIT compiler runs just before the application is executed, it does no have much time to do the compilation; otherwise, the users would become impatient before they had a chance to see the program itself. To save time, it is not possible to perform extensive and advanced optimizations—this would really speed up the code, but slow down the startup. HotSpot uses adaptive optimization to resolve the problems of JIT compilation by taking into account an interesting characteristic of most programs. Almost 100 percent of all programs spend most of their time executing a small part of their code. The relation between executed time and code part is about 80 to 20. About 80 percent of the time is spent on 20 percent of the code. Maybe you have already noticed that this relation has appeared several times throughout the book, in different situations. This particular relation is known as the Pareto principle or the 80/20 principle. More information on this topic can be found in Richard Koch's book, *The 80/20 Principle*.[30]

Instead of compiling the whole program when it starts, HotSpot runs the program immediately and tries to detect the critical areas of the program, which are called "hot spots." The global native-code optimizer then focuses on these hot spots. By avoiding compilation of infrequently executed code (on average, about 80 percent of the program), the HotSpot compiler can spend more time on the performance-critical parts of the program, without increasing the startup compile time. While the program is running, HotSpot monitors the activity of the program and adapts itself to the needs of the user. If, for example, someone is using a Java spreadsheet application, he may first do some calculations, so HotSpot will try to speed up this part of the application. Later, the user may be interested in presenting some graphics, so the code optimization moves on to this part of the application on the fly to support the user.

---

[28] http://www.camb.opengroup.org/openitsol/turboj/
[29] http://java.sun.com/products/hotspot/
[30] Richard Koch, *The 80/20 Principle*, Nicolas Brealey Publishing, Ltd., London.

Applications can also have some parts compiled dynamically, and other parts compiled through the native compiler. Hewlett-Packard, Sun, and Symantec[31] are developing tools to help users determine the best compilation strategies for their applications. No matter how the code is compiled, it can share the same runtime environment and interact with Java applets that come from anywhere in the organization.

If a JIT had time to perform a full optimization, it would be less effective than for other languages, like C, for the following reasons:

- **Type testing**—Dynamic type tests need to be performed frequently, because the virtual machine must ensure that programs do not violate language semantics or access unstructured memory.

- **Object allocation**—Object allocation rates are much higher for the Java language than for C++, because it allocates all objects on the heap.

- **Method invocations**—In Java, most method invocations are "virtual." This means that method invocation performance is more dominant and static compiler optimizations (especially global optimizations like in-lining) are much harder to perform for method invocations.

- **Dynamic loading**—Java programs can change on the fly due to the ability to perform dynamic loading of Java classes.

Table 12.7. Java Optimization Problems

As a rule, performance will depend on the application mix, but the Hewlett-Packard Java labs estimate that the optimized dynamic compiler offers five times the performance of the standard Java environments. The native compiler offers a boost of approximately six to seven times that of the standard Java environment.

To get the best performance from a Java-based configuration, it's not enough to tune just the Java applications. To improve performance, it is necessary to tune the entire configuration, including the Java runtime environment (JRE)

---

[31]http://www.symantec.com/

and the underlying operating system (see also table 12.7). Although hardware tuning may make sense in some cases, Sun's hardware Java chips failed, just as many other specialized chips, such as those for Pascal and other languages, failed before. The performance boost was too small to encourage users and developers to switch from multipurpose chips to highly specialized CPUs (central processing units). Some businesses, for example, have seen dramatic performance improvements by tuning the way Java applications make calls to other applications or databases.

Hewlett-Packard's Java Environment Tuning Center (JETC)[32] draws expertise from several HP lab organizations to evaluate and tune customers' applications and computing environments. One company to visit the JETC was Ariba.[33] By improving the way the Ariba applications made procedure calls across class libraries and fine-tuning calls to the Oracle database, performance was improved by about 250 percent. HP engineers from the Java organization worked with HP-UX kernel engineers and the Developer Alliance Lab to characterize the Ariba application performance and improve the overall implementation.

Other companies like IBM and Sun have similar organizations within their companies that help customers to speed up their Java development and improve the execution of their Java applications.

12.6.2 The 100 Percent Pure Java Initiative

The term "100 percent pure Java" means that an application is written completely in Java and does not rely on external class libraries or native code. It is possible to integrate third-party technologies, such as special classes, but they must be distributed with the applet or application so that the application can run on any computer supporting Java. With smaller third-party contributions, this works fine, but there are some problems with large third-party frameworks. The first problem is the size and the second problem is licensing issues. A third issue is that the technology used in the classes may be unknown and use proprietary technologies.

Java applications and applets should not rely on proprietary technologies, because these limit the program to a certain platform, which is opposed to Java's goal. Using the standard toolkits for the user interface, for example, allows customers to see your application on any given platform, without any restrictions. Although there were many deficits in Java 1.0, these deficits have been addressed and compensated in later versions. For example, proprietary extensions to build a modern-looking user interface are no longer needed.

The 100 percent pure Java initiative frees developers from incompatibility concerns and lets them take advantage of the full benefits of the Java platform. Because large third-party contributions are difficult to integrate into a

---

[32]http://www.hp.com/go/java/
[33]http://www.ariba.com/

100 percent pure Java application, many developers asked to expand the JDK to support the needs for the most commonly used components. This has the advantage of improved overall performance because they are more highly integrated.

12.6.3 Java Applet Security

Security is the major concern for many when going online. Many myths have contributed to this factor and new incidents seem to prove that the Internet as a whole is very insecure. Some companies block all types of applications, because they may contain viruses that can destroy information on a company computer.

Although viruses are a major concern, they are often associated with Java applets, and this is simply wrong. In theory, it is not possible to write Java applets that are malicious, because Java applets run in a so-called sandbox that does not have any connection to the resources on the client's computer. In practice, there have been some problems with the implementations of the browsers, which did not prevent all attacks.

To better understand why applets are secure, it is necessary to understand the differences between applets and applications. By design, applets are embedded into Web pages and do not run outside the Web page context. Applets are downloaded like HTML documents, but, unlike HTML documents, they are executed on the client computer.

Applets downloaded over the Internet are prevented from reading and writing files on the client file system. Although this would already be enough to secure the computer of the client, additional security has been built in to prevent someone misusing the client's computer as a gateway. This additional security allows Internet connections only back to the originating host.

Applets are also not allowed to start or access any application that has been already installed on the client, nor are they able to load libraries or define native method calls, preventing direct access to the operating system and its resources.

As you can imagine, these security restrictions also restrict the usability of the Java applets. By default, it is not possible to print or save documents. Java is able to print and save, but the Web browsers prevent these functionalities when an applet is loaded. The theory is that you cannot trust applets, because you do not know where they come from.

If your applet requires additional features, such as printing or saving, then you can ask the clients to allow these features. Adding access to local resources requires that the applet be signed. By signing the applet, the identity of the programmer is revealed. Once the applet has been loaded over the network, a browser requester pops up and asks the user if she wants to trust the applet of a certain person or company. Every additional resource should be accepted individually. Saving, printing, and loading would require three confirmations.

The signature, together with the confirmations, makes Java applets very secure.

Keep in mind that this is true only if the applet is loaded over the network. Applets that reside on the local hard disk are automatically trusted.

12.6.4 Java versus Active X

Active X and Java offer the possibility of adding functionality to static Web pages without additional server connections. When you download an Active X control or a Java applet, your Web pages become more dynamic and interactive.

This basic advantage also brings some problems. Active X and Java pose an additional security risk to the data on your computer. Downloading a program that contains back doors leave you open to unwanted access and the destruction of data on your computer. To make Java and Active X useful and accepted by the users, both approaches implement measures to ensure the security and privacy of your data.

Active X is supported natively in Internet Explorer and can be used in Netscape through a plug-in. Through the security settings, it is possible to accept Active X controls with or without warning or to refuse them altogether. If you decide to accept Active X controls, then you need to rely on your judgement, because there is no way to tell what the Active X control will be trying to do. Active X controls are like any other application, with all rights on the computer to read, delete, and modify data.

Active X controls may contain the author's digital signature. This digital signature tells you who has written the control and asks you to accept the control or to refuse it. In theory, digital signatures are a good idea, but after you have accepted an Active X control, it can take over the computer. And don't expect to remember all the signatures you have trusted in the past.

Java, on the other hand, restricts the access to local resources with untrusted applets. By default, all programs are run in the Java "sandbox," mentioned earlier. As long as no one finds a hole in the Java sandbox, you can be sure that your data and the resources on your computer (such as printers and hard disks) are protected.

Therefore, the major difference between accepting an Active X control and a Java applet is the level of damage that can be done by accepting unknown programs. Most Java applets and Active X controls are harmless, but one malicious piece of code can destroy all your data. As people download more Active X controls and Java applets that are harmless, they are more likely to trust the next one as well.

When you accept a Java applet, you do not permit access to local resources, but with Active X control, you are permitting access by accepting the download. If the Java security sandbox breaks down, then the Java applet will also gain access to all resources. The major difference is that you did not permit access to Java, but you did to Active X. If an Active X control tries to save a file to your hard disk and destroys some data by accident, you will have difficulties suing the company for destroying your data, because you granted access to it. With Java, it is quite clear that you did not permit access to the data.

To be safe, you should refuse all programs that are embedded into a Web page (although you'll decrease its value, because many applications rely on Active X controls or Java applets).

Signed Java applets offer a slight advantage over Active X because it is possible to partially trust programs. The the program is not able to see data on your hard disk just because it has permission to access the printer. Active X requires you to fully trust it or refuse it. Java, in general, also offers better protection against accidental damage caused by a bug in the program.

Due to the nature of Active X programs, it is possible to implement programming languages and let programs run in that environment. This is not restricted to Active X components; it is also valid for browser plug-ins. By accepting these programs, you are trusting only the plug-in or Active X control, but have no control over the programs that are run within it. Shockwave is such a plug-in; it executes applications created by Macromedia Director. If the plug-in or Active X control has a security problem, it can be exploited easily by the program that is running within the component.

Fortunately, few attacks are known through Java, Active X, or plug-ins. But no one can guarantee that this will last. The possibilities exist, and it is just a matter of time until someone writes some malicious code.

To reduce the risk, you should not trust a component by a single user or company. Every time you download a new component, think about its necessity. Is it really necessary to run it, or does it pose a security problem? To reduce the risk even further, trust only components that have a single functionality, such as displaying a new graphic format. If you trust a complex application, the risk is higher that something may go wrong, intentionally or unintentionally.

Always download the latest release of your favorite Web browser and look out for patches that close identified security holes. This will reduce the risk that the browser will be responsible for the accident. The computer that you use for Web browsing should not contain critical information that may be important for you or interesting for others. Keep these files on a server with password access, and you should be fine. If a program destroys the content of your hard disk, you should be up and running again fairly soon, if there is only standard software running on your system.

12.6.5   Moving from C++ to Java

Because Java is becoming more important every day, many companies want to port their existing code to Java in order to benefit from the object orientation and cross-platform abilities of Java. Java has significant advantages over C++ in terms of portability, power, and simplicity.

C++ was developed by Bjarne Stroustrop of AT&T Bell Labs during the

1980s. It was derived from the object-oriented language Simula and the procedural language C. C++ was developed to allow programmers to build object-oriented software without sacrificing C's efficiency. C++ is now widely used, its speed of adoption due to the fact that the transition from C to C++ was considered to be relatively simple. Another probable reason for success is that it is a hybrid language; you can use it in a procedural manner and/or an object-oriented manner.

But this is also the reason that C++ provides all the opportunities to shoot yourself in the foot, just as C did. Its Achilles heel is the freedom it gives the programmer in dealing with pointers. Pointer arithmetic, casting, and explicit memory management using "new" and "delete" are the major causes of bugs in C++ programs, as in C. This is not possible in Java, making it more foolproof than C++.

Many programs have been written in C++, so that object orientation is no problem, and it is not necessary to change the programming paradigm. These advantages are leading many people to consider replacing C++ with Java, not only for Web applets, but increasingly for client and server applications as well.

This subsection will highlight some of the most important things a programmer must think about when moving from C++ to Java. IBM has an excellent online tutorial[34] for people who require more information on this topic.

The major differences between C++ and Java are syntactic, so that the Java compiler will be able to discover the differences, in case you have forgotten to change them. The Java compiler is much more rigorous than that of C++, so much of the code that needs to be changed will be found by the compiler. But in some instances, the same code in C++ and Java has dangerously different consequences.

There are several differences that must be taken into account when moving code from C++ to Java. The Java language does not support three data types that are part of the C and C++ languages: struct, union, and pointer. These data types can be emulated in most cases. There are also some differences in how certain operators in the Java language work, as compared to both C and C++. And the command line arguments passed to a Java application are different in number and in type from those passed to a C or C++ program. Another important difference is string handling. In C and C++, strings are simply null-terminated arrays of characters. The Java language uses the String class provided in the java.lang package. In C++, you can have multiple-inherited classes, whereas Java has only single-inheritance. Other features not present in Java, but found in C++, include global variables, stand-alone functions, friend functions (everything in a package is a friend of everything else in the package), and nonvirtual functions.

A number of features have been added to Java to make it safer, including true arrays with bounds checking, concurrency, interfaces, and packages.

---

[34]http://www.ibm.com/java/education/portingc/

There is no need to explicitly allocate or free memory in Java, because this is handled by the garbage collector.

Because Java follows C++ conventions in many cases, large parts of the original C++ can remain unchanged. This includes variable names, the flow of control, names of primitive types, operators, and comments, for example. As in C++, Java allows you to write classes, override methods, overload methods, write constructors, and instantiate objects.

Moving from other languages may prove to be more difficult or, in some cases, easier. Languages belonging to the group of Wirth are very easy to convert to Java, because they follow a similar syntax. Moving programs written in Pascal, Modula or Oberon can be easily recompiled in Java, while Ada and Lisp require some in-depth review of the original source code before they can be moved to Java.

12.7   Avoiding the Java Wars

12.7.1   Hewlett-Packard

Through 1998, we saw two major fights over Java. Hewlett-Packard developed its own version of the Java API for embedded devices in conjunction with Intel and other partners, and Microsoft was sued for its implementation of Java in Internet Explorer 4. Many people were concerned that the Java standard would vanish after these wars, but actually the opposite happened. Likely due to the media attention on both fights, Java became even more popular.

After evaluating the draft specification of Sun's embedded Java implementation, Hewlett-Packard realized that practical considerations for manufacturing Java into these devices had not been taken into account. Because Sun is not producing embedded devices, they were not aware of the possibilities and problems of the embedded-devices market. Because of the unfortunate licensing scheme of Sun, HP would need to become a licensee of the Sun code and would have to renounce control over the intellectual property. Hewlett-Packard was not willing to participate in such a controlling process.

Hewlett-Packard wrote its own embedded virtual machine called Chai (Russian for Tea), and referenced published specifications to ensure compatibility with functional specs and upward compatibility with any enterprise Java implementation. The Hewlett-Packard virtual machine is a complete implementation, but the Java APIs are assigned to different devices based on the devices' function and memory. Microwave ovens and medical instruments, for example, require different functions and have different amounts of memory available. An embedded system requires flexibility. The original Sun embedded virtual machine required all devices to incorporate all APIs, which would add cost and memory overhead in the manufacturing process.

Java's automatic garbage collection is a big problem with Java for embedded systems. Garbage collection is used to automatically release memory from objects that are no longer needed. This makes it easy to write programs but occupies the system for an unpredictable period of time, making it unsuitable for real-time applications. Hewlett-Packard's modified version of the JVM uses a variant of the original garbage collection, called "incremental garbage collection," which allows for more determinacy than Sun's original implementation.

The paradigm of "write once, run anywhere" is much less important in embedded systems, where functionality is carefully defined in the design. Users normally do not program these devices; all software comes from the manufacturer. The real attraction of Java lies in its high-level object-oriented nature and the uniform development and target environment. Another problem lies in Sun's Java licensing model; because embedded devices are shipped in much higher volume, the price per device is too high to make it cost effective.

Many people thought that Hewlett-Packard wanted to go its own way, but the truth is that it wanted to show Sun how it should be done. Widespread approval of this approach and support from a range of leading real-time operating system vendors, such as Intel and Wind River, have influenced Sun to alter its original design.

Unfortunately, Sun halted halfway through. Shortly thereafter, the J Consortium[35] (see Figure 12.2) was formed by several companies including Hewlett-Packard, NewMonics,[36] and Plum Hall.[37] The J Consortium tries to push new features into the Java language for embedded devices independently of Sun. These companies have formalized an effort to define a standard for real-time extensions. The J Consortium is an open and democratic body organized as a not-for-profit consortium.

The J Consortium is an outgrowth of the Real-Time Java Working Group (RTJWG), which itself was an outgrowth of the NIST real-time requirements effort initiated in early 1998. The J Consortium specifications will be consistent with the NIST requirements. It can be seen as an incorporated version of the Real-Time Java Working Group. Incorporation gives the effort a better ability to set a real-time Java standard. The J Consortium wants to deal with the real-time extensions to Java, but won't change the rest of the Java technology. Their charter is to advance the creation of specifications and related activities for what we refer to as real-time and embedded extensions for Java Technologies.

Sun is not happy with this development, of course, because it creates two versions of the real-time extensions. The J Consortium members are unhappy about Sun, because the process of creating the real-time standard is controlled by Sun only. The J Consortium claims that Sun does not have enough knowledge in the area of real-time applications and devices.

In any case, this fight over Java clearly reveals Java's status in the industry. Every company tries to pull Java in its own direction to appear as the market leader in developing applications and devices. Although the fight over

---

[35] http://www.j-consortium.org/

[36] http://www.newmonics.com/

[37] http://www.plumhall.com/

Figure 12.2. J Consortium home page.

the real-time extensions won't change anything in the Java language standard, it shows where most companies see the future of computing. Pervasive computing will incorporate embedded devices. Therefore, gaining control over the programming language that will run on these devices will give the company the decisive advantage for the business of tomorrow. It seems that Java has won the race; now a new race will determine *which* Java is going to be used. More information on Java in embedded devices can be found in Chapter 16, which deals with the new paradigm of pervasive computing. There, embedded devices and Java play an important role.

In January 2001, the Object Management Group (OMG)[38] and the J Consortium established a liaison to promote rapid development of specifications for the real-time and embedded marketplace. Efforts include developing standards for real-time and embedded systems, such as sensors for the medical, avionics, amd automotive industries (among others), and moving toward computer controlled "appliances," ranging from smart refrigerators to automotive and aircraft engines.

The collaboration between OMG and the J Consortium will accelerate the availability of open vendor-neutral standards, which are essential to the development of the real-time, embedded systems being used to control modern, less expensive, more efficient automation. Examples of such systems are al-

---

[38]http://www.omg.com/

ready appearing in the medical and automotive fields and will soon be powering "smart" appliances.

Initial collaboration will occur between the J Consortium and OMG's Real-Time Special Interest Group (SIG), Telecommunications Domain Task Force (DTF), and the Manufacturing DTF. It is expected that other groups within OMG will participate also, such as the Transportation DTF and Healthcare DTF.

Because both OMG and the J Consortium are leaders in open vendor-neutral real-time and embedded standards development, and are also approved International Organization for Standardization (ISO) Publicly Available Specifications (PAS) submitters, this liaison will serve to bring to ISO real-time and embedded specifications with the broadest possible industry base.

These and other liaisons have made clear that the J Consortium has become an important player in the market. It remains to be seen if and how Sun will cooperate with the J Consortium. It doesn't make much sense to create two similar, but still different standards for real-time processing.

12.7.2 Microsoft

There was a different reason altogether for the fight between Sun and Microsoft. For Microsoft, the Java standard meant a threat to its market share, because the operating system suddenly became irrelevant. The operating system was the core business of Microsoft. Windows in all its flavors had more than 95 percent of the market share. But if people started to implement software in Java, it suddenly didn't matter which operating system they were using.

Nonetheless, Microsoft became a licensee of the Java language in order to incorporate Java into its Web browser Internet Explorer and its Software Development Kit (SDK) for Java.

In 1998, Sun sued Microsoft and asked them to remove Java from their products, because they did not seem to adhere to the Sun Java standard. Neither of the two programs passed the Java compatibility test, which meant that Java applications written with the Microsoft tools might not run on other platforms (such as the Mac OS) or in other browsers (such as Netscape Communicator).

Sun's complaint against Microsoft included trademark infringement, unfair competition, breach of contract, and false advertising. Sun's claim was that Microsoft was trying to break Java's success by tampering with its "write once, run anywhere" promise. Microsoft was suspected of adding Windows-specific code to the Java language that would inevitably break the cross-platform operability. See Table 12.8 for a list of differences in the implementations.

Although Sun's claims may have been accurate, the claims are also a sort of marketing gag. Few developers are using Microsoft tools to develop Java applications anyway, because there are much better tools on the market and

The Microsoft Software Development Kit for Java contained several alterations to the original specification provided by Sun. In January 1999, a patch was released by Microsoft that resolved the described changes.

- **New classes**—Sixteen new classes were introduced into java.awt that you should avoid.

- **New methods**—There are at least fourteen methods that you should not use unless you want to run your applications only on a Windows platform using IE.

- **New instances**—There are two instance variables for you to avoid also.

- **No portability**—Forget portability, if you choose to use the classes in com.ms.

- **Method missing**—A toString() method of ByteArray-OutputStream is missing.

- **Object locking**—This may be performed at a different level from the one you expect, so it may favor one platform over another.

Table 12.8. Modifications in Microsoft's Java

those who do not stay with the Java specification are not interested in achieving true cross-platform compatibility. Buying a reference book with the Java specification does not cost much, and the specification can even be downloaded from the Web. Microsoft, on the other hand, should not try to sell its software as 100 percent Java; it should write on its products "loosely based on Java" or something similar.

In January 1999, Microsoft had to put the Service Pack 2 for its developer products onto their Web site, which include patches to make its software compliant with the Sun specification. Microsoft lost that round of the fight in court.

It is true that developing new solutions with Java gives you the edge over your competitors, because it is the right tool for developing Internet services and products. With Java 2, Sun has opened the license of Java to allow others to modify the source code. If you do use Java, be sure to contact Sun and try to influence it to release Java as open source, which will make it the true and only standard for Internet applications for the future.

On January 23, 2001, Microsoft announced an agreement with Sun Microsystems to settle both the October 1997 lawsuit filed by Sun and the Microsoft countersuit in the dispute over the Java technology license agreement between the two companies.

The technology license and distribution agreement was signed by the parties in March 1996 and was due to expire in 2001. Under the terms of the settlement, the existing technology license agreement between the two companies is terminated. Microsoft can continue to ship all current products and those in beta containing Sun's technology for a period of seven years and in return agrees to pay Sun $20 million. Microsoft agreed not to use Sun's Java Compatible trademark, which it has not done since 1998. The license agreement and the settlement agreement confirm Microsoft's freedom to independently develop technology that competes with Sun's technology.

The settlement means that Microsoft is able to "enhance" the existing Java platform and continue to work on its .NET platform, which Microsoft hopes will become the best way to build, deliver, and aggregate Web services. Microsoft wants to help software developers build Web services with whatever programming language is most appropriate for their particular needs.

This basically means that Microsoft accepts the large market of Java and will continue to support it. At the same time, Microsoft is trying to push their new language and paradigm C#, which should replace Java over time for their platform. We shall see how successful Microsoft is with this strategy and how many developers move from Java to C#.

12.8   The Future of Java Computing

12.8.1   New Java Technologies

Many other Java technologies are emerging, among them additions like Java 3D, offering an API for developing applications with three-dimensional graphical objects. The Java 3D API gives developers a set of high-level constructs for creating and manipulating 3D geometry. Tools for constructing the structures used in rendering that geometry are also made available in the same package. Integration with other Web standards is also very important. The integration between Java and XML is an important step into the future.

Sun is developing a Java standard extension for XML. The basic functionality includes the reading, manipulating, and generating of XML text, which are the core features required to form the building blocks for developing fully functional, XML-based applications. This extension is planned to become a standard extension for Java, enabling every Java application to understand XML, if desired. By extending the JavaBeans architecture to understand XML, it becomes even easier to integrate it into existing applications.

XML is changing the way electronic business is implemented on the Internet. Together with Java, it is enabling a new generation of Internet applications. XML and Java together form a complete, platform-independent, Web-based computing environment that can produce portable "smart" data. Code written in Java can be embedded into an XML document. This allows data to be created with its own data manipulation application. Although XML enables the information exchange, Java is able to automate the exchange. XML contributes to platform-independent data in the form of portable documents and data, while Java contributes to platform-independent processing through portable object-oriented software solutions. IBM has created a dedicated vertical XML portal,[39] which contains many Java applications and example source code for business applications.

12.8.2 Outlook into the Future

Java 2 has been available for a while now, but it is still difficult to predict which direction it will take. To date, Sun has determined Java's fate. With the introduction of Java 2, the license has been made a little more friendly, allowing third parties to develop additions to the standard. One of the major contributors to new development in Java was IBM and its AlphaWorks[40] Web site.

Free implementations of Java appear regularly, making it possible to use Java without having to rely on Sun, which means it is truly an open programming language for anyone in every situation. But Java will become a standard for the future only if it becomes an official ISO standard.

Java won't make other programming languages superfluous, but it can be expected that new libraries for other languages will appear that will make cross-platform availability of the application easier. One such framework is FoundationWare, developed by Hewlett-Packard, which unifies and simplifies Windows NT and HP-UX development and deployment by bundling industry-leading middleware technologies with HP-UX. A set of common middleware services, such as CORBA ORBs and the LDAP Integration Kit, are made available for HP-UX or Windows through a set of APIs. This creates a single development environment for HP-UX and Windows NT applications.

The accompanying FoundationTools allow developers to use a single-source code stream for both Windows NT and HP-UX versions of an application. This common development environment and the single source code stream enable faster, easier, less costly development of robust, scalable applications that run immediately on Windows NT and HP-UX. The application can be developed in Visual C++ and then compiled at the same time for NT and HP-UX.

A similar product is Tributary by Bristol Technology.[41] Tributary enables software developers to use Microsoft Visual C++ as their integrated development environment for Sun Solaris and IBM OS/390. Tributary extends the

---

[39]http://www.ibm.com/developer/xml/
[40]http://www.alphaworks.ibm.com/
[41]http://www.bristol.com/

Visual C++ IDE (Integrated Development Environment), leveraging existing knowledge, to write, compile, link, and debug enterprise applications. The software allows developers to combine the power and reliability of Solaris and OS/390 with the ease of use of Visual C++ application development. The ability to integrate with third-party tools allows developers to write native Solaris and OS/390 applications from Visual C++, and to easily port Windows 32-bit applications and applications using the Microsoft Foundation Classes (MFC) to UNIX.

Similar products are under development by other companies to simplify the development and deployment of non-Java applications across several operating systems and types of devices. In addition to these new cross-platform compilers, new cross-language converters have been introduced that allow you to convert source code from one programming language to another. Many cross-language converters have been written to allow programmers to convert their code from Basic, Pascal, or C++ to Java to make the transition smoother and to combine new and old code more easily.

Java has put pressure on other programming languages to become cross-platform compatible and support the Internet. Java is still in the lead, but other languages are gaining popularity. We will have to wait and see what Java 3 will look like, but it is expected that Java 3 will remain in the forefront, as well.

Chapter 13

IMAGING ON THE INTERNET

13.1 Image Business

13.1.1 Reasons for Better Quality Images

It is easy to explain why a separate chapter has been devoted to images. Although many people browse the Internet for information, that information is primarily textual. The quality of pictures is poor compared to magazines, for example. This is the main reason most Internet users do not buy goods online that rely on high-quality pictures to show their design. Selling books, tickets, and CDs over the Internet is easy, because no one is really interested in the fabric of the cover or the information that is printed on the ticket. Content is more important than design in these cases.

But think about businesses that rely on design and not so much on content, and you'll realize that items bought on an emotional basis need good graphics on the Internet in order to sell. These emotive goods are bought not only because of their price or their features, but also because people like what they see.

If we look at the business opportunities on the Internet for high-quality imaging, we can identify two areas where with the greatest need:

- **E-Catalogs**—High-resolution images sell more products in e-commerce storefronts, especially for emotive goods.

- **E-Business Communications**—Newsletters, publishing, and banner advertising will also profit from the higher resolution of images.

Web sites using high-resolution imaging enhance communication, collaboration, and commerce. Customers on the Internet want better, more interactive experiences while browsing their preferred online shops. Online merchants, on the other hand, want to increase their volume of online sales; they want customers to say, "I can see the product." They want to reduce product return costs; they want customers to say, "It's what I thought it was." They want to increase the number of repeat orders per year; they want customers to say, "I like it, I'll do this again." This also allows the online merchants to sell higher-value goods online that would not have sold otherwise (e.g., cars, homes, jewelry, clothing).

13.1.2 Business Requirements

To realize the full potential of an image-rich Web site for business-to-business and business-to-consumer requirements, Internet imaging technology must meet the following requirements:

- **High resolution**—Viewing and printing of high-resolution images should be feasible for as many users as possible, without having the need for more resources on the client, server, and network sides.

- **Download speed**—Download times for high-resolution images must be kept to a minimum. Download times should be optimized for the output device, e.g., low resolution at 72 dots per inch (dpi) for the monitor and 600 dpi for a laser printer.

- **Universal format**—Use a multifunctional, information-rich format that allows a bandwidth efficient display on the Web and printout and doesn't need special plug-ins or additional software.

- **Universal access**—Users should be able to receive the pictures they desire from any source without being restricted by their own location.

- **Free choice of browser and image processing software**—Users should be able to use any browser or image processing software to download, print, or alter images.

- **Scalability**—Internet imaging solutions and technologies must enable companies and Webmasters to manage the fast-growing number of images quickly and efficiently.

- **Integration with existing solutions**—Every new imaging technology must enable the users to include downloaded images in existing applications.

- **Open standard and open source**—*Open standard* means that the format is developed in a public forum, and *open source* means that the source code of the viewer is free to use and be modified by anyone.

13.1.3 Example Business Cases

Having the technology to display high-resolution graphics can be achieved by creating new standards for the Internet. But more important is the business case. If the new standard or technology does not help us to sell more of our products online or reduce the costs of production, then there is no reason to use it. There are Internet examples in which people used hyped-up technology and subsequently failed because the business case was insufficient. So we will now develop four business cases and see if the technology adds value to each electronic business.

The Photographer

An artist wants to sell her artwork online. She is a photographer and a painter. Customers are able to connect to her site and look at the images. From static images, they can get a rough idea of what is in the picture. They send an email to the artist asking for a catalog in order to get a higher resolution of the desired picture. As you can see, this involves many additional steps before the deal can be closed. Why are customers unable to get higher-resolution images for the desired picture? Why can't they just print out a high-resolution image from within the Web page?

The Fashion Designer

A fashion designer needs new fabric for his designer clothes. He connects to the Web sites of several cloth factories to find out about their new material. He can easily compare the prices and the relative availability. But how about the fabric of the cloth? He sends email to ask if they can provide samples. Why can't the designer print out a high-resolution image of the fabric? In this case, of course, he still needs to order samples because he needs to feel the differences, but he can at least reduce the number of requests.

The Car Manufacturer

A car manufacturer wants to sell cars online. The customers connect to the Internet site of the manufacturer. They are able to find all the technical details about the car, see some pictures, and even buy it online. But if they want to do a test drive, they need to find the nearest car dealer (a little database on the Web site will do that). The next thing would be to check when it would best suit everyone for a test drive (an email to the dealer could be sent). But how about walking around the car while online? How about sitting in it and driving around without going to the car dealer at all?

The Retailer

A retailer has different means of transporting content to its customers: either sending out a traditional printed catalog, a brochure, a multimedia CD-ROM, or distributing information on the products via the Internet. Most retailers will have a unit working on the catalog, one working on the CD-ROM, and one working on the Web site. The reasons in the past were manifold, but the most important one was that the technology for producing these different types of media was too different. Wouldn't it be a good idea to unify the images and texts for all three media and get all the information from a single resource?

13.2   Image Concepts

13.2.1   Static Image Formats

If we now look at the commonly used formats on the Internet, we can see that only static image formats are directly supported by Web browsers. Here, *static* means that the image itself cannot change its colors, perspective, or resolution. All browsers understand the static file formats GIF, JPEG, and PNG. There are still some souls out there who put BMP graphics on their Web pages and do not notice that the majority of people see only a broken link. This section will give you a short overview of these formats and explain their advantages and disadvantages, before moving on to the dynamic formats that will enhance your Web presence tremendously.

If we look at the market share that GIF, JPEG, and PNG have, we will see that Portable Network Graphics, or PNG (pronounced "ping"), is not very common yet. But when creating Web sites with static images, you now should consider PNG to be the best solution.

Static images should be used to create a flashy layout on your site. When you try to sell something, you should consider moving on to dynamic formats.

So why bother with PNG when GIF and JPEG have been around for so long? Both of them have problems. GIF was developed by CompuServe and has a bad reputation for being the format of choice for pornographic images that were exchanged on the CompuServe network. GIF uses the patented LZW compression algorithm from Unisys, meaning that every GIF-supporting program should pay licensing fees. As far as I know, this was never enforced, but because this could change at any time, it is better not to rely on this format. GIF images support only up to 256 colors. This was fine until true color graphic cards became the standard in all computers.

JPEG, on the other hand, is a so-called *lossy* image format. Depending on the strength of compression, the image loses information. The compression algorithm tries to remove data that cannot be distinguished by the human eye, so that makes it a good format for viewing. But as soon as you try to change a JPEG image, you will notice that some information is missing. When applied to photos you won't notice the loss, but with clip art, text, and so on, you can see the difference immediately. The advantage of JPEG is that the files are compressed at a ratio of 1:10 or more, so that your 500 KB images become less than 50 KB to download.

When CompuServe announced in 1994 that the GIF format uses a patented algorithm, the Internet society started developing a new format (after the obligatory inflammatory weeks on Usenet) that would be free of charge and better than GIF and JPEG together. The PNG project is a perfect example of Internet cooperation and efficiency. Similar projects are Linux,[1] Mozilla,[2] and Apache;[3] see Chapter 15 for more information on open source projects. Using mainly email and newsgroups, developers from all over the world have designed and implemented this new standard. The goals for the new image format were the following:

- **Portability**—Make it portable across platforms, operating systems and implementations.

- **Network-friendly**—Make it network-friendly by reducing the size of the image.

- **New graphic format**—Create a new graphics format to replace GIF and partly JPEG.

PNG does not support animation. There is another format for animations called MNG (Multiple-Image Network Graphics). It is based on PNG and can do everything that GIF animations do and more (e.g., sprites, multimedia features).

PNG is directly supported since version 4 of Netscape Navigator/Communicator and Internet Explorer. Older browsers can be PNG-enabled by downloading a plug-in.[4] A Webmaster will want to find out how many customers still rely on older versions of browsers. If you are creating Web pages for your intranet and know that everyone uses Netscape 4.5 or higher, then it is quite easy to switch from GIF to PNG. Users with PNG-enabled browsers will notice the difference in image quality and faster download times. Always check the log files of your Web server and your user profile before moving to a new format (See Chapter 10 for more browser-related information), but today it should not be a problem anymore.

To get back to the business case. Static images are the best choice for images that do not contain content, but are for Web page design purposes only, for low-quality images, or for noninteractive pictures. Many companies now use static image formats for delivering high-quality and interactive imaging, but this requires a large overhead and limits use.

A simple example of the complexity involved in using static images is offering a small thumbnail of an image on a Web page. By clicking on the image, the user could get a higher resolution image of the same picture. Many people think that this may be a good solution, but it becomes highly complicated soon as there are thousands of images on the Web site and you want to offer them all in five different resolutions. A static format takes some good conversion tools, a database, and some other tools (CGI-scripts, content management systems,

---

[1]http://www.linux.org/
[2]http://www.mozilla.org/
[3]http://www.apache.org/
[4]http://browserwatch.internet.com/plug-in.html

The PNG image format is the new standard for static image files on the Internet. Officially, PNG stands for "Portable Network Graphics." The unofficial acronym for PNG is "PNG's Not GIF" (just like "GNU's Not UNIX," a recursive acronym). The most important features of PNG are:

- Greyscale images up to 16 bits (GIF and JPEG: 8-bit)

- True-color images up to 48 bits (GIF: 8-bit; JPEG: 24-bit)

- Up to 65,536 levels of transparency/translucency (GIF has one; JPEG none)

- Automatic "brightness" compensation across platforms (not supported by GIF or JPEG)

- Two-dimensional interlacing, which provides an initial impression of the image after just 1/64 of the data has arrived (GIF and JPEG: after 1/3 of the data has arrived)

- Free of patents, and better compression (1/3 of GIF; comparable to JPEG)

Table 13.1. What Is New in PNG?

etc.) to manage the site. The use of interactive image formats will simplify the administrative procedure, as we will see later.

Animations can be done quite easily with static image formats, but the size of the images will increase dramatically. Ask yourself if you really need to rotate the email button before uploading it to your Web site. The animation may attract more customers to click it, but if the download takes too long, fewer people will go to your Web site. Creating animations using dynamic image formats may require a little more work, but the files will be much smaller (e.g., a small ASCII text containing the co-ordinates of the movement of an object, instead of saving each frame of movement). The complexity of your Web page design should be driven by your customers' profiles (See Chapter 5 for more information on Web page design). Before developing a visual strategy, it is important to always decide on the purpose and the message of the site.

From a business point of view, static image formats will be important to Web designers but won't help increase sales over the Internet. The future of static image formats is PNG, and for animations, MNG, so use these formats to show that you are incorporating state-of-the-art technology. Static image formats become useless as soon as you try to create an interactive experience for the customers. It's not worth the effort. Looking at the assumptions made in the section "Business Requirements," it is easy to see that the requirements are not met by the static image formats.

13.2.2 Dynamic Image Formats

If we now look at dynamic image formats, we can see that there is a whole range of different products on the market right now. Dynamic image formats are able to change their resolution, the perspective, the lights, colors, etc. In the context of Internet imaging, dynamic does not mean Java applications, Director movies, or Active X controls that can also deliver dynamic and interactive image formats. They need additional programming. Dynamic image formats do not require programming. They do require design, though.

Dynamic images contain metainformation about the picture itself, allowing its appearance to be modified without having to create a new picture. For example, think of an apple that can be viewed from all sides without having to reload the Web page. Looking at an apple in GIF format, one cannot change the perspective of the apple; one cannot view the apple from the other side, because the GIF format hasn't stored any information on what the other side may look like. Adding metainformation to the data is crucial for processing it and for creating added value to the customer (as discussed in Chapter 6).

Most of the dynamic image formats use browser plug-ins or need special viewer programs. This limits the use of the formats if the plug-ins are not available for all target platforms. One of the few plug-ins that is available for all platforms is the Adobe Acrobat Reader plug-in,[5] making PDF files the standard for distributing documents over the Internet. Using Java applets will resolve the platform dependency, but this may require you to write a Java Web application (called *applet*). And that may be overkill. If you rely on browser plug-ins like Apple's QuickTime,[6] Platinum's CosmoPlayer,[7] or Real Networks' RealPlayer,[8] you have a good chance of being on the right track. All of these are installed with Netscape Communicator, for example. Let's explore some technologies that could enhance your online business case or enable a new business case to be taken online.

FlashPix, QuickTime VR, and VRML are three breakthrough technologies that have been chosen on the basis of business requirements for Internet imaging. There are many other formats, but none fits as well into the business requirements.

---

[5]http://www.adobe.com/
[6]http://www.apple.com/quicktime/
[7]http://www.cosmoworld.com/
[8]http://www.real.com/

13.2.3   Web-Safe Palette

Although the need for a Web-safe palette on standard Web browsers is decreasing over time, it is still important to mention the concept, because new devices come online that use only 256 colors. To make Web sites look good on all devices, it is important to understand how to create Web pages that look good with only a few colors. Always keep the low-end viewers in mind, people who surf the web on everything from text browsers and mobile phones to WebTV. If you design only for high-end systems, you'll be alienating a large portion of your audience.

There are some good reasons to use the Web-safe palette rather than either your default system palette or some different custom palette. Any 8-bit full palette has 256 colors—but not all platforms use the same 256 colors by default. When viewed on another computer in 256-color mode, the colors in your image may get replaced by a dithered approximation from that platform's palette. Because the 216 Web-safe colors are common to most platforms, using them will help your images appear the way you intend them to on the widest range of systems.

Several systems are used to describe colors. They're often targeted for a specific use; CMYK is used for color printing, while RGB usually refers to the colors your monitor is capable of displaying. Most of the time, when talking about Web graphics, you'll use the RGB system. The Web-safe palette cuts each axis of the RGB cube into 20 degree increments, for a total of six slices. With six different possible values in each of the three components, you have 216 different colors ($6 \times 6 \times 6 = 216$).

It's also helpful to pick the background colors for your web pages from the Web-safe palette. A little extra dithering in one area of a photo is distracting, but a screen full of dithering with text on top of it can be downright obnoxious.

If the audience is viewing a Web document on any display that shows them more than 256 colors at a time, the colors will appear correctly. The Web-safe palette isn't a cure-all. In many circumstances, you want to avoid it. Only use the Web-safe palette on images you were going to save as a GIF or 8-bit PNG anyway.

Most graphical applications allow you to save pictures using the web-safe palette. This ensures that the right colors are automatically selected. If you have only a PC at home, turn down the color depth of your graphics card to 256 colors and watch your Web site. You will probably see areas that do not look very good.

13.2.4   Color Scheme

Choose two or three main colors for your Web site and stick to them throughout the site. To check that your Web site has a good color design, print a page out on a black and white printer. If the page is still readable, you are doing it right. Depending on the focus of your site, you should know about the effect colors

---

To understand the problems and complexities of reproducing an image, it is essential to understand the different colorspaces, RGB and CMYK. Traditionally, photographers have worked in RGB colorspace and printers have lived in CMYK colorspace.

- **CMYK**—This colorspace is based on subtractive color. White, the presence of all colors, is the basis. Cyan, Magenta, and Yellow (hence CMY) pigments can be used to subtract from the light reflected off the printed page to make black. CMY colorspace is the theoretical opposite of RGB colorspace. You don't get black when you mix cyan, magenta, and yellow. You get a muddy brownish color. To overcome this problem, black ink is added. Black is the K in CMYK.

- **RGB**—This colorspace is based on additive color. Black, the absence of all colors, is the basis. Red, Green, and Blue (hence RGB) light can be added to make white. The human eye, a computer monitor, and film are all RGB colorspace devices.

Table 13.2. CMYK and RGB Colorspaces

have on the users. Some colors are more aggressive, while others are calming. The colors you choose should support the message of the Web page.

Colors can be used to influence the way users see a Web page. Red, for example, is a very aggressive color, full of energy, determination, and passion. It can be used to promote a new product aggressively. If you use orange, you invite your customers to remain longer on a given Web site and relax. The color orange represents happiness, courage, and success. Blue is tranquil, intuitive, and trustworthy, and is a preferred color for company logos.

Some Web pages talk about colors. Two excellent examples can be found on Myth.com[9] and on Artomatic.com.[10] Both sites explain colors and their meanings extremely well.

---

[9]http://www.myth.com/color/

[10]http://www.artomatic.com/color/

13.3   The FlashPix Format

13.3.1   Technical Overview

FlashPix (FPX) is unlike any other imaging technology available today. The key to FlashPix is a multi-resolution, tiled file format that allows images to be stored at different resolutions for different purposes, such as editing or printing. Each resolution is divided into 64 × 64 blocks, or tiles. Within a tile, pixels can be either uncompressed, JPEG compressed, or single-color compressed, depending on the network connection you have.

Highlights of the FlashPix format include:

- Resolution-independent coordinate system

- Multiple image representations

- Defines a standardized colorspace that keeps colors consistent when viewed across various displays and printers

- Contains compression header information shared between all files at all resolutions in all subimages, reducing file size dramatically

- Structured storage makes FlashPix easily accessible

- Allows creation of new extensions, such as an audio extension that allows you to attach audio data to an image in a single complete package

- Scalable and portable

- Specifies operations to be applied to image data acquired from a source

- Resulting image data can be cached independently of the source format

Table 13.3. FlashPix Features

FlashPix objects are stored in structured storage container files, and the image data is stored in defined colorspaces called sRGB, which are close to most commonly used RGB colorspaces, but which are calibrated to known color values. By defining the colorspace options and providing standard ICC color management profiles, FlashPix delivers consistent color on standard systems as well as with color managed systems.

Editing is easily handled, thanks to a set of image manipulation features known as the image view. The image view works like two coordinate systems: the source and the result coordinate system. Viewing parameters include area selection, a filtering parameter, a spatial orientation matrix, a color twist matrix, and a contrast parameter.

The FlashPix format is also rich in nonimage data definitions. This metadata includes information such as content description, camera information, and scan description. Finally, FlashPix has the ability to add numerous extensions. With FlashPix, applications can add new storage, streams, and/or property sets that can be maintained across editing sessions of the file. Audio, for instance, can already be embedded into FlashPix images.

The communication between Web browser and Web server is handled by the Internet Imaging Protocol (IIP). This new protocol, developed by the same team as the FlashPix format, is designed to communicate tiled image data and related information efficiently over network connections. To maximize performance over the Net, IIP reduces messaging overhead by bundling multiple requests into a single message that an IIP server can parse (for incoming messages) and format (for outgoing messages). This allows efficient access to multi-resolution images. IIP is designed to work well with images in FlashPix file format, but works with non-FPX files just as easily and transparently.

13.3.2 Checking the Business Cases

Looking at the examples from the first section, you can see that FlashPix is able to meet the expectations of the customers extremely well in the first two cases and the last one. The artist is able to deliver high-quality images to the customer using FlashPix technology. Using a conversion tool or a paint program (e.g., Adobe's PhotoShop), she is able to transform her artwork into high-resolution, Web-enabled images. The customers are able to surf the artist's Web page using low-bandwidth network access (e.g., via modem), looking at all the images online, but always with the possibility of high-resolution prints. The major issue with high-quality images is copyright protection. Digital watermarks have not proven to be effective so far. So additional protective measures should be taken. One measure should be that the name of the artist and the license scheme come with each picture. What is the end-user allowed to do with it? How many copies is the end-user allowed to print? These questions should be part of the license.

But this really depends on the type of artwork. If the image is large format pictures, there should be no need to add security because there are too few large format color printers around.

Poster designers and painters, creating small format pictures, on the other hand, have a problem giving out high-resolution images. It may ruin their business. In this case, they should consider selling the high-quality images over the Internet. Currently, it is not possible to limit the number of prints a user makes. But future releases of the FlashPix technology will eventually allow this type of licensing scheme. Two scenarios are possible:

1. **Prepaid**—Customers download a picture, pay for a certain number of printouts, and make the printouts whenever they want. As soon as they have reached the maximum number of printouts, the software refuses to print the image until the artist receives a new order from the user.

2. **Postpaid**—Encoded into the picture are the payment details (e.g., credit card, debit card, etc.). As soon as an individual prints out a picture, the information is sent to the artist via the Internet and a fee is collected for each printout. In conjunction with large-format printers, this could create a new dimension in selling art. A poster shop would consist of some terminals and a large format printer. Customers choose their preferred poster online and give this information to a shop assistant, who would print out the poster for the customer in the desired size. The customers could also access the poster shop from home and get the poster shipped. The customer is more satisfied because there is a greater choice of images, and the shop manager is happy because there is no need to buy a large quantity of posters in advance. The posters can be produced on demand.

The fashion designer in our second example is able to choose the color and fabric online without printing at all. While online, he can zoom into the pictures for more details, so that there is no need for a print. He can get a look at the details of the fabric and then decide which of them need to be examined in real life, saving him a lot of unnecessary work. Adding a "feel-device" may resolve the problem of not being able to touch and feel the cloth. Realistically, such a thing won't be available within the next few years, but maybe someone is creating just such a device. The fashion designer can use FlashPix himself for his online catalog, allowing users to take a closer look at the fashions presented online.

The third business case does not profit as much by the FlashPix technology. The only thing you can do with FlashPix for the car designer is to offer a selection of views of the car and let the user zoom into the details. It will be hard to create a 3D type of experience with the current versions of the FlashPix format. Future releases of FlashPix are expected to have a type of panoramic view built in that enables users to create 3D environments.

The retailer in the fourth business case could use FlashPix to generate a type of metacatalog for images. Just as with text, which will be basically the same for a catalog, CD-ROM, and Web site, the creators can join the image resolutions into a single database. Then they can extract the required resolution (e.g., 1200 dpi for the catalogue, 144 dpi for the CD-ROM, and 72 dpi for the Web site). The image will automatically be available in the required resolution.

Even without using the client software of FlashPix, the designers of the catalog can make a great impact on costs by using a unified source for images.

13.3.3 Online Experience

If we now look at the Web, we can see many companies already using FlashPix to deliver high-quality images to their customers. Fat Face,[11] a U.K.-based retailer of fashion for Generation X relaunched its Web site in November 1998 using FlashPix technology that was integrated into their existing InterShop shopping solution. More than 2,300 products are available in high resolution on the Internet. Customers now have the possibility to choose, for example, a pair of trousers and can zoom in and see embroideries, stitching, and other details.

Another fine example is the Web site of PowerDisc.[12] PowerPics, which is the online service of PowerDisc, is a digital stock photography site for business use in presentations, brochures, and newsletters. On the Web site, you can find images through keyword or category search engines. Images can be added to the shopping basket and are ready to be purchased. Customers can choose a resolution and a license agreement. The cost depends on both the resolution ("What size do I need?") and the license agreement ("What do I need the pictures for?"). PowerDisc formerly distributed images on CD-ROMs before moving its operation to the Internet.

Gallery-Net[13] uses the technology to show paintings in high quality. Figure 13.1 shows the difference in detail of FlashPix (left) and a JPEG (right) file, when zoomed in.

Pornographic Web sites were the first to adopt and use SSL encryption for credit card payments. After it proved to be a secure and viable way for Internet payment, other online businesses began using SSL encryption for doing secure business over the Internet. The use of HTML forms and SSL substantially reduced the cost for many companies. Suddenly, they could automate the whole payment process. FlashPix is in a similar position. It lowers costs for businesses using it, so soon it will be more widely adopted. The Digital Imaging Group has promised a simple freeware implementation of FlashPix, thus enabling everyone to use it.

13.3.4 Required Software

To view FlashPix images over the Internet, some software needs to be installed on the Web server. Among the server products available are Netgraphica/IIP Server by TrueSpectra, Inc,[14] Hewlett-Packard's OpenPix ImageIgniter,[15] and

---

[11]http://www.fatface.co.uk/

[12]http://www.powerpics.com/

[13]http://www.gallery-net.com/

[14]http://www.truespectra.com/

[15]http://image.hp.com/

Figure 13.1. Zoom on a picture by Nicolaj Romanov.

Live Picture's Image Server.[16] FlashPix images used to be displayed with a plug-in in older versions of the software servers. Newer releases of the server software allow the use of CGI-BIN applications, Java applets, ActiveX components, or even flat images. The most common way is to use a Java applet because it works on all platforms and does not require any additional software. In some cases, though, it may not be the fastest way to view the images.

An innovative feature has been introduced into Version 3.0 of OpenPix ImageIgniter. It automatically detects the type of browser and serves the images in the format that best suits the browser. Netscape browsers use a Java applet, Internet Explorer uses an Active X component, and all other browsers use a CGI-based solution. Although this is not the ultimate solution, it is the optimal solution for the current situation on the market, with different browsers adopting different standards. It would be ideal if all browsers would understand the same standards in the same way. The other companies producing server software are catching up and trying to top the feature list. For a complete list of FlashPix enabled products, you can always go to the Web site of the Digital Imaging Group.[17] There you will find an up-to-date list of products, ranging from digital cameras and scanners to image software that supports the FlashPix format and a freeware implementation of the FlashPix server software. Although it is far from being as powerful as the commercial products, it

---

[16]http://www.livepicture.com/
[17]http://www.digitalimaging.org/

enables companies to try out the power of the format without initially having to invest into the software.

13.4   QuickTime VR

13.4.1   Technical Overview

QuickTime was invented a few years back by Apple Computer and has since become the most popular environment for multimedia CD-ROM and Internet productions. QuickTime was designed to simplify the task of working with and integrating the widest possible range of digital media types, not just sound and video. The QuickTime Movie format is so popular that it has become the basis for the MPEG-4 standard.[18]

QuickTime consists of three distinct elements:

1. The QuickTime Movie file format, which features

   - a means of storing digital media compositions
   - a container format for storing not only media assets but also the description of the media composition

2. The QuickTime Media Abstraction Layer, which features

   - access to software tools and applications to the media support service
   - hardware acceleration for critical portions
   - a means for extending and enhancing media services

3. A rich set of built-in media services, which features

   - a comprehensive set of built-in capabilities to reduce development time
   - interoperability between QuickTime applications

Table 13.4. QuickTime Elements

QuickTime VR is the virtual reality component that allows the viewing of 360-degree panoramic images. Having panoramic images means that people

---

[18]http://www.mpeg.org/

can either look around from a point of view or that they can walk around a certain object, depending on what a company wants to display. In the first case, a webmaster could use it to show a room in the middle of which the users are standing. Depending on the quality of the image, customers can zoom into details like curtains, pictures on the wall, etc. The same method of zooming in and out can be applied to objects that can be viewed from all sides, e.g., a sports car.

Many games and educational software use QuickTime VR. But its use is not limited to these areas, as we will see in the next section.

13.4.2 Checking the Business Cases

If we now look again at our sample business cases, we can see that we have a hit for the first three cases.

In the first case, the artist would be able to present more than just images. She could put objects, sculptures, or installations online that can be viewed from every angle. The user could zoom in and out for more or less detail. The artist could take pictures of the gallery and let the users wander around the gallery. Using QuickTime VR, the user would be able to walk around and approach pictures. The advantage over the FlashPix format here is that after you have downloaded the QuickTime file, the speed is amazing; you zoom in and out in real time, you can walk around the object in real time as well. But this is also a disadvantage: You have to download the complete file first, and it will most likely be large for good quality examples (ranging from a few hundred kilobytes up to several megabytes). Downloading a 400 KB file using a 28.8 modem would take about two minutes, for example. This is something you can go for; most people will have the patience to wait that long for a cooler view of the world. But don't forget to mention on the Web page what the user should expect. Another disadvantage is that QuickTime VR does not adapt itself to the required resolution. QuickTime VR is a format that is made for onscreen viewing. It has no special features for printing, in contrast with FlashPix.

Looking at the second business case, the fashion designer, we discover some similarities. The fashion designer will not be really interested in "walking around the cloth," but the feature of zooming in is essential for him. The fabric manufacturer does not gain anything by using QuickTime VR over FlashPix, so he would stick to FlashPix. But the fashion designer can gain much through QuickTime VR. This technology enables him to present his fashions attractively on the Net. Just like having models wearing his clothing for a printed catalog, he can use them for creating 3D models on the Internet. The creation of QuickTime VR is a little more complex than just doing a photograph, but it will allow users to walk around the models and see what the clothing is like from all sides. QuickTime VR images actually consist of photographs of the same object from 12 or 24 different angles.

The third business model, the car manufacturer, profits from using Quick-

Time VR as well, and would profit even more when using QuickTime VR in conjunction with FlashPix technology. The car would be photographed from 24 different angles to create the 3D experience. The user could zoom in and out, and walk around the car. Clicking on certain points of the car—the wheel, for example—would cause the server to send a FlashPix image to replace the QuickTime VR image to give greater control on details. This could work for all objects that do not need a 3D experience, to reduce download times. If you need to turn the wheel, then the Web site would offer the option to download another QuickTime VR image or to use a VRML object (see section about VRML later in this chapter).

The fourth virtual business case, the retailer, cannot really gain anything by using QuickTime VR. He can create wonderful 3D experiences for the CD-ROM and the Web site, as described in the paragraph above. But he won't be able to create a unified image database with QuickTime VR, which was the business requirement for this case. A good layout and simple navigation will be more helpful to the retailer.

13.4.3   Online Experience

NASA[19] was of the most prominent users of the QuickTime VR format in July 1997, when Pathfinder[20] landed on Mars. A little rover called Sojourner drove around on the surface of Mars and took pictures. The pictures were taken in a form that enabled panoramic photographs to be created without additional overhead. Having panoramic photography meant that conversion to Quick-Time VR was just a matter of hitting some buttons. The QuickTime VR model allowed users to look around Mars, as if they were there themselves! They could zoom in on details, look around the landscape, and enjoy the strange red panorama of the planet. During the Pathfinder mission, NASA had to set up numerous mirror Web sites to maintain normal service on their main Web site, due to the huge demand for information. Most people didn't know that they were watching QuickTime VR because the necessary plug-in was already installed in their browsers. But still, this single event meant a huge boost in awareness for this technology (by the way, FlashPix and VRML technology became better known as a result of the same event, although it didn't have such a large impact on them). And even though NASA hasn't made any money from its multimedia images, the U.S. Congress has become more willing to spend money on space flights, due to the good coverage of the event.

Hewlett-Packard in Europe is showing its benchmark center on the company intranet using the QuickTime VR format. Visitors are able to wander around the benchmark center and see what equipment is available there (see Figure 13.2). A benchmark center is used to test the speed of hardware and software components and to fine-tune the whole architecture.

---

[19]http://www.nasa.gov/
[20]http://mpfwww.jpl.nasa.gov/

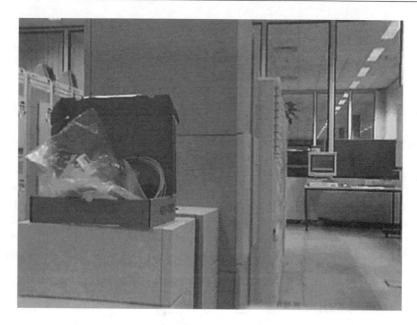

Figure 13.2. Hewlett-Packard's European Benchmark Center.

Another good example is Seiko Corporation[21] in Japan. Seiko uses Quick-Time VR to present its watches online.[22] At the time of this writing, Seiko is using its Web site for marketing purposes only, so using our definition from the introduction, we can classify its Web site in category 2. So far, you are not able to buy watches online. Although the technology of presenting watches is very good already, the only way to buy a watch is to select a country and send off an email to the country headquarters for more information on the nearest dealer. Checking available stock at a particular store is not possible, as it is on Hewlett-Packard's Web site.

Another beautiful Web experience is the Reebok[23] Web site for men's training shoes.[24] Here we have the same issue as with Seiko's online experience. It is a good marketing instrument, but there is no way for Reebok to measure whether it is increasing its market share. It gives the company the feel of being innovative, but a company should always try to reduce costs and/or increase profits when introducing a new technology. Depending on how important "coolness" is for a company, it could follow Reebok or Seiko and use technology just to show off. In most cases, this will not be enough for the company and its customers. QuickTime is more of a "feel-good" software than FlashPix is, due

---

[21]http://www.seiko-corp.co.jp/
[22]http://www.seiko-corp.co.jp/Kinetic/outer.html
[23]http://www.reebok.com/
[24]http://www.reebok.com/training/

to its speed, but FlashPix has the advantage of the well-defined business case. QuickTime has been used traditionally by creative people, whereas FlashPix is more the type of technology a business manager would choose.

13.4.4 Required Software

Software for developing QuickTime VR images can be obtained from Apple and third-party vendors. In contrast to FlashPix, QuickTime is not an open standard. Development and implementation are done entirely by Apple. The client software comes in the form of a standalone player and a browser plug-in, both free in the standard version. You can upgrade the standard to the professional edition, which features higher speeds. A small cost is involved, but it appears that no Web sites work only with the professional version, so you must weigh whether the upgrade is worth the expense.

On the Web server side, no additional software is needed. QuickTime files are stored in the path of the Web server documents to be retrieved by the browsers. To create QuickTime files, you need specialized authoring software. A complete list of tools can be found at Apple's QuickTime developer's home page.[25] To create QuickTime VR movies without interaction, you can download a freeware tool from Apple's Web site,[26] but it is available only for Mac OS. If you need to develop it on Windows, you have to use the commercial applications.[27]

13.5 VRML

13.5.1 Technical Overview

Virtual Reality Modeling Language (VRML) is the file format standard for 3D multimedia and shared virtual worlds on the Internet. It is an open specification for creating, viewing, and manipulating 3D objects and spaces. Just as HTML led to an explosion on the Internet by implementing a graphical interface and being the basis for the exchange of information, VRML adds the next level of interaction, structured graphics, and two extra dimensions to the online experience. The third dimension, depth, and the "fourth" dimension, time, are added to the flatlands of the Internet.

VRML is the most interactive format of the three discussed in this chapter. Having its own scripting language and interfaces to Java and JavaScript enables you not only to create 3D worlds, but to make them interactive as well. Using the fourth dimension of time, we can move things around or change them. Using one of the above-mentioned languages allows us to bring alive virtual people in a 3D world or to create virtual representations of people who

---

[25]http://www.apple.com/quicktime/developers/tools.html

[26]http://www.apple.com/quicktime/qtvr/

[27]http://www.apple.com/quicktime/authors/

VRML, which is pronounced either "vee-are-em-ell" or "ver-mul," is an abbreviation for Virtual Reality Modeling Language. You may see some references to "Virtual Reality Mark-up Language," which is what VRML was called at the beginning, taking its cue from HTML, the hypertext mark-up language. The main features are:

- **Open standard**—VRML was recognized as an international standard (ISO/IEC-14772-1:1997) in December 1997 by the International Organization for Standardization (ISO) and the International Electrotechnical Commission (IEC).

- **3D multimedia**—Long before its standardization, VRML became the de facto standard for sharing and publishing data between CAD, animation, and 3D modeling programs.

- **Shared virtual worlds**—Being able to talk and work in a 3D shared virtual space was one of the earliest motivations of the VRML pioneers.

- **On the Internet**—Unlike previous 3D applications, using the Internet to share 3D objects and scenes was built into VRML from the beginning.

Table 13.5. What Is VRML?

wander through the VRML scene. One could imagine having online meetings using VRML offices in the near future, whereby the quality of the human representation would improve with every meeting. The approach to VRML is totally different from the approach we have taken with FlashPix or QuickTime VR. You cannot just scan in an image and convert it to the VRML format. The format has evolved from the Inventor format designed by Silicon Graphics. The VRML language describes the objects you want to see on screen. The language contains constructs for displaying cubes, cylinders, spheres, and many other simple and not-so-simple geometric figures. The structure is similar to HTML. Using these relatively simple elements, you are able to build quite complex scenes. Architects, for example, use this method. Although the initial work is more complex than just drawing a two-dimensional picture, you can extract more information from the images afterward. Because you have the additional two dimensions, you can create complex 3D worlds where you are able to walk around and things may change over time. The only disadvantage of VRML is that it requires lots of processing time; that renders it unusable for low-end personal computers. More complex scenes require Pentium-II or PowerPC G3 chips that run faster than 400 MHz, supported by a fast graphics card. But as you know, it is just a matter of time until these processor speeds become low-end and available to low-budget consumers. Getting to know the VRML format now is strategic for the future of your company, if you are interested in close relationships with your customers.

13.5.2 Checking the Business Cases

VRML worlds offer advantages over "normal online shops." The dynamic virtual reality environment allows merchants to implement stronger marketing and branding initiatives. The retention period of a typical shopper is much longer in a 3D world, because there is much more to explore. It is much easier to create interaction between customer and merchant, and customers are able to see other customers and chat with them.

If we now look back to our business cases, we can see quite easily now where VRML fits and where it does not.

Getting back to our first case with our artist, you will see that we cannot enhance the quality of her paintings and photos at all. But we can build a virtual gallery around the pictures. Using textures, we can actually use scanned images for the VRML world. This allows users to walk up to a wall and see a picture. The quality of nonmoving pictures is better, but we can add some functionality that allows the user to view a high-resolution image by clicking on the textured image. As you can see, we cannot enhance the quality of the product presentation itself, but using VRML we can design a comfortable environment for online shopping. Using avatars, we would be able to see other visitors in the gallery and could even start to chat with them, just as in real life. In the Hindu religion, an avatar is an incarnation of a deity; here we mean, an embodiment or manifestation of an idea or greater reality. In virtual reality, an avatar is the visual "handle" or display appearance that a visitor uses to represent himself. On Worlds Chat,[28] The Palace,[29] and similar sites, you can be a unicorn, a bluebird, or any kind of creature or object that seems right. You can exchange opinions and experiences online. You may receive a price reduction for buying as a group and the site administrator could create personal agents to help customers.

If you now compare a 3D virtual reality shop with a standard HTML shop, you will find that most people would prefer the one in which they can actually talk to other people who are interested in the same things. Many shops already offer online chats, but using avatars increases the shopping experience.

---

[28]http://www.worlds.net/
[29]http://www.thepalace.com/

If we now remember the second business case (the fashion designer looking around for his preferred cloth), then we could imagine fabric manufacturers using programs to design the fabric and then converting the design of the fabric to VRML. This would allow the fashion designer to zoom in as far as he wanted. He could also use the VRML file to add the fabric to his clothes while designing them on the computer. In this case, the fashion designer could create virtual models wearing his latest fashion. They could walk around in a virtual shop and present the dresses, trousers, etc. Although this sounds highly unlikely today, it may be something real tomorrow. The reality of tomorrow is what we dream of today.

Our car manufacturer would gain significantly through VRML. He can transform his original CAD design files into VRML files for online viewing. Internet users would be able to create their cars online, by configuring them to their wishes. Changing the color or the type of tires would be very easy. After having configured the car you desire, you could choose a lovely place to go for a drive, like Tuscany. A virtual representation of the country roads could be reproduced on your screen, and you could drive around in your new car. Although this would never replace the real test drive, it would draw lots of people to the Web site. Although this scenario is still a little way off—today's computers are still too slow for such a simulation—we will eventually see this come alive.

If we look at the fourth case, the retailer, we can see a good use for VRML in the area of replacement pieces, for example. These are small parts designed on computers. They are normally stored in a CAD format. If we convert all these drawings into VRML files, we could use them for all three types of media. Depending on the resolution, we can output whatever may be required. Using VRML, we would be able to build a unified database of drawings. The advantage over other CAD formats would be the instant availability on the Internet.

Another example would be an architect selling architectural designs of houses. He has all the data in CAD format and converting it to VRML would enable his Web presence within minutes. With VRML, we must address the issue of copyright infringements; because we get the complete source code in readable form, any VRML file could be easily copied. Therefore, an architect or producer of replacement parts will use some type of conversion to reduce the high quality of the original drawings that will still be good enough for customers to view, but won't be good enough for competitors to copy.

13.5.3 Online Experience

Siemens KWU[30] in Germany is using VRML to speed up the development of new power plants. The new nuclear power plant EPR (European Pressurized Water Reactor) is built using the Internet for communication and the VRML standard for visualization. Siemens is exchanging information on new parts

---

[30]http://www.siemens.de/kwu/e/

within a power plant with customers and production partners. The Web clients are able to navigate through a virtual power plant and click on elements for more information. After an element has been chosen, it is possible to download CAD documents that need refinement. Siemens KWU completes only a raw design of the plant and lets selected partners develop the fine-grained version of the design. The VRML scenes are used to navigate through the documents on the server (see Figure 13.3).

Figure 13.3. Siemens KWU European Pressurized Water Reactor

After a partner has submitted the design of a particular piece of the building to Siemens, everyone involved in the construction phase can check that all components have been brought together in the right way, or if, for example, some pipes do not fit together. After having constructed the power plant on the Internet, the same system can be used to show potential customers what the power plant will look like. There is no shopping solution used here, and the 3D server does not handle payment. Having only a handful of customers and only a few power plants to select from online, shopping is not feasible because there is no fixed price for such a project and buying a nuclear power plant by credit card seems a little odd. Other business cases may involve payment options for all sorts of parts that need to be bought for the prototype, for example.

The quality of the VRML worlds is very high and demands lots of CPU power from the Web clients. In this case, where we have only a very few customers; setting up a high-end computer at each customer site is a problem that can be solved without spending much money. The first EPR is expected to go online in 2008 near Marseille, France.

This is also the reason why there aren't many examples of successful e-business applications on the Internet. The demand for resources is extremely high. Many companies use VRML for fun (and they sometimes call it marketing). Let's look at same examples. Skoda,[31] the Czech car manufacturer, uses it for a virtual showroom online, but walking around the showroom a customer will find that the animation is too slow or the quality is not high enough. Neither the customer nor the manufacturer really gains anything from this.

Lenin's home page in Russia[32] uses VRML, too. The Web site offers general information on Lenin and allows the visitor to view the famous mausoleum in Moscow, Russia. Visitors can tour the mausoleum virtually and learn more about the organizer of the 1917 October Revolution. It is possible to participate in a guided tour through the mausoleum or walk through it on your own.

In December 1997, a pan-European project consortium lead by Mellon Technologies,[33] a Greek company specializing in electronic payment systems, and the Greek software house, Exodus,[34] started an 18-month research project on "Virtual Reality Online Shopping."[35] The latest technologies were used to create an integrated environment for e-commerce using virtual reality and virtual communities. A virtual reality mall has been built with several virtual reality shops. You can shop in them and choose from a wide range of products. In addition to the shops, a whole environment has been built up around the shopping mall, where you can engage in conferences and watch street artists juggle balls. The project tries to emulate a real shopping experience, and it is quite intriguing to enter this virtual world. Still, the use of VRML right now is not perfect and complicates the Internet shopping experience. Instead of users finding certain goods immediately, they are left to wander around, just as in a real shopping mall, where the experience is more important than the shopping. Many high-resolution objects are used, so the process can become really slow if many objects are on the screen at the same time. Although the research project doesn't allow you to buy anything, many e-businesses will profit from the results of this project.

Activeworlds.com[36] is a 3D virtual reality environment featuring an online shopping mall called @Mart. Many 3D online stores have already been built using Activeworld's drag-and-drop store building technology. More than 100 online businesses like Amazon.com and Beyond.com[37] have already opened shops in @Mart. See Figure 13.4 for an example of Activeworld's work.

Shoppers walk around the @Mart virtual mall by pointing their mouse or using the arrow keys on their keyboard to proceed. Although the environment

---

[31] http://www.skoda-auto.cz/

[32] http://www.lenin.ru/

[33] http://www.mellon.gr/

[34] http://www.exodus.gr/

[35] http://www.vr-shop.iao.fhg.de/

[36] http://www.activeworlds.com/

[37] http://www.beyond.com/

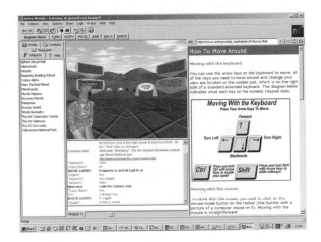

Figure 13.4. Walking around in the ActiveWorld.

is 3D, the merchandise is displayed in 2D. A detailed description of the products is displayed when clicking on one of the graphics. The actual purchase and payment process is then done on the merchant's Web site and not in the cyber mall, so that companies can add a fancy virtual shop, but do not need to replicate their existing infrastructure.

13.5.4   Required Software

All CAD software can design VRML objects and scenes. There are specialized VRML software products, but if you look at them, most are just stripped-down versions of CAD software. Interactivity cannot be designed with CAD software. That is accomplished using the programming interface, either Java or JavaScript. No software needs to be installed on the Web server, but the Internet customer needs to download one of the VRML plug-ins. In November 1998, Sony[38] released the Java source code of its VRML player, enabling other programmers to enhance the existing code. This open source initiative will enable more people to enjoy virtual reality on the Web.

13.6   Comparing Imaging Technologies

Now that we have looked at the three most promising technologies, let's review the business requirements from the second section. Table 13.6 describes which technology meets which requirement.

All three technologies have their advantages. If you look at the row called Software Integration, you can see where each of the technologies was originally

---

[38]http://www.sony.com/

	FlashPix	QuickTime VR	VRML
High Resolution	Yes	Yes	Yes, but requires a fast computer
Download Speed	Fast	Slow	Fast
Universal Format	Adapting itself to the browser	Requires plug-in	Requires plug-in
Universal Access	Yes	Yes	Yes
Free Choice of Browser	Yes	Yes, but requires plug-in	Yes, but requires plug-in
Scalability	Yes	Yes	Yes
Software Integration	Image processing	Multimedia	CAD
Open Standard	Yes	No	Yes
Open Source	No	No	Yes

Table 13.6. Comparison of Imaging Technology

positioned and has its roots. You can still mix the technologies or even choose a technology from one sector to deliver a solution in another. We have seen enough examples to prove this, but people tend to stay in the sector they feel comfortable with already.

Open standards and open source have become increasingly important. Having an open standard means that you do not have to rely on one company for the image format. There is a consortium behind the format that drives the development. Open source means that the source code can be adapted to the needs of the Webmasters and their clients, and that no license fees are paid. See Chapter 15 for more information on the Open Source Community.

13.7   The Future of Imaging

13.7.1   Fractal Compression

The future of imaging is manifold. One addition to the portfolio of important graphics formats is the use of fractal compression technologies. Many structures in nature follow repeating patterns, e.g., mountains, coastlines, or the leaves of plants. These self-repeating patterns can be used to save complex structures in rather simple equations. You can zoom into the structure without losing information. Fractal compression tries to save the whole picture in a transformation matrix. As a result, the image becomes resolution independent. No matter what resolution you require, it will be delivered to you. JPEG images are tied to pixels, but fractal compression images are tied to mathematical relations. Using these algorithms it is easy to print out a picture either as a thumbnail or as a poster, always having the highest resolution possible, using a very small image file.

The disadvantage of fractal compression is the time it needs to compress and decompress, because the transformation matrix is highly complex. The more detail the image has, the more complex the matrix will be. Eventually, faster hardware will become available, so we can expect a breakthrough in fractal compression technology. But better algorithms will also become available, we hope. Faster algorithms should always be preferred over faster hardware.

13.7.2   DjVu

AT&T[39] has invented a new format, the so-called DjVu pictures (pronounced "déjà vu"), that tries to overcome the deficits of using JPEG with scanned documents. The major problem with JPEG is that sharp contrasts cannot be reproduced perfectly. For example, black and white images and images with text should be saved in GIF or PNG format instead, due to this restriction.

AT&T has developed a format that separates the background information from the foreground image. The background and the foreground use different compression algorithms to achieve the best possible result. The compressed file is about five to eight times smaller than a comparable JPEG, but with a much better resolution than JPEG could achieve for scanned documents. A sample of a scanned document would take up 31.2 MB in TIFF Format, 604 KB in JPEG format, and only 134 KB in the DjVu format. The compression rates are extremely good, but limited to present scanned images on the Web. DjVu will never replace an all-purpose format like JPEG.

Conventional image viewing software decompresses images in their entirety before displaying them. This is impractical for high-resolution document images because they typically go beyond the memory capacity of many PCs, causing excessive disk swapping. DjVu, on the other hand, never decompresses the

---

[39]http://www.att.com/

Figure 13.5. Sharper Image in DjVu format.

entire image, but instead keeps the image in memory in a compact form, and decompresses the piece displayed on the screen in real time as the user views the image. Images as large as 2,500 pixels by 3,300 pixels (a standard page image at 300 DPI) can be downloaded and displayed on low-end PCs.

The DjVu format is progressive. Users get an initial version of the page very quickly, and the visual quality of the page progressively improves as more bits arrive. For example, the text of a typical magazine page would appear in just three seconds over a 56Kbps modem connection. In another second or two, the first versions of the pictures and backgrounds will appear. Then, after a few more seconds, the final, full-quality version of the page is completed.

More information on AT&T's DjVu format can be found at its research site.[40] At the time of this writing, a plug-in is required to view DjVu images, but this will be replaced by Java applets and native browser support in the future.

13.7.3   JPEG 2000

Of the existing standards, the JPEG standard, is being pushed at the moment. Code-named JPEG 2000,[41] an update for the existing JPEG format is in progress. Some of the planned features include the following: Grey-level images will be used; black and white pictures and computer generated images will have less distortion through the use of new algorithms in the lossy format; and a new lossless compression algorithm will be added to the basic set of compression algorithms. All this will result in better performance overall.

In the current version of JPEG, the compression used is called Direct Cosine Transformation (DCT), a system that defines 8×8 blocks of complete informa-

---

[40]http://djvu.research.att.com/

[41]http://www.jpeg.org/

tion, which means that a whole image cannot be viewed until it is entirely downloaded. By utilizing "wavelets" (logarithms that encode an image in a continuous stream), an Internet user will immediately see a low-grade version of the image, and the graphic details will improve as more data is progressively downloaded.

Wavelet compression is also less lossy than current JPEG and other current forms of compression, which often feature low-loss at best. JPEG 2000 can maintain data integrity throughout compression and transmission, a key feature for developers and other professionals.

The JPEG standard today offers only resolutions up to 65536×65536 pixels. Although this is more than enough for most applications, there still may be some who require an even higher resolution. Instead of supporting multiple decompression architectures as in the current version, JPEG 2000 will contain a unified decompression architecture.

Based on the JPEG standard, JPEG 2000 has new features that will move it closer to other formats, such as PNG.

- **Distortion Reduction**—Less distortion for highly detailed grey-level images.

- **Lossless compression**—Includes lossless and lossy compression in a single code stream.

- **Large images**—Support for images that are larger than 65536×65536.

- **Decompression architecture**—Creation of a single common decompression architecture.

- **Compensation for noisy environments**—Enhanced support for transmission in noisy environments to enhance the image.

- **Better performance**—Better performance on computer generated images.

Table 13.7. What's New in JPEG 2000?

There are a number of advantages for developers concentrated around the reduced file size. Smaller files translates into less storage requirements, which means that more graphics can exist within a confined space (such as on a Web page or within data storage). The small file size also helps ease the bandwidth concerns often associated with graphic file transmission and downloading.

Graphic artists will be satisfied to know that JPEG 2000 supports RGB palettes as well as CMYK palettes, a feature unavailable with current JPEG standards. Because the resolution of JPEG 2000 can be controlled on the consumer side, Web developers no longer need to create thumbnail images. Web users can zoom in, pan, and crop on their own, eliminating the need for several files for a single image.

Developers also have the new ability to incorporate meta-data as part of the file. Though currently a standard in many audio and video file formats, this is the first time this feature is available for compressed graphical files. Today, it is already possible to attach some information to JPEG files, but there is no standard way of doing it and not every application supports this feature.

Although called JPEG 2000, it is still not fully released in October 2001. But it is only a matter of time until the new format will be part of all graphics applications and incorporated into Web browsers. The standardization took longer than expected, but the results will make many tasks easier in the future, not only on the Web, but also for print publications and television productions.

Many other formats are in the pipeline, and we will see which will become a standard. Keep in mind that a standard can become highly successful only if it is supported by all the major browser software packages.

13.7.4 Scalable Vector Graphics

Scalable Vector Graphics, or SVG is a new Web image standard that will be radically different from both GIF and PNG. It is not based on pixels but rather on vectors. Vector images offer small file sizes and resolution-independent scalability. Both are very important in a heterogenous environment, in which download times are crucial and viewing platforms vary dramatically.

SVG is a language for describing two-dimensional graphics in XML. SVG allows for three types of graphic objects: vector graphic shapes (e.g., paths consisting of straight lines and curves), images, and text. Graphical objects can be grouped, styled, transformed, and composited into previously rendered objects. The feature set includes nested transformations, clipping paths, alpha masks, filter effects, template objects, and extensibility.

The advantages of vectors are so clear that a number of companies have already developed their own solutions. Corel Xara's WEB[42] and Deneba Canvas's Colada CVW[43] are examples of vector formats. Although these formats are good, there are some problems. In order to view them it is necessary to install a plug-in or a Java or Active X component. This restricts the use of the formats to some platforms and browsers only.

---

[42]http://www.corel.com/
[43]http://www.deneba.com/

Vector formats on the Internet have some important advantages over bitmapped formats.

- **Scalable**—Only one file per image.

- **Resolution independent**—Images can be resized to output device on the fly.

- **No background**—Images and backgrounds can be changed independently.

- **Cartoon-like**—Cartoons can be implemented very easily.

- **Metafiles**—Contain both raster and vector data.

Table 13.8. Advantages of Vector Formats

Therefore, the W3C[44] developed a new, open format for vector graphics. A couple of technical CAD-inspired formats were considered, but the two major submissions were Adobe's[45] PGML (Precision Graphics Markup Language) and Microsoft's[46] VML (Vector Markup Language). The two formats are very different. Adobe's approach was toward output quality, while VML stressed the importance of re-editability based on Microsoft experience. Still, both formats were based on XML, meaning that both are text-based languages acting to describe graphics in the same way that HTML describes Web pages. Therefore, the W3C combined the best of both approaches into the Scalable Vector Graphic (SVG) standard.

SVG drawings can be dynamic and interactive. The Document Object Model (DOM) for SVG allows for straightforward and efficient vector graphics animation via scripting. A rich set of event handlers, such as onmouseover and onclick, can be assigned to any SVG graphical object. Because of its compatibility and leveraging of other Web standards, features like scripting can be used on HTML and SVG elements simultaneously within the same Web page.

With a technology like SVG at its heart, the Web looks set to become the designers dream. It becomes visual, interactive, animated, and scalable.

---

[44]http://www.w3c.org/

[45]http://www.adobe.com/

[46]http://www.microsoft.com/

The scalable vector format has some interesting features that will make it a star on the Internet.

- **Colors**—Enhanced color control and accuracy

- **Dynamics**—Dynamic content, animation, and interactivity through scripting

- **Filters**—High-resolution gradients, drop shadows, and other filter effects

- **Independence**—Support for other devices, such as palmtops, GPS, and cellphones

- **Positioning**—Enables pixel perfect positioning

- **Typography**—Better typographic control including kerning, text on a path, and unlimited fonts

Table 13.9. Features of SVG

13.7.5   X3D

In February 1999, the Web3D Consortium[47] (formerly known as the VRML Consortium) announced that it had initiated the process to define X3D, a next-generation componentized 3D standard that includes integration with XML. Meaning "Extensible 3D," X3D is defined as an interoperable set of lightweight, componentized 3D standards that flexibly address the needs of a wide range of markets.

X3D incorporates a number of component specifications allowing extremely lightweight applications to be deployed on a variety of platforms, from workstations to set-top devices. Set-top boxes are small devices that enable TV sets to access the Internet and play multimedia content and games. Initial components include a lightweight 3D runtime engine with state-of-the-art rendering capabilities, a platform-independent 3D file format and integration with the XML standard. Additionally, by integrating real-time 3D graphics with text, along with 2D graphics and streaming sound and video, X3D will enable a wide range of Web- and broadcast-based applications including entertainment, on-line shopping, and enterprise data visualization.

X3D is building upon the VRML 97 ISO standard with clearly defined back-

---

[47]http://www.web3d.org/

ward compatibility with existing VRML content. X3D will be interoperable with other standards and technologies such as MPEG-4 and HTML. A prototype was released in mid-1999, and it is expected that X3D will replace VRML over the next few years. Companies are already shifting development focus from VRML to X3D.

As an extension to the X3D standard, in February 2001, the Web3D Consortium announced the Rich Media 3D (RM3D) initiative, which is developing an open standard to enable rich media content containing 3D graphics, video, and audio to be sent over the Internet and used in broadcast applications. RM3D is intended to enable an emerging category of media-capable Internet and broadcast devices and appliances to receive and optimally present advanced content, while simplifying the media authoring process. This initiative is being driven by a wide range of companies such as 3Dlabs, ATI, Eyematic, Shout Interactive, and Sony. The group intends to rapidly publish final specifications and initial physical implementations by December 2001.

The Web3D Consortium is working very closely with the MPEG-4 group. The RM3D initiative intends to work closely with MPEG-4 and to enhance the Consortium's contributions in bringing advanced 3D functionality to this important standard. RM3D will also be compatible with current Web3D technologies, such as X3D. The group's diverse mix of technology and content companies is intended to effectively enable new categories of highly interactive applications on a wide range of emerging visual platforms—from mobile devices to Internet terminals, game consoles, and set-top boxes.

Chapter 14

PAYING VIA THE NET

14.1   The Payment Business

14.1.1   Business Requirements

Electronic payments are becoming more important as the number of online business transactions continues to increase. New financial procedures and monetary structures have been introduced to reflect the technological possibilities and economic necessities of our time. Through globalization and the widespread use of the Internet, end customers and companies have changed the way they pay for goods and services.

Traditionally, *payment* means that a value is transferred using a variety of techniques, generally cash or documents. Cash has traditionally been provided in the form of bank notes and coins, which are mainly issued by national governments, and documents for payment have been provided in the form of bills of exchange, checks drawn on a bank, money orders written by an accepted authority such as a national post office, letters of credit, and payment card vouchers.

These payment mechanisms have differing characteristics. The extent to which the parties are identified ranges from total anonymity with cash to total identity with credit cards. The traceability and taxability of the transaction varies among the different payment methods. Many mechanisms exist because of the many different circumstances in which payments are exchanged. There is no single solution that can handle all types of payment. So each mechanism has created niche software markets, making it difficult to find the best solution for your payment problem.

As with traditional payment methods, the biggest challenge is ensuring that no one can copy your digital money or steal your credit card information. The financial transactions between banks have been digitized for some time. The SWIFT Network (Society for World-Wide Interbank Financial Telecommunication) is a private network, but more connections are being established with public networks such as the Internet. SWIFT is used by banks to exchange money between themselves. It is the backbone of the global finance industry.

Electronic payment systems on the Internet must fulfill certain requirements in order to emulate the properties of the existing payment schemes, so
they need to be flexible. They should support different payment models for different situations (such as credit card, cash, and check). Because the payment
models are so different, it is essential that the timing of the payment be agreed
upon by the parties involved. Does the money need to be transferred before the
goods are exchanged, at the same time as the exchange, or after the exchange?

An important feature to include in the payment system would be the option
to convert digital money from one system to another. If digital money cannot be exchanged among systems, the money becomes useless. There should
be a change office where individuals can exchange the digital currency of one
provider into the digital currency of another provider. Imagine travelling to
France with Russian rubles and no exchange office nearby. You cannot do anything with the Russian rubles in France. A payment infrastructure should
allow multiple forms of payment and digital currencies. Also, agreements with
providers of other digital and real funds should be signed to allow the conversion of funds into their system.

A successful payment infrastructure is widely accepted and easy for anyone
to use. Everyone should be able to pay with it or to cash in the money without
the need for an intermediary, such as a bank. The payment solution should be
an open standard that can be used by any business.

Buyers and sellers, as well as the transaction servers, should be independent of the standard. Anyone who wants to process the payment should be able
to do so. To be attractive to both customers and merchants, the customer and
merchant base needs to be large enough. The developers of the payment system
need to get as many merchants as possible on board to attract the customers.

All financial transactions could be performed via the Internet, but for security reasons, existing financial networks should be used for clearing. Every
transaction involves a buyer and a seller of products, information, or services.
To perform a financial transaction, a financial institution is required that enables the money transfer. In most cases, two financial institutions are involved.
The issuer is the financial institution used by the buyer, and the acquiring bank
is used by the seller. The acquiring bank has a business relationship with a
merchant and receives all credit card transactions from that merchant.

Electronic payments start with the communication between buyer and issuer, whereby the buyer asks the issuer to release money by withdrawing it
from a bank account or issuing a credit card, for example. The money is then
sent to the acquiring bank for clearing. If the acquiring bank validates the
money, a message will be sent on to the seller. The reseller can then start the
order processing, and the money is put into the seller's account.

Security is the most important issue with digital payment systems. Because
payments involve actual money, digital payment systems are a prime target for
criminals all over the world. In the real world, copying coins or bank notes is
hard, but not impossible, if you have the right equipment. But on the Internet,

To make a digital payment system successful, it needs to adhere to the following requirements:

- **Acceptability**—In order to be successful, the payment infrastructure needs to be widely accepted.

- **Anonymity**—If desired by the customers, their identities should be protected.

- **Convertibility**—The digital money should be able to be converted into other types of funds.

- **Efficiency**—The cost per transaction should be near zero.

- **Flexibility**—Several methods of payment should be supported.

- **Integration**—To support existing applications, interfaces should be created to integrate with the application.

- **Reliability**—The payment system needs to be highly available and should avoid single points of failure.

- **Scalability**—Allowing new customers and merchants into the system should not break down the infrastructure.

- **Security**—It should allow financial transactions over open networks, such as the Internet.

- **Usability**—Payment should be as easy as in the real world.

Table 14.1. Digital Payment Requirements

one must ensure that the payment system is secure; otherwise, it will not be accepted by the customers. The Internet is an open network that allows anyone to eavesdrop on the traffic, so modification of messages must be prevented by the use of digital signatures. Another important factor is that the money must arrive at the desired destination. If you pay in a shop, you give the sales assistant the money, but if you make payments via the Internet, transactions can be diverted to other bank accounts without anyone noticing it initially. Therefore, digital signatures and encryption technologies are required to make every financial transaction secure.

To make micropayments feasible, the payment system should not create additional costs or decrease performance. If you pay, for example, by credit card today in the real world, the merchant has to pay about four percent to the financial institutions involved, thus making credit card payments infeasible for small payments (so-called *micropayments*), such as paying for visiting a Web page.

After you have received digital money, you should always be able to pass it on to a bank or partner or keep it in a safe place. It should be accepted just as your credit card or cash. The acceptance rate should be so high that digital money will also be accepted by people who do not use the Internet. If digital money were highly accepted, you could walk into the local grocery store and pay for milk using digital cash instead a credit card. Your mobile phone could be used to transfer money from the Internet to the store cashier, for example.

Transactions via the Internet must be private. Third parties should never have the ability to intercept the transaction; if they do intercept it, they should not be able to read the transaction. And they won't, if it is encrypted. The buyer and seller—the only participants involved—should be the only ones privy to the information involving the transaction.

The integrity and authenticity of financial transactions must be maintained. The buyer message sent out to the seller should be signed to guarantee that no one else can withdraw money from the buyer's account or credit card without his or her consent. Every message should also be unique to guarantee that a financial transaction can be executed only once. After the transaction has been completed, the seller sends an acknowledgement to the buyer.

The availability and reliability of the financial system should be ensured. Hackers and online vandals will try to create denial of service (DoS) attacks, wherein payment services are premium targets. An interruption of the infrastructure could mean a loss to all participants. All parties should be able to perform their part in the financial transaction whenever they want or need to do so. For a transaction to be reliable, it must be complete. Either the payment is accepted or rejected, but there must never be any doubt regarding the status. The payment protocol must be able to handle cases in which the network or one of the participating computers breaks down. In most cases, the complete transaction becomes void and must be repeated, but some payment systems are able to continue and complete the transaction.

For cash-like payment systems, anonymity and untraceability need to be implemented, because these are the main advantages of real cash. This can be maintained only if no third party is required for the transaction. Anonymity allows the buyer to hide his or her identity, while untraceability means that different payments made by a single buyer cannot be linked, either to the buyer or to the other payments. It should be impossible to monitor an individual's spending patterns or determine that person's source of income. By encrypting all messages between the participants of a financial transaction, it is possible to make the transactions untraceable. On the other hand, it is also possible to implement anonymity and untraceability of the seller. When anonymity is important, the cost of tracking a transaction should outweigh the value of the information gained.

As the Internet expands, the demands placed on payment systems will grow as well. The payment framework should be able to handle a growing number of customers and merchants without adversely affecting performance. To keep the system alive, a distributed system should be preferred, wherein payment servers are placed in different locations on the Internet, in case one of the connections or servers breaks down.

The payment infrastructure should be able to support existing Internet applications through a programmable interface, so that little or no modification of the application is required.

As in the real world, several payment systems will coexist on the Internet. Depending on the value of the order, three types of payments have been established on the Internet:

- **Micropayments**—Transactions with a value of less than approximately $5. Suitable payment solutions are based on the electronic cash principle, because the transaction costs for these systems are nearly zero.

- **Consumer payments**—Transactions with a value between about $5 and $500. Typical consumer payments are executed by credit card transactions.

- **Business payments**—Transactions with a value of more than $500. Direct debits or invoicing seem to be the most appropriate solutions.

Table 14.2. Online Payment Categories

Each payment system described in Table 14.2 has different security and cost requirements. Micropayment systems are very similar to ordinary cash, while consumer payments are most likely done by credit or debit card. Business payments are executed in most cases by direct debit or invoice. The following sections give an overview of the possible payment methods. A common framework for Internet payment should be developed to support the above-mentioned requirements and payment systems. So far, many isolated solutions have been developed, and we'll explore some different types of payment frameworks here.

14.1.2   Psychology of Micropayments

Over the last few years, many developers have tried to push micropayment solutions to the Internet, but few have succeeded. The problem was never the technical implementation, but the Internet itself. Every company on the Internet gives away small pieces of information for free. This makes it hard to justify charging for small bits of information, even if the price is only a fraction of a cent. The other issue is psychological. If there is a choice of paying a one-time fee of $20, or paying 50 cents for every transaction, the majority would chose to pay a one-time fee, if the service is valuable to them. They don't have to think about payment again and can enjoy the service. If people who liked the service would be bothered everytime they use it with payment approvals, they would not use it in every instance. Ideally, both concepts should be available, in order to get the majority of people involved in the service.

Charging per transaction makes financial forecasts more difficult because you do not know in advance how much money the service will cost, especially if you may not know how often you will be using the service. Therefore, the subscription model is used most often on the Internet. It is preferred not only by the customers because the administrative overhead is reduced, but also by the e-business companies because they can better predict their financial future.

14.1.3   Minimizing the Risk

If you look at the number of transactions, you can imagine that these customers have already decided that payments handled throught the Internet are secure.

The number of transactions is rising significantly every year. But how secure is it to accept orders via the Internet? The explosive growth also adds an explosive risk to online retailers.

Although we will see that there are many different payment technologies available on the Internet that are thought to be secure, you should take precautions to protect yourself when accepting orders via the Web. Because the Internet offers automatic payment processes, it is important to realize that transmission errors can lead to great losses.

Credit card transactions via SSL do not guarantee that the credit card payment can be fulfilled successfully. Even if the money has been transferred into your account, the cardholder can enforce a charge-back to his account. Because Internet credit card transactions are classified as Card-Not-Present transactions, merchants are 100 percent liable for losses, even when the bank has authorized the transaction. Although electronic soft goods don't carry a high cost of goods, theft represents a loss of revenue and the potential for further fraud through illegal distribution.

The major problem is getting the information right in the first go. Therefore, your payment Web page should require certain information from the customers before they can send off the order: The credit card number and the expiration date are the most important items. Using a little JavaScript[1] I have written, it is possible to determine whether the checksum of the number is correct. Although this won't reduce the possibility of fraud, it does reduce the number of false entries.

An email address, the full postal address, and the name should also be present. Be sure to send the order confirmation to that email address. If the address turns out to be wrong, the order should be cancelled. The postal address can be verified by various online services. These first checks should be supplemented by a credit card check at the bank.

Internet customers often refuse a shipment for a few reasons. They may deny the transaction took place, so it is necessary to record all details of the transaction. Through the use of digital certificates, it is possible to enforce nonrepudiation. Others may claim that their credit card has been used fraudulently, because the card has been stolen or has been used without their authority. Another common problem is that customers claim that the goods never arrived, were defective, or were of poor quality.

Fraud has been simplified through the anonymity the Internet provides. Through simple measures, the risk of fraud can be reduced significantly.

Customers not known to a particular online business should have spending limits that are lower than for established customers. Another simple fraud preventing feature is implementing a confirmation Web page. On this page customers can verify their order details and accept the terms and conditions before accepting the order. If your company has any doubts about the credibility of a customer, you simply reject the order by sending out an email stating that it is not possible to serve them.

By accepting orders only when the customer and cardholder name match, you can further reduce the risk of fraud and confirm the order before fulfillment. You can even call or email the customer if you really want to play it safe. And always document the completed transaction for your own protection.

After a customer has placed an order, the goods should be shipped only to that particular address, never involving a third party. In order to keep control of your shipping, find a trustworthy logistics partner who enables you and your customers to track shipments after the goods have left your warehouse.

When shipping digital goods, ensure that a unique key identifying the customer is sent through a separate message. This enables you to ensure that only people who have paid will get access. In case of a charge-back, you can disable the key. This is especially important if you offer a subscription fee.

If you are afraid that these risks are too great for your small startup (or large corporation), then you can outsource the payment service completely. This lets you concentrate on your business and ensures that you get your money in the end. When you outsource the payment service, the subcontractor is responsible for getting back the money if there is a problem.

---

[1] http://www.net-factory.com/javascripts/

14.1.4   Internet Payment Methods

Just as in the real world, three different types of payment systems have been established on the Internet: prepaid, instant-paid, and postpaid systems. As the term prepaid suggests, you have to pay first and then can buy a product or service. Prepaid systems basically work by saving digital money to the hard disk or to a smart card. They could be seen as the digital equivalent of cash. The file containing the digital money is called a *virtual wallet*. The electronic money can be used at any time to pay for goods and services online. The advantage of electronic cash is that it is anonymous. No one is able to trace who paid for the service or goods, but after the goods are physically delivered, this advantage ceases to exist. The disadvantage is the actual storage on the hard disk or the smart card. If you lose the file the money is gone, just as if you lose your wallet. Anyone who "finds" the contents of the wallet can use it to pay for whatever suits them!

Instant-paid systems are based on the concept of paying at the moment of the transaction. Instant-paid systems are the most complicated to implement because they require direct access to the internal databases of banks to make the payment in an instant. Security must be implemented more strictly than in the other cases, because instant-paid systems are the most powerful systems. A payment limit for the instant-paid payment solution may make sense to reduce the possibility of fraud. This is already enforced with debit cards. In Germany, you can pickup only 200 euros per day with a debit card.

In prepaid transactions, access to a bank is done before the actual order process is executed. The instant-paid solution requires that the money be debited from the bank account at the same moment the transaction takes place. Postpaid systems, on the other hand, allow you to buy a product and pay afterward. Credit cards are one of the most common postpaid systems, both in the real world and in the cyber world.

Credit cards are appropriate in particular circumstances. They are, however, very expensive for companies to utilize. This is primarily because of the low level of security (which relies on embossing, magnetic strips, signatures, and stop-lists), and the resultant high and increased cost of fraud. In addition, transaction processing costs are significant.

Debit cards are highly secure, because they require the customer to confirm something that only the card owner should know: the PIN. But although the costs from error and fraud are very low, the communication costs associated with fully online transactions are high, which must be paid by the shop owner, for example.

14.1.5   Political Impact of Digital Currencies

Many concerns regarding the impact on the money supply and governmental control have been raised since the introduction of digital currency. In the short run, governments will retain control over the currencies by adjusting the control of the money supply. The reason is that companies mostly deal with invoices, and in most cases end customers use credit cards. These types of payments do not require a new currency; they use currencies that are under global market control. Customers who pay in dollars, euros, or yen won't influence the value of the currencies directly.

But new digital currency systems that are not directly linked to a physical currency may affect the monetary system in two ways. These currencies may influence the supply of money by changing the way money is multiplied. Price levels and interest rates could also be affected by digital currencies if they reach a critical mass.

Governments make money by issuing money, because the cost of printing a bank note is less than its actual value. This so-called "seigniorage" and interest-free lending to the government by the public are the revenues, which a government receives every year.

From early times, coinage was the prerogative of kings, who prescribed the total charge and the part they were to receive as seigniorage. Because the seigniorage and coinage charges were collected by withholding part of the bullion brought for coinage, the currency value of the coins received in exchange was often less than the bullion's market value. Eventually, merchants stopped providing bullion for the mint, and the supply of coins became inadequate. In England, all charges for coinage were abolished in 1666.

Because coins are now issued only as token money for domestic purposes, they no longer need to possess a high intrinsic value, and low-standard silver or certain base-metal alloys provide all the qualities required. A substantial margin usually exists between the cost of producing a coin and its statutory currency value.

Through the introduction of digital currencies, some portion of the government's revenue is taken away. Introducing digital currency by a private company is like printing private money. As a result, the central banks relinquish their legal monopoly to issue money or money substitutes.

Most states are not intending to issue electronic money. In most cases, private companies are offering the electronic cash. One exception is Finland, where an electronic wallet is being issued by a company wholly owned by the central bank.

If private companies are allowed to print money, the revenues related to seigniorage will be shared between the government and these companies. The acceptance of a currency depends on public confidence. If there is enough confidence in these companies, competitors will surely emerge. Unlike a government, which does not let consumers participate in the profits, private companies may distribute the profits to their customers, which will lead to totally new perspectives in the currency industry and new forms of convenience, service, and quality. Online banks, for example, could compete with the governments by paying interest on digital currency deposits.

At the time of this writing, no legal framework has been established allowing private companies to create commercial types of digital currencies. Many tests have been done, but governments fear that digital currencies will be used for criminal activities, such as money laundering. Digital currencies are not necessary for the Internet to succeed, but the Internet has deregulated many markets, including the currency market.

14.2   Fraud on the Internet

14.2.1   Introduction

The success of online commerce and e-business not only has propelled lots of money toward new online ventures, but also has attracted lots of criminals. Crime in cyberspace is basically traditional crime perpetrated through a new and powerful medium. The fraudsters have not changed. Web-based fraud claims are rising dramatically, accounting for two-thirds of all the fraud cases investigated by the Commercial Crime Service (CCS) of the International Chamber of Commerce for its business members in 2000.

According to eMarketer's[2] ePrivacy and Security Report, 87 percent of online fraud committed in 2000 was attributed to online auction sites, and the greatest percentage of users falling victim to online fraud are Generation X members and Baby Boomers, accounting for 50 percent of all cases. For most Internet users, the protection of personal information is a real and valid concern. Offerings of free services and promises of wealth lure participants into binding contracts. Unbelievable great deals entice consumers to buy products that never arrive or are of substandard quality.

According to the two largest credit card companies in the world, Visa and MasterCard, the rate of credit card fraud as a percentage of all credit card transactions is miniscule. Their records show that in 1999, 22 million fraudulent credit card transactions occurred out of an estimated total of 25 billion transactions.

It is important to understand what types of fraud are possible on the Internet and how to protect yourself and your company from fraud.

14.2.2   Fraud Detection

Fraud affects business productivity, because online businesses must invest in resources that manually scrutinize orders, track down bad transactions, and negotiate in case of trouble with the bank. Companies that implement fraud techniques that are too strict, on the other hand, will lose customers and revenue if they pose additional burden on the customer's side to ensure security and liability. Customers will most likely go to another online shop where paying is easier.

---

[2]http://www.emarketer.com/

To reduce the incidence of fraud, several companies have started to offer fraud detection programs. One of them is ClearCommerce,[3] which helps online merchants decrease the number of charge-backs and fraudulent transactions. Negative databases, with records of email addresses, card numbers, and phone numbers of those who have initiated charge-backs, make it easier to detect fraud. In addition, modules check the number of times an individual card is used in a single week. Limiting the purchases on a single card each week can reduce fraud significantly.

A charge-back is a credit card transaction that is billed back to the merchant who made the sale. This happens when a credit card holder disputes a charge on his bill by claiming that the product was never delivered or that he was dissatisfied with it in some way. Cardholders are supposed to try to obtain satisfaction from the merchant before disputing the bill with the credit card issuer.

Instead of monitoring the transactions manually, the FraudShield product by ClearCommerce allows companies to set up rules that validate the transactions automatically and lock out all transactions that are suspicious. The software checks online to verify that the cardholder's name and card number match with the corresponding bank and to determine whether the customer has enough credit to buy the goods. It offers real-time, automated fraud-checking that performs numerous Internet-specific checks that substantially reduce your risk of fraud while lowering your costs. Merchant-configurable fraud rules enable you to establish fraud screens tailored specifically to your business. ClearCommerce's fraud protection software enhances, rather than duplicates, checks performed by the card processor.

Fraud checks include guarding against processing invalid credit card numbers, checking for duplicate orders, recognizing suspicious spending patterns, and guarding against automatic card generator programs.

The fraud checklists let you establish criteria for lock-outs based on combinations of individual fraud checks for increased sophistication. These Boolean statements allow you to combine a number of variables in the rule. For example, you can set up a rule to be as specific as: "If the transaction occurs between midnight and 2:00 A.M. and includes item #579243 (leather coat) and is initiated by a Hotmail user and ships to Eastern Europe, then decline it."

Using address verification services makes it easy to verify whether a certain person lives at a certain address. This works quite well for individuals ordering services or goods from a Web site. In Germany, for example, the Deutsche Post[4] offers an address verification service for online businesses that are interested in selling goods in Germany. In the United States, Visa[5] offers an address verification check in conjunction with the credit card. The card number and the address can be sent off to Visa and they will check whether the shipping

---

[3] http://www.clearcommerce.com/
[4] http://www.post.de/
[5] http://www.visa.com/

or billing address match the address of the card owner. This guards against fraud by requiring the hacker to have not only a credit card number, but also additional information on the owner of the card.

Cabela's, Inc.,[6] a catalog and retail merchant for hunting and fishing equipment, uses real-time credit authorization and fraud detection to expand their customers' purchasing options to include the Internet. The payment back-end software was integrated with a storefront, the legacy systems in the company, and the bank to make it a cheap and efficient solution. This allowed Cabela's to integrate the payment services data from its bank and pass the data through the process to the settlement point, saving time. Also, this payment service arragement was customizable to the requirements of the Cabela's fulfillment system.

14.3 Example Business Cases

New standards on the Internet can be achieved by using advanced payment technologies. For a payment technology to be successful, it must support a solid business case. If the new standard or technology does not help to sell more products online or reduce the costs of production, then companies will not use it. There are many cases on the Internet where people have used hyped technology and have failed because the business case was not good enough. So we will now develop four business cases and see whether the technology adds value to that particular electronic business.

14.3.1 The Internet Bookshop

A bookstore is the standard example for online business. A digital shop has been set up where customers are able to browse through a large offering of books and can choose the desired ones. How should customers pay for the books?

14.3.2 The Translation Service

A freelance translator offers her services on the Internet. Customers send in their texts via email, FTP, or fax and receive a price quotation and the finished translation by the same means of communication. How should customers pay for the service?

14.3.3 The News Agency

A news agency delivers its content to the Web and is able to provide highly customized news to individual customers and portals. The news flashes can be provided to customers through push channels or email, or the agency may

---

[6]http://www.cabelas.com/

provide the content on a Web page. How should customers pay for this information?

14.3.4 The Software Company

A software company sells its products via the Web and offers updates, online help, and an online call center for the customers. What would be the most appropriate payment method for the software and the call center?

14.4 Postpaid Payment Systems

14.4.1 Credit Card Solutions

Credit card payments are the most common and preferred payment method on the Internet. Using credit cards is easy, and they are accepted worldwide. To shop with a credit card, customers browse through a Web site, decide what services or products they need, and enter their credit card information into an HTML-form. The information is sent to the Web site, where one of two things may happen. The information is either collected and sent once a day to the bank or the Web site owner has established a direct link to the bank, whereby it is possible to check on the fly whether the user has enough credit to pay for the goods.

The credit card payment system has some advantages over other forms of payment. Credit cards offer consumers the ability to collect all charges and pay the total at a later time (for example, at the end of the month). The credit card system provides good consumer protection, because customers have the right to give back goods within a certain time frame and to dispute charges, because they are not charged directly to the account of the customer. Credit cards are not bound to national currencies. No matter where people buy their goods and services, the currency conversion is done automatically.

In the credit card payment system, there are four players: the customer, the merchant, the issuer, and the acquirer. To use a credit card, the customer and the merchant need to establish relationships with the issuer with respect to the acquirer. The issuer gives the consumer a credit card. The merchant applies to an acquirer for the ability to accept one or more card brands. Customers who want to buy goods or services present their credit cards to the merchant. The merchant verifies the validity of the credit card by sending the credit card information to the acquirer. The request is then passed over the financial network to the customer's bank. The bank then verifies the information and returns the authorization to the merchant through the acquiring bank. This may sound highly complicated, but it works the same way if you go into a shop and buy something.

Although some companies want you to give them your credit card number without encrypting the transmission, most companies use encryption to protect private information about the credit card, the order, and the customer. Without encryption, it would be easy for hackers to intercept the messages and use or alter the information for their own purposes.

Using special programs called *sniffers*, criminals are able to copy the de-crypted information and use it to pay for other things. As long as you do not need a shipping address, the credit card information can be misused easily, for example, to pay for online services. Although stealing credit card information is nothing new, the Internet enables attackers to steal more systematically.

To make credit card payments secure, two standards have been established over the past few years: SSL encryption developed by Netscape and Secure Electronic Transactions (SET)[7] developed by Visa and MasterCard. The dif-ferences between SSL and SET are evident. SSL encrypts traffic only between the Web browser and the Web server (the user's computer and the merchant's computer). SET offers a complete payment solution, which involves not only the customer and the merchant, but also the bank, which is needed for credit card payment.

SET

SET was designed exclusively to secure Internet financial transactions, provid-ing a confidential method of payment and order information. SSL is a generic encryption system that can be used to transmit any data. SET combines exist-ing security technologies with public key encryption using digital certificates for both credit card holders and merchants. The public key infrastructure (PKI) is defined within the scope of SET. The PKI is used to verify that a participant in the transaction really is the person or institution he or she claims to be. This is important because the Internet provides no standard mechanism to verify a person or institution. Using this mechanism, it is possible to introduce the concept of nonrepudiation to Internet-based transactions. Customers who pay via SET cannot dispute afterward that they did not make the transaction, be-cause all orders are digitally signed, and the digital signature cannot be forged. PKI is also used to send encrypted information via the Internet. Using strong encryption, it is possible to transmit the credit card transaction over public networks, such as the Internet.

All information in a SET transaction is encrypted. The integrity of the transmitted data is ensured through the digital hash code, which is appended to every message and enables the receiver to verify that the message has not been altered in transit. By using digital certificates, it is possible to show that a cardholder is the legitimate user of the credit card. The authentication is also required for the merchant to be properly identified by the acquiring bank. The SET protocol is not dependent on transport security measures, such as additionally using SSL on top of the SET encryption, and does not prevent their use. Because SET programs are developed by several software vendors, interoperability is very important.

---

[7]http://www.setco.com/

SET was developed by MasterCard and Visa in 1996 and has been established as one of the leading standards in credit card payment via the Internet. The following are SET specifications:

- **High security**—The transmission of credit card information can be transmitted over public networks using strong encryption technologies.

- **Low visibility**—Only the information that a partner needs to see is displayed. The merchant does not need to see the credit card information, and the bank does not need to see what has been ordered.

- **Recognized standards**—Transaction flows, message formats, integrity, authentication, confidentiality, and encryption algorithms are all defined in the SET standard.

- **Nonrepudiation**—The SET standard defines a public key infrastructure that is used for verification of the participants and to encrypt/decrypt the messages sent between the partners. A digital signature is used to identify the participants.

Table 14.3. What Is SET?

SET provides some privacy features that make it harder to gain information about the customer. The only information revealed is just what the participants really need to see. A merchant, for example, does not really need to know a customer's credit card details. This information can be routed directly through to the bank, and the bank can confirm the validity of the information for the merchant and authorize the money transfer. SET defines more than just encryption. Transaction flows, message formats, and encryption algorithms are provided to guarantee the integrity and confidentiality of the messages, and the authentication of the users.

Additional security will be introduced in SET 2.0, when smart cards will be supported. Credit cards will then have an additional chip on the plastic card that will contain the digital certificate and the public and private key of the user that is required to perform a SET transaction. Currently, only debit cards have the chip. The chip card solution provides additional security and convenience for the cardholders. This will also enable more people to use it, as it is currently.

Using a chip card, customers will be able to use SET-enabled network devices anywhere. Home computers and TV set-top boxes, office computers, and public kiosks are examples of SET-enabled network devices. An additional benefit for the card industry is the similarity between SET transactions and conventional POS and ATM ones, when a chip card is used. This will surely simplify processing and operating procedures.

At the time of this writing, several pilots for the C-SET (Chip-secured Secure Electronic Transactions) are under way in the European Union. The European Commission has adopted C-SET as a recommended specification. The smart card provides authentication and encryption. The design also includes an enhanced banking gateway that handles most of the payment processing, thus reducing the cost and complexity for the merchant.

To resolve legal issues with the encryption, the cryptographic functions are implemented on the bank side to avoid regulations that prohibit widespread deployment of cryptographic software.

There are many other possible ways to pay via credit card, and we'll explore some of those solutions here. The disadvantage is mainly that they are not open and are bound to a certain service provider. Consumers cannot switch between providers easily. The following sections will give a short overview of three solutions.

WireCard

The WireCard[8] solution consists of several modules, making it suitable for business-to-consumer and business-to-business transactions. The secure online payment module allows the secure transmission of credit card information from the customer to the merchant, using a Java applet that encrypts the information with 2048 bits. The applet uses RSA and BlowFish algorithms for encryption, making it very secure. With today's technologies, it would take approximately 10^{22} (10,000,000,000,000,000,000,000) years to decode the credit card information.

Because the company resides in Germany, the software can be exported to any other country without restrictions. The solution is also not bound to a certain browser or operating system, making it a very good solution for online credit card payment, but data entered into the WireCard solution cannot be reused in another shop using a different solution.

After the credit card information has been entered, the applet encrypts the data and sends it to the server, which passes the information to a bank for validation. After the credit card has been validated successfully, the merchant will receive a notice to proceed with the transaction. The back-end validation is done by the clearing module, which allows credit cards to be checked in real time (which is more secure) or in a batch (which is cheaper).

---

[8]http://www.wirecard.de/

CyberCash

The CyberCash[9] solution encrypts credit card details, just as SSL and SET do, but the procedure is a little bit different. The credit card information is sent from the customer to the merchant and is encrypted in such a way that the merchant can't decrypt it. The merchant passes the information on to the CyberCash server, together with the sum of the customer order. From the CyberCash server, the payment is initiated through the financial networks.

First Virtual

First Virtual[10] was founded in 1994 and is the only online payment system that is secure without using any encryption technology. The First Virtual system guarantees security by requesting a confirmation email from the customer. If the customer does not respond in a given timeframe with a certain code, the order will not be executed. To prevent sniffing of credit card information, special IDs are exchanged instead of the credit card information. The credit card needs to be stored once on the First Virtual server and a VirtualPIN is assigned to the credit card number, which is used for transactions. The user must call First Virtual and tell them the credit card number; the information is never sent via the Internet. The First Virtual server initiates the payment transaction with the financial networks.

During the most successful phases in 1996, more than 2000 merchants and 200,000 customers were using the system to pay for goods on a global scale. In late 1998, First Virtual's credit card payment system was put on hold, because there was not enough demand. Many merchants invested in the general purpose SSL encryption technology and SET standard at that time, which was struggling to become the standard credit card payment system.

14.4.2   Invoices

Credit card transactions are very common in the business-to-consumer area, but invoices are more common in the business-to-business sector. In many cases, the business-to-business transaction volume is too high for credit card transactions. Suppose that your company needs to buy 100 computers, printers, and monitors. The sum would be too high for the limit of most credit cards. Buying each computer on its own would be possible via credit card, but this would certainly be more expensive than buying all at once, for both the buyer and the seller.

Another important reason to consider payment via invoice is that many companies traditionally have paid via invoice and changing the type of payment would require a reorganization of the process, which would cost too much. A third reason could be that the credit card companies want up to four percent

---

[9]http://www.cybercash.com/
[10]http://www.fv.com/

of the transaction in fees. For many smaller companies, this four percent can mean the difference between profit and loss. Although credit cards are now accepted world-wide, some countries still do not make much use of them. In these countries, payment via invoices is also a viable way to substitute online payment solutions.

Lufthansa Cargo[11] digitized its SameDay[12] service in January 1999. Same-Day allows you to send documents and small packages throughout Europe in a maximum of six hours, hence the name SameDay. Because this service is too expensive for private use, the target customers are businesses that need to send spare parts and documents throughout Europe very quickly. Most of their target customers have an infrastructure for paying via invoice, so in the first phase of the project, invoice was the only accepted form of payment. The next step for Lufthansa was to introduce a way to connect the financial systems of the customers and their own in order to send invoices electronically via electronic data interchange (EDI). Only then did they start to build an infrastructure for people who wanted to pay via credit card—mostly freelancers and small companies who do not use EDI or have an SAP R/3 installed.

To make invoices a good solution for the Internet, it is necessary to provide a secure solution. Therefore, some sort of user identification is necessary. In the Lufthansa example, a SameDay employee calls the customer to say when the courier will be picking up the package. For an expanding business, it is not practical to call all the customers. Actually, it is necessary to check the identity only when a customer uses the service for the first time. The next time the customer returns to the Web site, they would only need to enter a login and password for identification. Because the SameDay service involves nonelectronic procedures, such as picking up the goods at a certain address, the possibility of abuse is limited. With a totally digitized product or service, such as an online newspaper, much bigger problems can occur.

For these services, printed bills would mean extra costs that are larger than the purchasing price itself. Therefore, online billing can cut costs and automate manual processes. Two of the first banks to implement electronic billing were Bank One Corp[13] and Bank of America,[14] which have started to offer integrated electronic billing to their online banking customers. Another important advantage of online billing versus printed billing is the fact that billing errors can be reduced substantially.

Online billing creates a new service sector on the Internet: the online billing service. Instead of going to many different places for paying invoices, billing services can consolidate bills so the customer can pay all bills in a single location. These billing portal sites are interesting prospects for many companies because every customer will return to the site at least several times a month,

---

[11]http://www.lhcargo.com/
[12]http://www.sameday.de/
[13]http://www.bankone.com/
[14]http://www.bankofamerica.com/

making it easy to start cross-selling activities based on the user profile (which could include the billing information). Therefore, not only are banks trying to get into the online billing market but also traditional Internet portals such as Yahoo! and Excite.

Although end-customer billing will be the first step on the Internet, the real advantage lies in offering invoices to business customers on the Web. Business-to-business transaction costs will be lowered because of this new technology.

14.4.3 Internet Checks

Internet checks have no great importance on the Internet so far; still, it is important to understand how they can be used, because they may be of value for your particular business. Electronic checks work similarly to conventional checks. Customers receive digital documents from their banks and need to enter the amount of the payment, the currency, and the name of the payee for every payment transaction. Electronic checks must be digitally signed by the payer.

The use of checks in the U.S. and Europe differs significantly. Most existing electronic check solutions are based on the U.S. system, whereby the check must be signed by the payer and the payee. The payee brings the check to the bank and receives the money, and then the check is sent back through the bank to the payer. In Europe, checks are like cash. You write in the amount and the receiver can cash it in immediately or even pay for goods. There is no complicated process of signing and returning the check to the owner.

NetCheque

In 1995, the NetCheque system was developed by the Information Sciences Institute of the University of Southern California,[15] which implements all the requirements mentioned at the beginning of this chapter.

The buyer and the seller need to have accounts at NetCheque. To make it really secure, a Kerberos-identification and a password are used. To pay via check, it is necessary to install special client software, which works like a check book.

Kerberos is a secure method for authenticating a request for a service in a computer network. Kerberos was developed by the Athena Project at the Massachusetts Institute of Technology (MIT). The name is taken from Greek mythology; Kerberos was a three-headed dog who guarded the gates of Hades. Kerberos lets a user request an encrypted "ticket" from an authentication process that can then be used to request a particular service from a server. The user's password does not have to pass through the network.

This means in our case that NetCheque customers are able to send an encrypted check using this software to the merchant. The merchant is able to

---

[15]http://www.usc.edu/

get the money from a bank or to use the check for a transaction with a supplier. A special accounting network verifies the checks and gives an OK to the merchant, who then delivers the goods.

Although the system is also suitable for micropayments, it never really took off. The main problem is the public key infrastructure that is needed to exchange certificates and sign the checks. In 1995, this was not available, and at the same time credit card transactions became extremely popular. Another weakness of NetCheque was also its small initial customer and merchant base.

PayNow

The PayNow service developed by CyberCash supports micropayments in the form of electronic checks. The CyberCash Internet wallet contains the PayNow checks, which can be used in online shops that support the CyberCash standard. The electronic check works in a similar manner to stored-value chip card transactions where the consumer preloads a CyberCash wallet with value, though the real money remains in the bank.

E-check

The FSTC Electronic Check (e-check)[16] is currently being piloted at the U.S. Department of the Treasury. The e-check leverages the check payment system from the real to the virtual world with fewer manual steps involved. It fits within current business practices, eliminating the need for expensive process reengineering. The e-check system is highly secure and can be used by all bank customers who have checking accounts. Checking accounts do exist in the U.S., but are unknown in Europe. The whole concept of checking accounts and its associated processes does not exist in Europe.

E-checks contain the same information as paper checks and are based on the same legal framework. The electronic checks can be exchanged directly between parties and can replace all remote transactions where paper checks are used today. E-checks work the same way traditional checks work. The customer writes the e-check and gives it to the payee electronically. The payee deposits the electronic check and receives credit, and the payee's bank "clears" the e-check to the paying bank. The paying bank validates the e-check and charges the customer's account for the check sum.

E-checks offer the ability to conduct bank transactions in a safe way via the Internet. The validity of the e-checks can be verified automatically by the bank, which reduces fraud losses for all parties involved. Using the Financial Services Markup Language (FSML) and digital signatures and certificates makes the system highly secure.

---

[16]http://www.echeck.org/

14.4.4   Cash on Delivery

Another postpaid model that works offline is cash on delivery (COD). Customers can order goods and services online and pay when the goods or services arrive at their doorstep. Arktis,[17] one of Germany's largest retailers of Macintosh software, uses this system for its online business. Customers can browse through the online (or printed) catalog; order via telephone, fax, mail, or e-mail; and collect the goods delivered to their doorstep. The employee of the postal service who delivers the goods gets the money from the customer. The advantage here is that Arktis gets the money from the postal service and does not need to verify in every case that a customer is willing to pay for the goods. If the customer is unwilling to pay at the doorstep, the package is sent back to the sender and the postal service asks for a refund, if it already paid the sender.

This system makes it easier to sell goods and services to people whom you do not know and who are not willing to pay via credit card for one reason or another. And you do not have to wait until the customer pays the invoice to receive your money. COD is normally more expensive, because it involves the postal service, but these costs are normally paid by the customer.

14.4.5   Checking the Business Cases

Based on the economics of our first business case example, an Internet bookshop, we can see quite easily that all postpaid solutions are viable options for the online bookshop. Credit cards are most likely supported because the bookshop will use them if it has physical shops. If this is the case, the relationship to the bank has been established. Invoices are also very common in the bookshop business, because the goods are not so expensive that one customer's late payment would ruin the business. If the online bookshop is spending money on new technologies, it will most likely allow electronic checks or gift vouchers that can be exchanged for books. The advantage of this system is that a customer can purchase a check or a voucher and give it to someone as a present. Due to the large number of customers, a niche payment system such as electronic checks may still be useful to implement. The cash on delivery system also works well for bookshops, because the necessary infrastructure is already in place. The connection to the logistics partner has been established and can be used to receive the money from them.

The translation service, our second business case, won't use all the postpaid solutions as they are not suitable for freelancers. Freelancers won't accept credit card transactions, because they have far fewer financial transactions than a bookshop. Paying four percent credit card fees may be viable for a shop that has thousands of transactions a day, but translators will most likely have only a limited number of financial transactions a month. Setting up the credit

---

[17]http://www.arktis.de/

card infrastructure and then paying the credit card fees will be prohibitively expensive. A translator will most likely use invoices to initiate payments because this requires only a bank account and no interaction on the translation service side. All transaction costs are on the customer side. Electronic checks are not suitable for this type of business, because the number of customers is limited and it is not likely that many of the customers will have the technical infrastructure to support the system. Cash on delivery is also highly unlikely because the translation service is more business-to-business than business-to-consumer. And in the B2B world, it is not likely that companies have thousands of dollars or euros lying around just in case a business partner sends a completed translation by COD.

The news agency service, our third business case, can be paid by almost all postpaid systems. Two types of payment can be envisioned here. Either micropayment for every single news item or a subscription fee that is paid every week, month, or year. Credit cards are not designed for micropayments, but can be used to pay subscription fees. The same applies to invoices. Sending out invoices for every single electronic transaction would cost more than the transaction is worth. Electronic checks can be used to handle micropayments and subscription fees. This may be the most economic solution for the news agency and the customer, because the service and the payment are fully digital and do not require the switch to an analog medium. This reduces the error-rate and increases the processing speed. Cash on delivery is not an option, because the goods are delivered digitally. It would be possible to extend the cash on delivery model to the Internet by paying with electronic cash, of course. We will explore that possibility in the prepaid model later in this chapter.

Our fourth business case, the software company, would most likely support all postpaid payment systems. As with the news agency service, the online call center could be paid either by micropayments or through a subscription fee. As previously mentioned, credit card transactions are not suitable for micropayments, so if you have a credit card infrastructure, it would be easier to support the subscription model. The software itself would most probably be paid for by credit card. Invoices could be used for the software and the support through the online call center, if based on the subscription model. Just as with the news agency service, electronic checks will be an adequate solution for both selling software and offering online support. Cash on delivery would only make sense for the software, but not for the online support service.

14.4.6 Online Experience

Credit card payment is, without a doubt, the most successful payment system on the Internet. It is actually difficult to find a site that does not accept credit card payment. About 99 percent of all Web sites that accept credit cards use a simple SSL encryption to ensure the privacy of the credit card information.

On the Web site of Florists Transworld Delivery[18] and A Camelia Flores,[19] it is possible to select a bouquet of flowers and pay for it directly online with a credit card. All the customer has to do is to enter the credit card details, which are then transmitted electronically to the payment server using SSL encrypted communication. After the order has been authorized by the credit card company, the order will be sent to the local flower shop. The local flower shop accepts the order, the credit card is debited, and the order is executed by delivering the flowers to the recipient.

Discos Castello,[20] a compact disc online shop in Spain, uses the SET standard for accepting credit cards. The SET standard uses much stronger encryption by employing digital certificates and a public key infrastructure. For customers to pay with their credit cards, they need to ask their bank for a SET certificate that identifies them. In Spain, the credit card processor 4B[21] and more than 40 banks participate in the SET program and give out the certificates to their customers. After a customer has applied for the certificate and has loaded it into the electronic wallet (which needs to be installed on the customer's computer), the wallet can talk to the point of sale (POS) software installed on the Discos Castello's Web server. The wallet software encrypts the order information with the public key of the merchant, and the credit card information is encrypted with the public key of the bank. Using this mechanism, the merchant sees only the order, but not the credit card information. The merchant passes the credit card information to the bank, which authorizes the order and sends an OK back to the merchant, who then processes the order. Unlike the floral delivery service in the first example, the communication between merchant and bank is highly standardized and strongly supported by the credit card processors.

Another option is to use an online bank to ensure the accuracy of the credit card transaction. The *Internet Business Magazine*[22] in the UK uses this system for reader subscriptions. Readers who would like to subscribe to the magazine go to the Web site and are redirected to NetBanx,[23] where the credit card details are collected. In this case, the bank receives an up-front fee for every transaction, which is higher than if the magazine implemented it itself. The advantage for the online companies is that they do not need to think about digital certificates or install special software on their system for the payment process, because there is only one product that can be paid for.

The official Japanese Titanic home page[24] offers Titanic cups, t-shirts, and other goods that can be bought through CyberCash. The German Web site

---

[18]http://www.ftd.com/

[19]http://www.acameliaflores.com.br/

[20]http://www.discoscastello.es/

[21]http://www.4b.es/

[22]http://www.ibmag.co.uk/

[23]http://www.netbanx.com/

[24]http://www.titanic.co.jp/

Referate Online[25] offers reports for pupils who don't want to write their own for school. Through CyberCash payment, the pupils are able to download reports for any school subject.

The German online poster shop 3W Art[26] enables its customers to browse through an online catalog and select posters and other art-related articles. After customers have decided on the goods to order, they are asked for their addresses and the products are sent out. Together with the goods, an invoice is sent out asking the customer to pay via money transfer. This may seem risky, as there is no guarantee that the customer will pay in the end. But because the goods are not costly and need to be sent out to a real address, it is a risk that many companies, especially those in Europe, are willing to take. Many of them are connected to address databases provided by postal services, such as the Deutsche Bundespost.[27] Using these databases, it is possible to verify if a given person lives at a certain address. Because the price for the products is very low, sending out the goods via COD would increase the shipping significantly and reduce the number of people ready to buy online.

Billserv.com,[28] an online billing service, has created a billing portal called Bills.com,[29] where consumers are able to pay regular, monthly bills.

Travel Overland,[30] an online ticketing service, is another business that bills customers via invoice. Customers choose their flights online and book them directly into the systems of the airlines. The customers receive a confirmation via email, and the invoice is sent via normal mail. If the flight is booked more than four weeks in advance, then the customers need to pay 75 euros per person in advance. The balance must be paid ten days in advance of the departure date, and the tickets will be mailed to the customer thereafter.

NetCheques and PayNow have been out of business for quite a while. There are no curent real-life examples on the Web, but knowing that these solutions have failed and why they failed is important to prevent your business from failing. Having the right business idea and an excellent Web site is useless if people are not able to pay because the business is using a payment solution no one knows how to use or has access to.

Arlt,[31] a reseller of computer hardware, uses the cash on delivery method, but restricts it to Germany. With this payment option, customers pay an additional 10 DM (5 euros or dollars).

---

[25]http://www.referate.de/

[26]http://www.poster.de/

[27]http://www.post.de/

[28]http://www.billserv.com/

[29]http://www.bills.com/

[30]http://www.travel-overland.de/

[31]http://www.arlt.de/

14.4.7   Required Software

Accepting credit card payments using SSL encryption requires a digital certificate on the Web server that encrypts the traffic between customer and merchant. The certificate can either be created by a certificate server that can be installed on any system at the merchant site or can be bought from a company such as VeriSign.[32] These certificates are accepted in all browsers. For certificates that are created by nontrusted partners, such as a merchant, customers should acknowledge the certificate before using it the first time. The problem with SSL is that no standard mechanisms on the server exist that allow for communication with the bank. This issue needs to be resolved on an individual basis.

As previously mentioned many banks offer the outsourcing of payment methods. You set up your shopping site and let the bank take care of the payment. This is the best solution, especially for smaller shops. Besides services such as NetBanx, there are many other payment service providers, such as MasterMerchant,[33] which offer special payment services for things like sports books, adult Web sites, and online casinos.

The SET standard requires the installation of special software on the client computer, the merchant server, and the bank gateway. This software regulates the communication that is required for the credit card transaction between the parties involved. Hewlett-Packard and IBM offer complete solutions for the SET standard. Hewlett-Packard's solution is based on the Verifone[34] software, which they bought in 1997, and is called vSuite.[35] It contains four products, vWallet for the customer, vPOS for the merchant, and vGATE and Omnihost for the bank. IBM proposes its IBM Payment Suite,[36] which consists of the IBM Consumer Wallet, IBM Payment Server, IBM Payment Gateway, and IBM Payment Registry. There are many other smaller vendors of SET software. A complete list can be found at the SetCo site.[37]

Verifone has developed a new product called PayWorks, which can act as the foundation and central hub of any Integrated Payment Solution (IPS) application configuration (the IPS Switch application component that switches payment messages from one IPS component or option to another). The software handles a broad range of information, including credit transactions (via SET and SSL, for example), debit transactions, payments, and other payment-related messages. The IPS Switch is just one of many application components that are a part of IPS. IPS contains a wide variety of application components to handle credit and debit, draft capture and settlement, private label credit, issuer interfaces, and even Internet security. Through the modular design, it is

---

[32]http://www.verisign.com/

[33]http://www.mastermerchant.com/

[34]http://www.verifone.com/

[35]http://www.verifone.com/solutions/internet/

[36]http://www.software.ibm.com/commerce/payment/

[37]http://www.setco.org/matrix.html

possible to select the capabilities that match your business needs and build a powerful electronic payment system customized to your business requirements. When a business requires a new form of payment, it can plan for it and add it easily. The whole solution is based on Java and XML.

Traditional invoices require companies to get the information through their ERP system to a printer and then send the printouts to the customers. One provider of online billing software is BlueGill Technologies,[38] which has developed applications for four vertical industries. Edify[39] has built online billing into its banking platform software. E-Bill, developed by CheckFree,[40] allows banks to convert legacy billing data and present it on the Web.

All other payment solutions are proprietary. In summary, credit card payment is the way to go for postpaid transactions right now, because the technology is proven and there are many different vendors to choose from.

14.5   Instant-paid Payment Systems

14.5.1   Debit Cards

Debit cards are used frequently; in fact, they are used more in Europe than in the U.S. The difference between credit cards and debit cards is that debit cards require a personal identification number (PIN) and a hardware device that can read the information stored in the magnetic strip on the back. With a credit card, all the information contained in the magnetic strip is also printed on the front of the card. Of course, the other main difference is that you must have enough money in your bank account to cover the amount of the purchase if you want to use a debit card! Most banks allow customer to overdraw their accounts upto a certain level, but ask for high interest rates.

So far, business with debit cards is nonexistent on the Internet because no computer is equipped with a hardware terminal that can read the magnetic strip. As the prices for such devices drop, they will become a commodity that will be sold with every computer, replacing the floppy drive. The trend is moving away from magnetic strips to electronic chips on smart cards. Smart cards currently are used mainly for electronic cash, but in the future, they will replace debit and credit cards as well.

14.5.2   Direct Debit

Direct debit is another postpaid solution that is used in online transactions. The German ISP PureTec[41] uses this system for the payment of their services, which consists of domain name registration and Web site offerings. Instead of

---

[38] http://www.bluegill.com/
[39] http://www.edify.com/
[40] http://www.checkfree.com/
[41] http://www.puretec.de/

asking the user for his credit card number, PureTec (see Figure 14.1) asks the customers for their bank account number and the bank code.

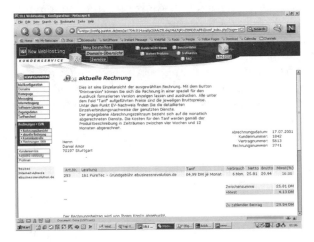

Figure 14.1. PureTec's Direct Debit Model.

The money can then be debited directly from the bank account. The only problem with this system is the signature. The bank pays out the money only if a valid customer signature appears on the same sheet as the order. Until legislation for digital signatures is established, it is necessary to print out the completed order, sign it, and fax it to PureTec.

Direct debit is not yet a fully instant-paid solution, but with digital certification laws in the making, it is just a matter of months until the first Web sites and banks will accept digital signatures from their customers to debit their accounts.

14.5.3   Mobile Payments

Payments via mobile phones are becoming more fashionable. As discussed earlier, you can already buy a soda in Helsinki via your mobile phone. This technology is very simple, because it merely requires the customer to be near the vendor machine. It shouldn't be surprising that new technologies have been developed to make mobile payments possible over the Internet.

Monkey Moneybox

Monkey[42] is short for "Mobile Network Key," a new technology that enables secure transactions and user identification via a mobile phone. The "moneybox" service is simple-to-use. A one-time registration takes only five minutes. When buying online, the customer selects the payment option "moneybox – payment

---

[42]http://www.monkeybank.com/

via mobile phone" and enters the mobile phone number. Within a few seconds, the mobile phone rings and the moneybox repeats the debitor's name and the amount. The customer enters a four-digit pin, and the payment is executed.

The company Monkey AG cashes in the money for products and services, and sends the money to the online shops. Just as with credit cards, online shops must pay a percentage per transaction (called disagio). In this case, the percentage is 2.5 percent, so it's cheaper than some credit cards. In addition to the the disagio, online shops have to pay a yearly fee of about 5 dollars/euros.

The moneybox system works with all mobile phones and all mobile service providers. The registration is done at Monkey's Web site. After customers are registered, they receive PINs and can instantly pay for goods and services via mobile phone.

Moneybox reduces customers' fears that they need to provide personal information and credit card numbers over the Web. Using moneybox, no such information is transmitted, making it more secure than traditional online payments. The moneybox server is in a trust-center to ensure that no one can steal data collected by the system. Have a look at table 14.4 for more information on Monkey's services.

The following services are provided by Monkey AG:

- **Internet 2 moneybox (voice)**—Online payment via voice, and PIN via touchtone

- **moneybox 2 moneybox (voice)**—Payment from mobile phone to mobile phone, and PIN via touchtone

- **Internet 2 moneybox (SMS)**—Online payment via SMS, and TAN via Web interface

- **moneybox 2 moneybox (SMS)** –Payment from mobile phone to mobile phone via SMS, and TAN via Web interface

- **monkey (voice)**—User identification via voice—for example, for telephone banking

- **monkey (SMS)** –User identification via SMS; password entry via Web interface

---

Table 14.4. Service Offerings of Monkey AG

14.5.4   Checking the Business Cases

Referring again to our first business case, the online bookshop would profit from the instant-paid model because the money would come in at the time of order, which would reduce the possibility of fraud. A disadvantage to post-paid models occurs in the case of a return. Because the postpaid payment systems are not debited immediately from a customer's bank account, the customer could potentially send back the books before any financial transaction had taken place. In the instant-paid model, the money needs to be credited back to the bank account. The major obstacle for debit cards is the implementation. There are no standards that are accepted on a countrywide, continent-wide, or worldwide level because debit cards differ greatly. With direct debit, we encounter a similar problem. Transferring money from your own account to someone else's is possible worldwide, but someone else debiting your account is not possible throughout the world because of the missing standards. On a national basis, this is possible, so if you limit your target group to a certain country, then the direct debit model will work.

For our second business case, the translation service, the same restrictions apply as with postpaid models. The implementation on the Internet would be far too expensive for the number of transactions, and the other limiting factors described in the bookshop example do not help with the business model.

The news agency, our third business case, may be compatible with the instant-paid model. Users could subscribe to a service and provide their bank details with the authorization to debit the account in the case of an information transaction. People would receive a free newsletter with short summaries of news stories, and would receive a login and password to identify themselves when entering the news Web server. At the Web server, they can read through the whole story and download it in their preferred format. Every time they do this, a fee would be debited from their bank account. The transactional costs would need to be low in order to make this an efficient method of payment. A better solution would be to charge a monthly fee for allowing the customers to read through all stories that come up in that particular month. This, of course, does not give you control over what a customer is able to see. Depending on the exact business model and the customer base, it must be decided which model is more useful.

In the final business case, the software company, the same rules apply as with the bookshop. The software company could handle all transactions by instant-paid systems in a very efficient way. If the online support is paid by subscription fee, it could be bundled into the product and sold in one transaction to the customer. Micropayments are possible, but it remains to be seen how much a single transaction would cost. As long as digital signatures are not accepted by banks, the manual process involved would hinder an efficient use of the payment model. Ideally, the software company would use an instant-paid system and add other payment solutions later.

14.5.5 Online Experience

No online shops use direct debit cards for online business at this time, but it will not take long until the first shops support this payment model because it is very useful for small to medium payments. Travel Overland,[43] which normally uses the invoice payment model, requires customers to use the direct debit model for special offerings and last-minute flights. The customer books the flight in the standard way, but is redirected to a special Web page for entering payment information. The page must then to be printed by the customer, signed, and faxed to Travel Overland. Travel Overland debits the card and sends out the tickets (if there is enough time). Alternatively, the tickets are left at the airport for pick up.

14.5.6 Required Software

No special software is required for direct debit, because digital signatures are not yet accepted by banks in most countries. In Germany, the HBCI standard has been established, which allows not only direct debit, but also other banking applications. The transmission of data is done by a net data interface, which is based on a flexible delimiter syntax (similar to UN/EDIFACT). A special Web form suffices to gather all relevant information from the customers, which they then print and fax to the merchant. The entire process is manual, but the data entered in the form can help save time, because the bank details are saved in digital form. The faxed form is used to authorize the money transfer. When digital signatures are accepted, special software on the merchant server will pass the transaction to the bank, where the money transfer will be initiated in an instant.

14.6 Prepaid Payment Systems

14.6.1 Electronic Cash

Electronic cash solutions use software to save the equivalent of cash onto a hard or floppy disk. Coins and bank notes are replaced by digitally signed files. The advantage of this system is that the cost of passing on the money is nearly zero (the only real cost is your Internet connection). To receive the money, you need to go to a virtual automatic teller machine on the Internet or to a real-world ATM, where you can get electronic cash by direct debit from the bank account or by credit card payment. The difficulty with electronic cash is ensuring that it is implemented in a secure way. And although the money is stored in files, you should note that by copying the files the value of the cash is not increased, nor should it be possible to alter the amount of the digital money on your hard disk. Electronic coins and notes should have digital marks that

---

[43]http://www.travel-overland.de/

make it impossible for them to be used more than once. The use of encryption technologies, digital signatures, and electronic signatures helps to reduce the possibility of fraud.

To emulate coins and bank notes, digital money should not reveal the identity of the person who has paid with it. Payment should not require a bank to be involved. Electronic money should be exchanged directly between the two partners involved. Splitting up the value is also very important. Instead of one digital bank note, you should be able to split it up into several bank notes and coins, which can be passed on to different people. The following are some implementations of electronic cash.

DigiCash

DigiCash[44] has a product called eCash. Bookshops, casinos, and online newspapers accept the money in exchange for goods, games, and information.

The DigiCash solution was once very successful. The Deutsche Bank[45] in Germany decided to become a partner and issues eCash to its customers. Some other banks around the world have become issuers as well, such as the St. George Bank[46] in Australia.

To use eCash, the customer must open an account at a participating bank, such as Deutsche Bank or Mark Twain Bank. The customer transfers a certain amount of money into that particular account and receives the money in the form of electronic cash, which can be stored on the customer's hard disk. The money is stored in the form of tokens. The electronic cash that customers get from their bank is also transferred to a special bank account from which the merchants are then paid for financial transactions. The eCash system is a one-way token system that allows the money to be used only once. Only one transaction can be executed between customer and merchant. The merchant cannot use a token to pay for something else. It must be brought back to the bank to be cashed in. Peer-to-peer transactions between customers are possible but require a bank in between to convert the tokens. Every token contains the sum it represents, a random number that is used as the serial number, and a digital signature of the issuing bank. The bank is able to validate the electronic cash without knowing who used it, allowing the anonymous use of the electronic money. This is achieved by using a system called *blind signature*. Table 14.5 explains in detail how this works.

The consumer is then able to go to a Web site that supports DigiCash and pay with the files on the hard disk. A merchant who wants to accept DigiCash money also needs to set up an account at a DigiCash supporting bank in order to cash the accepted money. The transaction costs are zero for the DigiCash model. In 1998, more than 150 Web sites accepted DigiCash money

---

[44]http://www.digicash.com/
[45]http://www.deutsche-bank.de/
[46]http://www.stgeorge.com.au/

> The blind signature is a patent-pending algorithm that was invented by David Chaum, the founder of DigiCash. To put it simply, a customer that acquires electronic cash creates raw tokens. A serial number is added to the token and sent to the customer's bank. The serial number is made invisible to the bank by multiplying it with another random number (the so-called *blinding factor*). The bank adds a digital signature to the token and sends it back to the customer. The customer is able to divide the serial number by the blinding factor and get the original serial number back. Using this mechanism, the bank is not able to trace the tokens to the customer, because the bank does not see the original serial number.

Table 14.5. What Is a Blind Signature?

until DigiCash went bankrupt in late 1998. Credit card transactions destroyed the business for DigiCash, although the company is seeking new investors to rebuild the service with a better business model.

A support site for German eCash shops[47] has been established, where you can find a list of shops that accept eCash from DigiCash. The eCash system has established itself in many different areas of online selling, such as providing information, entertainment, and digital goods such as software products; traditional online retailers also accept eCash.

NetCash

NetCash was developed by the University of Southern California in 1995, but is no longer in use. Although it was a very good implementation, it was introduced too early to be successful. It required a complex infrastructure that was too difficult to implement and use by many Internet users in the early days. Here's how the NetCash scheme worked.

NetCash provided anonymous payments on the Internet. It was an electronic currency that supported real-time electronic payments. To get money from a currency server, the customer needed an account on a NetCheque server. The NetCheque system discussed earlier provides a secure framework for online payment systems, which can be extended to include electronic cash. With the combination of NetCash and NetCheque, customers have the possibility of choosing their level of anonymity.

---

[47] http://www.ecash-shops.de/

The anonymity was not as great as in the DigiCash system, because the NetCash coins could be purchased only through NetCheque. The currency server used to distribute the NetCash coins could trace the customers who purchased the coins. Still, this was not likely to happen because the customers could freely choose which currency server they used.

After a customer purchased the coins, they could be passed to other customers or merchants without revealing the identity of the buyer, although a currency server was involved to ensure that the coins were valid. Only persons who wanted to exchange the NetCash coins for real currency needed to identify themselves at a currency server. In the NetCash scheme, it was possible to transfer coins without needing a currency server, but there was no assurance that a coin was valid.

CyberCoins

Besides the CyberCash credit card solution mentioned earlier in this chapter, there is also a system for micropayments called CyberCoins. CyberCoins enable merchants to sell, and consumers to buy, digital products via the Internet. CyberCoins can have a value ranging from $.25 up to $10, denominations too small for use in credit card purchases.

For every customer and merchant, special "cash containers" are provided on a special Internet server, which act as CyberCoin accounts. Using the CyberCash wallet, a customer can move money to her CyberCoin account. To pay with the wallet, a special command from the Web browser is sent to the wallet, which requires the customer to accept the payment. After the customer has accepted the money, it is transferred electronically from the customer's account to the merchant's. The communication is secured through encryption. The customer's order is sent to the merchant, who adds the merchant data to the order and sends the completed order to the CyberCash gateway, which then moves the money between the accounts.

IBM Micro Payment

The system developed by the payment division of IBM Israel in Haifa[48] is a micropayment system that allows the alteration of simple HTML links into payment links. Therefore, it is necessary to put ISPs between customers and merchants. The system uses the existing payment infrastructure of the ISPs. The clicks on a certain link are registered in the log files of the merchant and can be attributed to a certain customer. The required payment is then passed on to the ISP, which debits the money from the customer's bank account. So far, only some pilots are available on the Internet. Due to the rather complicated structure of the solution, with ISPs as go-between, it never succeeded in the market.

---

[48]http://www.hrl.il.ibm.com/mpay/

MilliCent

MilliCent[49] was developed by DEC (Digital Equipment Corporation). It is based on a system of vouchers, which allow payment below the cent limit, allowing true mini-payments at a very small level. These vouchers are called *scrips*. A broker, typically an ISP or financial institituion, sells broker scrips to customers and manages the merchants' scrips. Scrips are different for every merchant. A customer exchanges a broker scrip for a merchant-specific scrip when he wants to buy something. The scrips are managed in the MilliCent wallet. Using a merchant scrip, the customer is able to pay for goods, information, and services from a certain merchant without the interaction of a third party. This makes MilliCent a cheap solution for micropayment businesses. Although several pilots are on the way, it is not clear if the system will have a future, especially because the system does not guarantee anonymity.

14.6.2 Smart Cards

Smart cards are very popular in Europe and their acceptance is increasing in the United States. Phone cards, health care cards, and debit cards have embedded chips that contain money, health information, and account information. Every debit card issued in Europe (called an EC Card) contains information on the owner and the account. In addition to these pieces of information, systems have been developed to store cash on the chip.

The money on the card is saved in an encrypted form and is protected by a password to ensure the security of the smart card solution. Smart cards must be run through a hardware terminal to complete a transation. The device requires a special key from the issuing bank to start a money transfer in either direction.

Smart cards give shop owners the advantage of not having large amounts of cash on hand. Instead, they can transmit the money electronically to their bank accounts at the moment of payment. Actually, virtual money that has been used to pay for the goods can be transmitted in an instant to the merchant's bank. The major advantage of smart cards is that it is possible to use them in both worlds, real and cyber. A smart card can be "loaded" at a bank and used to make purchases on the Internet. The other way around is just as feasible. Offer a service on the Internet, charge your customers who transfer their money to your card, and then cash the money in at your bank or pass the money on to pay for another service. Electronic cash as described in the last subsection can be used only on the Internet. Smart cards can act as a bridge. Online auctions can profit a lot from the use of smart cards, because people can exchange money directly, without an intermediary.

The great advantages of smart cards are relative security, and simple, offline operation. Together, these translate into low transaction costs. In Eu-

---

[49]http://www.millicent.digital.com/

rope, two standards have been established: the Mondex card in the United Kingdom and the GeldKarte in Germany.

Mondex

The Mondex company, a subsidiary of MasterCard International, has become established in the United Kingdom and is becoming increasingly popular in the U.S. Money can be transferred by smart card readers that are attached to telephones, ATMs, and through special electronic wallets. The reader is able to dial into a bank and enable the transfer between user and bank. After your money is loaded onto your smart card, you can transfer the money to your business partners using electronic wallet. Using the wallet, ATMs, and Mondex telephones, you can check the balance on the card. Money can be exchanged between anyone in possession of a Mondex card. The Mondex system supports up to five different currencies on the card at the same time, which can be exchanged at a bank for any other currency. So far, no mechanism on the card itself converts a given currency into another one, because the smart card does not contain information about current exchange rates.

It is not necessary to have a bank as an intermediary in every case. The system guarantees anonymity just as real cash does, but this is also a disadvantage, because it is not possible to track criminal transactions. Few sites accept the Mondex card today, but soon more sites will, because it offers a great possibility to implement micropayments with no transaction costs (users pay a monthly fee of about two dollars/euros).

The Mondex system utilizes some strong security features that make it virtually impossible to forge the money. Mondex uses the Value Transfer Protocol (VTP), which uses strong cryptography to protect the movement of the money. Mondex values can be moved only between Mondex cards, which makes it a closed system.

The Mondex system allows customers to lock the value on a given card, in case of a loss. Banks are then able to offer a reward system as an incentive to return a card to its rightful owner. The persons who find the card can't do much with it, because it requires entry of a PIN to operate.

GeldKarte

In 1997, banks in Germany started issuing new debit cards with an embedded chip. This chip contains the functionality of electronic cash called the Geld-Karte (MoneyCard). Because debit cards are replaced every two years, by the beginning of 1999, every debit card in Germany had become a smart card. The main difference, compared to Mondex, is the way the cards are loaded with money. A special teller machine is necessary to get the money.

To pay with the smart card, existing devices need to be enhanced. Hardware devices for personal use are not planned. This would allow a person to log all transactions between smart cards. If more money is coming from the card than originally had been loaded onto the card, it would be inactivated. This also allows you to recover money in the case of a loss. Privacy is an issue with the log files, but the banks give assurances that they do not misuse the logging information. Sellers do not see personal information from the buyer; all they see is the number of the smart card, which then can be used by the bank to identify the user.

There are no sites that accept the MoneyCard at the time of writing due to its infrastructure, but its acceptance rate in shops and ticket machines is very high. The MoneyCard is a very attractive alternative for electronic businesses. Unlike credit card companies, which charge approximately four percent of the transaction, the MoneyCard enables banks to charge only 0.3 percent (or a minimum of 0.01 euro). Because of the low transaction costs, the MoneyCard is ideal for micropayments, such as small fees for Web pages, documents, and pictures. In addition, the merchant receives the money during the ordering process, not after. The process is completed only if enough money is on the smart card.

The disadvantages of the MoneyCard for customers are that they have to preload the money onto the smart card (as with all prepaid solutions) and risk losing interest earned on the money if it had been left in a bank account. Another drawback of the system is that it is only a national solution. So far, only Germany is using it. To make it really successful, other European countries need to adopt it, or it will be replaced by other international systems, such as the Mondex card. Even more important is that smart card readers become a commodity integrated into the keyboard, without imposing additional costs on customers. So far, money can only be downloaded at the bank; with smart card readers, it would be possible to perform this action at home.

Technical specifications for the use on the Internet were issued in 1998, but only pilots have been set up thus far. The major obstacle is the wide use of smart card readers.

VisaCash

VisaCash, the electronic wallet, has been tested in several countries. Two different cards are available: the one-way card, which works like a telephone card; and a card that can be reloaded, which works like the Mondex card and the GeldKarte.

The VisaCash card works on the Internet, but only a prototype has been demonstrated (at the CardTech/SecurTech Conference in Orlando, Florida). Even though it was the preferred payment method during the 2000 Olympic Games in Atlanta, not much has happened with VisaCash. The effort to reload the cards was too high for many people to handle.

14.6.3   Checking the Business Cases

Prepaid solutions are the preferred solutions of banks and online shops because they require the user to pick up the money in advance. This is good for the bank, because it does not have to pay interest on the money anymore, and is good for the user, who can hand the funds over to the online shop the instant the product is purchased. This helps to prevent digital fraud. The system works just as in real shops, where people come in and buy products for cash. It is easy to understand, especially for people who do not have much knowledge in the area of payment.

Our first business case, the bookshop, would most probably accept electronic cash, as long as the books do not become too expensive. Due to the fact that the money is on the hard disk of the customers, they won't pick up hundreds of dollars or euro and store them until they find what they were looking for. Ideally, the bookshop would accept mixed payments, in that one part is paid using a credit card and the other part is paid with electronic money. Smart cards would not be accepted right away because the necessary readers are not available with every computer and there is no established standard accepted on a continentwide or worldwide basis. Technically, there is no issue holding smart cards back, but it will take some time before smart card payments are fully established. After a standard is establish, the bookshop will most likely pick up this payment method.

For our second business case, the translator, this would not be a viable solution, because the cost for building up the infrastructure would be too high. The amount of money paid for the services would also normally be higher than the prepaid solutions are suitable for. The translator does not provide services that can be paid with micropayment solutions, nor are most of the translations in a price range below $200.

For the third business case, the news agency, prepaid solutions would fit perfectly if the business model is based on fees for every single transaction. The pay per view model works perfectly together with the micropayment solutions that are offered by the prepaid models. Even with a subscription model, this would make sense, as long as the subscription fee is reasonably low.

The fourth business case, the software company, would accept prepaid payment solutions for smaller software packages and, of course, for the online call center. Typically, micropayments and prepaid solutions are supported by end customers but not by businesses because they need an invoice first to pay for a certain article.

14.6.4   Online Experience

The DPunkt Bookshop[50] in Germany allows customers to download books in an electronic format. The content can be downloaded chapter by chapter, and

---

[50]http://ecash.dpunkt.de/

customers pay per chapter. They can use digital money to pay for chapters. Every chapter is available in PDF (Adobe Acrobat) format, which can be viewed on any platform. In addition, DPunkt has a database of images and textures which can be bought online.

NetCash and CyberCoins had been widely used until 1998, when new standards came into effect, shutting down the NetCash and CyberCoins option. In 1997, the First Union Bank[51] in the U.S. had started a pilot with CyberCoins and had even built a mall on the bank's Web site where people could shop for CyberCoins. Research on the Internet lead to many dead links for these payment schemes. But still, they are worth mentioning because they have had a large impact on the Internet, and they will help you understand which payment schemes are available and useful.

Currently no online businesses accept smart-card-based systems such as Mondex or the GeldKarte, although there are several trials underway. One example is the University of Exeter in the U.K., which has developed a set of tools to deal with Mondex cards on the Internet.[52]

14.6.5 Required Software

These solutions are not based on open standards. Therefore, it is necessary to contact the companies that have developed the standards for particular software. Refer to the above mentioned URLs for further information. Because the payment solutions mentioned in this chapter do not embrace the open source standard, they really cannot be recommended here.

14.7 Comparing Payment Technologies

14.7.1 Overview

Now that we have looked at the three types of online payments, we need to review the business requirements from the second section. Table 14.6 shows which technology meets which requirement.

It becomes quite clear that postpaid systems score the highest marks, because they have been established on the Internet for a while. Prepaid and instant-paid systems are not as common on the Internet. The standards for these have not been settled yet, and many things are still changing. Although this may seem bad, it is actually good, because it opens up the possibility of integrating new technologies and paradigms. It is because SSL-based credit card payments are so established that other standards like SET fight difficult uphill battles.

---

[51]http://www.firstunion.com/
[52]http://www.ex.ac.uk/ecu/mondex/JTAP/

	Postpaid	Instant-paid	Prepaid
Acceptability	High	Low	Low
Anonymity	Low	High	Middle
Convertibility	High	High	High
Efficiency	Low	High	High
Flexibility	Low	Low	Low
Integration	High	Low	Middle
Reliability	High	High	High
Scalability	High	High	High
Security	Middle	High	Middle
Usability	High	Middle	Middle

Table 14.6. Comparison of Payment Technology

14.7.2 Problems in the B2B Environment

Although many of the electronic payment systems mentioned here work well and have been evolving over the last few years, several B2B marketplaces cannot make use of them, because they are too simple for complex businesses. For example, GlobalFoodExchange.com,[53] a marketplace for the perishable-food supply chain, has assessed many e-payment systems, but none meets the company's needs.

Their problem is the disparity between the purchase-order price and the invoice price because perishable food items have a wide range of quality or suffer some type of degradation during shipping. No e-payment system can handle that kind of discrepancy efficiently. Most platforms do not go beyond the purchase order.

Therefore, the GlobalFoodExchange.com is developing its own payment and settlement software. For now, marketplace members must work out invoice disputes as they always have—typically through time-consuming phone conversations. The coordination of purchase-orders and invoice tracking is the main challenge for such a payment system. To make this work, custom integration with each of its members is required.

Many other marketplaces must to go the same route and develop their own custom payment solutions, because the standard solutions do not work well in the complicated business-to-business world. Another company that had problems with packaged solutions is Packexpo.com,[54] a marketplace for the pack-

---

[53]http://www.globalfoodexchange.com/
[54]http://www.packexpo.com/

aging industry, which uses at least six financial exchange models. Depending on the goods sold, member companies may need an open-account model, a financed model, or other methods. These cannot be easily delivered as a standard product. Custom integration is always required to automate the whole process.

Although not impossible, there are still some issues that must be resolved individually to make B2B payments successful.

14.8   The Future of Payment

14.8.1   SEMPER

In the future, highly integrated frameworks will help to conduct secure business via the Internet. Payment solutions will be only one segment in the infrastructure, because currently payments do not address the broader "trading" process in an open, extensible way. Trading is more than making payments and includes additional factors, such as promotional offers, receipts, proof of delivery, and customer care. Consumers demand in the real world, but these must be available in the virtual world. This section will focus on two projects for the business-to-consumer area (SEMPER and the Open Trading Protocol) and two for the business-to-business transactions (Global Trust Enterprise and OBI). I will also identify the payment solutions used therein.

SEMPER (Secure Electronic Marketplace for Europe)[55] is a research project founded by the European Union to allow payment with electronic money via the Internet. The SEMPER project tries to identify the required infrastructure for such an environment. Its predecessor project, CAFÉ (Conditional Access for Europe), already identified the technical requirements for electronic passports, digital driving licenses, and cyber money in real-world applications. Terminals and teller machines are able to identify the user and allow the storage of electronic money.

As we have already seen in this chapter, many different and incompatible Internet payment systems compete with one another. Most online shops accept only a limited subset and some accept only one payment system. Ideally, every online shop should be able to support any available method of payment, but without increased costs on the merchant side. Without a unified framework for payment, the solution architect for an online business needs to implement every payment method, one after the other, but this is costly. A general payment service framework, is necessary to separate the business model from the payment model. The framework needs to make different payment models transparent to the business application.

The SEMPER framework consists of a security kernel and different services that surround it. The services are divided into modules. At the time of this

---

[55]http://www.semper.org/

writing there are modules for encryption, certification, and payment. These modules can be called from business applications through the security kernel by using a special application programming interface (API).

The connection between the payment and the business process must be defined through a hierarchy of APIs that represent payment models, such as credit card payment systems or electronic cash solutions. Some features need to be implemented to complement the APIs. Payment models need to be selected automatically, so that applications do not need do this. The applications should have to consider only the value and the recipient of the payment. And tools will need to be created that allow the incorporation of payment models into this generic payment service.

A Java-based generic payment service has been created for the SEMPER system. It can be extended fairly easily, by adding new classes to the generic payment service class. So far, SET and DigiCash have been implemented so that users of the generic payment service are able to exchange financial transactions with people who use either SET or DigiCash. It is just a matter of time until other modules become available and make the whole system valuable. Through the modularity of Java and the open framework, implementation is not a big issue. It is more difficult convincing owners of propriety standards to support an open standard infrastructure, because they have to reveal their source code.

14.8.2   The Open Trading Protocol

The Open Trading Protocol (OTP)[56] complements today's electronic payment protocols by addressing the process of doing business. The OTP provides a means to negotiate trade and to buy and sell by invoking the underlying payment protocols, which can be one of those previously mentioned.

The aim of OTP is to lower the cost of trading. This is accomplished by using the Internet as a distribution channel that is consistent, inexpensive, and secure. The required framework is described as part of OTP. OTP enables new models of trade that are available only on the Internet. The framework allows payment models with two (direct payment) or three (indirect payment) parties. The protocol is open, flexible, extensible, robust, and vendor-neutral, making it ideal for the Internet. As you will recall, "open" means that the specifications are not secret, and the flexibility allows the creation of differentiated service offerings to be created. The extensibility means that new or enhanced trading and payment models can be integrated without disrupting the service of the other components. The robustness of the protocol means that the whole infrastructure is able to cope with errors or downtime of the participating servers and clients. Because the protocol is open, any interested independent software vendor (ISV) is able to create software that adheres to the standard. This offers businesses the ability to choose from a range of products with similar feature

---

[56]http://www.otp.org/

sets and makes it independent of the ISV.

Costs for customer care can be lowered significantly by using OTP, because it has a flexible, but standard way of providing information about a certain payment. The information can then be extracted to resolve issues of payment. OTP supports the delivery of goods both digitally and physically. The whole trading chain is linked by the information, so that the delivery data can be brought together with the payment information.

14.8.3   Open Buying on the Internet

OBI,[57] Open Buying on the Internet, is a freely available framework for business-to-business transactions. The standard contains a detailed architecture, concise technical specifications, guidelines, and information on compliance and implementational issues. Any organization or individual can acquire a copy of the OBI standard and use it to build a product, service, or solution.

The OBI architecture is based on the idea that process owners should be responsible for the information associated with their business processes. For example, suppliers should be responsible for the prices and content of their online catalogs, and purchasing organizations should be held responsible for profile information and account codes.

The architecture normally involves three organizations: the supplier, the purchaser, and the payment authority. Part of the purchaser organization is the requisitioner who actually places the orders via the Internet. To identify the requisitioner, a digital certificate is used. The purchaser is the owner of the OBI server, which is responsible for receiving order requests and returning orders, and can be used to handle profile information of the buyers. The purchasing department also maintains the relationship with the suppliers and deals with pricing.

The payment authority provides the processes needed for the authorization of the payment between the purchaser and the supplier. A payment authority in most cases is a financial institution, such as a bank. If the payment is done via bulk invoice, the responsibility for authorizing payment could also be the supplier's.

The supplier maintains a dynamic electronic catalog that presents accurate product and price information for every purchaser. The information needs to be kept private—one purchaser should not be able to see the prices and product range of the other purchasers. The product and price information are displayed as agreed on in the contract with a buying organization.

Communication between the trading partners is done over standard HTTP and through the use of SSL encryption using standard Web browsers to reduce costs on the purchaser side. Not surprisingly, the information is transported via the Internet. As more companies adopt the OBI standard, a purchasing order will become cheaper. By 1999, some OBI pilots had started, but no real

---

[57] http://www.openbuy.org/

OBI is designed for business-to-business purchasing, which is different from consumer purchasing and is built on the following principles:

- **Common vision**—The OBI standard is based on the expectations for B2B solutions of the participants and the common issues that arise. The standard tries to be as general as possible.

- **Cost effectiveness**—Maintenance costs need to be reasonable, and OBI solutions need to integrate easily with the existing IT infrastructure.

- **Flexibility**—The standard needs to be flexible enough to accommodate variations of different implementations and upcoming business needs.

- **Robust infrastructure**—The infrastructure needs to be able to process transactions securely and reliably.

- **Value-added services**—Service providers have the possibility of differentiating themselves through value-added services with protocol and message formats.

- **Vendor neutrality**—To encourage a diversity of product offerings from a variety of software vendors, the standard is open and includes interoperability tests.

Table 14.7. Properties of OBI

implementations have been spotted on the Internet. In 2001 many companies are doing business via OBI. You can find a list on the OBI home page.

14.8.4   Global Trust Enterprise

Global Trust Enterprise was developed by CertCo[58] in the U.S., together with many partner banks throughout the world, including the HypoVereinsbank[59] in Germany. The main reason for building this service was to create a powerful enabler for business-to-business transactions. The idea is founded on the prin-

---

[58]http://www.certco.com/
[59]http://www.hypovereinsbank.de/

ciple of broad participation by financial institutions, and more banks are taking part in the initiative. Unlike business-to-consumer transactions on the Internet that rely on one-to-one authentication models, the global trust enterprise seeks to extend this model into a multilateral (many-to-many) environment, because most businesses have more than one employee.

The major obstacle to implementing worldwide business-to-business networks is the issue of identity trust. But through the new system, companies doing electronic business will be able to identify the trading partner. CertCo is issuing identity warranties that enable buyers and sellers to manage the risk. This confidence in the business partners enables enterprises to conduct high-integrity, authenticated, and trusted business-to-business transactions via the Internet with known and unknown trading partners. As mentioned earlier, payment in the business-to-business area is mostly done via invoice, so the problem is not sending out the invoice. The problem is that companies need to be sure about the identity of the business partner.

International trade, corporate purchasing, and content delivery represent some of the typical business-to-business transactions covered by the global trust enterprise. As an example of global trust at work, consider a Danish ice cream company that wants to expand its market reach, minimize its costs, and conduct business with several importers in the Americas and Asia. Digital certificates issued by participating banks allow the exporters and the importers to trust each other as they negotiate the prices and sign the contracts. The certificates can also be used to audit the transactions. After the participating companies have obtained the certificate from their banks, they are able to conduct business with any other company that has registered at any of the participating institutions via the Internet.

The reason CertCo chose to work with financial institutions to provide the authentication of business partners is easily explained. Banks are experienced in identifying corporate customers and their employees for the online initiation of electronic transactions, because they have done this for years on the private financial networks. Signature guarantees, check verification, and credit card verification are tasks that banks already perform and are able to extend easily to the Internet. It naturally follows that trading partners on the Internet will trust the identity of others because they trust the financial institution with which they work.

Using the global trust enterprise framework, corporate customers will be able to use services provided by participating banks. A typical buy-sell transaction would require the seller to ask the financial institution to verify the buyer's digital signature. The seller's and the buyer's banks would automatically contact each other through the network and exchange the required information. In this case, the buyer's bank would verify the signature and send back an attestation that the signature is valid. Likewise, the buyer may ask to verify the digital certificate of the seller.

A standardized system and process has been established to facilitate communication between the participants. The global trust enterprise will act as a root certification authority for the financial institutions and will be able to perform an audit to monitor the adherence to a set of predefined system rules and business practices.

The global trust enterprise differs in several ways from previous efforts:

- **Interoperability**—Businesses are not dependent on a particular software vendor or financial institution, because the identity trust is based on common business practices and open technical specifications.

- **Support**—The framework is sponsored by financial institutions throughout the world, making it an efficient way of doing business via the Internet.

- **Digital identity**—Businesses will require only one digital certificate for all their virtual business activities.

Table 14.8. Advantage of the Global Trust Enterprise

The global trust enterprise addresses the elements of identity trust based on common legal and business practices. The foundation is created by establishing a uniform set of identification and operating practices. The global trust enterprise provides the technology to identify trading partners in real time via the Internet. The digital signatures and hash codes are used to verify that the information transmitted has not been changed during the transmission. Through these technologies, nonrepudiation can be guaranteed, and they provide strong legal evidence of the existence of the message, including additional information such as the signature, time and date, and the certificate of the sender.

The global trust enterprise does not require participants to obtain special proprietary standards. It is built on open standards to facilitate interoperability between the participants. Digital signatures, certificates, and business practices are shared throughout the framework to expand the business-to-business transactions.

Although the processes are standard banking and payment processes, new technologies can enhance these processes and standards by reducing cost and increasing speeds. Therefore, the subject of online payments is very important and must be taken into account for every e-business project.

Part IV

The Present Future

Chapter 15

THE OPEN SOURCE COMMUNITY

15.1 Information Wants to Be Free

15.1.1 Free Software

On the Internet, people have been willing to share information, programs, and media files for free. This happened long before the current open source movement. The so-called free software movement, made up of public domain software, freeware, cardware, mailware, giftware, and shareware, is the movement in the programming era that dominated the Web before large companies decided to give away their software for free.

For programmers, placing a program into the public domain meant that others could grab their programs, use them, and even modify them without even mentioning the original author. Few programs have been released as public domain software. But the educational value of having such programs is very high. The source code can be used by others to understand how to program something and can be used for their own projects.

Freeware is a little more strict, in that it allows users to use a program for free, but the author retains the copyright and does not allow the commercial use of the program. In many cases, the source code is not available, and when the source code is available, you must obtain the original author's permission before using the code in other programs. Giftware, cardware, and mailware are special types of freeware, in which the author requests a gift, a postcard, or a letter from the users. These requests are never enforced, but the author is happy about every reaction from the user.

The intention of these types of free programs is to provide a service to the online community and to become known in the community. Most projects have been based on programs that solved a personal computing problem and were then extended to solve problems of the general public. Freeware programmers work for fun, not for economic purposes. They are not interested in money, but in the beauty and utility of their programs.

Shareware is a little different. The author releases the software for free, but requests that the users pay a fee if they like the program. Freeware programs do not enforce this payment. Others use special keys that allow potential customers to use a certain program only for 30 days or restrict the functionality (for example, saving is not allowed). Today, these programs are called evaluation copies. The shareware concept allowed many people to earn some money without the need (or cost) of building a company. Homegrown programs could be easily distributed over the Internet without much marketing. The chat client mIRC,[1] for example, is distributed as shareware. Anyone can download the software, try it out, and then decide to keep it or to delete it. Much pirated software is used only once before it is removed from customers' computers. The shareware concept enables customers to test a product legally, for free, instead of buying the product to test it (distributing a demo or evaluation version via floppy or CD always involved replication costs).

Another good example of shareware is the Group-Graphic Editor by Kessler-Design,[2] which allows owners of Nokia mobile phones to create graphics, upload them to their phones, and share them with their friends, customers, and partners. The software was written by a student in his spare time. The Internet is the only channel for marketing and distribution. Customers can download a 30-day version of the tool and need to pay a fee to receive a key that will allow them to continue using the tool. Without the Internet, such a business could not be operated.

"Free" has two meanings in English: without cost, and freedom. Free software actually means both: it is free to use, but even more important the user is free to change the source code, redistribute it, and extend it by improving the source code. Richard Stallman of the Free Software Foundation (FSF)[3] has a concise definition of free software on his Web page: "Think free speech, not free beer." Everyone is allowed to speak out, but not everyone may receive free beer forever.

Free software means that users have the freedom to look at the source code, are allowed to copy the programs, and can change or enhance the applications to meet their needs. This does not mean that software needs to be available free of charge. Free software in the sense of the FSF may also be sold.

The reason software should be free in this sense is that a computer program can be compared to a recipe. Both describe steps that lead to a certain result. Just as exchanging recipes is something very common, the exchange of software should also be free. Who would want to prohibit the exchange of recipes? Although this is a good definition of free software, a new term has been introduced: open source software, which is similar but not the same.

---

[1] http://www.mirc.co.uk/
[2] http://www.kessler-design.com/wireless/
[3] http://www.fsf.org/

15.1.2 The Impact of the Internet

Software that can be used for free and contains the complete source code is gaining market share and will eventually dominate the market. Therefore, it is necessary to understand what free software means and what it implies. The Apache[4] Web server and the Linux[5] operating system are the fastest-growing free software packages for their respective market segments. Apache accounts for more installations than all other server packages combined, and its market share is growing. The Linux operating system is the fastest-growing competitor for the still Windows-dominated world. The software can be downloaded for free, and it is even possible to participate in the development of new releases.

The Internet has become so successful because its standards are free—free of charge and freely extensible. Anyone can download the specifications and use them to implement new applications or even enhance them by submitting a new request for comment (RFC).[6] But a problem has arisen with the Internet. It has become fairly easy to copy programs. A person can circumvent copy-protection and put a program onto a Web site, where millions of people have the opportunity to download a certain file. Making money from programs has become more difficult. To make money from software, it is necessary to give it away for free. This may sound illogical, but it was the only way Netscape could survive the threat of Microsoft.

To retain its market share, Netscape had to release its browser software for free, just as Microsoft did a few months earlier. But Netscape topped Microsoft's free offer by offering the source code for free as well, making Netscape the "good guy" in the browser war. In an instant, thousands of people were downloading and reviewing the source code. They found bugs in the source code that the developers at Netscape had not. Thousands of eyes see more than two. Even if a company is able to pay for thousands of testers, free source code is better, because it enables the testers to rewrite the code and present the bug fix to the Internet community, which then flows into the next update of the program.

The major difference between software development in a company and on the Internet is that the Internet community is more chaotic, so the development cannot be managed in a traditional way. Product design on the Internet is not driven by a predefined time line or a traditional top-down or bottom-up design. It is driven by the ideas of the programmers involved and can be bottom-up and top-down at the same time. These ideas make it more difficult to have a product ready at a certain time, but enable innovation and bring new ideas to the product that may seem too unconventional and too costly for a company.

---

[4] http://www.apache.org/
[5] http://www.linux.org/
[6] http://www.ietf.org/rfc/

15.1.3   The Cathedral and the Bazaar

In 1997, Eric Raymond, one of the most prominent evangelists for the open source movement, gave a keynote speech at the Perl (another open source product) conference. Titled "The Cathedral and the Bazaar,"[7] it compares traditional software development methods with the new open source paradigm. The cathedral stands for a closed group software development method, in which the design and the implementation are done within the group, with limited or no interaction with outsiders.

The members of the bazaar work in a loose-knit collective in a public way that allows people to move in and out during the process. Old-style programming depends on a group of programmers, each with a certain task, that may not necessarily be interchanged with the work of the others. All traditional software companies use the cathedral model; even older open source movements such as the Free Software Foundation[8] are considered to work in the cathedral method, because not everyone is permitted to work on the source code.

The management style of the new open source movement is quite different. Instead of managing a tight group of experts, the managers of the open source communities try to get as many people on board as possible, generating a much larger effect, because new ideas flow more freely. This results in finding bugs more easily, because everyone can inspect the source code and improve it. The motivation for people to take part in an open source project is a craving for recognition.

Many people fear that open source software will lead to the balkanization of a program, which means that many different versions of the original software appear on the market, confusing users. The owners may start a battle over which version is better and this could drive users away. This has not yet happened, due to centralized integration of new source code. The chaos and confusion have not appeared, but malicious programmers will always try to create confusion. With good control over the integration process, however, this won't happen.

15.1.4   Microsoft's Shared Source

Microsoft[9] ignored the open source movement for a long time, but Apache and Linux have become predominant on the Web (see monthly statistics on NetCraft[10]) in the past two years because of that movement. In April 2001, Microsoft vice president and software analyst Craig Mundie announced the availability of a new concept called "shared source". In this model, Microsoft shares the source code with certain companies but denies them the ability to

---

[7]http://www.tuxedo.org/ẽsr/writings/cathedral-bazaar/
[8]http://www.fsf.org/
[9]http://www.microsoft.com/
[10]http://www.netcraft.co.uk/

modify it. According to Microsoft, this approach takes the best of open source, by sharing the knowledge with others, but reduces the risk of incompatibility by not allowing other people to modify to source code and creating forked developments. If you look closely, you will discover that the shared source philosophy is nothing but the status quo for Microsoft, and Microsoft is trying to make shared source sound like open source even though it is not.

Microsoft's position on open source is that research and development can be done only if the intellectual property can be sold afterward. Microsoft claims that research and development is founded on the principle "the importance of intellectual property rights." Open source puts intellectual property into the public domain, making it impossible to make money from the property and eliminating the chance to finance innovation. So charging for intellectual property is good for the economy.

Many open source activists responded to this approach, among them Linus Torvalds and Alan Cox. Their take on this approach is manifold. First, Microsoft seems to be interested in profit only, which is good for Microsoft and its shareholders, but not necessarily for the whole industry. As we will discover later in the chapter, it is very easy to make money from open source products, by moving into the services space. If you look at Microsoft, you will discover that Microsoft relies heavily on products and has invested very little in providing services.

Torvalds reminds the world in an article about all the work done by people like Albert Einstein, Niels Bohr, Leonardo da Vinci, and others who have done more for humanity than most companies have ever done. Those people were driven by an idea. Most of them were able to profit from their inventions eventually, but the idea was the starting point, not how much they could earn with it. It appears that Microsoft is just trying to jump onto the open source bandwagon without really contributing to this great idea.

15.1.5 Building a Successful Open Source Project

If we look at the successful open source projects on the Web, it is easy to see what makes them so outstanding. First, they require a modular design. To allow many developers to work on different parts of the project, it is necessary to create modules that work independently. This makes the project very strong, because it allows everyone to work at his own speed, without breaking up the whole project. The communities are also able to exchange programmers much more easily, because the modules tend to be small and easy to understand. The modules should be so small that a programmer can finish within a reasonable time before moving to the next module or project.

A leader must to coordinate the efforts of the different groups working on the project. A flat hierarchy is necessary, otherwise chaos will prevail. The leaders also inspire the developers who are providing their skills and time for free. A leader needs both good technical and interpersonal skills. Perl has

Larry Wall to supervise developments, while Linus Torvalds is the leader of the Linux project. Apache works differently, with a committee of thirteen people forming the leadership. No matter how the leadership looks, a project succeeds only when the leadership is clear.

To make the project a success, the software product should solve a general problem. An operating system, a Web server, or an online library are projects that interest many people. A program for measuring network devices will not attract many developers, but could be part of a larger project.

15.1.6   Open Source Definition

The portal site of the open source movement[11] defines open source in the following way. To qualify a program as open source, it needs to be freely redistributable, include the source code, allow modifications, and protect the integrity of the original version. Further, the license should not discriminate against any person, groups, or fields of endeavor. Redistribution should be possible without additional interaction, and the license should not be specific to the product, nor place restrictions on bundling it with other software packages. Reliability and quality are guaranteed through independent peer review and the rapid evolution of source code.

This means that the license may not restrict any party from selling or giving away the software as a component in a software package. No fee will be paid for such a sale. The source code must be distributed with the executable. If the source code is not included in the distribution pack, a way of freely downloading the source must be documented. The source code should not be obfuscated, and intermediate forms such as the output of a preprocessor or interpretable bytecode are not considered as source code.

The author must allow modification of the original source code and the distribution under the same terms and conditions of the original software. The author may restrict the distribution of the modified source code without changing the name or version of the original source code, to prevent the liability for a piece of software that has been modified by a third party.

The author must not discriminate against any person or groups by preferring or neglecting someone. The software may also not be restricted for a certain form of business. It must be allowed for private and commercial use without any restrictions. To make a license valid, it should not depend on a particular software and not place restrictions on other products.

15.1.7   Free Games

In the next chapter, we will see quite a few software solutions based on free software or open source software base, but no major games have been released in this way. Many games have been released as freeware or shareware, but

---

[11]http://www.opensource.org/

few of them provide source code. Only this would ensure that the game will
be developed in a collaborative environment allowing new ideas to be included.
Most freeware games are programmed by individuals in a hobby environment.
Few open source games have been noticed by the general public and for good
reason.

If you try to use the open source ideas that have been formulated by Eric
Raymond and others on computer games, you will soon notice that it probably
means that not all parts of the game will be developed in open source. Computer games have a set of properties that make them special in the software
world.

One of the major reasons to implement a piece of software as open source is
the fact that the collaboration of many ensures, the stability and quality of the
software. The difference between a game and an operating system is that the
operating system will be used every day, all day long. Games tend to be used
only a few times and then are replaced by a new game. Another very important
point is that games are simple to install, simple to play, and simple to remove
(in most cases), so it is difficult to build up a set of services around a game that
supports an industry. Due to the short period of interest for the player, there
is often no need to update or enhance a game. The collaborative approach can
actually hinder the development of a good game.

Games, like music and films, are dependent on the idea of a single person
or a small group of people. The more people try to modify this idea, the more
difficult it becomes to produce the game with this idea in mind. The whole idea
of open source is to move toward a service industry. With games, it becomes
more difficult, but this does not mean that games are not part of this exciting
movement.

The open source movement has started to infiltrate the entertainment industry. Not the games themselves, but the underlying technologies. Game
engines and libraries to create games have been very successful in the past,
and many open source projects have contributed to this fact. The open graphics engine Genesis 3D[12] and Crystal Space,[13] for example, offers everything
that is required for programming state-of-the-art games.

The difference between the actual game and the game engine is that the
game engine can be reused for many games, making it worthwhile to add features, remove bugs, and create value-added services around it. Game companies can reduce costs massively by using a game engine or library and invest
more into the design and the idea of the game. Internet games have become
very popular and the need for new games is immense.

Things are slowly changing in the games industry. Commercial game companies have released the source code of their products. The popular games
Doom and Quake, for example, are available in source-code form today. The

---

[12]http://www.genesis3d.com/
[13]http://www.crystalspace.com/

games industry is not the only part of the software industry that cannot benefit immediately from the open source movement, but creative people will make open source part of the whole software industry. Other sections of the software industry are moving slower, because the open source movement has not reached them yet. The whole software industry will eventually become a service industry.

15.2   Free Software Projects

15.2.1   The Gutenberg Online Library

One of the oldest movements on the Internet is Project Gutenberg.[14] It started in 1971 when Michael Hart typed the "Declaration of Independence" into a mainframe computer. The philosophy behind Project Gutenberg was to create electronic texts (such as information, books, and illustrations) that everyone in the world could read, in the simplest, easiest form. The Gutenberg Online Library has 10,000 books available in 2001, which enables users to read, use, quote, and search these documents over the Internet. People should easily be able to look up quotations from conversations, films, songs, other books, with any text editor that supports a search functionality.

Therefore, the electronic texts in the Gutenberg online library are made available in the standard ASCII format. These files can be read by any computer, because they do not contain any layout information. Italic, underlining, bold-faced words have been replaced by capital letters. Having the electronic texts in this format guarantees that no matter how old or new the computer is, if it can display text, then it will be able to display Gutenberg's electronic texts.

Just as with the file format, the Gutenberg Project tries to reach 99 percent of the general public by offering texts that most people want and use. Texts that are interesting for only a small group are not considered for inclusion into the electronic library. The same applies to the editions that Gutenberg puts on the Web site. Content is king, punctuation is not as important, and the people at Gutenberg won't get into any debates about whether a colon is more appropriate than a semicolon in a particular case.

After the copyright of an edition has expired, the work enters the public domain. The copyright normally expires at a certain time after the death of the author, depending on the country of origin. In the United States, for example, the copyright expires 50 years after the death of the author. After a work is in the public domain, the Gutenberg staff enters it into a computer and releases it to the Internet community.

The Gutenberg online library is divided into three sections (see Table 15.1). The "light literature" section contains books such as *Alice in Wonderland* and *Peter Pan*. It is designed to get readers interested in computer-based texts. It

---

[14]http://www.gutenberg.org/

To qualify for Project Gutenberg a book, text, or piece of information needs to fit into one of the following three categories:

- **Light literature**—Stories for anyone, who is interested in reading such as *Peter Pan* and *Aesop's Fables*.

- **Heavy literature**—Literate highlights, such as *Moby Dick* and *Paradise Lost*.

- **References**—Books that do not contain literature, but are references such as dictionaries and encyclopedias.

Table 15.1. Project Gutenberg

can provide a reference for people who want to read the book of a movie they have seen. These are books that everyone knows by name, but may never have read.

The second section is the so-called "heavy literature" section, which contains books such as the Bible and the collected works of William Shakespeare and Victor Hugo. This section is provided for the power user who needs to look up quotations and sections in these books. The books can also be used to create a new printed edition by adding the layout to the text.

The third section is the references section, which contains many useful resources, such as Roget's Thesaurus, dictionaries, and almanacs, that provide support for anyone involved in creating new texts.

15.2.2 The Linux Operating System

The now famous Linux[15] operating system was started by Linus Torvalds, a student at the University of Helsinki, Finland. Work started in 1991, when Linus started to enhance the UNIX derivate Minix. In 1994, the first version of the Linux kernel was released. Linux started to become more and more popular, first in the scientific community, because it offered the power of UNIX on low-cost Intel-based hardware. Small ISPs use Linux systems, because the investment in hardware is much lower and the software is available for free. Linux has evolved into a completely new operating system that is similar but not identical to UNIX.

The term Linux originally referred to the kernel, the core of the operating system, but now it is used for the complete package, just as many people think

---

[15]http://www.linux.org/

that Office 98 is an operating system when it's actually Windows 98. The complete packages on top of the Linux kernel are called distributions.

Although the source code is freely available to everyone through the GNU General Public License, the distributions are put together by companies who may charge for the collection of software. The GNU public license allows the reselling of the configured software packages, with the limitation that the source code must be published with the sold package. This limitation also means that all software created on top of the Linux kernel must be available in source code form as well, if the kernel is required in any form.

Today, several commercial companies are offering distributions, such as Red Hat,[16] Caldera,[17] and Suse.[18] These companies started with compiling and configuring the software available for Linux, but now they are actively writing software to add value to their distributions.

Linux is available on all major platforms and runs on Intel-based Pentiums that are normally used to run Windows, PowerPC-based computers that normally run the Mac OS, and most UNIX hardware platforms.

One of Linux's earlier problems was the missing commercial applications. Today, the situation has changed; all major vendors of software support Linux. Corel Draw, WordPerfect, Star Office, and Netscape Communicator are just a few of the applications that run on Linux. WABI,[19] a Windows emulator, allows 16-bit Windows applications to run on Linux.

The Linux community has its own mascot, the penguin, which was selected by Linus to represent the image he associates with the operating system. Due to the popularity of Linux, the merchandising business is up and running, and it is possible to buy T-shirts, mugs, mouse pads, and other items that proudly display the Linux penguin logo.

15.2.3   The Open Directory

The Open Directory project[20] evolved from the NewHoo directory, which was developed and maintained by some free spirited minds who wanted to create an alternative to the Internet's commercial search engines. In November 1998, Netscape bought NewHoo and included it in its open source Web site, Mozilla. The goal is to provide a comprehensive directory of the Web by relying on a vast number of volunteer editors.

Commercial directories that rely on humans to do the categorizing are unable to handle the thousands of submissions they receive each day. Adding an entry into Yahoo! takes months. Therefore, the quality and comprehensiveness of the commercial directories has suffered lately. Although Web crawlers often

---

[16]http://www.redhat.com/

[17]http://www.caldera.com/

[18]http://www.suse.de/

[19]http://www.wabi.com/

[20]http://www.dmoz.org/

retrieve thousands of documents, few of them are really relevant to the search query.

To regain the quality and the comprehensiveness of a directory, the Open Directory project tries to provide a means for the Internet to organize itself. With the fast pace of the Internet, the number of users is also growing—some of whom can be recruited to do a little work at the Open Directory. It provides the opportunity for everyone to contribute. Every person has certain areas of interest, in which she or he collects information and links. Open Directory editors can use this knowledge to add a URL to a certain zone and organize the zone. They are responsible for an up-to-date zone that does not contain bad links.

So simple is the project that everyone who is able to use a browser can become an editor and instantly add, change, or reject entries.

15.2.4 The TeX Typesetting System

TeX is a typesetting system written by Donald E. Knuth intended for the "creation of beautiful books—and especially for books that contain a lot of mathematics." And although *this* book contains very little mathematics, it has been set in TeX, because the system creates a pleasant and consistent layout that can be used directly by printers. It also reduced the amount of stress put on the author, because the text is plain ASCII and can be written in any text editor, reducing the risk of system crashes by overblown and buggy word processors.

Knuth developed a system of "literate programming" to write TeX, and he provides the literate source of TeX free of charge, together with tools for processing the source into something that can be compiled and something that can be printed. By offering the source for free, TeX can be ported to virtually any operating system and platform. The system itself is highly portable, as are the documents that are created.

The TeX typesetting system consists of a macro processor, which offers powerful programming capabilities, making the system also rather complex to use. To support TeX, Knuth has written two additional packages, called Metafont and Metapost. TeX is able to define the layout of the glyphs on a page, but Metafont is able to define the relationships between the shapes of the glyphs, detail the sizes of the glyphs, and detail the rasters used to represent the glyphs. In information technology, a glyph is a graphic symbol that provides the appearance or form for a character.

Over the years, Knuth and many others have designed many sets of fonts using Metafont. Fortunately, TeX is not restricted to these, and is also able to use any TrueType or PostScript font, after it has been converted to the TeX format.

Metapost, on the other hand, is used to implement a picture-drawing language that outputs PostScript, which can be incorporated into documents.

Because TeX is rather complex, more advanced macros have been written.

The most famous macro package is LaTeX, which provides a document processing system. Similar to HTML, LaTeX allows markup to describe the structure
of a document. The author does not need to think about presentation, because
this is handled automatically by the system. The layout can be controlled using a document class or add-on package. LaTeX tries to balance the required
functionality of the author with ease of use. This book was written in LaTeX,
which made the process that much smoother.

TeX is free, because Knuth wanted it to be. This decision was made long
before anyone talked about Linux or open source, and Knuth did not mind if
others earned money by selling TeX-based services and products. Unlike many
other projects, the development of TeX has come to a halt. The decision was
made soon after TeX 3.0 was released. Knuth is continuing to fix bugs in the
current version, and every bug-fix release adds a digit to the version number,
slowly approaching the number π. The release of TeX used to write this book
was 3.14159, which has a copyright notice of 1982! This is something very
unique. Most software that we use is no more than one year old!

The source code license agreement is also very special. When Knuth dies,
he wants TeX to be frozen at version π. Thereafter, no further changes may be
made to the source code. Metafont is bound to a similar license agreement, but
the version numbers are reflected in the Euler number e, which is currently at
2.718.

These restrictions haven't stopped the development of new projects in this
area. People have already started to develop a successor to TeX, one of them
being the Omega Project. The Omega Project is an extension of TeX supporting
Unicode, which allows authors to use any alphabet in the world (e.g., Cyrillic
or Kanji). Omega uses a powerful concept of input and output filters that work
with existing transliteration schemes. At the same time, LaTeX 3 is becoming
the new standard for document processing.[21] People will probably use LaTeX
3 and Omega at the same time for a while before switching completely to the
Omega Project.

15.3 Open Source Projects

15.3.1 The Jabber Instant Messaging System

Jabber[22] is an instant messaging system, providing online status and instant
message delivery to participating users via the Internet. It is similar in functionality to ICQ,[23] IRC,[24] and AIM,[25] which are already used by millions of
users on the Internet.

---

[21]http://www.latex-project.org/latex3.html
[22]http://www.jabber.org/
[23]http://www.icq.com/
[24]http://www.irchelp.org/
[25]http://www.aol.com/aim/

The developers of Jabber offer an alternative to these two commercial systems by providing an open source initiative and have overcome first generation problems and the commercial attitude of those systems. The key features of Jabber include an architecture of distributed servers, which allows customers to connect to their nearest server, reducing the traffic to the outside world and speeding up the connection. Jabber will provide ISP-level service, similar to most other Internet services. The protocol is based on the XML standard for the data exchange, and although simple in functionality, it allows pervasive clients to be created, which can be easily embedded or extended. The major advantage of this system is that it tries to maintain back-end compatibility with other instant messaging systems, such as ICQ, IRC, and AIM, thus creating a unified instant messaging solution for the Internet.

The Jabber team integrated the Jabber instant messaging engine into Mozilla to make the browser even more useful.

15.3.2 The Jikes Compiler

Jikes[26] is a Java compiler developed by the T.J. Watson Research Center at IBM. It has been rewritten from scratch in C++ and translates Java source files into byte-code.

The original Java compiler by Sun was written in Java and is slow. The Jikes compiler speeds up the compilation, but has no effect on the execution of the program afterward. It has been created as a replacement for the original compiler and can also be used to verify that your source code conforms to the specification. If your program can be compiled by Sun's and IBM's compilers, chances are very high that it conforms to the Java standard.

The reason IBM released Jikes as open source was mainly that people were asking for a Linux version (until then, only a Windows binary was available). In July 1998, IBM released the Linux version of Jikes, and the response was overwhelming! Not only was the Linux version very successful, but the Windows version also became more popular.

IBM received many bug reports, and people started to ask for the source code, especially people who have Linux installed. So IBM Research released the source code to make Jikes more reliable and accessible. Since then, many people have ported the source code to other platforms, and the compiler has become faster and more bug-free.

IBM also used Jikes to learn more about open standards and the open source movement. Although it is highly unlikely that IBM will release all software as open source, the very successful example of Jikes may eventually lead to other open source projects coming from IBM. IBM is, for example, already cooperating with the Apache open source movement, and it has integrated the Apache Web server into its product line.

---

[26]http://www.research.ibm.com/jikes/

Mailing lists and newsgroups are used to offer support for users and developers. The source code has been published in CVS form, which helps IBM to track changes to the source code and enables volunteers to contribute to the source code. The Concurrent Versions System (CVS) is a program that lets a code developer save and retrieve different development versions of source code. It also lets a team of developers share control of different versions of files in a common repository of files.

15.3.3   The KDE Graphical Desktop Environment

The graphical desktop environment K Desktop Environment (KDE)[27] is an add-on for operating systems that use X11[28] as the graphical user interface. X11 is used by all UNIX implementations. The commercial UNIX systems have a graphical desktop called CDE (common desktop environment), which makes using and administering the UNIX system much easier.

Because CDE is commercial, it is not available for free UNIXes, such as FreeBSD,[29] NetBSD,[30] or Linux.[31] KDE has been created as a free substitute for CDE. Today, KDE offers more functionality than CDE.

The KDE project is being developed by several hundred enthusiasts from all over the world. The complete KDE code is made available under the LGPL/GPL (GNU Public License) licenses. This license allows anyone to modify and distribute KDE code freely, under the condition that it remains free of charge.

Although X11 is very powerful, there is a need for KDE, because users want a common feeling for all platforms. X11 does not have a common drag-and-drop protocol, meaning that different applications provide different means and processes for drag-and-drop. The desktop configuration cannot be done through an easy-to-use, dialog-based interface. Another problem is that there is no unified application help system, which is common for Mac or Windows operating systems.

KDE overcomes these problems and offers some great new features. The desktop can be easily adjusted to the wishes of the customer through so-called themes. Besides many newly invented themes, it is possible to install a Windows 95 or MacOS theme, giving UNIX applications the look and feel of a Windows PC or Apple Macintosh computer. Although this may seem like a toy for UNIX users, it will help newcomers become accustomed to the new operating system. A consistent feel and look also makes it easier to learn new applications. Menus, toolbars, keybindings, and color schemes, for example, are standardized. KDE is fully localized and available already in more than 25 languages. Any application that runs on X11 will also run on KDE, but to

---

[27] http://www.kde.org/
[28] http://www.x.org/
[29] http://www.freebsd.org/
[30] http://www.netbsd.org/
[31] http://www.linux.org/

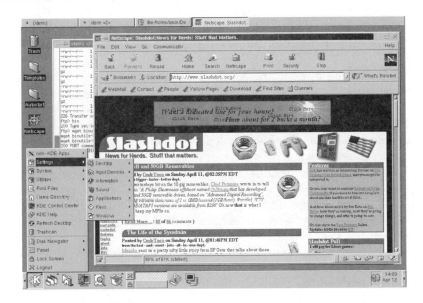

Figure 15.1. KDE Desktop running on HP-UX.

exploit the possibilities of KDE, more applications appear that run exclusively on KDE, such as an Office Suite.

In Figure 15.1, you can see KDE running on a computer equipped with HP-UX 10.20 and nicely replacing the CDE desktop.

15.3.4   The Mozilla Browser

In January 1998, Netscape made two announcements that changed the browser market. From then on, the Netscape browser was free of charge and at the same time, the source code of Netscape Communicator was released to the general public. These two announcements came out of Netscape's desperate attempt to survive in the browser war against Microsoft. The decrease in market share was stopped and new, more stable browser versions have been released since then.

When Netscape announced the release of the browser source code, the Swiss newspaper *Neue Zürcher Zeitung (NZZ)*[32] called this a new type of software communism. The newspaper meant communism in its negative sense of being a dictatorship in which everyone received little, but almost for free. Free software has nothing to do with communism, but deals with the freedom of the individuals to do whatever they like with a piece of software. Although the wording may be a bit strange, it showed the general change in attitude regarding software. Newspapers like the *NZZ* that were not interested in free

---

[32]http://www.nzz.ch/online/01_nzz_aktuell/internet/internet1998/nzz980306kommunismus.htm

software suddenly became very interested in this new development. Interest increased not only in Mozilla, but also in other open source or free software projects.

To coordinate the work on the source code, Netscape sponsored a Web site[33] and named the open source effort "the Mozilla Browser," which opened in March 1998. The mission of the Web site was to allow the product to grow and mature and continue to be useful and innovative. The various changes made by disparate developers across the Web needed to be collated, organized, and brought together as a cohesive whole.

Unlike other open source efforts, in which the originating company retreats from the development, Netscape created a special Mozilla division that was chartered to act as a clearing house for the newly available Netscape source. The Mozilla people from Netscape are the code integrators. The Mozilla organization provided a central point of contact and community for those interested in using or improving the source code. Those behind the Mozilla organization collect changes, help to synchronize the work of the submitting authors, and release the source code on the Web site.

Mailing lists and discussion forums have been set up in order to speed up development and allow the exchange of ideas between the developers. The Mozilla organization tries to help people reach consensus and steer them in the right direction, by coordinating the efforts of the different developer communities. The Web site contains roadmaps to the code, coordinates bug lists, and keeps track of the work in progress.

The open source project lead by Netscape is trying to base its principles on the bazaar style proposed by Eric Raymond, discussed earlier in this chapter. The development is done in a distributed manner, while the integration is done at a central point, the Mozilla Web site.

Netscape calls its system a meritocracy—the more code participants contribute, the more responsibility they will gain. Becoming a member of the team is simple: just write some code. The code is then reviewed by the Mozilla core team, who decides if the code can be included into the source tree or not.

Figure 15.2 shows a version 0.9.6 of the Mozilla browser. The displayed version was compiled on November 20, 2001 and is nearly finished. Version 1.0 is expected to be released in early 2002.

Although Mozilla is not (yet) the market leader in 2001 as some have predicted, it has changed the browser market significantly. Mozilla has produced many offsprings, the most famous probably being Netscape 6 and Konquest. The browser market has become more diverse than ever before, offering users more and better choices and increasing the general adoption of standards in a much faster way.

---

[33]http://www.mozilla.org/

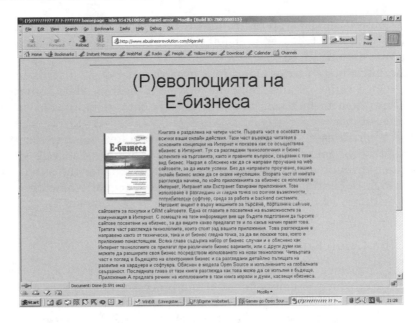

Figure 15.2. Mozilla 0.9.6, Bulgarian E-Business (R)Evolution Home Page.

15.3.5   The Ohaha System

One of the hottest topics on the Internet are P2P networks and applications (see also Chapter 9). Propelled by the rapid proliferation of higher-bandwidth, always-on connections in people's homes (through DSL and cable modems), the Internet's topology is changing to enable a new class of network applications and services: They are called "peer-to-peer" and use everyone's computing devices (not just traditional PCs) as servers, in addition to their conventional use as application clients.

Most P2P systems remain incomplete in key parts, lacking scalability, or simply without end-user implementation that is sufficiently easy to use to be of wider appeal. In particular, one such system, Gnutella is a decentralized, file-sharing protocol that is still in an early development stage, with certain key scalability issues not being addressed yet, lacking an efficient search algorithm, and having no systematic way of managing index information. Another, Freenet, is a distributed, file-storage effort that is big on anonymity, but rather thin on elementary functions such as querying.

The Ohaha System[34] is an open-source architecture that takes decentralized data sharing to the next level by combining the simplicity of the Gnutella approach with certain key redundant, data-caching ideas from the Freenet system. But it adds a protocol for managing index information and collections as

---

[34]http://www.ohaha.com/

first-class objects in the system. To make the system more scalable, a smart algorithm for data distribution and indexing has been added to efficiently manage data in a decentralized way.

Ohaha introduces a set of algorithms used in "queryless" distributed proxy caching, which relies on an intelligent method of hashing data, queries, and index information to locations in a way that is both globally consistent and locally computable.

These algorithms make searching much faster, requiring one step to data access, instead of going through a Gnutella-style crawling search, which requires going through all connected devices and checking for the availability of a certain file. Updating the virtual global index is equally efficient through these algorithms.

15.3.6   The Open Firmware ROM Code

The Open Firmware (OF) initiative provides nonproprietary open standard boot firmware, which is independent of the processor or bus type. The specification defines a device interface, which allows peripheral cards to identify themselves and uses a boot driver that works on any CPU supported by the OF initiative. To facilitate programming, a user interface is provided that allows powerful scripting and debugging. An API (Application Programming Interface) has been developed that allows the operating systems and their loaders to make use of services provided by OF to assist in the configuration and initialization process.

Although the firmware is only a small piece of software within the computer, the computer would not do anything without it. Therefore, it is very important, and several companies have started implementing the OF specifications. One such company is FirmWorks[35] in Mountain View, California. The FirmWorks solution provides a processor-independent configuration and booting support for plug-in devices. The ANS Forth interpreter is used for programming, debugging, and configuration. A range of drivers is already included in the package, and a framework for creating new drivers is included.

15.3.7   The OpenPGP Cryptography Framework

OpenPGP[36] software uses a combination of strong public-key and symmetric cryptography to provide security services for electronic communications and data storage. These services include confidentiality, key management, authentication, and digital signatures. The standard is defined in an RFC (request for comment), which is "the Internet way" of openly publishing new standards. All basic standards, such as mailing, news, and HTTP, are available as RFCs.

---

[35]http://www.firmworks.com/
[36]http://www.ietf.org/rfc/rfc2440.txt

The idea for OpenPGP was born after Phil Zimmermann released his program, PGP, which allowed the encryption and signature of files. The OpenPGP project tries to implement these ideas in a public standard, so that anyone is able to create programs based on the OpenPGP standard to exchange encrypted information with other applications. The OpenPGP standard describes the encryption/decryption, and the complete infrastructure necessary to operate. OpenPGP is based on PGP 5.x.

15.3.8 The OpenSSL Toolkit

OpenSSL[37] was started as a response to the commercial implementations of the SSL protocol. OpenSSL is a robust, full featured toolkit for secure sockets layer (SSL versions 2 and 3) and transport layer security (TLS version 1). The source code is available and is based on the open source paradigm. It provides a full-strength cryptography for the whole world, because it has been developed outside of the United States and does not need an export license from the United States.

Volunteers from all around the world are working on the OpenSSL project and use the Internet to communicate, plan, and develop the toolkit and the documentation related to the project. The OpenSSL project is based on SSLeay, which is a library for including support for the SSL protocol into any program.

The project is managed by a small core team of developers that coordinate the efforts of the OpenSSL community.

15.3.9 The Zope Web Application Platform

Zope[38] is an object-based, open source Web application platform, which allows powerful, high-performing, and dynamic Web applications to be easily built. It uses an integrated object database, which provides a facility for servicing content managers and Web application developers.

The Zope architecture competes with commercial products, such as Cold Fusion,[39] Netscape's Application Server, and SilverStream.[40] But unlike products aimed at systems programmers and relational databases, Zope uses a scripting model and the built-in object-oriented database.

The Zope platform consists of several components, namely the Z Publisher, which provides a means for publishing objects, and integrates with common Web servers using a number of protocols, such as Zope's Persistent CGI. In addition to the Z Publisher, the Z Framework exists, which contains the foundation for the environment and built-in objects such as folders, documents, and images.

---

[37] http://www.openssl.org/
[38] http://www.zope.org/
[39] http://www.coldfusion.com/
[40] http://www.silverstream.com/

Dynamic page generation is handled through the Z Template system. The integrated Z Object Database is able to handle large volumes of files and is tightly integrated with the object model of Zope. The Z SQL Methods and Z Database Adapters provide the integration of the object-oriented data in relational SQL servers.

Unlike many other software products presented here, Zope was not created by some people in their free time, but by a company called Digital Creations.[41] The product was a commercial product with a price tag before the company decided to move from being a product company to a consulting company. Digital Creations offered two versions of their software: Bobo, a free, open source toolkit for Web-object applications, and Principia, which is its commercial cousin. These products were maintained in different groups, splitting the engineering efforts. In an effort to consolidate the two software projects, the company found that the real value of the product could be better exploited by joining the best features of both products and releasing the new software for free.

At the beginning, there was resistance within the company because the value of the intellectual property of the software was considered an important asset to the company. But it was not hard to convince the critics that open source can actually increase the value of the company, because it brings some advantages. By marking the well-known software as open source, the user base can be multiplied within little time, which leads to a better-known brand. This leads to more activities in the consulting area and an increased valuation of the company.

By moving the product to open source, it became available for more platforms and could be easily extended by other people, adding more capabilities much faster and with fewer errors. By fostering a product community, an army of messengers was created, which extended the marketing of the product (and the consulting as well) and made it more pervasive.

The investment in releasing the source code of the application made it easier for the company to grow, because it could spend less on engineering and marketing and put more efforts into building up a consulting force. Another important issue for customers of such a small company was the longevity of the software lifecycle. By placing it in the open source community, the software could live forever, and by supporting an open source community, the company is able to add technologies much faster.

By moving to open source, Zope has established itself as an alternative to Cold Fusion, which had previously dominated the market. There truly was no other way for Zope to get so much market share in such short time and with such little investment.

---

[41] http://www.digitalcreations.com/

15.4   Moving Your Company from Products to Services

15.4.1   Supporting the Software

As we have seen in the Zope example, open source software does not automatically mean that a company cannot profit. Although the companies behind the open source software are not always very well known, they provide the missing parts that make the software project a product. In the early years of the software business, the software was the core product to sell, but now the prices are dropping, and more companies are releasing the source code, because it becomes too complex to maintain within their own company.

The major advantage for software developers in the open source arena is that they can freely create their software without having to cope with support for customers and can concentrate on the program. But the major issue preventing companies from using free software is that no matter how good a product is, if no 24-hour support is available, they are very reluctant to use it. Internet-born software has lots of support, but this support differs from the traditional software support, where you can call someone for one-on-one guidance.

Newsgroups and online chats offer great support to the free software communities. You can ask a question, and within a few hours, you will most likely have the answer to your problem. In many cases, you may even have the answer to a problem that has not occurred yet. Web pages with in-depth information, FAQs, and other resources offer everything a customer may need. But the support cannot be guaranteed. Basically, no one and everyone is responsible for your receiving an answer to your question, and this is not well received by companies using certain products. Still, Cygnus Software[42] offers support, documentation, and customization for software that is released under the GNU public license, and Red Hat Software[43] offers technical support for the Linux operating system. Both companies charge for support and services around the software.

15.4.2   Improving the Software

As a result of Cygnus' efforts, for example, the GNU C Compiler was adapted to other CPU architectures and brought back into the original source code stream in order to provide a sound basis for the core product. However, Cygnus is the only one making money from the adaptation by delivering not only the adaptation, but also the knowledge that is required for support. The open source community has nothing against profit, as long as it comes from add-on value that these companies provide and distribute for free.

Apache is creating business for several companies. The commercial version

---

[42]http://www.cygnus.com/
[43]http://www.redhat.com/

of Apache called Stronghold, developed by C2Net,[44] is one offspring of Apache. The company combines the free Web server Apache with the free SSL software SSleay, to create a secure Web server and the necessary infrastructure around it. A Web-based administration part, scripting, an integrated search engine, and digital certificates have been added by C2Net. The company also developed support for SSL v3, integrated it into Stronghold, and then gave the source back to the developers of SSleay, which had developed only the code to support SSL v2.

Organic Online,[45] another company led by one of the chief developers of the Apache team, provides Web site services to large customers using Apache as the core product.

Caldera[46] is a company in the Linux business that integrates software and creates a simplified administration interface for Linux. Instead of selling Linux to customers, Caldera provides solutions for different market segments. It is possible to buy a server with the software (such as a Web server, DNS server, and mail server) preintegrated for Web hosting, or a general purpose workstation with Netscape Communicator and WordPerfect preinstalled.

15.4.3   Integrating the Software

Netscape is using Open Directory on its portal. Instead of investing in resources to build up the directory, it uses the free time of the people on the Internet. This lowers the investments for the company while providing a useful service for free. Anyone can get the data behind the open directory and include it in their own site. Anyone who wants to provide a portal can use the data and extend the service section.

The latest to profit from open source software are the hardware companies. In late 1998 and early 1999, almost all large computer manufacturers in the Wintel (Microsoft Windows/Intel) world announced their support of Linux as an alternative operating system. The most prominent examples are Corel Computer[47] (a division of the software developer Corel), which introduced a complete line of computers that exclusively run with Linux, and Hewlett-Packard, which introduced a 24-hour support hotline for Linux. These and other companies responded to the market by offering the open operating system on their existing hardware. More reasons for introducing Linux: There is no charge for a license for the operating system, and development for hardware drives was done by third-party companies without financial support from the hardware vendors.

---

[44]http://www.c2.net/

[45]http://www.organic.com/

[46]http://www.caldera.com/

[47]http://www.corel.com/

15.4.4   Problems with Open Source

But there are also problems with the open source paradigm. Caldera, for example, has access only to the integration, but no influence on the implementation of the underlying software. If a bug appears in the operating system and breaks down the service on one or more of the installed computer bases, Caldera can only submit a bug report to the Linux community and hope that the bug will be resolved. The same applies to the introduction of new hardware devices. Caldera is not in the position to write drivers for new hardware devices, so it must wait until the Linux community responds to the request. There is no way to be proactive without investing in developers who know the source code and are able to react in the case of an emergency. But this is still cheaper than maintaining the whole source code.

On the Internet, the cost of replicating software is zero, and protecting programs has become almost impossible. Therefore, more companies are releasing their software as open source. If the Internet community accepts the open source philosophy, it guarantees the software product a long life, while companies are able to provide the services around the core product. Because the services are individual to the customer, the companies are able to charge more per customer, and software pirates have no means of copying the services.

Netscape retains some control over its software by actively contributing to its development and providing the forum, but other open source projects, such as Linux, are developed totally independent of any company and provide their own funding for the infrastructure.

A company that wants to release a program's source code to the public needs to be aware that just releasing the source code isn't enough. Someone may pick it up, rip off some of the code, and use it for something else. But this is not the expected result for the company that released the code. Keeping control over the source code is essential in developing a high-quality software product.

15.4.5   Releasing New Open Source

The reasons for releasing the code can be manifold. In Netscape's case, it was necessary to improve the quality of the program and to stabilize the market share of the browser software. Other companies may be forced to release the source code because the people who knew the source code left the company or it is no longer strategic to improve the code. Other open source software is developed by employees in their free time and then placed on the Internet for everyone's benefit and used to build new services within the company.

To make the open source project work it is necessary to set up a Web site, newsgroups, and mailing lists. Software for code management and bug tracking is also necessary. All the required software can be found for free on the Internet, so the investment is not very high. In addition to the installation of software and hardware, processes need to be set up to allow developers to retrieve the code and submit the changes.

If the infrastructure is not in place, the project will fail. In addition to the infrastructure, it is necessary to electrify the community and support them in the first phase to get the open source project up and running. If the program has a base of developers who use it to develop services on top of the program, then they can be invited to embrace the source code and continue development. If the program is designed for end users without developers in between, someone should be nominated to lead the effort—either someone who is working on a similar product or someone from within the company.

15.5   Introduction to Open Hardware

15.5.1   Differences between Open Hardware and Open Software

Open hardware is the logical extension of open source software. Unlike software, hardware is much more difficult to reproduce. Hardware companies spend billions of dollars for the construction of new chip production plants. For that reason, it would appear that few people would invest time in creating open hardware. But my investigations on the Internet proved this reasoning wrong. Actually, there are many projects in progress.

Like software, hardware requires more time upfront to design a new product and only a small percentage to distribute it afterward. To develop a successful open hardware project, all the requirements of the open source are valid, but depending on the type of hardware, it is necessary to find a partner who will be able to reproduce the hardware design. Typically, universities and research institutes provide the facilities for the test phase, and commodity manufacturers provide a forum for mass reproduction.

The first step will most likely be to create virtual hardware that runs on existing hardware and can be used to verify the design and start to implement applications for that particular hardware, because it is always difficult to convince someone to use a certain hardware product if no applications are available. On the other hand, the application designers won't start programming if no one buys the hardware.

Like software, hardware is always designed using software that speaks a hardware description language, such as VHDL[48] or Verilog.[49] These products allow not only design, but also circuit testing before they are prototyped or produced.

The problems begin after testing. To verify the correctness of the chip design, it is necessary to create a physical representation of the design to create benchmarks and allow bug tests. This requires a partner. Fortunately, most universities already have the capability to produce basic circuit boards, and many are able to create circuit boards of a higher complexity. Students involved in an open hardware project are able to use these facilities to create the

---

[48]http://www.vhdl.com/
[49]http://www.verilog.com/

necessary hardware.

Examples of open hardware projects could be the following. Special chips that support hardware acceleration of certain applications could be created. An open-design kit could be created, which has several interfaces that connect an FPGA (field-programmable gate array) board with your computer. Specially designed compression/decompression and encryption/decryption chips could be implemented. General-purpose processors could also be the target of open hardware developers. Signal processors to support audio applications, such as speech recognition and music synthesis, could also be targeted by the hardware developers.

15.5.2   Open Hardware Projects

The Common Hardware Reference Platform

The common hardware reference platform (CHRP) architecture specification provides hardware-to-software interface definitions. Although the chips are based on the PowerPC processor architecture (which is copyrighted), the interface definitions are free. Though the PowerPC microprocessor is the most widely used RISC processor, substantial legacy software exists and a mechanism for running the major part of this legacy software is a requirement. The system address map has been defined with a specific objective of assisting efficient x86 emulation. Additionally, the PowerPC microprocessors support Bi-Endian operation, which is a key attribute important to running the supported operating systems and applications.

An important feature of the architecture is the ability to freely implement below the designed interfaces through device drivers, the use of open firmware, a runtime abstraction service (RTAS), and a hardware abstraction layer (HAL).

The idea of the architecture is to combine leading-edge technologies to create a superior computing platform by supporting a wide range of computing needs. The goal is that as many operating systems as possible are able to run on this system. The architecture was developed with support for legacy hardware without restricting itself to it. It helps protect the customer's investment while moving on to a more advanced computing platform. Systems based on this architecture are expected to offer price/performance advantages and to address the expected growth in computing performance and functionality.

Apple was the first to implement the CHRP architecture in its PowerMac product line. By opening up its systems, standard peripherals could be used more easily, but before the first system was due to appear, Apple changed its mind, and remained with its proprietary architecture. In August 1999, IBM released an open-source CHRP board to support the PowerPC-Linux community. Although IBM does not sell the boards, it enabled third-party vendors to build dedicated Linux computers based on the PowerPC chip, which is built by IBM.

The Freedom CPU

The first chip developed in the Freedom CPU line is the F1-CPU. Freedom, as the architecture is called, can be used in the GNU/GPL sense, in which you are free to take the design and masks and manufacture your own chips. The developers of the F1-CPU opposed the idea of calling it O-CPU (where "O" stands for open), as requested by some people, because they do not like the definition of open source. They prefer to be part of the original free software (and hardware) movement, making it rather difficult to use it in commercial products.

The basic idea of the F1-CPU is to create a RISC processor with increased performance. To solve performance issues, it is necessary to remove bottlenecks, such as the context switch latency, caused by saving and restoring register sets. The F1-architecture provides near-zero context switch latencies by providing a memory-to-memory architecture as opposed to the register-to-register architecture implemented by many RISC processors.

The design of the F1-CPU will have an external floating point unit (FPU) due to space restrictions on the die. The sequel chip F2, which will be implemented in a higher density will most likely have four FPUs on the die working in parallel.

To support multiple processors working together, the Freedom CPU team opted to implement a NUMA-style multiprocessing architecture, which allows both shared memory and message-passing. Symmetric multiprocessing (SMP) as used by Intel is not supported, because it creates a new bottleneck.

The goal of the F1-CPU is to provide an alternative to the upcoming Merced processor. Although the F1-CPU will run at lower clock rates than Merced, it will be faster because of optimizations on the chip and in software (especially compilers). It is expected that integer performance will be comparable to or better than the Merced. FPU performance will basically depend on the number of FPUs plugged into the CPU bus. With two FPUs, the F1 will probably provide better performance than the Merced. With four FPUs, it should be much faster than the Merced.

Linux will be the first operating system to run on the F1-CPU with other operating systems following later on. A Linux port is being developed at the same time as the F1-CPU development.

Open Design Circuits

The ideas for the open design circuits (ODC)[50] architecture have not been implemented so far, but present a typical approach to open hardware. ODC chip designs are openly shared among developers and users, similar to the open source software. The ODC approach captures the advantages of open-source software and applies them to hardware. The approach by ODC avoids the large

---

[50]http://circu.its.tudelft.nl/

initial investments usually needed for hardware development, and it allows for the rapid design sharing, testing, and user feedback that are key to open-source software success.

ODC offers an approach that differs quite a bit from other open-design hardware initiatives. They resemble more closely open source software. Open design circuits are very close to reality, even though no development community exists for them at the time of this writing.

The fabrication costs of chips are particularly high for the relatively small quantities needed for development versions. Also problematic are the long fabrication delays and the effort required to get test boards working on many sites. And manufacturers are very secretive about their fabrication processes and cell libraries, while documentation is necessary to create open-source design tools.

The reason the initiators chose the name "open design circuits" over "open design hardware" is that the latter term is too general. The ODC approach is specific to designing digital circuits for chips. Writing device drivers for existing hardware or creating new motherboard designs are not part of the initiative.

To avoid the above mentioned problems, there are two fairly obvious alternatives to manufacturing. A simulator is often used to test a design. By distributing the simulator and the design and masks as open-source software, it is possible to simulate the results and detect logical errors. The problem arises when it comes to performance testing. A simulator does not offer the possibilities to test the amount of time a certain program needs to execute, because the simulator is bound to the underlying hardware and software.

Field programmable gate arrays (FPGAs) provide an interesting alternative, because they contain large numbers of programmable logic blocks (logic gates and registers) and a programmable interconnect. These chips are like typical gate array chips and can be programmed without the need for a wafer processing plant. SRAM FPGAs are interesting for ODC development, because the configuration is stored in RAM on the chip. This enables the developers to re-program the chip simply and fast. When developers using FPGAs have hardware to test, it is possible to measure hardware performance without the need for a large up-front investment by producing silicon wafers. Still FPGAs are relatively expensive for someone who just wants to play around a little bit with a design. By developing open chips over the Internet, prices for FPGA will decrease and the development will take off.

To push the open chip development, it is necessary to create interesting ideas for open design activities, to connect a group of people with the appropriate FPGA hardware, and to create a better price/performance ratio for the hardware to attract more people. Many people have at least basic knowledge in the software area, but few know anything about hardware design and manufacturing.

Several technical issues need to be addressed in order to spread the ODC initiatives. Because the ODC initiatives use FPGA devices, it is necessary to rely on some important properties. The devices should have an open specification to connect them to the design tools that may be written by the initiative. The devices should be robust and not break with design mistakes. Portability is also an issue; in order to make designs portable, the hardware should not use proprietary extensions that would cause the design to break on a future hardware device.

The development process for ODC is divided into several phases, which are also common in open source software. A small group of people connects over the Internet to build a virtual community that sets the goals for the open design tools, data formats, and hardware. They set up a Web site that promotes their activity and create newsgroups and mailing lists for technical and administrative discussions. Before starting the design, this group selects tools and integrates them into a basic package that every interested developer can download from the Web page. If the required tools are not available, then the team will evaluate the effort for developing a new tool or changing the design. After the tools and the design have been decided on, the appropriate FPGA devices are selected for initial development.

With the information and better open design tools available, more people will be joining the initiative and working on comprehensive design libraries and large designs. As soon as interesting designs become available, more people will begin buying FPGA boards, and testing and improving the designs.

Universities and smaller companies will then come on board and use the tools and designs in courses, in-house applications, and even in product development. These low-cost solutions won't replace the mainstream hardware, but will find many niches where they can play an important role. A new type of consultant will emerge: the open design circuit consultant. On the hardware side, FPGA manufacturers and ODC initiatives will try to improve the performance of the hardware.

After the solutions have matured and become comparable to commercial offerings, the open design community will have established a movement with a large number of designers, and larger corporations will integrate the open technology into their own products.

Although these ideas are still wishful thinking, they could become reality. Just as Linux is becoming more important than some commercial operating systems, the same could happen to an open design chip.

15.5.3 The Open Hardware Certification Program

The Open Hardware Certification Program[51] is for hardware manufacturers who would like to certify their hardware devices as open. This means that a manufacturer promises to make available a set of documents for programming device-driver interfaces for the particular hardware device.

Although this does not guarantee that a driver will be available for every

---

[51]http://www.openhardware.org/

piece of hardware, it will ensure that people who are interested in writing a driver will have the resources to do so. Hardware manufacturers can go through a simple self-certification procedure and use the open hardware logo on their packaging.

Although the certification program does not ensure the development of new hardware or access to the design documents of the chip, it allows anyone to access the functionality of the hardware. This makes it accessible for open source programs, such as Linux (which has a constant lack of drivers), because many companies only develop drivers for Windows.

15.5.4 The Open Hardware Specification Project

The Open Hardware Specification Project (OHSpec) is an attempt to respond to the hegemony of Wintel (Microsoft Windows/Intel). Its goal is to create a truly free and open hardware design to compensate for the decreasing impact of alternative architectures on the market, such as the Sun and SGI chip architecture for low-end workstations.

OHSpec does not try to attempt to license or register hardware components whose interfaces are available publicly, such as the open hardware certification program, but to create a new computing platform as an alternative to the existing platforms. It will be released under a variation of the GNU General Public License, adapted to hardware projects.

The OHSpec project tries to create a new hardware design from scratch, which requires dedication and hard work. The goal is to overcome the limits and design flaws of the current computers. The design tries to integrate with existing hardware without restricting itself to these paradigms. If a choice must be made between support for existing hardware compatibility and introducing a better hardware paradigm, the OHSpec will choose the latter.

To let as many people as possible participate in the project, the most important design principle is simplicity, in order to constantly extend and improve the OHSpec platform. The OHSpec team is still in its early stages and is trying to define how far they want to break away from current hardware designs and which standards will be used to implement the system.

Other than software development, hardware manufacturing is not a cost-free venture. Therefore, some sort of funding must be established to maintain a supply of necessary components. OHSpec wants its funds controlled by a nonprofit organization, such as the Free Software Foundation. Funds could conceivably come from printed documentation, production of reference platforms, or support from research and industry.

Development is organized via the Web site and mailing lists that let developers exchange ideas and information.

15.6   Outlook into the Future

The future of free software looks promising. More companies offer the source code of their programs for free, and some new programs are directly developed for free. The move to free software and hardware is a move away from the Industrial Age to the Information Age, where money is made in services such as customizing and consulting and not so much in product sales.

Prices for software replication have dropped to zero with the introduction of the Internet, and prices are dropping constantly for hardware replication. In the ideal world, both hardware and software will be free in the future and people will offer their services for free. As the ideal world is unlikely to happen, we will still have to pay for most hardware and software in the future, but with fierce competition from activists for free products.

Currently the free product movements are not well coordinated. In the near future, the open source and free software movements will grow, but won't form a uniform industry. Although the basic idea is similar, the implementation of a free product is diverse.

Free hardware will be boosted by new inventions that make replication an easy and low-cost operation. The lower the cost for a certain piece of hardware and the more standardized the hardware is, the more services can be run on top of it and the larger the market for such services and solutions is.

Vertical open source portals, such as Mozilla.org or Linux.com, and horizontal open source portals, such as SourceXChange,[52] will become more important in the future. SourceXChange, for example, is designed to let companies tap into the pool of open-source programmers while letting those developers get paid for their efforts.

The Web site lets programmers bid for projects that companies don't want to do on their own. Companies can offer a variety of compensation, including cash or free equipment, and the resulting software will be released to the open-source community. Projects will have formal schedules and milestones, and will eliminate some of the remaining excuses people have for not using the open-source development model.

SourceXChange is hosted by O'Reilly and Associates[53] and will be backed by Hewlett-Packard and other companies. O'Reilly will get a part of the proceeds that change hands, similar to the online auction Web site, eBay,[54] which receives a fraction of every transaction. The developers and the organizations sponsoring the research will be able to rate each other. In the near future, we will see other similar initiatives coming up on the Internet.

---

[52]http://www.sourcexchange.com/
[53]http://www.ora.com/
[54]http://www.ebay.com/

Chapter 16

PERVASIVE COMPUTING

16.1 Internet Services

16.1.1 Enabling Technologies

Pervasive computing is slowly becoming a reality. The concepts have been available for several years now, and the companies that are driving the Web recognize the value of an extended Internet—a universal network. IBM[1] calls it "The next generation of e-business focusing on the integration and infrastructure complexities of B2B by leveraging the benefits of Internet standards and common infrastructure to produce optimal efficiencies for intra- and inter-enterprise computing."

Some companies already fear the end of personal computer-based computing. The hardware manufacturers can relax; this won't happen, but the growth rates will drop. Not everyone wants to have a personal computer with Windows or MacOS on their desktops. In many cases, people would prefer to connect to the Internet through their mobile phones or TV sets. The Nokia Communicator[2] (see figure 16.1) offers not only Web access, but also email and file transfer capabilities. Many companies have started to provide access to the Internet through so-called set-top boxes, allowing Web content to be viewed on a TV—users compose and send e-mails without having to know about device drivers or DLL files. These Internet appliances have been around for quite a while, but basically they just take the functionality of a PC into another device.

Pervasive computing goes a step further. It not only replicates the standard functionality of the Web into embedded devices, but also offers services provided by the device to other entities on the Internet. The idea is to reap the benefits of ever-broader networks without having to deal with obtuse, unwieldy technology. The first generation of embedded devices were passive, meaning that they relayed existing services to other devices, such as a TV. The second generation of embedded devices is more intelligent and can look for services on the Internet, collect them, and bundle them into a meta-service, such as a

---

[1]http://www.ibm.com/
[2]http://www.nokia.com/

fridge that provides information about its contents.

Today, companies are forced to build their entire offering virtually from scratch. Online businesses have to provide all services required for the complete e-business solution; they cannot easily outsource parts of it, because the integration between components is rather complex.

Amazon.com[3], for example, provides the service of selling books to its customers. All services required for selling books have been implemented by Amazon.com and are maintained by them, making their Web site proprietary, massive, and costly.

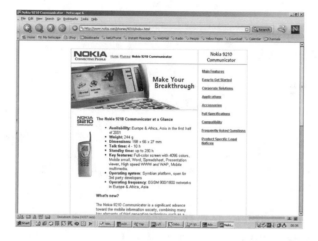

Figure 16.1. Nokia Communicator.

Companies focused in the past on providing customers with solutions that help manage the proliferation of data between the end-user and a business application over any network to any device. From the concepts of screen-scraping and Web clipping to the importance of transcoding content to any device to support the benefits of a thin-client architecture, the emphasis is on front-end interactions.

Inventory management, distribution, billing, and Web store management are all services required by most online retailers in order to implement the service of selling goods on the Internet. Although not part of their core business, these services need to be implemented, maintained, and operated by the online retailer. Next generation online retailers will be able to outsource these services to inventory management, billing, distribution, and Web store management solution providers, who are able to provide these services at a lower price and a better quality.

To make the outsourcing of services feasible on the Internet, every service needs to be able to communicate with the other. The concept of service is, on

---

[3]http://www.amazon.com/

this level, rather abstract. The service of billing can then be further divided into several more simple services. One of them will be physical printing of the bill. The bill is printed on the retailer's local printer and then sent to the customer. The bill could be printed at a local billing office, which reduces the cost of shipment. If the customer's printers have a direct Web connection, the bill could be printed at the customer site, which eliminates the shipping cost for the billing company. Costs could be reduced even further if the bill is entered directly into the company's ERP system and paid automatically.

To make this new paradigm work quickly and efficiently, all levels of service need to be integrated. While the Internet enabled the communication between different services and HTML/XML enabled the data exchange between different services, a new layer needed to be added to enable services to accept other service to connect and create new meta services. This new layer also made it possible to broadcast the availability of a new service to the network.

Because today's networking capabilities are too cumbersome or limited for the next generation of applications that are about to appear, several companies have created technologies that connect everything from light switches to supercomputers in one ubiquitous network. The race is on to create the standard for the next generation of the Internet, and as often happens with high-technology efforts in their infancy, companies will compete to establish their own vision of the universal network.

Sun and its Jini technology are probably the best-known promoters of the universal network, otherwise known as pervasive computing vision. But many other well-known companies have started to create similar technologies and have incorporated the idea of the universal network into their corporate vision. Hewlett-Packard, IBM, Lucent Technologies, and Microsoft have technologies and paradigms available for their customers to take them to the next level of computing, pervasive computing.

This chapter provides an overview of the available technologies and the visions of the companies behind them. The race has just started and it is impossible to say who will win in the end. It may be worth noting that most technologies presented in this chapter are inspired by the *Star Trek* television and film series, and relate to trying to bring part of the 23rd-century Star Trek vision to the beginning of the 21st century.

The technologies are part of the corporate vision or company strategy, so it cannot be expected to spread rapidly throughout the world. The tactical goal of these new technologies is, in most cases, to make the companies developing the software and architecture to appear as innovative as possible, while driving sales of more traditional products such as operating systems, servers, and printers. But the strategic goal will change many current products in the long term.

Companies that use these technologies can reduce time-to-market significantly and reduce costs as well. This allows them to be more mobile, flexible, and modular, and enables them to react more quickly and precisely to changes in the market. These modular services can be used by anyone connected to the Internet. People and companies can combine several modular services to form a new service, or add own components to the service to make it more valuable. Every company becomes both user and provider of services on the Internet.

16.1.2 Business Opportunities

The new paradigm of Internet services allows businesses and consumers to use the Internet as a cost-effective access to a wide range of high-quality, dependable services. Areas will include traditional Internet services such as financial management, procurement, marketing, travel, and data storage, but new digital services will also be created, such as partner collaboration services and health care monitoring.

Therefore, time-to-market is increased, the costs are decreased, and it becomes easier to adapt to market change. These advantages also mean a growing opportunity for businesses to become Internet service providers themselves. Software suppliers, for example, have already started to make their products available on a usage basis over the Internet, rather than through the traditional software licensing model.

Pervasive computing will take the Internet far beyond the one-way Web to a rich, collaborative, interactive environment. Pervasive computing will harness a constellation of applications, services, and devices to create a personalized digital experience. It will constantly and automatically adapt itself to your needs and those of your family, home, and business. It means a whole new generation of software that will work as an integrated service to help you manage your life and work in the Internet Age.

Consumers will experience the simplicity of integrated services; unified browsing, editing, and authoring; access to all your files, work, and media online and off; a holistic experience across devices; personalization everywhere; and zero management. It means, for example, that any change to your information, no matter whether the data resides on your computer, your mobile phone, or your television, will instantly and automatically be available everywhere you need it.

Knowledge workers, people who add value to information, and businesses will benefit from unified browsing platform, editing, and authoring; rich coordinated communication; a seamless mobile experience; and powerful information management and e-commerce tools that will transparently move between internal and Internet-based services, and support a new era of dynamic trading relationships.

Independent software developers will have the opportunity to create advanced new services for the Internet Age—services that are able to automatically access and leverage information either locally or remotely, working with any device or language, without having to rewrite code for each environment. Everything on the Internet becomes a potential building block for this new generation of services, while every application can be exposed as a service on the Internet.

16.1.3 Internet Services Standards

To make Internet services just as successful as the World Wide Web, it is necessary to create standards that are just as widespread and accepted as HTML. The standards include protocols and APIs for accessing and deploying services on the Internet that need to be added to these content-oriented Internet standards.

The standards need to support the core functions of electronic services, such as the description and virtualization of the Internet services. On the Web, catalogues, icons, files, and entire Web pages represent actual products, databases, or organizations. The creation of virtual representations of Web objects is proliferating rapidly, yet there is no one standard. Many of the methods are home-grown or less than functional. A component that virtualizes Web objects lies at the center of many current and new commerce, content, and collaborative services.

To add value to the Internet service, it must support tracking and monitoring of delivery of services and goods. This functionality is crucial to the commercial viability of Internet-based services. It needs to be built into the core components to allow a quick deployment of intelligent Web services. Results can be observed easily, and the quality of service can be guaranteed by making adjustments it to the usage of the service and changes in business and technology.

Another important point that needs to be provided by the core functionality of an electronic service standard is to ensure the security and privacy of the service. A core Internet services platform function needs to support building blocks for rapid security and privacy.

These core functions are provided by an Internet service engine that are required to operate a service on the Internet. They support and integrate with the services and embed core capabilities within the services themselves. It is, for example, possible to create services directories that allow users to track activities, virtualize objects, and identify service components, access types, and participants. By monitoring and adjusting the quality of service, it is possible to guarantee service level agreements (SLA). Another important feature that becomes available instantly is billing. This supports secure transactions and authentication of the participants. By giving service customers and service providers tools for the interaction, they are able to negotiate service level agreements and transactions. This also allows access to be virtualized.

Virtualization means that a service, such as a file, that you want to be visible to certain people gets a virtual name on the computer of every person who is allowed to view it. The source name and target name are different, making it possible to move the original location of the file without having to change the name at the destination or even notify users of the change.

16.1.4 Moving Applications to the Web

The first step in pervasive computing has already taken place. More services and applications are now available on the Web. Online email and calendar services are very popular and will become the standard in the near future. By putting these services onto the Web, any device that contains a Web browser can be used to access these services. People using a cell phone, a handheld PDA, a notebook, and a desktop computer are all able to access email, for example, from any place.

The problem is that not all files are currently on the Web. A text written in Star Office, for example, is saved in most cases on a local hard disk and is not available from other computers or embedded devices. By moving applications such as word processors to the Web, the files can be easily saved on a Web server. This allows customers to access their data from any Internet-enabled device.

Moving a word processor to the Web is no trivial task, so companies are looking for other ways to access documents distributed all over the place through a Web interface. FusionOne[4], for example, has built an Internet-based technology that recognizes and updates information across a personal network of unrelated devices of different sizes and platforms. A traveler using an Internet-connected kiosk, for instance, could call up FusionOne's site and access documents that reside in that personal network.

FusionOne has developed a software called Internet Sync, which allows customers to indicate which files they want to access on their personal network and allows the seamless synchronization of the digital information. Internet Sync allows customers to access the most recent updates to almost any file on their own personal hard drive back at the office, including word processing documents, spreadsheets, MP3 music files, browser cookies, as well as calendar and contact information. This allows content to be moved to any device the customer is using at the moment. However, it does not allow the user to move applications.

While sharing files over the network is fine, it does not help to have a certain image file if the device you are using at the moment is not able to display or change the image. Pushing applications to the screen of any device will require changing the paradigm of programming to allow for automatic detection of the capabilities of embedded devices. A framework for programming applications for different devices needs to be established, as does a standard to allow the creation of such an application without creating additional overhead for the programmer.

---

[4]http://www.fusionone.com/

16.1.5 Open Internet Services

By using open standards, businesses can offer their Internet-based services to as many people as possible. At the same time, the single service can be combined to work together with other services to create an even more valuable feature. Service providers will also benefit because the costs of standards-based products are lower. The emerging standards are described later in this chapter.

In the past, clear standards have not been available as to providing the core functionality for Internet services. Putting an additional layer on top of traditional standards, such as HTML, will not help the effectiveness of the proposed services and will make them dependent on these other standards. The new standards should propose a way to provide the basic features without requiring intensive technology engineering to shield the user from the pain of learning proprietary solutions.

Although the Internet and Web are clearly based on layered protocols, the profusion of non-standard technology and engineering to adapt proprietary solutions to generic usability are all-too-familiar themes within the computer industry. The Web's accelerated growth and continued success continues to be an opportunity to change industry patterns. In fact, the rapid pace of adoption often rules out time to specify the complex solutions of the past. New services have to be deployed instantly. They must be created with the assurance that core functions will be in place to support them.

By deploying a standard-based Internet service solution, customers will experience a more valuable and more personalized service, while businesses will be able to provide more efficient and mission-critical services to their customers without having an overhead on complex technologies. Service providers can create new services more quickly, because the core functionality is already provided. These new standards will drive more traffic to the electronic services, as more people are able to use and find it, and will allow faster, lower-cost deployment of value-added services with partners or independently.

The ultimate goal of pervasive computing is making service the prime directive on the Internet, while extending it to reach out for devices that were previously not connected. Several companies have started to build technologies and visions to reach this goal, and the rest of this chapter explains which company has already done what and how they have implemented their visions.

16.2 Programming Models

16.2.1 Introduction

For devices to communicate with each other, it is necessary to create a whole new environment. Part of this environment is also a new programming paradigm that allows all devices to share information and services. Some of the most important issues around pervasive or nomadic programming are described in this section.

There are a number of ways to connect these devices, but depending on what you want to do, different approaches should be taken. First, it is important to find out whether a certain device is used to display information only or whether it is part of the service chain—providing services to other devices and to humans. Another important factor to consider is whether a device is connected constantly to a network or only when necessary. If the second is true, it needs to contain some memory to review cached data. Displaying information is one of the first problems that must be resolved. Most devices do not provide a 1024×768 resolution, as most computers provide today. Handhelds provide a 40×20 resolution, and a television displays at 736×512 pixels. To display the information correctly, it is necessary to create a device-independent data model that can serve all existing and future devices. By having such a model, we not only support current devices, but also older models with very limited display capabilities. Therefore, the end-user does not need to buy the latest version of all devices, but can use adapters for older devices to view the same content. This device-independent device model requires an intelligent, render-device-oriented translation mechanism to provide the optimal output for all devices. This translation mechanism is called transcoding.

The problem is simple to express, but difficult to resolve. In the past, most applications were written for a certain target system, and no one cared about running them on other systems. But in the world of pervasive computing, all business-processing systems should be as deployment transparent as possible. If the consumer accesses a system via a connected computer or a Web browser with high resolution and rich color, we want to take advantage of that. Conversely, if the access to the systems is via a voice recognition system or a palm-computing device, the service should take advantage of the strengths of that computing device. The most important feature is to provide transparency of access in computing systems. Most companies understand that a Web presence is not enough to survive in today's digital jungle. Many companies have started to provided WAP access to their services, along with a call center. These additional channels to their service have been costly. But based on a new application paradigm, this cost can be greatly reduced in the future.

One of the easiest ways of achieving this level of presentation independence is the use of XML, XSL, and HTML/DHTML. This type of independence would move the presentational elements to the client device, with the more advanced mechanisms providing a level of client-side edit checking and list selection. The various client-side rendering technologies are responsible for both presentation and simple edit checking. Instead of concentrating on the rendering for newer devices that support context rendering via XML, XSL and HTML/DHTML, the focus can shift to providing a rendering engine for older devices that may need to be part of the service chain. The integration of new devices is easy, if the above-mentioned standards are used.

DHTML can define a presentation layout that rivals that of traditional client/server computing and execute it within a browser frame. If our pervasive device is capable of this type of rendering and processing, this is a powerful way of extending application functionality to the focused device. Many DHTML-aware devices allow you to work off-line, drawing content from the browser's page cache. This would allow for a limited form of roaming with the portable device. Although far from perfect, it is a first step toward a pervasive environment.

A rich component specification will help this scenario greatly. It could be used as input to a transcoding engine for use as a template in defining the source material. By modeling the specifications using advanced UML concepts, you can export those specifications via one of the XML-based UML schema expressions such as XMI.

This makes it possible to convert the component specification into a machine-readable format. Therefore, the transcoding engine (transcoder) is able to understand the format and the behavior of the interfaces and their operations. If a device service is interested in executing operations of a given interface only and viewing the results, there is little additional work to do.

If the portable device is better served by the implementation of more involved processes, then script code can be written to execute on the application or Web server(s) to facilitate the collaboration of multiple operations or components, with the results provided to the transcoding engine in an expressive fashion.

Previous programming models have focused on a single system, even attempting to mask interactions with other systems to look like local interactions. Pervasive computing technologies need to be explicitly designed to allow the integration or orchestration of any group of resources on the Internet into a single solution. With today's technologies, this type of integration is extremely complex and costly. New programming models will have to make all software development intrinsic, because the solutions of the future require an integrated approach.

16.2.2   Manufactured component objects

Most devices will not be permanently online, so a more powerful programming model is required. This means that bandwidth and connections are reduced to a minimum, and the device becomes network transient. This allows the user to roam freely, meaning that the user is no longer restricted by wires or certain mobility providers. To support free roaming, a richly specified component-based solution becomes an especially powerful ally.

Component-based development requires a formal separation of specification and implementation. If this can be achieved, a device using a certain component may utilize any implementation of this component knowing that every implementation in the world adhering to the given specification would be feature-compatible with each other. The user could move around the world with access to the same services.

This means that a system designed to execute with one set of topological constraints, such as a traditional client/server system, could be re-hosted to different devices with minimal impact on the overall system. Likewise, given a component with multiple implementations, each implementation would be capable of providing the same output, given the same set of input conditions. The key point of contention is the location of the persistent data used to disconnect the life-cycle of a given component object—an instance of a component—from the life-cycle of an application's execution. The persistence issue must be solved to restore the node independence we require in nomadic computing.

The basic premise of the architectural pattern is that one component object—referenced by a number of different consumers—is responsible for the manufacturing and management of many individual component objects of interest to the consumer. More importantly, the architectural component object manages the persistence of the overall collection of component objects, while the manufactured component objects manage the processing of business rules against their individually encapsulated state value. This sharing of responsibility ensures that the node responsible for management of state may be different than the node(s) responsible for enactment of business rules. The prudent application of a pattern or two means our portable devices are once again free to roam.

16.2.3　Design Guidelines

By introducing component-based development guidelines and applying them to pervasive computing, the programming model needs to separate the "process" from the "persistence." If you want to review these types of component dependencies, have a look at the UML specification and how it is implemented in modeling tools such as Rational Rose.

To create a good pervasive computing service, concentrate on defining behavioral interfaces that achieve business goals, independent of the persistence. Do not assume that each boundary represents a disparate node; instead, initially view the separation as a delineation of roles.

More importantly, look to fully resolve one or more business goals in a consistent package. Ensure that there is a single interface, factored to one or more components, capable of satisfying the needs of each use case identified during analysis. Although difficult to achieve, it can still be helpful when designing interfaces. This single goal will ensure that your business components are both detached from the persistence issues and supportive of the resolution of business, and not technical, goals. You may be concerned that implementing this type of architecture may cause performance problems. Keep in mind that network performance and computing capacity will continue to increase, while application design lasts for the life of the application. What may seem like a potential performance problem today will seem trivial in 18 months. But in a truly nomadic network, you don't know what type of devices will connect to your services. You cannot guarantee bandwidth or computing power in a distributed network, so do not rely on these variables. Expect the worst, and do your best.

16.2.4 Basic Building Blocks

By providing pre-fabricated components, developers have the ability to focus fewer resources on where or how an application runs and more on what it does, especially on the part that really adds value. Today, more than 50 percent of the time is spent on things that are related to the application you want to do, but not the core functionality itself. Instead of writing a letter, people are messing around with font sizes and colors, for example. By using components, you can address some of the biggest challenges developers face today, wrestling with the tradeoff between functionality and manageability. It allows, for example, application hosting on a higher level, enabling the integration of hosted applications with other applications, whether hosted or not. It makes it also easier to customize these applications to the needs of the single user. Standard interfaces also make it easier to increase and enhance functionality and allow you to run the applications, both online and offline.

By providing a set of basic building blocks, developers can leverage and customize services in their own applications and services, reducing the effort required to create compelling products. These services do not necessarily have to be available in source code form for the developers. They could be rented or leased from service providers that develop and operate these basic services.

Some of the most important building blocks are the following: availability, directory, identification, notification, personalization, and unification.

- **Availability**—An important building block is the availability of information about a certain user. This information can be stored in a powerful calendar and accessed through different services, depending on the needs. This becomes especially important as people use more devices more often, and as users and services interact more richly. The pervasive computing platform needs to provide the basis for securely and privately integrating your work, social, and home calendars so that they are accessible to all your devices and, with your consent, other services and individuals.

- **Directory**—A very important building block is the service directory. It includes all available services on a local network and interfaces with other directories on the Internet and other local networks. This makes it possible to find services and people with which to interact. These directories are more than search engines or "yellow pages." They can interact programmatically with services to answer specific schema-based questions about the capabilities of those services. They can also be aggregated and customized by other services and combined with them.

- **Identification**—To customize a service to a specific user, strong authentication and authorization of the user is required. This means that before using any service in the pervasive computing world, the user (or a service) needs to identify herself (or itself). This can be done through simple login/password procedures, using one-time passwords or smartcards and biometric devices. The identification service should work on two levels, the identification itself and the interface toward the user or the service. Every device will have other ways of offering identification services. The television may go for eye scan, the mobile phone for finger prints, and a kiosk for smart cards. This requires a good database in the back-end offering all the required information against which to match. These databases should be controlled by the government or a trusted third-party. A service requiring identification should not need to have the complete database available. It should pass the credentials on to the identification service and receive only the required data back. By offering identification services, devices are able to provide not only personalization but also privacy to their customers.

- **Notification**—Notification works on several levels and with several objectives. It allows users to send messages back and forth on a network. Any type of communications will notify the user as soon as it arrives at a certain device, and the user is logged on. This allows the integration of any type of messaging. If you use a device with a text display, you should be able to convert an audio message into text. On another level, notification can be used to notify devices about automatic upgrades of their software and increased functionality of other devices connected to the same network. This can happen without user installation or configuration. Pervasive computing technologies proactively adapt to what you want to do on any of your devices. This inversion of the traditional installation-dependent application model is a necessity in a world where users will enjoy the benefits of services on multiple devices.

- **Personalization**—After a customer has been identified, personalization plays a big role. It allows the device to create rules and preferences that implicitly and explicitly define how notifications and messages should be handled, how requests to share your data should be treated, and how your multiple devices should be coordinated (e.g., always synchronize my laptop computer with the full contents of my storage service). It also provide a personal profile of the users, including their likes and dislikes.

- **Unification**—Unification of information can be achieved only if the pervasive computing architecture foresees a universal language and protocol that describes what a particular piece of information means. This enables data to maintain its integrity when being transmitted and handled by multiple services and users. The result is that services can interact and exchange and leverage each other's data. This also means that the pervasive computing platform needs to provide unique storage for user related information. A central storage area is essential to maintain correct data. Each of the devices can access this, optimally replicating data for efficiency and offline use. Other services can access the stored data with the user's consent. After data has been replicated for offline use, it should not be able to be modified through a different device. All other devices would have read-only access and have to wait for that particular device to upload the information again to maintain data integrity.

These basic distributed services need to be available both online and off. A service can be invoked on a stand alone machine not connected to the Internet, provided by a local server running inside a company, or accessed via the Internet. Different instances should be able to cooperate and exchange information, allowing organizations to decide whether to run their own infrastructure or host it externally without compromising their control or access to services across the Internet, or when not connected to the Internet. So, for example, a corporate directory service can federate with a service in the Internet cloud.

Today, only two companies offer the full set of basic functionalities that are required to set up a complete pervasive computing infrastructure: Hewlett-Packard and Microsoft. You can find out more about their offerings later in this chapter. If they are truly pervasive, they will also work with each other. There are doubts regarding Microsoft's offering, because it runs only on Windows, but if implemented in an open architecture, it could run as part of the E-Services initiative by Hewlett-Packard. Actually, some companies are trying to port Microsoft's initiative to Linux. Sun and IBM are ramping up their offerings to match those of Hewlett-Packard and Microsoft, so we will see a fierce competition in the future. If done right, we will be able to use Sun's directory service, Hewlett-Packard's infrastructure, IBM's personalization, and identification features, and Microsoft's calendar, for example. But this would require all companies to work together to make sure that the components are based on the same architectural design.

16.2.5 The Future

The move to pervasive computing, together with the convergence of digital technologies into devices of ever changing form, will become predominantly important over the next few years. So it is important to understand that a shift in programming paradigms is necessary to support these new needs. A new architecture is needed to support the new business models and technological advances.

This does not mean that current investments are a waste of money, but that a shift will soon happen. What we see today as foundation blocks of a given service solution will become building blocks for a new foundation to support any type of pervasive computing in the near future. New adaptors will be required to support the translation of information and services to the new device-driven network, but most of the current Internet infrastructure and services will be included in future offerings. The new foundation layer will ensure that the applications we build today are ready to support the topologies of tomorrow.

By implementing the components model, it is possible to use different devices to achieve the same goal, no matter where you are or what type of device you are using. By introducing pervasive components, developers can build services according to the needs of the users, and not the other way round. There is a bright future if programmers and solution architects adapt to these new paradigms.

16.3   Device-to-device Communication

16.3.1   Introduction

A set of technologies has been introduced to allow devices to communicate with each other. These technologies allow the connection of devices to an existing network, such as the Internet, and allow the set-up of local area networks for the exchange of information and services, such as in an office or at home.

This is the lowest layer in the pervasive computing technology architecture. It defines how the communication is established, how the information is transported, and how the connection is terminated. It does not specify how the information needs to be structured or what a service is. ChaiServer, Inferno, Universal Plug and Play, and Jini are technologies that have been developed respectively by Hewlett-Packard, Lucent Technologies, Microsoft and Sun. Bluetooth is a new company-independent standard that allows the ad-hoc creating of wireless local area networks.

16.3.2   ChaiServer

Hewlett-Packard also has a similar vision of connected devices working together to provide services to end users, and announced it in March 1998 with ChaiServer. As we saw in Chapter 12, Hewlett-Packard contested the implementation of Sun's Java for embedded devices. The reason was that embedded devices have different requirements and Sun's Java implementation does not take this into account. Embedded devices can be simple requiring minimal or no administration, such as a palmtop, or more complex, requiring administrative and management features, such as printers.

Chai, the name of Hewlett-Packard's implementation of the Java Virtual Machine, means "tea" in many languages such as Russian, Czech, Turkish, and Hindi, and it means "life" in Hebrew. Tea is one of the most popular drinks throughout the world, so Hewlett-Packard decided to call its virtual machine and embedded technologies family of products "Chai" to convey the notion of a world where virtually every device, processes, or service (analogous to the pervasiveness of tea) is improved (that is, given life) just by virtue of being empowered by Chai. Another reason for calling the product Chai is the connection to Java, which is a type of coffee. With Chai, these devices, process, or services are able to combine measurement, computing, and communications capabilities to attain a new level of local sophistication and intelligent interoperability.

Unlike Sun's embedded Java Virtual Machine, ChaiVM takes the differences in embedded devices into account and enables manufacturers of embedded devices to get the maximum out of the hardware. The ChaiServer[5] adds new functionality to ChaiVM by extending it to allow Web-based connections to other devices on the network. The connectivity is implemented using existing Internet protocols and technology standards and extends the capabilities of the embedded devices. HP ChaiServer has a scalable architecture that allows appliance designers to install only those portions required by the appliance. It provides a scalable, compact, robust Web server with a very small ROM footprint (the appliance's memory size), ranging from about 200KB to 400KB, making ChaiServer perfect for embedded applications with footprint constraints.

The ChaiServer creates information appliances that are able to manage appliances and devices remotely through the World Wide Web. The appliance downloads new diagnostic routines in devices, runs them remotely, and receives notification of events in the devices, so it can take action on them. The embedded devices are able to upgrade software dynamically in the devices with new releases.

By adding the ChaiServer to embedded devices, it is possible to add additional capabilities to a device with little additional cost, because most of the existing infrastructure and software can be retained. Every device is able to have its own Web pages that may contain information on the functionality of the device or could be used to securely manage and administer the device through a set of dynamic Web pages.

ChaiServer also provides an execution environment that allows users to update the appliance with platform-independent, dynamically loadable, plug-in objects called Chailets. A Chailet is an HP ChaiServer object written in Java that performs functions ranging from creating a home page to complex operations (such as diagnostics, measurements, or computations) based on input from remote devices. Chailets implement one or more methods that may perform some computations and then send information to, and retrieve it from, a host. A Chailet communicates with other network entities using protocols like HTTP and SMTP (electronic mail), or through the ChaiServer Notifier Chailet. Chailets can be loaded at runtime using the Loader, and they can interact with the host device(s) via the I/O interface. Chailets have their own Uniform Resource Locator (URL) with which they can be directly accessed via the Internet using any browser. Chailets may also include native code using standard Java Native Interfaces (JNIs). Chailets require the ChaiServer to run, which in turn

---

[5]http://www.chai.hp.com/

runs on any Java-enabled platform ranging from a small embedded device to a large Unix server.

Some of the main features of ChaiServer are the support for HTTP 1.1 (ChaiWeb is an HTTP daemon that enables a Web browser to access the functionality of Chailets), the installation, update, and loading of remote Chailets, and event notification and propagation. Chailets can be used to generate dynamic Web pages.

16.3.3   Inferno

Inferno,[6] developed by Lucent Technologies,[7] is one of the oldest technologies available. The first version of Inferno appeared in March 1997. The technology consists of a small footprint operating system that can connect to networks or run programs within a virtual machine. It was designed with smart phones, Internet appliances, or set-top boxes in mind and supports programs written in two languages: the Limbo language developed by Lucent technologies, which translates Java applications on the fly, and Personal Java, the stripped down version of Java, developed by Sun for embedded devices.

Inferno can run directly on hardware platforms or hosted on standard operating systems such as Windows NT and Linux. It is a distributed architecture-independent network operating system, which models all available resources as files. The virtual machine is used to hide the differences in hardware, and the namespaces are personalizable. Security is one of the strongholds of the Inferno architecture. Security mechanisms are built into the architecture, enabling encrypted communication between the devices and the Limbo language. This makes Inferno a good solution for enabling particular applications in the universal network. Inferno was developed with the telecom world in mind and is not a general solution for the converging universe of computers and information appliances. For the telecom world, it offers one of the best solutions by providing a common API, which enables the exchange of information and services.

The idea of treating all resources in a universal network as files may make it easier for users to access them in the end, but requires lots of overhead and makes it difficult to exploit all the features of the single resource. Inferno is a good native operating system for embedded devices and network appliances. To make Inferno a full blown implementation of a pervasive computing framework, it is necessary to add, for example, dynamic extensibility, scalable lookup and brokerage services, identity through attribute descriptions, and an inter-machine trust and interaction model.

Another problem with Inferno is that almost no one knows about it. Although it is well designed and works well in the above mentioned niche markets, Lucent has spent no time marketing the solution. Inferno fits well into

---

[6]http://www.lucent-inferno.com/
[7]http://www.lucent.com/

today's architectural needs, but lacks vision for the future of the Internet. It enables embedded devices to participate in a network, but does not allow other services or applications to exploit the resources of these embedded devices.

Lucent has three target sectors for its Inferno technology: the network element manufacturers (such as Cisco[8]), the consumer electronics manufacturers (such as Philips[9]), and network service providers, allowing them to introduce a wide array of new devices and new customer-focused service offerings. Inferno-based services offer the possibility of increased customer satisfaction and strengthened customer loyalty. The Inferno system is backed by a complete infrastructure that supports highly interactive applications. Lucent has developed scenarios for sending and receiving email on mobile phones or receiving pay per view films over a set-top box connected to any type of network.

Lucent has introduced a new firewall concept, based on Inferno technology, allowing network devices to talk to the firewall software on a server and making it easier to detect intruders and prevent attacks. Philips introduced the first Inferno-enabled mobile phone, the IS-2630, that can connect to the Internet. Intel and UMEC[10] have also announced reference designs for a Web phone, a telephone with a Web browser and e-mail program built in.

The advantage of Inferno is its maturity. At the time of this writing, Lucent had released version 2.3 of the Inferno software package, making it a stable solution. It runs on most personal computer operating systems, making it easy to develop applications for it. Every developer receives a CD-ROM with a reference manual and many examples, making it easy to build new services. The downside of Inferno is that the software and the CD are not free of charge. Within the three target markets, Lucent has a long list of well-known partners, which will help to guarantee the success of the product. Another factor that will help to bring Inferno to a broader audience is the well-organized "University Partners" program, which ensures that many students will have access to the technology and are able to develop applications for it. A seed financing program for Inferno projects tries to get independent software vendors onboard.

In short, Inferno is a device-centric software solution, making it difficult to implement complex services that require the co-ordination of several types of devices and their services.

16.3.4   Universal Plug and Play

Universal Plug and Play (UPnP)[11] by Microsoft is another technology that allows the creation of networks for the exchange of services and information. It is an extension of the plug-and-play hardware recognition system, which was introduced with Windows 95 (and is also known as plug and pray), allowing

---

[8]http://www.cisco.com/
[9]http://www.philips.com/
[10]http://www.umec.com/
[11]http://www.upnp.org/

people to tie devices together without a computer. Devices are able to announce themselves and their capabilities when plugged into a network.

Universal Plug and Play is designed to work with "smart objects" such as light switches or volume controls and intelligent appliances such as Web-enabled telephones or computers—devices not currently connected to a network. Unlike the other approaches described in this chapter, UPnP is an evolution of an existing technology, taking on the burden of the underlying technology. This makes UPnP more complex and less innovative and elegant. Microsoft calls this approach more secure because it leverages a big heritage of existing technologies and brings Internet technologies into a new class of devices. The conservative approach is typical for Microsoft.

UPnP works only with devices that are based on one of the Microsoft operating systems. This makes the system not truly universal as the name tries to suggest, and tries to further the market reach of the Microsoft products into the embedded devices market. Microsoft has found support from Compaq, Intel, ATI, 3Com, AMD, Kodak, and others.

UPnP, which is conceptually related to Jini, works nicely as a complementary technology to Jini, because UPnP could handle much of the grunt work required to secure blocks of IP addresses. This would allow Jini to concentrate on the interaction between the intelligent appliances themselves and the network.

Microsoft extended the reach of UPnP by creating the Universal Plug and Play Forum. Formed in June 1999, it is a group of companies and individuals across the industry who intend to play a leading role in the authoring of specifications for Universal Plug and Play devices and services. The association consists of over 350 consumer electronics, computing, home automation and security, home appliance, computer networking and other leading companies working together in an open process to design schema and protocol standards for UPnP.

The goals of the Forum are to enable the emergence of easily connected devices and to simplify the implementation of networks in the home and corporate environments. The Forum will achieve this by defining and publishing UPnP device control protocols built upon open, Internet-based communication standards.

16.3.5   Jini

Jini[12] is maybe the best-known component of the pervasive computing technology, thanks to the marketing efforts of Sun.[13] Jini is part of the pervasive computing initiative by Sun Microsystems, which allows all types of devices to be connected into so-called impromptu networks. Jini allows access to new network services and can create a network consisting of all types of digital devices

---

[12]http://www.sun.com/jini/
[13]http://www.sun.com/

without extensive planning, installation, or human intervention. Each device broadcasts the services it offers to all other devices in the community, which then can be used by all members of the network.

An impromptu community is created when two or more devices create a network to share their services. They do not need to have prior knowledge of each other in order to participate. The communication is established dynamically and does not require the devices to exchange drivers to offer their services to the other devices in the community. Jini is designed to bypass computers altogether. The only requirement is that Java reside someplace on the network.

Other than traditional networks, an impromptu community will most probably consist of information appliances, such as mobile phones, television sets, and personal digital assistants. Every electronic device can handle information and contains a certain type of microprocessor. Jini adds the functionality to connect to a network and exchange information and services. It enables the discovery of any device or program on the network and makes that device or program seamlessly available to authorized users.

Jini makes it possible to associate devices, such as printers and scanners, to people and places. Suppose that you need to print out a text in another office. You simply press print, and it will be printed on the printer that is next to you, no matter what type of printer it is and to whom it belongs. Jini allows instant access to any network program or service by providing an object-oriented approach to distributed computing.

The most significant feature in Jini is called Federations (another *Star Trek* reference), a bunch of loosely connected devices that are regulated in a decentralized manner. It is assumed that every device connected is friendly. This concept makes it easy to integrate new devices into the impromptu network, but also creates security issues. The first release of Jini did not include distributed security features.

The main benefit of Jini is that it is not necessary to invest in new equipment to realize the vision of pervasive computing. Jini runs on all types of devices that can be fitted with a Java Virtual Machine and allows dynamic change of the network. Dynamically changing the network means adding and/or removing devices during operation. Jini heavily depends on the existence of an underlying operating system. This requires that embedded devices install and load an operating system; a certain amount of memory is required as well. Because Jini works as an add-on, it is rather easy to program applications and services on standard personal computers with Java and Jini installed. If users connect Jini-enabled devices to their personal computers, no drivers need to be installed in addition to the Jini software on the computer.

One possible application of Jini could be to tap multiple processors across a network to work in parallel and resolve highly complex computations. This type of clustering enables computers on the network to use the available capacities to a maximum. Imagine that 20 computers are connected to each other. A user starting a computing-intensive application on one system will broadcast the request for processing power to the other computers. Every computer that has processing time available will donate it to the application. This, of course, requires a rewrite of traditional single-processor applications.

Scalability is one of the major issues with the current implementation of Jini. It can run only in workgroups of up to 200 objects. This makes Jini a workgroup solution in which participants share the same security model. Jini does not scale well to a wide area network (WAN), nor does it provide functions to cross firewalls that protect company networks from the rest of the Internet. The reason for the lack of scalability is that all changes are expected to be consistent. An additional drawback to scalability is that all members of an impromptu network need to share a single clock by which they operate. If one device gets out of sync, it must be resynced to share its services and data. This takes time and resources. It also means that devices in such a network cannot drop out and reconnect whenever they wish. They must be online all the time to share their information and services.

A lesser problem is its dependency on Java. It is difficult to enable devices to talk in the "Jini way" of network communication if they are not Java enabled. But because Java is available for almost any type of hardware, it should not be a problem. It may be more of a problem to introduce Jini into a company with no knowledge of Java. Jini's meta data system requires that suppliers and consumers of services agree on a common description of the services and devices to find each other. Java supports only a global namespace, making it impossible to create local names for devices and services that are located in other locations. Therefore, the whole name must be used to address such a service or device.

Jini can work as an extension to CORBA (Common Object Request Broker Architecture), just as most solutions presented in this chapter. Actually, most of the solutions presented here were built at a time when CORBA was not as powerful as it is today. Jini can be viewed as a Java directory and lookup service, which are also available in CORBA. But this can also be said of most solutions provided in this chapter. The difference with Jini is that for the first time all types of devices are able to exchange information and services in a standardized manner.

Jini is a good device architecture due to its installable interface, and many companies have started to license the technology to create new devices and services. Cisco,[14] for example, has created a Jini-powered cable modem, and Quantum[15] has demonstrated a free-standing Jini hard disk.

---

[14]http://www.cisco.com/
[15]http://www.quantum.com/

16.3.6 Bluetooth

Bluetooth[16] was first introduced in May 1998 as a result of several companies working together to provide a solution for wireless access to computing devices. The five companies instrumental in the development of Bluetooth were Ericsson, IBM, Intel, Nokia, and Toshiba. Each company helped Bluetooth become the product it is today. Ericsson was instrumental in developing the Special Interest Group (SIG). Since its inception in 1998, more than 1,000 companies have become involved with the SIG.

The codename Bluetooth traces back to 10th-century Denmark. Harold Bluetooth, King of Denmark, was filled with Christianity from his mother from an early age. At the loss of his father, Harold inherited rule over Denmark. In a time of war and destruction, Harold found himself in charge of rebuilding the churches and belief of Christianity throughout Denmark. In doing so, Harold Bluetooth was credited with uniting the provinces of Denmark under a single crown. Just as Harold joined a country on one belief, Bluetooth technology unites different computerized devices to one standard. Hence, the codename Bluetooth was adopted.

The idea behind Bluetooth is to allow wireless communication between two entities without the hassle of connecting wires. Cellular phones can automatically send email to your computer when you come within 10 meters of the computer. This is the concept of Bluetooth technology.

Bluetooth is the specification for small form factor, low-cost, short range radio links between mobile PCs, phones, and other portable devices. From its cable replacement to radio link and data transfer times, Bluetooth is actually simple to understand. It is comprised of a 9×9 mm chip that is inserted into two devices so that they can communicate with each other. Bluetooth uses the frequency band of 2.45 GHz and is designed to switch among 79 channels in this band at 1,600 hops per second. The rate at which data is transmitted and received is 1 Mb/s. The Bluetooth baseband protocol is a combination of circuit and packet switching. Each packet is transmitted in a different hop frequency. This band is available globally with exceptions in a few countries. The fact that this frequency band is free and unregulated precedes the availability of global expectations by the Federal Communications Commission (FCC). The range in comparison with its competitors can reach 10 meters or 40 feet. Bluetooth can be outfitted to make longer connection distances, if desired.

Bluetooth contains a maximum of three voice channels and seven data channels per piconet. Security has been administered at the link layer. Each link is encoded and protected against both eavesdropping and interference. In fact, Bluetooth can be considered a secure, short-range wireless network, because it uses encryption of up to 64 bits. One of the main advantages of using Bluetooth is that it provides a universal bridge to existing networks. Installation of Bluetooth has grown from only the PC and mobile phone to many other

---

[16]http://www.bluetooth.org/

devices such as fax machines, keyboards, mice, and joysticks.

There are different reasons for using Bluetooth. There is also the question of why to use Bluetooth in the first place. The problems foreseen with Bluetooth are cost, privacy, accessibility, security, and future. Future aspirations for Bluetooth are immeasurable because of the acceptance it has received from many big companies. One concern is privacy and whether transmissions will be secure. Security on transmissions has been questionable since the evolution of Bluetooth, due to its underlying architecture.

Business solutions can be one of the most important reasons why Bluetooth will take off so well in the business market. The ability to check e-mail without the hassle of connecting wires will be widely received, as will printing from across the room without having to plug in a cable. All of these simple solutions will help businesses perform at higher quality. There is no limit to what Bluetooth can help the average business do. As long as both your PC and cellular phone are equipped with Bluetooth technology, they can "talk" continuously.

Imagine receiving email when your computer is not even on; with Bluetooth this is possible. When someone leaves voice mail on your cell phone, it automatically sends it to your PC for e-mail availability also. Bluetooth allows for easy access to any or all of your electronic devices that can send or retrieve data. Printers, keyboards, mice, and fax machines can all work with Bluetooth.

Widespread adoption of Bluetooth will eventually determine whether it becomes global. Already able to be used globally in devices, Bluetooth's marketing strategy will determine whether it becomes a worldwide phenomenon. Bluetooth will allow other countries to have the same business success that the United States has if it is incorporated properly.

E-business will definitely get a boost with Bluetooth. People can buy and sell stocks while out of the office. Bluetooth can also link e-wallet to POS terminals for payment using e-cash.

The Finnish manufacturer of tyres, Nokian[17] has developed a new business model for Bluetooth. In the future, sensors will be built into the tyres that are able to send warning messages to the driver's mobile phone. This development has been done in conjunction with the Finnish manufacturer of mobile phones, Nokia. The first generation of tyres will roll out in 2001 and will work with all mobile phones that support Bluetooth. The first generation has been developed especially for trucks and race cars. In later versions, additional measurements will be performed, in order to prevent aquaplaning, for example.

Sales of Bluetooth technology are likely to exceed two billion dollars/euros by 2005, according to research carried out by Allied Business Intelligence.[18] The ABI report concludes that Bluetooth technology will replace cables joining user devices with a short-range radio link that is universally compatible. Bluetooth will enable a wireless connection between virtually any electronic device

---

[17]http://www.nokianrenkaat.fi/
[18]http://www.abi.com/

over a distance of up to 10 meters. Broadcasting at the 2.4 GHz ISM band, Bluetooth microtransceivers take advantage of the recently formalized IEEE 802.11 specification for wireless LANs. The sales projections are based on the assumption that Bluetooth will be used in many user devices including notebook, desktop, and handheld computers, PDAs, cellular/PCS handsets, pagers, printers, fax machines, modems, wireless LAN and LAN access devices, headsets, and thermostats. Early adoption is likely to be highest among business users of mobile phones and notebook computers.

16.4 Information Exchange

16.4.1 Introduction

The middle layer of the pervasive computing architecture is responsible for the exchange of data between devices. While the bottom layer connects the devices and the top layer connects the service providers with the service customers, the middle layer is responsible for the flow of information between service provider and service customer. Hewlett-Packard (with JetSend), IBM (with T Spaces), Lucent Technologies (with InfernoSpaces), and Microsoft (with Millennium) offer solutions for solving the problem of inconsistent types of data. The problem with data is that it is saved on every device in a different format, making it difficult to transport the information to another device that does not understand that format exactly. The middle layer provides a means for devices to negotiate the appropriate format in advance. For example, it would be possible to choose the JPEG format for the communication between a scanner and a printer. Another function of the middle layer is the creation of a device-independent format that can be understood by all participating devices. XML, for example, could be used for the communication between a word processor and the hard disk. The following technologies promise to solve this problem.

16.4.2 JetSend

Hewlett-Packard[19] introduced the JetSend[20] technology in 1997 to reduce the complexity in handling different document formats. The technology complements most of the solutions presented here, such as E-Speak, Jini, and Universal Plug and Play.

The idea behind JetSend is to allow devices to negotiate the best way to share documents. A JetSend-enabled scanner could send images to a JetSend-enabled printer directly, for example, without the interaction of a personal computer in between. Another example could be a cable television operator who sends out video on demand to its customers and does not need to worry about the format of the film. The operator's and customer's JetSend-enabled

---

[19]http://www.hp.com/
[20]http://www.hp.com/go/jetsend/

devices are able to determine the right format automatically. The two devices involved must be on the same network and will negotiate through the JetSend protocol, which is known to both of the devices and is used to interchange the information without any data.

Hewlett-Packard offers a wide range of printers, scanners, and digital cameras, and it is obvious that these devices were the first to learn the JetSend protocol. Computers now support the protocol. This will allow them to take over JetSend communications for non-JetSend-enabled devices.

Hewlett-Packard is trying to position JetSend as the Esperanto of the computing world, promising universal viewability of content. The JetSend technology already has been licensed by several companies, including Panasonic, Minolta, Siemens, Xerox, and Canon, which are all producing printers, scanners, and cameras.

16.4.3 T Spaces

T Spaces,[21] developed by IBM[22] works on a Java-based technology that allows computers and embedded devices to share data, such as email or database queries. T Spaces is just one of IBM's many projects and tries to complement Sun's Jini to achieve the common goal of pervasive computing.

As IBM puts it: "T Spaces allows you to connect all things to all things, whereby a thing is a chip-based device. It is a network communication buffer with database capabilities and enables communication between applications and devices in a network of heterogeneous computers and operating systems." The technology makes it easy for resources such as printers, scanners, fax machines, or software services to be shared across networks with lots of different kinds of computers. T Spaces is designed for the local area network (LAN) and will help to reduce the hardware costs in homes and small offices first. T Spaces has not been designed for thousands of devices attached to a single network. There is also no way to cross firewalls without compromising security.

IBM's vision is to target the home market, unlike Hewlett-Packard, which tries to create a global pervasive computing vision. Pervasive computing in every household requires a dedicated server, which controls the flow of information and services between the devices, and IBM hopes to be the company that will sell these hubs to homeowners of the next century. IBM is looking at a way to provide a virtual terminal and a broker between resources, but so far only on a local level.

T Spaces has many advantages over other technologies. Data is de-coupled from programs, meaning that data can outlive its producer (because after it's produced, it lives in n-tuple space) and can be produced before the receiver exists. The communication is anonymous, and the sender does not need to know anything about the receiver (and vice-versa). Sender and receiver need only

---

[21] http://www.almaden.ibm.com/cs/TSpaces/
[22] http://www.ibm.com/

know about tuple space, which mediates all communication. The communication is also asynchronous, whereby the sender and receiver do not have to be on the network at the same time for the communication to happen. The producer produces when it's ready, and the consumer consumes when it's ready.

T Spaces has been implemented in Java and consists of a small core, which can be loaded into most embedded devices with little memory on board. Persistent data repository and database indexing and querying capabilities are the strongholds of the T Spaces implementation. New operators can be defined dynamically and used immediately, making the whole system very dynamic and interactive. Event notification is also integrated into T Spaces, making it possible to react immediately to changes on the network.

T Spaces has been available for several years and has matured over time. Still, some flaws are visible. It does not perform well on Windows NT, and the built-in HTTP server will fail if there is no network connection, e.g., on a laptop that has been disconnected from the network.

16.4.4 InfernoSpaces

The InfernoSpaces technology provides a framework for building distributed computing applications. It extends many of the Inferno namespace capabilities to non-Inferno platforms and allows application deployment across a heterogeneous environment, independent of the hardware platform, the network protocols, the programming languages, and the operating systems. InfernoSpaces contains a set of software libraries that allow, for example, legacy applications to take advantage of a distributed computing environment. An application created with InfernoSpaces will be able to interoperate with other Inferno or InfernoSpaces applications.

InfernoSpaces is a flexible, scalable, and distributed-computing technology that allows any device to be connected seamlessly and easily with any other device. In addition, the creation and sharing of network services and devices becomes much easier. It can be used to create any type of distributed application in a network and can be used with almost any programming language and operating system. InfernoSpaces supports C, Java, Limbo, Windows, Solaris, and InfernoOS at the time of writing. InfernoSpaces is free of charge, making it accessible to anyone with an Internet connection.

InfernoSpaces is simple, so you can learn it in just days. It is based on a file model known to all developers. Its flexibility allows the developers to separate application design from the underlying network configuration and the software scales from the smallest embedded device to large network elements and servers. Through its design model, it is possible to write networking application without writing specific networking code. The simple-to-use and elegant framework allows even beginners to develop networked applications.

Some of the applications that can be written with InfernoSpaces are IP telephony and distributed call processing. Internet Games and instant messaging solutions can be also developed without much hassle. Directory services and online billing solutions are also typical applications for the InfernoSpaces architecture.

InfernoSpaces is a highly sophisticated technology that will work well in conjunction with other pervasive computing products presented here.

16.4.5 Millennium

To complement Microsoft's pervasive computing strategy, a next-generation distributed operating system called Millennium has been developed that lets computers share tasks across a network, automatically adjusting to new components being added or removed. The goals of this technology include seamless distribution, worldwide scalability, transparent fault tolerance, security, resource management, and resource discovery.

The prototypes that have been implemented so far are Borg, Coign, and Continuum. The first prototype, Borg (a reference to Star Trek), is a stripped down version of the Java Virtual Machine, using the Microsoft flavor of Java (see Chapter 12) that can create a cluster of computers that looks like a single one when running Java programs. The discovery of new devices in the network is based on a notification-oriented system.

The second prototype, Coign, is an automatic distributed partitioning system (ADPS). It can automatically convert local COM applications into distributed client-server applications without access to source code. Using a scenario-based profiling system, Coign discovers the internal structure of an application and cuts the application into client and server components; choosing a distribution that minimizes communication between client and server. Coign supports Microsoft's flavor of Java, as well as Visual Basic and C++ based on the distributed COM architecture written by Microsoft. After a program is started, Coign decides how to distribute a program and automatically accomplishes that task in a way that maximizes the network performance. This is combined with a discovery protocol that measures bandwidth availability, latency, and the speed of the available CPUs.

Continuum (another reference to Star Trek) has the same functionality as Borg and Coign, and is not restricted to a particular application, but will work with any application. The designers of Continuum have had the ambitious goal of distributing the Windows API to create a single computing environment (i.e., one single system image) across multiple machines. The goal of Continuum is to provide a distributed single system image environment to a large class of applications regardless of their source language.

The advantage of this system is that it allows application designers to continue with their existing applications, and the underlying Millennium component will take care of the distribution. The distribution is handled automatically after the application has been written. This approach is far easier than with Jini or CORBA, which both require the application to adapt to the new paradigm during the development.

The downside of the system is that it is released only as developers' pre-releases, and the prototypes run only on Windows. Millennium is built on top of Microsoft's Component Object Model (COM), and future releases will rely on COM+, which will be strictly limited to the Windows platforms, making it a homogeneous environment with a central server.

16.4.6 InfoBus

InfoBus, just like Jini, is part of the pervasive computing initiative of Sun. InfoBus allows the cooperation of applets or JavaBeans. They can exchange data through the InfoBus architecture. JavaBeans can become "data providers" and "data consumers," which are defined in the InfoBus architecture. A JavaBean that acts as a provider connects to a database and offers the data to the InfoBus. JavaBeans that act as data consumers are able to retrieve the data from the bus and process it. The advantage of InfoBus is that participating objects do not need to understand data formats and instead can concentrate on the implementation of the data processing. The concept of segregating provider from consumer is extremely powerful in that it enables applications to be independent of their data.

The InfoBus specification provides a set of interfaces that allows you to share and exchange dynamic data. It is possible to create so-called "data flows" between co-operating components. The semantics of the data flow are based on the interpretation of the data content, which flows across the InfoBus interfaces as opposed to responding to names of parameters from events or names of call-back parameters.

InfoBus complements Jini, which allows device-to-device communication, by implementing a way to exchange data over a standard interface. Through Jini and InfoBus, it is possible to extend the functionality of the Web to other devices, without introducing a new paradigm.

16.5 Service Broadcasting

16.5.1 Introduction

The top layer of the pervasive computing architecture is the service layer, which allows the exchange of services over a network. Services that reside on a device can broadcast their existence and then become available to other devices, business objects, or human beings. While Jini offers some basic functionality for local service exchange, it lacks the scalability and the security to make it a product for the Internet. Products like SOAP and the E-Speak product by Hewlett-Packard scale well on the Internet. This means that it does not matter whether thousands or millions of people use the service. It is designed to always run smoothly.

16.5.2   E-Speak

Jini's vision is not unique to Sun. Many in the industry today and over the last several years have had a vision of interconnecting devices.

HP's E-Speak technology, code-named Fremont, takes this vision even further by adding new, dynamic capabilities such as scalability, security, and heterogeneity. Jini is an architecture for device interaction in a small, trusted workgroup (LAN) or home environment, whereas Fremont is an architecture for service interaction in a large, unsafe, distributed environment, such as the Internet. It offers services that include computing resources, information, and even access to applications on a pay-per-usage basis, in a similar way that information has been available for some time on the Web.

The difference between the old Web and the new infrastructure is that the availability and the quality truly become the most important aspects of the service. It is not necessary to know how it is managed, who provides the service, or where it is installed and configured. The Fremont technology handles the service-related issues on the Internet.

Fremont is a network middleware layer that lies on top of the operating systems, making services independent of the operating system. One could call this type of solution "install once, serve anywhere," in addition to Java's "write once, run anywhere."

Fremont is designed to make any computing resource (disks, files, Java objects, legacy applications, and device drivers) available as services over the network. It also allows these electronic services to advertise their capabilities and discover new ones as they are added or become available anywhere on the network. Fremont provides unique mechanisms and protocols for negotiation, brokering, bidding, and billing between these electronic services. The management, monitoring, and fine-grained, dynamic access controls and security make it easy to create service solutions that are powerful and secure. The Fremont architecture makes it easy to combine electronic services, thus creating a new service in a modular way.

These meta services do not need to reside on a single device. It is possible to combine services from different devices to create a new service. Imagine a weather report service that uses different devices such as a thermometer and a barometer. If each of these devices were Fremont-enabled, it would be easy to present the actual weather data on a Web page with little programming knowledge (mainly HTML).

Fremont links services, not just repositories of data, making a real leap in the future of computing. It has been designed to be a universal language and protocol for electronic services. Hewlett-Packard sees Fremont as a technology platform for open services. An open service is a state in which end-user services can be dynamically composed of best-in-class and competitive service components and resources using standardized, non-proprietary interfaces.

In a nutshell, Fremont is a federated software infrastructure that runs on

Hewlett-Packard's E-Speak Technology offers very interesting features.

- **Independence of Language**—Unlike other pervasive computing implementations, E-Speak does not depend on a single programming language, such as C++ or Java.

- **Meta data System**—Attribute-based lookup is supported, making it easy to exchange information and services.

- **Name Virtualization**—The virtualization of resources makes it easy to move the original resource without reconfigurating the clients.

- **Revocation of Privileges**—Fremont can configure itself to revoke access to materials lists and other secure information.

- **Scalability**—Unlike Jini, for example, Fremont can handle resources on the Internet, not just on an Intranet or closed network.

Table 16.1. E-Speak Overview

top of an operating system. It is similar to the Web, and is a living system, similar to an operating system. Unlike most middleware such as CORBA, which consists basically only of a set of tools, it simplifies and secures the creation, management, and access of services over the Internet.

Most pervasive computing technologies enable device-to-device connectivity, but this is not sufficient to enable electronic services. ChaiServer allows devices to talk to each other, but it does not specify how to do this. To create electronic services, it is necessary to advertise, broker, compose, and maintain the service. The broker, for example, is able to handle sets of services, sets of data types, and sets of access devices.

Fremont allows the creation of instant extranets, providing collaboration among business partners. On a case-by-case basis, it becomes possible to allow partners access to single services on your intranet, if necessary, without compromising security. The ability to connect services spontaneously allows people to collaborate in a far more direct and efficient way than we know today. The creation of an extranet takes months to decide and implement. With Fremont,

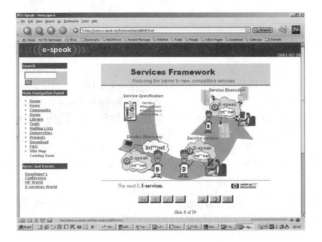

Figure 16.2. Facts about E-Speak.

particular services can be relayed in a secure way to the Internet, making the service available only to the partners who are allowed to see and use it. This reduces the risk of someone breaking into your corporate network.

Partners who use the Internet to share services need to start up a client application. It represents an interface to the originator. This interface allows the originator to choose a file from a directory on his machine and make it available to a partner who is running the client application. A "gateway" process, running on the originator's machine, presents the client application with its interface to the FireScreen service. The FireScreen gateway is responsible for "pushing" shared information to the external FireScreen "connector" and for retrieving requests found at the connector site.

A "connector" process, running on a separate host, somewhere on the Internet, will allow gateway processes to "post" information. Gateway processes will post one of three types of information to the connector: "availability" messages (which represent sharing authorizations), "consume" messages (which represent file transfer requests), and the actual file contents (during a transfer). A second gateway process, running on the consumer's machine, acts in much the same role as the gateway process on the originator's machine and provides the consumer with information about file availability. This gateway will also post "consume" or fetch requests as directed by the consumer's client application. A second client application, running on the consumer's machine, will allow the user to see the files made available with his identity and retrieve those files. This application will actually be identical to the application run by the originator. The consumer and originator simply use different features as they exchange roles.

This concept allows businesses to create next generation portals, which are also called electronic service brokers (ESBs). ESBs allow online services to charge other systems for ESBs resources and create a new business channel for the delivery of electronic services in the following ways.

An ESB creates additional revenue opportunities for telephone companies by allowing them to provide services beyond basic connections to consumers and creates new business opportunities for companies who want to deliver electronic services to their customers. Consumers can gain access to a wider range of functionality without having to purchase or install applications on their own, and an ESB lowers the cost barrier for access to sophisticated capabilities. This allows customers to access services without having to pay for the underlying infrastructure. Instead of buying applications that need to be installed locally, for example, you rent them over the Internet for the time you need them.

Fremont (aka E-Speak) sits on top of other consumer-device focused technologies, such as Jini, ChaiServer, or Universal Plug and Play. While Sun promotes Java everywhere and Microsoft promotes Windows everywhere, Hewlett-Packard does not care about the operating system nor about the implementation language for accessing the electronic services. It can use any of the mentioned technologies to implement these services.

Several E-speak pilots are under development, such as at Uniscape,[23] Captura,[24] and Helsinki Telephone.[25] At Uniscape, for example, E-speak is used to find translators and allow them to bid for services. Customers can select translators based on speed, quality, and price.

16.5.3 Salutation

Salutation is a service discovery and session management protocol developed by leading information technology companies. Salutation is an open standard, independent of operating systems, communication protocols, and hardware platforms. Salutation was created to solve the problems of service discovery and utilization among a broad set of appliances and equipments in an environment of widespread connectivity and mobility. The architecture provides applications and services, and formulates a standard method for describing and advertising their capabilities, as well as finding out the capabilities of others. The architecture also enables applications, services, and devices to search for a particular capability, and to request and establish interoperable sessions with them.

The Salutation architecture defines an entity called the Salutation Manager (SLM) that functions as a service broker for services in the network. Different functions of a service are represented by functional units. Functional Units represent essential features of a service (e.g. fax, print, scan, etc.). Furthermore, the attributes of each Functional Unit are captured in the Functional

---

[23]http://www.uniscape.com/
[24]http://www.captura.com/
[25]http://www.hpy.fi/

Unit Description Record. Salutation defines the syntax and semantics of the Functional Unit Description Record (e.g. name, value).

Salutation Manager can be discovered by services in a number of ways:

- **Static Tables**—Using a static table that stores the transport address of the remote SLM.

- **Broadcast**—Sending a broadcast discovery query using the protocol defined by the Salutation architecture.

- **Inquiry**—Acquiring the transport address of a remote SLM through a central directory server. This protocol is undefined by the Salutation architecture; however, the current specification suggests the use of Service Location Protocol (SLP).

- **Specification**—The service specifies the transport address of a remote SLM directly.

Table 16.2. Discovery of Services

The service discovery process can be performed across multiple SLMs. An SLM can discover other remote SLMs and determine the services that are registered there. Service Discovery is performed by comparing required service types, as specified by the local SLM, with the service types available on a remote SLM. Remote Procedure Calls are used to transmit the required Service types from the local SLM to the remote SLM and to transmit the response from the remote SLM to the local SLM. The SLM determines the characteristics of all services registered at a remote SLM by manipulating the specification of required service types. It can also determine the characteristics of a specific service registered at a remote SLM or the presence of a specific service on a remote SLM by matching a specific set of characteristics. Salutation, unlike Jini, is a lightweight protocol and makes the least assumption of the underlying protocol stack and computing resources. Hence, it can easily be ported to low power handheld devices.

16.5.4 SOAP (Simple Object Access Protocol)

Dynamically generated HTML content works fine in Web browsers, but can be a nightmare for anyone trying to utilize that data with other programs. For example, you can easily view an auction site in a browser, but an application would require a complex HTML parser to read the status of your bid from the same site. Worse, you would need a different parser to track a different auction site, and the simplest redesign of either site could throw off your program.

Web services solve this problem with a consistent and easy method for accessing online information. As more online services are offered, new applications can be built to interact directly with them. For example, that Web-based auction site could let you write software that automatically updates your bids based on the status of a bid on a different auction site. Or you could edit your Web log with your favorite word processor if the site and application were both speaking the same language. Web services could potentially create a whole new type of Web.

SOAP provides a simple, lightweight mechanism for exchanging structured and typed information between peers in a decentralized, distributed environment using XML. SOAP does not itself define any application semantics such as a programming model or implementation specific semantics; rather, it defines a simple mechanism for expressing application semantics by providing a modular packaging model and encoding mechanisms for encoding data within modules. This allows SOAP to be used in a variety of systems, ranging from messaging systems, to RPC. SOAP consists of three parts:

- **Envelope**—Defines an overall framework for expressing what is in a message, who should deal with it, and whether it is optional or mandatory.

- **Encoding Rules**—Defines a serialization mechanism that can be used to exchange instances of application-defined datatypes.

- **RPC Representation**—Defines a convention that can be used to represent remote procedure calls and responses.

Although these parts are described together as part of SOAP, they are functionally orthogonal. In particular, the envelope and the encoding rules are defined in different namespaces to promote simplicity through modularity.

Table 16.3. SOAP Components

The Simple Object Access Protocol (SOAP) is a standard for encoding inter-machine function calls in XML so they can be passed among heterogeneous systems. It enables any client application to call a function on any server machine, no matter what operating system each is running on or what language each is written in.

SOAP is a lightweight protocol for exchange of information in a decentralized, distributed environment. It is an XML-based protocol that consists of three parts: an envelope that defines a framework for describing what is in a message and how to process it, a set of encoding rules for expressing instances of application-defined datatypes, and a convention for representing remote procedure calls and responses. SOAP can potentially be used in combination with a variety of other protocols.

The protocol has been drafted by UserLand, Ariba, Commerce One, Compaq, Developmentor, Hewlett-Packard, IBM, IONA, Lotus, Microsoft, and SAP. It is backed by Compaq and others, giving a big push. SOAP exchanges application data over HTTP in XML encoding. Because HTTP is ubiquitous and XML parsers are widely available, SOAP can be easily adopted and quickly developed. The trade-off is speed; SOAP won't replace lower-level technologies, but it works where interoperability is paramount. SOAP toolkits are already available for most popular development environments, including Python, Java, Visual Basic, and Perl. Programmers experienced with remote procedure call APIs, such as Java's RMI or Microsoft's COM+, will find the SOAP toolkits familiar.

16.5.5   UDDI (Universal Description, Discovery, and Integration)

Within a more distributed model of the business part of the Internet, a flexible, open, yet comprehensive framework is required to embrace this diversity, encouraging agreement on standards, but also stimulating the innovation and differentiation that fuels the growth of e-business. The framework also needs to allow businesses to describe the business services that their Web sites offer, and how they can be accessed globally over the Web. A global solution must go beyond traditional directories, to also define standards for how businesses will share information, what information they need to make public, and what information they choose to keep private.

The solution is the creation of a service registry architecture that presents a standard way for businesses to build a registry, query other businesses, and enable those registered businesses to interoperate and share information globally in a distributed manner, just as the Internet was intended to be used. A Web services framework and public registry will enable buyers and sellers and marketplaces around the world to share information, connect Web services at low cost, support multiple standards, and prosper in the new digital economy.

To address this challenge, a group of technology and business leaders came together to develop the Universal Description, Discovery, and Integration (UD-

DI) specification, a sweeping initiative that creates a global, platform-independent, open framework to enable businesses to discover each other, define how they interact over the Internet, and share information in a global registry that will more rapidly accelerate the global adoption of e-business.

The UDDI specification provides a common set of SOAP APIs that enable the implementation of a service broker. The UDDI specification was outlined by IBM, Microsoft, and Ariba to help facilitate the creation, description, discovery, and integration of Web-based services. The motivation behind UDDI.org,[26] a partnership and cooperation of more than 70 industry and business leaders, is to define a standard for B2B interoperability.

UDDI is also a framework for Web services integration. It contains standards-based specifications for service description and discovery. The UDDI specification takes advantage of World Wide Web Consortium (W3C) and Internet Engineering Task Force (IETF) standards such as eXtensible Markup Language (XML), HTTP, and Domain Name System (DNS) protocols. Additionally, cross-platform programming features are addressed by adopting early versions of the proposed Simple Object Access Protocol (SOAP) messaging specifications found at the W3C Web site.

16.5.6 WSDL

The Web Services Description Language (WSDL) is an XML vocabulary that provides a standard way of describing service IDLs. The Interface Definition Language (IDL) is the prevalent language used for defining how components connect together. WSDL is the resulting artifact of a convergence of activity between NASSL (by IBM) and SDL (by Microsoft). It provides a simple way for service providers to describe the format of requests and response messages for remote method invocations (RMI). WSDL addresses the topic of service IDLs, independent of the underlying protocol and encoding requirements. In general, WSDL provides an abstract language for defining the published operations of a service with their respective parameters and data types. The language also addresses the definition of the location and binding details of the service.

As communications protocols and message formats are standardized in the Web community, it becomes increasingly possible and important to be able to describe the communications in some structured way. WSDL addresses this need by defining an XML grammar for describing network services as collections of communication endpoints capable of exchanging messages. WSDL service definitions provide documentation for distributed systems and serve as a recipe for automating the details involved in applications communication.

A WSDL document defines services as collections of network endpoints, or ports. In WSDL, the abstract definition of endpoints and messages is separated from their concrete network deployment or data format bindings. This allows the reuse of abstract definitions: messages, which are abstract descriptions

---

[26]http://www.uddi.org/

of the data being exchanged, and port types which are abstract collections of operations. The concrete protocol and data format specifications for a particular port type constitute a reusable binding. A port is defined by associating a network address with a reusable binding, and a collection of ports define a service.

It is important to observe that WSDL does not introduce a new type definition language. WSDL recognizes the need for rich type systems for describing message formats and supports the XML Schemas specification (XSD) as its canonical type system. However, because it is unreasonable to expect a single type system grammar to be used to describe all message formats in the present and future, WSDL allows the use of other type definition languages via extensibility.

In addition, WSDL defines a common binding mechanism. This is used to attach a specific protocol or data format or structure to an abstract message, operation, or endpoint. It allows the reuse of abstract definitions.

16.6   The Vision

16.6.1   Introduction

Although pervasive computing is being implemented by several companies, it can be successful only if the company has a vision. A vision will align all organizations within the company to ensure that it becomes reality. So far, only IBM, Hewlett-Packard, Microsoft, and Sun have tried to present a complete vision of the future of computing.

These new flexible, Internet-based applications and services will allow companies to create new products and services faster than existing methods can reach new customers and add new relationships economically. In the future, existing relationships will change dynamically, allowing the engagement in multiple e-business models simultaneously and providing customized experiences for both partners and customers.

Some benefits include a significantly faster time to market, convergence of disparate e-business initiatives, significant reduction in total cost of ownership (TCO), real-time updating and dynamic linking of partner and client systems, and easy-to-use software tailored for business people rather than for IT staffs.

New technologies will automate the process of linking constituents and their core competencies across a value chain quickly and efficiently on the Internet. These technologies offer a new style of application based on Web services that can be shared among all members of an extended value chain. Members can interconnect applications and Web services, and new members can join the value chain dynamically.

The idea is to enable the business processes that link these partners (content, data, business logic, pricing, and so on) to be updated dynamically, thereby reducing costly, time-intensive manual programming. This enables the dynamic assembly of loosely coupled components (Web services, legacy data, and other systems), which is very different from the traditional hard-wired approach of developing applications that resist change. This technology provides consumers and businesses access to up-to-date, real-time information—any time or any place. The information is provided through applications that dynamically link data and transfer it back and forth between members within the value chain using XML and other standards-based technologies.

This will have broad implications for all companies, but it is ideally designed for companies that have rapidly changing applications, data, systems, and partners. Historically, companies had to update these complex relationships using manual programmers and hard-coding single-use applications and relationships, but today these can be done using automation technology.

16.6.2 Brazil

Because other companies have defined a strategy and a vision for the future, Sun[27] did not want to stand back while other companies advanced. Sun defined a more complete vision of the future than with Jini. This vision is called Brazil. The Brazil project is a Web-based infrastructure that securely links people to information, computers, and other devices leveraging existing standards and protocols.

This framework enables standalone systems to work together within the Web space. A strong authentication architecture allows extranets to access intranets in an open environment without compromising security. The approach extends the endpoints to new applications and smaller devices; yet it also can adapt legacy applications into this architecture. Corporations can take advantage of Web-based computing to dynamically control access to, and management of, corporate information systems and other digital data that represents a state in physical space, door status, room temperatures, camera inputs, and so on. Each of Sun's initiatives tries to explore the possibilities expressed by this infrastructure.

The core component of the Brazil project is the Brazil Web application framework. It began as an extremely small footprint HTTP stack, originally designed to provide a URL-based interface to smart cards, so the smart cards could be accessed more easily from an ordinary web browser. Along the way, it grew to provide a more flexible architecture for adding URL-based interfaces to arbitrary applications and devices.

The Brazil toolkit interfaces are based on the Java language because of its strong typing. However, the Brazil Handlers communicate with each other with no type-checking involved. This makes it possible to reuse handlers for other purposes. The Brazil toolkit uses its own Brazil Scripting Language (BSL) to use the information communicated between Handlers for dynamic HTML generation.

---

[27] http://www.sun.com/tech/features/brazil/

The Brazil architecture is defined by four main characteristics:

- **Toolkit**—A rich toolkit of powerful, reusable parts

- **Modularity**—Large applications achieved by combining simple parts in consistent ways

- **Simplicity**—Small applications that are simple to build

- **File System Neutral**—No preconceived notion or rigid structure of file systems

---

Table 16.4. The Brazil Technology Architecture

BSL allows for the separation of the Java language Handlers from the HTML Web page look and feel. The Handlers never generate HTML, and the page's HTML is just that. The advantage here is that making changes in the HTML doesn't require a programmer looking over the shoulder of the Web developer to avoid or correct mistakes inadvertently made to the Java technology code in the process, and vice versa. No longer does the content server have to produce both the content and its presentation (look and feel). They're easily separable.

Although Brazil is very strong on the technology side, it lacks the business vision that the other two contenders offer today. It will be very attractive to IT departments, because it uses standard languages and is based on reusable components, but without the business vision, it will be difficult to convince the corporate world.

16.6.3 E-Services

Hewlett-Packard has created a unique vision based on the above-mentioned products, which is HP's so-called e-services strategy. Hewlett-Packard is forecasting an explosive growth of specialized, modular electronic services that pervade the fabric of life and is aligning all of its organizations, resources, and expertise to make their customers take full advantage of the e-services vision.

It's no longer only Web sites or portals that matter. Of increasing importance are electronic services that are integrated into all kinds of devices and utilities and are made available via brokers. An e-service is a service or resource that can be accessed on the Net by people, businesses, and devices, such as computers and mobile phones. Several e-services can be combined automatically to perform virtually any kind of task or transaction.

Hewlett-Packard is working on the mass proliferation of e-services. These services will be modular and combine and recombine to solve problems, complete transactions, and make life easier. Some will be available on Web sites, but others will be delivered via your TV, phone, pager, car, email in-box, or virtually anything with a microchip. Some will even operate behind the scenes, automatically working on your behalf.

Hewlett-Packard sees three trends becoming very important in the near future: apps-on-tap, e-service portals, and dynamic brokering of e-services. The proliferation of apps-on-tap will enable companies to take full advantage of pay-as-you-go software for many key functions: accounting, payment systems, payroll, ERP, and purchasing. The birth of new e-services portals will create vertical portals, such as OpenSkies[28] in the travel industry, and horizontal portals, such as Ariba.com's[29] procurement portal. The dynamic brokering of e-services will enable consumers and businesses to send out requests for services via the Net. E-services will bid to fulfill those requests, giving companies the opportunity to reach their customers anywhere they are.

To better understand the new opportunities, it is necessary to look at today's business on the Internet. Most Internet business is based on Web servers and browsers that communicate and exchange information and follow pre-defined processes. Web enabled start-ups rock entire industries by reaching out for customers that were not accessible to small companies before. Amazon.com is the perfect example of a start-up that no one took seriously in the beginning, and it suddenly became the biggest fish in the pond. Traditional book companies, such as small bookshops, large chains of bookshops, publishing houses, and large resellers suddenly had to start their own online ventures to counter the attacks of the Internet start-ups. Slowly, companies have started to think about their businesses differently. They adapt the rules of the start-ups and redefine their customer service. Customer-centric business has become more important, and through the Web, customers have been enabled to serve themselves.

Extranets have helped to unify communities of partners and have saved the participating companies lots of money. New services appear on the Internet every day. But the problem with today's Web sites is the fact that each company has built its services in a proprietary, massive, and costly way. The companies were forced to create their entire offerings from the ground up.

The open service paradigm developed by Hewlett-Packard makes electronic services more modular, which allows them to be assembled on the fly because they are based on the open-services interface. They can be combined more easily to offer new types of services. The paradigm of "do-it-yourself" evolves into "do-it-for-me," because the services can talk to each other without human interaction by using the open-services interfaces. The interface allows for inte-

---

[28]http://www.openskies.com/
[29]http://www.ariba.com/

gration of any type of device into an e-service.

It is expected that the shift in this paradigm will be followed in the business world and the IT area. Web sites will become less important. The automated services will work more likely in the background. Most people would rather only think about all the things they want to get done, not how they get done. With e-services, this will become reality.

The first set of e-services provided by Hewlett-Packard will most likely include the following services:

- **Storage e-services**—Providing storage on demand over the Internet

- **MIPs on demand**—Providing computing power whenever it is necessary

- **Payment processing e-services**—Creating independent payment processing services to support e-business

- **Imaging and publishing e-services**—Making printing and publishing through specialized e-service providers easier

---

Table 16.5. E-Services

By implementing e-services, it has become possible to offer traditional services such as banking to more people via a wider variety of devices. Business-to-business Web sites will profit from the new paradigm, because it will become easier to implement billing systems, automated supply-chain management, procurement solutions, and a modular ERP system. All kinds of business-to-business transactions can now be handled by combinations of intelligent e-service systems.

The IT department will also be able to benefit greatly from the introduction of e-services. Certain services, which are not required daily and are not part of the core business, can be outsourced, such as processing power, data storage. and data mining. E-services will help to ensure the availability and security of these services. E-services will give companies much more flexibility in the way they manage their IT infrastructures, making more efficient use of both in-house and outside resources. The IT department will transform into a service provider, which will use outsourcing strategically to lower costs and gain flexibility. It will enable e-services of all types and plan profitable e-services solutions, such as extended supply chains, and ensure the quality of service and the consistency of user experience. Everything on the Net (both inside the enterprise and the outside world) is treated as an online service.

The most important battle is the long-term one. In an e-services world, there is going to be more choice, and thus more competition. Customer loyalty will be based on the reliability of your systems, how easy they are to use, and how useful they are.

Another interesting field for the paradigm of e-services is the pay-per-use service. All types of consumers are able to pay for services on demand, such as software, video, or audio services. Pay-per-use e-services will be tightly woven into daily life. People will plug into them via e-service utilities, such as corporate networks, phone companies, and ISPs, using a variety of devices. And they can take advantage of a much wider range of services, because they'll pay only for what they use.

E-services are highly modular, making them attractive to customers who do not want to buy enormous, monolithic systems. Customers are able to subscribe to the specific services they want to use. This reduces the initial cost for accessing a service, and companies will be able to generate more stable profit streams because the money is coming on a more regular basis and from more customers. The basis for the profit is broadened, and by streamlining whole chains of transactions, companies are able to save costs. Another advantage of e-services is that services can be developed, tested, and put on the market much more quickly because of their modular architecture.

E-services make it possible to focus on the real work and neglect the underlying technology and processes. End users will be able to take advantage of much more sophisticated services because they don't have to buy the whole thing. They can just subscribe to the services they need, paying for some of them on a pay-per-use basis. The aim of Hewlett-Packard is to turn any service or computing resource into a building block for e-services.

16.6.4   Microsoft .NET

Microsoft[30] is another company providing a comprehensive vision of the future of the Internet. Microsoft is creating an advanced generation of software that melds computing and communications in a revolutionary new way, offering developers the tools they need to transform the Web and every other aspect of the computing experience. Microsoft .NET will allow the creation of truly distributed Web services that will integrate and collaborate with a range of complementary services to serve customers in ways that today's Internet companies can only dream of. Microsoft .NET will be an important player in the Next Generation Internet. It tries to make information available any time, any place, and on any device.

The idea behind Microsoft .NET is that the focus is shifting from individual Web sites or devices connected to the Internet to constellations of computers,

---

[30]http://www.microsoft.com/

devices, and services that work together to deliver broader, richer solutions. People will have control over how, when, and what information is delivered to them. Computers, devices, and services will be able to collaborate with each other to provide rich services, instead of being isolated islands where the user provides the only integration. Businesses will be able to offer their products and services in ways that let customers seamlessly embed them in their own electronic fabric.

Microsoft .NET will help drive a transformation in the Internet toward HTML-based presentation augmented by programmable XML-based information. XML is the key to the Next Generation Internet, offering a way to unlock information so that it can be organized, programmed, and edited; a way to distribute data in more useful ways to a variety of digital devices; and a way to allow Web sites to collaborate and provide a constellation of Web services that will be able to interact with each another.

Microsoft .NET includes the .NET platform from Microsoft, .NET products from Microsoft, and third-party .NET services. The .NET platform includes .NET infrastructure and tools to build and operate a new generation of services. It offers a unique .NET user experience to enable rich clients; .NET building block services, a new generation of highly distributed megaservices; and .NET device software to enable a new breed of smart Internet devices.

The .NET products from Microsoft features a new version of its operating system named Windows.NET that includes a core set of pre-integrated services, such as MSN.NET, personal subscription services, Office.NET, Visual Studio.NET, and bCentral for .NET.

MSN.NET will become the new .NET platform by combining the leading content and services of MSN.[31] The new MSN.NET will enable consumers to create a single digital personality and leverage smart services to ensure consistent, seamless, and safe access to the information, entertainment, and people they care about any time, any place, and on any device.

The personal subscription services will add premium consumer-oriented services on the .NET platform. These personal services are targeted toward the consumer market and will build on existing Microsoft entertainment, gaming, education, and productivity products. Today, these products are software applications that you buy on CD and install locally on your personal computer. In the future, these software packages will be online services that will give people the power of traditional desktop applications with the flexibility, integration, and roaming support of the new .NET family of user experiences.

Office.NET will replace today's office software package that includes Word, PowerPoint, Excel, Outlook, and other tools. Office.NET will provide tighter integration of these applications by providing a so-called universal canvas technology that combines communication, browsing, and document authoring into a single environment, enabling users to synthesize and interact with informa-

---

[31] http://www.msn.com/

Microsoft will create a set of core services to support its .NET concept. These services will be treated as plug-ins or add-ons to the new Windows.NET operating system.

- **MSN.NET**—Internet platform for content and services.

- **Personal Subscription Services**—Set of premium consumer-oriented services, such as entertainment, gaming, education, and productivity products.

- **Office.NET**—Communications and productivity tools, including universal canvas technology that combines communication, browsing, and document authoring into a single environment.

- **Visual Studio.NET**—XML-based programming model and tools.

- **bCentral for .NET**—Subscription-based services and tools for small and growing businesses.

Table 16.6. .NET services

tion in a unified way. Instead of having separate applications for word processing and browsing, a single service will replace all of these applications. New collaboration capabilities provide the means to communicate and collaborate with people inside and outside of their companies. This new service will be accessible through a new so-called smart client that will replace the current browser technology to provide rich functionality, performance, and automatic deployments on any device.

Visual Studio.NET will provide a new environment for developers. This new service will support an XML-based programming model and tools. They will be supported by MSDN, the Microsoft Developer Network, providing newsgroups and tools to support developers. This enables the easy delivery of highly distributed, programmable services that run across standalone machines, in corporate data centers, and across the Internet.

And last but not least, bCentral for .NET will provide a range of subscription-based services and tools for small and growing businesses. These hosted services include messaging and e-mail, enhanced commerce services, and a new customer relationship management service built on the .NET platform. These services will enable small businesses to better serve their customers online.

The proposed functionality will include support for rich hosted catalogs and the ability to track interactions with customers to enable personalized service.

The third-party .NET services are provided by a vast range of partners and developers who have the opportunity to produce corporate and vertical services built on the .NET platform.

The Microsoft .NET platform uses XML and standard Internet protocols. This concept allows the creation of XML-based Web services. Whereas today's Web sites are hand-crafted and don't work with other sites without significant additional development, the Microsoft .NET programming model provides an intrinsic mechanism to build any Web site or service so that it will federate and collaborate seamlessly with any others.

Microsoft also is creating an entirely new set of development tools, designed from the ground up for the Web, and spanning client, server, and services. These tools will enable developers to transform the Web from today's static presentation of information into a Web of rich, interactive services. Microsoft's Visual Studio allows the creation of Internet services in XML. Microsoft also provides tools for BizTalk, to allow the visual programming of business processes by composition of services, enabling business analysts to develop solutions the same way developers do.

Microsoft promises that .NET services can be used on any platform that supports XML, but unfortunately, .NET servers run only on Windows platforms, meaning that not every device can become a service provider. Devices that do not run Windows need to create an interface to a Windows platform and use a proxy service to promote their services in a .NET world.

In Microsoft's long-term vision, all application software will likely be provided as a service, subscribed to over the Internet. This will allow service providers to offer better customer service, transparent installation and backup, and a positive feedback loop into the product-development process. Software delivered as a service would also allow developers to respond more swiftly with backups and antivirus protection.

This means that most software applications will become subscription services over time. These subscription services will be part of the next generation desktop platform based on Windows.NET. It will provide a tight integration with a core set of .NET building block services, integrated support for digital media and collaboration, and personalization. Another feature is that it can also be programmed by .NET services, meaning that existing subscription services can extend the platform easily without having to install additional components on the platform itself.

With its .NET platform, Microsoft promises that it will revolutionize computing and communications in the first decade of the 21st century by being the first platform that takes full advantage of both technologies. The company from Redmond promises to make computing and communicating simpler and easier than ever. It will spawn a new generation of Internet services and enable tens of thousands of software developers to create revolutionary new kinds of online services and businesses. It will put you back in control and enable greater control of your privacy, digital identity, and data.

Microsoft's business philosophy has always been to produce low-cost, high-volume, high-performance software that empowers individual and business users, and creates opportunities for customers, partners, and independent developers. That philosophy is what sets Microsoft apart from its competitors, and Microsoft .NET takes it to a new level. As you can see from its philosophy and the services provided in the first generation .NET services, Microsoft's vision is targeted toward consumers and small-to-medium businesses. Large corporations are not mentioned in their vision. To make .NET a truly universal idea, several things need to change.

First, it needs to take into account all types of individuals and businesses. It needs to extend its business model beyond its successful office products and support all types of platforms, regardless of whether or not the platform is running Microsoft products. If Microsoft adapts its vision to become truly universal, it has a good chance of becoming a major supplier of services in the next Internet generation.

16.6.5 IBM Web Services

IBM defines Web Services as self-contained, modular applications that can be described, published, located, and invoked over a network—generally, the Web. Essentially, dynamic e-business envisions an Internet where business entities can manage electronic interactions within their own domain and between trading partners programmatically. From the discovery of new partners to the integration of another business entity, dynamic e-business puts the emphasis on program-to-program interactions instead of the customer-to-program interactions that dominated the early phases of e-business.

IBM provides an architecture for dynamic e-business. The Service-Oriented Architecture (SOA) is a conceptual architecture for implementing dynamic e-business. Today, most of the systems and applications running in the business world are made up of tightly-coupled applications and subsystems. The drawback with this is that a change to any one subsystem causes breakage in a variety of dependent applications. This brittle aspect of existing systems is partly responsible for the high cost of system maintenance and the limitations around the number of trading partners one can manage. In the Web Services architecture, each component is regarded as a service, encapsulating behavior and providing the behavior through an API available for invocation over a network. This is the logical evolution of object-oriented techniques (encapsulation, messaging, dynamic binding, and reflection) to e-business.

The potential concept of SOA was found to have merit by companies like IBM and Microsoft who recognized that, for SOA to succeed where other distributed computing concepts had failed, it must be implemented on open standards. Thus, these companies have recently cooperated on recommended stan-

A number of basic principles will surface to help articulate what must be done to address the complexities of e-business integration in the future to make it dynamic and automatic. The following principles are required:

- **Loose Integration**—Integration between software resources should be loosely coupled.

- **Universal Access**—Service interfaces for software resources should be universally published and accessible.

- **Open Standards**—Program-to-program messaging must be compliant with open Internet standards.

- **Outsourcing**—Applications can be constructed by stitching together core business processes with outsourced software components/resources.

- **Granularity**—An increase in the availability of granular software resources should improve the flexibility and personalization of business processes.

- **Efficiency**—Reusable outsourced software resources should provide cost and/or productivity efficiencies to service consumers.

Table 16.7. Web Services

dards like UDDI and WSDL. Regardless of the implementation, SOA is comprised of three participants and three fundamental operations:

- **Service Provider**—A service provider is a network node that provides a service interface for a software asset that manages a specific set of tasks. A service provider node can represent the services of a business entity, or it can simply represent the service interface for a reusable subsystem.

- **Service Requestor**—A service requestor is a network node that discovers and invokes other software services to provide a business solution. Service requestor nodes will often represent a business application component that performs remote procedure calls to a distributed object, the service provider. The provider node may reside locally within an intranet, or it could reside remotely over the Internet. The conceptual nature of

SOA leaves the networking, transport protocol, and security details to the specific implementation.

- **Service Broker**—The service broker is a network node that acts as a repository, yellow pages, or clearinghouse for software interfaces that are published by service providers. A business entity or independent operator can represent a service broker.

These three SOA participants interact using three basic operations: publish, find, and bind. Service providers publish services to a service broker. Service requesters find required services using a service broker and bind to them

After you comprehend the concept of SOA, reflect on some of the basic principals of dynamic e-business to understand how best to implement it. A fundamental aspect of a successful implementation is the reliance on open Internet standards. The dynamic e-business strategy is founded on a core set of emerging technologies that reflect the work of researchers and consultants from a variety of companies and industry organizations.

IBM incorporates XML, SOAP, WSDL, and UDDI into its vision of the future. These enabling technologies collectively reflect on the set of Web services technologies offered by IBM. Over time, extensions and additions to this set will arise, but all such changes will arise from an ongoing reliance and cooperation with open industry efforts.

IBM has put together a very strong proposition, and it can be expected that they will have a say in what the future will look like. Still, it remains to be seen whether IBM can implement the ideas presented here.

16.7   Comparison of Pervasive Computing Technologies

The following tables give a short summary on the functionality of the different pervasive computing technologies. It is difficult to tell which technology will prevail. Two or three technologies will probably fight for the next few years to become the standard for pervasive computing, but due to the nature of pervasive computing, this does not really create a problem. If it is truly pervasive, the technologies will not only live side-by-side, but also create many connections to create a new technology built from the best components of every technology. If this reminds you of the Borg in Star Trek, then you understand the concept of pervasive computing. But pervasive computing is not supposed to be hostile. Resistance is not futile, if you do not like it. If you do not know the Borg, don't worry :-). You still should be able to grasp the concept of a single entity containing all information and services.

As we have seen, pervasive computing technologies can be divided into three layers. The bottom layer is responsible for the device-to-device communication, the middle layer is responsible for the exchange of data between

- **BlueTooth**—Technology to create wireless local area networks

- **ChaiServer**—Java Virtual Machine extended to allow Web-based connection to other devices on the network

- **Inferno**—Small-footprint network operating system to let any type of device plug in to the network

- **Jini**—Devices that are able to share services for "spontaneous networking" with other Jini devices

- **Universal Plug and Play**—A technology that extends hardware recognition and connection of any type of device

Table 16.8. Device-to-Device Communication

devices, and the top layer is the service level, which allows the exchange of services between devices. These three layers need to be present to make pervasive computing successful. The above-mentioned technologies often represent more than one layer in the layer model. By using the layer model, it is also possible to integrate technologies from different vendors. It is, for example, possible to use Jini in conjunction with E-Speak, or T Spaces with ChaiServer. The reason is that most of the technologies are based on Java. Microsoft is the exception, and it has created a new programming language called C#, which should have interfaces to connect Java-based pervasive computing technologies.

Mobile phones, video cameras, CD players, car stereos, and other electronic mobile devices, which already use lots of technology, most likely will be the first devices to be connected to the Internet. Refrigerators, microwave ovens, and other household devices eventually will become connected to the rest of the world. Security issues must be resolved before every device can participate in the Internet. But companies like Hewlett-Packard and Lucent Technologies have thought about security, resulting in a more secure infrastructure for any type of device. A universal authentication module will need to be implemented that is independent of the technologies used, and it should be independent of the authentication method. Retina scan, finger scan, voice recognition, login/password, smart card, or any other technology should be connected without problems. This will make sure that any service will be able to use the authentication module.

- **InfernoSpaces**—Allows distributed computing applications to be built, independent of the platform.

- **InfoBus**—Allows cooperation of applications across devices and exchange of data

- **JetSend**—Lets networked devices negotiate common file formats for data exchange

- **Millennium**—Lets collections of computers automatically divide up computing tasks across networks

- **T Spaces**—Allows any type of device to share messages, database queries, print jobs, or other network services

Table 16.9. Information Exchange

- **E-Speak**—Architecture for service interaction in a large, unsafe, distributed environment, such as the Internet

- **Salutation**—Service discovery and session management protocol

- **SOAP**—Standard for encoding intermachine function calls in XML so they can be passed among heterogeneous systems

- **UDDI**—Technology that enables the implementation of a service broker

- **WSDL**—XML vocabulary that provides a standard way of describing service IDLs

Table 16.10. Service Broadcasting

The vision of Microsoft,[32] Sun,[33] and Hewlett-Packard[34] are mainly used to

---

[32] http://www.microsoft.com/
[33] http://www.sun.com/
[34] http://www.hp.com/

demonstrate knowledge in these technologies and business cases. It remains to be seen which vision will be realized, but it is safe to assume that all of them will be implemented, because they are so similar. It is even probable that these visions will merge into a single strategy over time, after more knowledge and experiences about the technologies are available.

- **Brazil**—Web-based infrastructure to link people and resources over the Internet

- **E-Speak**—Architecture for service interaction in a large, unsafe, distributed environment, such as the Internet

- **.NET**—Vision of next-generation operating system using subscription services over the Internet

- **Web Services**—Self-contained, modular applications that can be described, published, located, and invoked over a network

---

Table 16.11. The Vision

If we look at the various vision presented here, we can easily detect that Microsoft and Sun are building a technology-driven vision with lots of good ideas in mind, but they don't offer a solution for businesses. To make a business successful, it needs a business vision, marketing vision, product vision, and many other parts of a corporate vision. Although HP does not target all of these parts, it does address businesses with many business cases that can be found on the HP Web site. We will see which of these visions will prevail. It is likely that all three of them will be accepted, because they address three different target markets. Hewlett-Packard is targeting the business managers in the big accounts, Sun targets the technology managers in the big accounts, and Microsoft targets the small-to-medium enterprises technology manager. The big issue will be transforming these partial visions into a singular vision about the Universal Network.

16.8   The Future of Pervasive Computing

The future is still wide open; with new standards about to develop, it is hard to predict what the future of pervasive computing will bring. One thing is clear today: It will change the way we use computers in many ways.

Software, for example, won't necessarily be installed anymore on a computer. We will be able to use a certain piece of software on many different devices, meaning that software becomes a service, that is paid for on demand. A request will be sent out, and the appropriate service will send back the answer. This paradigm is true for any type of information or service. Information and services will become available whenever there is need for them. Think again of the car from the preface. It does not need to have a petrol station search engine built in. It is enough to know that one is available and how to get to it when the petrol is low.

This may change the way we work. It will certainly require lots of changes in the working world, because everything is moving to the just-in-time paradigm. Products, for example, won't be built and then sold at a time when the customer is ready to buy. The products will be built when the customer is paying, and services will be offered at the time the customer needs them.

Pervasive computing may also change the way we see advertising. Just as spontaneous networks can be created, spontaneous advertising will be available to match the needs of the customer on the fly. By personalizing advertising, consumers will get the feeling that the ads are valuable information and feel less disturbed by the information flow.

Pervasive computing also makes it easier for freelancers (or e-lancers) to make money on a world-wide basis. Through pervasive computing, it is possible to deliver a small building block in a highly specialized area to other services to make them more sophisticated, without interfering with their business. This will also mean that we are moving from software developers to service developers. The quality of the service idea becomes more important than a particular implementation.

Therefore, two types of new entrepreneurs will be around for the next few years: service developers and service providers. The service providers of today will eventually merge to the service providers of tomorrow, but it gives start-up companies the chance to take away market share from traditional service providers, because they may be slow to move to the next generation of services. If you are interested in more information on this topic, please check out my book dedicated to this topic, *Internet Future Strategies*[35], and keep an eye on the book's Web site[36] for updates on this topic.

---

[35] Daniel Amor, Internet Future Strategies, Prentice Hall, 2001
[36] http://www.internetfuturestrategies.com/

Chapter 17

BEYOND PERVASIVE COMPUTING

17.1 Technical Outlook on the Future

17.1.1 Opening Internet Access

If we look at a future where pervasive computing has been fully implemented, we can only wonder what will happen next. Although this may be 10 to 15 years away, it is still important to think about the future and how we can help to design it. This chapter presents some ideas about how the future may evolve; these ideas may be completely wrong, but the goal is to provide a realistic vision. The time frame may be off, meaning that the vision may be reality in 5 years or as far away as 50 years. In any case, this chapter may help you to develop new ideas on how to create the future. A forum for the exchange of these new ideas can be found on the Web site[1] for this book.

Pervasive computing will change the way we work and live. But it will be a transition rather than a revolution, from a technological point of view. Just as the telephone did not replace direct human communication and the television did not replace the cinema, pervasive computing will not replace current computing technologies. Desktop computers will still be part of everyday life, but they won't be "hot" technology anymore. The big business will move on to new paradigms, technologies, and devices.

Pervasive computing will add a new facet to our lives, giving us the opportunity to do more things more easily and in less time. Many services will become instant and will be able to anticipate the customer's need and act appropriately.

The cost for accessing the Internet will drop to nearly zero for most parts of Europe and Northern America, and other countries will be able to catch up with the Internet as new devices become available, such as the PDSL (power digital subscriber line) technology from Northern Telecom.[2] This allows Internet ac-

---

[1]http://www.ebusinessrevolution.com/
[2]http://www.nortel.com/

cess over power lines instead of telephone lines, and reduces the investment in infrastructure for poorer countries.

BellSouth[3] is about to release its passive optical network (PON), which is already available in Atlanta, Georgia, to selected customers, and will offer a bandwidth of 100 MBits/s to its customers. The new standard does not require active network components to be installed at the customer's site. Lucent Technology[4] and Oki Electric[5] provide the network termination module. This module translates not only the network traffic from ATM to Fast Ethernet, but also automatically extracts radio and television content, so that radios and television sets can be used in their usual ways without any additional hardware components. The test installation allows the transmission of 100 MBits/s, 120 digital and 70 analog television programs, and 31 digital audio channels at the same time. The new access is available for about $60 a month. This is a huge advancement.

Wireless communication will also become more important, making an individual even less dependent on a certain location, certain device, or certain software. Even more important, the bandwidth will become adjustable so that anyone will get the speed he or she needs at a given moment. Delays and disconnects will become errors of the past. Quality of service will become a standard on the Internet allowing customers to buy certain service level agreements from their content access providers.

In the future, companies will not distinguish themselves via faster or more advanced processors. A successful company is a company that is able to connect to all other devices, enabling the consumer the freedom of choice. The biggest change in technology will not be providing advanced and faster processors or new operating systems, but providing the free choice of technology. It suddenly will not matter how fast your computer at home is or which operating system you are using. Through Internet services, you will acquire processing power for a short period of time, whenever necessary, which will then be much cheaper than buying a new computer; the operating system will not matter, because the services offered over the Internet will no longer depend on a certain piece of hardware or software. The services will adapt to the environment of the customer and always offer the best performance.

17.1.2 Consumer Device Integration

With the unlimited availability of bandwidth, we will also see a total convergence of media over the next few years. Instead of having a radio, television set, compact disc player, and computer, which most people have today, only one device will be needed, and it will replace all of these consumer devices. Physical media, such as compact discs and video cassettes, will become obsolete. Still,

---

[3]http://www.bellsouth.com/
[4]http://www.lucent.com/
[5]http://www.oki.com/

the covers may remain, since they usually contain the lyrics and photos of the artists. You might buy these in person in a shop or have them shipped to your home. In addition to the usual booklet information, the former CD booklet will contain an access code to download the music from the Internet to your local audio device. The audio or video will be saved onto a local or remote hard disk in a format similar to MP3, but with better compression and security features built-in, to prevent the illegal copying of music. It won't prevent the copying of the music, but if the music is copied from one device to another one, the price will be deducted from the credit card of the owner of the target device. Traditional compact disc and video sellers have a few years remaining before they need to change their business to support the new paradigm.

Television and radio will become just another set of packets on the Internet. They won't disappear, but the diffusion over the air will disappear. Instead of an aerial, you will need a broadband Internet connection to watch digital television. The same will happen to radio, which is already today one of the most popular services on the Internet. Personally, I love to listen to Radio Deejay[6] from Milan, Italy, Capital Radio[7] from London, England, and CoolFM[8] from Belfast, Northern Ireland, at work. By moving television and radio to the Internet, aerial frequencies that were once blocked by the television and radio transmissions become available. This will allow new sorts of devices to communicate with each other in a wireless manner.

Due to broadband Internet access, the next obvious device to move from being a separate entity to an integral part of the "new media center" will be the telephone. Today, ISDN already offers the possibility of not only hearing but also seeing the other participant. With broadband access (such as DSL) and this new media center, you will be free to choose between audio only or audio/video calls.

The next generation of cellular phones is expected to have a bandwidth of 2 MB/s, allowing it to serve more information over the mobile phone than ever before. Right now, the GSM standard is restricted to approximately 9 KB/s, making it even unusable for larger e-mail and Web sites. As we saw in Chapter 3, there are ways around this limit. The MegaCar is the first mobile media and business center, which allows high-speed Internet connection on the road. It achieved the high-speed connection by multiplexing 16 GSM channels. Imagine multiplexing 16 channels of the new standard of 2 MB/s, making it possible to transfer 32 MB/s to and from a moving car. Phone calls, television, radio, computer applications, electronic services, audio, and video will become available anytime, anywhere—as long as your media center supports the output. The next generation of mobile phones will have color displays, making it easy to display video and live transmissions. Imagine your phone acting as a projector to increase the size of the image.

---

[6]http://www.deejay.it/
[7]http://www.capitalradio.co.uk/
[8]http://www.coolfm.co.uk/

With the migration of the traditional consumer electronic devices to the new media center, consumers get rid of another problem that was rather annoying in the past—the format problem. Remember the Beta versus VHS video cassette war, the MPEG versus AVI movie format war, or the compact disc versus the minidisc war. A long list of format wars has wasted time in the past, because they did not allow the further development of technologies. With the integration of consumer electronics, you will get the electronic content you requested, and you won't have to know which format it is in and how it has been transported to your screen or your speakers. If a new format is required, the appropriate software will be delivered with it on the fly.

Other devices in your household won't likely merge—a dishwasher is not capable of washing your clothes, nor is a refrigerator able to act as a stove. But, pervasive computing will still have an impact on these devices. These devices are already fitted with computer chips, so connecting them to a local network will be the next logical step. Control from a central point may be useful, but there is still manual work involved, like putting the clothes into the washing machine or taking the dishes out of the dishwasher. It will also most probably not be of interest to you how much energy was spent on washing the clothes. But this information may be of interest to your energy broker, who tries to get you the lowest energy prices available. The future will bring along a rich set of brokers.

By handing out all the relevant information regarding your usage of energy, the energy broker can determine which power supplier will be the most cost efficient, and may even offer advice on how to lower the cost even more. The energy broker could tell you that you may reduce costs to switch on the washing machine on Monday evening, because there seems to be a surplus of energy, which can be bought at a low price for that particular action. The broker will update your local database with this information, which in turn will trigger your washing machine at the right time. This still requires you to load it with dirty clothes, but when you do it may not make a big difference. In any case, the energy broker will check with your Internet-based calendar to see if this conflicts with an evening at the cinema.

Another example could be the refrigerator, which is connected to your food broker, who selects the shops where you can buy your preferred food at the best price and quality. You may be buying your food on Saturdays, but this may change in the future, because the price won't be fixed for food anymore. It will depend on the demand of the market. Therefore, the food broker will try to match your food preferences with the offerings on the market and buy the food that costs less. You will have to be a bit more flexible to get the lowest prices for your food or eventually pay a bit more for exactly what you requested.

17.1.3   Privacy and Security in the Future

Every device collects data on your spending and usage, so one-to-one marketing can become even more effective. The more information about you that becomes available to merchants, the easier they can make the appropriate offers to you. The disadvantage is that you may eventually lose your privacy if you give out all this information to every merchant that passes by on the Internet.

"Big Brother" from George Orwell's book *1984* could easily become reality now, but not exactly as Orwell envisioned it. It will most probably not be the government stealing your privacy, but the advertising and marketing agencies interested in your profile in order to convince you to buy even more things you do not need. This tendency can be seen already on many Web sites today.

To prevent such a situation, a new form of trust needs to be built. The brokers mentioned in the previous section won't be humans, but more likely intelligent agents sitting in the media center and controlling the flow into and out of the house. They will be the only ones to see your detailed profile. The energy broker, for example, won't send out your profile to every power supplier in the world to get the best prices. Instead, to retain your privacy, the broker will ask the power suppliers to provide a detailed price list with up-to-date information so that your needs can be compared with the price lists of the suppliers.

There will probably be a constant connection between power suppliers and energy brokers, so that the energy brokers are able to get instant power and the lowest prices for say, the washing machine, which is switched on once a week, whenever the customer switches on an additional digital device. The communication between energy broker and power supplier needs to be encrypted to make sure the transaction is not intercepted. Because the energy broker will most likely buy energy from several power suppliers at the same time, they won't be able to get the full picture of the customer. But by intercepting the communication with all power suppliers, someone would be able to benefit from this information. Encryption technologies should be allowed on a worldwide basis at a high level, making break-ins impossible.

Security also becomes very important. If the energy broker orders energy whenever it is required, it is critical to ensure that nobody can break the energy broker or its connection to the power suppliers. The whole installation should be highly redundant and highly available, meaning that the envisioned "five nines" of Hewlett-Packard (99.999 percent, which is equal to five minutes down-time a year) will need to increase to at least six or seven nines. Only if this high level of availability can be guaranteed can the technology be used on a day-to-day basis. Otherwise, hackers would find ways to black out whole towns with a few commands.

To maintain your privacy and ensure that no one else can switch devices in your household on or off, a next generation type of firewall will be required that allows secure access to your devices, while you are on vacation, for example, but prohibits any other access to them. New forms of authentication will be required making it impossible for penetrators to appear as someone else.

Digital and biometrical authentication and authorization methods will be combined to form a new biodigital form of access to your home, car, and anything else that should restrict public access.

17.1.4   Next Generation Internet

The future of the Internet will be tightly integrated with the technological advances and the change of business models in the future. Several programs are in progress to create new Internet technologies, such as the Internet 2 initiative[9] in the United States. This brings us to the infrastructure that is required to build up highly-interconnected homes and will allow us to bundle all types of media into a single media center.

The World Wide Web that dominates today's online business will evolve into a more interactive and multimedial place. Many services that are available on the Internet have already become part of the World Wide Web. Group calendar services, online chats, and newsgroups are all merging to the Web platform making it easy to integrate all other types of services. The teletext system, which is part of your television, will be replaced by the Web, allowing you to view a television program in a more interactive manner. You will be able to choose a show, read information on it, and then set a reminder so that the television will provide you with a reminder five minutes before the show starts. You will be able to click on everything that you can see during the show and get more information on it. Imagine a scene in a kitchen, where you are able to get more information on the stove and order it directly over the Internet. If you think the last James Bond film was overloaded with advertising, think again. The next generation of Internet will allow you much more direct or indirect advertising over the different channels it will provide.

A similar paradigm will be available for the radio. Listen to the radio, and click on a button if you like a certain song. This will lead you to the Web site of the singer, where you can get additional information and buy the recording. Radio and television will become streaming content on the Internet.

The Web as we know it today will likely disappear or at least become less relevant. The simple linking of pages will be substituted by a more powerful way of linking content to each other. Multiple targets will become common, meaning that clicking on one link will provide you with more than one resource at a time. This will eliminate link lists. Instead of providing a list of links on a certain subject, you provide one link with the possibility to specify the content and the right content will automatically be selected for you. Although this is already possible through search technologies, it will become available to anyone through a simple command in HTML.

Searching on the Web will also become easier as search technologies evolve

---

[9]http://www.internet2.edu/

and become more mature. Instead of typing in cryptic keywords, natural sentences and search engines with built-in voice recognition will ask you to clarify the search request. They will become the new standard on the Internet.

17.2 Looking into the Future of Business

17.2.1 Content Brokers

In the future, new intermediaries will appear in between consumers and providers. They will either provide content, products, or services. Unlike traditional intermediaries, the new brokers will have access to all providers at the same time and will most probably have fixed contracts with one or a few providers, as we have seen in the past. They will be free to choose whatever may be the best for their customers and will earn their money by receiving a percentage of each transaction. Half of a broker's fee will probably be paid by the content provider for the chance to have a new customer, and half by the customer for the opportunity to have the best provider.

The content providers will deliver the content to the new media center that will replace all the consumer electronics in most households. The content will be delivered on top of broadband Internet access, meaning that Internet networking and content standards will be used. New technologies will be necessary to ensure the same quality of service customers have received from traditional television and radio services, for example.

The traditional model of selling goods at a fixed price will also change from the pay-once standard toward the pay-per-use model. Advanced technologies in billing will allow companies to charge customers on a pay-per-use basis, incurring very low costs for both customers and suppliers. Digitized products and services will benefit most from the new model, because they can be easily uploaded and removed from the premises of the customer. Digital certificates and one-time passwords will allow access to content once, for example, and then the content will be automatically deleted or locked until the customer enters a new valid one-time password.

New rights management and metering systems will allow copyright holders to implement these new pricing models. The metering systems will allow for charging on a microtransaction basis, if the copyright holder wishes and if the user agrees. These microtransactions would entail any or all of several operations, including searching within the content, modification, duplication, printing, exporting from the controlled environment, browsing, and transmission to others. Instead of using pricing models based on subscriptions or units, content providers, authors, and publishers could choose to charge a small amount for small transactions. Instead of downloading a complete book, you would pay as you read each chapter that is delivered to your doorstep, in whatever form, either as a file or as a printout or as an audio file. The same may apply to magazines. You would pay only for the articles that you are really interested in reading.

The transaction-based revenue stream will eventually exceed the revenue stream of traditional print products. To succeed, content providers will have to cannibalize their existing print, subscription, and connect-time businesses. If they don't, startups will most likely take over the lead in content providing. A problem is how to move from traditional pricing to the transaction-based pricing without destroying the traditional business. To make this move, it is important to take a longer period of declining revenues into account. Many traditional companies will be reluctant to move forward, but they will benefit by getting a stable transaction-based set of businesses. New and small companies will have fewer barriers into a market, as technology becomes more open and enables them to be much quicker than large corporations with their legacy systems.

17.2.2 Product Brokers

By now it should be apparent that the future of business will be bright, but only for companies that adapt to the new paradigm of service and selling. The Internet revolutionized computing and adapted business, and pervasive computing is the logical extension of Internet computing. That said, it truly provides a revolution in the business area.

Remember the example from the introduction, where a car automatically selects the cheapest gas station nearby for refueling. This is a basic product broker, which is also location sensitive due to the fact that the car cannot get the gas from just anywhere, but requires it within the next 10 miles. The request for gas and the demand will eventually set the price the driver has to pay.

From this example, you can see that the most important change will be that fixed prices will disappear over the next 10 to 15 years. If we look at the prices of the flight tickets of Lufthansa[10] or British Airways,[11] you will see they do not have fixed prices anymore. A flight from Stuttgart to London can cost anywhere from 100 to 800 dollars/euros. The initial prices that were set by the company will start to move either up or down immediately after they have been released, depending on the demand for that particular flight. If it is a flight that no one wants to take, you will see ticket offers near the 100 dollars/euros price, while almost full flights will cost up to 800 dollars/euros. Sometimes, there is no price difference between economy class and business class. The reason is that if economy class is booked, no matter which class you chose, you paid business class and would fly business class. The airline could have easily said that economy was full, but many companies pose restrictions on the use of business class. By offering an economy class ticket, the travel department would be buying it, because it is normally cheaper than business

---

[10]http://www.lufthansa.com/
[11]http://www.britishairways.co.uk/

class and the traveler would arrive in London at the desired time.

As prices start to become fluid, it will become harder for end customers to handle because the prices become less transparent. Therefore, a new set of intelligent agents will be introduced that will help to decide which offering is the best in a particular situation. We are already seeing the first generation of intelligent shopping agents appear on the Web, with DealPilot,[12] being one of the most prominent examples for buying books. These intelligent shopping agents will be refined over the next few years to give you even lower prices. Imagine that you need to buy a certain book, but do not necessarily need the book tomorrow. In this case, the shopping broker will be given a week to find the cheapest offering. During that week, the prices may go up and down at a single shopping site because of the varying demand, but the shopping broker will accumulate orders from different customers. After three days, the shopping broker may have found 10 people who are interested in the same book and place a bid for 10 books at every single online bookshop. The shops would then reply with their price to the shopping broker, which then would further negotiate prices and get the best price for your request.

17.2.3 Service Brokers

Besides shopping brokers, a new class of service brokers will appear, which will be able to handle mass-customized services, such as a television program, and highly-individualized services, such as translations. In addition to television channels with a preset selection of programs, the future will bring highly-customizable films and shows that you can view at any give time. This is already possible in some areas, such as closed hotel television systems, but this sector will grow very fast in the future. Because the showing of a film or show does not require any additional service other than broadcasting, it can be easily mass-customized. Again, prices will vary. Top titles will be rather expensive, while older films may have lower prices assigned to them, depending on the preference of the customers.

In addition, films that no one wants to see will be free of charge. This may seem unorthodox, but as no one is viewing them, nobody is losing money by offering these films free of charge. Offering films for free will get the attention of the customers, and eventually demand will start to rise for these films, and the price will increase over time. If no one is interested in the films, keeping them in the archives won't cost much, because memory prices will drop with every month, just as they currently do.

Service brokers for translators will use a similar schema to determine a price. It will be based on the quality, reputation, and availability of the translator. Imagine a company that needs 20 pages of technical text translated within a week and two translators bidding for the contract through the translation broker. There is a young translator, inexperienced and seeking work, who is

---

[12]http://www.dealpilot.com/

offering his service at \$1 per line translated as a base price. The more experienced translator offers her service at \$2 per line translated. The number of pages and the time frame until it needs to be completed determine the real price of the bid. This is still a partly manual process. First, both translators need to check whether they have time for 20 pages, which would take about two days. Due to the fact that the text is of a technical nature, then the price of the first translator rises to \$1.75 and the second to \$2.10. The difference in increase is linked to the experience in that particular field. The experienced translator has already done several translations on that particular technology, while the other one has never done such a translation. If we now look at the availability, the young translator has many other translations to do in that particular week, so it would be difficult to do this translation as well. Therefore, his price rises to \$2.40 per line, because he is reluctant to take on this work as well. The more experienced translator revises her calendar also and finds it also difficult to include it into the time schedule, but is willing to take on the extra work in the evening, so the price rises only slightly to \$2.30.

The translator broker will pass these two prices to the company who requested the translation service and they will be able to determine which offering is the better one. The choice will not be made only on the basis of the price, but also on the existing relationships with the translators. It could well be that they will choose the young and more expensive translator for that particular case, because they know him well and he knows the company, while the other one may be a very good translator, but hasn't had any experience with the company.

As you can see, service brokerage will not be able to make automated decisions on who should provide the service, but it offers a good way to determine the market price at the moment a service is required and reduces the overhead for finding the right service for that particular moment. Prices will vary depending on demand and offerings on the market. At another given time, it may be possible that 200 translators will bid for a single translation.

As you can imagine, this will increase the competition in an already competitive market. It can be expected that manufacturers, retailers, and content producers will all need to change the way they do business. Instead of offering complex products, they will only offer small building blocks that are compatible with the offerings of the competition. Car manufacturers, for example, will most likely disappear in their current form. Over the last few decades, they have evolved from manufacturers to parts assemblers. The parts come from third parties, which are tightly integrated into the supply chain of the car manufacturer. Today, the car manufacturer decides on the design and the technical specifications of a car and assembles the car from prebuilt parts. In the future, it is possible that car manufacturers will evolve into car assemblers that accept parts from any third-party vendor.

Customers will then be able to use a highly-sophisticated online configurator to build a personalized car. Imagine a future in which you will be going to

BMW's[13] Web page, selecting the chassis of a Ferrari[14] and the motor of a Rolls Royce.[15] In this future, all parts will be compatible, just as services are becoming compatible in Hewlett-Packard's E-Services vision; this is something car manufacturers will have to embrace. This not only applies to the automotive industry, but also to any other industry that builds complex products from pre-built components. The computer industry will not be much different; today, we can already see the dominance of the computer platform decreasing through the Internet, HTML, and Java. Computers will become commodities, offering the basic computing service, which can be enhanced in real time over the new Internet. The boxes that you buy in the future will contain a computing broker that will get the appropriate resources over the network for you. Additional memory, hard disk space, or processing power will be made available to you whenever you need it. This will reduce the cost of the computing broker to a minimum, making it possible for anyone to get such a box, which will deliver the basic functionality required to connect to the Internet.

The move from agriculture to the Industrial Age to the service era will be completed within the next 10 to 15 years. This does not mean that we will be able to live without agriculture and industry, but they will become commodities that are expected to be in place with technological advances occurring in the future, requiring even fewer people in these particular areas. The service industry will become the place to make big money.

It seems the biggest problem is imagining a postservice era. What will come after service? Maybe that is like asking for the fourth dimension of space, which may be mathematically easy to prove, but almost impossible to imagine. Maybe there is nothing after service, but it seems the world should dedicate some resources to defining a new type of business culture and model that will lead us through the 21st century. Those who can best predict the postservices area will become the new millionaires over the next 20 years.

17.2.4 Broker Software

While auctions have always played an important role in all economies around the world, the Internet has brought us to a new level, in which the paradigm of auctions has started to dominate the economies. The Internet reduced the high costs for receiving information on an auction, and participating is free. The Internet makes it possible to reduce the transaction costs to such an extent that almost anything can be sold through the auction/broker model over the Internet. Typical auctions are used for the following market segments: Last-minute tickets, electronic components, used goods, and consumer products.

The Internet is the ideal platform because it removes the limits of traditional auctions, such as a short time for the offer and the low number of bid-

---

[13]http://www.bmw.de/

[14]http://www.ferrari.it/

[15]http://www.rollsroyce.co.uk/

ders. To offer an auction service on the Internet, a broker information system must be installed at the auction site. One solution is the Auction Server, developed by AIT GmbH,[16] which provides a complete infrastructure for developing online auction and brokering services. Anything from a small auction to a complete auction server can be implemented by the Auction Server software.

The software offers more than just a simple bidding process. Automatic bidding agents are able to act on behalf of customers who have no time to attend the auction themselves. The bidding agents can be programmed to bid up to a maximum price automatically. The first site that used the Auction Software from AIT GmbH was QuickM@rket,[17] which acts as an "auction mall," where small and large customers are able to create auction services.

The German eBay[18] site uses auction software from Living Systems,[19] which is built on a multithreaded service architecture. The Auction Broker uses advanced features such as JIT compilation and caching that ensure high performance on the most demanding sites. The deployment platform supports multiserver clusters with native load balancing and fail over to reliably serve high-volume, transaction-intensive applications.

The Auction Broker Software allows companies to create and design their own customized auction and/or virtual store. It's a user-friendly auction tool with an e-commerce solution. It is designed to be simple to navigate. It offers flexibility for any size of business. The back-end administrator (Auction Control Center) has features to customize the software to the needs of the company. The Auction Broker Software is available for rent or purchase, making it possible to run the business yourself or to outsource it to Living Systems.

17.2.5 Total Automation of Business

The use of next generation brokers will eventually lead to a complete automation of business, making human resources superfluous for electronic services. Searching for the best price will become an automatic feature of your company, requiring fewer resources on the sales side and on the procurement side. Although production may still need human resources, the administrative part of the company will reduce itself to the minimum required.

The introduction of global Internet laws will make it easy for intelligent agents to discuss contracts with each other without any human interaction. Human intelligence will only be required to feed the intelligent agents and to use the service in the end. As more fully automated services run in the background, the need for human business is reduced, leaving the field open to new ideas.

As more people are superfluous in large companies, they will eventually be-

---

[16]http://www.aitgmbh.de/
[17]http://www.quickmarket.de/
[18]http://www.ebay.de/
[19]http://www.living-systems.de/

come electronic freelancers who offer a set of highly specialized services and work on multiple jobs at the same time. Through the Internet, one person and some high-speed hardware will be able to handle many thousands of requests simultaneously, instead of one at a time. This will reduce the number of people in the freelancer space as well. Few people will have jobs in agriculture, production, and the service area. Most people will have time to do whatever they like, exploring new things and making new discoveries.

The total automation of business may make large companies collapse because they are too expensive to maintain, which will put the electronic freelancers in a perfect position to produce goods or services, both online and offline. Smaller manufacturers may find it easier to produce highly specialized goods at a good price, as opposed to large companies that produce many types of goods at the same time.

The Internet will allow for the creation of virtual value chains instantly for the production of certain goods, which can be highly personalized. The need for rock-solid value chains will be reduced, and the power in business will be reshuffled accordingly.

17.3   The Societal Impact

17.3.1   The Transition Phase

Advances in technology will always influence society, but not merely in a positive or negative way. Politicians should think about ways to give everyone in this new society a role that allows them to be happy. National politics will lose control completely over the global network economy in the future, so the national politicians have plenty of time to think about new social structures and programs to help people in the transition phase.

With hope, after the transition phase, people will have found a new sense in life and will have a new income stream to support themselves and their families. The major obstacle for such a future are politicians who do not know much about technology and are slow to respond to the changing needs of the ever-faster evolving world. But a new generation of politicians will eventually appear that has grown up with the Internet and will know what to do with the opportunities that surround them.

Internet technologies offer huge opportunities for the world to concentrate on the important things in life and forget about the day-to-day work that is done better by computers. The downside of this example is that if the world depends so much on technology, it will have an enormous problem if the power supply fails at any given time. Therefore, the free time that has become available should be used to show people how things worked in a world without electricity, computers, and networks. Although it may not shut down all the network, it can impact people in certain areas very badly.

Farmers should learn how to produce food without the help of machines, just as everyone should learn how to write with a pen and learn how to cook or make fire without high-end technology. Already today this knowledge is getting lost, because school children have seen cows only on television and think milk is made in the supermarket. Technology may make life easier, but the roots should not be forgotten and should still be taught in school.

While technology advances, people should think about how to simplify the use of technology. Operating a VCR is often a very complicated mission, as is changing the time on the car stereo. Technology should enable everyone to use it, not just the highly educated specialists. A mobile phone is a good example of a simple-to-use technology that hides all the complexity from users.

17.3.2   Responsibility for the Society

The Internet has already become the major form of communication for educational institutions and businesses all over the world. Governments are catching up fast, and we need to ensure that everyone will get access to the Internet. This means that everybody should be provided with the hardware, the software, and the necessary knowledge to make use of the content and services on the Internet. This type of knowledge is called *information literacy*.

Print literacy is still a major problem around the world. In many countries, many people cannot read or write. Obviously, before they can go on to learn how to use the Internet, this problem must be solved. Otherwise, the Internet becomes an elite information infrastructure, accessible only to those who have the resources, skills, and knowledge. This would further increase the gap between the rich and the poor.

To ensure global access to the Internet, the education standards around the world need to be raised. New paradigms of accessing information need to be implemented that allow the less-fortunate to access the basic services via graphical symbols, for example. Many Web-based services need to be accessed over a standard phone to allow people without Internet access or reading skills to access electronic services.

17.3.3   Next Generation Work Life

Through the automation of standard business processes, the amount of work as we know it today will be reduced significantly. This poses a huge problem for many people who built their life around work. For the next generation, the importance of work to make enough money to live a decent life is decreased. In an automated business world, products and services will be available at the fraction of the current costs, making them available to virtually anyone who desires them.

It remains to be seen whether the reduced amount of work will be distributed evenly among the work force or whether it will become a status symbol for the new information elite. The current trend is moving toward a working elite, and this won't be stopped unless politicians do something about it. This will require a shift from a work-life balance to a new form of making sense of life. The Internet may create psychological dependencies on networked communication, thus reducing the demand for relationships in real life. The Internet allows people to hide their identity every time they connect. People may associate more freely online because they are not bound to geographical or temporal limits.

It may well be that people will still work, not to earn a living, but to stay occupied. In a positive future, this will mean that work shifts to scientific research, art, music, and sports, which are all jobs, but not necessary to survive, because they do not provide food. Still, it also may have a negative impact, in which a government might force people to work to keep them out of trouble.

17.3.4   Politics in the 21st Century

Governments and politics have always been bound to geographical limits. The limits defined the governments' areas of influence. Laws are enforced within these limits, and taxes must be paid by the people living within these limits. The taxes are used in part to pay for infrastructure and security of the inhabitants of a country defined by its borders.

The globalization of the economy has also created a situation in which companies reside in a certain country, but pay taxes in another country. BMW,[20] for example, a German company, does not pay any taxes in Germany. There is also no way to force them to pay, because they would move the whole production to another country, causing employees to lose their jobs. The New Economy has a large impact on politics, much more than ever before. The Internet increases this dilemma for national governments. Governments will still be needed to keep up public safety, for example, but influence of governments on the economy will soon vanish.

The European Union is one example of a transnational government, which sets rules on a transnational level. Although taxes still differ among the members of the union, the laws are merging. At the same time as we see the creation of a transnational government, the influence of national governments is largely reduced. But the influence of regions has increased over the same period of time. The European Union has become less a union of national states, and more a union of regions, whereby the local identity becomes more important than the national identity.

The economies of these regions are competing against each other, and each region can be seen as a single economy competing against other economies under the same law and taxation system.

Politics will have to focus on regional and transnational issues to survive. The existing national states will not have a bright future if they do not adapt to the changing environment.

---

[20]http://www.bmw.com/

The Internet and its technologies have already changed the way people communicate and interact. Although it is impossible to predict the future, we can expect an invasion of new technologies that will try to emulate the real-world in new ways. You should not forget that the Internet and its technologies are just models of the real-world. In many cases, these are idealistic models, which cannot represent the complexity of life. Therefore, remember that when dealing with businesses and people over the Internet, it may not be real, but only a very realistic model of the transaction.

Appendix A

GLOSSARY OF E-BUSINESS TERMS

This appendix contains a list of all the buzz words and acronyms used throughout the book. You can use this glossary while reading the book, or keep it as a future reference.

3G The acronym stands for third (or next) generation of wireless technology beyond personal communications services. The World Administrative Radio Conference assigned 230 megahertz of spectrum at 2 GHz for multimedia 3G networks. These networks must be able to transmit wireless data at 144 kilobits per second for mobile user speeds, 384 kbps for pedestrian user speeds, and 2 megabits per second for fixed locations. See also *UMTS*.

802.11 The Institute of Electrical and Electronics Engineers standard for wireless local area network interoperability.

ACID An acronym and mnemonic device for learning and remembering the four primary attributes ensured to any transaction by a transaction manager (also called a transaction monitor). These attributes are: Atomicity, Consistency, Isolation, and Durability.

Acceptable Use Policy (AUP) A former set of formal rules that govern how a network, application, or piece of information may be used. See also *Netiquette*.

Access Code Each baseband packet starts with an Access code, which can be one of three types, CAC, DAC, and IAC. The CAC consists of a preamble, sync word and trailer, and its total length is 72 bits. When used as a self-contained message without a packet header, the DAC and IAC do not include the trailer bits and are a length of 68 bits.

ACL See *Asynchronous Connectionless Link*.

Active Box Loudspeaker box with built-in power amplifier or output amplifier (also for loudspeakers with separate amplifiers for high, middle, and bass frequencies).

Active Termination One or more voltage regulators for terminating voltage (ensures a uniform signal level over the entire bus).

Active X Software technology developed by Microsoft that helps designers include applications in HTML pages. Its lack of security causes many people to prefer Java over Active X.

Active X Controls A set of interfaces that access Windows resources; small additional modules, called controls, that can be embedded in a program. The module concept was standardized by Microsoft and dubbed Active X (for example, a calendar element provides programs with standard calendar functions, eliminating the need for programming them on your own).

ADC Acronym for analog-to-digital conversion. This is an electronic process in which a continuously variable (analog) signal is changed, without altering its essential content, into a multi-level (digital) signal.

Address An address on the Internet is described as a URL, or Uniform Resource Locator, which can be used for any type of addressing, such as email (mailto:info@gallery-net.com), Web pages (http://www.news.com/), and FTP sites (ftp://ftp.netscape.com/pub/communicator). Instead of using domain names, it is also possible to use IP addresses. See also *Electronic Mail, File Transfer Protocol, Transmission Control Protocol/Internet Protocol, Uniform Resource Locator*.

Address Resolution Protocol (ARP) Used primarily with IP—Network Layer to resolve addresses.

ADR See *Astra Digital Radio*.

Ad Server A program or server that is responsible for handling the banner advertisements for several Web sites. These servers offer statistics about visits and movements of customers. They also offer functionality, such as banner rotation, so that a single customer will not see a certain banner twice during a single visit to a Web page.

ADSL See *Asymmetric Digital Subscriber Line*.

Ad Transfer The successful arrival of a customer at the site of the banner advertisement.

Advanced Mobile Phone Service (AMPS) An analog cellular phone service standard used in the USA and other countries. Compared to other standards, such as GSM, it is not really advanced.

Advanced Research Projects Agency Network (ARPANet) A computer network that was developed in the late 1960s by the U.S. Department of Defense to allow communication in a postnuclear war age. Predecessor of the Internet. See also *Internet*.

Advanced SCSI Programming Interface (ASPI) Standard for developing SCSI drivers. The ASPI manager ensures that all devices connected to the SCSI controller function properly.

Advanced Television Enhancement Forum (ATVEF) Consortium of hardware manufacturers and program vendors interested in creating a single standard from various procedures of interconnecting TV and Internet under one name. ATVEF is also aimed at the home-network market, particularly because the interfaces defined in the standards proposals call for controlling much more than TVs and computers.

AFK Net language for "away from keyboard."

Air Interface The standard operating system of a wireless network; technologies include AMPS, TDMA, CDMA, and GSM.

Agent Application that helps a customer by completing transactions, seeking information or prices, or communicating with other agents and customers.

AI See *Artificial Intelligence*.

Aliasing Distortion of video images (or other analog information) as a result of digitizing analog information or processing information by digital means with an insufficiently small sampling rate (see *Sampling*). To reproduce the information properly, the sampling rate must be at least twice as large as the resolution of the original.

Alternate call Allows the user to switch back and forth between two calls.

American Standard Code for Information Interchange (ASCII) A standard for the representation of upper- and lowercase Latin letters, numbers, and punctuation on computers. There are 128 standard ASCII codes that are represented by a 7-digit binary code ($2^7 = 128$). The other 128 bit codes are used differently on most computers. To display non-Latin codes, Unicode is used in most cases. See also *Unicode*.

AMPS See *Advanced Mobile Phone Service*.

Anonymous FTP Anonymous access to FTP server. See *File Transfer Protocol*.

ANSI See *American National Standards Institute*.

Answer call Allows the user to take a call.

Anti-aliasing Suppressing the effects of aliasing by filtering out rough, "step-like" edges or smoothing the edges by mixing colors to form transitions (interpolation). It is the standard process used to remove jagged edges in computerized graphics.

API See *Application Program Interface*.

Applet Java programs that are embedded into HTML pages. Applets are restricted in such a way that they are, for example, not allowed to read and write to the hard disk of the user without explicit permission. See also *HyperText Markup Language, Java, Servlet*.

Application A program that is self-contained and that executes a set of well-defined tasks under user control.

Application Program Interface (API) Interface that allows the communication between programs, networks, and databases.

Application Service Provider (ASP) A service provider that makes applications available on a pay-per-use basis. ASPs manage and maintain the applications at their own data center and make the applications available via the Internet to subscribing businesses.

APS See *Automatic Programming System*.

Archie Software for finding files on anonymous FTP sites. It searches only for filenames, and has been replaced by more powerful Web-based search engines. See also *File Transfer Protocol*.

Architecture In terms of data processing or information technology, a general term for the structure of all parts of a computer system (hardware and software).

ARP See *Address Resolution Protocol*.

ARPANet See *Advanced Research Projects Agency Network*.

Artificial Intelligence (AI) A branch of computer science that studies how to endow computers with capabilities of human intelligence.

ASCII See *American Standard Code for Information Interchange*.

ASP See *Application Service Provider*.

ASPI See *Advanced SCSI Programming Interface*.

Assistant (also referred to as "Expert" or "Wizard") A tool designed to help users create programs (e.g. databases).

Asymmetric Digital Subscriber Line (ADSL) The alternative to an ISDN line. It allows much higher bandwidths over a standard digital telephone line. It needs to be configured similar to a leased line in such a way that it can connect only to ISPs that are near you. A typical ADSL setup allows download speeds up to 1.5 megabits per second (about 200 kilobits per seconds), but upload is restricted to 128 kilobits per second (similar to two ISDN lines). ADSL works asynchronously, hence the different upload and download speeds. See also *Binary Digit*, *Bits Per Second*, *Integrated Services Digital Network*, *Leased Line*.

Astra Digital Radio (ADR) Transmission procedure for digital radio stations that have been broadcasting since 1995 via ASTRA satellites. It is based on the data compression procedure Musicam / MPEG-1. The data rate is 192 Kbit/s (including error correction at 256 Kbit/s). In addition, 9.6 Kbit/s are used as overhead to transmit Radio Data Signals (RDS), conditional access (access control for Pay Radio), and other signaling data.

Asynchronous Connectionless Link (ACL) One of the two types of data links defined for the Bluetooth Systems, it is an asynchronous (packet-switched) connection between two devices created on the LMP level. This type of link is used primarily to transmit ACL packet data. The other data link type is SCO.

Asynchronous Transfer Mode (ATM) A fast, intelligent hardware switch that can support voice, data, image, and video. Cell-switching (as opposed to packet) technology replaces variable-length packets now in use with uniform (53 byte) cells. It promises any-to-any connectivity and networks that scale easily from a few nodes to global deployment. Combines packet-switching's efficient use of bandwidth with circuit-switching's minimal delays.

@ The commercial a—also referred to as the "at" sign. It has become a symbol recognized the world over as a separator in email addresses.

AT Attachment (ATA) ANSI version of the IDE interface.

ATA See *AT Attachment*.

Atapi See *AT-Bus Attachment Packet Interface*.

AT-Bus Attachment Packet Interface (Atapi) Interface for AT-Bus hard disk but also for CD-ROM drives or CD recorders that "understand" the IDE controller.

ATM See *Asynchronous Transfer Method*.

Attached File A file—for example, an application, image, or sound—that is embedded into an email message. See also *Electronic Mail*.

ATVEF See *Advanced Television Enhancement Forum*.

Audio Video Interleaved (AVI) Windows format for saving video with sound.

Audiovision Combination of sounds and images.

AUP See *Acceptable Use Policy*.

Authentication The process of verifying a person is who he or she claims to be.

Authorization The process of allowing system access to a person.

Auto PC An in-vehicle combination AM/FM radio, Windows CE-based computer, compact disc and CD-ROM player, wireless phone, and navigational system. The units are about the size of a typical car stereo.

Automatic Programming System (APS) Automatically assigns all receivable television stations to the TV's preset positions when the TV is switched on for the first time.

Automatic Vehicle Location (AVL) Combining a location-sensing device (such as a GPS receiver) with a wireless communications link to provide a home office or dispatcher with the location of a vehicle or mobile asset (such as a trailer or heavy machinery).

Avatar Three-dimensional representation or digital actor of a customer in a Web shop or chat room.

AVI See *Audio Video Interleaved*.

AVL See *Automatic Vehicle Location*.

Backbone The top level of a hierarchical network. Major pathway within a network offering the highest possible speed and connecting all major nodes. The main pipes along which data is transferred. See also *Network*, *Node*.

Back-end The "side" of a client/server program that supplies data (typically, a database server. See also *Front-End*.

Bandwidth The maximum amount of information that can be sent through a connection at a given time. Usually measured in bits per second (bps). See also *Binary Digit*, *Bits Per Second*, *T-1*.

Bandwidth on Demand A component in the DECT-MMAP standard that provides the required channel capacity—dependent on the current service and data load.

BASIC See *Beginners All-purpose Symbolic Instructional Code*.

Baud Commonly used in the same way as bits per second. See also *Binary Digit*, *Bits Per Second*, *Modulator Demodulator*.

BBS See *Bulletin Board System*.

BCC See *Blind Carbon Copy*.

Beginners All-purpose Symbolic Instructional Code (BASIC) Invented at Dartmouth University, a computer language that is easy to learn and highly flexible.

Beta A prerelease of an application that is made available for the purposes of testing.

Binary Mathematical base 2, or numbers composed of a series of zeros and ones. Because zeros and ones can easily be represented by two voltage levels on an electronic device, the binary number system is widely used in digital computing.

Binary Digit (Bit) A single digit number in base 2 (therefore 0 or 1). The smallest unit for computerized data. See also *Byte*, *Kilobyte*, *Megabyte*.

Binary Hexadecimal Algorithm to convert binary files into ASCII text. Used mainly on Macintosh computers. See also *ASCII*, *Binary*, *Multipurpose Internet Mail Extensions*, *UNIX-to-UNIX Encoding*.

Binhex See *Binary Hexadecimal*.

Biometrics The science and technology of measuring and statistically analyzing biological data.

Bit See *Binary Digit*.

Bits Per Inch (BPI) Describes the data density on magnetic media in bits per inch.

Bits Per Second (BPS) A unit for measuring the data transmission rate, for example, the transmission path of a modem. The fastest modems operate today at 56 KBPS. An ASCII letter consists of 8 bits; theoretically speaking, a 56 K modem can transfer 7,000 characters (nearly 2.5 pages of standard letter-size pages) per second. See also *Bandwidth*, *Binary Digit*.

BLER See *Block Error Rate*.

Blind Carbon Copy (BCC) Copies people onto emails without showing their names to the person to whom the email message was originally addressed. See also *Carbon Copy*, *Electronic Mail*.

Block Error Rate (BLER) Number of data blocks, contained in one or more errors at the lowest level of error correction.

Bluetooth The Bluetooth consortium introduced the open Bluetooth standard 1.0 (available as a PDF file from www.bluetooth.com) in 1999, led by the founding companies Ericsson, Nokia, Toshiba, IBM, and Intel. Bluetooth was developed especially for economical, short-range, wireless links between PDAs, laptops, cellular phones, and other (mobile) devices. Bluetooth devices are capable of detecting each other automatically and setting up a network connection. Using a modulation frequency of 2.4 GHz, data is transferred from one adapter to another, whereby the signals do not have a pre-defined direction and can, in principle, be received from any other device. Bluetooth functions with spread-spectrum modulation, combined with frequency hopping (1600 frequency hops per second). There are 79 usable hopping frequencies available between 2.402 GHz and 2.480 GHz spaced at 1 MHz. A unique ID plus data encryption ensures that only "authorized" devices can communicate with each other. The maximum data rate is 750 Kbit/s, and the range is limited to 10 meters. However, the standard also permits 100 meters with increased transmission power. Bluetooth also enables devices to communicate with each other on the basis of JINI Technology without being connected by cable. Many of the typical Bluetooth fields of application overlap with those of the IrDA standard for infrared data transmission. The first hardware and software products equipped with Bluetooth were introduced at the end of 1999. Experts predict that by 2005, nearly 700 million of these devices will be in use.

BOFH Net language for "bastard operator from hell."

Bookmark A file that contains references to Web pages that you have already visited, which then can be organized and used to return to a particular page.

Boolean Search A search allowing the inclusion or exclusion of documents containing certain words through the use of operators such as "AND," "NOT," and "OR."

Boot To startup or reset a computer. When a computer is booted, the operating system is loaded. There are two different ways of booting a computer. A cold boot means that the computer needs to be powered up from an off state, and a warm boot means that all data in the memory is erased and the operating system is loaded from start. See also *Operating System*.

Bot Net language for "robot." A piece of software, usually run from a shell account. Most bots are harmless, and simply keep channels open for their owners, while they are not on IRC. There are some malicious bots, however, made to take over channels, etc. A popular and usually friendly bot series is called "Eggdrop." See also *IRC*.

Bozo Filter A feature to screen out incoming email and news postings from those whose correspondence is not valued. See also *Electronic Mail*, *Spam*.

BPI See *Bits Per Inch*.

BPS See *Bits Per Second*.

Broadband Describes a communications medium capable of transmitting a relatively large amount of data over a given period of time. A communications channel of high bandwidth.

Brokering The general act of mediating between buyers and sellers. In the universal network, brokering technologies, such as E-Speak, will enable universal service-to-service interaction, negotiation, bidding, and selection. See *E-Speak*.

Browser Client application that is able to display various kinds of Internet resources. See also *Client*, *Home page*, *Uniform Resource Locator*, *World Wide Web*.

BSIG Bluetooth Special Interest Group, with over 1,500 member companies and organizations.

BTW Net language for "by the way."

Bug A programming error that causes a malfunction of the computer software or hardware. Not synonymous with *Virus*.

Building Automation Describes the sum of all automating measures in buildings (including rented housing and private homes). Building automation makes it possible to control and regulate technical systems to ensure efficiency, primary energy savings, productivity, and comfort.

Bulletin Board System A computer-based system that allows people to discuss topics, upload and download files, and send and receive email. Bulletin boards can either run independently on a single computer to which people dial in, or can connect to other bulletin boards to form a network, such as the FidoNet. See also *Electronic Mail*, *Network*.

BWOTD Net language for "bad word of the day."

Byte Eight bits in a byte, which is used to represent a single ASCII character, for example. See also *Binary Digit*.

Cache A small, intermediate memory area for exchanging or transferring data, for example, between the hard disk and central processing unit. A cache accelerates hard disk access.

Carbon Copy (CC) When people use the CC function of their Web browser, they use it to copy additional recipients to an email. See also *Blind Carbon Copy*, *Electronic Mail*.

Carrier A company that provides a communications service.

CASS See *Conditional Access Sub-System*.

CBT See *Computer-based Training*.

CC See *Carbon Copy*.

CCIR See *Comité Consultatif Internationale des Radiocommunications*.

CCITT See *Comité Consultatif Internationale de Telegraphie et Telephonie*.

CD-DA See *Compact Disc-Digital Audio*.

CDMA See *Code Division Multiple Access*.

CDMA2000 A third-generation wireless technology proposal submitted to the International Telecommunication Union, which is based on the IS-95, or cdmaOne, standard.

CDPD See *Cellular Digital Packet Data*.

CEBus See *Consumer Electronics Bus*.

Central Processing Unit (CPU) The main chip inside every computer that is used to run the operating system and the application software.

Cellular Digital Packet Data (CDPD) Also referred to as "wireless IP" and a method of sending and receiving information via mobile devices. CDPD allows information to be sent in "packets" or blocks over the existing analog cellular network. It is best suited for short, periodic bursts of information. CDPD is a wireless transmission method that uses the analog cellular network, also known as Advanced Mobile Phone System (AMPS). CDPD allows information to be transmitted on idle cellular voice channels.

CERN European Laboratory for Particle Physics in Geneva, Switzerland, the birthplace of the World Wide Web.

Certificate Authority (CA) Issuer of digital certificates; used for encrypting communication and signing documents. See also *Digital Certificate*.

CGI See *Common Gateway Interface.*

Chai A product-family name for a group of HP products supporting intelligent interaction among embedded devices through the use of the Java programming language and today's Web standards.

Chat Direct communication over the Internet with multiple persons. Unlike email, responses are made in real time. See also *Internet Relay Chat.*

Checksum A special calculation applied to validate the transmission of a piece of information. If the information is transmitted and the calculation achieves the same result, then the transmission was successful.

Chip Term for complex, integrated circuits that can contain several hundred thousand semi-conductor circuits (transistor/diodes, etc.). By creating structures as small as one thousandth of a millimeter, higher levels of integration can be achieved.

Class In object-oriented programming, a category of objects, or the applet file itself. For example, there might be a class called shape that contains objects that are circles, rectangles, and triangles.

Clear Call Allows the user to terminate a call.

Clear Connection Allows the user to terminate an individual call. This service is required if the user wants to terminate a call to only one conference participant within a telephone conference.

Client Application that resides on the customer's computer and contacts a server to communicate. Examples: IRC clients, Web clients. See also *Internet Relay Chat, World Wide Web.*

Client/Server Databases in a network often administered from a central location by a server. Client software installed on the user's computer retrieves required data from the server.

Clipboard A piece of memory that stores information temporarily.

CODEC Program or device that COmpresses/DECompresses digital video.

Code Division Multiple Access (CDMA) A spread spectrum air interface technology used in some digital cellular, personal communications services, and other wireless networks.

Comité Consultatif Internationale des Radiocommunications (CCIR) International consultative committee for radio and TV standards, based in Geneva, Switzerland.

Comité Consultatif Internationale de Telegraphie et Telephonie (CCITT) An international consultative committee for international telecommunication protocol standards, based in Geneva, Switzerland.

Common Gateway Interface (CGI) A standard that describes how a Web browser passes information to a Web server. CGI programs read the information, process it, and pass the results back to the Web browser.

Common Interface An interface specified by DVB, e.g., as PCMCIA interface in set-top boxes for connecting a conditional access module. This enables the user to add a decoder module to a generic set-top box with a common interface for receiving the services/programs offered by a pay-TV provider. See also *DVB*.

Compact Disc-Digital Audio Standard for audio CDs (defined in the Red Book drafted by Philips and Sony).

Compiler A program that translates a programming language into machine code.

Compression Technology to reduce the size of files and save bandwidth. See also *Bandwidth*.

Computer-Based Training (CBT) A way of learning that uses a computer and a software package as the delivery mechanism, offering information on a certain subject and a test for the pupil.

Computer Telephone Integration (CTI) Describes the integration of telephones and computers. This enables solutions that go far beyond the limitations of standard telephones. A classic example is using a telephone in combination with a PC database.

Concept Search Instead of searching for documents that contain a given keyword, a concept search will search for documents related conceptually to a given keyword.

Conditional Access In the framework of the European project DVB, a European transmission standard, DVB/MPEG-2, was passed. There are various systems (e.g., Irdeto, Beta, Conax, Cryptoworks, Seca, Syster Digital, and Viaccess) used in Europe for the additional encoding required by pay-TV channels.

Conditional Access Sub-System (CASS) System of access authorization to (digital) TV and radio services that can only be descrambled (see *Descrambling*), i.e., viewed or heard, for certain user groups or if a service fee has been paid.

Conference Call Allows the user to converse with several parties on one line. The maximum number of conference members are limited by the PBX. See also *PBX*.

Connection Established path for exchanging information.

Constraints Logical rules stored in a database. These rules check certain conditions at the table level, for example, whether a particular range of values was violated for numerical fields.

Content Information that has a tangible aspect because it has been collected and contained in a content object. Content can be unstructured (usually text) or structured (in a database). Content can be collected at differing levels of granularity.

Content Management The process of developing, maintaining, organizing, and deploying Web content to efficiently support the collaborative activities of content creators, site administrators, and users.

Consultation Call Allows the user to consult (call) a third party while the second party is still on the line.

Consumer Electronics Bus (CEB) Communications standard for home networks developed by the Electronics Industry Association (EIA) and the Consumer Electronics Manufacturer Association (CEMA).

Control Prog/Monitor (CP/M) Operating system created by Gary Kildall in the 1970s.

Controlled Vocabulary A predetermined list that specifies the acceptable terms that can be used to describe a particular information resource. Control of these terms is necessary to solve two common problems: (1) users employ different terms to describe the same resource (oil, petrol, petroleum, gas), or (2) a term can have multiple meanings (musical pitch, pitch the ball, sales pitch, etc.).

Cookie Piece of information that is stored in the browser and can be retrieved by the server that placed the information there. This piece of information can be used to identify a user.

CORBA Common Object Request Broker Architecture is an architecture and specification for creating, distributing, and managing distributed program objects in a network. It allows programs at different locations and developed by different vendors to communicate in a network through an "interface broker."

CP/M See *Control Prog/Monitor*.

CPU See *Central Processing Unit.*

CRC See *Cyclical Redundancy Check.*

Credit Card Processor Offers services for electronic businesses to process credit card transactions and verify credibility of customers.

Crossposting A message that is sent simultaneously to several newsgroups. See also *Newsgroup.*

CTI See *Computer Telephone Integration.*

Cyberculture A collection of cultures and cultural products that exist on and are made possible by the Internet, along with the stories told about these cultures and cultural products.

Cyberspace First used in the book *Neuromancer*, by William Gibson, published in 1984. It is used to describe the Internet. See also *Internet.*

Cyclical Redundancy Check (CRC) Checksum for correcting errors that occur during data transmission.

DAB See *Digital Audio Broadcasting.*

Daemon A background process waiting for a client to start up the service, such as the POP3 daemon, which runs continually, but is activated only when people retrieve email using an email client.

Data Dictionary Area of memory in which all information on a database and the accompanying programs are stored and managed. This includes information on tables, triggers, constraints, relations, and indices.

Database A term with several meanings: refers to a DBMS (Database Management System) as well as a file that contains, for example, customer addresses or other data. A database can combine several tables into one file. Often only one table is allowed per database file for PC databases. In this case, the user can still create a link to other tables from various files (see *Referential Integrity*).

Data Encryption Key (DEK) A string used to mathematically encode a message so that it can be decrypted only by someone with either the same key (see *symmetric encryption*) or with a related key (*asymmetric encryption*).

Data Encryption Standard (DES) Encryption scheme developed by IBM in the 1970s.

Data Header Data structure at the beginning of a data packet header.

Data Packet Data is generally transmitted within networks in the form of data packets. These packets contain the header, the actual data (user data), and redundant data (CRC) for error correction on the receiving end.

Data Rate Also known as data transfer rate. Indicates the number of data units per specified time interval in bit/s (bits per second).

Data Record Combines all the data for a specific table entry into a logical entity. Using a file-card box as an analogy, a record would be the equivalent of one file card.

Data Throughput Transmission rate of the actual user data (excluding redundant data for error correction or data for delimiting individual data blocks, e.g., header). Specified in cps (characters per second).

DCOM See *Distributed Component Object Model*.

Decryption The reconstruction of encrypted data.

DECT See *Digital Enhanced Cordless Telecommunication*.

DECT-MMAP DECT Multimedia Access Profile. A further development of the DECT standard as a "virtual cable" for mobile data devices; typically used for wireless Internet or intranet access within the transmission range of the base station with data rates of up to 2 Mbit/s. The most important DECT-MMAP features include service negotiation, dynamic resource management, and bandwidth on demand. See also *DECT*.

Dedicated Line A phone line that connects two computers permanently to keep up service.

Deflect Call Forwarding an incoming call without having to actually answer the call.

Demilitarized Zone Zone in multilayered firewalls that contains public Internet services.

DES See *Data Encryption Standard*.

Descrambling See *Decryption*.

DHCP See *Dynamic Host Configuration Protocol*.

DHTML See *Dynamic HyperText Markup Language*.

Dial-up A temporary connection between two computers established over a phone line.

Digerati The digital elite; invented by *Wired* magazine. Derived from the word *literati*.

Digital Audio Broadcasting (DAB) System for digital terrestrial transmission of radio and multimedia data services. The MUSICAM system is used for data compression—from 1.411 Mbit/s to 192 Kbit/s.

Digital Certificate File containing information about its owner that can be used to identify the owner. See also *Certificate Authority*, *Secure Sockets Layer*.

Digital Enhanced Cordless Telecommunication (DECT) The cordless telephone represents the most common application of DECT standards. Wireless, digital communication DECT-MMAP operating at ISDN speed (64 Kbit/s) or faster is growing in significance. The effective radiated power specified for DECT of 250 mW provides an effective range of up to 50m in buildings and 300m outdoors. The voice signal is 32 Kbit/s. Germany uses the 1.9 GHz band, whereas other frequencies between 1 and 10 GHz, commonly between 1.5 and 3.6 GHz, are also used. The access method used by DECT known as TDMA (Time Division Multiple Access, time multiplex) allows up to 100,000 simultaneous users in a single cell.

Digital Home See *Intelligent Home*.

Digital Satellite Equipment Control (DSEC) System for controlling satellite receiver equipment. Conventional satellite equipment uses a 14/18 volt switching voltage to switch between polarization levels (horizontal or vertical). An additional 22 kHz frequency on the input voltage line signals the direction of the satellite antenna to specific orbit positions. In contrast, DiSEqC uses a universal control concept, because the 22 kHz signal not only switches equipment on and off, but also samples frequencies. This allows a number of commands (including polarization switching) to be transmitted within the DiSEqC system. DiSEqC level 2 also features bi-directional communication. Thus, the satellite receiver sends commands to the peripheral components capable of logging on to the receiver. Plug and Play in satellite receiver technology is an example.

Digital Signal Processor (DSP) A separate processor, built into some sound cards, that relieves audio processing from the computer's CPU.

Digital Subscriber Line (DSL) General description (also referred to as "xDSL") for high-speed, broadband data transmission over copper wires (i.e. "twisted pair" cables). See also *ADSL*, *HDSL*.

Digital Versatile Disk (DVD) A new standard for recording video on CD-ROMs using MPEG2, thus boasting better-than-broadcast TV quality. Costing about the same as a CD, DVD-ROMs hold 8 to 40 times more data. DVD will replace videocassettes, laserdiscs, CD-ROMs, and audio CDs.

Digital Video Broadcasting (DVB) Initially conceived as the European Launching Group (ELG) in 1991, the DVB project was founded in 1993. It comprises nearly 180 companies, institutions and organizations, equipment manufacturers, TV and radio stations, network providers, research institutions, and authorities from 23 countries. "The objective of the DVB, a project financed solely from membership dues without significant subsidies, is the shared and coordinated development of systems and standards in order to make digital television in Europe possible by means of satellite, cable, and terrestrial broadcasting (German Platform for HDTV and New Television Systems). Although DVB was originally set up as a European project, a number of companies from Japan, South Korea, Canada, and the USA have since joined". DVB can be used for more than digital TV and radio broadcasting. This technology can be applied as a generic "data highway" offering transfer rates of up to 36 Mbit/s. As a result, there have been proposals to rename the system Digital Versatile Broadcasting instead of Digital Video Broadcasting. DVB encompasses the following standards: DVB-S, DVB-C, DVB-CS, DVB-T, DVB-MS, DVB-MC, DVB-SI, DVB-TXT, DVB-CI, DVB-Subtitling, DVB-RCC, DVB-RTC, DVB-NIP, DVB-IPN.

DiSEqC See *Digital Satellite Equipment Control*.

Disk Operating System (DOS) Outdated operating system with a command-line interface. See also *Operating System*.

Distributed Component Object Model (DCOM) A set of Microsoft concepts and program interfaces in which client program objects can request services from server program objects on other computers in a network.

Dithering In computer graphics, if a color is not available, it can be made from the available colors by placing a pattern of colors next to each other to mix visually. For instance, the illusion of orange can be made by placing red and yellow pixels next to each other.

DMZ See *Demilitarized Zone*.

DNS See *Domain Name System*.

Domain In an Internet address, the domain names separated by dots are listed according to the protocol and service (e.g., "http://www"). An example is "ebusinessrevolution" (sub-domain) and "com" (top-level domain). The top-level domain can contain a country code ("fr" for France) or an abbreviation indicating the type of server (for example, com for commercial companies, org for organizations, or edu for educational institutions).

Domain Name The name of a computer connected to the Internet. The domain name is used to form a URL. See also *Uniform Resource Locator*.

Domain Name System (DNS) Database that links IP addresses and domain names. See also *Domain Name*, *Transmission Control Protocol/Internet Protocol*.

Domotik Widespread industry solution designed to connect products such as security, telecommunications, household appliances, and heating systems by means of an integrated residential wiring system. All electrically controlled devices are networked via the European Installation Bus (EIB) and controlled by a multimedia PC. Domotik can also be operated with the HomeAssistant multimedia program used for entering the various functions. HomeAssistant runs on standard multimedia PCs. The user-friendly graphical interface is to a large extent self-explanatory.

DOS See *Disk Operating System*.

Download Information (e.g., PDF files) or programs can be copied from a server (e.g., the Internet) to the computer's hard disk or other data media. Common examples of downloaded data include drivers for hardware components or updates for software applications.

Downstream The data flow from the server to the client or from the provider to the subscriber/customer. See also *Upstream*.

Dropout Error (on the magnetic coating of a magnetic tape or on other magnetic media) caused by dirt or surface damage. Dropouts can cause—depending on their size and severity—read errors or data loss.

DSL See *Digital Subscriber Line*.

DVB See *Digital Video Broadcasting*.

DVB-C A standard compatible to DVB-S for distributing digital programs or services in a cable network. To convert the data transmitted from satellites to a channel-compatible 8 MHz bandwidth, QPSK must be transcoded into 64-QAM (Quadrature Amplitude Modulation with a bandwidth efficiency of [64 = 26] 6 Bit/s/Hz).

DVB-CI DVB "Common Interface"—common interface for Conditional Access and other programs.

DVB-CS A DVB-C or DVB-S adapted standard for cable or satellite-supported reception of DVB signals via community antenna systems.

DVB Developments Further specifications and procedures are in preparation or being developed for data radio via DVB, synchronization of single-frequency-networks, interfaces between the DVB world and ATM or SDH networks, Digital Satellite News Gathering (DSNG) based on DVB, bi-directional communication in GGA and terrestrial networks, networking DVB terminal equipment, and integration of HDTV and DVB.

DVB-IPN Gateways from DVB to the telecom world.

DVB-MC Specification for Microwave Multipoint Distribution Systems (MVDS) in the frequency range below 10 GHz. The procedure that is also used on the ground is based on the standards defined for digital channel transmissions (DVB-C) and thus uses similarly equipped receivers/decoders. (DVB-MS and DVB-MC are also referred to as "specifications for wireless broadband cabling").

DVB-MS (Digital Multipoint Video Distribution System/MVDS) uses microwaves for the terrestrial transmission of a larger number of TV channels directly to the audience. The microwaves are bundled and broadcast to receiver antennas that are positioned in the "visible area" of the transmitter antenna. Although they pertain to terrestrial broadcasting, the DVB-MS specifications are based on those for DVB-S. That is why DVB-MS signals from standard DVB satellite receivers can be received via small rooftop antennas, but a corresponding MVDS frequency converter is used instead of the LNCs (Low Noise Converter).

DVB-NIP Network-independent protocols for interactivity (protocols, that permit communication in the form of a data stream).

DVB-RCC Specification for interaction channels (forward and backward channels) in broadband cable networks.

DVB-RTC Specification for interaction channels (backward channels) via telephone and ISDN.

DVB-S System for satellite transmission with an 11/12 GHz bandwidth; it can be configured for various transponder bandwidths and transfer rates. The type of modulation is a four-phase shifting (QPSK, Quadrature Phase Shift Keying). At a constant amplitude, the modulated signal can assume one of four phase conditions, of which each can transmit 2 bits of information (given a bandwidth efficiency of 2 Bit/s/Hs).

DVB-SI The Service Information System is designed to transmit data within the transport data stream. It is used for the self-configuration of the DVB decoder (set-top box), for designing the user interface and for identifying programs and services.

DVB-Subtitling Tools for subtitles and displaying the graphics.

DVB-T Standard for terrestrial television; this transmission procedure uses a bandwidth efficiency comparable to DVB-C for 7-8 MHz terrestrial channels and is based on a COFDM system (Coded Orthogonal Frequency Division Multiplex). In this multi-carrier procedure, the channel spectrum is divided into several thousand subcarriers each of which is modulated with a part of the data stream.

DVB-TXT DVB specification for monitoring Teletext (in special data packets).

DVD See *Digital Versatile Disk*.

Dynamic Host Configuration Protocol (DHCP) Internet standard, based on RFC 1541, for the automatic allocation of IP addresses.

Dynamic HyperText Markup Langauge (DHTML) An extension to HTML that allows for better user interaction and introduces dynamic Web page creation.

Dynamic Resource Management Frequency-economic adaptation of the channel bandwidth to the current traffic load DECT-MMAP.

E911 911 service becomes E911 when automatic number identification and automatic location information is provided to the 911 operator.

EBCDIC See *Extended Binary Coded Decimal Interchange Code*.

E-Cash See *Electronic Cash*.

ECC See *Error Correction Code*.

ECMA See *European Computer Manufacturers Association*.

EDGE See *Enhanced Data GSM Environment*.

EDI See *Electronic Data Interchange*.

EHS See *European Home System*.

EIB See *European Installation Bus*.

EIBA See *European Installations Bus Association*.

E-ide See *Enhanced Integrated Drive Electronics*.

Email See *Electronic Mail*.

Electronic Cash Electronic money that can be exchanged on the Internet for goods, information, and services. It is mostly used for micropayment solutions. See also *Micropayments*.

Electronic Data Interchange (EDI) A standard for the interorganizational computer-to-computer exchange of structured information.

Electronic Mail Exchange of digital documents via the Internet.

Emoticon Sideways "face" that expresses emotions without words on the Internet using special characters on the keyboard. The best-known emoticon is the smiley :-). If you can't see the face, turn your head to the left and look again. Other emoticons include the smiling pirate .-) and the sad person :-(.

Encryption Procedure to render a message illegible to anyone who is not authorized to read it.

Enhanced Data GSM Environment (EDGE) A faster version of the Global System for Mobile (GSM) wireless service designed to deliver data at rates up to 384 Kbps and enable the delivery of multimedia and other broadband applications to mobile phone and computer users.

Enhanced Integrated Drive Electronics (EIDE) Advanced development of the IDE standard offering higher data transfer rates and support for newer drives.

EPOC Operating system designed for small, portable computer-telephones with wireless access to phone and other information services. EPOC is based on an earlier operating system from Psion, the first major manufacturer of personal digital assistants (PDAs).

Error Correction Code (ECC) Redundant data that helps detect errors and eliminate them through recalculation. ECC on-the-fly means that hardware error correction for hard disks takes place while the data is being transferred. See also *On the Fy*.

E-Service An electronic service available via the Net that completes tasks, solves problems, or conducts transactions. E-services can be used by people, businesses, and other e-services and can be accessed via a wide range of information appliances.

E-Speak The universal language of e-services. To accelerate the creation of an open e-services world, HP has engineered E-Speak technology. The E-Speak platform provides a common services interface, making it easier and faster to create, deploy, manage, and connect e-services. Through the process of dynamic brokering, E-Speak lets an e-service discover other e-services anywhere on the Internet and link with them on the fly—even if they were built using different technology. See also *Brokering*.

ESPRIT European Strategic Program for Research and Development of Information Technology.

Ethernet Standard for connecting computers on an intranet, also known as IEEE 802.3. See also *Bandwidth*, *Intranet*.

European Computer Manufacturers Association (ECMA) Association of computer manufacturers with the goal of defining common standards.

European Home System (EHS) Created under the auspices of the EU project ESPRIT (European Strategic Program for Research and Development of Information Technology). It uses electrical wiring as the installation bus and offers a data throughput of up to 2.4 Kbit/s. A separate two-wired cable can also be used instead of an electrical cable. This increases the potential data throughput to a maximum of 48 Kbit/s. EHS and EIB are to be united into a common standard.

European Installation Bus (EIB) Network technology for residential wiring. EIB is designed for two-wire cable only. EIB versions for electrical cables as well as wireless systems for radio and infrared (as a functional proto-type) have recently become available. The Siemens "Instabus" complies with the guidelines of the EIB standard, as well as Domotik developed by Bosch. The version EIB.net can also use normal data networks in accordance with IEEE 802.2, with transfer rates of up to Ethernet 10 Mbit/s. The extension EIB.net 'i' allows forwarding, for example, via the normal IP router and thus the EIB connection via the Internet. Maximum EIB data transfer rate is 9.6 Kbit/s.

European Installations Bus Association (EIBA) The EIB Association is a widespread manufacturer association dedicated to establishing the EIB standard. Over 100 manufacturers and more than 8,000 licensers throughout Europe offer nearly 5,000 EIB components.

European Telecommunication Satellite Organization (Eutelsat) A European agency founded in Paris in 1977 for managing satellite communication services.

Eutelsat See *European Telecommunication Satellite Organization*.

Extended Binary Coded Decimal Interchange Code IBM's 8-bit extension of the 4-bit Binary Coded Decimal encoding of digits 0-9 (0000-1001).

Extensible Markup Language (XML) A flexible way to create common information formats and share both the format and the data on the Internet.

Extranet Extended intranets used to share information with business partners over the Internet in a very secure way. See also *Intranet*.

FAQ See *Frequently Asked Questions*.

Fast-SCSI Transmission protocol compliant with SCSI-2 that allows data transmission of up to 10 Mbyte/s on a 8-bit bus.

FAT See *File Allocation Table*.

FDDI See *Fibre Distributed Data Interface*.

Fibre Channel A technology for transmitting data between computer devices at a data rate of up to 1 Gbps (one billion bits per second). (A data rate of 4 Gbps is proposed.) Fibre Channel is especially suited for connecting computer servers to shared storage devices and for interconnecting storage controllers and drives.

Fibre Distributed Data Interface (FDDI) Standard for computer connections on optical fibre cables at a rate of 100 Mbit. See also *Bandwidth, Ethernet, T-1, T-3*.

Field The smallest unit in a record in a database. Each field has a specific data type that contains, for example, text, dates, currencies, etc.

File Allocation Table (FAT) The data table at the beginning of a partition used in operating systems such as DOS and Windows 95/98. The data table stores the information about where files are located on the disk.

File Transfer Protocol (FTP) Internet protocol to move files from one Internet site to another one. Public FTP servers allow the upload and download of files, creating public file archives.

Finger Tool to locate people on other UNIX servers. It helps to see if a certain person is online.

Firehunter A comprehensive solution for measuring, monitoring, and reporting on Internet services.

Firewall A tool to separate an intranet from the Internet by disallowing connections on certain ports, keeping the intranet very secure. See also *Intranet, Network*.

FireWire See *IEEE 1394*.

Firmware Commands stored in a ROM chip for controlling the hard disk. This data can usually be updated (known as flashing the ROM).

Flame A crude or witless comment on a newsgroup posting or email. See also *Flame War*.

Flame War Instead of discussing positions in an online discussion, personal attacks (or flames) against the debators are exchanged. See also *Flame*.

Flat File A database in ASCII format that separates records by a special character. See also *American Standard Code for Information Interchange*, *Database*.

Flooding On IRC, when a person sends many messages in a very short period of time. You are normally limited to 1 line every second. So if you send 10 lines in 3 seconds, you are flooding. Bots in channels have the authority to remove users from the channel for flooding. See also *Bots*.

Font Typographic style, such as Times Roman or Helvetica.

Forward Sending an email on to a third person. See also *Electronic Mail*.

Frame Frames make it possible to divide the Browser window into several sections and independently configure and control their contents. Thus, a fixed menu can be shown in one frame while scrolling text, images, or animations can be displayed in another. See also *Browser*, *HyperText Markup Language*.

Frame Relay Wideband, packet-based interface used to transmit bursts of data over a wide-area network. Seldom used for voice.

Freenet Internet access provided on a nonprofit basis.

Freeware Software that is available to anyone without paying a fee, while the author retains the copyright.

Frequently Asked Questions (FAQs) Many home pages and nearly all newsgroups offer FAQ lists to answer questions frequently asked by users. To save time, it is often sufficient to refer to the list of FAQs to determine whether specific questions have already been answered.

Front-End Refers to a part of a program that allows user to access the database. See also *Back-End*.

FTP See *File Transfer Protocol*.

Full-Duplex Transmission protocol for the simultaneous transfer of data and signals in both directions.

Full-Text Index Database containing every word of every document, including stop words. See *Stop Words*.

Fuzzy Search Finds matches even if the keyword is misspelled or only partially spelled.

FWIW Net language meaning "for what it's worth."

FYI Net language meaning "for your information."

Gamma Correction Because not all screens or printers are the same, colors have to be adjusted from the computer's idea of "normal" before they are displayed.

Gateway Architecture for bridging between two networks that work with different protocols.

General Packet Radio Service (GPRS) A packet-based wireless communication service that promises data rates from 56 up to 114 Kbps and continuous connection to the Internet for mobile phone and computer users.

Geographic Information System (GIS) Enables you to envision the geographic aspects of a body of data. Basically, it lets you query or analyze a relational database and receive the results in the form of some kind of map.

GIF See *Graphic Interchange Format*.

Gigabyte 1,024 Megabytes, but some round it off to 1,000 Megabytes, because it is easier to calculate with. See also *Byte*, *Megabyte*.

GIS See *Geographic Information System*.

Glitch Small malfunction in the hardware or software that does not cause an interruption.

Global Positioning System (GPS) A series of 24 geosynchronous satellites that continuously transmit their position. Used in personal tracking, navigation, and automatic vehicle location technologies.

Global System for Mobile Communication (GSM) A digital mobile telephone system that is widely used in Europe and other parts of the world. GSM uses a variation of time division multiple access (TDMA) and is the most widely used of the three digital wireless telephone technologies (TDMA, GSM, and CDMA).

Glyph Glyph is from a Greek word for "carving." A glyph is a graphic symbol that provides the appearance or form for a character. A glyph can be an alphabetic or numeric font or some other symbol that pictures an encoded character.

Gopher Internet protocol for presenting menus of downloadable documents or files. It is still around, but has no real importance anymore. See also *HyperText*, *HyperText Transport Protocol*, *World Wide Web*.

GPRS See *General Packet Radio Service*.

GPS See *Global Positioning System*.

Granularity The level of complexity of a content object. There are coarsely grained content objects (e.g., sites, databases, applications, collections) and finely grained content objects (e.g., documents, audio clips, drawings). More coarsely grained content objects contain more different types of content objects. Examples: (towards finer granularity) book—chapter—page—paragraph—sentence—word—letter; video—story—event—shot—frame.

Graphic Interchange Format (GIF) Very common image format on the Internet. See also *JPEG*.

Graphical User Interface (GUI) Graphical environment to simplify the use of the operating system and applications.

Grep UNIX command to scan files for patterns; also used as a synonym for fast manual searching.

GSM See *Global System for Mobile Communication*.

GUI See *Graphical User Interface*.

Guru Synonym for expert.

Hacker Skilled computer programmer or engineer who loves a challenge. Not synonymous with "computer criminal" or "security breaker."

Handheld Device Markup Language (HDML) Written to allow Internet access from wireless devices such as handheld personal computers and smart phones. Derived from *HyperText Markup Language*.

HAVi See *Home Audio-Video Interoperability*.

HDML See *Handheld Device Markup Language*.

HDSL See *High-data-rate DSL*.

HDTV See *High Density Television*.

Header Contains information about the type and/or meaning and/or structure of the subsequent data packet. The header forms the beginning of a data packet, so it can also be used to mark the end of the previous data structure.

Hello World! The program that every computer student learns first; program outputs "Hello World!"

High-data-rate DSL Transmission procedure capable of a transmission rate of 1,544 Kbit/s (T1) or with 2,048 Kbit/s (E1) with pulse-code modulation via dual copper wires.

High Definition Television (HDTV) High-resolution television (i.e. doubled horizontal and vertical resolution).

Hit The download of an element on a Web page. If a Web page consists of HTML text, two images, and a sound file, then there have been four hits on the Web server. It is a way to measure the load of the server. See also *HyperText Markup Language*.

Home Audio-Video Interoperability (HAVi) The goal of the HAVi consortiums (Grundig, Hitachi, Matsushita, Philips, Sharp, Sony, Thomson, und Toshiba) is the development of a home network architecture for the (consumer) electronics and multimedia industries. Philips represents the eight companies as a primary contact for licensing issues. According to the HAVi version 1.0b standards (which can be downloaded as a PDF file from www.havi.org), user programs are capable of detecting and controlling HAVi-compatible equipment from different manufacturers. These programs can also control individual components within various systems independent of their physical location. The HAVi standards refer to a IEEE 1394-supported, digital AV-environment. The key specifications include components used for exchanging messages and events via IEEE 1394, the registration and detection of device capabilities via the network and the management of digital AV streams and devices. Available features include a security system for virus protection, a component that supports functions such as pre-programmed (audio/video/data) recording as well as standard programming interfaces for controlling equipment functions.

Home Automation See *Building Automation*.

Home page Starting page, i.e., page 1 of a Web site (WWW). It usually contains a table of contents and links to other areas or pages on the site.

Home Phoneline Networking Alliance (HPNA) Consortium promoting the use of telephone lines for data transfers of up to 10 megabits per second without restricting parallel telephone usage (members: AMD, Compaq, 3COM, IBM, Intel, and Lucent).

HomeWay Multimedia cabling system offered by Corning for apartments, houses, and home-offices. The system requires only one cable and a universal wall receptacle for telephone, fax, PC, TV, home automation, and multimedia programs. The multimedia cabling system consists of a control center, a broadband cable, and a standard wall socket. All external wiring is connected to the control center. A broadband cable networks all rooms, and the wall socket provides connections for multimedia terminal devices. In terms of design, the sockets are tailored to the various switch programs. Their modular structure ensures that all services are available at any point in the residence. The inserts can be easily replaced if the socket is to be used in another way, for example, for a cable TV connection in another room. An integrated component of HomeWay is home automation based on the already available Instabus EIB (European Instabus). HomeWay also meets the specifications recommended by major providers including ASTRA, Deutsche Telekom, and property management companies.

Host See *Server*.

HTML See *HyperText Markup Language*.

HTTP See *HyperText Transfer Protocol*.

Hyperband In the service channel network, the frequency used for distributing TV stations (300 - 470 MHz). It is the range of choice for digital transmissions according to DVB-C.

HyperText Web documents that contain links to other documents.

HyperText Markup Language (HTML) The language for developing documents for the World Wide Web. See also *Client*, *Server*, *World Wide Web*.

Hypertext Taxonomy Taxonomy composed of hyperlinks that enable the non-sequential retrieval of related information, allowing users to follow associative trails within or between taxonomies in order to quickly locate specific resources.

HyperText Transfer Protocol (HTTP) The protocol for transporting files from a Web server to a Web browser. See also *Client*, *Server*, *World Wide Web*.

IBT See *Internet-Based Training*.

Icon Mnemonic convention to replace functional names by images.

IDE See *Integrated Drive Electronics*.

IDL See *Interface Definition Language*.

IEEE See *Institute of Electrical and Electronic Engineers*.

IEEE 1394 The P-1394 bus technology originally developed by Apple became the industry standard IEEE 1394/1995 in 1995—commonly known as "FireWire." The IEEE 1394 technology describes a serial interface for computer and video devices for transmitting digital data up 400 Mbit / sec. In 1997, Sony introduced their "i.Link" logo for identifying standardized IEEE-1394 interfaces.

IES See *Integrated Reception System*.

IMAP See *Internet Mail Access Protocol*.

IMHO Net language for "in my humble opinion."

Index A searchable database of documents created automatically or manually by a search engine.

Information Architecture The design of information organization, labelling, navigation, and indexing systems to support both browsing and searching in order to minimize the time that users spend looking for information.

Information Management The application of information science principles to the administration of corporate information to ensure that information is captured, formatted, maintained, and disseminated across the organization to support decisioning and future use. See also *Information Science*.

Information Science Generally refers to the study of the production, collection, classification, storage, manipulation, retrieval, dissemination, use, and measurement of information. Distinct from Computer Science and Information Systems, which focus primarily on the study of technology and the design of hardware and software, Information Science examines the interaction among people, technology, and information.

Infranet Communication structure for networking equipment in the household or in other applications such as gas stations, restaurants, medicinal technology, or agriculture (a supplement to Internet and Intranet).

Infrared Data Association (IrDA) An industry-sponsored organization set up in 1993 to create international standards for the hardware and software used in infrared communication links. In this special form of radio transmission, a focused ray of light in the infrared frequency spectrum, measured in terahertz, or trillions of hertz (cycles per second), is modulated with information and sent from a transmitter to a receiver over a relatively short distance.

Integrated Drive Electronics (IDE) A 16-bit parallel interface transferring only data. Cheaper than ESDI medium-range capacity (40-200Mb). It can't perform a physical (low-level) format because it is not a device-level interface.

Integrated Receiver/Decoder (IRD) Receiver/decoder unit for digital data or TV services. IRD describes the same device known internationally as "set-top box" or "Digital Decoder."

Integrated Reception System (IRS) With the structure of the IES—promoted by the satellite operator ASTRA and, for example, implemented by WISI—existing distributor and communication structures (cable, terrestrial systems, telephone) can be supplemented through community Sat-reception. The accompanying wall socket combines antennas and telephone connections.

Integrated Services Digital Network (ISDN) Digital version of the good, old analog telephone line and integrates several different services.

Intelligent Home Control signals for building automation or transmitting multimedia signals. The forerunners of today's modern concepts: Professor Ken Sakamura's Tron house in Tokyo in the 1980s and Chriet Titulaer's Huis van de Toekomst in Rosmalen (Holland).

Intelsat See *International Telecommunications Satellite Organization*.

Interface Definition Language (IDL) The prevalent language used for defining how components connect together. Beyond its use in CORBA systems, it has proven a popular way to describe platform and language-neutral connection interfaces, including the core API for XML—the Document Object Model (DOM). Even variations on IDL, such as that used by Component Object Model (COM), tend to be similar to IDL. Understanding IDL brings about key insights to many of the techniques of component programming.

Interleave / Interleaving 1. Multi-level, interleaved storage of user data for simplifying error correction. Interleaving is also used for digital television (DVB) as a means of splitting code. Bytes from a defined number of successive data packets are selected in memory in such a way that the successive bytes originate from various data packets. Through this interleaving, which is reversed in the receiver, transmission errors that have corrupted a longer section of the digital data stream are parsed into single errors that are easier to correct. 2. Arranging the sectors in a similar way on a hard disk cylinder.

International Organization for Standardization (ISO) A federation of national standards bodies such as BSI and ANSI.

International Telecommunications Satellite Organization (Intelsat) An organization of over 150 member countries promoting intercontinental telecommunications via satellite.

Internet Worldwide conglomeration of data networks. Initially intended for military use, the Internet was increasingly used for exchanging research data among universities and institutes. Today, online service providers and network providers have made the Internet available to everyone. It is the computer network for business and leisure based on the TCP/IP protocol. All other computer networks have become irrelevant. Evolved from ARPAnet. See also *Advanced Research Projects Agency Network, Network, Transmission Control Protocol / Internet Protocol*.

Internet-Based Training (IBT) Evolution of computer-based training; offers real-time learning over the Internet with a teacher. See also *Computer-Based Training*.

Internet Mail Access Protocol (IMAP) RFC 1730[-33] IMAP4 allows a client to access and manipulate electronic mail messages on a server. This should be viewed as a superset of the POP3. The IMAP4 server listens on TCP port 143. IMAP is definitely an emerging technology, and it completely outperforms the older POP environment functionally.

Internet Protocol (IP) See *Transmission Control Protocol / Internet Protocol*.

Internet Protocol Number Unique address for every computer connected to the Internet. Currently each is composed of a series of four numbers, separated by dots. Example: 127.0.0.1. Domain names refer to IP numbers. See also *Domain Name, Internet, Transmission Control Protocol / Internet Protocol*.

Internet Relay Chat (IRC) Multiuser chat facility on the Internet. Many servers around the world are interconnected to allow hundreds of thousands of users to chat at the same time. Special IRC clients are necessary to connect.

Internet Server API (ISAPI) Programming interface for Internet server programs that use the Microsoft Internet Information Server (MIIS) in conjunction with Windows NT.

Internet Service Provider (ISP) A company that provides individuals and other companies access to the Internet and other related services such as personal mail boxes. An ISP has the equipment and the telecommunication line access required to have points-of-presence on the Internet for the geographic area served.

Internet Society (ISOC) Nongovernmental international organization for global cooperation and coordination of the Internet and its technologies and applications.

Intranet Private network that is based on the same technologies as the Internet, but is restricted to a certain user group. See also *Internet, Network*.

IP See *Internet Protocol, TCP/IP*.

IP Address Address of a single computer in the Internet. The IP address consists of four numbers from 0 to 255, each separated by dots (example: 123.27.1.155). To make this system more practical for users, IP addresses are converted into alphanumeric names. IPv6 will extend the range from four numbers to six numbers, thus making many more IP addresses available for appliances.

IPv6 The latest level of the Internet protocol (IP) and is now included as part of IP support in many products, including the major computer operating systems.

IRC See *Internet Relay Chat*.

IRC-Op IRC operators who administrate the IRC servers on an international level. These operators have access to additional commands unavailable to normal users.

IRD See *Integrated Receiver / Decoder*.

IrDA See *Infrared Data Association*.

ISAPI See *Internet Server API*.

ISDN See *Integrated Services Digital Network*.

ISO See *International Standards Organization*.

ISOC See *Internet Society*.

ISP See *Internet Service Provider*.

JAR See *Java Archive*.

Java Programming language developed by Sun with cross-platform neutrality, object-orientation, and networking in mind. See also *Applet, Java Development Kit*.

Java Archive (JAR) A file format used to bundle all components required by a Java applet. JAR files simplify the downloading of applets because all the components (.class files, images, sounds, etc.) can be packaged into a single file.

Java Development Kit (JDK) Basic development package from Sun distributed for free in order to write, test, and debug Java programs. See also *Applet, Java*.

Java Intelligent Network Infrastructure (JINI) Sun Microsystems introduced JINI technology in the summer of 1998. It is based on Java and can "spontaneously" network connected devices. In other words, devices that are dynamically connected to the network are immediately detected throughout the entire network. JINI regulates the communication between computers and other devices in the network and allows peripherals to be connected to the network without special configurations and used immediately. The self-identifying devices transmit their technical specifications and eliminate the need the for "manual" driver selection. In contrast to Ethernet systems, JINI automatically allocates resources.

JavaScript Scripting language developed by Netscape that allows interaction within HTML pages. See also *HyperText Markup Language*.

JDK See *Java Development Kit*.

JetSend A device-to-device communications protocol that allows devices to intelligently negotiate information exchange. The protocol allows two devices to connect, negotiate the best possible data type, provide device status, and exchange information, without user intervention.

JINI See *Java Intelligent Network Infrastructure*.

JIT See *Just-In-Time*.

Joint Photographic Experts Group (JPEG) One of the most popular graphic formats. The JPEG format frequently used in digital photography compresses large or color-intensive pictures to a fraction of their original size. This reduces storage requirements and file transfer time (i.e., on the Internet).

JPEG Image format for the Internet using lossy compression algorithms. See also *Joint Photographic Experts Group*.

Just-In-Time (JIT) The concept of reducing inventories by working closely with suppliers to coordinate delivery of materials just before their use in the manufacturing or supply process.

Kill File File that contains rules for filtering unwanted messages.

Kilobyte 1,024 bytes, or sometimes 1,000 bytes. See also *Binary Digit*, *Byte*.

Knowbie Expert in computer networking.

Knowledge Facts or ideas acquired by study, investigation, observation, or experience. Within the framework of Information Science, knowledge results from the contextual analysis of information, which can be used repeatedly to inform decision making.

Knowledge Management The discipline of gathering, organizing, managing, and disseminating the corporation's structured and unstructured information resources in order to improve corporate decision making and maximize staff productivity. See also *Structured Information, Unstructured Information*.

Lag The delay caused by high traffic congestion or other overloading between IRC servers or Internet provider sites, resulting in slow communications.

LAN See *Local Area Network*.

Last Mile Technology Last-mile technology is any telecommunications technology, such as wireless radio, that carries signals from the broad telecommunication infrastructure along the relatively short distance (hence, the "last mile") to and from the home or business.

LCN See *Local Control Network*.

LDAP See also *Lightweight Directory Access Protocol*.

Leased Line A permanently established phone line that is used to offer 24-hour access to the Internet.

Lightweight Directory Access Protocol A technology that provides access to X.500 for PCs.

Link The World Wide Web, a link that allows the user to branch from one Web page to another. Links are usually displayed as underlined text on HTML pages. Clicking these links makes it possible to "surf" the World Wide Web.

LMDS See *Local Multipoint Distribution Service*.

Local Area Network (LAN) Computer network limited to a certain location. See also *Ethernet, Wide Area Network*.

Login Account name to gain access to a system. See also *Password*.

LOL Net language for "laughing out loud."

LNS See *LonWorks Network Services*.

Local Control Network (LCN) An installation bus developed by Issendorff GmbH for residential and functional buildings. Conventional installation elements such as switches, pushbuttons, sensors, are replaced or supplemented by "intelligent" modules. All modules in the building are connected to an additional wire in the installation cable (actually, a 4-wire electrical cable that uses an added wire as a data channel). The data transfer rate is 9.6 Kbit/s.

Local Multipoint Distribution Service (LMDS) Located in the 28 GHz and 31 GHz bands, LMDS is a broadband radio service designed to provide two-way transmission of voice, high-speed data, and video (wireless cable TV).

LON See *Local Operating Network, LonWorks*

LonWorks The field bus system originally developed by Echelon Corporation (Palo Alto, California) for production control. According to company information, it is the most widely used field bus system in the world for building automation (reference installations in Germany: Reichstag Building and Debis administration offices in Berlin). This technology was developed in 1988 and launched on the German market in 1991. In a LON (Local Operating Network), every bus participant or "network node" has its own microprocessor or "neuron processor." The separate network nodes work independently and do not communicate with other nodes until it becomes necessary. A LON can be operated with two-wire cables, coaxial cable, electrical cables, or as a wireless system. Depending on the transmission path, the data rate is 10 Kbit/s (electrical cable) up to a theoretical maximum value of 1.2 Mbit/s (1,200,000 bits per second). According to press reports, integration into known data networks—for example, through cooperation with the Internet specialist Cisco—is the most widespread configuration. Using LNS (LonWorks Network Services), LON systems can be integrated via gateways into Ethernet installations and the Internet.

LonWorks Network Services (LNS) Allows the user to integrate LON systems into the Internet and Ethernet installations via gateways.

Look-up Service Also known as "spontaneous networking" because each device is detected immediately (as soon as it is connected to the network). A component of the JINI system architecture that registers every active JINI device in the network, together with its technical characteristics in a table, and makes it available to authorized users (example: a handheld computer that has been registered in the look-up service detects available printers, free memory space on a hard disk in a desktop computer, or an Internet connection).

Magneto-Resistive Heads Write/read head in hard disks that can supply a stronger signal level when reading data from the disks due to a magneto-resistive element.

Make Call Enables the user to set up a call.

Mailing List A system to redistribute mail from one person to many other people who are interested in that mail. Mailing lists are used to create online discussion, similar to newsgroups; however, the mail is sent automatically, while newsgroups require the user to actively retrieve the information. See also *Electronic Mail*, *Newsgroup*.

MAPI See *Messaging Application Programmable Interface*.

Masking-Pattern-Adapted Universal Subband Integrated Coding And Multiplexing (MUSICAM) Complies with MPEG-1 Audio, Layer II. It reduces the data rate of audio signals from 1,411 Mbit/s (audio CD) to 192 Kbit/s.

MediaFusion US company that has announced a major breakthrough in transmitting data over electrical cables (www.mediafusionllc.net). The company received a patent for a system that can theoretically transfer 2.5 Gbit/s—more than fibre-optic cable—and bridge distances of over 3,000 kilometers without a regenerator. The high-frequency carriers are microwaves from a maser (a "laser" for the microwave range) that are fed into the power supply. According to MediaFusion, the magnetic field surrounding the cable encapsulates the waves and transports them to the receiver.

Megabyte 1,024 Kilobytes, or sometimes 1,000 Kilobytes. See also *Binary Digit*, *Byte*, *Kilobyte*.

Message Messages or private messages refers to messages sent to one or more IRC participants. These messages can only be read by the recipient and the sender.

Message Handling System X.400 series of recommendations of abstract services and protocols used to provide electronic mail services in an OSI networking environment. X.500 is a series of recommendations that provide a distributed, user-friendly subscriber directory to help users address X.400 messages. These services are called simply "the directory."

Message Transfer Agents (MTA) Part of the X.400 OSI stack. Responsible for the actual transport of the message between user agents. MTAs typically reside on separate machines.

Messaging Application Programmable Interface (MAPI) Microsoft standard for accessing mail on a server, similar to IMAP. See also *Internet Mail Access Protocol*.

Metadata Assigned information "tags" or key words that help index documents or resources by providing background information, such as creation date, author, and date of last update. Metadata is not necessarily visible to the user, but rather works in the background to ensure that documents are properly indexed for searching. It can be stored in fields in the document itself or in a relational database, which "fills" document fields with associated metadata when a particular document or resource is retrieved by a user.

MHP See *Multimedia Home Platform*.

MHS See *Message Handling System*.

Micropayments Payments that have a value between a fraction of a cent and roughly 10 dollars (or euro).

Microwaves Frequencies in the range above 3 GHz (Gigahertz = billion Hertz). Microwaves can also be used to distribute digital TV services and are sometimes referred to as "wireless cable."

MIME See *Multipurpose Internet Mail Extensions*.

Mirror Site Site that contains exact copy of the original site. They are used to spread the load over several sites and to speed up the download for the customers by placing the server nearer to them.

Modem See *Modulator/Demodulator*.

Modulator/Demodulator (Modem) Device between computer and phone line that converts computer signals to a form that can be used to transport the data over telephone networks.

Monitor Device A PBX is requested to forward all events at a particular extension (device) to a file server. A caller with the number XXX-XXXX is assigned the to the extension.

Motion Picture Experts Group (MPEG) A common workgroup—Working Group 11 (WG11), also known as the international MPEG laboratory—of the International Standards Organization (ISO) and the International Electrotechnical Commission (IEC). MPEG was founded in 1988 by over 100 companies to negotiate proposals and define standards in specific expert groups (requirement or system groups).

MPEG See *Motion Picture Experts Group*.

MR Head See *Magneto-Resistive Heads*.

MTA See *Message Transfer Agents*.

MUD See *Multiuser Dungeon*.

Multi Channel Feed Data compression, encoding, and modulation processes are optimized for minimum bandwidths in Digital Video Broadcasting (DVB) resulting in a relatively large number of transmission channels.

This is why a program can be transmitted over several channels from several cameras simultaneously. Viewers can view the event from a selected camera angle (and not necessarily from the perspective of the director). Typical applications include simultaneous broadcasts of Formula 1 racing events from inside different vehicles, from a helicopter, or from the pit lanes. Symbols displayed on the screen show the viewer which button to press and which perspective will be shown.

Multimedia Home Platform (MHP) The MHP software package is the open, technical solution for all new multimedia programs and services within the framework of the DVB standard (digital television). MHP connects radios, the Internet, TVs, and computers. Essentially, a standard system for all services. With MHP, the DVB project has a uniform standard for the software interface (API) of universally applicable DVB receivers. By implementing the standardized software interface (DVB-J) based on the program language Java, all services and programs can be implemented in set-top boxes in the future. An interface available to all program and service providers, MHP opens the door to manufacturing receivers that are compatible with all current and future standards. MHP will be implemented in DVB receivers and multimedia PCs.

Multipurpose Internet Mail Extensions (MIME) Format for attaching binary files to email. Enables multipart/multimedia messages to be sent over the Internet. This standard was developed by the Internet Engineering Task Force (IETF). See also *Binary Hexadecimal, UNIX-to-UNIX Encoding*.

Multiuser Dungeon (MUD) Environment for multiuser role playing games. Every user plays a different role in the game and is able to communicate and interact with others. Connect to a MUD, for example, via "telnet 130.149.19.20 7680."

MUSICAM See *Masking-Pattern-Adapted Universal Subband Integrated Coding And Multiplexing*.

National Television System Committee (NTSC) US TV signal with 60 Hz vertical frequency, a 4:3 screen format, and a resolution of 767×575 pixels.

Near Video on Demand (NVoD) A TV program broadcast in, for example, 20 minute intervals on additional channels. Audiences can then watch a program practically at any time starting within the 20-minute time frame.

Netiquette Code of behavior on the Internet.

Netizen Responsible citizen on the Internet.

Network The connection of two or more computers in order to share resources.

Networked House House or apartment with a cabled or wireless intelligent network used to support the inhabitants. See also *Intelligent Home*.

Network News Transport Protocol (NNTP) Standard protocol for exchanging postings and newsgroups over the Internet.

Newsgroups The "blackboards" of the Internet. Includes thousands of public information and discussion forums sorted according to topic. Participants can read and submit messages. Discussion group on USENET. See also *USENET*.

NICAM A transmission mode employed in various countries for two digital audio signals (stereo or bi-language) in the analog TV channel.

Node A device connected to a network.

NNTP See *Network News Transport Protocol*.

NTSC See *National Television System Committee*.

NvoD See *Near Video on Demand*.

Object-Oriented Programming (OOP) Art of programming independent pieces of code, which are then able to interact with each other. This program philosophy was made popular through Smalltalk, Object Pascal, and C++.

ODBC See *Open Database Connectivity*.

Offline Not connected to the Internet.

Online Connected to the Internet.

On-Screen Display (OSD) A screen menu providing user instructions and simplifying operation.

OOP See *Object-Oriented Programming*.

Open Database Connectivity (ODBC) Interface defined by Microsoft for database systems. With an ODBC driver installed on a PC, the user can access other formats such as dBase, Oracle, Paradox, or Access.

Operating System (OS) Software that is loaded right after the boot time. It provides the basic functionality to run applications, based on a single set of instructions. An operating system manages, for example, the resources and processes, input/output controls, file system, and the user interface.

OS See *Operating System*.

OSD See *On-Screen Display*.

Packet The smallest unit for transmitting data over the Internet. Data is broken up into packets, sent over the network, and then reassembled at the other end.

PALplus A system introduced in 1994 that is backward compatible to the PAL standard system for analog transmission of TV programs in the 16:9 Widescreen format aspect ratio. Coordinated by Germany's ZDF network, PALplus was developed by a consortium of industrial companies, TV stations, and research institutes. On conventional screens (4:3 format), PALplus programs appear in the letterbox format with black strips along the upper and lower edges of the screen.

Partial Response Maximum Likelihood (PRML) Digital procedure for interpreting the data stored as analog information on magnetic data media.

PASC See *Precision Adaptive Subband Coding*.

Password Secret code to identify a user when logging onto a system.

Pay-TV Subscription television. Audio and video signals can only be received (unscrambled) after a fee has been paid to the program provider. See *Encryption*.

PBX See *Private Branch Exchange*.

PCMCIA See *Personal Computer Memory Card Industry Association*.

Perl Powerful scripting language, often used to write CGI scripts.

Personal Computer Memory Card Industry Association (PCMCIA) Originally designed as a memory expansion card for laptop computers, this interface is used today for miniature modems or for digital TV descrambling systems.

PGP See *Pretty Good Privacy*.

Phrase Search A search for documents on the Internet containing an exact sentence or phrase specified by a user.

Picture In Picture (PIP) An additional picture displayed within the TV picture. This system is used to simultaneously view a second TV channel or monitor the image from a remote camera.

PIP See *Picture In Picture*.

Plain Old Telephone Service (POTS) Another name for traditional wired, land-based telephone service.

PLC See *Powerline Communications Forum*.

Plug-ins Software that adds functionality to commercial applications, such as the Netscape browser or Adobe's Photoshop.

Plug and Play Procedure for automatically configuring computer expansion devices or cards.

Point of Presence (POP) Local access to the services of an ISP. See also *Internet Service Provider*.

POP See *Point of Presence*.

POP3 See *Post Office Protocol*.

Port Interface for accessing services on a server.

Portal Point of entry; Web site to the Internet.

Postmaster Administrator of the mail server. In case of problems, you can contact the postmaster. The postmaster of someone@foobar.org is postmaster@foobar.org, for example.

Post Office Protocol Protocol for receiving mail via a client.

POTS See *Plain Old Telephone Service*.

PowerLine Systems that use the electrical network for data transfer. See also *PLC*, *MediaFusion*.

Powerline Communications Forum (PCF) A consortium founded in 1997 by members of the telecommunications industry and energy suppliers. This group tests applications and services supplied to homes via electrical cables to determine their feasibility and efficiency. See also *PowerLine*, *MediaFusion*.

Precision Adaptive Subband Coding (PASC) Similar to MUSICAM. Coding and data compression process for audio signals. It offers a data rate of 384 Kbit/s and is used for DCC (Digital Compact Cassettes).

Pretty Good Privacy Encryption algorithm developed by Phil Zimmerman.

Private Branch Exchange (PBX) A private telephone network used within an enterprise. Users of the PBX share a certain number of outside lines for making telephone calls external to the PBX. Most medium-sized and larger companies use a PBX because it's much less expensive than connecting an external telephone line to every telephone in the organization. In addition, it's easier to call someone within a PBX because the number you dial is typically just 3 or 4 digits.

PRML See *Partial Response Maximum Likelihood*.

Protocol Rules controlling how computers and applications interact.

Proxy Server A proxy server retrieves documents on demand from a server and passes them to a client. The advantage with a proxy server is that it normally caches documents. It is considerably faster to retrieve documents from the proxy rather than directly from a Web server, especially if someone else has already retrieved that particular document.

PSTN See *Public Switched Telephone Network*.

Public Switched Telephone Network (PSTN) The worldwide voice telephone system, also called the Bell System in the United States.

Push Technology Also referred to as "Web-casting" or "channel-casting," this technology broadcasts personalized information to subscribers.

Pulse Width Modulation (PWM) A standard means of encoding data read by a laser beam from optical media (CD, DVD).

PWM See *Pulse Width Modulation*.

QAM See *Quadrature Amplitude Modulation*.

Quadrature Amplitude Modulation (QAM) Digital modulation procedure. QAM is used, for example, for digital TV broadcasting via broadband cable.

Quadrature Phase Shift Keying (QPSK) Digital modulation procedure. QPSK is used, for example, for TV broadcasting via satellite.

Quality of Service (QoS) The idea that transmission rates, error rates, and other characteristics can be measured, improved, and, to some extent, guaranteed in advance.

Query Request for information from a database.

Query-by-example Find search results similar to a search result the user finds particularly useful.

Queue Sequence of objects.

QoS See *Quality of Service*.

QPSK See *Quadrature Phase Shift Keying*.

RAM See *Random Access Memory*.

Random Access Memory (RAM) Memory that is used for executing applications and storing documents while working on them.

Readme A text file containing information on how to use the file you want to access.

RealAudio Software tool that supports transmissions of real-time, live, or prerecorded audio.

Referential Integrity For databases, referential integrity in its simplest form means that, when a record is deleted from a main table, all related subordinate records in other tables will also be automatically deleted.

Relational Database A database that does not have a pre-defined link structure. This allows the user to create new relationships between tables dynamically, i.e., during the course of operation. For example, you can link customer names with invoices using the customer ID number.

Remote Login Logging into a computer system from a remote location, meaning from another system on the network.

Request for Comments (RFC) The process for creating an Internet standard. New standards are proposed and published in the form of a request for comments document. When a new standard has been established, it retains the acronym RFC and a number is added, such as RFC1029.

Residential System Technology See *Building Automation*.

Residential Wiring Technology See *Building Automation*.

Resource Manager A component of the HAVi system capable of managing a number of operations. It resolves conflicts between devices, coordinates the programming of scheduled events (such as timer recordings on a digital recorder), and monitors the network to determine whether reserved devices are still in place. See also *HAVi*.

Retrieve Call A caller has parked an earlier call and terminates his current call. Retrieve call makes it possible to return to the first caller.

RFC See *Request for Comments*.

Root The administrator account that has super-user rights on a system. See also *Sysop*.

ROTFL Net language for "rolling on the floor laughing."

Router A device to handle the connection between two or more networks. See also *Network*.

RTFM Net language for "read the f*cking manual." Answer to a question that users could have answered themselves by reading the manual.

Runtime Module Allows the user to execute a database program without requiring the entire database development system required to create the program.

Sampling Scanning analog signals, in which samples of the current amplitude are taken at the sampling frequency and digitized. The quality of the digital signal depends on the sampling frequency (twice as high as the frequency of the digitized analog signal).

Scrambling Encryption of TV images to make them unrecognizable. In reference to pay-TV, programs that are scrambled can be received only by subscribers who have agreed to pay a fee for the program and have a descrambling unit (decoder) connected to their TVs.

SCSI See *Small Computer System Interface*.

Search Engine Databases containing information about documents available on the World Wide Web, i.e., the "reference works" or "indices" of the Internet. Search engines are created manually or automatically by computers.

Searching A method for finding information using keyword location systems (search engines) that index resources in an information repository. Common search types include known-item, exploratory, and comprehensive searches.

Secure Electronic Transaction (SET) Payments are encrypted and sent via a (trusted) third party—a bank, for example. Then they are checked, and the customer identity is verified.

Secure Sockets Layer (SSL) Protocol invented by Netscape to encrypt communication between Web browsers and servers. It provides privacy, authentication, and integrity.

Server A device that provides one or more services to several clients over a network. See also *Client, Network*.

Service Negotiation A component in the DECT-MMAP standard for negotiating the minimum and maximum data rates for a particular service.

Service on Demand A provision of services that are available whenever required.

Servlet A Java application that runs on a server. The term usually refers to a Java applet that runs within a Web server environment. This is analogous to a Java applet that runs within a Web browser environment.

SES See *Société Européenne des Satellites*.

SET See *Secure Electronic Transaction*.

SGRAM See *Synchronous Graphics RAM*.

Shareware Programs that can be copied for testing purposes. Users who decide to use the program are required to register the software and pay a fee to the author. Shareware programs can often be used without restriction—based on the presumption that users are honest. Sometimes, however, they are limited in function or expire after a certain period of time.

Shopping Cart Keeps track of all the items that a customer wants to buy, allowing the shopper to pay for the whole order at once.

Short Message Service (SMS) A feature of GSM phones that allows users to receive and sometimes transmit short text messages using their wireless phones.

Simple Mail Transfer Protocol (SMTP) The protocol to send electronic mail over the Internet. See also *Electronic Mail*.

Simple Network Management Protocol (SNMP) Protocol to manage and monitor devices connected to a network.

Simple Object Access Protocol (SOAP) A way for a program running in one kind of operating system (such as Windows NT) to communicate with a program in the same or another kind of an operating system (such as Linux) by using Hypertext Transfer Protocol (HTTP) and Extensible Markup Language (XML) as the mechanisms for information exchange.

Simulcrypt Several CA systems (CASS) are transmitted simultaneously in a program packet. A decoder with one CA system suffices for reception. Example: a Seca or Viaccess decoder is required for the French ABsat-Packet.

Small Computer System Interface (SCSI) Standardized interface for connecting peripheral devices to a PC.

Smart Card Plastic card of credit-card size with an embedded microchip. The chip can contain digital money and personal information about the owner.

Smart Home See *Intelligent Home*.

SMDS See *Switched Multimegabit Data Service*.

Smiley See *Emoticon*.

SMPTE See *Society of Motion Picture and Television Engineers*.

SMS See *Short Message Service*.

SMTP See *Simple Mail Transport Protocol*.

SNMP See *Simple Network Management Protocol*.

SOAP See *Simple Object Access Protocol*.

Société Européenne des Satellites Company that operates Astra satellites.

Society of Motion Picture and Television Engineers (SMPTE) Organization that developed a time code for controlling the synchronization of images and sounds.

SoD See *Service on Demand*. See also *VoD*.

Spam Inappropriate use of e-mail and postings by sending information and advertising to people who did not request them.

Spider See *Web Crawler*.

SQL See *Structured Query Language*.

SSL See *Secure Sockets Layer*.

Stop Words Conjunctions, prepositions, articles, and other words that appear often in documents yet alone may contain little meaning.

Structured Information Information that is created and maintained in distinct and inflexible formats. Common examples include financial transaction records and operational databases.

Structured Query Language (SQL) The preferred programming language for communication with databases.

Switched Multimegabit Data Service (SMDS) A proposed new standard for very high-speed data transfer.

Symbian Joint venture between Ericsson Inc., Motorola Inc., Nokia Corp., and Psion to develop new operating systems based on Psion's EPOC32 platform for small mobile devices including wireless phones or handheld personal computers.

Symbol A data block consisting of a defined number of bits (the most well-known example of a symbol is a byte consisting of 8 bits).

Synchronous Graphics RAM (SGRAM) High-speed video memory for video signals.

Sysop See *System Operator*.

System Operator (Sysop) Person who is responsible for the operations of a computer system or network resource.

T-1 A leased line with a bandwidth of 1,544,000 bits per second (about 1.5 Megabits/s). See also *Bandwidth, Binary Digit, Byte, Ethernet, T-3*.

T-3 A leased line with a bandwidth of 44,736,000 bits per second (about 44 Megabits/s). See also *Bandwidth, Binary Digit, Byte, Ethernet, T-1*.

Table Combines identical records together in columns (fields) and rows (records).

Tagged Information File Format (TIFF) A compressed graphic file format developed by Aldus as an international standard format. Unfortunately, there are different versions of TIFF around, notably the MAC and PC versions, which have differing ways of compressing the data.

TAPI See *Telephony Application Programming Interface*.

TCP/IP See *Transmission Control Protocol / Internet Protocol*.

TCS-AT A set of AT-commands by which a mobile phone and modem can be controlled in the multiple usage models. In Bluetooth, AT-commands are based on ITU-T recommendation v.250 and ETS 300 916(GSM 07.07). In addition, the commands used for fax services are specified by the implementation. TCS-AT will also be used for dial-up networking and headset profiles.

TDMA Time Division Multiple Access is a technology used in digital cellular telephone communication to divide each cellular channel into three time slots in order to increase the amount of data that can be carried.

Telephony Application Programming Interface (TAPI) The Windows telephony interface developed by Microsoft and CTI.

Telematics The integration of wireless communications, vehicle monitoring systems, and location devices.

Telnet Program to perform a remote login to another computer.

Terabyte 1,024 or 1,000 Gigabytes. See also *Byte, Kilobyte*.

Thesaural Browser A hybrid searching and browsing tool that indexes all available corporate resources and provides users with a comprehensive list of resources that have synonymous, hierarchical, and associative relationships with a particular search term.

Thin Client A cut-down network terminal with no local processing power.

TIFF See *Tagged Information File Format*.

Transaction Ensures that any modification to a database is carried out either completely (i.e., for all records) or not at all.

Transfer Call Allows the user to forward a call to another phone.

Transmission Control Protocol/Internet Protocol (TCP/IP) A set of protocols that are the foundation of the Internet and which enable the communication between computers. Technical basis for transmitting data on the Internet. It divides the contents of a Web page into small packets and sends them along different paths, if necessary, to the receiver where TCP/IP then reassembles the packets in their original order.

Transponder Satellite transmission technology. Combination of a receiver that receives signals from a terrestrial station (uplink) and a transmitter that beams down the signals as a satellite TV program to the earth (downlink). The term is a combination of transmitter and responder.

Triple-dub Net language for "WWW."

Trojan Horse A program that seems to be harmless, but starts harmful functions after it has been installed.

Ultra-SCSI Extension of Fast-SCSI that allows a data rate of up to 20 Mbyte/s by doubling the clock frequency.

Ultra-Wide SCSI Extension of Wide-SCSI, that allows a data rate of up to 40 Mbyte/s by doubling the clock frequency.

UMTS See *Universal Mobile Telecommunications System*.

Unicode Text encoding scheme including international characters and alphabets.

Uniform Resource Locator (URL) Addressing scheme on the Internet to locate Internet resources. A URL consists of a server name, possibly a directory name or full pathname, and the document title (example: http://www.ebusinessrevolution.com/blgarski/).

Universal LNB A receiver unit located in the focal point of a parabolic antenna (dish-shaped or satellite antenna). LNB (Low Noise Block Converter) is also used to describe an LNC (Low Noise Converter). In the LNB, the signals received from a satellite are converted into a lower frequency range before they are forwarded via cable to the satellite receiver in or next to the TV set. The term "Universal" indicates that the LNB can be used for both analog TV (10.7-11.7 GHz) and digital TV (11.7-12.75 GHz) frequencies.

Universal Mobile Telecommunications System (UMTS) Europe's approach to standardization for third-generation cellular systems.

Universal Plug and Play (UPnP) Windows 9x and Windows 2000 offer "Plug and Play" technology for automatically detecting all compatible devices within a PC. Universal Plug and Play is designed to expand this technology to include devices in an (external) network. After devices are connected to a network supporting Universal Plug and Play, they automatically configure themselves, which eliminates the need for set-up and configuration. UPnP detects the devices along with the relevant product characteristics including communication protocols. For example, a camera can automatically detect a printer in the network, determine its ability to print in color, and print a photo.

Universal Serial Bus (USB) Serial interface that allows connection of up to 127 devices at speeds of either 1.5 or 12Mbits/s. It supplies power for those devices and allows the devices to be added and removed without rebooting. Thanks to the hot-plugging function, any number of devices can be switched on, plugged into different sockets, or removed while the PC is in operation. The USB host detects the change and renumbers the device addresses. Windows 98 is the first operating system to fully support the Universal Serial Bus. In version 1.1, the USB operates at a maximum data rate of up to 12 Mbit/s. USB Version 2.0 will offer data rates that are 20 times faster (i.e., 240 Mbits per second) and will be backward compatible. Devices are connected with a four-wire cable with standardized plugs that are polarized to prevent them from being inserted in the wrong direction. The cable can also supply current, if necessary, to connected peripheral devices. The devices are chained to the bus via passive hubs, which can also be integrated into separate USB devices such as keyboards or monitors. The maximum cable length between hub and peripheral is five meters. Intel introduced a USB system 2.0 early in 2000 that offers a maximum data rate of 480 Mbit/s—40 times faster than version 1.1.

Universal Wireless Communications Consortium (UWCC) An industry group supporting IS-136 time division multiple access and IS-41 wireless intelligent network technology.

UNIX Operating system that was developed in the early 1970s.

UNIX-to-UNIX Copy (UUCP) Software to exchange email and news on a store-and-forward basis.

UNIX-to-UNIX Decoding Method of converting text files to binary files. See also *Binary Hexadecimal*, *Multipurpose Internet Mail Extensions*.

UNIX-to-UNIX Encoding Method of converting binary files to text files. See also *Binary Hexadecimal*, *Multipurpose Internet Mail Extensions*.

Unstructured Information Information that is produced and stored in multiple, non-specified formats. Common examples include e-mail documents, memos, and reports.

UPnP See *Universal Plug and Play*.

Upstream The data flow from a client to a server or from a subscriber/customer to a provider; the opposite of downstream.

URL See *Uniform Resource Locator*.

USB See *Universal Serial Bus*.

USENET A decentralized worldwide system for newsgroups. See also *Newsgroup*.

UUCP See *UNIX-to-UNIX Copy*.

UUDECODE See *UNIX-to-UNIX Decoding*.

UUENCODE See *UNIX-to-UNIX Encoding*.

UWCC See *Universal Wireless Communications Consortium*.

VESA See *Video Electronics Standards Association*.

Video on Demand (VoD) Procedure in which TV programs can be directly accessed by a subscriber via a back channel from a video server. The transmission, which requires special switching equipment with distributed structure and bi-directional channels from and to the subscriber, is enabled after payment has been made. Similar services are being discussed, such as Audio on Demand, Software on Demand and others that are outlined under the heading. See also *Service-on-Demand*.

Video Random Access Memory (VRAM) High-speed video memory.

Video Server Hard disk storage for video signals with computer-controlled file management. In contrast to magnetic tape cassettes, this type of storage offers fast random access to specific scenes or images. In conjunction with Video on Demand (VoD), proposed video servers will provide storage capacity for hundreds, or possibly thousands, of video clips and films. Instead of gigabytes, these storage capacities are being measured in Terabytes (1 Terabyte = 1024 Gigabyte).

Viewtime The time during which a banner advertisement is visible on a Web page.

Virtual Memory System (VMS) A multiuser, multitasking, virtual memory operating system for the VAX series from Digital Equipment.

Virtual Reality Modeling Language (VRML) A programming language for displaying 3-D spaces on the Internet. VRML allows the user to design virtual landscapes or 3-D games. Current browsers are capable of displaying such data. Numerous browser plug-ins offer 3-D functions.

Virus Malicious piece of code that can be hidden in programs to destroy data on a computer.

Visit A complete session of accesses to a certain Web site conducted by one person. A visit is concluded when the customer hasn't viewed any page for a certain period of time (60 seconds in most cases).

VMS See *Virtual Memory System*.

VoD See *Video on Demand*.

Voice mail Similar to Email, voice mail is a message sent or received within a network as audio data.

VoIP A term used in IP telephony for a set of facilities for managing the delivery of voice information using Internet Protocol (IP).

VoxML Voice Markup Language. A technology from Motorola for creating a voice dialog with a Web site in which a user can call a Web site by phone and interact with it through speech recognition and Web site responses.

VRAM See *Video Random Access Memory*.

VRML See *Virtual Reality Modeling Language*.

WAIS See *Wide Area Information Servers*.

WAN See *Wide Area Network*.

WAP See *Wireless Application Protocol*.

W-CDMA See *Wideband CDMA*.

Web See *World Wide Web*.

Web Crawler Service that scans Web documents and adds them to a database. After having indexed one page, it follows all links and indexes them as well. See also *Search Engine*.

Webmaster The person in charge of a Web server. Most Web servers will allow mail to be sent to the webmaster. The webmaster of http://www.foobar. org/ can be reached at webmaster@foobar.org, for example. See also *Postmaster*.

WebQoS See *Web Quality of Service*.

Web Quality of Service (WebQoS) A product that assures consistent quality of service on shared systems by preventing surges in online customer demand from overloading the server. It also allows service providers to safely host multiple sites on a single system by preventing busy sites from impacting each other's performance.

Web Server A computer that provides World Wide Web services on the Internet (or intranet). It includes the hardware, operating system, Web server software, TCP/IP protocols, and the Web site content. The term may refer to just the software that performs this service, which accepts requests from Web browsers to download HTML pages, other document, images, etc. It can also execute related server-side scripts that automate functions such as searching a database.

What You See Is What You Get (WYSIWYG) The promise that what you see on screen will also be what you get when you print out the document. Few software packages are able to fulfill this promise.

Wide Area Information Servers (WAIS) Software package that allows the indexing of large quantities of information. Uses a separate protocol from HTTP and is not used very much anymore. See also *HyperText Transfer Protocol, Search Engine*.

Wide Area Network (WAN) A network that is distributed over several locations. See also *Local Area Network*.

Wideband CDMA The third generation standard offered to the International Telecommunication Union by GSM proponents.

Widescreen TV screen format with an aspect ratio of 16:9 (width/height). This adapts to the perspective of human vision in which the horizontal range is wider than the vertical range. Widescreen images reduce eye strain, particularly for larger screen formats. From a technical standpoint, the 16:9 format can be implemented in conventional analog TVs (PALplus) as well as digital TVs (DVB).

Wide-SCSI Transmission protocol compliant with SCSI-2 that defines an extension of the bus width to 16 bit and thus requires special cables and plugs. Wide-SCSI is normally used with Fast-SCSI and is capable of data transmission of up to 20 Mbyte/s.

Window-RAM Special type of VRAM with high bandwidth used by Matrox, Number Nine, and other video card manufacturers.

Wintel The majority of computers today run the Wintel combination: the Windows operating systems and Intel processors.

Wireless Using the radio-frequency spectrum for transmitting and receiving voice, data, and video signals for communications.

Wireless Application Protocol (WAP) A specification for a set of communication protocols to standardize the way that wireless devices, such as cellular telephones and radio transceivers, can be used for Internet access, including email, the World Wide Web, newsgroups, and Internet Relay Chat (IRC).

Wireless IP The packet data protocol standard for sending wireless data over the Internet.

Wireless LAN (WLAN) Local area network using wireless transmissions, such as radio or infrared instead of phone lines or fibre-optic cable to connect data devices.

Wireless Markup Language (WML) Formerly called HDML (Handheld Devices Markup Language), a language that allows the text portions of Web pages to be presented on cellular phones and personal digital assistants (PDAs) via wireless access.

WML See *Wireless Markup Language*.

World Wide Web (WWW) The part of the Internet that is accessible through a Web browser. The Web is not the Internet, but a subset.

Worm A program that is designed to replicate itself over a network. Although not all worms are designed to destroy, most of them will try to attack your resources.

WRAM See *Window-RAM*.

WRT Net language for "with respect to."

WWW See *World Wide Web*.

WYSIWYG See *What You See Is What You Get*.

Xanadu Bill Gates' networked home uses a variety of methods for electronic house control. According to press reports, the house has over 100 PCs connected to thousands of sensors and activators used to regulate lighting, air, and temperature. They also use chip cards to identify the whereabouts of people in each room. After the person has been identified, his music and video preferences can be pre-selected.

xDSL Designation for digital subscriber line technology enabling simultaneous two-way transmission of voice and high-speed data over ordinary copper phone lines.

XML See Extensible Markup Language.

Xpresso A processor designed for the Java-Engine by Zucotto Systems. It is used for broadband access to handheld devices via an integrated Bluetooth connection. The Xpresso core is formed by Sun architecture (KVM, Kernel Virtual Machine) around which the proprietary data slice (service layer in Consumer Electronics) was programmed.

Yahoo! The original and most famous Web directory. The name Yahoo! is an acronym for "Yet Another Hierarchical Officious Oracle."

YMMV Net language for "your mileage may vary." A warning that not everything described in a manual will work exactly the way it is promised to.

Appendix B

EXAMPLE INTERNET BUSINESS ARCHITECTURE

This appendix provides a real-world example, in which we try to implement many parts of the lessons that were provided throughout the book. The example is simple but can be easily expanded for larger companies. The basics are always the same.

B.1 The Business Idea

The following is based on ideas I developed for my father's business. After working for several years as a freelance editor for a large publishing company in Germany, my father wanted to restart his editing, translation, and recording service, which he had almost dropped in favor of large contracts for the publishing company. The proposed solution here has not been implemented at the time of writing; it has been developed during the writing of this book and will be implemented after the book is finished. You will find the link to this Web site on this book's home page.[1]

To restart the business and reach out to new customers, it was necessary to build a Web site that represents his service and shows customers what he and his potential partners are able to do. Although my father had been using e-mail for several years, he did not have a Web site with information about his company, ETS.

If you remember the six phases from the introduction, you will notice that we were at Phase 0. In this phase, the Internet is used only passively by the company. There is no Web presence. Some basic Internet knowledge was available, such as using email and a Web browser, but there was really no available information on how to build a web site.

To see how the online business could be created, it was necessary to take a closer look at the services offered. Editing, translating, and recording are all tasks that cannot be done in real time over the Internet, because these

---

[1]http://www.ebusinessrevolution.com/

tasks are far too unique for software to handle. The Internet can only be used to market and promote these services. It cannot be used to automate these services. But the Internet allows us to create value-added services on top of these basic services.

To create a successful the Web site, ETS had to build a business portal for each of these services. By offering the value-added service for each of the services, it becomes easy to guide a large number of people to these sites and generate new profit streams, such as banner advertising.

We will develop one of the three business portals as an example. If we look at the recording service ETS wanted to offer over the Internet, we need to understand exactly what the job consists of. Until now, companies who had a German promotional image or training film called ETS and asked if my father was available to voiceover the translated text in English. In many cases, ETS would also do the translation work before the actual recording. The recording work is done in various studios in the region. While it would be quite easy to make the deal on the Internet, the actual recording would still have to take place in a studio. Therefore, it would not be very useful to offer the recording service to companies outside of the region (southern Germany and bordering areas) if they have their own sound studios.

This brings us to the point of which we must consider our target market. Who are the potential customers and where are they located? It would not be feasible for my father to travel the whole world for recordings that may take only a few hours to complete. Because the Internet allows content to be viewed by anyone all over the world, it needs to be stated clearly that the services are not offered on a world-wide basis. Because companies have their preferred suppliers (in this case, studios), it is difficult to work in these studios all around the world.

Imagine companies from Australia, Russia, and South Africa selecting the services of ETS. They will most likely have their preferred local sound studios, and traveling would take up too much time to be cost effective. So they would be forced to choose a sound studio proposed by ETS. By making agreements with several sound studios in the region, ETS would be able to attract international customers who are in need of a native English speaker for promotional films.

To offer additional value on the Web site, the business portal needs to be built. In this case, it would be a vertical portal regarding all facets of recording. There needs to be a directory of recording Web sites and resources, possibly links to books on recording (although I haven't seen any), and links to recording studios and speakers. The portal can offer multiple recording studios and speakers so that customers have a choice. To maintain the business with ETS, the speakers and recording studios would need to pay a transaction fee for every customer that comes from the business portal. This guarantees that the speakers are not taking away business from ETS and ensures a high quality of speakers because they are hand-picked. The directory could also consist of two parts. A general section would include all available resources, and in a more specialized part, ETS would propose selected studios and speakers. Because ETS specializes in English-speaking recordings, supporting speakers for other languages will increase the value of the Web site without reducing the amount of work ETS receives in the end. The final goal may be to delegate all the work and use the Web site as a transactional site for other speakers, including native English speakers.

B.2 Marketing on the Web

To market the capabilities of ETS, the service needs to be explained in detail on the Web site. The Web site is first and foremost the business card of ETS. In addition to a written description, which is similar to the document ETS used to send out to customers, the Internet offers additional possibilities. Many companies request a tape in order to hear the voice before deciding to make use of the service. Instead of sending out the document with the service description and the tape, it is possible to set up a few Web pages that give the same result.

In addition to the service description, sample Web pages could be set up that contain the audio in conjunction with the speaker's text. Five different texts for five different situations would be enough to give most customers a good idea of how the voice would work in their film.

To market the Web site efficiently, it needs a domain name that reflects its content. Actually, two domain names would be suitable, one of which carries the name of the company—in this case, "ets," and one for the content of the business portal, something connected to recording. Before deciding on the exact second-level domain name, we need to should think about the top-level domain. As you know by now: If the offering is regional, then a country domain would be more suitable, but if it is a general worldwide service, then a ".com" would probably be more suitable. As we've seen, ETS's service can be offered to the whole world, so a ".com" top-level domain would be suitable. In addition to this, we would try to target the German market in particular, so the complete Web site would be English and German, and the German Web site would get a ".de" domain to make it a more regional offering for Germany.

We looked at the Web site of Internet Solutions[2] in the United States and Ripe.net[3] in Europe to find out which ".com" and ".de" domain names were available.

The most obvious domain names—ets.com, ets.de, and ets.net—were already taken, so we had to look for similar names that made it easy for customers to find the site and remember the domain name. The same applied to recording.com, speakers.com, aufnahme.de, and sprecher.de. Finding a solution for the second domain name was easier, because attaching something like -net was easy, making it recording-net.com. But choosing a top level do-

---

[2]http://www.internetsolutions.com/
[3]http://www.ripe.net/

main name was more difficult to resolve. How should the domain name for the company name be chosen if the most appropriate names were already taken? PureTec[4] offers a service that proposes up to thirty domain names, if the domain name that you wanted to use is already taken. In the end, my father decided to take a totally different domain name encompassing all fields of work: text-projects.de.[5]

The ".de" at the end indicates where the company is located and the English domain name provides an idea of the type of work he does. As you can see, choosing a domain name can be difficult if you do not have a well-known brand name or well-known products. See Figure B.1 for a view of the English home page.

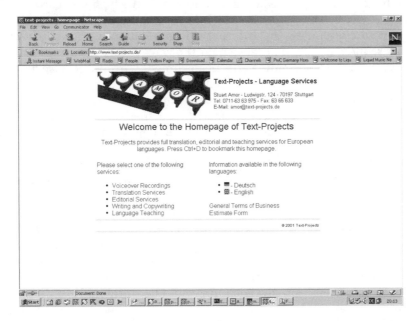

Figure B.1. Home page of Text-Projects.

After we decided on the domain name, we needed to create the site and publish the address in as many locations as possible. First, the URLs need to be put into the footers of the e-mail sent out to existing customers, so that they can look at the site. The next step is to submit the URLs to as many search engines as possible. This will ensure that people who are looking for that particular service through a search engine will be able to find ETS's site.

On the Web, there are many sites dedicated to recording, so a banner and link exchange with these sites will increase the traffic directed to ETS's Web site. To keep visitors and customers returning to the site, it needs to be updated

---

[4]http://www.puretec.de/
[5]http://www.text-projects.de/

on a regular basis. A news section should keep the customers informed about changes on the site, and news from the recording industry should keep them coming back at regular intervals.

A frequently asked questions (FAQ) page will help customers answer the most common questions regarding the service, thus reducing the load of questions coming in through email. At the same time, it is important to set up a feedback page, allowing customers and visitors to express their opinions and wishes, and making it easier for the company to extend the service in the right direction and meet customer demand individually and dynamically.

Known customers should be able to login and receive personalized information. It would be possible, for example, to handle all the communication via the Web site instead of email, making it easier for both parties to track the comments of the other. The personalized Web site can also offer special information or updates on work in progress.

In addition to the actual service and documents around the service, a mailing list and newsgroup could be set up to allow the exchange of ideas between customers, sound studios, and speakers. In this case, four newsgroups would work quite well, one more general and three dedicated lists for customers, sound studios, and speakers. The content would most likely be about the business and new technologies shaping the business, but it would not be restricted to these topics.

B.3   Implementation of the Service

To implement the service on the Internet, it is necessary to buy the domain names, which costs about 35 euros or dollars per domain name, per year. In addition to the domain name, we must to decide whether the Web site should be hosted on its own system or put onto a Web server hosted by an ISP. In this case, ETS is a small company with no resources dedicated to Internet technology, so it would not make sense to set up a computer locally and lease a phone line to connect to the Internet. Maintenance would be a problem. Therefore, outsourcing the Web server option to an ISP is the simplest and cheapest solution. A typical ISP Web server hosting solution would cost about 20 to 30 euros or dollars per month, for about 30 MB of Web space and unlimited traffic per month. This basic Web server package normally includes a POP3 email address and unlimited email aliases for that particular address. One such ISP could be cihost.com[6] in the United States; many other providers throughout the world offer similar services at similar prices.

The one POP3 e-mail address will allow ETS to retrieve email from the server and read it in an email program, while the email aliases will help customers to speak to the right person within the company. ETS would be able to set up multiple email addresses easily. Typical email addresses for a com-

---

[6]http://www.cihost.com/

pany include webmaster@domain.com, which deals with questions regarding the technical implementation; info@domain.com, for general requests about the Web site and the service; orders@domain.com for ordering inquiries and status updates; and stuart@domain.com for personal mail.

The different domain names would all link to a single Web server, but to other directories. The ".de" domain would show the site in German, while the ".com" site would present the content in English. Through a simple HTML link, the customer would have the ability to switch between languages at any time.

In this case, the aliases all link to one e-mail address, making it easy for ETS to respond to any type of query from a single mail program without the need for setting up multiple configurations. For the customers it looks like there are many different people working for the company, which may be true in the future, but for a startup, the aliases make it easier to appear as an important and quality company.

To facilitate easy communication between customers and company, the customers would use a Web-based form for sending email to the company. This makes it easier for the customer to decide to whom the email is sent by selecting the appropriate email address and function and by guiding the customers to information that gets a qualified response in a very short time. In the recording business, information about the recording will help to qualify the type of recording and its price. Because the service is very individual, it is not possible to put up a price list on the Web site. A Web form could include fields for the length of the film, the type of film, and other details that are of interest in determining the price. An upload button for adding the text and sending it automatically for review to ETS could also be easily implemented. By disallowing new customers to send email directly to ETS, it is easier to classify email and respond to customers.

The business portal, which should contain a directory of recording and speaker related sites, can be built quite easily by extracting the relevant parts from the Open Directory[7] project, which allows other sites to take the complete database or parts of it and include it on their own Web site. We would need to search for the relevant parts for our vertical business portal and define a way to automatically extract these parts on a regular basis to keep the data up-to-date. A Perl[8] script can be used, for example, to extract the necessary parts on a monthly basis and put them into the Web page design of the Web site. The license of the Open Directory asks for a link back to the original and the add site link, which also leads automatically back into the database. These two links are created easily and voluntarily because the Open Directory is an invaluable service for any portal.

In addition to Open Directory, database sound studios and other speakers

---

[7]http://www.dmoz.org/
[8]http://www.perl.org/

need to be integrated into the site. This leads us to the next step: the design of the Web pages. Because ETS had no knowledge of Web page design, this work needed to be outsourced to a Web design company that creates the initial set of Web pages according to the company design. The cost of the Web design is high, so the company won't be used for the ongoing business. A short introduction to the Web and HTML should be sufficient to let ETS staff maintain, update, and operate the site.

Therefore, a tool needs to be selected that enables ETS to change the Web site at any given time—moving pages around, changing content, adding new pages, or deleting pages—without having to know how HTML works and how the update process works to move the changed site to the Internet. For this purpose, we have chosen NetObjects Fusion,[9] which makes it easy to change the Web site after the basic templates have been created. The program uses an interface that is similar to desktop publishing systems and word processors, making it easy for a nontechnical person to understand how to change, delete, or add pages. The software offers a staging area where the changed Web pages can be viewed before they are uploaded to the production server, making sure that only correct Web pages are uploaded. The editing process is very easy to understand. And the software costs less than 200 euros or dollars.

Payment won't occur over the Internet in this business-to-business scenario. Invoices will be sent after the recording has been completed, so there is no need to implement an online payment system for this Web site. To create additional revenue streams, the Web site should carry banner advertising. The banner advertising can be organized on a one-to-one basis, meaning that ETS would have to negotiate, or it is possible to go to one of the many online banner advertising offices. To lessen ETS's workload in this area, we chose an online banner advertising office.

The personalization of the Web site can be managed through a set of Perl scripts that need to be written to allow access to private parts of the Web server that are dedicated to single customers. These private directories may contain documents—such as contracts, texts, sound files, and video files—that need to be exchanged before and after the recording session. The private sessions should be controlled by login and password, which is a standard functionality of all Web servers. If the material contained in these directories is sensitive, such as contracts, the Web server should exchange the data encrypted, so SSL encryption needs to be switched on, which is also a standard functionality of all Web servers. To enable SSL encryption, a digital certificate needs to be purchased, which is available for 100 to 200 euros or dollars on the Web. A local search engine for the Web site is integrated into most Web servers, and if not, Perl scripts are available that offer this service. Problems with cultural differences are not expected, because the Web site is business-to-business only and contains only business-related information.

---

[9] http://www.netobjects.com/

The site of ETS is now between phase three and phase four from the introduction, which I called "Trying E-Commerce" and "Doing E-Business." The company is trying to sell a service online. The system is not connected to the real databases on the intranet. This would not make sense in this case, because a one-man company would not require an intranet.

Startup costs are about 1,000 to 2,000 euros or dollars, depending on the cost of the Web design agency. The ongoing costs are very low in this model. After the site is up and running online, the Web space and the domain name need to be paid for, but the maintenance work on the Web site is done by ETS. Because the site is very specialized and much of it is automated, the need for change is not very great.

The personalized Web site offers security through standard login and password authentication and the communication is secured through SSL encryption. Implementation and operating costs are low, so it is easy to focus on the actual work, which results from the customer deals, made over the Web or through traditional channels.

B.4   Outlook into the Future

The site has now been live for about two years. So far, it has only been a marketing web site providing information about the services that my father offers. In addition to marketing material, it offers a communication option, using the Web form. So far, there has been no need to expand the business any further, because my father is already swamped with work and every additional function would create even more work. But still, many options remain for the future, especially when you think about expanding from a one-man business toward a small company.

If we look at the future and pervasive computing, there are good chances to integrate the recording service into the new paradigm. The new paradigm connects all sorts of devices and integrates them into the Internet. In our case, we could envision a future in which the customer provides the film, the sound studio, and the recording equipment, and the speaker sits at home using a microphone. The film is broadcast to the sound studio and the speaker at the same time, allowing the speaker to add the text and the sound studio to record the text.

This requires the speaker to have a dedicated room for recording, equipped with a microphone, a computer, and a television set. Each device is connected to the Internet. The computer is used as a teleprompter, which shows the text in real time, while the microphone sends the voice to the sound studio, which records and alters the voice to fit into the film. The television set shows the film from the customer in real time. This enables each of the participants to deliver the best possible service without having to worry about how these devices connect and how content is delivered. After the film and the voice are synchronized and the customer is happy, the film can be sent off to a video copying firm that can instantly produce video cassettes, and at the same time the company can make the film available on its intranet, enabling the employees to see the film before it is used or even making it public on the company's Web site.

Everything is available the moment it is needed. Instant private business networks will become more important in the future, in which most of the business will be conducted over the Internet.

Appendix C

USEFUL WEB ADDRESSES

The following is a selection of my favorite sites. I collect keywords in my memory, because I don't feel the facilities for administering bookmarks in the browsers are adequate. The URLs change so quickly that it does not make any sense to remember them. To find information, I rely on metasearch engines, so that I only have to remember the keywords in order to find a certain site again. Have fun with the following sites. Please bear in mind that Web sites appear and disappear at light-speed on the Internet, so I cannot guarantee that these sites will still work by the time you try to access them.

C.1 Business

This section provides some links to highly valuable business sites on the Internet.

http://www.daytraders.org/ Here's a professional, live, free chat room for day traders. Online since 1996.

http://www.etrade.com/ One of the best known online investment and financial services comes with a portal site for financial matters.

http://www.idealab.com/ The Idea Lab focuses on new business models. Some of their incubated businesses are eToys, CarsDirect, CitySearch, and Goto.com.

http://www.stock-world.com/ Here's another investing portal with a great deal of information.

http://www.turtletrader.com/ TurtleTrader teaches the Turtle trading techniques. These trading techniques are used by some of today's most successful traders and can help all traders earn above-average profits in most futures and stock markets going both long and short.

C.2 Comics

The following are some of my favorite comic sites on the Web. They deal with
lost souls, either in the working or Internet world.

http://www.dilbert.com/ The Dilbert Comic Zone is a must-read for everyone
working for a cubicle company.

http://www.eeggs.com/ The Easter Egg Archive provides amusing secret tid-
bits hidden in software, movies, music, TV, books, and art.

http://www.thehungrysite.com/ One former employee of a failing dot-com
solicits donations to avoid returning to the New Economy and cubicle hell.

http://www.kimble.org/ The mighty Kimble fights against the evil powers of
the world.

http://www.pcweenies.com/ This is the comic strip with typical nerds.

http://www.userfriendly.org/ Here's the daily UNIX-friendly comic strip.

http://www.webcomics.com/ This portal site features online comics on a variety of topics.

C.3 Computers

These Web sites are always useful to find out more information about the hardware you are using.

http://www.amiga.de/ Although they lost the battle, some lost souls still hope
for a new Amiga.

http://www.apple.com/ Here's the ultimate user-friendly computer. If you
want an easy-to-use computer, take a Mac.

http://www.compaq.com/ Compaq is of the largest PC makers in the world
and is (probably) now part of the new Hewlett-Packard (probably).

http://www.digital.com/ Compaq bought Digital.

http://www.hp.com/ The inventor of the open systems has moved to become
the company of open services.

http://www.ibm.com/ It's Big Blue, and you know who they are.

http://www.sun.com/ The inventor of Java always has some interesting new
ideas, concepts, and pieces of software.

http://www.sgi.com/ The former Silicon Graphics has evolved from a graphic
processor company to a general computer company with lots of interesting
hardware.

C.4 Fun

These fun Web sites provide no value other than a good laugh.

http://theportal.to/area52/ This is the site that Area 51 doesn't want you to know about. It includes alien pictures, alien FAQs, and bogus sightings.

http://www.thenia.com/ The Nerd Intelligence Agency provides all computer users with very important information.

C.5 Hacking-Related Sites

Even if you're not a hacker, you will find these resources interesting. Anyone interested in Internet security will find information here to make his or her systems more secure. Only when you are aware of the threats can you do something about them.

http://www.antionline.com/ AntiOnline's mission is to educate the public about computer security and hacking-related issues.

http://www.hackers.com/ This is a complete resource for hackers.

http://www.l0pht.com/ This commercial site provides security tools, plus hacking info, exploits, and news.

http://catless.ncl.ac.uk/Risks/ This is a forum on risks to the public in computers and related systems.

http://www.technotronic.com/ Technotronic Security Information provides the network administrator with up-to-date, security-related information.

C.6 Internet Organizations

The following organizations have influenced the Internet and its standards. To discover what the Internet will look like in the future, have a look at the following sites.

http://www.iesg.org/ The Internet Engineering Steering Group is responsible for technical management of IETF activities and the Internet standards process.

http://www.ietf.org/ The Internet Engineering Task Force is the driving force for new Internet standards. It is an open international community of companies that design and operate networks, research new technologies, and sell products based on these technologies. Although it is open to anyone, the task force is driven by companies that try to agree on new standards that enable new services on the Internet while running more smoothly. Internet Standards proposed by the IETF are the so-called Requests for Comments (RFC).

http://www.isoc.org/ The Internet Society is an organization of Internet experts who comment on policies and practices. It oversees a number of other boards and task forces dealing with network policy issues.

http://www.w3.org/ The World Wide Web Consortium is the inventor of the World Wide Web.

C.7   Mailing Lists

Interesting mailing lists provide you with up-to-date information in your mailbox. No need to surf the web anymore!

http://www.allEC.com/ The all E-Commerce mailing list provides news and updates in the e-commerce sector.

http://www.geek-girl.com/bugtraq/ BugTraq is the mailing list for security relevant bugs and flaws in applications and operating systems. This site is a must for anyone connected to the Internet who is concerned about security.

http://www.alistapart.com/ Here's a lively mailing list on all topics around the Web.

http://www.nua.ie/ This site provides free weekly email contributing to a philosophy for the Digital Age.

C.8   News

These online news sites are all concerned about the Internet, related technology, the New Economy, and the "webified" society. Each of these sites also offers a free newsletter.

http://www.news.com/ Here's a leading source of computer- and Internet-related information.

http://www.techweb.com/ This news center has lots of interesting information on computers and the Internet.

http://www.slashdot.org/ This news service is for extreme geeks.

http://www.wired.com/ Here's your news source for Internet, computer, and political issues.

C.9   Search Engines

While more search engines appear on the Internet every day, I prefer metasearch engines that search across several search engines.

http://www.google.com/ This is the search engine without comprise. It's small, fast, and the best!

http://www.metacrawler.com/ My favorite metasearch engine usually provides good results.

http://www.savvysearch.com/ If I cannot find something with metacrawler, then I look here for the missing pages. If I cannot find a Web page in metacrawler and savvysearch, it probably does not exist.

http://www.metager.de/ Here's my third option when metasearching.

C.10   Software Development

These sites are for those who are in need of a piece of source code or hints on programming.

http://www.developer.com/ This is the metaresource for developers; it covers all important programming languages.

http://www.cgi-resources.com/ If you are looking for CGI scripts to pep up your Web site, then this is the right resource.

http://developer.netscape.com/ This site provides all the information that a person on the Internet needs regarding JavaScript, HTML, and Netscape products.

http://developer.java.sun.com/ Here's the ultimate Web site on Java technology.

Appendix D

INTERNATIONALIZATION OF
WEB SITES

This appendix is not intended as a complete guide to internationalization, but rather as a reference to some of the most common issues regarding the technicalities of its implementation. For basic concepts on internationalization and localization, please check out Chapter 5.

D.1 Introduction

When the Web first began back in 1991, all texts were in English. The character set it was built on, called ISO-8859-1 (also known as Latin-1), contains all characters for most Western European languages. As a result the Web spread first toward Western Europe. Early on, Web pages put up by Japanese or Greek companies or individuals were also in English as well, but over time the Web has become accessible to almost anyone, so the need for native language support has steadily increased. And these days, the content of a Web page isn't the only thing in another language; in many cases, a different character set and font are used.

HTML is now widely used with other languages, using other coded character sets or character encodings through various ad hoc extensions. This originally resulted in many different versions of a Russian Web page, for example, making things difficult for the reader, who had to install all sorts of extensions to be able to see all Russian language Web pages.

In the past, various communities got into the habit of sending out their documents with a Content-type: text/html (i.e. without an explicit character set specification) on the assumption that the reader would have already set their browser correctly. This was always a technically incorrect thing to do: Documents should be sent out with a Content-type that specifies the correct character set. Earlier versions of HTML (2.0 and 3.2) were based on the default character set being ISO-8859-1, whereas HTML 4.0 explicitly states that there is no default character set. So under either specification, an explicit character set is required.

Unfortunately, some earlier browsers did not work properly when sent a Content-type header that included an explicit character set, and refused to display the document at all. So users in these communities got accustomed to configuring those (now-obsolete) browsers to use a different font, so that the 8-bit characters would look right, and ignored the character set issue entirely. (Note that this procedure usually means that the browsers render &entity; and &#number; representations incorrectly, but those old browser/versions were incapable of anything better.) Now, the supporters of this procedure would tell the reader to use their browser's character-set override feature to select the correct repertoire. While this procedure might be understandable in relation to those older browsers (and some communities still insist they need to run old browsers because of their low-powered machines), it should be noted that this isn't (and actually never was) in accord with the published specifications. It is a pity that there were browsers that failed to implement the specs correctly.

ISO-8859-1/Latin 1 supports special characters for German, French, Spanish, and Scandinavian languages. This means that special characters for West European languages, like ñ, Ü, or ß, may be rendered using regular HTML code rather than by using <meta> tags, attributes, or other solutions (such as using images of text, .pdf files, or transliteration). Because special characters may be indicated by using regular, old HTML, this method is likely to provide the least number of problems. That is, most browsers on most machines will be able to display these characters correctly. These characters are individually encoded so that the browser will display them in all their glory. For instance, française is encoded as <française>. Special characters may be encoded this way in the text that comes between any tags.

Table D.1. Special Characters

In the mean time, internationalization of HTML has taken place at two levels. First, the characters in the text (apart from the markup) should be able to represent non-western alphabets, such as Cyrillic, Arabic, Hebrew, Japanese, etc. And second, for correct display and other operations, it is sometimes necessary to explicitly set the language of a text fragment. This led to two important developments. All browsers now support the ISO-8859 family of character sets. In addition, all versions of HTML (beyond 3.2) use Unicode (or ISO 10646), which means that some 34,000 of the world's characters are available.

As if the problem with old web browsers wasn't bad enough, increasing numbers of Web pages are being provided by authors who have neither the necessary level of support from their provider, nor the expertise themselves, to know how to send out pages with a proper character set header. They typically use a META HTTP-EQUIV in their HTML documents instead.

One of the biggest problems in the area of internationalization is that not all problems are universal. For example, many scripts do not have diacritic marks such as accents and cedillas, and people whose native scripts have no diacritic marks tend to not consider the problems of using them; similarly, many scripts do not contain capital letters, and people whose native script doesn't have capital letters have less understanding of where these characters can cause problems.

D.2   Bad Habits

Many people have tried to solve the language problem on the display level by replacing the font to display the words in the desired language. Some people use the symbol font on Windows to display Greek characters. This habit has been unfortunately transformed to the Web in HTML documents by using <FONT FACE=Symbol> and such to select a different repertoire of displayable characters. As far as HTML is concerned, this is at entirely the wrong protocol level. The transmitted octets, &name; entities, and &#number; representations have meanings defined by HTTP and HTML protocol standards. That meaning could be displayed by cosmetically different fonts, but to select a font that produces a quite different displayed character is entirely contrary to the intentions of HTML.

Although it might appear to produce the effect intended by the author, in a limited range of viewing situations, this can also produce all kinds of deleterious consequences, including undiagnosed but incorrect display in other viewing situations, such as a different browser, or even a different operating system. If you change the language factor only on the display level, you have to assume that all other users have the same infrastructure below this level. This means that others who want to read the text have the same fonts installed and probably the same version of the browser. The author of a Web page should not need to know anything about the machinery that exists in a client platform for turning coded characters via font resources into a screen display: The device used for viewing HTML pages should be treated as a black box as far as the HTML author is concerned. Another nasty side effect is the search robots' incorrect indexing. Russian search engines won't understand the text on a given Web site if it does not adhere to the standards. Because all letters will probably be in the wrong place, the search engines do not even detect that it meant to be Russian. Braille or speech browsers will certainly fail as well, because they rely on meta-information (i.e., additional information about the Web page) that is not given in these cases.

To display text properly, the browser must recognize the meaning (e.g., &#bignumber;) of HTML markup and make whatever font selection is needed internally for displaying that meaning to the reader. It should be no part of an HTML author's job to second guess what fonts the reader might have at his disposal and to interfere in the browser's selection of fonts.

D.3   ISO 8859 and Unicode

There are several ways to tell a browser which language or character set is used. The easiest way of doing this is to use the ISO 8859 and Unicode settings in the browser.

The ISO 8859 character sets were designed in the mid-1980s by the European Computer Manufacturer's Association (ECMA) and endorsed by the International Standards Organization (ISO). The ISO 8859 character set is an extension of ASCII code, which is only 7-bit and leaves 128 characters unused. These 128 characters are reused for different purposes. The ISO 8859 standard is a full series of 15 standardized multilingual single-byte coded (8-bit) graphic character sets for writing in alphabetic languages:

1. **ISO 8859-1**—Also known as Latin-1, this set covers most West European languages, such as French (fr), Spanish (es), Catalan (ca), Basque (eu), Portuguese (pt), Italian (it), Albanian (sq), Rhaeto-Romanic (rm), Dutch (nl), German (de), Danish (da), Swedish (sv), Norwegian (no), Finnish (fi), Faroese (fo), Icelandic (is), Irish (ga), Scottish (gd), and English (en). In addition to the European languages, it also covers Afrikaans (af) and Swahili (sw), and in effect the entire American continent, Australia, and much of Africa. The most notable exceptions are Zulu (zu) and other Bantu languages using Latin Extended-B letters, and of course Arabic in North Africa, and Guarani (gn) missing GEIUY with tilde. The lack of the ligatures for Dutch IJ, French OE, and German quotation marks is considered tolerable. The lack of the new C=-resembling Euro currency symbol has opened the discussion of a new Latin0.

2. **ISO 8859-2**—Also known as Latin-2, this set covers the languages of Central and Eastern Europe: Czech (cs), Hungarian (hu), Polish (pl), Romanian (ro), Croatian (hr), Slovak (sk), Slovenian (sl), and Sorbian.

3. **ISO 8859-3**—Also known as Latin-3, this set is popular with authors of Esperanto (eo) and Maltese (mt), and it covered Turkish before the introduction of Latin5 in 1988.

4. **ISO 8859-4**—Also known as Latin4, this set introduced letters for Estonian (et), the Baltic languages Latvian (lv, Lettish) and Lithuanian (lt), Greenlandic (kl), and Lappish. Latin4 was followed by Latin6.

5. **ISO 8859-5**—This set provides Cyrillic letters that let you type Bulgarian (bg), Byelorussian (be), Macedonian (mk), Russian (ru), Serbian (sr), and pre-1990 (no ghe with upturn) Ukrainian (uk). The ordering is based on the (incompatibly) revised GOST 19768 of 1987 with the Russian letters except for ё sorted by Russian alphabet (ABVGDE).

6. **ISO 8859-6**—This is the Arabic alphabet, but only the basic alphabet for the Arabic (ar) language. It does not contain the four extra letters for Persian (fa), nor the eight extra letters for Pakistani Urdu (ur). Therefore, it is not well-suited for text display. Each Arabic letter occurs in up to four presentation forms: initial, medial, final, or separate. To make Arabic text legible, you'll need a display engine that analyzes the context and combines the appropriate glyphs on top of a handler for the reverse writing direction shared with Hebrew. Additional software is required to make text written in ISO 8859-6 legible.

7. **ISO 8859-7**—This set is modern monotonic Greek (el) that is not accented. It was formerly known as ELOT-928 or ECMA-118:1986. Unfortunately, it does not provide accented characters, oversimplifying the Greek language.

8. **ISO 8859-8**—This is the script used by Hebrew (iw) and Yiddish (ji). Like Arabic, it is written leftward, but does not require an additional display engine because the Hebrew script is much simpler than the Arabic counterpart.

9. **ISO 8859-9**—This is also known as Latin-5 and replaces the rarely needed Icelandic letters in Latin1 with the Turkish ones.

10. **ISO 8859-10**—Also known as Latin-6, this set rearranged the Latin4 characters, dropped some symbols and the Latvian ŗ, added the last missing Inuit (Greenlandic Eskimo) and non-Skolt Sami (Lappish) letters, and reintroduced the Icelandic letters to cover the entire Nordic area.

11. **ISO 8859-11**—This is the Thai standard TIS620 Latin/Thai (th). It contains some combining vowel and tone marks that have to be written above or below the consonants. Thai also requires a complex rendering engine to show the glyphs at the right place within the word.

12. **ISO 8859-12**—This is currently unused. It is expected that this number will be used in future for the ISCII Indian standard.

13. **ISO 8859-13**—Also known as Latin-7, this set covers the Baltic Rim, reestablishes the Latvian (lv) support lost in Latin-6, and introduces the local quotation marks.

14. **ISO 8859-14**—Also known as Latin-8, adds the last Gaelic and Welsh (cy) letters to Latin-1 to cover all Celtic languages.

15. **ISO 8859-15**—Also known as Latin-9, this set aims to update Latin-1 by replacing the less needed symbols with forgotten French and Finnish letters and placing the Euro sign in the cell of the former international currency sign.

The ISO 8859 character sets are not even remotely as complete as Unicode, but they have been around and usable for quite a while. They were the first registered Internet character sets for use with MIME and have already offered a major improvement over plain 7-bit US-ASCII. You can specify the character set by putting a line like this in the <head> of the document:

```
<META HTTP-EQUIV=Content-Type" content="text/html; charset=iso-8859-15">
```

Unicode (ISO 10646) will make this whole chaos of mutually incompatible character sets superfluous, because it unifies a superset of all established character sets and aims to cover all the world's languages. Today, most computers are based on the ISO 8859 standards, and a transition is happening slowly. Latin1 has also been adopted as the first page of ISO 10646 (Unicode). Latin1 is HTML's base character set, but HTML has now been globalized through RFC 2070. MacOS X from Apple, for example, is already fully Unicode compliant; other operating systems are trailing behind.

D.4   ISO 639 Language Codes

The ISO 639 language codes are defined for some 150 of the world's several thousand known languages. The 1998 edition of the ISO-8859 Latin alphabets comes with a table of languages covered. A survey of each language's characters was started by Harald Alvestrand. A more complete but less computerized survey is Akira Nakanishi's colorful book *Writing Systems of the World*.[1]

Instead of specifying the type of character set, it has also become common to describe the language attributes to indicate the language of a document. Rather than indicating Polish to the browser using a font, such as Times CE or Warsaw, or a character set, such as ISO-8859-2, you can specify "PL" in the <meta> tags. The advantage is that search engines are able to identify a language much more easily than through the character set. A Latin-1 character set could be anything from English to Italian to German. By using the language attribute, this can be set more specifically. With language attributes, you can label documents with an abbreviation for the language in which they are written. Some browsers don't care, but more advanced browsers, and especially editors with spelling checkers, can use the information. More Web applications

---

[1]Akira Nakanishi, *Writing Systems of the World*, ISBN 0-8048-1654-9

will be able to use the information, including search engines that will search for documents in a particular language. You can specify the language by putting a line like this in the <head> of the document:

```
<META HTTP-EQUIV=Content-Language CONTENT=en>
```

The character set needs to be defined, so it should always be set, but language attribute gives additional information, and should be always included as well. Ideally, you select the character set Unicode and use the attributes to describe parts of a document. If certain sections of your document are in a different language, put a label on the elements concerned. For example, to mark that a certain quote is in Italian:

```
<P>... And here is a quote from Giovanni Scholare: \\
<BLOCKQUOTE lang=it>\\
<P>Non so chi e', ma credo che sia una persona buona.\\
</BLOCKQUOTE>
```

Often, it is necessary to create and maintain a document in multiple languages. There may be a master document with (automatic or human-made) translation or several language originals to be aligned or compared. When a document is available in a variety of languages, and the translations are more or less aligned, it should be possible to create links (half-)automatically between the different versions, or multi-headed links that target all the versions at the same time. HTML versions 3.2 and higher provide a simple scheme to allow adding links to translations (or just to related documents in other languages) in the <head> of your document. The simple scheme works like this. Imagine you've written an article called "Sports in Europe," and you had it translated into Italian and German. You can add this to the <head> of your document:

```
<LINK REL=alternate HREF=mydoc-it.html LANG=it TITLE="Lo Sport in Europa">
<LINK REL=alternate HREF=mydoc-de.html LANG=de TITLE="Sport in Europa">
```

This adds two links to your document, one to an Italian (LANG=it) document and one to a German (LANG=de) document. REL=alternate means they are equivalent documents to the current one, but in some alternative form—in this case, in a different language.

D.5   International URLs

URLs are used to address and locate resources. URLs are the technology that makes the Web work because they provide the uniform interface to distributed resources accessible via a large number of protocols. Part of the success of the Web is that URLs can be used universally. And even though people might not be able to read the URL, nearly everyone stands a pretty good chance of having a keyboard that allows them to enter ASCII characters and URLs.

The URL standard is currently moving through the Internet Engineering Task Force (IETF) standards process and as part of its review, a number of people have suggested that URLs should be extended to incorporate support for either multiple character sets, or more practically, Unicode rather than plain ASCII. They argue that this will allow non-English speaking users to use URLs that contain strings that mean something to them. To deal with the problem of the large amount of software that already handles ASCII URLs, they have suggested that non-ASCII characters from the Unicode character set can be "percent-escaped" in the same way as "reserved" characters from the normal ASCII character set are. Some example URLs and processing software (such as servers that generate Unicode URLs from localized filenames) have been produced and are currently under discussion.

At this point, it is still not clear whether the advantage of being able to support localized character sets in URLs for specific groups will outweigh the clumsiness and possible difficulty of entering them on existing, non-internationalized systems. We are seeing a clear drifting away from an English-only Internet, so localization becomes very important. The probability is high that we will see localization fully implemented over the next few years. English will soon be a minority on the Internet, and the earlier you know how to handle sites with multiple languages, character sets, idioms, and icons, the better off you will be.

Appendix E

DOT.COM DEATH ANALYSIS

E.1 Introduction

In 1999 and 2000, the stock market rocketed to new heights. Small Internet companies became big players in the market. Netscape and eBay multiplied their value by 4,000, and it seemed that nothing could stop the Internet business boom. "This time next year, we'll be millionaires," was the popular wave of thought that so many people broke out of their corporate shackles and started e-businesses. Those who didn't have their own dotcom ideas, simply stole the ideas of others, and then claimed to be running an innovative start-up.

Far too many thought that they had the skills needed to become successful entrepreneurs. Everyone was getting funding. As long as a business plan included the words "Internet," "e-business," or any related term, funding was almost guaranteed. This lead to a storm to the stock markets. People with no knowledge about the stock market started buying stocks of Internet start-ups, which further fuelled the stock prices.

In the mid-90's the dotcom fever had hit the market hard. This hype was not much different from others in the past. Important elements of hype include mass participation, the role of the media, and the extent of the inflation. The stock market bubble was the result of an irrational exuberance. Periods of wild overvaluation of equities were nothing new and had historically coincided with "new era" sentiment. In other words, every so often a new technology comes along that will clearly make some people lots of money at some point in the future—and may even revolutionize the way we do business. We have seen this with the steam engine, the introduction of electricity, and more recently the introduction of personal computers. See also my article for JITTA[1] called *The Industrialization of the Internet Gold Rush*[2] for more information on similar historic events.

This confidence in a sure-fire bet on the future obscures such pithy matters as who will win, the size of their bounty, and when it will be secured. In 1999, a company just needed to announce that it would offer its products and ser-

---

[1] http://www.jitta.org/
[2] http://home.ust.hk/jitta/journal/volume3_4/ec200109amor.pdf

vices on the Internet in order to increase the share prices. Companies expected explosive growth of their business through the Internet.

Although explosive growth seems more interesting than a slow growth rate, you should take the base figures into account. Although companies like Yahoo! and eBay have rocketed from zero to billion dollar businesses, they often lacked the ability to provide a profitable business. Many Internet companies have just burnt cash along the way. For example, Webvan, a now defunct online grocery store, burned 1 billion dollars of investment money. While companies grow exponentially, investors hope that at some point they would make a profit.

And then consider that, in the short term, the market rewards those who anticipate what everyone else will do, and you have a recipe for froth. But the degree of frothiness can be exploited as cover for incompetence and mismanagement, and can be directly or tacitly whipped up by interested parties. Due to the hype surrounding e-business, mass media such as radio and television started to provide regular updates on the stock market. Financial news received a similar status to sports events on the news.

The sports-style coverage of business issues in the mass media, particularly in the US, has given rise to superstar analysts. Though the quality of their research is not in doubt, their objectivity is questionable. Banks are unlikely to issue "sell" advice in a high-growth business when they, too, are touting for lucrative contracts.

At the heart of the hype was the contention that the Internet and related information industries were a revolution in the way companies and sectors organize themselves. It was more than just the emergence of a new industry; it was a so-called "disruptive technology" that would cut costs and fatten profits across the economy.

Much of the Net's value was thought to be enmeshed within existing corporations, specifically in the telecommunications and media sectors. Share valuations soared, and the companies borrowed and did deals on the back of those soaring valuations.

Even if you go back a couple of years to when there were very few Internet firms, demand for their shares was high. It is this imbalance between supply and demand that pushed prices so high, attracting even more interest in companies with little or no financial record. And this speculative bubble was whipped up even more by marketing, publicity, and hyperactive PR. Those companies that did come to market restricted the supply of stock and managed the release, guaranteeing a stellar first-day performance, and yet more attention.

Eventually, a sufficient number of pure Internet firms came to market for buyers to become discerning and, predictably, share prices slumped. Venture capitalists pulled the plug on investment funding in Boo.com, which we will discuss in more depth. Companies from News Corp to Disney reined in their investments and slashed jobs.

Telecom companies were hit with an unexpected bill of billions of dollars for 3G (third-generation) licenses (the high watermark of irrational exuberance), and their credit ratings were downgraded. Like the Asian tigers in 1998, they found that with confidence undermined, capital markets are reticent when they are most needed. The Asian tigers are countries like Malaysia and Thailand, which seemed to become industrialized countries in the early 1990s, but lost much of the drive after the Asian market collapsed in 1998.

E.2   Dot.com Failures

Many companies have failed over the last year, but few had a large impact on the overall business. One of the companies that affected the Internet industry was Boo.com. When Boo.com failed, it was like an earthquake in the Internet industry.

Boo was set up by the Swedish pair, Ernst Malmsten and Kajsa Leander, who became overnight stars with their book-selling venture Bokus.com. The company had an impressive list of backers, including banking giant Goldman Sachs and Bernard Arnault, chairman of Christian Dior and the French luxury goods company LVMH.

Boo was 18 months old when it imploded in May 2000, having spent more than 80 million dollars and incurring debts totalling 20 million dollars. At one point, the company was wasting 400,000 dollars a week on the operations of the Web site, advertising, and human resources. The expensive advertising campaign was particular suicidal for a company that saw trendy twentysomethings as its target market.

The much-hyped Web site, which is said to have cost 20 million dollars to put together, allowed visitors to try on clothes in a virtual dressing room. The three-dimensional stock images cost 250,000 dollars alone. The site could take orders in 7 languages and 18 currencies, but in the end, was too complex and jammed customers' computers.

Boo was ahead of its time with the Web site, because you needed access to a powerful modem and broadband capabilities to run it. Although one of the best-known sites, it could not attract enough buyers to lead to a profit-making company. Boo's business sins are not unique, but its meteoric rise and fall is a remarkable Internet horror story.

Boo's idea of selling street fashion to young Internet users was viable, but everything else was a disaster. The amount of money it spent was appalling. Boo.com spent about one billion dollars, but in order to be successful Boo would have needed more aggressive, accountable cash management. Boo.com is not the only party responsible for the disaster.

Also to blame are the venture capitalists who made billions of dollars in the mid-1990s from the likes of AOL and Netscape in the US and then tried to repeat the success in Europe. The venture capitalists are to blame because they should have said it was time to stop. Instead of stopping new Internet start-ups from emerging onto the market, they put even more money on the table to make a quick win at the stock market. But these companies take the portfolio approach of investing in 20 companies and making all their profit from a single success.

After Boo.com failed, many others followed en suite: living.com, pets.com, and eToys.com had to give up (just to name a few). Most of these companies were badly run from a business point of view and focused too much on technology. The cash burn rate was extremely high without turning any profit. Some companies spent one million dollars a week while earning only 10,000 dollars during the same time period. While many start-ups failed, traditional retailers have taken over and now run quite successful online ventures.

E.3   Successful Examples

Despite the failure of many start-ups, there are notable successes. AOL, for example, was the senior partner in the merger with Time-Warner at the beginning of 2001. And the online auctioneer eBay is valued at 10 billion dollars, thanks to its dominance of a high-margin, high-growth business. It has succesfully fought off competitors, claiming 88 percent of the market, and has the rare status of being a profitable consumer e-commerce company.

There are many other successful online companies, such as Amazon.com and Metropolis.de. To be successful, it is important to follow the rules detailed in Chapters 1 and 2. Successful companies have understood that the Internet is a new infrastructure for existing business cases (in most cases). You must realize that only very few companies can create new business cases and be successful. Most successful online businesses have used a successful business case and introduced a new communication and transaction channel with the Internet. Remember, 80 percent of a successful online business is comprised of a business plan, business processes, and online content. A maximum of 20 percent of the success can be contributed to the underlying technology.

E.4   The Future

Many thought that after the start-up crash in 2000, the Internet and e-business were dead. Things have just started to become interesting. To make Internet technology pervasive, it needs to become a commodity. A first step toward commoditization of the Internet has already taken place. No matter which ISP you use, we all access the Internet in the same way. Internet access has become genuinely transparent.

As a result, the ISP market has really become consolidated over the past few years, and few global players can be considered competitive. And while there is always a market for niche players, the market is less fragmented than it was a few years ago, when every ISP provided a different set of services.

Through the industrialization of Internet access services, the margins are lower, but due to the larger market that is accessible now, companies are able to grow at a steadier rate. The early years can be considered as explosive growth, but with less reliable forecasts. While some companies are trying to jump onto the next bandwagon, many will try to stabilize their business through the adoption of standards in technology and processes. After this phase has been completed, we will see a commodity layer of services on the Internet.

The move toward commodities of Internet services or e-services will change the way companies work in the near future. Commodities on the Internet allow companies to choose from an e-service instead of building up their own infrastructure to accommodate all sorts of services.

The major advantage of this approach is that complexity is considerably reduced. Companies can focus on their core competencies and expect these additional services that are required to come from reliable third-party sources without having to worry about integration. E-services will be one of the major growth areas on the Internet over the next few years. In the end, it will turn around more money than all current e-business services together can.

This new generation of e-services will generate a new hype over the next few years, and we will see another shakeout afterward. One strategy would be to wait until after the shakeout, but my suggestion would be to get into e-services now with moderate investments and let the others be pioneers in business models and technologies.

SUBJECT INDEX